TRADITIONAL DETAILS

FOR BUILDING RESTORATION, RENOVATION, AND REHABILITATION

TRADITIONAL DETAILS

FOR BUILDING RESTORATION, RENOVATION, AND REHABILITATION

From the 1932–1951 Editions of

ARCHITECTVRAL GRAPHIC STANDARDS

Editors

JOHN BELLE, FAIA, RIBA
JOHN RAY HOKE, Jr., AIA
STEPHEN A. KLIMENT, FAIA

JOHN WILEY & SONS, INC.
New York / Chichester / Brisbane / Toronto / Singapore

Copyright © 1991 by John Wiley & Sons, Inc.

Library of Congress Cataloging-in-Publication Data:

Ramsey/Sleeper ; traditional details for building restoration,
  renovation, and rehabilitation from the 1932–1951 edtions of
  Architectural graphic standards / editors, John Belle, John R. Hoke,
  Jr., Stephen A. Kliment.
      p.   cm.
  Includes bibliographical references (p.   ) and index.
   1. Buildings—Details—Drawings.   2. Buildings—Repair and
reconstruction.   I. Ramsey, Charles George, 1884–1963.
II. Sleeper, Harold Reeve, 1893–1960.   III. Belle, John.   IV. Hoke,
John Ray, 1950–   .   V. Kliment, Stephen A.   VI. Ramsey, Charles
George, 1884–1963.   Architectural graphic standards for architects,
engineers, decorators, builders, draftsmen, and students.
VII. Title: Traditional details for building restoration,
renovation, and rehabilitation, from the 1932–1951 edtions of
Architectural graphic standards.
   TH2031.R37   1990   692'.2–dc20   90–13050
                                                                                         CIP

   ISBN 0-471-52956-7

Printed in the United States of America

10 9 8 7 6 5 4 3 2 1

CONTENTS

PUBLISHER'S NOTE

In his Foreword to the 1st Edition of Charles G. Ramsey and Harold R. Sleeper's *Architectural Graphic Standards,* Frederick L. Ackerman wrote in 1932 that the goal of the book was "to confine within a book of reasonable dimensions the essential factual references required by the architect, draughtsman, and builder in the course of the day's work." The success of that attempt may be judged by the seven editions which have followed and the many hundreds of thousands of copies sold since that time. Many have called it "the Bible of architectural practice."

Following the publication of the 4th Edition in 1951, the revision process for succeeding editions of *Architectural Graphic Standards* has included a careful winnowing out of material adjudged no longer useful for modern construction. Thus hundreds of pages have been deleted and replaced by more modern content, to the point where in the 8th Edition (1988), only two-thirds of a single page remain from the illustrations in the original 1932 book.

As a perhaps inevitable consequence of this process, much material has been deleted from past editions which might be extremely useful to architects, engineers, interior designers, and contractors engaged in the restoration, renovation, and rehabilitation of historic structures. Although a chapter on Historic Preservation was added to the 8th Edition in recognition of the role this subject has assumed in current practice, this cannot begin to cover the scope of the deleted material, now numbering in the many hundreds of pages. Thus, we began to hear increasing requests for republication of the "best of" *Graphic Standards* particularly those details useful to designers working with older, existing structures.

Hence this volume, in which designers and contractors engaged in the work of rebuilding and renovating structures designed and built in decades past will find many of the details and much of the information utilized by the original architects and builders. As the editors pored over the many hundreds of pages deleted from past editions, there was one single criterion for inclusion in this volume: would the information be of use to a modern designer in approaching the restoration, renovation, or rehabilitation of an older building?

This volume restores to the practicing professional illustrations and standards that are once again relevant to active design practice. We are proud to continue to build on our legacy in architectural publishing. And we're glad you, the professional, are a part of it.

August 1990

TRADITIONAL DETAILS

FOR BUILDING RESTORATION, RENOVATION, AND REHABILITATION

INTRODUCTION

John Belle

The astonishing expansion over the past decade of restoration, renovation, and reconstruction activities in the construction industry has led to the publication of this special edition of Ramsey and Sleeper.

When Charles Ramsey and Harold Sleeper first published *Architectural Graphic Standards* in 1932, they carefully defined for whom they expected the book to have some useful purpose. "For Architects, Engineers, Decorators, Builders, and Draftsmen" they noted on the title page.

Their expectations have been exceeded over the past half century as one edition or another of their work has become a permanent fixture in design studios everywhere. Years ago, working as a young architectural assistant in the London office of Maxwell Fry, I remember seeing a copy of *Graphic Standards* sitting on the book shelves. Knowing of Max's far-flung network of architectural colleagues, I surmised it has come from one of them. Perhaps Gropius has sent it to him after departing for greener pastures? I'll never know.

As a reference source it seems to turn up in some unlikely places, from the offices of international architects such as Fry to one that I saw recently in a plumbing supply house in Riverhead, Long Island!

I suspect this special edition, devoted especially to traditional details, is likely to find a home not only in the offices of architects involved in restoration, but also in such places as state Historic Preservation Offices and Landmarks Commissions.

Just one short decade ago, when this "Bible" of construction detail was into its 7th edition, no one would have predicted there would be the need to publish an edition exclusively devoted to the technology of "old buildings." Yet when one examines the contents of the first four editions, published in 1932, 1936, 1941, and 1951, and compares them with the 8th edition, published in 1988, it becomes evident that valuable and useful information about traditional construction had been left on the sidelines long ago by the press of details spawned by modern construction technology.

Where could the architect restoring a slate roof with a hipped dormer go to look at the traditional detailing of such a component? (See page 131). Or perhaps to check out the connections in standard mill construction (see page 88).

A second phenomenon of the 1980s has been the growing interest in architectural drawing. And as that interest has grown and encouraged greater experimentation in contemporary drawings, so has an interest and curiosity about previous techniques and even the style of architectural drawings from past eras. The styles illustrated in the 1932 and 1936 editions were fine examples of a technique that had prevailed for over a quarter of a century—crisp lines, firm corners, clear unmannered freehand lettering. It is a style that in a "cottage industry" way has much in common with contemporary CAD generated drawings, which also have the same no-nonsense yet distinctive style. At their best, the architectural drawings of both eras are direct and unaffected by fashion or mannerisms. (See Perspective, pages 9–11).

Our efforts as editors began with a review of the first four editions (1932, 1936, 1941, and 1951), which revealed a great deal of technical information on traditional detailing that was no longer readily available in current sources.

Next the issue of its usefulness needed to be addressed. Unlike the typical edition of Ramsey and Sleeper with its emphasis on contemporary practices or applications, a case was made for including examples of traditional information and details which, though they did not meet current regulatory requirements—such as energy codes or access for the handicapped—can still be encountered in the course of working on an old building. Therefore, whether or not there was the need to add insulation to an exterior framed wall in order to meet energy codes, it seemed useful to have a source that would clearly tell how the wall was originally detailed in an era that predated such concerns.

Having winnowed down some 1354 pages to a more manageable number and feeling assured that the information would be useful to someone engaged in restoration, renovation, or reconstruction activities, the final editorial function was to organize the material. This turned out to be the easier task because of Ramsey and Sleeper's original work in organizing their material in sections "from foundation to furniture" as they wrote in their first edition preface. We have followed the same sequence—omitting sections that are not relevant (for example, reinforced concrete does not appear) and simply bracketing this conventional Ramsey and Sleeper sequencing with two sections—a General Planning and Design section at the beginning, and a Mechanical, Electrical, and Plumbing section at the end.

The pagination is obviously different from the original since the information was originally published in one of four editions. Aside from that slight but important change, the reader will be seeing a page as Ramsey and Sleeper originally conceived and organized it. For the more curious or persistent reader, the index references the edition in which the information first appeared.

We trust that this latest volume of the venerable Ramsey and Sleeper series will serve the user well by providing a comprehensive source of traditional details in a graphic style both distinctive and memorable.

1

GENERAL PLANNING AND DESIGN DATA

LETTERING

ABCDEFGHIJKLMN
OPQRSTUVWXYZ &
USED FOR TITLES

ABCDEFGHIJKLMNOPQRSTUVWXYZ
ABCDEFGHIJKLMNOPQRSTUVWXYZ

ABCDEFGHIJKLMNOPQRSTUVWXYZ
ABCDEFGHIJKLMNOPQRSTUVWXYZ

abcdefghijklmnopqrstuvwxyz
abcdefghijklmnopqrstuvwxyz
used for subtitles as Plan · Elevation

ABCDEFGHIJKLMNOPQRSTUVWXYZ - PLAN - POOL
PLAN TRANSVERSE SECTION ELEVATION

ABCDEFGHIJKLMNOPQRSTUVWXYZ~1234567890
THIS · IS · ANOTHER · TYPE · USED · FOR · SUB-TITLES
ABCDEFGHIJKLMNOPQRSTUVWXYZ - SLOPING

abcdefgghijklmnopqrstuvwxyz   This type is often used for notes
abcdefghijklmnopqrstuvwxyz,   an upright variation of the foregoing

ABCDEFGHIJKLMNOPQRSTUVWXYZ - NOTES OR SMALL SCALE TITLES
ABCDEFGHIJKLMNOPQRSTUVWXYZ - A SLOPING VARIATION OF ABOVE

abcdefghijklmnopqrstuvwxyz   an upright type of lettering which may be used for notes
abcdefghijklmnopqrstuvwxyz   Type of lettering used throughout this book for notes etc.

LETTERING

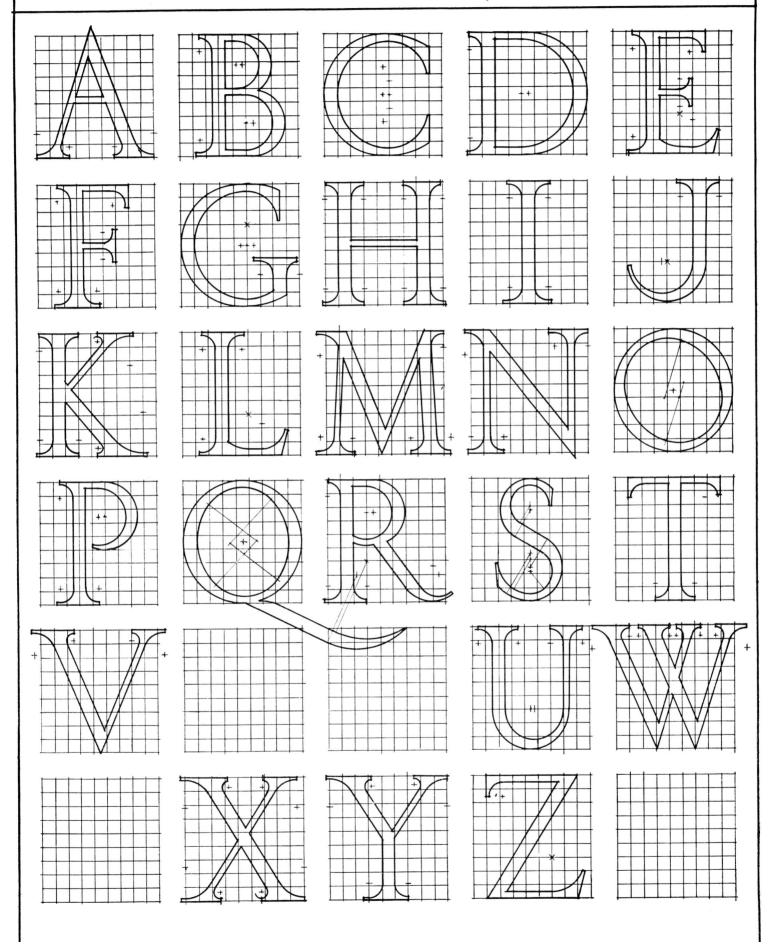

ELLIPSES

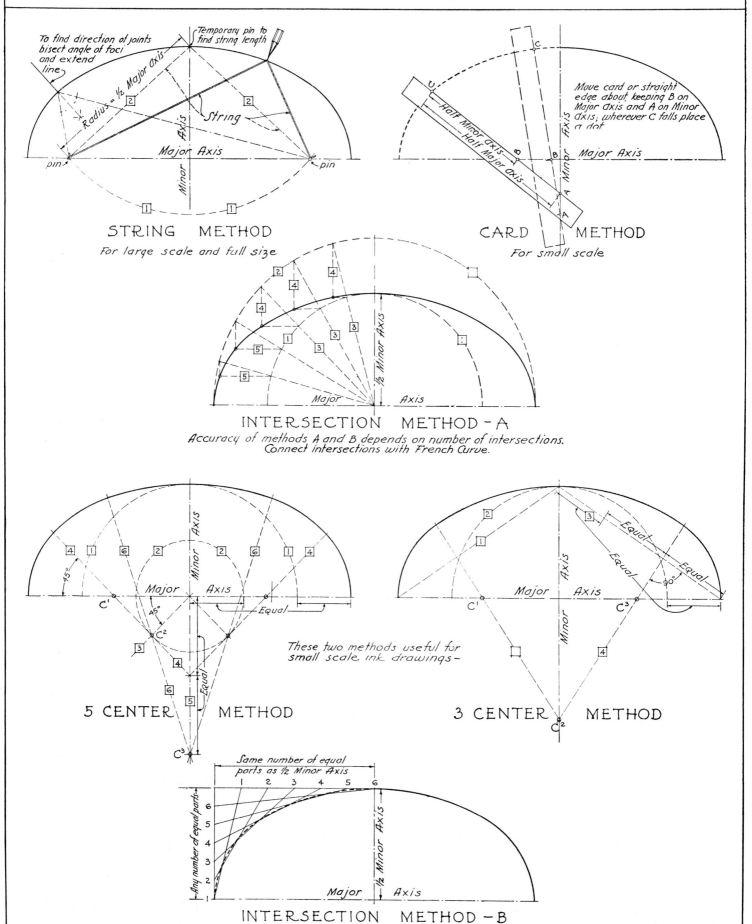

STRING METHOD

For large scale and full size

To find direction of joints bisect angle of foci and extend line

Temporary pin to find string length

Radius = ½ Major Axis

Axis

String

Minor

Major Axis

pin   pin

CARD METHOD

For small scale

Move card or straight edge about, keeping B on Major Axis and A on Minor Axis; wherever C falls place a dot.

Half Minor Axis   Half Major Axis

Minor Axis

Major Axis

INTERSECTION METHOD – A

½ Minor Axis

Major   Axis

Accuracy of methods A and B depends on number of intersections.
Connect intersections with French Curve.

5 CENTER METHOD

45°

Minor Axis

Major   Axis

45°

Equal

C¹   C²

Equal

C³

These two methods useful for small scale ink drawings –

3 CENTER METHOD

Equal   Equal

Equal

Minor Axis

Major   Axis

90°

C¹   C³

C²

INTERSECTION METHOD – B

Same number of equal parts as ½ Minor Axis

1 2 3 4 5 6

Any number of equal parts

½ Minor Axis

Major   Axis

For procedure in laying out ellipses, follow numbers consecutively from No. ☐. For compass methods use centers C¹, C² & C³

ENTASIS, VOLUTE, RAKE MOULDS and POLYGONS

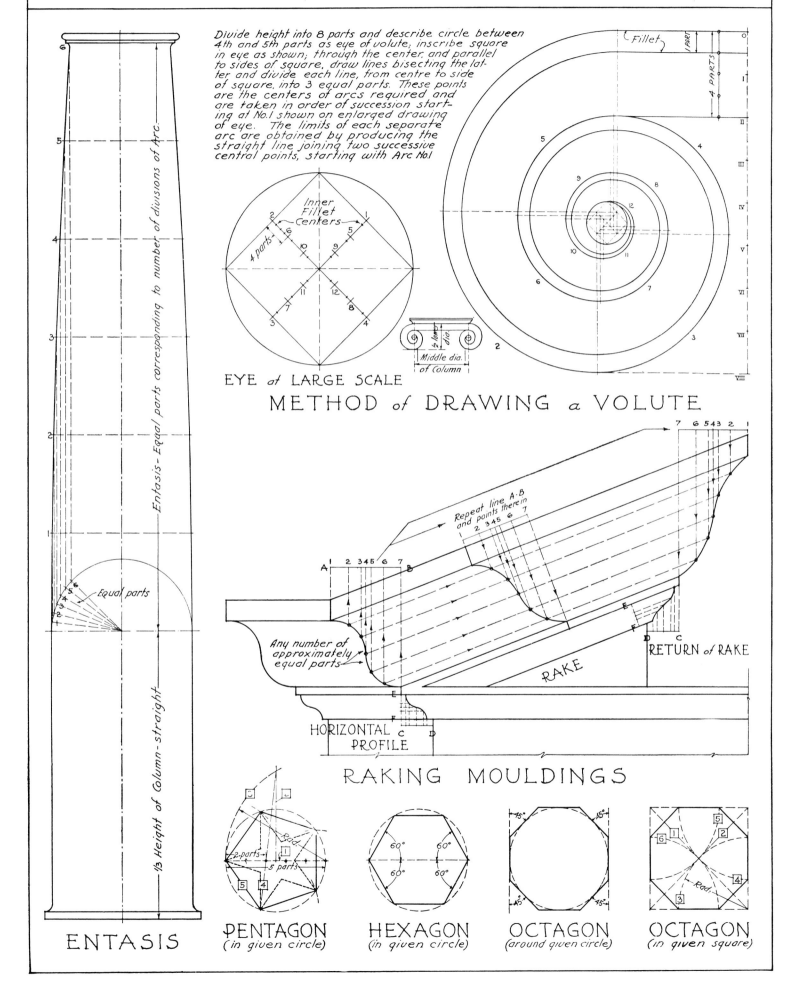

Divide height into 8 parts and describe circle between 4th and 5th parts as eye of volute; inscribe square in eye as shown; through the center, and parallel to sides of square, draw lines bisecting the latter and divide each line, from centre to side of square, into 3 equal parts. These points are the centers of arcs required and are taken in order of succession starting at No.1 shown on enlarged drawing of eye. The limits of each separate arc are obtained by producing the straight line joining two successive central points, starting with Arc No.1

EYE at LARGE SCALE

METHOD of DRAWING a VOLUTE

ENTASIS

RAKING MOULDINGS

HORIZONTAL PROFILE

RETURN of RAKE

RAKE

PENTAGON
(in given circle)

HEXAGON
(in given circle)

OCTAGON
(around given circle)

OCTAGON
(in given square)

PARABOLA & ENTASIS

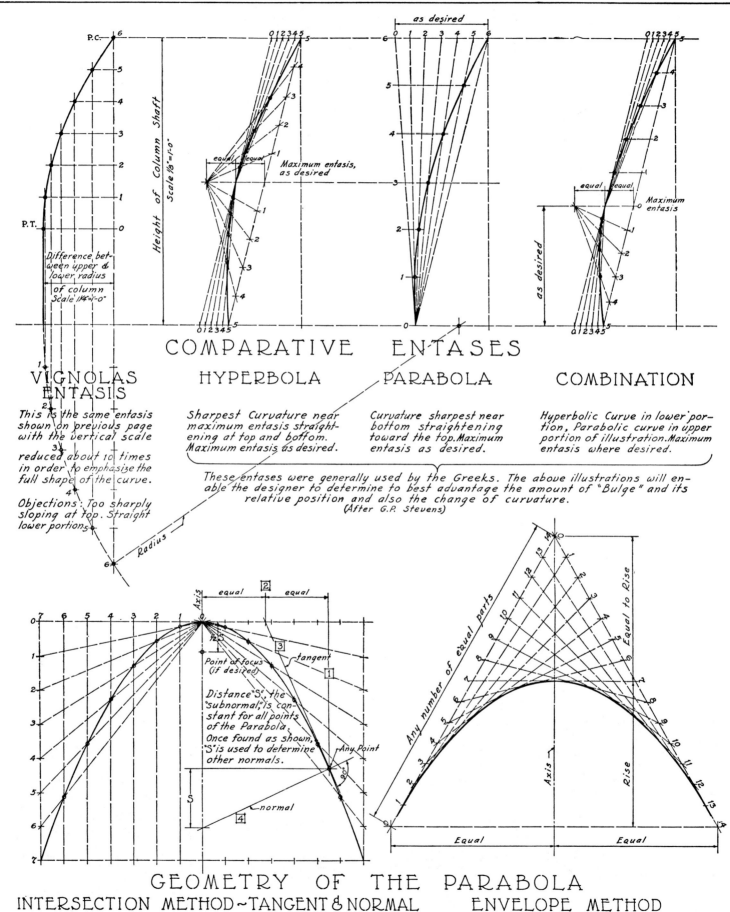

COMPARATIVE ENTASES

as desired

P.C. 6

P.T. 0

Height of Column Shaft
Scale 1/8"=1'-0"

Difference between upper & lower radius of column
Scale 1 1/4"=1'-0"

equal equal
Maximum entasis, as desired

as desired

Maximum entasis

equal equal
Maximum entasis

VIGNOLAS ENTASIS

This is the same entasis shown on previous page with the vertical scale reduced about 10 times in order to emphasize the full shape of the curve.

Objections: Too sharply sloping at top. Straight lower portions.

Radius

HYPERBOLA

Sharpest Curvature near maximum entasis straightening at top and bottom. Maximum entasis as desired.

PARABOLA

Curvature sharpest near bottom straightening toward the top. Maximum entasis as desired.

COMBINATION

Hyperbolic Curve in lower portion, Parabolic curve in upper portion of illustration. Maximum entasis where desired.

These entases were generally used by the Greeks. The above illustrations will enable the designer to determine to best advantage the amount of "Bulge" and its relative position and also the change of curvature.
(After G.P. Stevens)

Axis

equal equal

Point of focus (if desired)

tangent

Distance "S", the "subnormal", is constant for all points of the Parabola. Once found as shown, "S" is used to determine other normals.

Any Point

90°

S

normal

Any number of equal parts

Equal to Rise

Axis

Rise

Equal Equal

GEOMETRY OF THE PARABOLA

INTERSECTION METHOD ~ TANGENT & NORMAL

This is comparable to the intersection method for the ellipse shown on previous page, & is equally good for inscribing a parabola in a parallelogram.

ENVELOPE METHOD

This method does not give points on the curve, but a series of tangents which outline the parabola directly.

Compiled by Andre Halasz A.I.A.

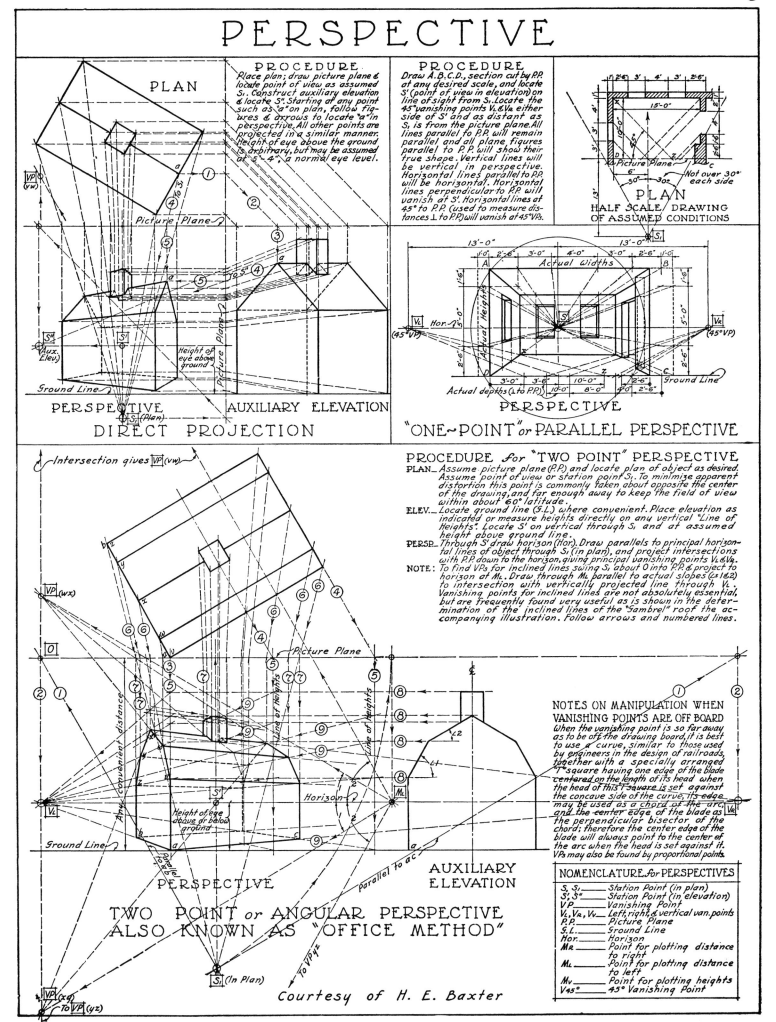

PERSPECTIVE

PERSPECTIVE ~ PLAN METHOD

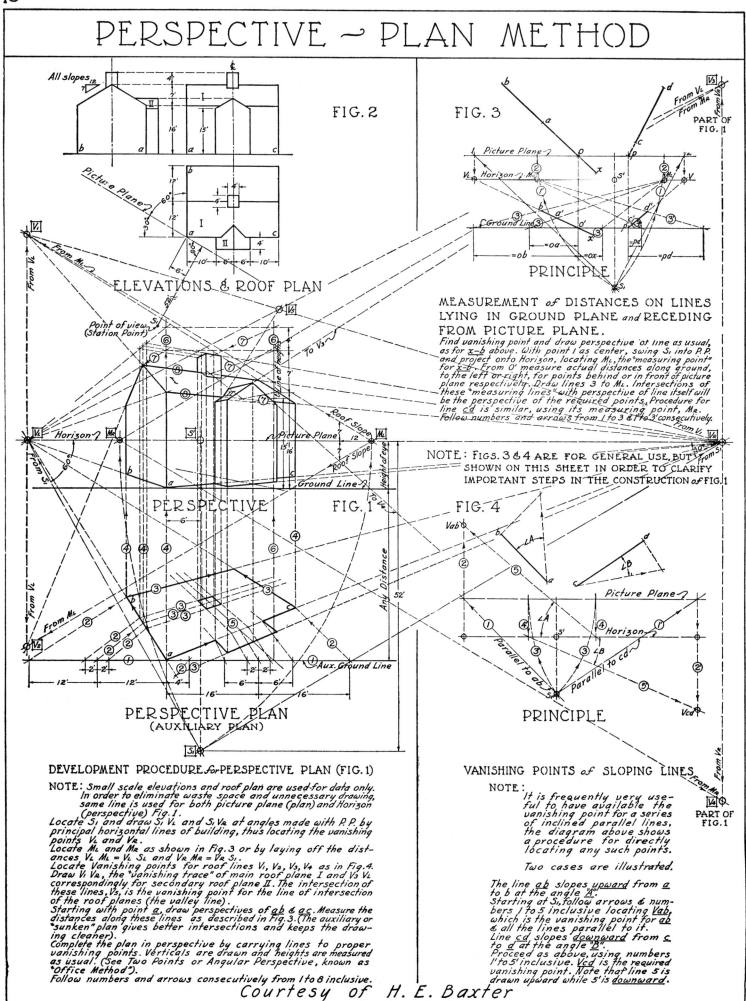

Courtesy of H. E. Baxter

PERSPECTIVE ~ THREE POINT

FIG. 3

Horizon

Ground Line

PERSPECTIVE

DEVELOPMENT PROCEDURE for ILLUSTRATION ABOVE

Assume ground line and center line where convenient. Locate
Vv & Mv as shown in Fig. 2. Horizontal lines and measurements,
and hence the plan, are handled exactly as in the "Perspective
Plan" method. Vertical lines pass through the corresponding
points in plan and converge at Vv. To get any point such as
"a" in perspective, draw through "a," (plan of "a") to VL and continue to intersection with ground line at "b". Through "b" draw
one line, (bc) parallel to VL Vv, and another through Vv (bVv).
Scale off actual heights above (or below) ground along bc. Draw
cMv to "d" and draw dVL. Where dVv intersects Vv a, is the perspective point of "a".

FIG. 1-A

FRONT ELEVATION

FIG. 1-B

SIDE ELEVATION

FIG. 2

FIG. 1

PLAN

NOTE: Plan & Elevations are drawn
to ½ F.S. Used for data only.

DEVELOPMENT PROCEDURE

Small Scale layout diagram
showing method (¼ F.S.)

DEVELOPMENT PROCEDURE NOTES for EVOLUTION of PERSPECTIVE

(Note: See Fig.2 above). Draw center line ① and ground line ② at will. Using these as
vertical and horizontal planes as seen in profile, assume station point Ⓢ as desired. Draw
line of sight ③ from Ⓢ toward "center of interest" of the object, and through Ⓧ draw P.P. ④
at right angle to ③. Follow arrows and numbers through ⑨. Swing Ⓢ about into P.P. &
then about Ⓧ into ₵ locating Ⓢ. Draw ⑫ and ⑬ through Ⓢ at angles plan makes
with ground line (∠s B and C), locate VL and VR, and from these find ML and MR.
Draw (VL and Vv) and on it locate Mv by following numbers or by making Vv Mv = SY.

Courtesy of H. E. Baxter

BUILDING CUBE

CUBAGE *includes the following volumes taken in full:*
Bays, oriols, dormers, chimneys, Pent house, tanks, vaults, pits, trenches (if of masonry), enclosed porches in full, and the cubic content of the actual space enclosed within the outer surfaces of the outside walls and contained between the outside of roof and bottom of basement floor slab.
    This includes the following volumes in part:
        a. Non-enclosed porches :- If built within house proper and having no screens or sash _____ 2/3 Volume
                             If built as extension to house and having no screens or sash _____ 1/2 volume
                             If built as extension to house and having screens and sash _____ Full volume
        b. Areaways: _____ 1/2 Volume
        c. Parapets - If they are of excessive height (3'-0" or over) take excess as :- _____ Full Volume
    The cubage does not include the following volumes : Outside steps, terraces, light shafts, cornices, parapets, footings, piles, caissons, deep foundations, exterior garden walls; Special foundations, etc., should be allowed for in $

    CUBIC FOOT COST *equals net cost ÷ the above total cubage.*

    NET COST *includes the following according to usual practice :*
Building construction, mechanical trades, hardware, lighting fixtures, elevators, sprinklers, signal systems.
    The following items are usually excluded from net costs :-
Furnishings, and equipment such as ranges, laundry and kitchen equipment, clocks, organs, lockers, files, hangings, shades, awnings, Venetian blinds, furniture not built in. Also roads, walks, exterior walls, terraces, steps, landscape work sewage disposal system, power plant, wells, water supply, services to building, etc. Also Architect's and Engineer's fee.

    The above is similar to the A.I.A. Standard #230-1928, except that it suggests treating cubes of open porches, enclosed courts and shafts and the square foot area of stoops, balconies, terraces as supplementary information.

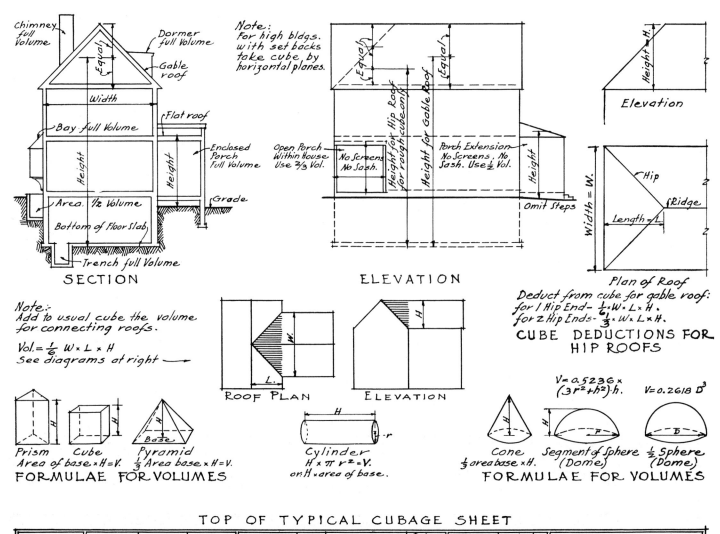

SECTION

ELEVATION

Plan of Roof

Note:
For high bldgs. with set backs take cube by horizontal planes.

Note:-
Add to usual cube the volume for connecting roofs.

$Vol. = \frac{1}{6} W \times L \times H$
See diagrams at right ⟶

ROOF PLAN   ELEVATION

Deduct from cube for gable roof:
for 1 Hip End- $\frac{1}{6} W \times L \times H$.
for 2 Hip Ends- $\frac{1}{3} W \times L \times H$.
CUBE DEDUCTIONS FOR HIP ROOFS

Prism
Area of base × H = V.

Cube

Pyramid
$\frac{1}{3}$ Area base × H = V.

FORMULAE FOR VOLUMES

Cylinder
$H \times \pi r^2 = V.$
or H × area of base.

Cone
$\frac{1}{3}$ area base × H.

$V = 0.5236 \times (3r^2 + h^2) \cdot h.$
Segment of Sphere (Dome)

$V = 0.2618 \ D^3$
½ Sphere (Dome)

FORMULAE FOR VOLUMES

TOP OF TYPICAL CUBAGE SHEET

Unit	Length	Width	Height	Area	Factor	Cube	@¢ per CU. FT.	Cost $	Total Cost.	(Diagram here):
A	20	16	32	320		10,240	.50	5,120		
B	10	5	10	50	½	250	.50	125		
C	25	12	30	300		9,000	.50	4,500	$9,745	

ARCHITECTURAL SYMBOLS

ALL SYMBOLS ARE FOR PLANS AND SECTIONS UNLESS MARKED "ELEVATION"

BRICK
* Common   *Face-on Common. Firebrick-on common   Elevation

CONCRETE
* Stone   Cinder   Cast Block   Cement   Terrazzo

EARTH, ETC.
* Earth   * Rock   Cinders   Sand

GYPSUM
Plaster   Gypsum Tiles   Solid Plaster Part'n
Adding adjacent line to masonry indicates plaster

GLASS
Large Scale   Structural Glass   Metal Studs & Plaster   Small Scale

ABBREVIATIONS
Aluminum — AL
Asbestos — Asb
Brass — Br
Cast Iron — cI
Cast Stone — cs
Cement — Cem
Concrete — Conc
Copper — Cop
Galvanized Iron — GI
glass — gl
Hollow Metal — HM
Kalamein — Kal
Limestone — l-s
Plaster — pl
Terra-cotta — tc
Waterproofing — wp
Wire glass — w-gl
Wrought Iron — w.I

INSULATION
Loose Fill   Boards or Quilts   Insulation-Solid

MARBLE
WATERPROOFING FELT FLASHING ETC.

METALS
Usually used for all Metals
* Steel-Iron   Brass-Bronze   Aluminum   Sheet Metal   Small Scale

STONE
Cut Stone   Rubble   Cast Stone   Cut Stone   Rubble   Slate, Bluestone & Soapstone
Elevations

TERRA-COTTA & HOLLOW TILE
Top line is large scale
Clay Hollow Tile   Glazed Block, and Tile   Hollow Tile Floor Arch   Architectural tc on Brick   Architectural tc closed back on brick

TILE (CERAMIC)
Large Scale   Small Scale   Elevation
Large Scale   Small Scale   **GLASS BLOCK**

WOOD
* Finish   Rough   Shingles or Siding (Elev.)

EXAMPLES
Face Brick   Exterior side of Wall Brick   Cast stone   Cut Stone   Architectural tc   Exterior side of Wall Cut stone   Rubble
Rubble   Clay Hollow Tile   Brick   Concrete-stone   Plaster   Brick   Concrete Block   Glazed Face Hollow Tile
Interior   Interior

PLANS of EXTERIOR WALLS

Solid Plaster   Concrete Block   Clay Hollow Tile   Glazed Block & Tile   Brick-plastered   Gypsum Block   Stud

PLANS of PARTITIONS

Tile   Marble   Wood   Terrazzo   Cement   Stone   Brick

SECTIONS of FLOOR FINISHES

*A.S.A. and A.S.M.E. Standard

13

14

CONVENTIONS

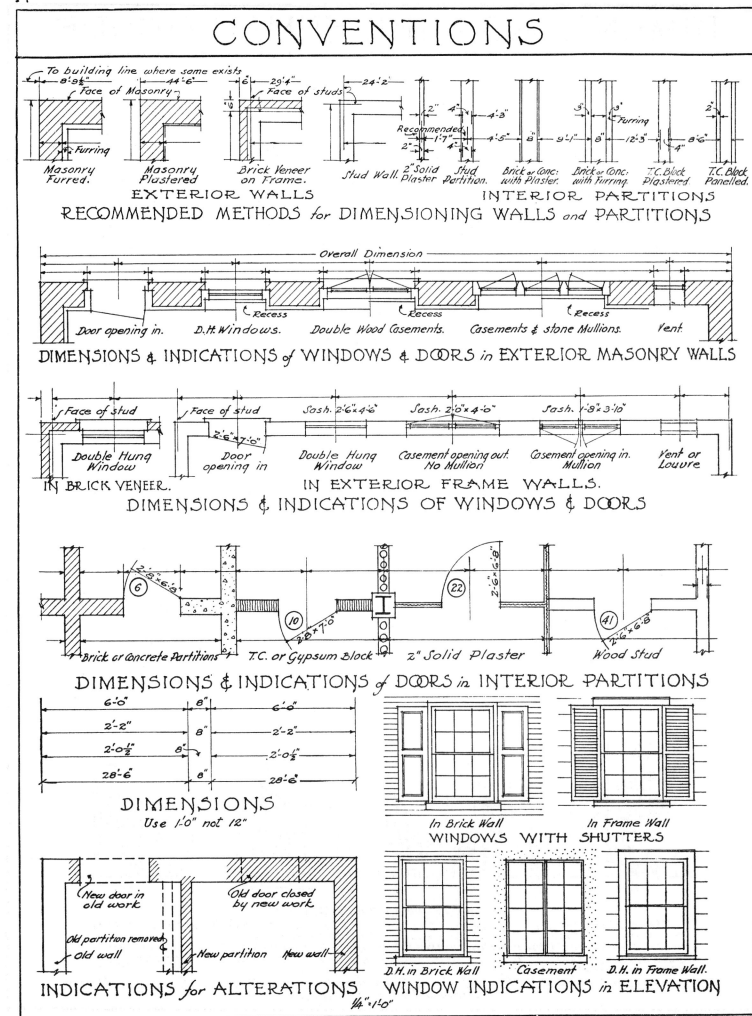

To building line where some exists

Furring — Masonry Furred.

Masonry Plastered

Brick Veneer on Frame.

Stud Wall.

2" Solid Plaster

Stud Partition.

Brick or Conc. with Plaster

Brick or Conc. with Furring

T.C. Block Plastered

T.C. Block Panelled.

EXTERIOR WALLS

INTERIOR PARTITIONS

RECOMMENDED METHODS for DIMENSIONING WALLS and PARTITIONS

Overall Dimension

Door opening in.   D.H. Windows.   Double Wood Casements.   Casements & stone Mullions.   Vent.

Recess   Recess   Recess

DIMENSIONS & INDICATIONS of WINDOWS & DOORS in EXTERIOR MASONRY WALLS

Face of stud   Face of stud   Sash 2'-6"x4'-6"   Sash 2'-0"x4'-0"   Sash 1'-8"x3'-10"

Double Hung Window   Door opening in   Double Hung Window   Casement opening out. No Mullion   Casement opening in. Mullion   Vent or Louvre

IN BRICK VENEER.   IN EXTERIOR FRAME WALLS.

DIMENSIONS & INDICATIONS OF WINDOWS & DOORS

Brick or Concrete Partitions   T.C. or Gypsum Block   2" Solid Plaster   Wood Stud

DIMENSIONS & INDICATIONS of DOORS in INTERIOR PARTITIONS

6'-0"   8"   6'-0"
2'-2"   8"   2'-2"
2'-0½"   8"   2'-0½"
28'-6"   8"   28'-6"

DIMENSIONS

Use 1'-0" not 12"

In Brick Wall   In Frame Wall

WINDOWS WITH SHUTTERS

New door in old work   Old door closed by new work

Old partition removed   Old wall   New partition   New wall

INDICATIONS for ALTERATIONS

D.H. in Brick Wall   Casement   D.H. in Frame Wall.

WINDOW INDICATIONS in ELEVATION

¼"=1'-0"

DIMENSIONS of THE HUMAN FIGURE

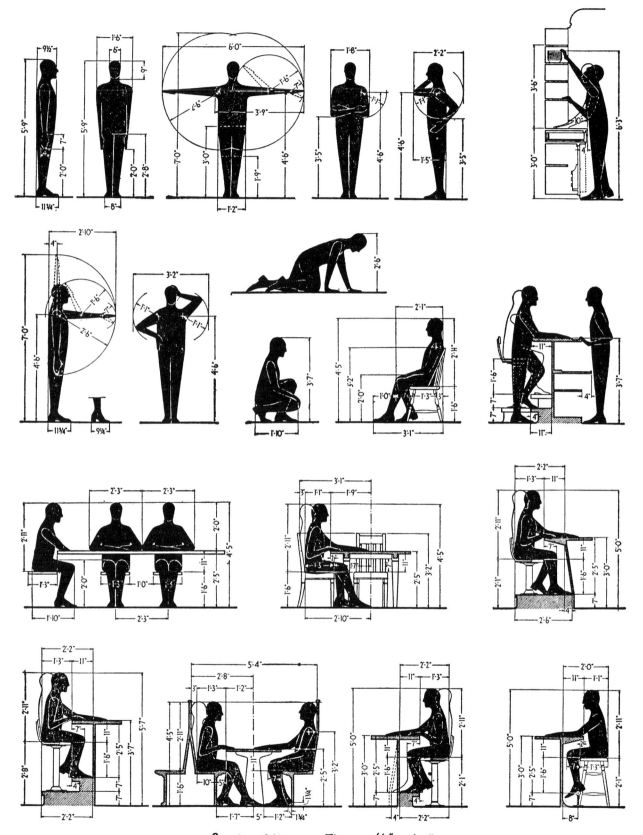

Scale of Human Figure 1/4" = 1'-0"

These dimensions are based on the average or normal adult. As clearances are minimum they should be increased when conditions will allow.

Table, desk, and other sitting work-top heights are shown 2'-5"; however some authorities prefer 2'-6" or 2'-6½". See sheets titled "Children's Furniture," for their size and furniture.

Drawings by Ernest Irving Freese

LIBRARY EQUIPMENT

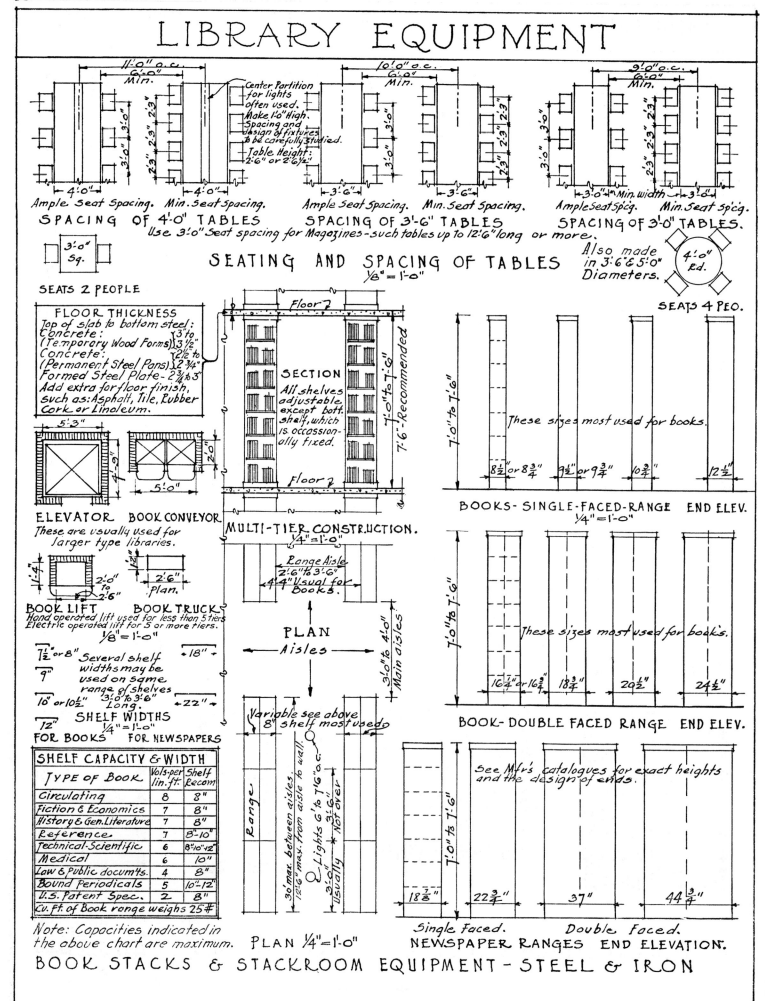

SPACING OF 4'-0" TABLES   SPACING OF 3'-6" TABLES   SPACING OF 3'-0" TABLES.

Ample Seat Spacing.   Min. Seat Spacing.   Ample Seat Spacing.   Min. Seat Spacing.   Ample Seat Sp'cg.   Min. Seat sp'cg.

Use 3'-0" Seat spacing for Magazines - such tables up to 12'-6" long or more.

SEATING AND SPACING OF TABLES
1/8" = 1'-0"

Center Partition for lights often used. Make 1'-0" High. Spacing and design of fixtures to be carefully studied. Table Height: 2'-6" or 2'-6½".

3'-0" Sq.   SEATS 2 PEOPLE

Also made in 3'-6" & 5'-0" Diameters.

4'-0" Rd.   SEATS 4 PEO.

FLOOR THICKNESS
Top of slab to bottom steel:
Concrete: (Temporary Wood Forms) 3" to 3½"
Concrete: (Permanent Steel Pans) 2½" to 2¾"
Formed Steel Plate - 2¾" to 3"
Add extra for floor finish, such as: Asphalt, Tile, Rubber Cork or Linoleum.

ELEVATOR   BOOK CONVEYOR
These are usually used for larger type libraries.

5'-3"   5'-0"   2'-0"   4'-9"

BOOK LIFT   BOOK TRUCK
2'-0" to 2'-6"   2'-6" Plan.
Hand operated lift used for less than 5 tiers. Electric operated lift for 5 or more tiers.
1/8" = 1'-0"

7½" or 8"   Several shelf widths may be used on same range of shelves 3'-0" to 3'-6" Long.   18"
9"
10" or 10½"   22"
12"   SHELF WIDTHS   1/4" = 1'-0"
FOR BOOKS   FOR NEWSPAPERS

SECTION
All shelves adjustable except bott. shelf, which is occasionally fixed.

Floor   7'-0" to 7'-6" - Recommended   Floor

MULTI-TIER CONSTRUCTION.
1/4" = 1'-0"

Range Aisle 2'-6" to 3'-6" 4'-4" Usual for Books.

PLAN Aisles

3'-0" to 4'-0" Main Aisles

Variable see above 8" shelf most used.

Range   30" max. between aisles. 12'-6" max. from aisle to wall.   2 Lights 6' to 16' o.c. 3'-0" Usually   3'-6" Not over

PLAN 1/4" = 1'-0"

SHELF CAPACITY & WIDTH

Type of Book	Vols. per lin. ft.	Shelf Recom.
Circulating	8	8"
Fiction & Economics	7	8"
History & Gen. Literature	7	8"
Reference	7	8"-10"
Technical-Scientific	6	8"-10"-12"
Medical	6	10"
Law & Public docum'ts.	4	8"
Bound Periodicals	5	10"-12"
U.S. Patent Spec.	2	8"
Cu. Ft. of Book range weighs 25#		

Note: Capacities indicated in the above chart are maximum.

BOOKS - SINGLE-FACED-RANGE   END ELEV.
1/4" = 1'-0"

7'-0" to 7'-6"   These sizes most used for books.

8½" or 8¾"   9½" or 9¾"   10¾"   12½"

BOOK - DOUBLE FACED RANGE   END ELEV.

7'-0" to 7'-6"   These sizes most used for books.

16¼" or 16¾"   18¾"   20½"   24½"

See Mfr's catalogues for exact heights and the design of ends.

7'-0" to 7'-6"

18⅞"   22¾"   37"   44¾"

Single Faced.   Double Faced.

NEWSPAPER RANGES   END ELEVATION.

BOOK STACKS & STACKROOM EQUIPMENT - STEEL & IRON

MINIMUM SIZES *for* BATHS *and* TOILETS

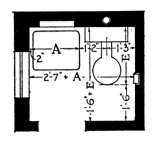
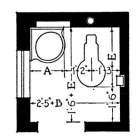
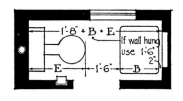
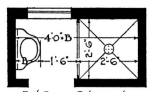

End Recess Tub may be
used in place of Shower

TWO FIXTURE TOILETS

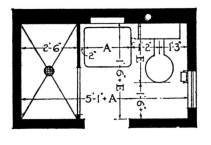
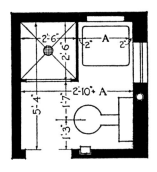
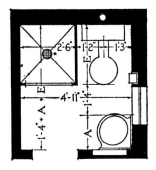
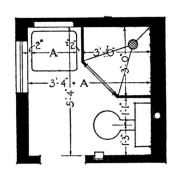

THREE FIXTURE BATHROOMS *with* CLOSET, LAVATORY *and* SHOWER

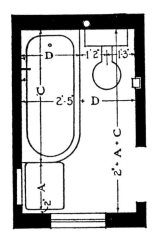
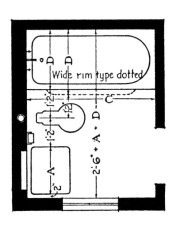
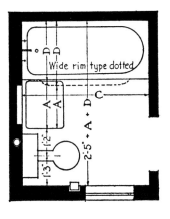
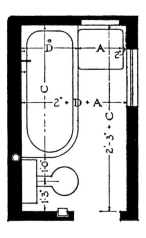

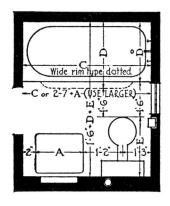
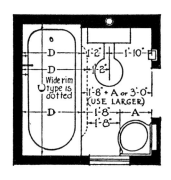
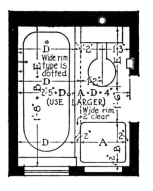
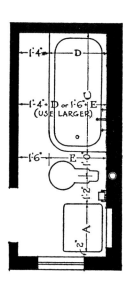

THREE FIXTURE BATHROOMS *with* CLOSET, LAVATORY *and* BATH TUB

Scale ¼" = 1 Foot

STAIRS

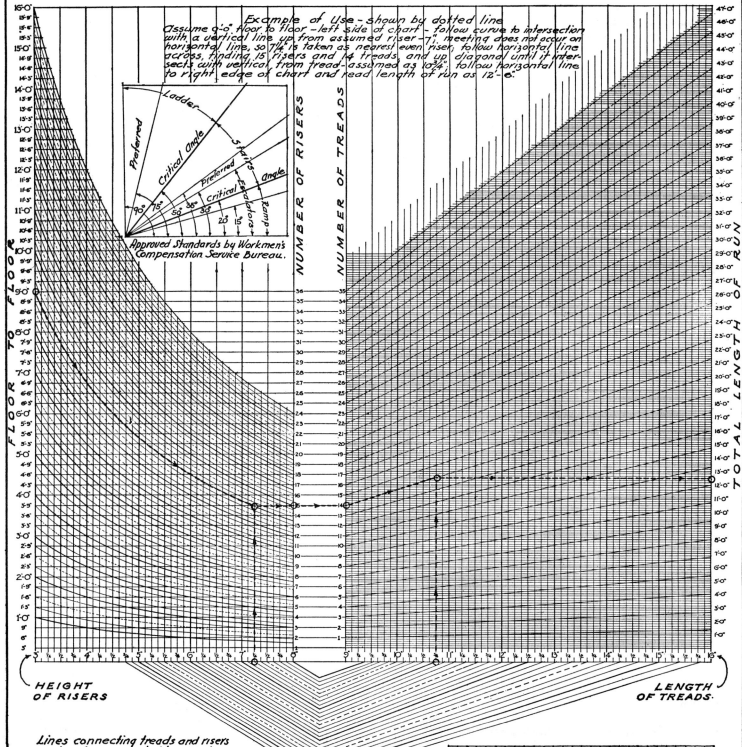

Example of Use - shown by dotted line

Assume 9'-0" floor to floor - left side of chart - follow curve to intersection with a vertical line up from assumed riser - 7"; meeting does not occur on horizontal line, so 7¼" is taken as nearest even riser; follow horizontal line across, finding 15 risers and 14 treads, and up diagonal until it intersects with vertical from tread - assumed as 10¾"; follow horizontal line to right edge of chart and read length of run as 12'-6".

Approved Standards by Workmen's Compensation Service Bureau.

NUMBER OF RISERS

NUMBER OF TREADS

FLOOR TO FLOOR

TOTAL LENGTH OF RUN

HEIGHT OF RISERS

LENGTH OF TREADS.

Lines connecting treads and risers are based on product of tread & riser = 75 (about); these lines may be disregarded and any other rule substituted. They do not apply to exterior stairs.

Another rule commonly used is:—
Run + Riser = 17½; Run equals tread less nosing.
Recommendations:—
Minimum width of tread with nosing = 11", except stairs with open risers.
Maximum width of tread with nosing = 15". Maximum height of riser = 7¾"; minimum = 6".

Table of stair proportions using Formula $\frac{R}{T} = Tan(R-3)8°$

Riser	Tread	Riser	Tread	Riser	Tread
4"	28.3"	5¾"	14.2"	7½"	10.3"
4¼"	24.1"	6"	13.5"	7¾"	9.9"
4½"	21.2"	6¼"	12.8"	8"	9.5"
4¾"	19.1"	6½"	12.2"	8¼"	9.2"
5"	17.4"	6¾"	11.7"	8½"	8.8"
5¼"	16.2"	7"	11.2"	8¾"	8.5"
5½"	15.1"	7¼"	10.7"	9"	8.1"

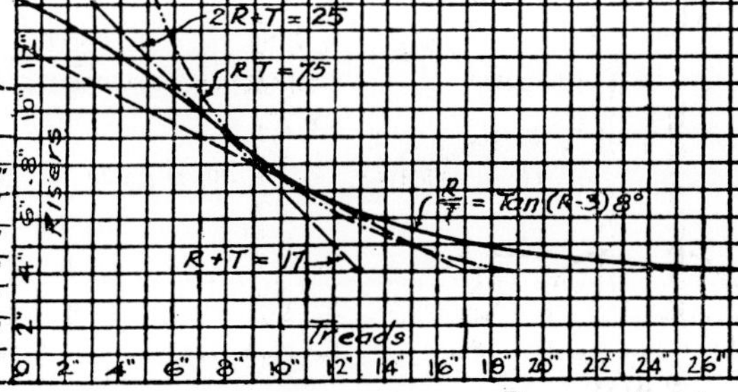

STAIR PROPORTIONS USING FORMULA $\frac{R}{T} = TAN(R-3)8°$

Formula devised by Jamieson Parker. A.I.A.
Reprinted by permission of "Architecture"

Conceived by Frederick L. Ackerman. Architect.

PARK EQUIPMENT

PICNIC BENCHES

2"×6"
2'-6"
7/8 Fascia
1'-6"
1'-6"
2"×4"
2-5/16 bolts
END
1'-0" 10" 1'-0"

6'-0"
4"×4" framing members halved at corners.
2" pipe
2"×6"
2"×6"
Grade
Concrete footings
FRONT
1'-0" 4'-2" 1'-0"
2'-2"

TREE GUARD
10"
PLAN
3/4"=1'-0"
3/4"×3/16 W.I.

GARDEN EDGING
1/4"×4 W.I.
4"×5 steel in 16' lengths
steel stakes

ELEVATION
6'-0"
Equal Equal
Grade
2"×4"
1'-6"

MOVABLE PLAY TABLE
4'-0"
1/4" Joints
2" pipe
Grade
END

6'-0"
2"×6"
1-8"
1 1/2 pipe
FRONT

WICKET GUARD
3/4"=1'-0"
Weld
Spring Line
Weld 1 1/2 long - both sides
Grade
6"
6"×6"×6" con. footing at each end at junction of lengths, and not more than 8'-0" on centers.

C.I. PORCH BENCHES
1'-5 1/4"
2 1/4"×3/4"
1'-6"
1-4 1/4"
END
9'-0"
1/2"ø steel rod
1'-6"
FRONT

BACKLESS BENCHES
2'-0"
A
1'-6"
3/8 round bars 4 to each standard
1'-5"
2'-6"
1'-0"
END

6'-0"
1 1/4"×3/4" wood slats, 1/4" radius rounded edges
10" 4" 3'-8" 4" 10"
Precast concrete standards set in concrete
6" min.
FRONT

BENCH SECTION A
3"=1'-0"
3/8 R.H. brass screw 2" long
Wood plug
Brass expansive screw anchor

FIXED PLAY TABLE
4'-0"
7/8 Fascia
2" pipe
END
1'-0" 2'-2" 1'-0"

6'-0"
4"×4" framing halved at corners
concrete footing
2'-2"
FRONT
1'-0" 4'-2" 1'-0"

FIXED BENCHES
3'-0"
A
A
1'-5 3/4"
5 3/4"
3/8"ø bars, 4 to each standard
2'-5"
4"
END
Grade
4 1/2" 4" 3'-1 1/2" 4" 3'-1 1/2" 4" 4 1/2"
1 1/4"×2 1/2" slats, rounded edges
3/8"ø bars
Precast concrete standards set in concrete
6" min.
1'-0"
FRONT

Scale 3/8"=1'-0" except as noted

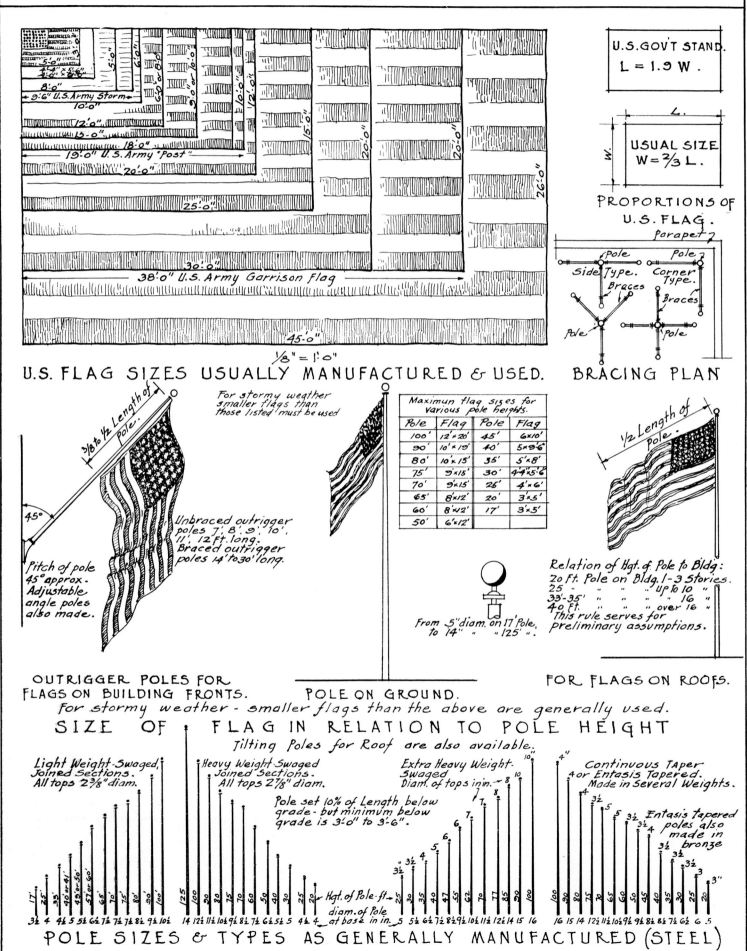

FLAGS & POLES

BOATS & CANOES

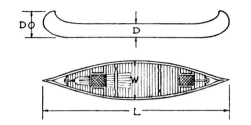

1/8" = 1'-0"

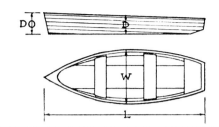

TYPES	L	W	D	DO
One man	9' to 15'	2'-10½"to 3'-0"	11" to 12½"	
Standard	16' to 18'	2'-9" to 3'-1"	12" to 13"	24"
Safety	16' to 18'	3'-5" to 3'-7"	12" to 13"	to
Guides	18' to 20'	3'-0"to 3'-3"	13" to 13½"	28"
War Canoes				
11 Paddles	25'	3'-5"	14½"	
21 ,,	34'	3'-8"	15"	

CANOES

TYPES	L	W	D	DO
Many Types and designs	8'-0" to 16'-0"	3'-8" to 4'-7"	1'-2" to 1'-8"	2'-0" ±
Skiffs are of similar design and sizes, may be of lighter construction				

ROW-BOATS

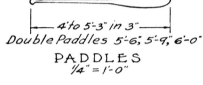

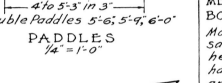

4' to 5'-3" in 3"

Double Paddles 5'-6", 5'-9", 6'-0"

PADDLES
1/4" = 1'-0"

STORAGE REQUIRE-MENTS FOR SAIL-BOAT EQUIPMENT.
Mast spars, sheets, sails (usually in heated space) halyards, buoys, anchor, pump, oars, life preservers, cushions.

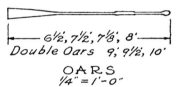

6½", 7½", 7⅞", 8'

Double Oars 9', 9½', 10'

OARS
1/4" = 1'-0"

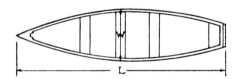

1/8" = 1'-0"

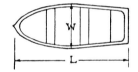

TYPE	L	W	D	DO
Life Saving	18'-0"	4'-6"	20"	23"
Fisherman's	14'-0"	4'-1"		
Average sizes shown				

DORY

L	W	D
7'-6" to 14'-0"	42" to 54"	18" to 20"
Wood or Canvas Covered		

DINGEY or TENDER

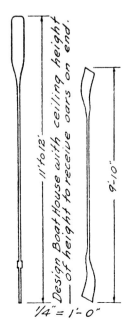

11' to 12'

9'-10"

Design Boat House with ceiling height of height to receive oars on end.

1/4" = 1'-0"

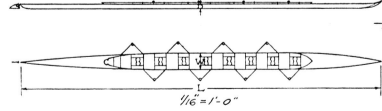

1/16" = 1'-0"

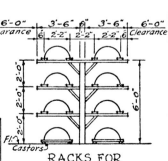

6'-0" Clearance 3'-6" 3'-6" 6'-0" Clearance
6" 2'-2" 2'-2" 2'-2" 6"

2'-0", 2'-0", 2'-0", 2'-0" 6'-0"

Castors

RACKS FOR EIGHTS & FOURS
1/8" = 1'-0"

Notes:
All dimensions minimum
Racks 15'-0" apart
3 for an eight

TYPE	L	W	D	WEIGHT
Single Racing	25' to 27'	12"	6½"	30#
Double ,,	31' to 35'	16"	7"	60#
Four Oared	38' to 47'	21"	8½"	120#
8 Oared Shell	56' to 63'	24"	10"	270#
Practise Gigs	Gigs in all classes, same depth but shorter and wider than shells.			

RACING SHELL & GIG ~ ROWING

MOTOR VEHICLE DATA

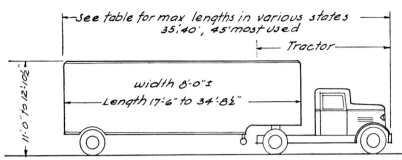

See table for max lengths in various states
35', 40', 45' most used

Tractor

width 8'-0"±

Length 17'-6" to 34'-8½"

11'-0" to 12'-0½"

Max. length	States
40'	Indiana
45'	Ala. Iowa Mass. N.H Pa. Va. Conn. Kans. Minn. N.J. R.I. W.Va. Ga. Ky. Miss. N.D. Tenn. Wis. Ill. Me. Mo. Ohio Tex.
50'	Ark. Fla. Neb. S.C. Del. La. N.Y. S.D. N.C.(48) D.C. Mich. Okla. Vt.
60'	Cal. Mont. Wash. Colo. Ore. Wyo. Md.(55') Idaho Utah
65'	Ariz., N.M. Nevada (no restriction)

In many Western states, combinations of truck and full trailer & tractor-semi-trailer and full trailer
are used to full legal length.

SEMI·TRAILER & TRUCK·TRACTOR
Turning radius of trailer depends on radius of tractor (24'-43')

MAX. STATE LIMITS for
TRUCK·TRACTORS & SEMITRAILERS
(as of April 1, 1948)

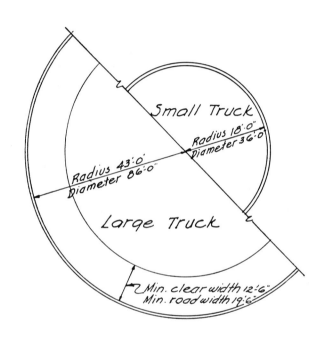

Small Truck

Radius 18'-0"
Diameter 36'-0"

Radius 43'-0"
Diameter 86'-0"

Large Truck

Min. clear width 12'-6"
Min. road width 19'-6"

MOTOR TRUCK
TURNING RADII
Radius is assumed a wall higher than mudguard

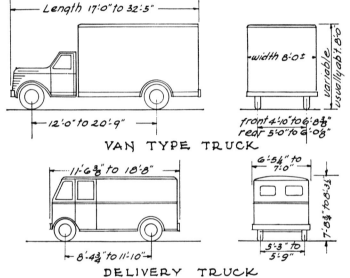

Length 17'-0" to 32'-5"

width 8'-0"±

variable usually abt. 8'-0

front 4'-10" to 6'-8⅜"
rear 5'-0" to 6'-0⅝"

12'-0" to 20'-9"

VAN TYPE TRUCK

11'-6⅜" to 18'-8"

6'-5¼" to 7'-0"

7'-8¾" to 8'-3¼"

8'-4¾" to 11'-10"

5'-3" to 5'-9"

DELIVERY TRUCK

Car
Trailer
Terrace

30'
40'

℄ of town

3' sidewalk

TYPICAL LOT for
A TRAILER PARK *
For trailer coach sizes see
"Automobile Data" page.
1 acre land recommended
for every 25 trailer coaches.

*Recomm. of Trailer Coach Manufacturers Association

DIMENSIONS of MOTOR VEHICLES

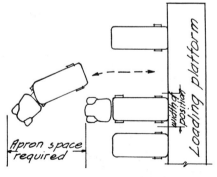

Apron space required

Loading platform

waiting position

Tractor-trailer length	Width of position	Apron space required
35'	10'	46'
	12'	43'
	14'	39'
40'	10'	48'
	12'	44'
	14'	42'
45'	10'	57'
	12'	49'
	14'	48'

Apron space required for one
maneuver into or out of position
for tractor-trailer.

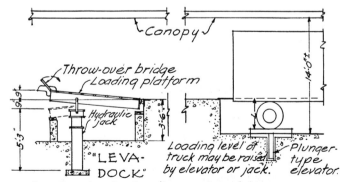

Canopy

Throw-over bridge
Loading platform

Hydraulic jack

14'-0"±

5'-3" 9'-9"

3'-6"

"LEVA-DOCK"

Loading level of
truck may be raised
by elevator or jack.

Plunger-type elevator

Loading levels of trailers ("L") variable from
44" to 50" (48"-50" for heavy-duty units). For
van-type trucks 38"-44" (41"-42" average).
For delivery trucks 25" to 31".

LOADING of MOTOR VEHICLES

MOTOR VEHICLE DATA

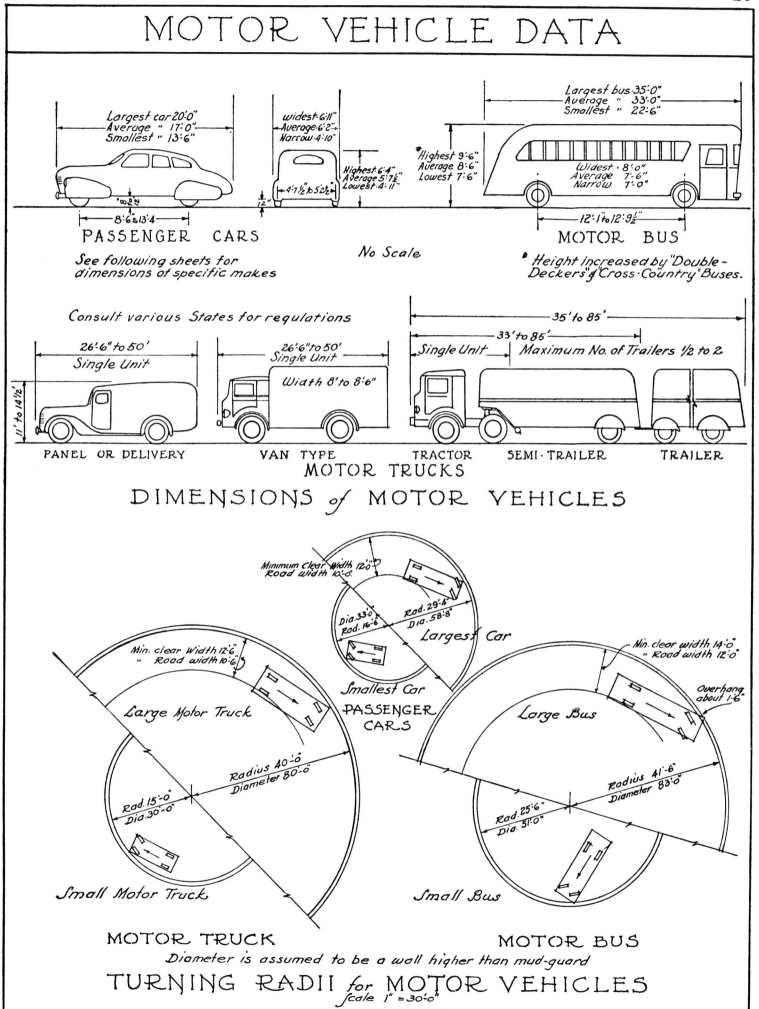

PASSENGER CARS

See following sheets for dimensions of specific makes

No Scale

MOTOR BUS

* Height increased by "Double-Deckers" & "Cross-Country" Buses.

Consult various States for regulations

PANEL OR DELIVERY

VAN TYPE

TRACTOR   SEMI-TRAILER   TRAILER

MOTOR TRUCKS

DIMENSIONS of MOTOR VEHICLES

PASSENGER CARS

Smallest Car

Largest Car

Large Motor Truck

Small Motor Truck

Large Bus

Small Bus

MOTOR TRUCK

MOTOR BUS

Diameter is assumed to be a wall higher than mud-guard

TURNING RADII for MOTOR VEHICLES

Scale 1" = 30'-0"

CARS, TRAILERS and MOTORCYCLES

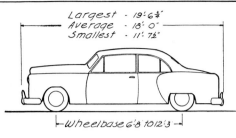

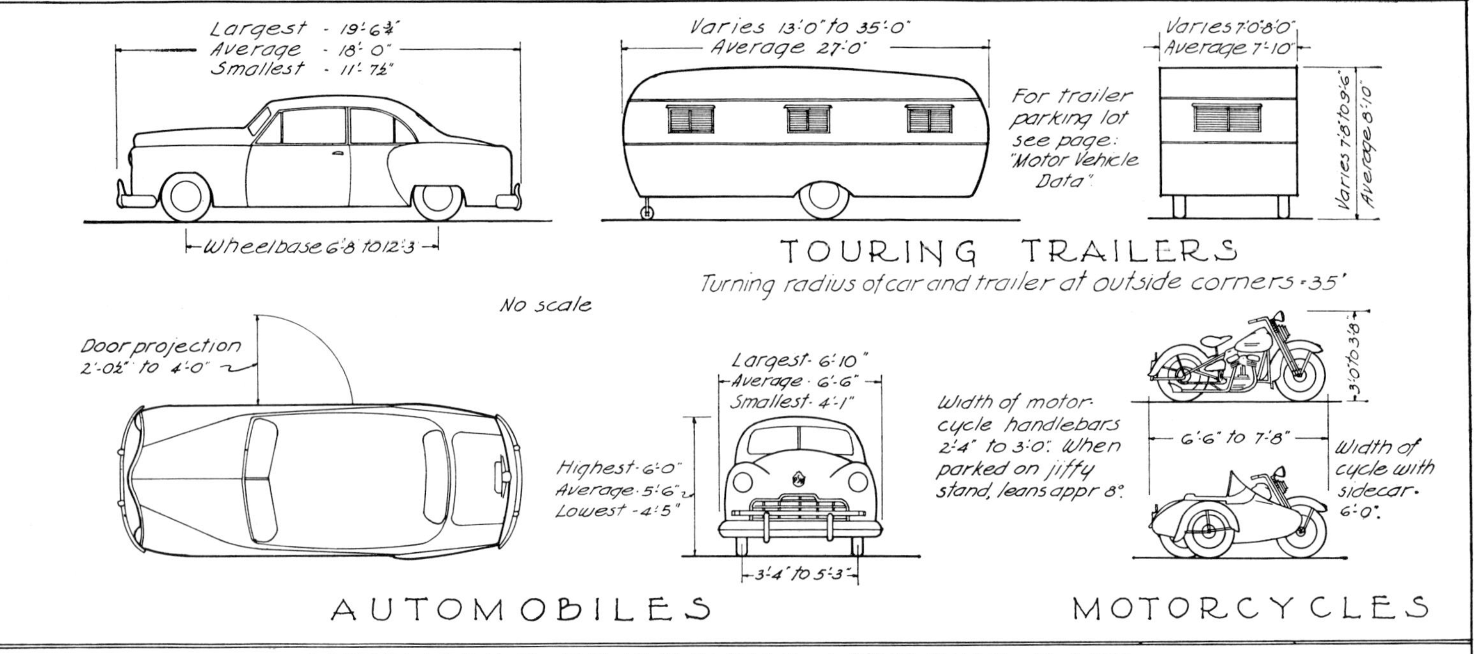

Largest - 19'-6¾"
Average - 18'-0"
Smallest - 11'-7½"
Wheelbase 6'-8" to 12'-3"
Varies 13'-0" to 35'-0"
Average 27'-0"
Varies 7'-0" - 8'-0"
Average 7'-10"
For trailer parking lot see page: "Motor Vehicle Data"
Varies 7'-8" to 9'-6"
Average 8'-10"
TOURING TRAILERS
Turning radius of car and trailer at outside corners = 35'
No scale
Door projection 2'-0½" to 4'-0"
Largest - 6'-10"
Average - 6'-6"
Smallest - 4'-1"
Highest - 6'-0"
Average - 5'-6"
Lowest - 4'-5"
3'-4" to 5'-3"
Width of motorcycle handlebars 2'-4" to 3'-0". When parked on jiffy stand, leans appr 8°.
3'-0" to 3'-6"
6'-6" to 7'-8"
Width of cycle with sidecar - 6'-0".
AUTOMOBILES
MOTORCYCLES

AUTOMOBILE DIMENSIONS & TURNING RADII

	MODEL	YEAR	LENGTH	WIDTH	HEIGHT	T.T.	W.B.	T.R.	D.P.
Austin	A-40		12'-9"	5'-1"	5'-2½"	4'-1½"	7'-8½"	19'-0"	
	A-125		16'-0"	6'-1"	5'-7"	5'-0"	9'-11"	21'-6"	
Bentley			16'-0"	5'-9"	5'-4"	4'-8"	10'-0"	21'-3"	
Buick	Special 40	1948	17'-3½"	6'-5½"	5'-6¾"	5'-2"	10'-1"		
	Super 50	1948	17'-8½"	6'-6¾"	5'-5"	5'-2"	10'-4"		
	Roadm 70	1948	18'-1¼"	6'-6¾"	5'-5¼"	5'-2½"	10'-9"		
	Series 40	1949	17'-3½"	6'-5½"	5'-6¾"	5'-2"	10'-1"	21'-7¼"	3'-11"
	" 50	1949	17'-5½"	6'-6½"	5'-5¼"	5'-2¼"	10'-1"	21'-4¾"	3'-11"
	" 70	1949	17'-10¼"	6'-6½"	5'-5¾"	5'-2¼"	10'-6"	22'-2½"	3'-11"
Cadillac	6	1948	17'-10"	6'-7"	5'-7½"	5'-3"	10'-6"		
	62	1948	17'-10"	6'-7"	5'-7½"	5'-3"	10'-6"		
	60S	1948	18'-9½"	6'-6¼"	5'-7½"	5'-3"	11'-1"		
	75	1948	18'-10"	6'-8¼"	5'-11¼"	5'-2½"	11'-4¼"		
	6107, 6207	1949	17'-11"	6'-8"	5'-2"	5'-3"	10'-6"	23'-4¾"	3'-10½"
	6169, 6269	1949	17'-11"	6'-7"	5'-3½"	5'-3"	10'-6"	23'-4¾"	3'-1"
	6267	1949	17'-11"	6'-8"	5'-1¼"	5'-3"	10'-6"	23'-4¾"	3'-10½"
	6069	1949	18'-10¾"	6'-6¼"	5'-3½"	5'-3"	11'-1"	24'-3½"	3'-1½"
	Series 75	1949	18'-10"	6'-10"	5'-8¼"	5'-2½"	11'-4¼"	24'-4¾"	2'-5"
Chevrolet	FJ-FR	1948	16'-5¾"	6'-0¾"	5'-9½"	5'-0"	9'-8"		
	Styleline	1949	16'-5"	6'-2"	5'-6"	4'-10¾"	9'-7"	20'-10½"	3'-0¾"
	Fleetline	1949	16'-5"	6'-2"	5'-6"	4'-10¾"	9'-7"	20'-10½"	3'-1¼"
	Sta. Wagon	1949	16'-7"	6'-2"	5'-8"	4'-10¾"	9'-7"	20'-10½"	2'-9¾"
Chrysler	C-38	1948	17'-6¾"	6'-5¾"		5'-0¼"	10'-1½"		
	C-39	1948	18'-0¾"	6'-5¾"		5'-1¼"	10'-7½"		
	C-40	1948	19'-6¾"	6'-5¾"		5'-2"	12'-1½"		
	C-45	1949	18'-6¾"	6'-2¾"	5'-8¾"	5'-3"	11'-7½"		3'-10½"
	C-46	1949	18'-6¾"	6'-8"	5'-6"	5'-3"	10'-11½"		3'-10"
	C-47	1949	19'-2¼"	6'-8"	5'-9¼"	5'-3¾"	12'-1½"		
Crosley		'48 & '49	12'-1"	4'-1"	4'-9"	3'-4"	6'-8"	15'-0"	3'-5"
Daimler	8		18'-6"	6'-2"	6'-0"	5'-3"	12'-3"		
	27		17'-9"	6'-2"	6'-0"	5'-3"	11'-6"		
DeSoto	S-11	1948	17'-3¼"	6'-3¾"		5'-0¼"	10'-1½"		
	S-13	1949	18'-6¾"	6'-2¾"	5'-8¾"	5'-3"	11'-7½"		3'-11"
Dodge	D-24	1948		6'-3¾"		5'-0¼"	9'-11½"		
	D-29	1949	16'-5¼"	6'-0½"	5'-5"	4'-9"	9'-7"		3'-11"
	D-30	1949	18'-4¾"	6'-2¾"	5'-8¾"	5'-3"	11'-5½"		3'-11"
Ford	87 HA	1948	16'-4¼"	6'-1¼"	5'-6¼"	5'-0"	9'-6"		
	89 A	1948	16'-6"	6'-1¼"	5'-6¼"	5'-0"	9'-6"		
		1949	16'-4¾"	6'-0¾"	5'-4¾"	4'-8"	9'-6"	21'-10¾"	3'-3"
	Sta. Wagon	1949	17'-4"	6'-4½"	5'-10½"	5'-0"	9'-6"	21'-10¾"	3'-6¼"
Frazer	F485-F486	1948	16'-11"	6'-1"	5'-4½"	5'-0"	10'-3½"		
	All	1949	17'-3½"	6'-1"	5'-4½"	5'-0"	10'-3½"	22'-6"	2'-11"
Hillman	Minx		13'-3¼"	5'-1¾"	5'-0"	4'-0¾"	7'-9"	16'-6"	2'-9¼"
Humber	Pullman		17'-6½"	6'-2½"	5'-9"	5'-2¼"	10'-11"	24'-0"	2'-6¼"
Hudson	6481-482	1948	17'-3½"	6'-5½"	5'-0¼"	4'-10½"	10'-4"		
	8,482-483	1948	17'-3½"	6'-5½"	5'-0¼"	4'-10½"	10'-3"		
	490	1949	17'-3½"	6'-5"	5'-0"	4'-10½"	10'-4"	21'-10"	3'-9½"
Jaguar	1½ litre		15'-1"	5'-6"	5'-0"	4'-7"	9'-4½"		
	2½ & 3½ litre		15'-6"	5'-6"	5'-1"	4'-8"	10'-0"	19'-0"	
Kaiser	K481-K482	1948	16'-11"	6'-1"	5'-4½"	5'-0"	10'-3½"		
	All	1949	17'-2½"	6'-1"	5'-4½"	5'-0"	10'-3½"	22'-6"	2'-11"
Lancia	Aprilia		12'-11"	4'-9½"		4'-2"	9'-0½"		
Lincoln	876 H	1948	18'-2"	6'-5¾"	5'-7¼"	5'-0¾"	10'-5"		
	–	1949	17'-9"	6'-4½"	5'-5"	5'-0"	10'-1"	28'-7¼"	3'-3¾"
	Cosmopol.	1949	18'-4½"	6'-5¾"	5'-3¾"	5'-0"	10'-5"	28'-7¼"	3'-6½"
Mercury	89 M	1948	16'-9¼"	6'-1¾"	5'-9"	5'-0"	9'-10"		
	–	1949	17'-2¾"	6'-4½"	5'-4¾"	5'-0"	9'-10"	27'-2"	3'-3¾"
	Sta. Wagon	1949	17'-9¼"	6'-4½"	5'-7½"	5'-0"	9'-10"	27'-2"	3'-4½"
M.G.	Midget		11'-7½"	4'-8"	4'-5"				
Nash	600-4840	1948	16'-8"	6'-2½"	5'-8¼"	4'-11¾"	9'-4"		
	Amb. 4860	1949	17'-5¼"	6'-3½"	5'-9¼"	5'-0½"	10'-1"		
	600-4940	1949	16'-9"	6'-5½"	5'-2"	4'-11¾"	9'-4"	20'-2"	3'-5"
	Amb. 4960	1949	17'-6"	6'-5½"	5'-2"	5'-0½"	10'-1"	21'-4"	3'-5"
Oldsmobile	60-66	1948	17'-0"	6'-3¼"	5'-7¾"	5'-1½"	9'-11"		
	70-76	1948	17'-9"	6'-4"	5'-5"	5'-1½"	10'-5"		
	60-68	1948	17'-0"	6'-3¼"	5'-7¾"	5'-1½"	9'-11"		
	70-78	1948	17'-9"	6'-4"	5'-5"	5'-1½"	10'-5"		
	98	'48 & '49	17'-9"	6'-6¾"	5'-4"	5'-1½"	10'-5"	21'-0"	4'-1"
	76	1949	16'-10"	6'-3¼"	5'-2½"	4'-11"	9'-11½"	20'-0"	3'-4"
	88	1949	16'-10"	6'-3¼"	5'-3½"	4'-11"	9'-11½"	20'-0"	3'-4¼"
Packard	8	1948	17'-0¾"	6'-5½"	5'-4"	5'-0½"	10'-0"		
	Super 8	1948	17'-0¾"	6'-5½"	5'-4"	5'-0¾"	10'-0"		
	Custom 8	1948	17'-8¾"	6'-5½"	5'-4"	5'-0¾"	10'-7"		
	8 & Super 8	1949	17'-0¾"	6'-5½"	5'-4¼"	5'-0¾"	10'-0"	23'-4"	4'-0"
	Custom 8	1949	17'-8¾"	6'-5½"	5'-4¼"	5'-0¾"	10'-0"	23'-10"	4'-0"
Plymouth	P-15	1948	16'-2¾"	6'-1¾"		5'-0¼"	9'-9"		
	P-17	1949	15'-5¾"	5'-11"	5'-5"	4'-8"	9'-3"		3'-8¾"
	P-18	1949	16'-4"	5'-11¾"	5'-7½"	4'-8"	9'-10½"		3'-8¼"
Pontiac	6-25	1948	16'-0½"	6'-3¾"	5'-6"	5'-1½"	9'-11"		
	6-26	1948	16'-6¼"	6'-4¾"	5'-5¼"	5'-1½"	10'-2"		
	8-27	1948	16'-0½"	6'-3¾"	5'-6"	5'-1½"	9'-11"		
	8-28	1948	16'-6¼"	6'-4¾"	5'-5¼"	5'-1½"	10'-2"		
	All	1949	17'-0"	6'-2"	5'-6½"	4'-11"	10'-0"	21'-9"	3'-5"
Renault	4 C.V.		11'-9½"		4'-9"		6'-10½"		
	49		11'-9½"	4'-8"	4'-8"	3'-11"	6'-11"		
Rolls Royce			17'-6"	6'-0"	6'-0"	4'-10"	10'-7"	22'-6"	
Studebaker	7G	1948	15'-10¾"	5'-9½"	5'-0¾"	4'-8¼"	9'-4"		
	15 A	1948	16'-4½"	5'-9½"	5'-1¾"	4'-7"	10'-3"		
	8G	1949	16'-0"	5'-9½"	5'-1¼"	4'-10½"	9'-4"	21'-8½"	3'-1¼"
	16A-Comm.	1949	17'-1½"	5'-9½"	5'-1¾"	4'-8¼"	9'-11"	21'-4"	3'-1¼"
	16A-La.Cr.	1949	17'-5½"	5'-9½"	5'-1¾"	4'-7"	10'-3"	22'-0¾"	2'-7¼"
Willys	663	1948	14'-8½"	5'-8¾"	6'-0¼"	4'-9"	8'-8"		
	Jeep	1949	10'-2¾"	4'-11"	5'-9½"	4'-0¼"	6'-8"	19'-0"	2'-0½"
	Sta. Wag.	1949	14'-6¾"	5'-8"	5'-11"	4'-9"	8'-8"	18'-6"	2'-2"

Where not noted, sizes are for largest models by each manufacturer. Abbreviations used: T.T. = tire tread (c. to c.); W.B. = wheelbase; T.R. = turning radius of smallest walled-in circle in which car can turn; D.P. = projection beyond width of car of one door when fully open. If difference exists between door projections, tire treads, or turning radii for any one model, largest size is shown.

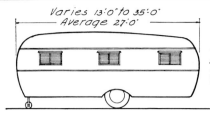

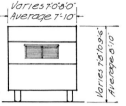

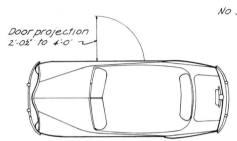

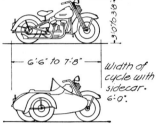

BUS DATA

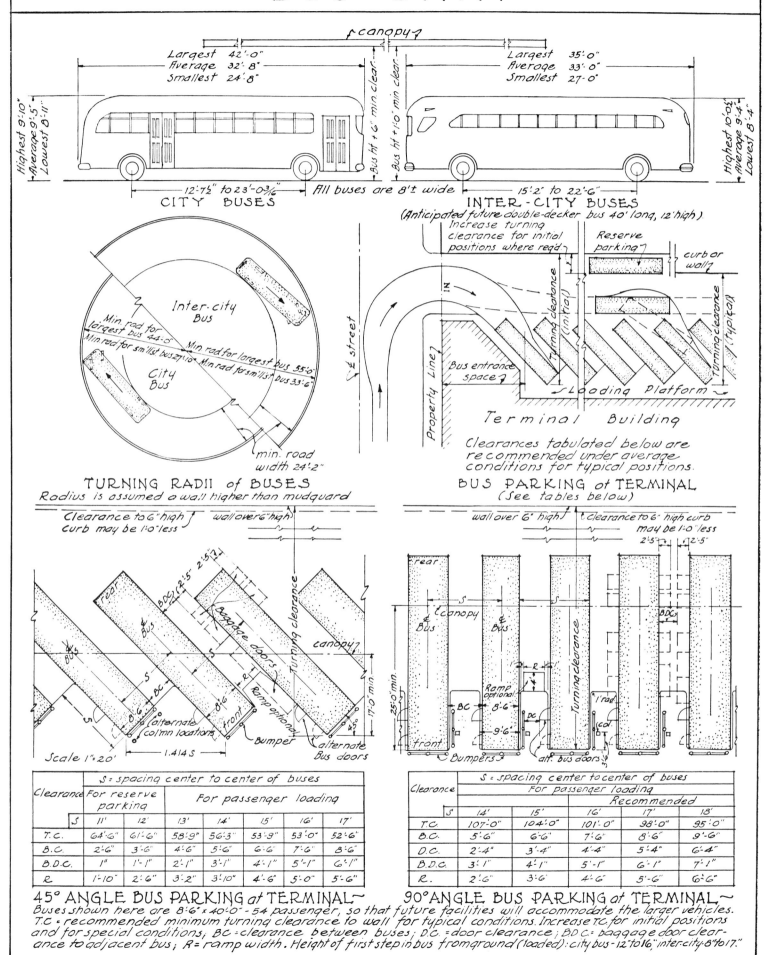

CITY BUSES

Largest 42'-0"
Average 32'-8"
Smallest 24'-8"

Highest 9'-10"
Average 9'-5"
Lowest 8'-11"

12'-7½" to 23'-0 3/16" All buses are 8'± wide

INTER-CITY BUSES
(Anticipated future double-decker bus 40' long, 12' high)

Largest 35'-0"
Average 33'-0"
Smallest 27'-0"

Highest 10'-0"
Average 9'-4"
Lowest 8'-4"

15'-2" to 22'-6"

TURNING RADII of BUSES
Radius is assumed a wall higher than mudguard

Inter-city Bus — Min. rad for largest bus 44'-0" — Min rad for sm'llst bus 27'-10"
City Bus — Min rad for largest bus 55'-0" — Min rad for sm'llst bus 33'-6"
min. road width 24'-2"

BUS PARKING at TERMINAL
(See tables below)

Clearances tabulated below are recommended under average conditions for typical positions.

45° ANGLE BUS PARKING at TERMINAL~

Clearance	For reserve parking		For passenger loading				
S	11'	12'	13'	14'	15'	16'	17'
T.C.	64'-6"	61'-6"	58'-9"	56'-3"	53'-9"	53'-0"	52'-6"
B.C.	2'-6"	3'-6"	4'-6"	5'-6"	6'-6"	7'-6"	8'-6"
B.D.C.	1"	1'-1"	2'-1"	3'-1"	4'-1"	5'-1"	6'-1"
R	1'-10"	2'-6"	3'-2"	3'-10"	4'-6"	5'-0"	5'-6"

90° ANGLE BUS PARKING at TERMINAL~

Clearance	S = spacing center to center of buses For passenger loading Recommended				
S	14'	15'	16'	17'	18'
T.C.	107'-0"	104'-0"	101'-0"	98'-0"	95'-0"
B.C.	5'-6"	6'-6"	7'-6"	8'-6"	9'-6"
D.C.	2'-4"	3'-4"	4'-4"	5'-4"	6'-4"
B.D.C.	3'-1"	4'-1"	5'-1"	6'-1"	7'-1"
R.	2'-6"	3'-6"	4'-6"	5'-6"	6'-6"

Buses shown here are 8'-6" x 40'-0" - 54 passenger, so that future facilities will accommodate the larger vehicles. T.C.= recommended minimum turning clearance to wall for typical conditions. Increase T.C. for initial positions and for special conditions; B.C.= clearance between buses; D.C.= door clearance; B.D.C.= baggage door clearance to adjacent bus; R= ramp width. Height of first step in bus from ground (loaded): city bus-12" to 16", inter-city-8" to 17".

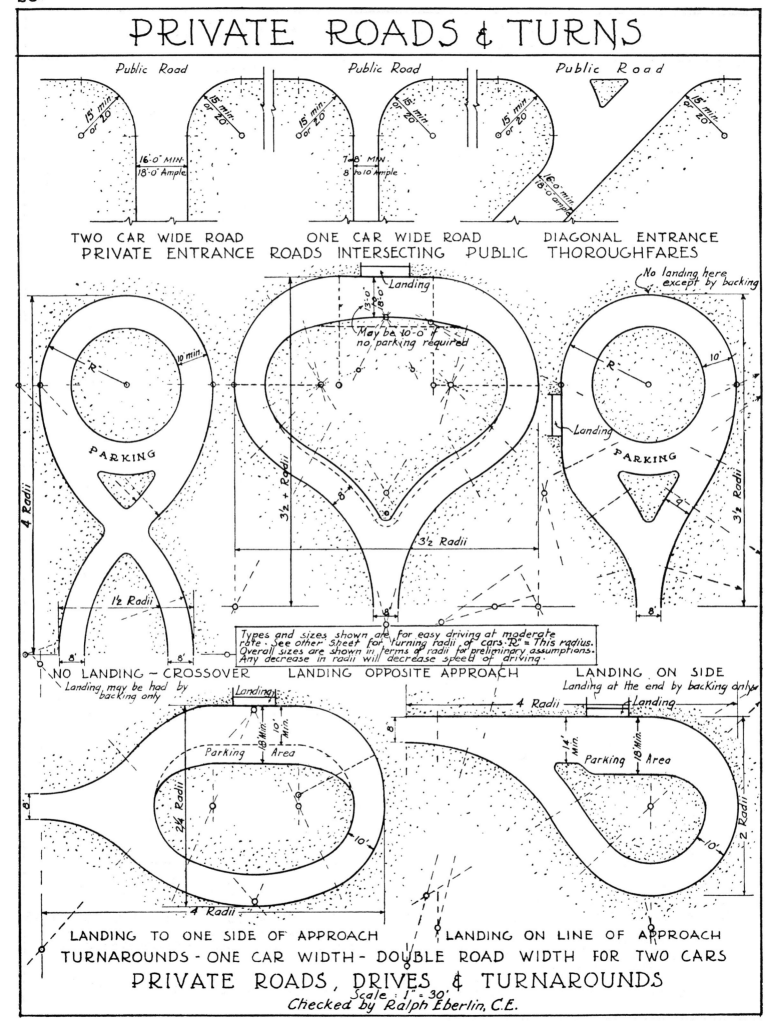

PRIVATE ROADS & TURNS

PRIVATE ROADS, DRIVES & TURNAROUNDS
Scale: 1" = 30'
Checked by Ralph Eberlin, C.E.

27

GARAGE ROADS & TURNS

Note:
All turns require 1'-6" clearance beyond road line shown. These turns are for easy driving with average size car. Larger radii will permit faster & easier driving. Smaller radii should be used for small cars only.

This dimension equals wheelbase—between 8'-7" & 12'-7" for most cars less than 11'-0"

"Y" TURN FOR BACKING IN
Dotted line shows route going in
Scale: 1/16" = 1'-0"

"Y" TURN FOR BACKING OUT
Dotted line shows route going out
Scale: 1/16" = 1'-0"

Employed only where space limitations demand its use.

Wheelbase Minimum 8'-7"
do. Maximum 12'-7"
normally under 11'-0"

MINIMUM TURNING SPACE-BACKING THREE TIMES

Do not use curbs on narrower runways as trucks often have 5'-10" to 6'-0" wheel gauge

MINIMUM

AVERAGE

WIDE

5'-0" Average Gauge

CONCRETE RUNWAYS TO GARAGES
Widen for all turns

DOUBLE Y TURN REQUIRING BACKING BOTH WAYS
Exact size depends on car. This is for average car
Employed only where space limitations demand its use.

ROADS AND TURNS FOR PRIVATE GARAGES

STABLES

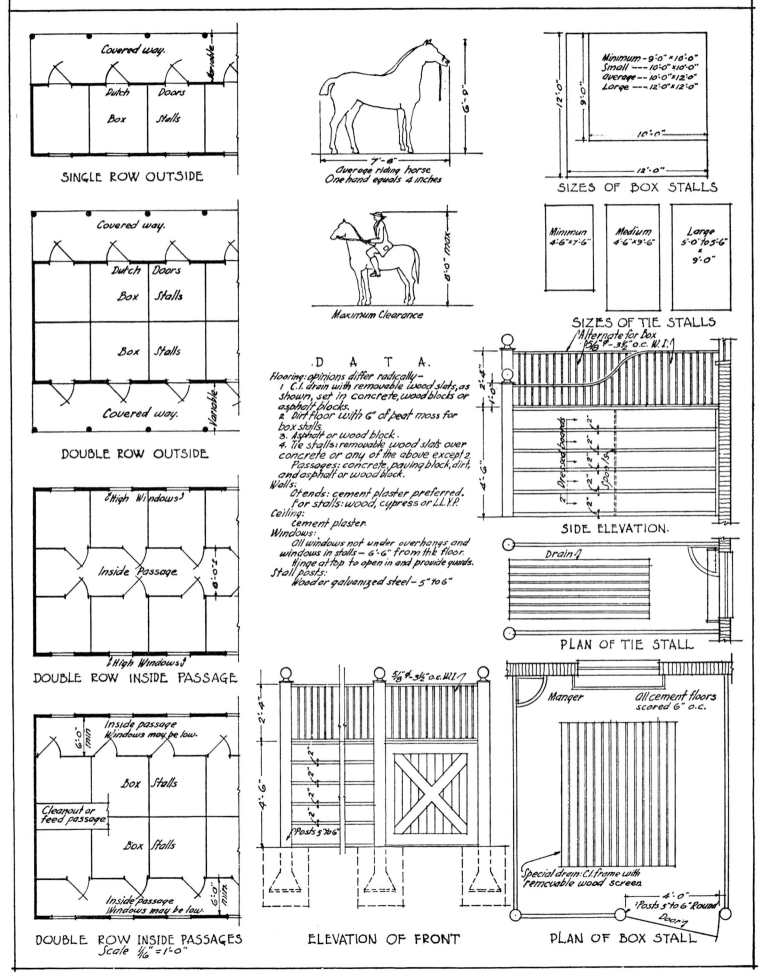

SINGLE ROW OUTSIDE

Covered way.
Dutch Doors
Box Stalls

DOUBLE ROW OUTSIDE

Covered way.
Dutch Doors
Box Stalls
Box Stalls
Covered way.

DOUBLE ROW INSIDE PASSAGE

High Windows
Inside Passage
High Windows

DOUBLE ROW INSIDE PASSAGES
Scale 1/16" = 1'-0"

Inside passage
Windows may be low.
Box Stalls
Cleanout or feed passage
Box Stalls
Inside passage
Windows may be low.

Average riding horse
One hand equals 4 inches

Maximum Clearance

.D A T A.

Flooring: opinions differ radically—
1. C.I. drain with removable wood slats, as shown, set in concrete, wood blocks or asphalt blocks.
2. Dirt floor with 6" of peat moss for box stalls.
3. Asphalt or wood block.
4. Tie stalls: removable wood slats over concrete or any of the above except 2.
Passages: concrete, paving block, dirt, and asphalt or wood block.
Walls:
At ends: cement plaster preferred.
For stalls: wood, cypress or L.L.Y.P.
Ceiling:
cement plaster.
Windows:
All windows not under overhangs and windows in stalls — 6'-6" from the floor.
Hinge at top to open in and provide guards.
Stall posts:
Wood or galvanized steel — 5" to 6"

SIZES OF BOX STALLS

Minimum — 9'-0" x 10'-0"
Small — 10'-0" x 10'-0"
Average — 10'-0" x 12'-0"
Large — 12'-0" x 12'-0"

SIZES OF TIE STALLS

Minimum 4'-6" x 7'-6"
Medium 4'-6" x 9'-6"
Large 5'-0" to 5'-6" x 9'-0"

SIDE ELEVATION.

Drain
PLAN OF TIE STALL

Manger
All cement floors scored 6" o.c.

Special drain: C.I. frame with removable wood screen.
Posts 5 to 6" Round
Door
PLAN OF BOX STALL

ELEVATION OF FRONT

2

FOUNDATIONS AND SITEWORK

PILES

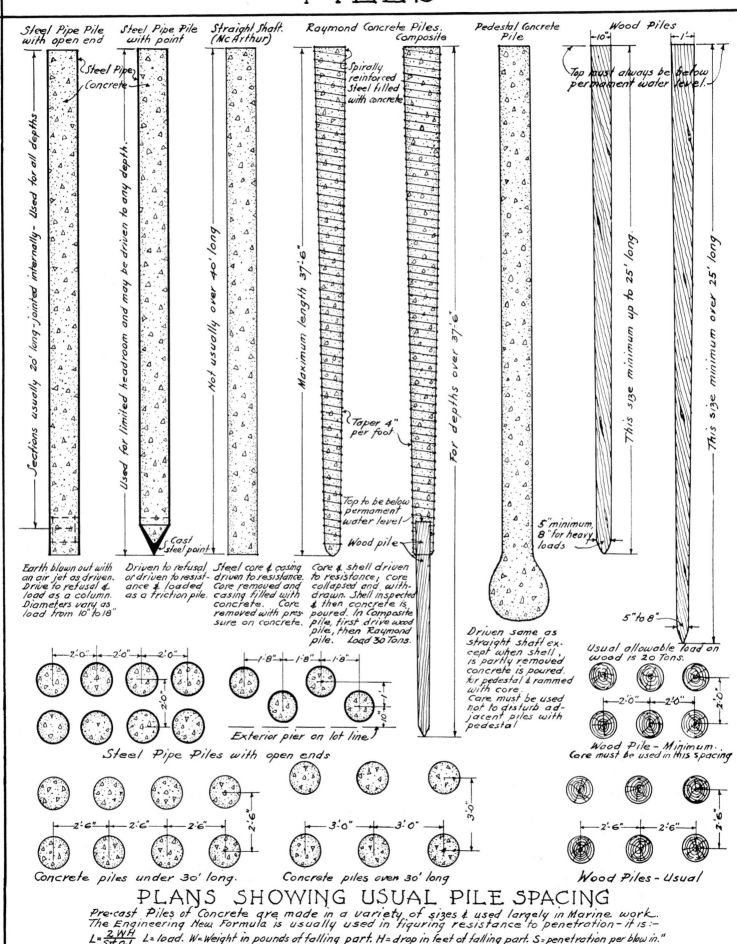

Steel Pipe Pile with open end

Sections usually 20' long-jointed internally - Used for all depths

Steel Pipe · Concrete

Earth blown out with an air jet as driven. Drive to refusal & load as a column. Diameters vary as load from 10" to 18"

Steel Pipe Pile with point

Used for limited headroom and may be driven to any depth.

Cast steel point

Driven to refusal or driven to resistance & loaded as a friction pile.

Straight Shaft. (McArthur)

Not usually over 40' long

Steel core & casing driven to resistance. Core removed and casing filled with concrete. Core removed with pressure on concrete.

Raymond Concrete Piles.

Spirally reinforced Steel filled with concrete

Maximum length 37'-6"

Taper 4" per foot

Top to be below permanent water level

Wood pile

Core & shell driven to resistance; core collapsed and withdrawn. Shell inspected & then concrete is poured. In Composite pile, first drive wood pile, then Raymond pile. Load 30 Tons.

Composite

For depths over 37'-6"

Driven same as straight shaft except when shell is partly removed concrete is poured for pedestal & rammed with core. Care must be used not to disturb adjacent piles with pedestal

Pedestal Concrete Pile

5" minimum, 8" for heavy loads

Wood Piles

10'

1'

Top must always be below permanent water level.

This size minimum up to 25' long.

This size minimum over 25' long.

5" to 8"

Usual allowable load on wood is 20 Tons.

PLANS SHOWING USUAL PILE SPACING

2'-0" 2'-0" 2'-0"

2'-0"

Steel Pipe Piles with open ends

1'-8" 1'-8" 1'-8"

10'

Exterior pier on lot line.

Wood Pile - Minimum. Care must be used in this spacing

2'-6" 2'-6" 2'-6"

2'-6"

Concrete piles under 30' long.

3'-0" 3'-0"

3'-0"

Concrete piles over 30' long

2'-0" 2'-0"

2'-0"

2'-6" 2'-6"

2'-6"

Wood Piles - Usual

Pre-cast Piles of Concrete are made in a variety of sizes & used largely in Marine work.
The Engineering News Formula is usually used in figuring resistance to penetration - it is :-

$$L = \frac{2WH}{S+0.1}$$ L = load. W = Weight in pounds of falling part. H = drop in feet of falling part. S = penetration per blow in."

A #1 Steamhammer has weight of 5000 lbs falling 36". A #2 steamhammer has weight of 3000 lbs falling 30"

Approved by Elwyn E. Seelye, Consulting Engineer.

1/4" = 1'-0"

BRICK PAVING

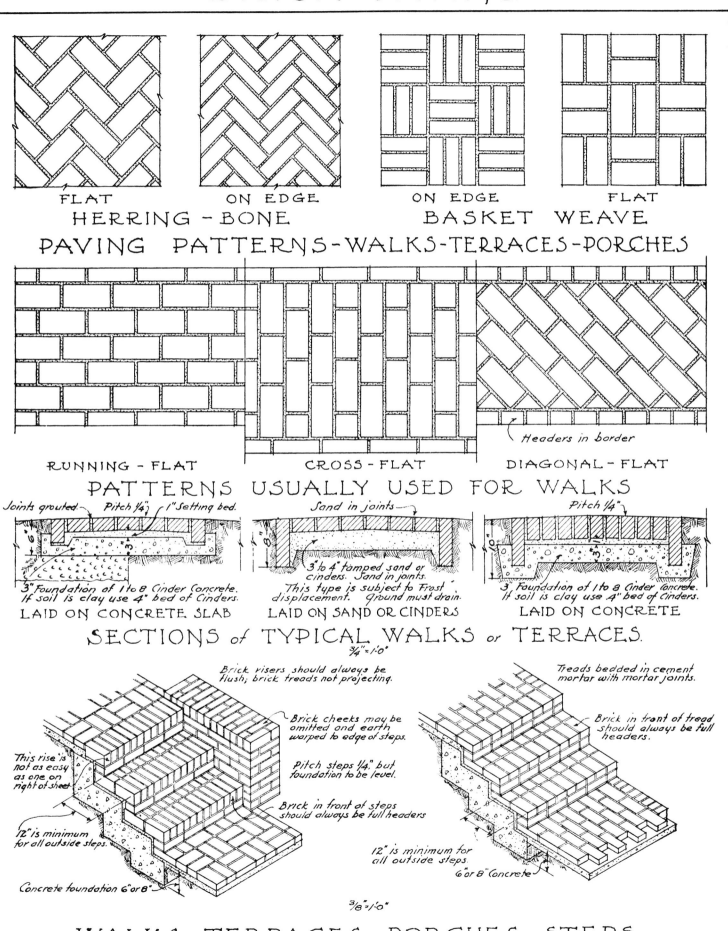

FLAT   ON EDGE   ON EDGE   FLAT

HERRING - BONE   BASKET WEAVE

PAVING PATTERNS - WALKS - TERRACES - PORCHES

Headers in border

RUNNING - FLAT   CROSS - FLAT   DIAGONAL - FLAT

PATTERNS USUALLY USED FOR WALKS

Joints grouted.   Pitch 1/4"   1" Setting bed.   Sand in joints   Pitch 1/4"

3" Foundation of 1 to 8 Cinder Concrete. If soil is clay use 4" bed of Cinders.

3" to 4" tamped sand or cinders. Sand in joints. This type is subject to Frost displacement. Ground must drain.

3" Foundation of 1 to 8 Cinder Concrete. If soil is clay use 4" bed of Cinders.

LAID ON CONCRETE SLAB   LAID ON SAND OR CINDERS   LAID ON CONCRETE

SECTIONS of TYPICAL WALKS or TERRACES.

3/4" = 1'-0"

Brick risers should always be flush; brick treads not projecting.

Treads bedded in cement mortar with mortar joints.

Brick cheeks may be omitted and earth warped to edge of steps.

Brick in front of tread should always be full headers.

This rise is not as easy as one on right of sheet

Pitch steps 1/4" but foundation to be level.

Brick in front of steps should always be full headers

12" is minimum for all outside steps.

12" is minimum for all outside steps.

6" or 8" Concrete

Concrete foundation 6" or 8"

3/8" = 1'-0"

WALKS - TERRACES - PORCHES - STEPS.

Recommendations of the Common Brick Manufacturers Association of America.

RETAINING WALLS

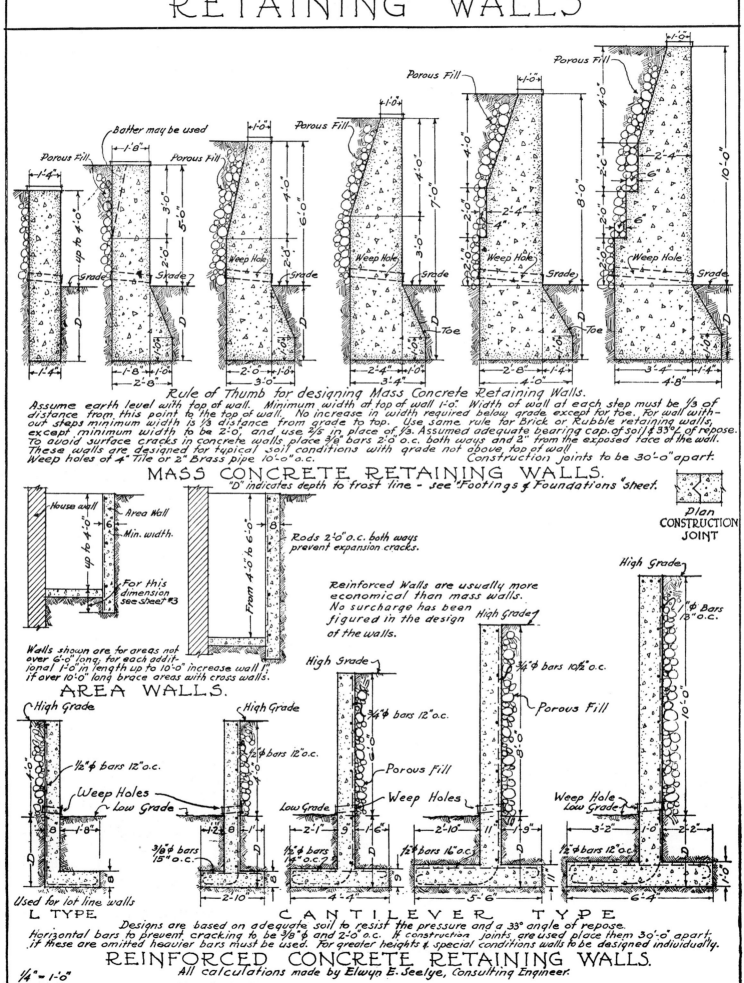

Rule of Thumb for designing Mass Concrete Retaining Walls.

Assume earth level with top of wall. Minimum width at top of wall 1'-0". Width of wall at each step must be ⅓ of distance from this point to the top of wall. No increase in width required below grade except for toe. For wall without steps minimum width is ⅓ distance from grade to top. Use same rule for Brick or Rubble retaining walls, except minimum width to be 2'-0", and use ⅖ in place of ⅓. Assumed adequate bearing cap. of soil & 33°∠ of repose. To avoid surface cracks in concrete walls place ⅜" bars 2'-0" o.c. both ways and 2" from the exposed face of the wall. These walls are designed for typical soil conditions with grade not above top of wall.
Weep holes of 4" Tile or 2" Brass pipe 10'-0" o.c.   Construction joints to be 30'-0" apart.

MASS CONCRETE RETAINING WALLS.
"D" indicates depth to frost line – see "Footings & Foundations" sheet.

Plan CONSTRUCTION JOINT

House wall   Area Wall   Min. width.
For this dimension see sheet #3

Rods 2'-0" o.c. both ways prevent expansion cracks.

Reinforced Walls are usually more economical than mass walls. No surcharge has been figured in the design of the walls.

Walls shown are for areas not over 6'-0" long; for each additional 1'-0" in length up to 10'-0" increase wall 1"; if over 10'-0" long brace areas with cross walls.

AREA WALLS.

High Grade   High Grade   High Grade   High Grade   High Grade

½"∅ bars 12"o.c.   ½"∅ bars 12"o.c.   ¾"∅ bars 12"o.c.   ¾"∅ bars 10½"o.c.   1"∅ Bars 18"o.c.

Weep Holes   Low Grade   Porous Fill   Porous Fill

⅜"∅ bars 15"o.c.   ½"∅ bars 14"o.c.   ½"∅ bars 16"o.c.   ½"∅ bars 12"o.c.

Used for lot line walls
L TYPE   **CANTILEVER TYPE**

Designs are based on adequate soil to resist the pressure and a 33° angle of repose. Horizontal bars to prevent cracking to be ⅜"∅ and 2'-0" o.c. If construction joints are used place them 30'-0" apart. If these are omitted heavier bars must be used. For greater heights & special conditions walls to be designed individually.

REINFORCED CONCRETE RETAINING WALLS.
All calculations made by Elwyn E. Seelye, Consulting Engineer.

¼" = 1'-0"

ROADS & PAVING

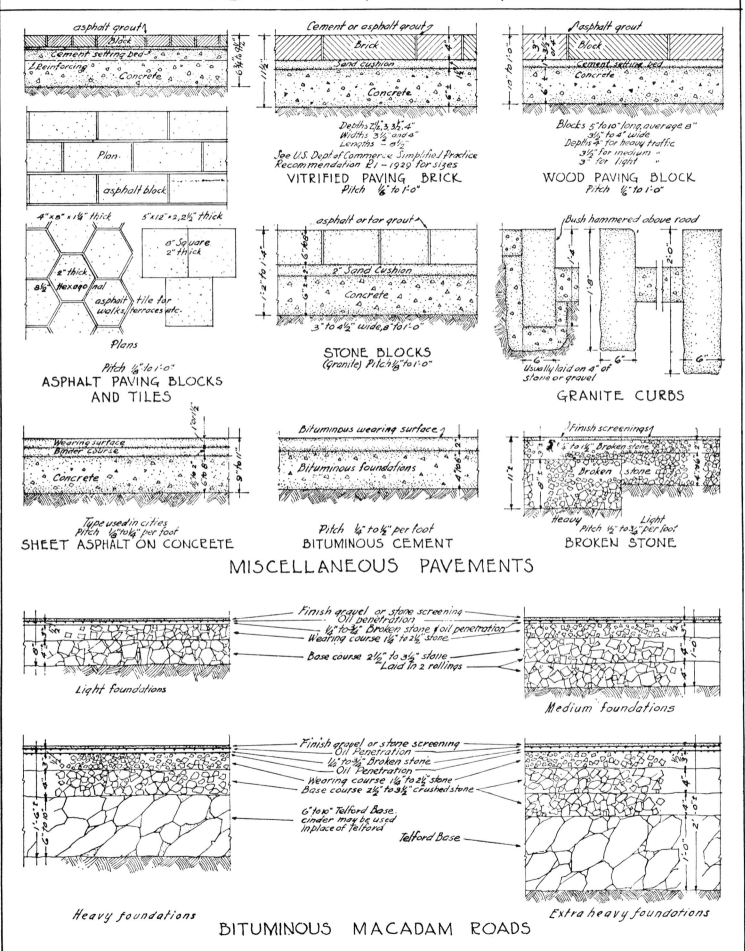

ASPHALT PAVING BLOCKS AND TILES

asphalt grout
Block
Cement setting bed
Reinforcing
Concrete

Plan.

asphalt block

4"x8" x1¼" thick
5"x12" x2,2½" thick

8" Square
2" thick

2" thick
8½" Hexagonal

asphalt tile for walks, terraces etc.

Plans

Pitch ⅛" to 1'-0"

VITRIFIED PAVING BRICK
Pitch ⅛" to 1'-0"

Cement or asphalt grout
Brick
Sand cushion
Concrete

Depths 2½", 3, 3½", 4"
Widths 3½" and 4"
Lengths - 8½"
See U.S. Dept of Commerce Simplified Practice
Recommendation R1 - 1929 for sizes

WOOD PAVING BLOCK
Pitch ⅛" to 1'-0"

asphalt grout
Block
Cement setting bed
Concrete

Blocks 5" to 10" long, average 8"
3½" to 4" wide
Depths 4" for heavy traffic
3½" for medium "
3" for light "

STONE BLOCKS
(Granite) Pitch ⅛" to 1'-0"

asphalt or tar grout
2" Sand Cushion
Concrete

3" to 4½" wide, 8" to 1'-0"

GRANITE CURBS

Bush hammered above road

Usually laid on 4" of stone or gravel

MISCELLANEOUS PAVEMENTS

SHEET ASPHALT ON CONCRETE

Wearing surface
Binder course
Concrete

Type used in cities
Pitch ⅛" to ¼" per foot

BITUMINOUS CEMENT

Bituminous wearing surface
Bituminous foundations

Pitch ¼" to ½" per foot

BROKEN STONE

Finish screenings
Broken stone
Broken stone

Heavy   Light
Pitch ½" to ¾" per foot

BITUMINOUS MACADAM ROADS

Light foundations

Finish gravel or stone screening
Oil penetration
¼" to ¾" Broken stone & oil penetration
Wearing course 1¼" to 2½" stone
Base course 2½" to 3½" stone
Laid in 2 rollings

Medium foundations

Heavy foundations

Finish gravel or stone screening
Oil Penetration
¼" to ¾" Broken stone
Oil Penetration
Wearing course 1¼" to 2½" stone
Base course 2½" to 3½" crushed stone
6" to 10" Telford Base,
cinder may be used
in place of telford

Telford Base

Extra heavy foundations

TREES and SHRUBS

DECIDUOUS TREES – SCALE 1" = 80'

Silhouettes indicate specimens of typical form, height & spread, grown in ideal open conditions. Spacing is distance o.c. for usual row planting & may be varied for conditions. Hedge & screen spacing should be considerably less, depending on size of plant used. Arranged alphabetically. (with exceptions).

Tree	HEIGHT MATURE	DIA. TRUNK	SPREAD	SPACED O.C.
AILANTHUS — Ailanthus glandulosa	50'-75'	2'-3'	40'-60'	30'-40'
APPLE — Malus sylvestris	20'-40'	1'-2'	20'-40'	25'
ASH, WHITE — Fraxinus americana	70'-80'	2'-3'	35'-50'	40'-50'
BEECH, AMERICAN — Fagus americana	50'-75'	1½'-4'	40'-50'	30'-40'
BEECH, EUROPEAN — Fagus sylvatica	50'-75'	3'-4'	50'-70'	50'-60'
BIRCH, WHITE (European) — Betula alba (See small trees for Grey Birch.)	50'-75'	1'-3'	30'-50'	30'-40'
CATALPA, WESTERN — Catalpa speciosa	80'-100'	3'-4'	50'-60'	50'-60'
GINKGO BILOBA — Maidenhair tree	60'-80'	2'-3'	50'-60'	50'-60'
ELM, AMERICAN — Ulmus americana	80'-100'	4'-8'	70'-80'	60'-70'
ELM, ENGLISH — Ulmus campestris	75'-100'	3'-4'	50'-60'	50'-60'
HORSECHESTNUT — Aesculus hippocastanum	60'-70'	2'-3'	40'-50'	40'-50'
LOCUST, BLACK — Robinia pseudoacacia	40'-70'	2'-4'	30'-40'	30'-40'
LOCUST, HONEY — Gleditsia triacanthos	40'-60'	2'-3'	20'-30'	30'-40'
LINDEN — Tilia (species)	70'-90'	2'-4'	50'-60'	40'-50'
MAGNOLIA (cucumber tree) — Magnolia acuminata	70'-90'	3'-4'	60'-70'	50'-60'
MAPLE, NORWAY — Acer platanoides	60'-80'	2'-3'	60'-70'	50'-60'
MAPLE, RED — Acer rubrum	50'-75'	2'-3'	40'-50'	40'-50'
MAPLE, SUGAR — Acer saccharum	70'-100'	2'-4'	50'-60'	50'-60'
OAK, PIN — Quercus palustris	60'-80'	3'-4'	40'-50'	40'-50'
OAK, RED — Quercus rubra	60'-80'	2'-6'	60'-70'	50'-60'
OAK, WHITE — Quercus alba	80'-100'	3'-6'	80'-100'	100'
PLANE TREE (EUROPEAN) (Sycamore, Buttonwood) — Platanus orientalis	70'-80'	3'-4'	50'-60'	50'-60'

Prepared with the assistance of Leo Novick of the office of A. Carl Stelling. Drawings by Alice Recknagel.

TREES and SHRUBS

DECIDUOUS TREES (Continued) — SCALE 1" = 80'
See notes on previous page

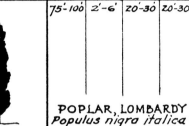

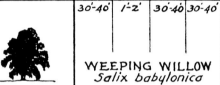

	HEIGHT MATURE	DIA. TRUNK	SPREAD	SPACED O.C.
POPLAR, CAROLINA — Populus eugenei (deltoides)	75'-100'	3'-5'	40'-50'	30'-40'
POPLAR, LOMBARDY — Populus nigra italica	75'-100'	2'-6'	20'-30'	20'-30'
SWEET GUM — Liquidambar styraciflua	80'-120'	3'-5'	40'-50'	40'-50'
TULIP TREE — Liriodendron tulipifera	100'-120'	3'-4'	50'-60'	50'-60'
WALNUT, BLACK — Juglans nigra	75'-150'	3'-5'	50'-75'	50'-60'
WEEPING WILLOW — Salix babylonica	30'-40'	1'-2'	30'-40'	30'-40'

SMALL DECIDUOUS TREES — SCALE 1" = 40'

For large deciduous trees see previous sheet

COMMON NAME / Botanical name / Height / Dia. Trunk / Spread / Spacing O.C.	GREY BIRCH	CRABAPPLE, FLOWERING	DOGWOOD, FLOWERING	HAWTHORNE	MAGNOLIA, SAUCER
Botanical name	Betula populifolia	Malus (species)	Cornus florida	Crataegus (species)	Magnolia soulangeana
Height	20'-35'	15'-20'	20'-25'	15'-30'	20'-25'
Dia. Trunk	clumps, stems, under 1'	Less than 1'-0"	Less than 1'-0"	6" to 1'-0"	9" to 1'-0"
Spread	15'-20'	20'-25'	25'-35'	20'-40'	20'-25'
Spacing O.C.	10'-20'	20'-30'	20'-30'	20'-30'	20'-30'

For large deciduous trees see previous sheet

SMALL EVERGREEN TREES — SCALE 1" = 40'

For larger Evergreen trees see following sheet

COMMON NAME / Botanical name / Height / Dia. Trunk / Spread / Spacing O.C.	ARBOR VITAE	BOX TREE	HOLLY, AMERICAN	JUNIPER (Red Cedar)
Botanical name	Thuja occidentalis	Buxus sempervirens	Ilex opaca	Juniperus virginiana
Height	25'-50'	20'-30'	40'-50'	25'-50'
Dia. Trunk	1'-2'	1'-2'	1'-2'	1'-2'
Spread	10'-20'	25'-30'	25'-35'	10'-15'
Spacing O.C.	10'-20'	20'-25'	30'-40'	20'-30'

Spacing for hedges may be much closer than that below

INDICATIONS FOR SHRUBS AND TREES

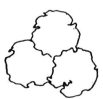

TREE
1" = 40'

Deciduous   Evergreen
S H R U B S
1" = 20'

HEDGES

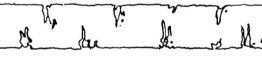

SPACING FOR HEDGES

Type of Hedge	Height	Single row	Staggered double row
Barberry	1'-6"	1'-0"	1'-3"
Privet (Amurense)	3'	1'-6"	2'-0"
Yew (Hicksi)	2'	1'-0"	1'-3"

Prepared with the assistance of Leo Novick of the office of A. Carl Stelling. Drawings by Alice Recknagel

TREES and SHRUBS

H = HEIGHT
D = TRUNK DIA.
S = SPREAD
O.C. = SPACING

EVERGREEN TREES – SCALE: 1" = 80'
See notes at top of Deciduous Tree sheet

H = HEIGHT
D = TRUNK DIA.
S = SPREAD
O.C. = SPACING

	H	D	S	O.C.
BALD CYPRESS *Taxodium distichum* (Mature tree / Young Tree)	100'–150'	3'–5'	50'–100'	60'–70'
DOUGLAS FIR *Pseudotsuga taxifolia* (Mature tree / Young tree)	100'–200'	10'–12'	50'–60'	50'–60'
YEW, IRISH *Taxus baccata fastigiata*	50'–60'	4'–6'	30'–40'	30'–40'

	H	D	S	O.C.
CYPRESS, SAWARA *Chamaecyparis pisifera (varieties)*	20'–40'	9"–15"	15'–20'	20'–30'
FIR, WHITE *Abies concolor*	100'–150'	3'–4'	50'–60'	50'–60'
HEMLOCK, CANADA *Tsuga Canadensis*	60'–100'	2'–4'	40'–60'	40'–50'
LARCH, EUROPEAN *Larix europa*	50'–60'	1'–3'	30'–40'	40'–50'

	H	D	S	O.C.
MAGNOLIA, SOUTHERN *Magnolia Grandiflora*	70'–80'	2'–3'	50'–60'	50'–60'
LIVE OAK *Quercus Virginiana*	50'–60'	4'–6'	60'–70'	60'–70'
PINE, AUSTRIAN (NORWAY) *Pinus nigra*	60'–80'	2'–3'	30'–40'	40'–50'
PINE, MONTEREY *Pinus radiata*	50'–60'	4'–6'	50'–60'	50'–60'

	H	D	S	O.C.
PINE, RED *Pinus resinosa*	60'–80'	2'–3'	30'–40'	40'–50'
PINE, WHITE *Pinus strobus*	80'–100'	4'–5'	60'–80'	50'–60'
SPRUCE, COLORADO *Picea pungens*	70'–90'	1½'–3'	30'–40'	40'–50'
SPRUCE, NORWAY *Picea excelsa*	50'–100'	2'–3'	40'–50'	40'–50'

DECIDUOUS SHRUBS

	H	S		H	S
MYRTLE CRAPE *Lagerstroemia indica*	15'–20'	15'–25'	LILAC, COMMON *Syringa vulgaris*	12'–15'	10'–12'
MOCK-ORANGE *Philadelphus (species)*	8'–10'	6'–8'	ROSE OF SHARON *Hibiscus (varieties)*	10'–12'	8'–10'
PRIVET, REGALS *Ligustrum ibata regelianum*	5'–6'	4'–5'	HONEYSUCKLE *Lonicera (species)*	6'–12'	6'–12'
SPIREA, VAN HOUTTE *Spirea van houttei*	5'–6'	5'–6'	SNOWBALL, JAPANESE *Viburnum tomontosum plicatum*	6'–8'	6'–8'
COTONEASTER *Cotoneaster horizontalis*	2'–3'	6'–9'	HYDRANGEA, SNOW HILL *Hydrangea arborescens*	4'–5'	5'–6'

	H	S
WHITE FRINGE TREE *Chionanthus virginica*	10'–15'	10'–15'
ARROW-WOOD *Viburnum dentatum*	10'–12'	10'–12'
FORSYTHIA, DROOPING *Forsythia suspensa*	6'–8'	8'–10'
BLUEBERRY, HIGHBUSH *Vaccinium corymbosum*	6'–8'	6'–8'
BARBERRY *Berberis thunbergi*	4'–5'	4'–6'

EVERGREEN SHRUBS

	H	S	O.C.
HOLLY, JAPANESE *Ilex crenata*	15'–20'	10'–15'	8'–10'
BOX, DWARF *Buxus suffruticosa*	10'–12'	10'–15'	variable
YEW, JAPANESE *Taxus cuspidata*	12'–15'	12'–15'	variable
PITTOSPORUM TOBIRA	6'–10'	6'–10'	4'–6'

	H	S	O.C.
RHODODENDRON *Rhododendron (species)*	6'–30'	6'–15'	5'–15'
OLEANDER *Nerium oleander*	7'–15'	7'–12'	6'–10'
PINE, MUGHO *Pinus montana mughus*	6'–8'	8'–12'	10'–15'
LAUREL *Kalma latifolia*	4'–10'	4'–8'	4'–8'
JUNIPER, PFITZERS *Juniperus chinensis pfitzeriana*	6'–8'	6'–8'	5'–10'

PALMS

	H	D	S	O.C.
DATE PALM *Phoenix canariensis*	80'–100'	3'–5'	50'–60'	50'–60'
COCONUT PALM *Cocos nucifera*	40'–100'	12"–18"	40'–50'	40'–50'
FAN PALM *Washingtonia robusta*	60'–90'	3'–4'	25'–35'	20'–40'
ROYAL PALM *Oreodoxa regia*	100'	1½'–2'	30'–40'	40'–50'

Prepared with the assistance of Leo Novick of the office of A. Carl Stelling. Drawings by Alice Recknagel.

3

MASONRY

BRICK COURSES

	2 1/4" + 1/8" JOINT	2 1/4" + 1/4" JOINT	2 1/4" + 3/8" JOINT	2 1/4" + 1/2" JOINT	2 1/4" + 5/8" JOINT	2 1/4" + 3/4" JOINT
1	2 3/8"	2 1/2"	2 5/8"	2 3/4"	2 7/8"	3"
2	4 3/4"	5"	5 1/4"	5 1/2"	5 3/4"	6"
3	7 1/8"	7 1/2"	7 7/8"	8 1/4"	8 5/8"	9"
4	9 1/2"	10"	10 1/2"	11"	11 1/2"	1'-0"
5	11 7/8"	1'-0 1/2"	1-1 1/8"	1'-1 3/4"	1'-2 3/8"	1'-3"
6	1'-2 1/4"	1'-3"	1-3 3/4"	1'-4 1/2"	1'-5 1/4"	1'-6"
7	1'-4 5/8"	1'-5 1/2"	1-6 3/8"	1-7 1/4"	1'-8 1/8"	1'-9"
8	1'-7"	1'-8"	1-9"	1'-10"	1'-11"	2'-0"
9	1'-9 3/8"	1'-10 1/2"	1-11 5/8"	2'-0 3/4"	2'-1 7/8"	2'-3"
10	1'-11 3/4"	2'-1"	2'-2 1/4"	2'-3 1/2"	2'-4 3/4"	2'-6"
11	2'-2 1/8"	2'-3 1/2"	2'-4 7/8"	2'-6 1/4"	2'-7 5/8"	2'-9"
12	2'-4 1/2"	2'-6"	2'-7 1/2"	2'-9"	2'-10 1/2"	3'-0"
13	2'-6 7/8"	2'-8 1/2"	2'-10 1/8"	2'-11 3/4"	3'-1 3/8"	3'-3"
14	2'-9 1/4"	2'-11"	3'-0 3/4"	3'-2 1/2"	3'-4 1/4"	3'-6"
15	2'-11 5/8"	3'-1 1/2"	3'-3 3/8	3'-5 1/4"	3'-7 1/8"	3'-9"
16	3'-2"	3'-4"	3'-6"	3'-8"	3'-10"	4'-0"
17	3'-4 3/8"	3'-6 1/2"	3'-8 5/8"	3'-10 3/4"	4'-0 7/8"	4'-3"
18	3'-6 3/4"	3'-9"	3'-11 1/4"	4'-1 1/2"	4'-3 3/4"	4'-6"
19	3'-9 1/8"	3'-11 1/2"	4'-1 7/8"	4'-4 1/4"	4'-6 5/8"	4'-9"
20	3'-11 1/2	4'-2"	4'-4 1/2"	4'-7"	4'-9 1/2"	5'-0"
21	4'-1 7/8"	4'-4 1/2"	4'-7 1/8"	4'-9 3/4"	5'-0 3/8"	5'-3"
22	4'-4 1/4"	4'-7"	4'-9 3/4"	5'-0 1/2"	5'-3 1/4"	5'-6"
23	4'-6 5/8"	4'-9 1/2"	5'-0 3/8"	5'-3 1/4"	5'-6 1/8"	5'-9"
24	4'-9"	5'-0"	5'-3"	5'-6"	5'-9"	6'-0"
25	4'-11 3/8"	5'-2 1/2"	5'-5 5/8"	5'-8 3/4"	5'-11 7/8"	6'-3"
26	5'-1 3/4"	5'-5"	5'-8 1/4"	5'-11 1/2"	6'-2 3/4"	6'-6"
27	5'-4 1/8"	5'-7 1/2"	5'-10 7/8"	6'-2 1/4"	6'-5 5/8"	6'-9"
28	5'-6 1/2"	5'-10"	6'-1 1/2"	6'-5"	6'-8 1/2"	7'-0"
29	5'-8 7/8"	6'-0 1/2"	6'-4 1/8"	6'-7 3/4"	6'-11 3/8"	7'-3"
30	5'-11 1/4"	6'-3"	6'-6 3/4"	6'-10 1/2"	7-2 1/4"	7'-6"
31	6'-1 5/8"	6'-5 1/2"	6'-9 3/8"	7'-1 1/4"	7'-5 1/8"	7'-9"
32	6'-4"	6'-8"	7'-0"	7'-4"	7'-8"	8'-0"
33	6'-6 3/8"	6'-10 1/2"	7'-2 5/8"	7'-6 3/4"	7'-10 7/8"	8'-3"
34	6'-8 3/4"	7'-1"	7'-5 1/4"	7'-9 1/2"	8'-1 3/4"	8'-6"
35	6'-11 1/8"	7'-3 1/2"	7'-7 7/8"	8'-0 1/4"	8'-4 5/8"	8'-9"
36	7'-1 1/2"	7'-6"	7'-10 1/2"	8'-3"	8'-7 1/2"	9'-0"
37	7'-3 7/8"	7'-8 1/2"	8'-1 1/8"	8'-5 3/4"	8'-10 3/8"	9'-3"
38	7'-6 1/4"	7'-11"	8'-3 3/4"	8'-8 1/2"	9-1 1/4"	9'-6"
39	7'-8 5/8"	8'-1 1/2"	8'-6 3/8"	8'-11 1/4"	9'-4 1/8"	9'-9"
40	7'-11"	8'-4"	8'-9"	9'-2"	9'-7"	10'-0"
41	8'-1 3/8"	8'-6 1/2"	8'-11 5/8"	9'-4 3/4"	9'-9 7/8"	10'-3"
42	8'-3 3/4"	8'-9"	9'-2 1/4"	9'-7 1/2"	10'-0 3/4"	10'-6"
43	8'-6 1/8"	8'-11 1/2"	9'-4 7/8"	9'-10 1/4"	10'-3 5/8"	10'-9"
44	8'-8 1/2"	9'-2"	9'-7 1/2"	10'-1"	10'-6 1/2"	11'-0"
45	8'-10 7/8"	9'-4 1/2"	9'-10 1/8"	10'-3 3/4"	10'-9 3/8"	11'-3"
46	9'-1 1/4"	9'-7"	10'-0 3/4"	10'-6 1/2"	11'-0 1/4"	11'-6"
47	9'-3 5/8"	9'-9 1/2"	10'-3 3/8"	10'-9 1/4"	11'-3 1/8"	11'-9"
48	9'-6"	10'-0"	10'-6"	11'-0"	11'-6"	12'-0"
49	9'-8 3/8"	10'-2 1/2"	10'-8 5/8"	11'-2 3/4"	11'-8 7/8"	12'-3"
50	9'-10 3/4"	10'-5"	10'-11 1/4"	11'-5 1/2"	11'-11 3/4"	12'-6"
51	10'-1 1/8"	10'-7 1/2"	11'-1 7/8"	11'-8 1/4"	12'-2 5/8"	12'-9"
52	10'-3 1/2"	10'-10"	11'-4 1/2"	11'-11"	12'-5 1/2"	13'-0"
53	10'-5 7/8"	11'-0 1/2"	11'-7 1/8"	12'-1 3/4"	12'-8 3/8"	13'-3"
54	10'-8 1/4"	11'-3"	11'-9 3/4"	12'-4 1/2"	12'-11 1/4"	13'-6"
55	10'-10 5/8"	11'-5 1/2"	12'-0 3/8"	12-7 1/4"	13'-2 1/8"	13'-9"
56	11'-1"	11'-8"	12'-3"	12'-10"	13'-5"	14'-0"
57	11'-3 3/8"	11'-10 1/2"	12'-5 5/8"	13'-0 3/4"	13'-7 7/8"	14'-3"
58	11'-5 3/4"	12'-1"	12'-8 1/4"	13'-3 1/2"	13'-10 3/4"	14'-6"
59	11'-8 1/8"	12'-3 1/2"	12'-10 7/8"	13'-6 1/4"	14'-1 5/8"	14'-9"
60	11'-10 1/2"	12'-6"	13'-1 1/2"	13'-9"	14'-4 1/2"	15'-0"

BRICKWORK

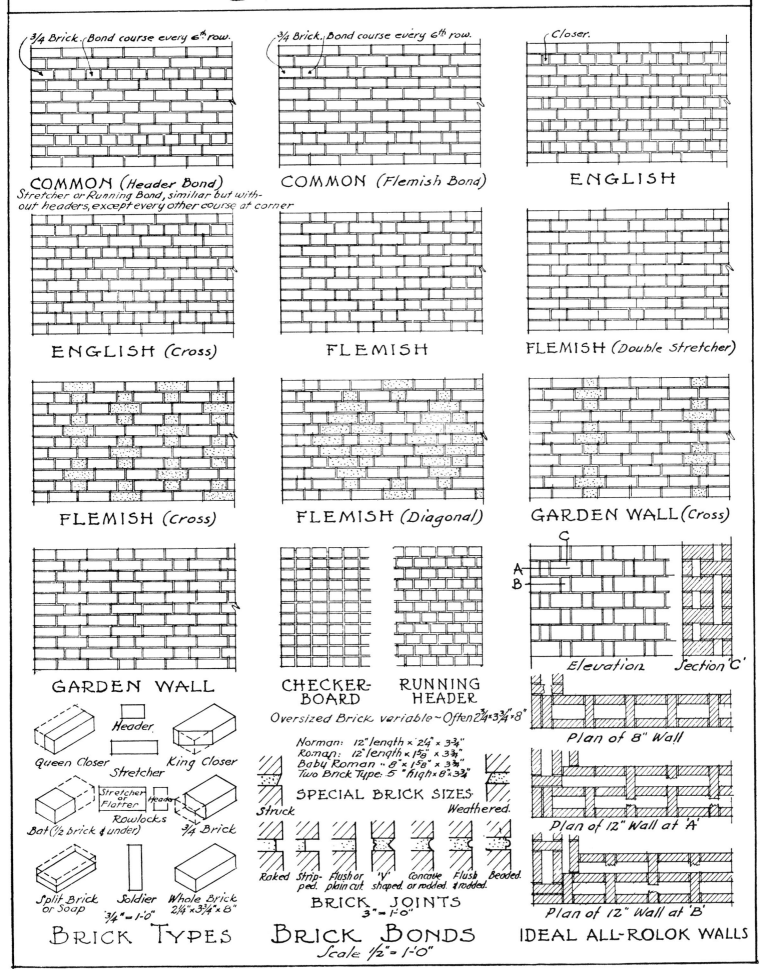

3/4 Brick. Bond course every 6th row.

COMMON (Header Bond)
Stretcher or Running Bond, similar but without headers, except every other course at corner

3/4 Brick. Bond course every 6th row.

COMMON (Flemish Bond)

Closer.

ENGLISH

ENGLISH (Cross)

FLEMISH

FLEMISH (Double Stretcher)

FLEMISH (Cross)

FLEMISH (Diagonal)

GARDEN WALL (Cross)

GARDEN WALL

CHECKER-BOARD   **RUNNING HEADER**

Oversized Brick variable ~ Often 2¾"×3¾"×8"

Norman: 12" length × 2¼" × 3¾"
Roman: 12" length × 1⅝" × 3¾"
Baby Roman " 8" × 1⅝" × 3¾"
Two Brick Type: 5 "high×8"×3¾"

SPECIAL BRICK SIZES

Header
Queen Closer   Stretcher   King Closer

Stretcher or Flatter   Header
Bat (½ brick & under)   Rowlocks   ¾ Brick

Split Brick or Soap   Soldier   Whole Brick 2¼"×3¾"×8"
¾"=1'-0"

BRICK TYPES

Struck   Weathered.

Raked   Strip-ped.   Flush or plain cut.   'V' shaped.   Concave or rodded.   Flush & rodded. Beaded.

BRICK JOINTS
3"=1'-0"

BRICK BONDS
Scale ½"=1'-0"

C
A
B

Elevation   Section 'C'

Plan of 8" Wall

Plan of 12" Wall at 'A'

Plan of 12" Wall at 'B'

IDEAL ALL-ROLOK WALLS

BRICK WALLS

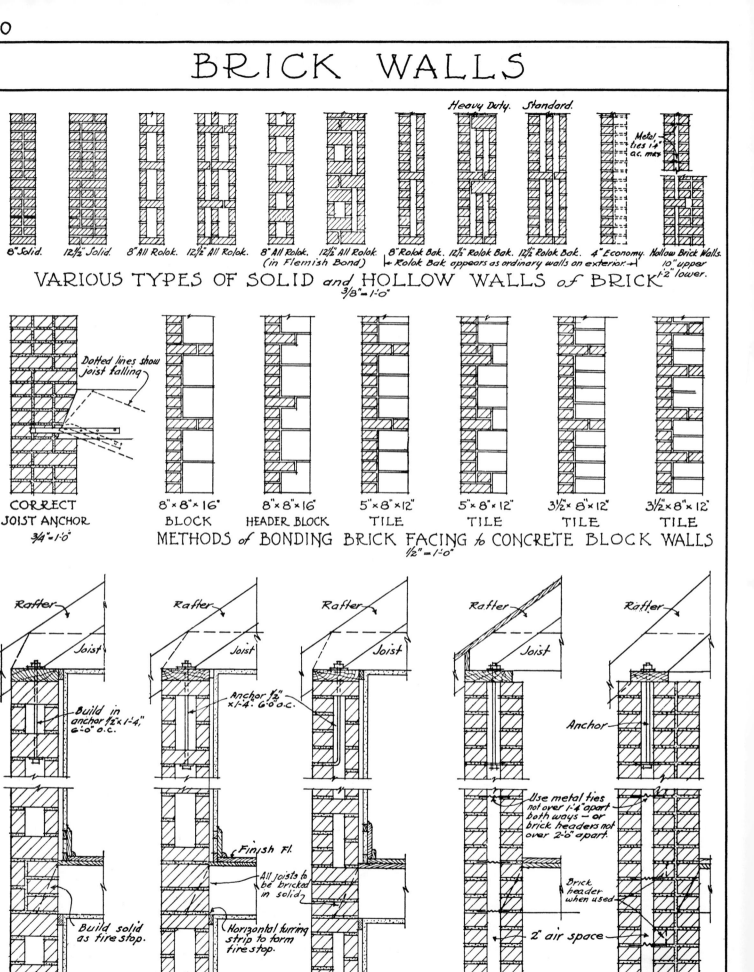

Heavy Duty. Standard.

8" Solid. 12½" Solid. 8" All Rolok. 12½" All Rolok. 8" All Rolok. 12½" All Rolok. 8" Rolok Bak. 12½" Rolok Bak. 12½" Rolok Bak. 4" Economy. Hollow Brick Walls.
(in Flemish Bond) ← Rolok Bak appears as ordinary walls on exterior → 10" upper 1'-2" lower.

VARIOUS TYPES OF SOLID and HOLLOW WALLS of BRICK
3/8"=1'-0"

CORRECT JOIST ANCHOR 3/4"=1'-0" — Dotted lines show joist falling

8"×8"×16" BLOCK — 8"×8"×16" HEADER BLOCK — 5"×8"×12" TILE — 5"×8"×12" TILE — 3½"×8"×12" TILE — 3½"×8"×12" TILE

METHODS of BONDING BRICK FACING to CONCRETE BLOCK WALLS
½"=1'-0"

ALL-ROLOK WALL IN FLEMISH BOND. — ALL-ROLOK-WALL — ROLOK-BAK WALL — 10" THICK — 1'-2" THICK HOLLOW OR VAULTED BRICK WALLS

(See "Brick Cavity Walls" for details)
3/4"=1'-0"

GLAZED BRICK

Stretcher · **Header** · **Quoin** · **Double Header** · **Double Quoin** · **Header Bat**

Quoin Bat · **Soap Stretcher** Same 3⅞" long · **Soap Quoin** Same 6" long Same 3⅞" long · **Soap Bond Quoin** Same 3⅞" long · **6" Bond Brick** Same 3⅞" long · **8" Bond Brick**

STRETCHERS, HEADERS AND QUOINS

Bullnose Same 3⅞" long · **Double Bullnose** · **Soap Bullnose** Same 6" long Same 3⅞" long · **Soap Bond B.N.** Same 3⅞" long · **Internal-External Bullnose Combination** · **Internal Bullnose**

Right & Left Bullnose Starter · **Double B.N. End** Same 3⅞" long · **Ext. 30° Octagon Ext. 45° Octagon Ext. 60° Octagon** · **Int. 30° Octagon Int. 45° Octagon Int. 60° Octagon** · **Chamfer Brick**

BULLNOSE, OCTAGONS AND CHAMFER CORNER UNITS

Flat Bullnose Stretcher (cored for lintel rods when required) · **Flat B.N. Header** Same 3⅞" long · **Right & Left Flat B.N Quoin** · **Right & Left Flat B.N Ext. Round** · **Right & Left Flat B.N. Internal Corner Square** · **Right & Left Flat B.N. Internal Corner Round**

Right & Left Bullnose Mitre · **Right & Left B.N. Header Mitre** · **Right & Left B.N. Sill & Jamb Mitre** · **Right & Left Standard B.N. Sill Mitre** · **Right & Left Rowlock B.N. Sill Mitre**

SILL, JAMB, LINTEL AND COPING UNITS

Two-Brick units shown, single bricks available in similar shapes. See following sheet for other shapes

GLAZED BRICK

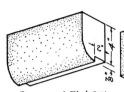 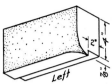 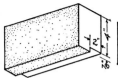 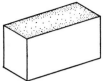 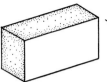 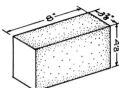

Recessed Flat B.N. Same 3⅞" long   Right & Left Recessed B N Mitre   Recessed Stretcher Same 3⅞" long   Flat Stretcher Same 3⅞" long   Flat Quoin Same 3⅞" long   Sill Lintel Stretcher Same 3⅞" long

SILL, JAMB AND LINTEL UNITS (cont'd)

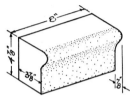 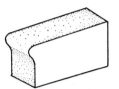 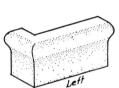 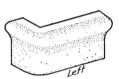 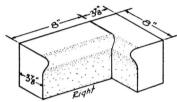

Cap Mould Stretcher Glazed on Head also   Cap Mould Header Same 3⅞" long   Right & Left Cap Mould Quoin   Right & Left Cap Mould Ext. Round   Right & Left Cap Mould Internal Mitre

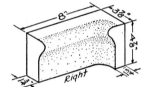 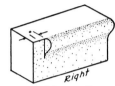 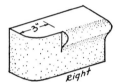  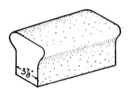

Right & Left Cap Mould Internal Corner Round   Right & Left C.M. Starter Quoin Head Glazed also   Right & Left Cap Mould Starter Bullnosed   Double Cap Mould Coping End Same 3⅞" long   Double Cap Mould Stretcher Same 3⅞" long

CAP MOULD AND COPING UNITS

 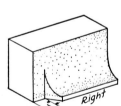 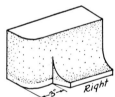  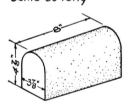

Double Bullnose Coping End Same 3⅞" long   Right & Left Cove Base Starter Head Glazed also   Right & Left Cove Base Starter Bullnosed   Double Cove Base End   Double Bullnose Coping Stretcher Same 3⅞" long

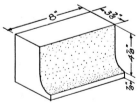 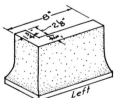 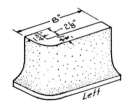 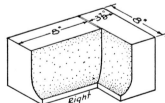 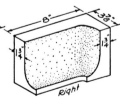

Cove Base Stretcher Same 3⅞" long Head Glazed also   Right & Left Cove Base Quoin   Right & Left Cove Base Ext. Round   Right & Left Cove Base Internal Mitre   Right & Left Cove Base Internal Corner Round

COVE BASE UNITS

NOTES

Two-brick units shown. Standard dimensions 4⅞"×8"×3⅞" full unit. 4⅞"×8"×1¾" Soap. Bull nose 2", and 1" also made. Cove radius 2" and 1¾" also made.
Standard brick also made in similar shapes. Standard dimensions 2¼"×8"×3⅞" full unit. Soap unit 2¼"×8"×1¾"
Shapes here shown are generally available but are not standard and may vary according to manufacturer used.
Units are generally cored but same are not shown as they vary according to the manufacturer selected.

Hollow clay tile manufacturers make similar glazed units with detail variations and limited number of shapes. See preceding sheet for other shapes.

BRICK-CAVITY & SERPENTINE WALLS

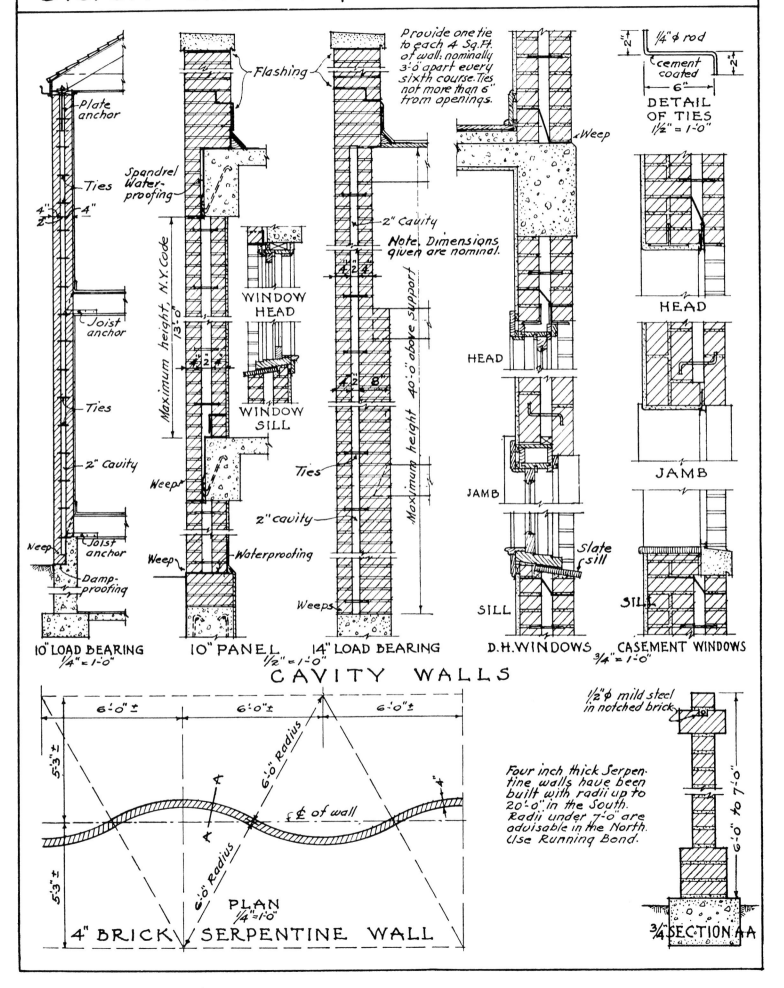

Plate anchor

Ties

4" — 4"
2" —

Joist anchor

Ties

2" Cavity

Weep — Joist anchor

Damp-proofing

10" LOAD BEARING
1/4" = 1'-0"

Flashing

Spandrel Water-proofing

Maximum height, N.Y. Code 13'-0"

WINDOW HEAD

4" 2" 4"

4" 2" 4"

WINDOW SILL

Weep

Weep

Waterproofing

10" PANEL
1/2" = 1'-0"

Flashing

Provide one tie to each 4 Sq.Ft. of wall; nominally 3'-0" apart every sixth course. Ties not more than 6" from openings.

2" Cavity

Note. Dimensions given are nominal.

4" 2" 4"

4" 2" 8"

Ties

2" cavity

Weeps

Maximum height 40'-0" above support

14" LOAD BEARING

CAVITY WALLS

Weep

HEAD

JAMB

Slate sill

SILL

D.H. WINDOWS
3/4" = 1'-0"

HEAD

JAMB

SILL

CASEMENT WINDOWS

2"
2"

1/4" ⌀ rod

cement coated

2"
2"

6"

DETAIL OF TIES
1/2" = 1'-0"

6'-0"±   6'-0"±   6'-0"±

5'-3"±

6'-0" Radius

A

6'-0" Radius

₵ of wall

6'-0" Radius

4"

A

5'-3"±

PLAN
1/4" = 1'-0"

4" BRICK SERPENTINE WALL

1/2"⌀ mild steel in notched brick

6'-0" to 7'-0"

Four inch thick Serpentine walls have been built with radii up to 20'-0" in the South. Radii under 7'-0" are advisable in the North. Use Running Bond.

3/4 SECTION A-A

BRICK VENEER

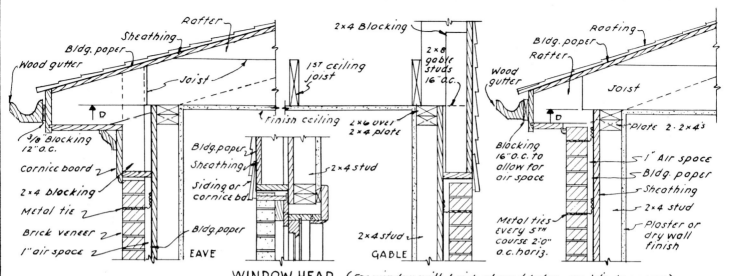

Rafter
Sheathing
Bldg. paper
Wood gutter
Joist
3/8 Blocking 12" o.c.
Cornice board
2×4 blocking
Metal tie
Brick veneer
1" air space
EAVE

2×4 Blocking
1st ceiling joist
2×8 gable studs 16" o.c.
Finish ceiling
2×6 over 2×4 plate
Bldg. paper
Sheathing
Siding or cornice bd.
Bldg. paper
2×4 stud
2×4 stud
GABLE

Roofing
Bldg. paper
Rafter
Wood gutter
Joist
Plate 2- 2×4's
Blocking 16" o.c. to allow for air space
Metal ties every 5th course 2'0" o.c. horiz.
1" Air space
Bldg. paper
Sheathing
2×4 stud
Plaster or dry wall finish

WINDOW HEAD *(For window with brick above & below, see Window pages.)*

EAVES, GABLE and WINDOW

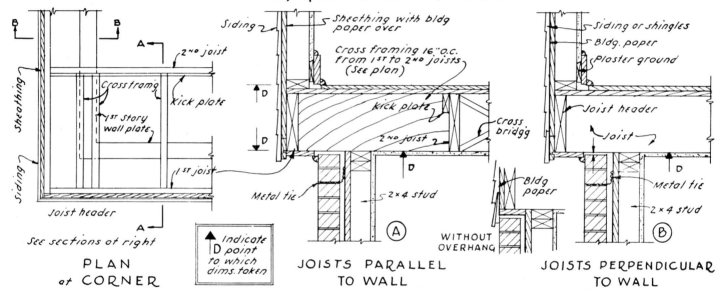

B
B
Sheathing
2nd joist
Cross framg
Kick plate
1st story wall plate
Siding
1st joist
A
A
Joist header
See sections ot right
PLAN ot CORNER

▲ Indicate D point to which dims. taken

Siding
Sheathing with bldg paper over
Cross framing 16" o.c. from 1st to 2nd joists (See plan)
kick plate
2nd joist
cross bridgg
Metal tie
2×4 stud
Ⓐ
WITHOUT OVERHANG
Bldg paper
JOISTS PARALLEL TO WALL

Siding or shingles
Bldg. paper
Plaster ground
Joist header
Joist
Metal tie
2×4 stud
Ⓑ
JOISTS PERPENDICULAR TO WALL

BRICK VENEER with WOOD SIDING on SECOND STORY

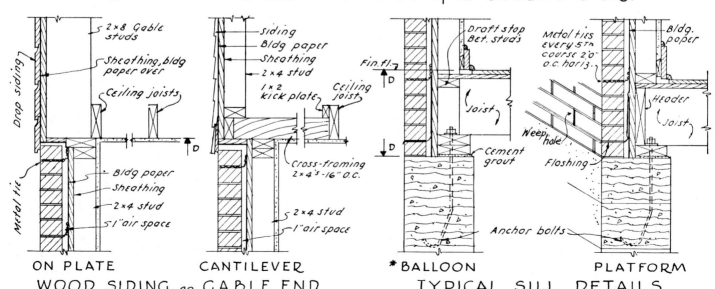

2×8 Gable studs
Drop siding
Sheathing, bldg paper over
Ceiling joists
Metal tie
Bldg paper
Sheathing
2×4 stud
1" air space
D
ON PLATE

siding
Bldg paper
Sheathing
2×4 stud
1×2 kick plate
Ceiling joist
Cross-framing 2×4's -16" o.c.
2×4 stud
1" air space
CANTILEVER

Draft stop bet. stud's
Fin. fl.
Joist
Cement grout
Anchor bolts
D
D
*BALLOON

Metal ties every 5th course 2'0" o.c. horiz.
Bldg. paper
Weep hole
Header
Joist
Flashing
PLATFORM

WOOD SIDING on GABLE END
If veneered, brick is continued up to louver of apex

TYPICAL SILL DETAILS
Preferred for 2 story bldgs, due to less shrinkage.

Scale: 3/4"=1'-0"
Adapted from data by National Lumber Manufacturers Association

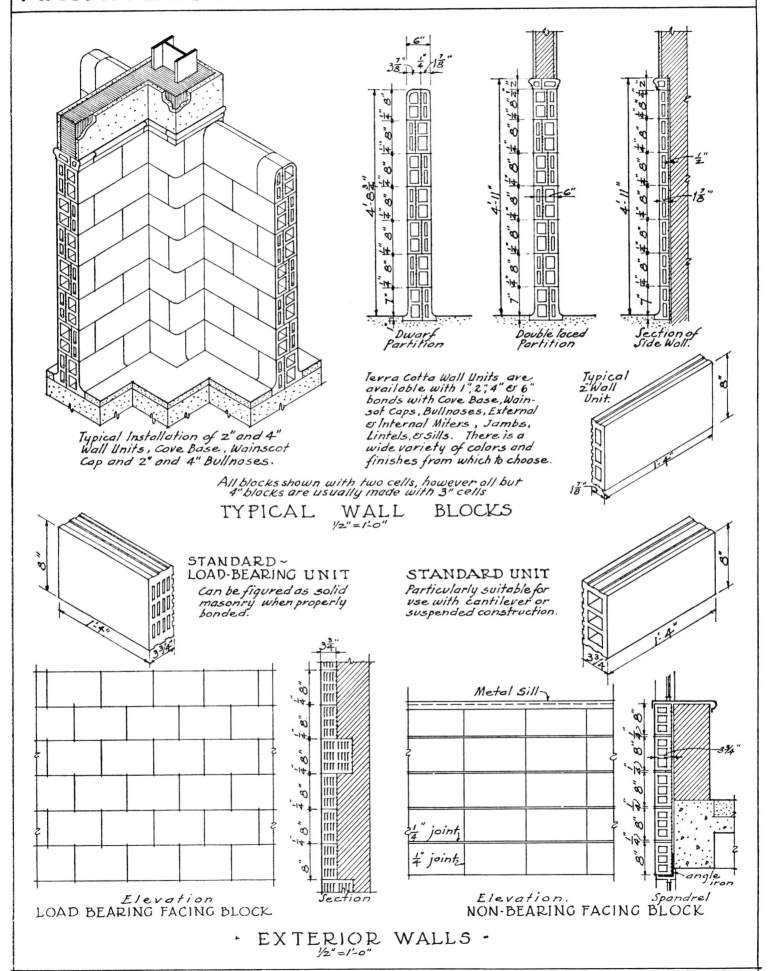

Dwarf Partition

Double Faced Partition

Section of Side Wall.

Terra Cotta Wall Units are available with 1", 2", 4" & 6" bonds with Cove Base, Wainscot Caps, Bullnoses, External & Internal Miters, Jambs, Lintels, & Sills. There is a wide variety of colors and finishes from which to choose.

All blocks shown with two cells, however all but 4" blocks are usually made with 3" cells

TYPICAL WALL BLOCKS
1/2" = 1'-0"

Typical 2" Wall Unit.

Typical Installation of 2" and 4" Wall Units, Cove Base, Wainscot Cap and 2" and 4" Bullnoses.

STANDARD~ LOAD-BEARING UNIT
Can be figured as solid masonry when properly bonded.

STANDARD UNIT
Particularly suitable for use with cantilever or suspended construction.

Metal Sill

2 1/4" joint
1/4" joint

angle iron

Elevation
LOAD BEARING FACING BLOCK

Section

Elevation.
NON-BEARING FACING BLOCK

Spandrel

· EXTERIOR WALLS ·
1/2" = 1'-0"

ARCHITECTURAL TERRA COTTA – EXTERIOR

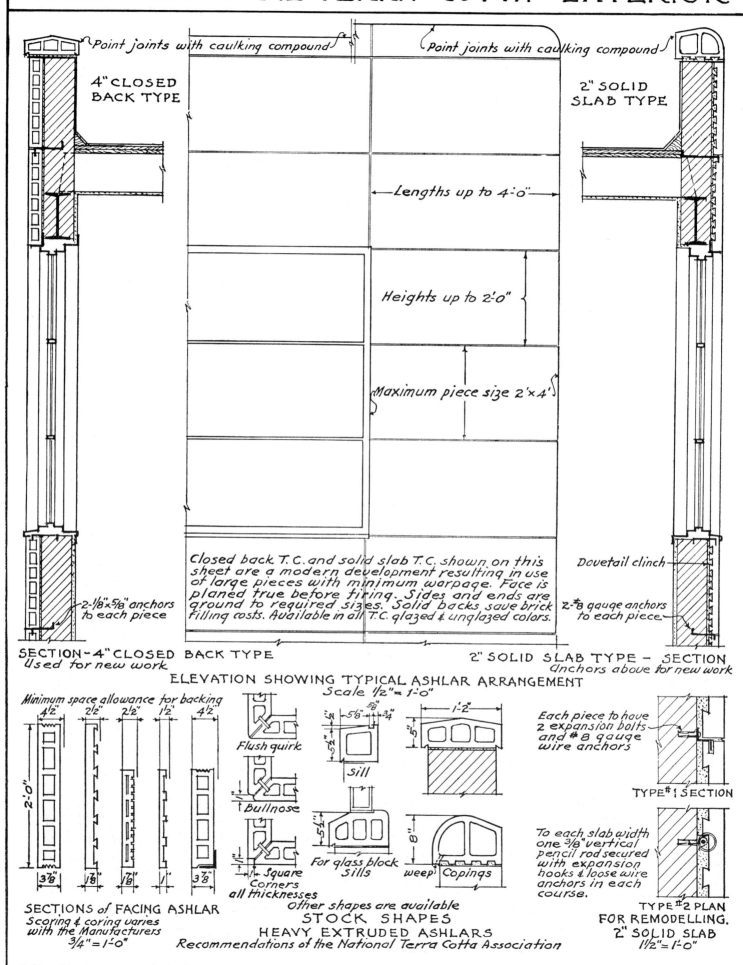

Point joints with caulking compound

4" CLOSED BACK TYPE

Point joints with caulking compound

2" SOLID SLAB TYPE

Lengths up to 4'-0"

Heights up to 2'-0"

Maximum piece size 2'x4'

Closed back T.C. and solid slab T.C. shown on this sheet are a modern development resulting in use of large pieces with minimum warpage. Face is planed true before firing. Sides and ends are ground to required sizes. Solid backs save brick filling costs. Available in all T.C. glazed & unglazed colors.

2-1/8"x5/8" anchors to each piece

Dovetail clinch

2 #8 gauge anchors to each piece

SECTION–4" CLOSED BACK TYPE
Used for new work

2" SOLID SLAB TYPE – SECTION
Anchors above for new work

ELEVATION SHOWING TYPICAL ASHLAR ARRANGEMENT
Scale 1/2" = 1'-0"

Minimum space allowance for backing
4 1/2" 2 1/2" 2 1/2" 1 1/2" 4 1/2"

2'-0"

3/8" 1/8" 1/2" 1" 3/8"

SECTIONS of FACING ASHLAR
Scoring & coring varies with the Manufacturers
3/4" = 1'-0"

Flush quirk

Bullnose

Square Corners all thicknesses

sill

For glass block sills

weep   Copings

Other shapes are available
STOCK SHAPES
HEAVY EXTRUDED ASHLARS
Recommendations of the National Terra Cotta Association

Each piece to have 2 expansion bolts and #8 gauge wire anchors

TYPE #1 SECTION

To each slab width one 3/8" vertical pencil rod secured with expansion hooks & loose wire anchors in each course.

TYPE #2 PLAN
FOR REMODELLING.
2" SOLID SLAB
1 1/2" = 1'-0"

ARCHITECTURAL TERRA COTTA

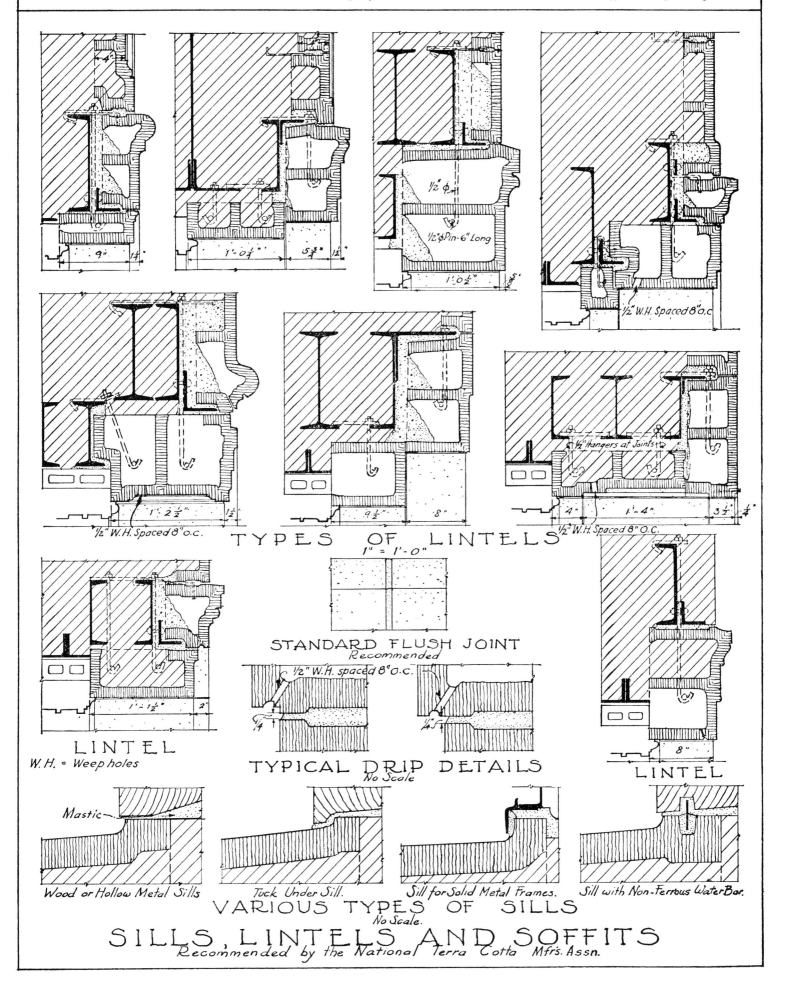

½" ϕ

½" ϕ Pin - 6" Long

½" W.H. Spaced 8" o.c.

½" W.H. Spaced 8" o.c.

½" hangers at Joints

½" W.H. Spaced 8" O.C.

TYPES OF LINTELS
1" = 1'-0"

STANDARD FLUSH JOINT
Recommended

½" W.H. spaced 8" o.c.

TYPICAL DRIP DETAILS
No Scale

LINTEL
W.H. = Weepholes

LINTEL

Mastic

Wood or Hollow Metal Sills.   Tuck Under Sill.   Sill for Solid Metal Frames.   Sill with Non-Ferrous Water Bar.

VARIOUS TYPES OF SILLS
No Scale.

SILLS, LINTELS AND SOFFITS
Recommended by the National Terra Cotta Mfrs. Assn.

ARCHITECTURAL TERRA·COTTA

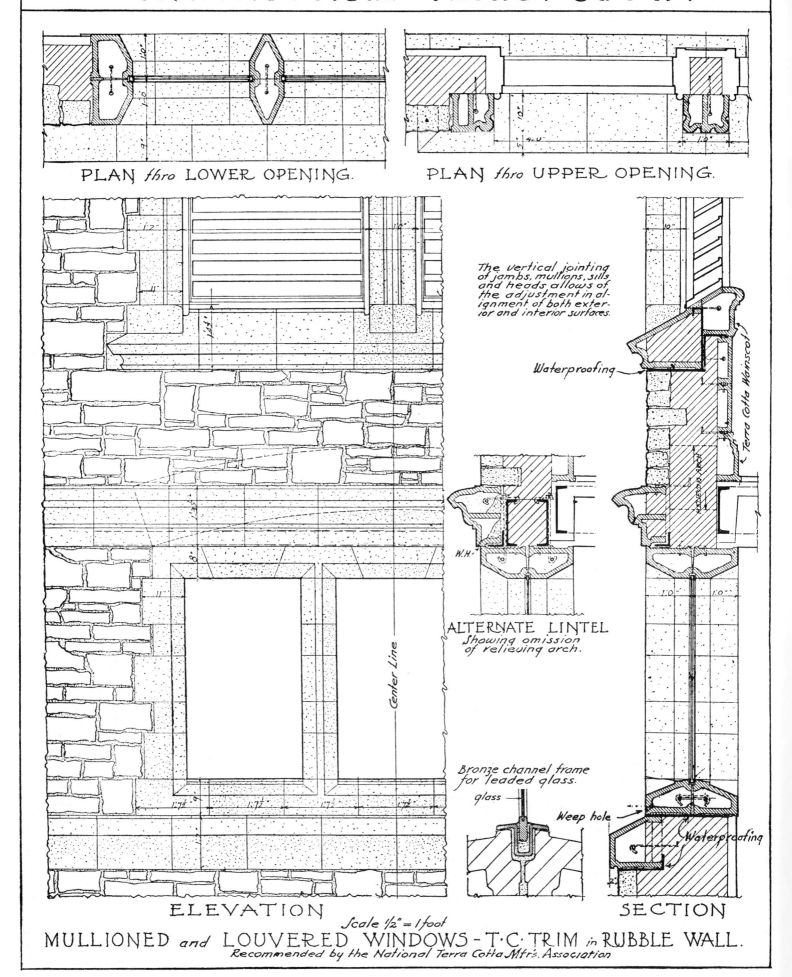

PLAN *thro* LOWER OPENING.

PLAN *thro* UPPER OPENING.

The vertical jointing of jambs, mullions, sills and heads allows of the adjustment in alignment of both exterior and interior surfaces.

Waterproofing

ALTERNATE LINTEL
Showing omission of relieving arch.

Bronze channel frame for leaded glass.
glass

Weep hole

Waterproofing

ELEVATION

SECTION

Scale ½" = 1 foot

MULLIONED *and* LOUVERED WINDOWS – T·C· TRIM *in* RUBBLE WALL.
Recommended by the National Terra Cotta Mfrs. Association

ARCHITECTURAL TERRA COTTA

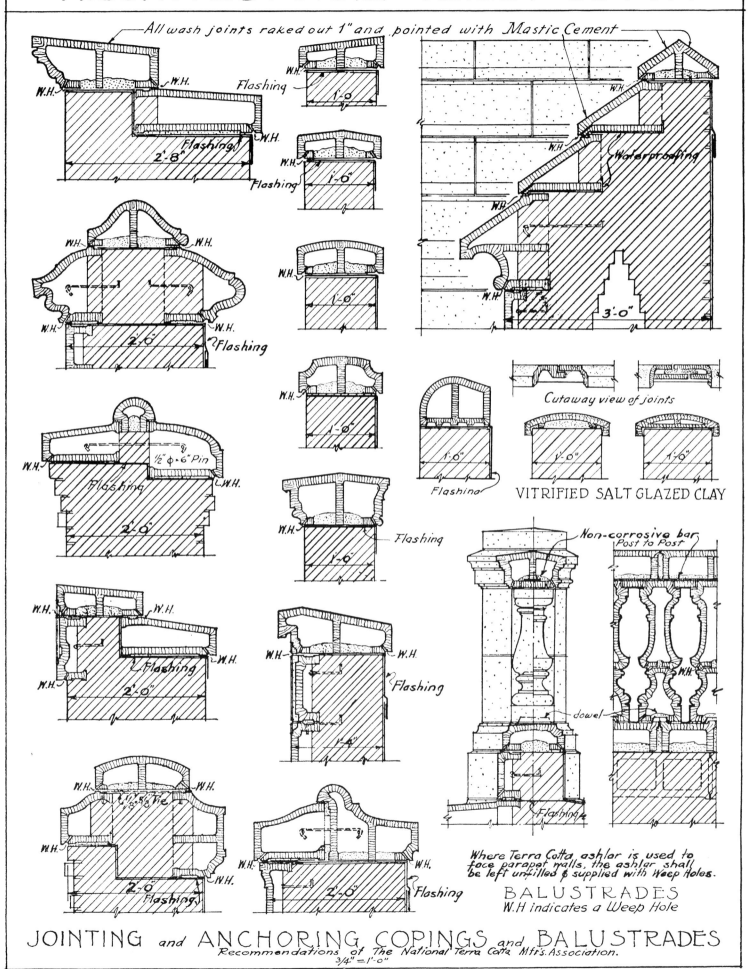

All wash joints raked out 1" and pointed with Mastic Cement

Flashing

W.H.

Waterproofing

Cutaway view of joints

VITRIFIED SALT GLAZED CLAY

Non-corrosive bar
Post to Post

dowel

Flashing

Where Terra Cotta ashlar is used to face parapet walls, the ashlar shall be left unfilled & supplied with Weep Holes.

BALUSTRADES
W.H indicates a Weep Hole

JOINTING and ANCHORING COPINGS and BALUSTRADES
Recommendations of The National Terra Cotta Mfr's Association.
3/4" = 1'-0"

ARCHITECTURAL TERRA COTTA

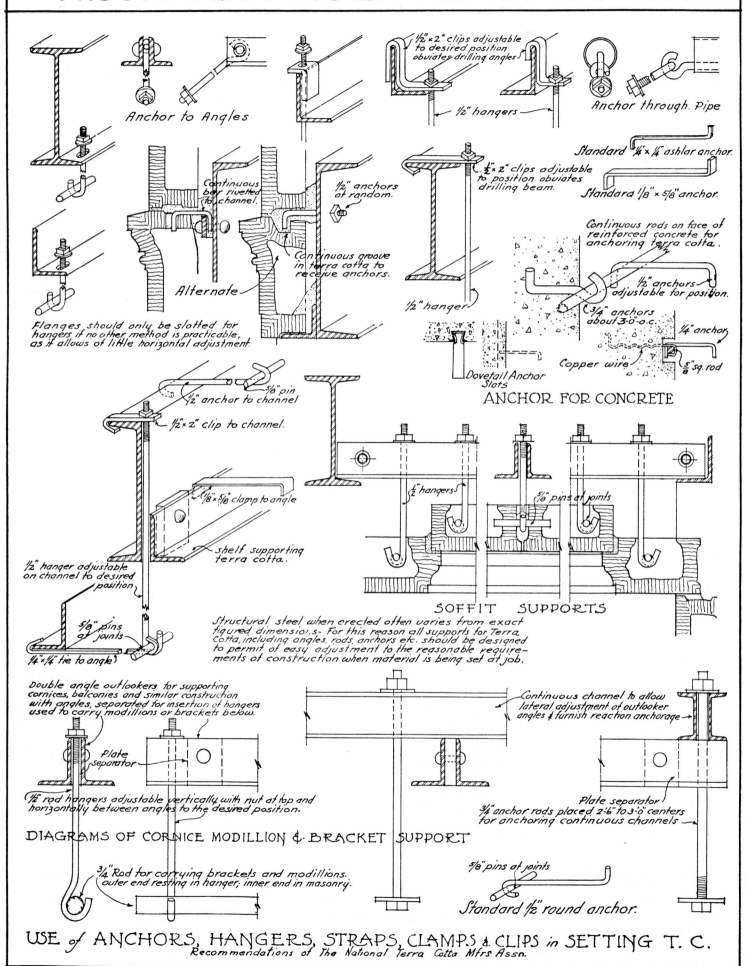

Anchor to Angles

½"×2" clips adjustable to desired position obviates drilling angles

½" hangers

Anchor through Pipe

Continuous bar riveted to channel.

½" anchors at random.

Standard ¼"×¼" ashlar anchor.

½"×2" clips adjustable to position obviates drilling beam.

Standard ⅛"×⅝" anchor.

Continuous groove in terra cotta to receive anchors.

Alternate

½" hanger

Continuous rods on face of reinforced concrete for anchoring terra cotta.

½" anchors adjustable for position.

¾" anchors about 3'-0" o.c.

¼" anchor

Copper wire

⅝" sq. rod

Flanges should only be slotted for hangers if no other method is practicable, as it allows of little horizontal adjustment.

Dovetail Anchor Slots

ANCHOR FOR CONCRETE

½" anchor to channel

⅝" pin

½"×2" clip to channel.

⅛"×⅝" clamp to angle

shelf supporting terra cotta.

½" hangers

⅝" pins at joints

½" hanger adjustable on channel to desired position

⅝" pins at joints

¼"×¼" tie to angle

SOFFIT SUPPORTS

Structural steel when erected often varies from exact figured dimensions. For this reason all supports for Terra Cotta, including angles, rods, anchors etc. should be designed to permit of easy adjustment to the reasonable require-ments of construction when material is being set at job.

Double angle outlookers for supporting cornices, balconies and similar construction with angles, separated for insertion of hangers used to carry modillions or brackets below.

Plate separator

Continuous channel to allow lateral adjustment of outlooker angles & furnish reaction anchorage

Plate separator

½" rod hangers adjustable vertically with nut at top and horizontally between angles to the desired position.

¾" anchor rods placed 2'-6" to 3'-0" centers for anchoring continuous channels

DIAGRAMS OF CORNICE MODILLION & BRACKET SUPPORT

¾" Rod for carrying brackets and modillions. outer end resting in hanger; inner end in masonry.

⅝" pins at joints

Standard ½" round anchor.

USE of ANCHORS, HANGERS, STRAPS, CLAMPS & CLIPS in SETTING T.C.

Recommendations of The National Terra Cotta Mfrs. Assn.

HOLLOW TILE

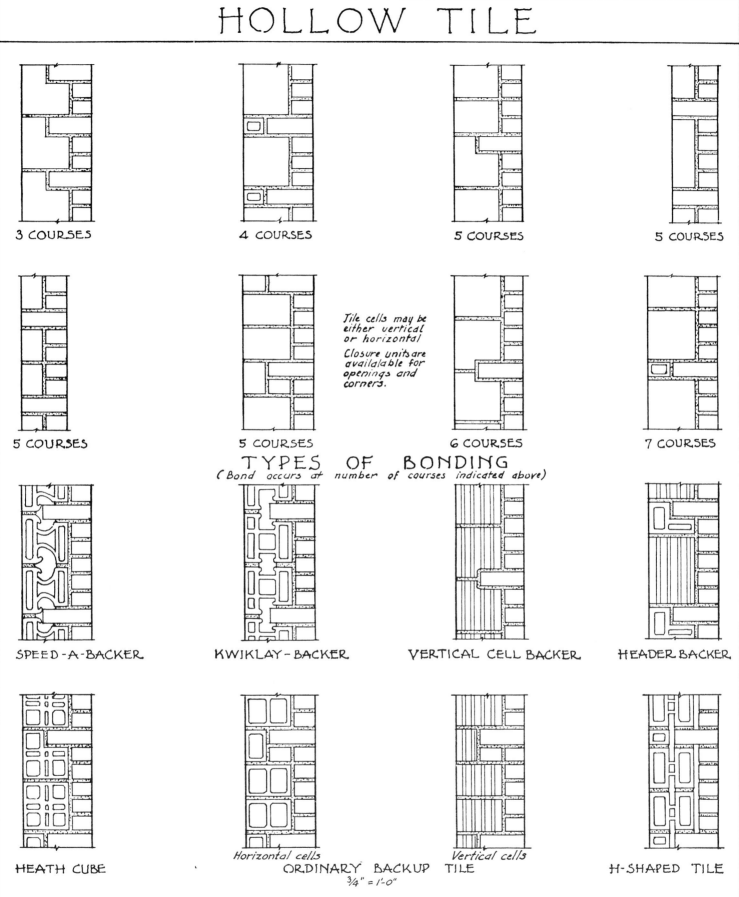

3 COURSES   4 COURSES   5 COURSES   5 COURSES

Tile cells may be either vertical or horizontal

Closure units are available for openings and corners.

5 COURSES   5 COURSES   6 COURSES   7 COURSES

TYPES OF BONDING
(Bond occurs at number of courses indicated above)

SPEED-A-BACKER   KWIKLAY-BACKER   VERTICAL CELL BACKER   HEADER BACKER

HEATH CUBE   *Horizontal cells* ORDINARY BACKUP TILE *Vertical cells*   H-SHAPED TILE

¾" = 1'-0"

Scoring not indicated on sections — — Walls are shown 12" thick but tile is made by most Manufacturers to make walls 10", 12", 14" and 16" thick.

Mortar for both brick and back-up tile to be 1 part Portland Cement – 1 part lime and 5 to 6 parts clean sharp sand; mortar beds to be ½" thick; ½" parging recommended back of Brick or surface of tile — All heights shown are standard for ½" mortar joint and 2¼" brick, other heights are available as standard.

STANDARD STRUCTURAL CLAY HOLLOW TILE for COMBINATION BRICK & TILE WALLS
Recommendations of the Structural Clay Products Institute-1941

HOLLOW TILE

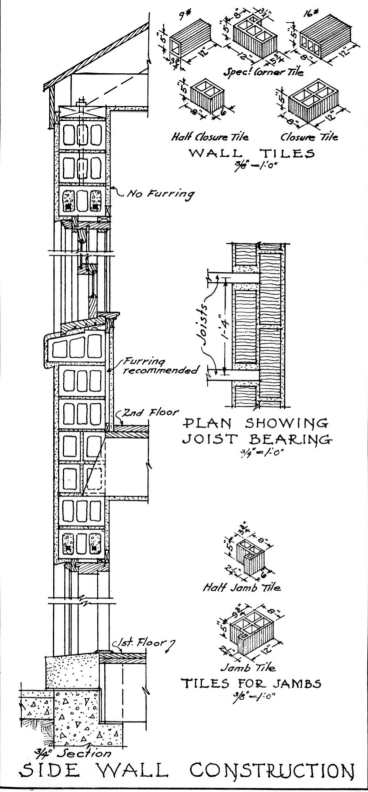

No Furring

Furring recommended

2nd Floor

PLAN SHOWING JOIST BEARING
3/4" = 1'-0"

9#   8#   16#
Spec! Corner Tile

Half Closure Tile   Closure Tile

WALL TILES
3/8" = 1'-0"

Half Jamb Tile

Jamb Tile

TILES FOR JAMBS
3/8" = 1'-0"

1st Floor

3/4" Section

SIDE WALL CONSTRUCTION

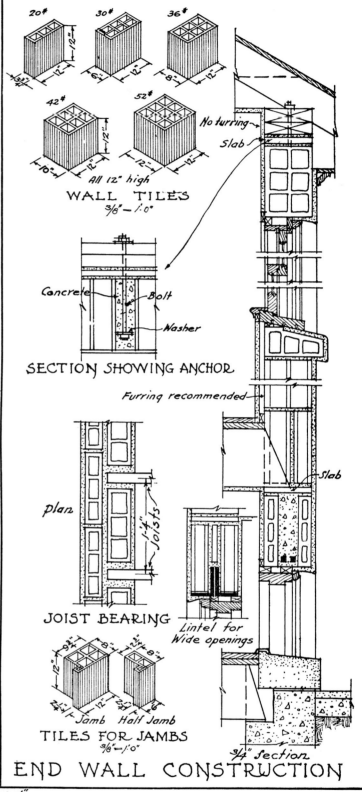

20#   30#   36#
42#   52#
All 12" high

WALL TILES
3/8" = 1'-0"

Concrete   Bolt
Washer

SECTION SHOWING ANCHOR

No furring
Slab

Furring recommended

Plan

Joists

JOIST BEARING

Slab

Lintel for Wide openings

Jamb   Half Jamb

TILES FOR JAMBS
3/8" = 1'-0"

3/4" Section

END WALL CONSTRUCTION

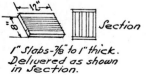

1" Slabs-7/8" to 1" thick. Delivered as shown in Section.

Section

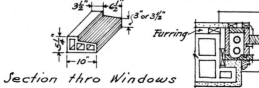

Furring

Section thro Windows

Door Jamb

DETAILS THAT APPLY TO BOTH TYPES OF WALLS

EXTERIOR WALL CONSTRUCTION with STUCCO FINISH

Recommendations of the Structural Clay Products Institute 1941

HOLLOW TILE

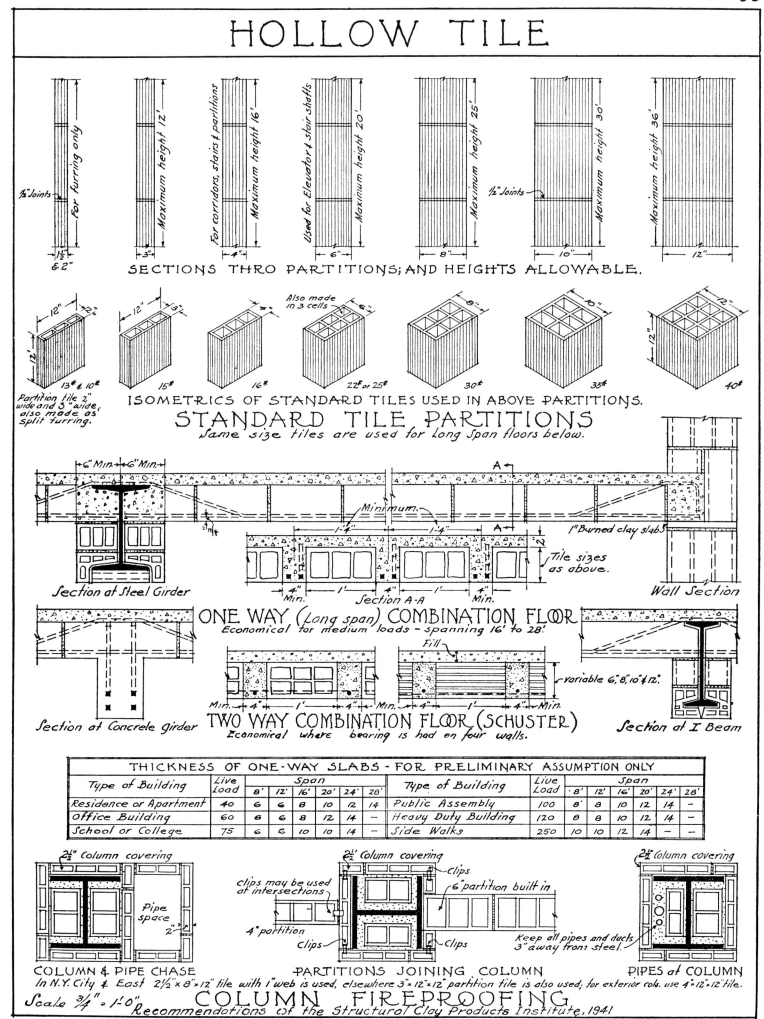

SECTIONS THRO PARTITIONS; AND HEIGHTS ALLOWABLE.

ISOMETRICS OF STANDARD TILES USED IN ABOVE PARTITIONS.

STANDARD TILE PARTITIONS
Same size tiles are used for Long Span floors below.

Section at Steel Girder — Section A-A — Wall Section

ONE WAY (Long span) COMBINATION FLOOR
Economical for medium loads - spanning 16' to 28'

Section at Concrete girder

TWO WAY COMBINATION FLOOR (SCHUSTER)
Economical where bearing is had on four walls.

Section at I Beam

THICKNESS OF ONE-WAY SLABS - FOR PRELIMINARY ASSUMPTION ONLY														
Type of Building	Live Load	Span						Type of Building	Live Load	Span				
		8'	12'	16'	20'	24'	28'			8'	12'	16'	20'	24'	28'
Residence or Apartment	40	6	6	8	10	12	14	Public Assembly	100	8	8	10	12	14	-
Office Building	60	6	6	8	12	14	-	Heavy Duty Building	120	8	8	10	12	14	-
School or College	75	6	6	10	10	14	-	Side Walks	250	10	10	12	14	-	-

COLUMN & PIPE CHASE — PARTITIONS JOINING COLUMN — PIPES at COLUMN

COLUMN FIREPROOFING
In N.Y. City & East 2½"x8"x12" tile with 1" web is used, elsewhere 3"x12"x12" partition tile is also used; for exterior cols. use 4"x12"x12" tile.

Scale ¾" = 1'-0" Recommendations of the Structural Clay Products Institute, 1941

CUT STONE

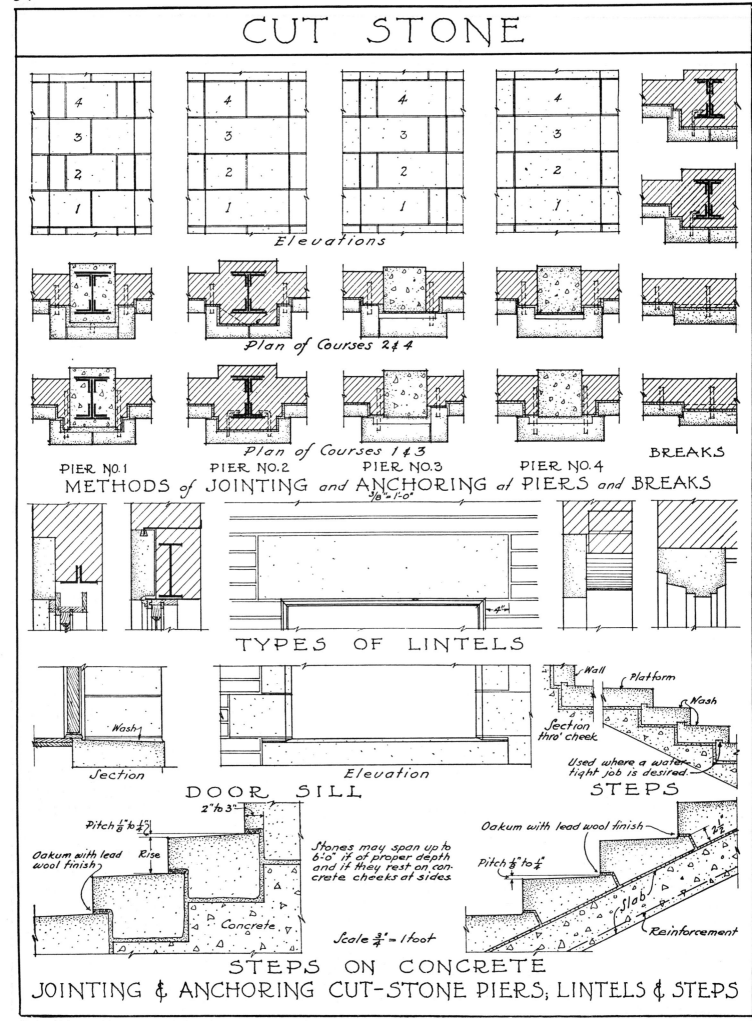

Elevations

Plan of Courses 2 & 4

Plan of Courses 1 & 3

BREAKS

PIER NO.1   PIER NO.2   PIER NO.3   PIER NO.4

METHODS of JOINTING and ANCHORING at PIERS and BREAKS

$3/8" = 1'-0"$

TYPES OF LINTELS

Wash

Section

Elevation

DOOR SILL

Wall

Platform

Wash

Section thro' cheek

Used where a water-tight job is desired.

STEPS

Pitch $1/8"$ to $1/4"$

2" to 3"

Oakum with lead wool finish

Rise

Stones may span up to 6'-0" if of proper depth and if they rest on concrete cheeks at sides.

Concrete

Scale $3/4" = 1$ foot

Oakum with lead wool finish

Pitch $1/8"$ to $1/4"$

$2\frac{1}{2}"$

Slab

Reinforcement

STEPS ON CONCRETE

JOINTING & ANCHORING CUT-STONE PIERS, LINTELS & STEPS

CUT STONE

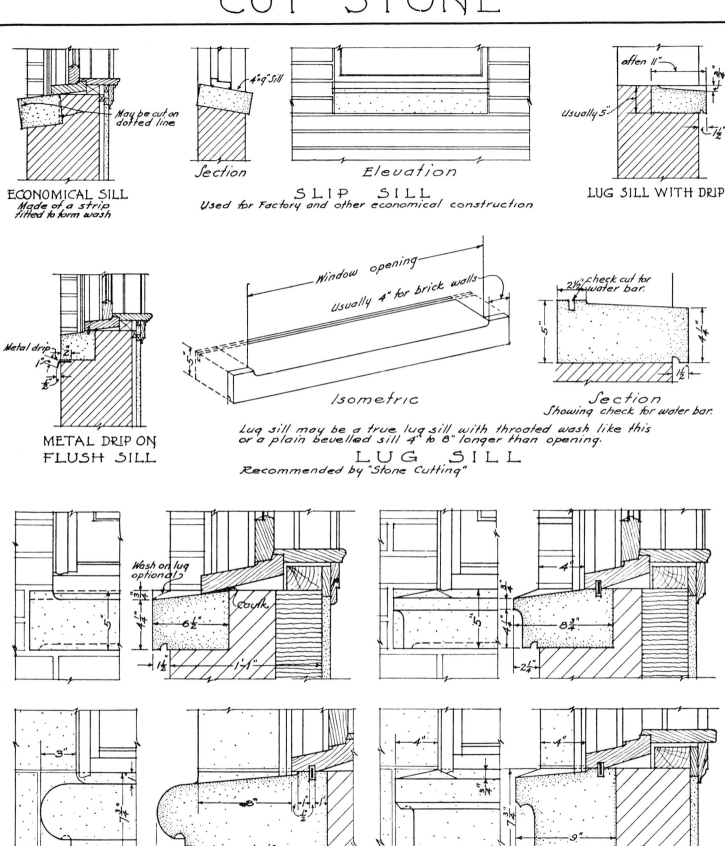

ECONOMICAL SILL
Made of a strip fitted to form wash

SLIP SILL
Used for Factory and other economical construction

LUG SILL WITH DRIP

METAL DRIP ON FLUSH SILL

LUG SILL
Recommended by "Stone Cutting"

Lug sill may be a true lug sill with throated wash like this
or a plain bevelled sill 4" to 8" longer than opening.

VARIOUS TYPES OF SILLS SHOWING DRIPS & WASHES
Recommendations of the Indiana Limestone Co.

CUT STONE WINDOW SILLS

Scales ¾" & 1½" = 1'-0"

CUT STONE

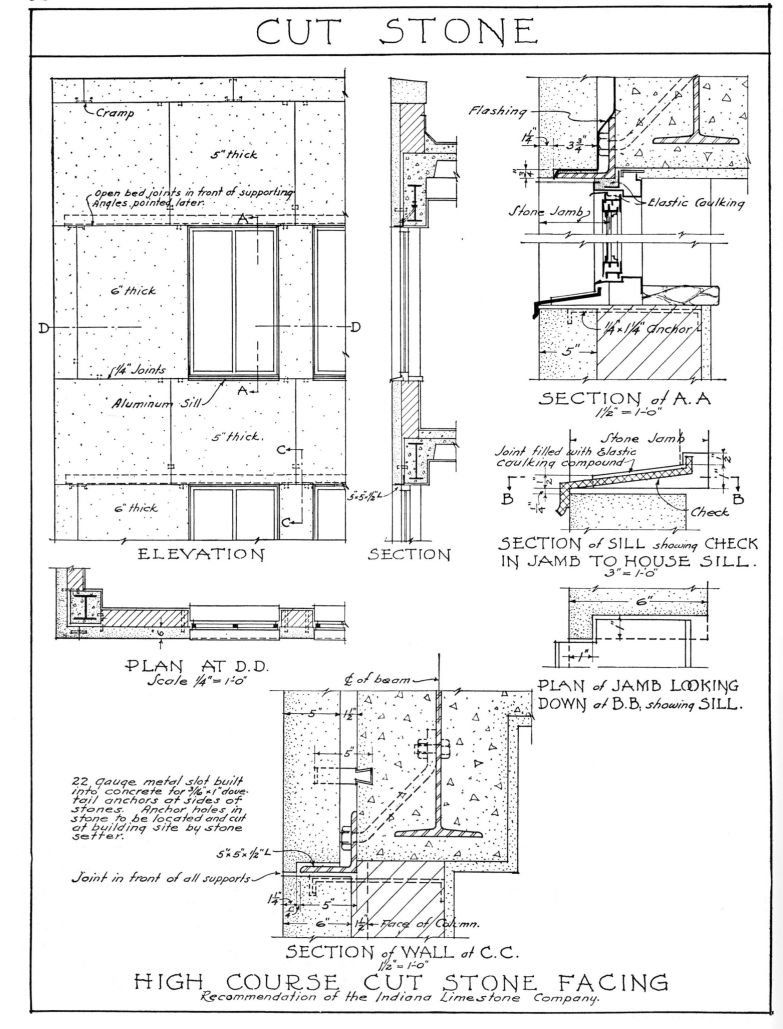

Cramp

5" thick

open bed joints in front of supporting
Angles, pointed later.

6" thick

1¼" Joints

Aluminum Sill

5" thick.

6" thick

ELEVATION

SECTION

5"×5"×½"L

Flashing

1¼"   3¾"

¾"

Stone Jamb

Elastic Caulking

¼"×1¼" Anchor

5"

SECTION of A.A
1½" = 1'-0"

Stone Jamb

Joint filled with Elastic
Caulking compound

Check

**SECTION of SILL showing CHECK
IN JAMB TO HOUSE SILL.**
3" = 1'-0"

6"

1"

**PLAN of JAMB LOOKING
DOWN of B.B, showing SILL.**

PLAN AT D.D.
Scale ¼" = 1'-0"

6

₵ of beam

5"   1½"

5"

22 gauge metal slot built
into concrete for ³∕₁₆"×1" dovetail anchors at sides of
stones. Anchor holes in
stone to be located and cut
at building site by stone
setter.

5"×5"×½"L

Joint in front of all supports

1¼"

5"

6"   1½" Face of Column.

SECTION of WALL at C.C.
1½" = 1'-0"

HIGH COURSE CUT STONE FACING
Recommendation of the Indiana Limestone Company.

CUT STONE

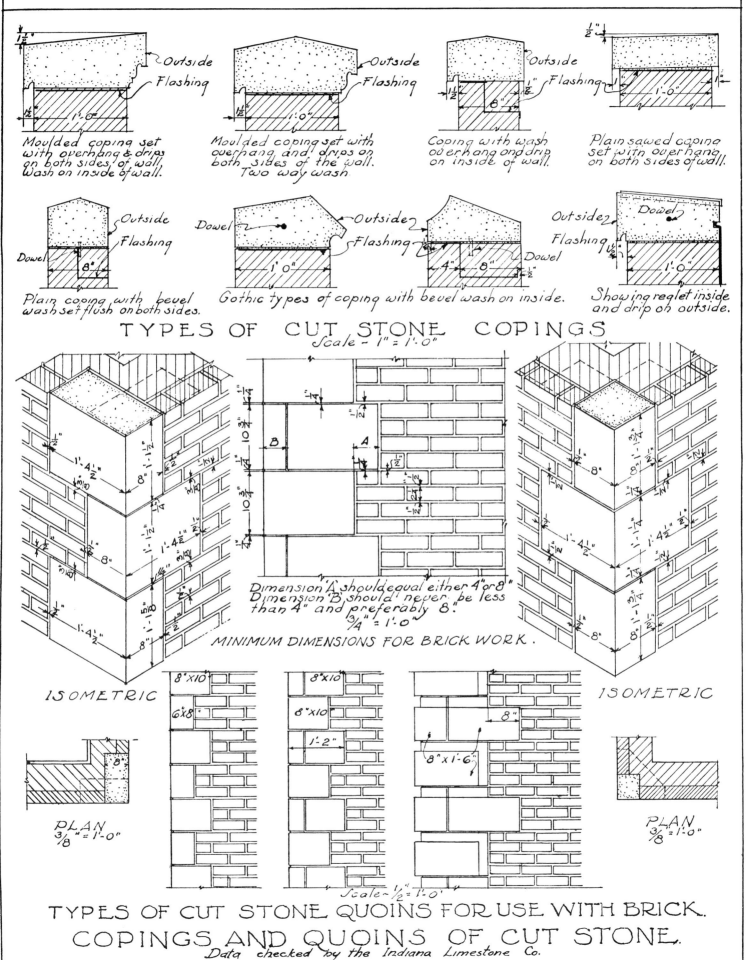

Moulded coping set with overhang & drips on both sides of wall. Wash on inside of wall.

Moulded coping set with overhang and drips on both sides of the wall. Two way wash.

Coping with wash overhang and drip on inside of wall.

Plain sawed coping set with overhang on both sides of wall.

Plain coping with bevel wash set flush on both sides.

Gothic types of coping with bevel wash on inside.

Showing reglet inside and drip on outside.

TYPES OF CUT STONE COPINGS
Scale - 1" = 1'-0"

Dimension 'A' should equal either 4" or 8". Dimension 'B' should never be less than 4" and preferably 8".
3/4" = 1'-0"

MINIMUM DIMENSIONS FOR BRICK WORK.

ISOMETRIC

ISOMETRIC

PLAN 3/8" = 1'-0"

PLAN 3/8" = 1'-0"

Scale - 1/2" = 1'-0"

TYPES OF CUT STONE QUOINS FOR USE WITH BRICK.
COPINGS AND QUOINS OF CUT STONE.
Data checked by the Indiana Limestone Co.

CUT STONE

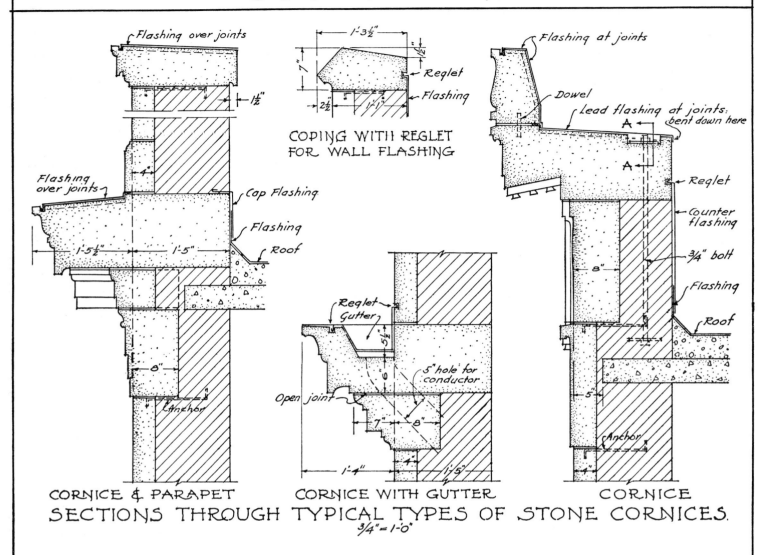

Flashing over joints

1'-3½"

COPING WITH REGLET
FOR WALL FLASHING

Reglet
Flashing
2½"   1'-1"

Flashing at joints

Dowel

Lead flashing at joints
bent down here

Reglet

Counter flashing

¾" bolt

Flashing

Roof

Anchor

Flashing over joints

Cap Flashing

Flashing

Roof

1'-5½"   1'-5"

8"

Anchor

CORNICE & PARAPET

Reglet
Gutter

5" hole for conductor

Open joint

7"   8"

1'-4"   4"   1'-5"

CORNICE WITH GUTTER

CORNICE

SECTIONS THROUGH TYPICAL TYPES OF STONE CORNICES.
3/4"=1'-0"

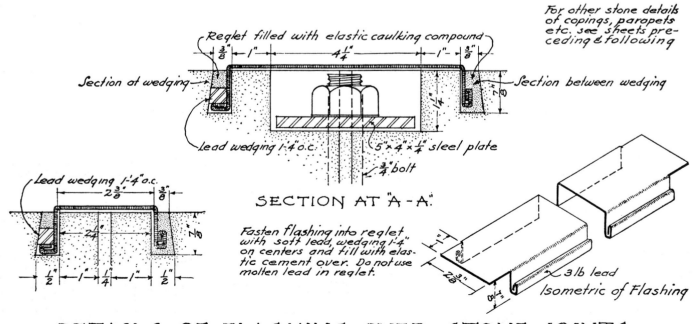

For other stone details of copings, parapets etc. see sheets preceding & following

Reglet filled with elastic caulking compound

⅜" 1"   4¼"   1"   ⅝"

Section at wedging

Section between wedging

Lead wedging 1'-4" o.c.

5"×4"×¼" steel plate

¾" bolt

SECTION AT "A-A"

Fasten flashing into reglet with soft lead, wedging 1'-4" on centers and fill with elastic cement over. Do not use molten lead in reglet.

Lead wedging 1'-4" o.c.

2⅜"   ⅜"

2¼"

½" 1" 1¼" 1" ½"

3 lb lead
Isometric of Flashing

DETAILS OF FLASHING OVER STONE JOINTS
LIMESTONE CORNICES SHOWING FLASHING
Recommendations of the Indiana Limestone Co

STONE WORK

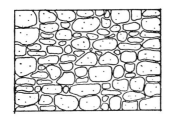
UNCOURSED FIELDSTONE
ROUGH OR ORDINARY.

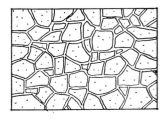
POLYGONAL, MOSAIC
OR RANDOM.

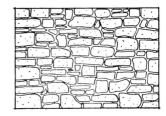
COURSED

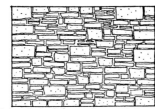
Laid of stratified stone fitted on job.
It is between rubble & ashlar. Finish
is quarry face, seam face or split.
Called rubble ashlar in granite.

TYPES OF RUBBLE MASONRY

SQUARED-STONE MASONRY.

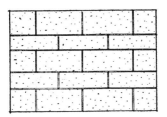
RANGE.
Coursed

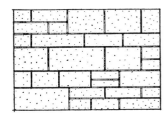
BROKEN RANGE.

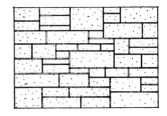
RANDOM RANGE.
Interrupted coursed

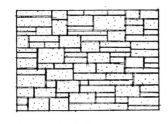
RANDOM RANGE.
Coursed (Long stones)

TYPES OF ASHLAR MASONRY
This is stone that is sawed, dressed, squared or Quarry faced.

ELEVATIONS SHOWING FACE JOINTING FOR STONE.

Draft line
For both hard and
soft stones.
Rock or Pitch Face.

Smooth, but saw mark
visible. All stones.
Sawed Finish (Gang).

More marked than
sawed. Soft stones.
Shot Sawed (Rough).

Smooth finish with some
texture. Soft stones.
Machine Finish (Planer).

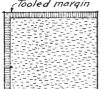
Tooled margin
May be coarse, medium or
fine. Usually on hard stones.
Pointed Finish.

After pointing on
hard stones.
Pean Hammered.

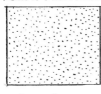
For soft stones
Bush-hammered.

All stones. Used much on
granite. 4 to 8 cut in 7/8".
Patent Bush-hammer.

For soft stones.
Drove or Boasted.

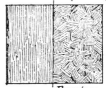
For soft stones.
Hand Tooled.

Tool marks may be 2 to 10 per inch.
Machine Tooled.

For soft stones.
Tooth-chisel.

Random
For soft stones.
Crandalled.

Textured by machine
For Limestone
Plucker Finish.

Very smooth.
For Limestone.
Done by machine
Carborundum Finish.

Smooth
All stones. May use
sand or carborundum.
Rubbed (Wet).

Very Smooth
Marble, granite. For
interior work. Soft stones.
Honed (rubbed first).

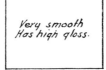
Very smooth
Has high gloss.
Marble and granite.
Polished (honed first).

STONE FINISHES.
Seam face and split face (or quarry face) not shown as they are not worked finishes.

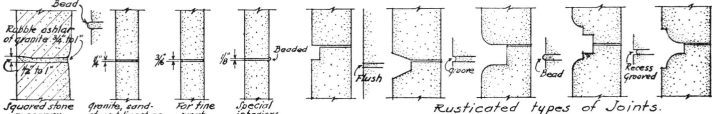
Bead
Rubble ashlar
of granite 3/4 to 1"
Squared stone masonry
1/2 to 1"

1/4
granite, sandstone & limestone
ashlar. general use.

3/16
For fine work.
Limestone

1/8
Beaded
Special interiors

Flush

Groove

Bead

Recess Grooved

Rusticated types of Joints.

STONE JOINTS

TYPES, FINISH AND JOINTING OF STONE MASONRY.
A perch is nominally 16'-6" long, 1'-0" high & 1'-6" thick = 24¾ cu.ft. In some localities 16½ & 22 cu.ft. are used.

STONE WORK

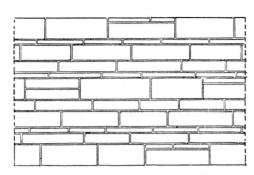

· FOUR UNIT, LONG TYPE RANGE WORK ·
Average length of Stones four times height
· BROKEN RANGE ·

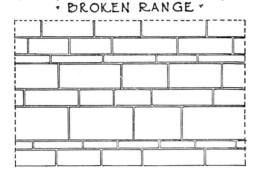

· FOUR UNIT, MEDIUM TYPE RANGE WORK ·
Average length of Stones about 2½ times their height.
· RANGE ·

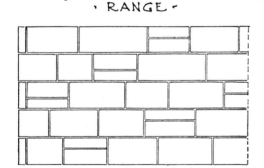

· EQUAL COURSE HEIGHTS ·
With occasional units divided by horizontal joints.
· BROKEN RANGE ·

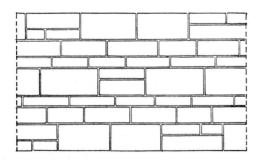

· · THREE UNIT RANGE WORK ·
With occasional Horizontal joints in the higher Courses.
· BROKEN · RANGE ·
This type of Stone is delivered in strips & jointed to length at the job. Joints all ½" except where noted ¾".
· RANGE & BROKEN RANGE ·

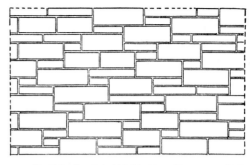

· TWO UNIT, MEDIUM TYPE RANDOM ASHLAR ·
Average length of larger Stones is three times height.

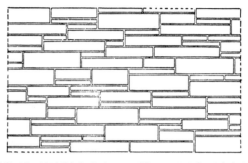

THREE UNIT, LONG TYPE RANDOM ASHLAR ·
Average length of Stones 4 times height or more .

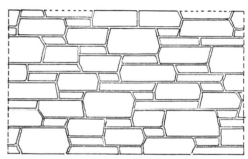

· THREE UNIT RANDOM ASHLAR; ANGULAR BROKEN END ·
Average length of larger Stones 2 times their height.
Joints ¾" thick.

· THREE UNIT MEDIUM TYPE RANDOM ASHLAR ·
· *Average length of larger Stones about twice the height.*

· RANDOM RANGE ·

· Scale:- ¼"=1'0" ·
· JOINTING · OF · STRIP · LIMESTONE · ASHLAR ·
Recommendations of the "Indiana Limestone Co."

STONE WALLS

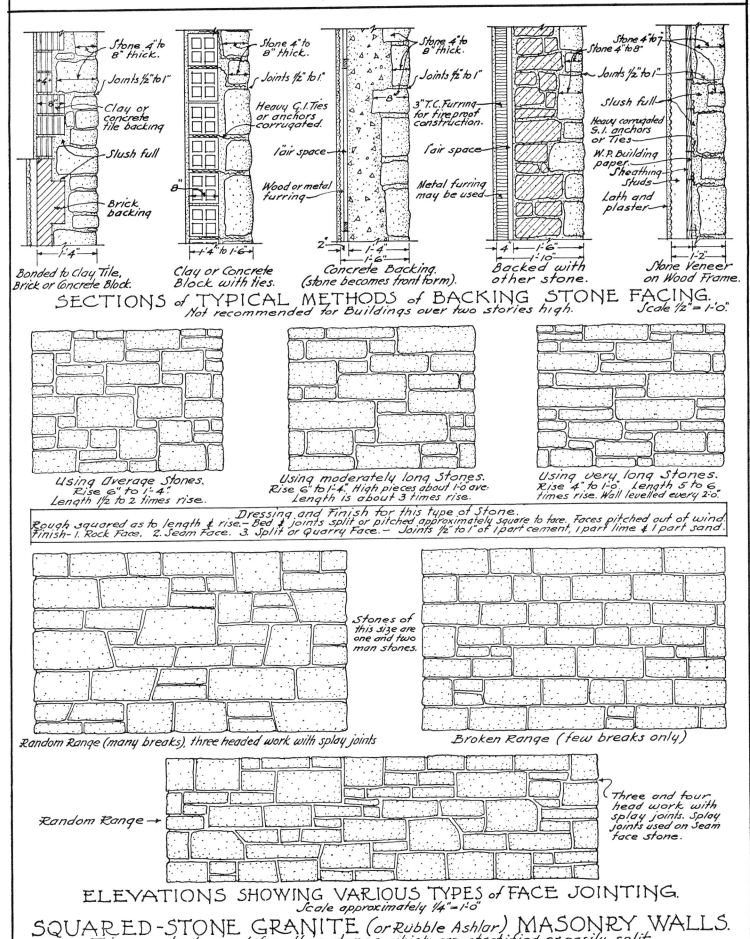

Stone 4" to 8" thick.
Joints 1/2" to 1"
Clay or concrete tile backing
Slush full
Brick backing

Bonded to Clay Tile, Brick or Concrete Block.

Stone 4" to 8" thick.
Joints 1/2" to 1"
Heavy G.I. Ties or anchors corrugated.
1" air space
Wood or metal furring

Clay or Concrete Block with ties.

Stone 4" to 8" thick.
Joints 1/2" to 1"
3" T.C. Furring for fireproof construction.
1" air space
Metal furring may be used

Concrete Backing. (stone becomes front form).

Stone 4" to 7"
Stone 4" to 8"
Joints 1/2" to 1"
Slush full
Heavy corrugated G.I. anchors or Ties
W.P. Building paper.
Sheathing
Studs
Lath and plaster

Backed with other stone.

Stone Veneer on Wood Frame.

SECTIONS of TYPICAL METHODS of BACKING STONE FACING.
Not recommended for Buildings over two stories high.
Scale 1/2" = 1'-0".

Using average Stones. Rise 6" to 1'-4". Length 1 1/2 to 2 times rise.

Using moderately long Stones. Rise 6" to 1'-4". High pieces about 1'-0 ave. Length is about 3 times rise.

Using very long Stones. Rise 4" to 1'-0". Length 5 to 6 times rise. Wall levelled every 2'-0".

Dressing and Finish for this type of Stone.
Rough squared as to length & rise.— Bed & joints split or pitched approximately square to face. Faces pitched out of wind.
Finish— 1. Rock Face. 2. Seam Face. 3. Split or Quarry Face.— Joints 1/2" to 1" of 1 part cement, 1 part lime & 1 part sand.

Random Range (many breaks), three headed work with splay joints

Stones of this size are one and two man stones.

Broken Range (few breaks only)

Random Range →

Three and four head work with splay joints. Splay joints used on Seam face stone.

ELEVATIONS SHOWING VARIOUS TYPES of FACE JOINTING.
Scale approximately 1/4" = 1'-0"

SQUARED-STONE GRANITE (or Rubble Ashlar) MASONRY WALLS.
This may also be used for other stones which are stratified or easily split.

GRANITE

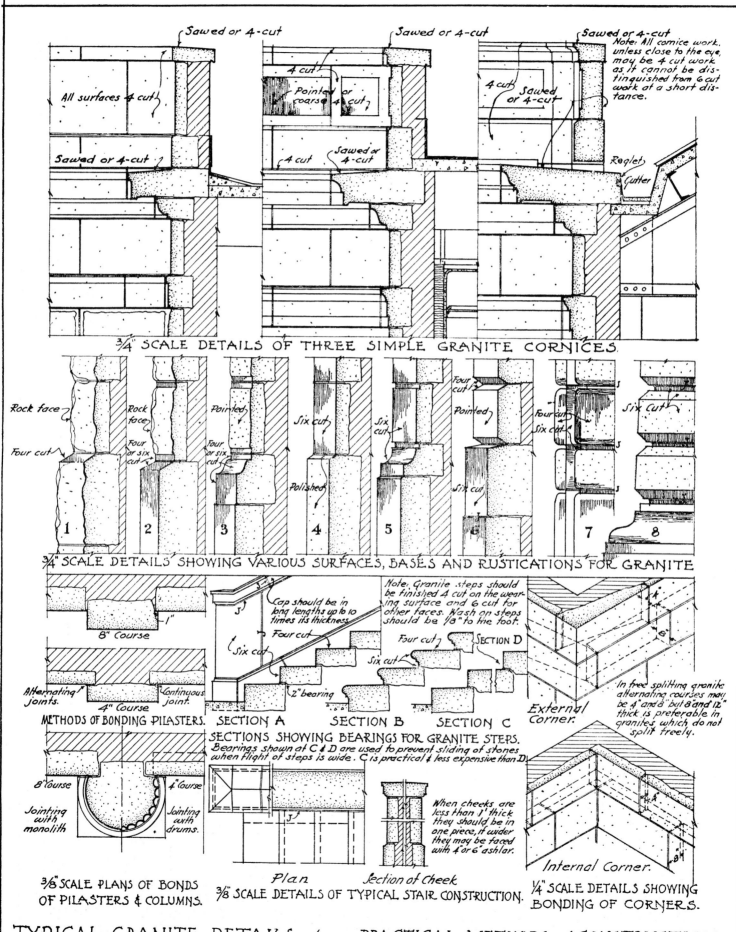

Sawed or 4-cut

All surfaces 4 cut

Sawed or 4-cut

Sawed or 4-cut

4 cut

Pointed or coarse 4 cut

4 cut

Sawed or 4-cut

Sawed or 4-cut

4 cut

4 cut

Sawed or 4-cut

Note: All cornice work, unless close to the eye, may be 4 cut work as it cannot be distinquished from 6 cut work at a short distance.

Reglet

Gutter

¾" SCALE DETAILS OF THREE SIMPLE GRANITE CORNICES.

Rock face

Four cut

Rock face

Four or six cut

Pointed

Four or six cut

Six cut

Polished

Six cut

Pointed

Six cut

Four cut

Six cut

Four cut

Six cut

1   2   3   4   5   6   7   8

¾" SCALE DETAILS SHOWING VARIOUS SURFACES, BASES AND RUSTICATIONS FOR GRANITE

1"

8" Course

Alternating joints.

4" Course

Continuous joint.

METHODS OF BONDING PILASTERS.

8" course

4" course

Jointing with monolith.

Jointing with drums.

3/8" SCALE PLANS OF BONDS OF PILASTERS & COLUMNS.

Cap should be in long lengths up to 10 times its thickness.

Four cut

Six cut

2" bearing

SECTION A

Note: Granite steps should be finished 4 cut on the wearing surface and 6 cut for other faces. Wash on steps should be ⅛" to the foot.

Four cut

Six cut

SECTION B

SECTION C

Four cut

SECTION D

Six cut

SECTIONS SHOWING BEARINGS FOR GRANITE STEPS.

Bearings shown at C & D are used to prevent sliding of stones when flight of steps is wide. C is practical & less expensive than D.

Plan

Section of Cheek

When cheeks are less than 1" thick they should be in one piece, if wider they may be faced with 4" or 6" ashlar.

3/8" SCALE DETAILS OF TYPICAL STAIR CONSTRUCTION.

External Corner.

In free splitting granite alternating courses may be 4" and 8" but 8" and 12" thick is preferable in granites which do not split freely.

Internal Corner.

¼" SCALE DETAILS SHOWING BONDING OF CORNERS.

TYPICAL GRANITE DETAILS showing PRACTICAL METHODS of CONSTRUCTION.

Recommendations of the National Building Granite Quarries Association.

ANCHORING of STONEWORK

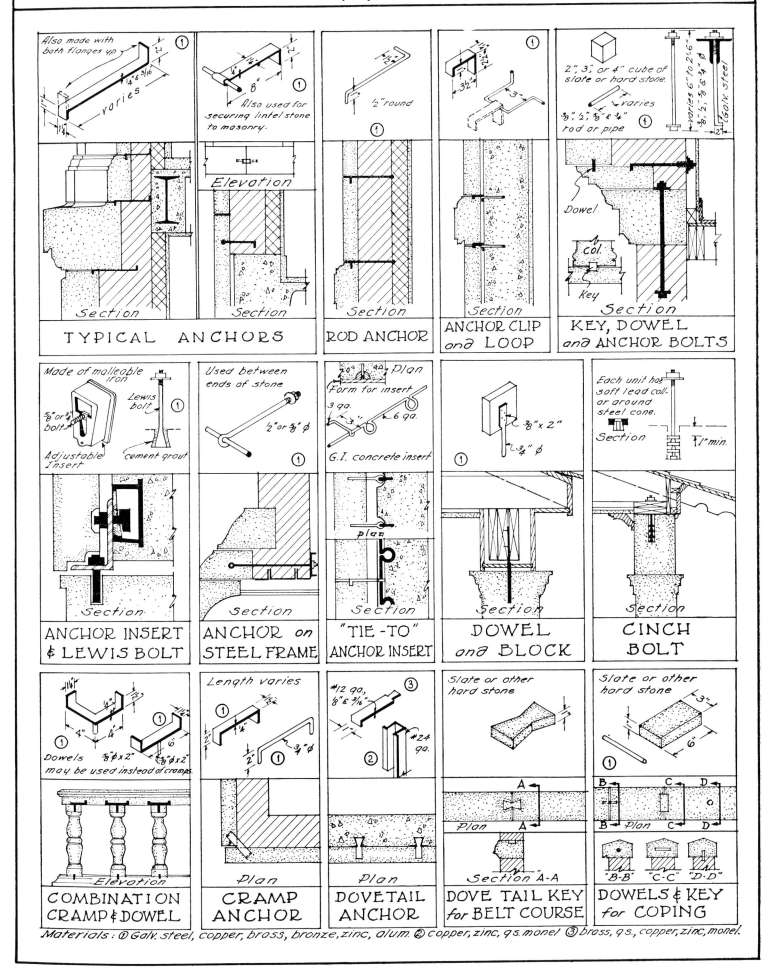

TYPICAL ANCHORS

ROD ANCHOR

ANCHOR CLIP and LOOP

KEY, DOWEL and ANCHOR BOLTS

ANCHOR INSERT & LEWIS BOLT

ANCHOR on STEEL FRAME

"TIE-TO" ANCHOR INSERT

DOWEL and BLOCK

CINCH BOLT

COMBINATION CRAMP & DOWEL

CRAMP ANCHOR

DOVETAIL ANCHOR

DOVE TAIL KEY for BELT COURSE

DOWELS & KEY for COPING

Materials : ① Galv. steel, copper, brass, bronze, zinc, alum. ② copper, zinc, g.s. monel ③ brass, g.s., copper, zinc, monel.

MASONRY ARCHES

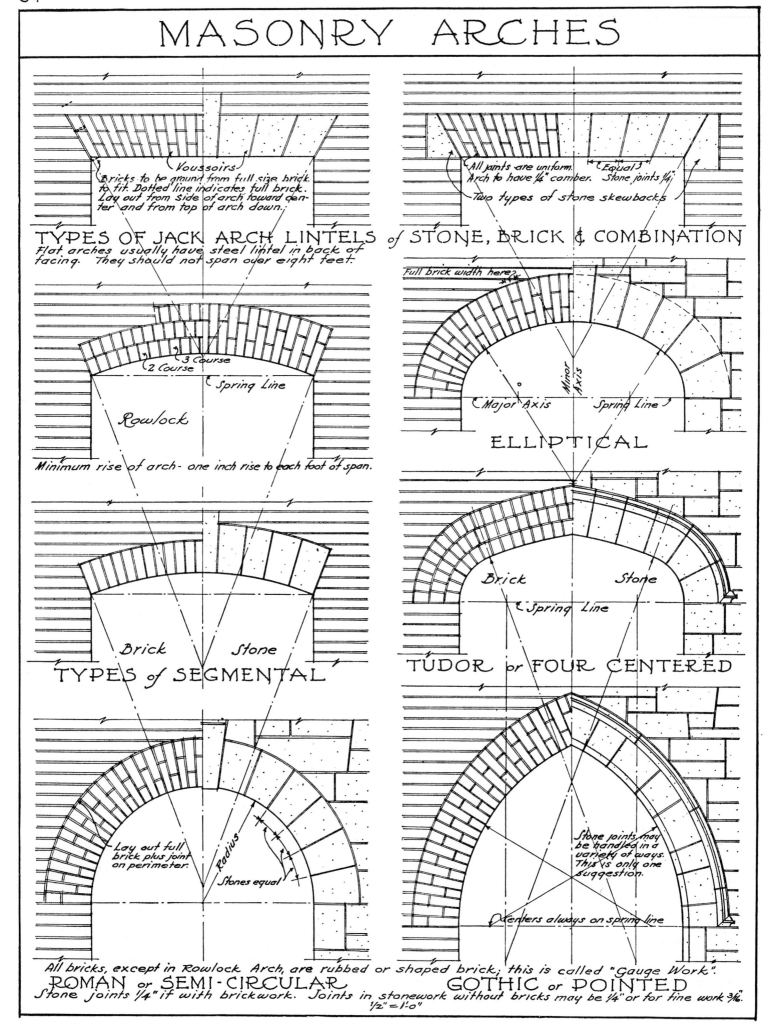

Voussoirs

Bricks to be ground from full size brick to fit. Dotted line indicates full brick. Lay out from side of arch toward center and from top of arch down.

TYPES OF JACK ARCH LINTELS *of* **STONE, BRICK & COMBINATION**

Flat arches usually have steel lintel in back of facing. They should not span over eight feet.

3 Course / *2 Course* / *Spring Line*

Rowlock

Minimum rise of arch - one inch rise to each foot of span.

All joints are uniform. *Equal* Arch to have 1/4" camber. Stone joints 1/4. Two types of stone skewbacks

Full brick width here?

Minor Axis / *Major Axis* / *Spring Line*

ELLIPTICAL

Brick *Stone*

TYPES of SEGMENTAL

Brick *Stone* / *Spring Line*

TUDOR *or* **FOUR CENTERED**

Lay out full brick plus joint on perimeter. *Radius* / *Stones equal*

ROMAN *or* **SEMI-CIRCULAR**

Stone joints may be handled in a variety of ways. This is only one suggestion.

Centers always on spring line

GOTHIC *or* **POINTED**

All bricks, except in Rowlock Arch, are rubbed or shaped brick; this is called "Gauge Work". Stone joints 1/4" if with brickwork. Joints in stonework without bricks may be 1/4" or for fine work 3/16.

1/2" = 1'0"

SPANDRELS

For specific details see pages, "Precast Masonry for Walls", "Facing & Curtain Wall Panels" & "Aluminum Spandrels".

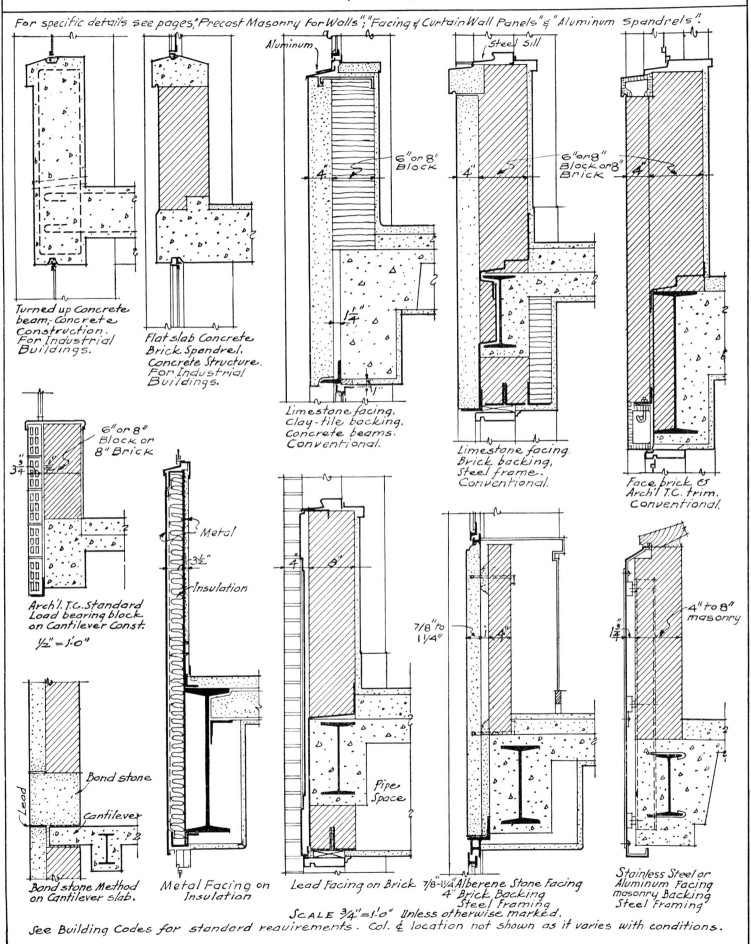

Turned up Concrete beam. Concrete Construction. For Industrial Buildings.

Flat slab Concrete Brick Spandrel. Concrete Structure. For Industrial Buildings.

Limestone facing. Clay-tile backing. Concrete beams. Conventional.

Limestone facing. Brick backing. Steel frame. Conventional.

Face brick & Arch'l T.C. trim. Conventional.

Arch'l. T.C. Standard Load bearing block on Cantilever Const. ½" = 1'-0"

Bond stone Method on Cantilever slab.

Metal Facing on Insulation

Lead Facing on Brick

Alberene Stone Facing 4" Brick Backing Steel Framing

Stainless Steel or Aluminum Facing masonry Backing Steel Framing

SCALE ¾" = 1'-0" Unless otherwise marked.

See Building Codes for standard requirements. Col. & location not shown as it varies with conditions.

MASONRY FLOORING & PAVING

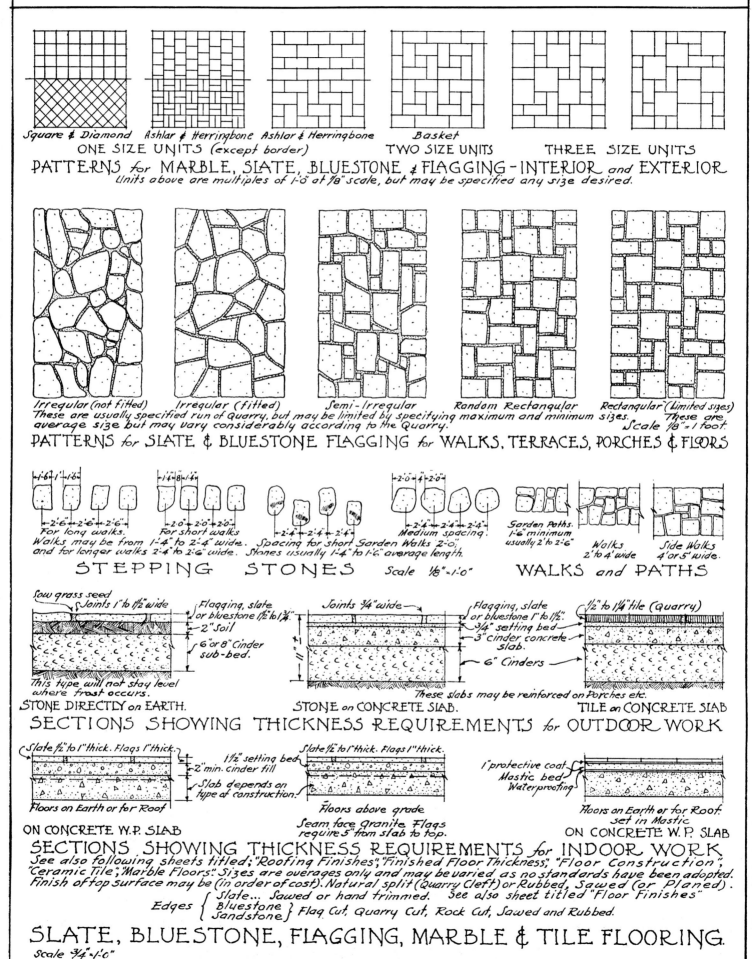

Square & Diamond | Ashlar & Herringbone | Ashlar & Herringbone | Basket
ONE SIZE UNITS (except border) | TWO SIZE UNITS | THREE SIZE UNITS

PATTERNS for MARBLE, SLATE, BLUESTONE & FLAGGING – INTERIOR and EXTERIOR
Units above are multiples of 1'-0 at 1/8" scale, but may be specified any size desired.

Irregular (not fitted) | Irregular (fitted) | Semi-Irregular | Random Rectangular | Rectangular (limited sizes)
These are usually specified run of Quarry, but may be limited by specifying maximum and minimum sizes.
These are usually specified by average size but may vary considerably according to the Quarry. Scale 1/8" = 1 foot

PATTERNS for SLATE & BLUESTONE FLAGGING for WALKS, TERRACES, PORCHES & FLOORS

STEPPING STONES   Scale 1/8"=1'-0"   WALKS and PATHS

SECTIONS SHOWING THICKNESS REQUIREMENTS for OUTDOOR WORK

STONE DIRECTLY on EARTH. | STONE on CONCRETE SLAB. | TILE on CONCRETE SLAB

SECTIONS SHOWING THICKNESS REQUIREMENTS for INDOOR WORK

ON CONCRETE W.P. SLAB | | ON CONCRETE W.P. SLAB

See also following sheets titled; "Roofing Finishes", "Finished Floor Thickness", "Floor Construction", "Ceramic Tile", "Marble Floors". Sizes are overages only and may be varied as no standards have been adopted. Finish of top surface may be (in order of cost). Natural split (Quarry Cleft) or Rubbed, Sawed (or Planed).
Edges { Slate... Sawed or hand trimmed.   See also sheet titled "Floor Finishes"
Bluestone / Sandstone } Flag Cut, Quarry Cut, Rock Cut, Sawed and Rubbed.

SLATE, BLUESTONE, FLAGGING, MARBLE & TILE FLOORING.
Scale 3/4"=1'-0"

CONCRETE BLOCK

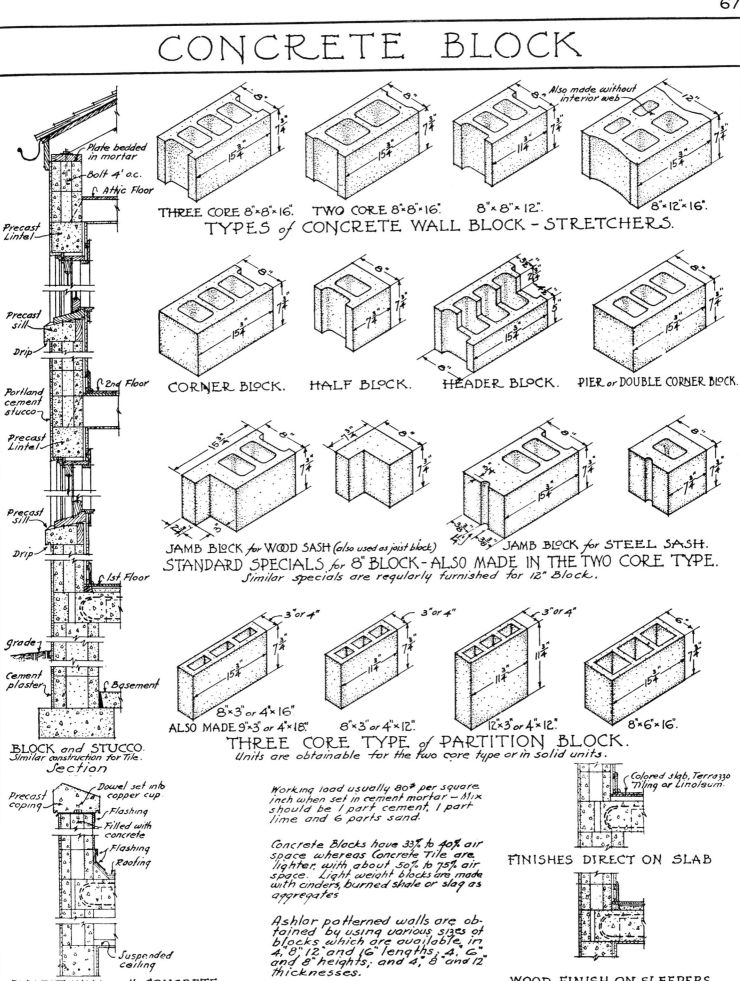

Plate bedded in mortar
Bolt 4' o.c.
Attic Floor
Precast Lintel
Precast sill
Drip
Portland cement stucco
2nd Floor
Precast Lintel
Precast sill
Drip
1st Floor
grade
Cement plaster
Basement

BLOCK and STUCCO.
Similar construction for Tile.
Section

THREE CORE 8"x8"x16".   TWO CORE 8"x8"x16".   8"x8"x12".   Also made without interior web   8"x12"x16".

TYPES of CONCRETE WALL BLOCK - STRETCHERS.

CORNER BLOCK.   HALF BLOCK.   HEADER BLOCK.   PIER or DOUBLE CORNER BLOCK.

JAMB BLOCK for WOOD SASH (also used as joist block)   JAMB BLOCK for STEEL SASH.

STANDARD SPECIALS for 8" BLOCK - ALSO MADE IN THE TWO CORE TYPE.
Similar specials are regularly furnished for 12" Block.

3" or 4"   3" or 4"   3" or 4"
8"x3" or 4"x16".   8"x3" or 4"x12".   12"x3" or 4"x12".   8"x6"x16".
ALSO MADE 9"x3" or 4"x18".

THREE CORE TYPE of PARTITION BLOCK.
Units are obtainable for the two core type or in solid units.

Precast coping
Dowel set into copper cup.
Flashing
Filled with concrete
Flashing
Roofing
Suspended ceiling

PARAPET WALL with CONCRETE ROOF

Working load usually 80# per square inch when set in cement mortar – Mix should be 1 part cement, 1 part lime and 6 parts sand.

Concrete Blocks have 33% to 40% air space whereas Concrete Tile are lighter, with about 50% to 75% air space. Light weight blocks are made with cinders, burned shale or slag as aggregates

Ashlar patterned walls are obtained by using various sizes of blocks which are available in 4", 8", 12" and 16" lengths; 4", 6" and 8" heights; and 4", 8" and 12" thicknesses.

Colored slab, Terrazzo Tiling or Linoleum.

FINISHES DIRECT ON SLAB

WOOD FINISH ON SLEEPERS

CONCRETE BUILDING BLOCKS
Recommendations of the Portland Cement Association

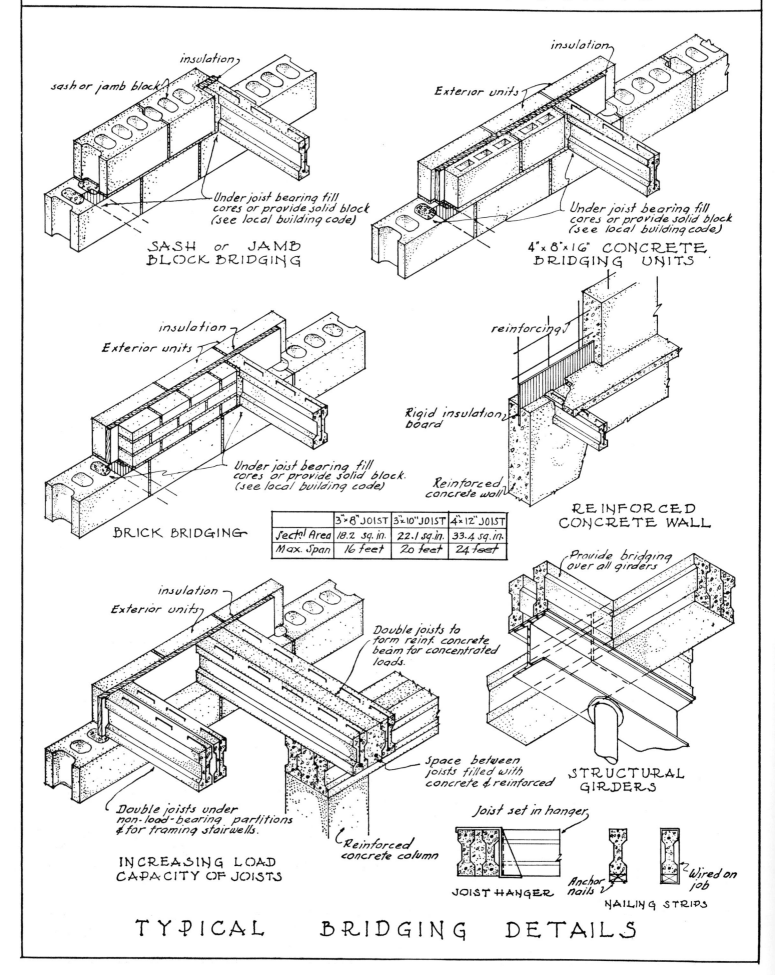

PRECAST CONCRETE JOISTS

68

SASH or JAMB BLOCK BRIDGING

4"x 8"x 16" CONCRETE BRIDGING UNITS

insulation
sash or jamb block
Under joist bearing fill cores or provide solid block (see local building code)

Exterior units
insulation
Under joist bearing fill cores or provide solid block (see local building code)

BRICK BRIDGING

Exterior units
insulation
Under joist bearing fill cores or provide solid block. (see local building code)

REINFORCED CONCRETE WALL

reinforcing
Rigid insulation board
Reinforced concrete wall

	3"x8" JOIST	3"x10" JOIST	4"x12" JOIST
Sect'l Area	18.2 sq.in.	22.1 sq.in.	33.4 sq.in.
Max. Span	16 feet	20 feet	24 feet

INCREASING LOAD CAPACITY OF JOISTS

insulation
Exterior units
Double joists to form reinf. concrete beam for concentrated loads.
Double joists under non-load-bearing partitions & for framing stairwells.
Space between joists filled with concrete & reinforced
Reinforced concrete column

STRUCTURAL GIRDERS

Provide bridging over all girders

JOIST HANGER
Joist set in hanger
Anchor nails
NAILING STRIPS
Wired on job

TYPICAL   BRIDGING   DETAILS

PRECAST MASONRY *for* WALLS

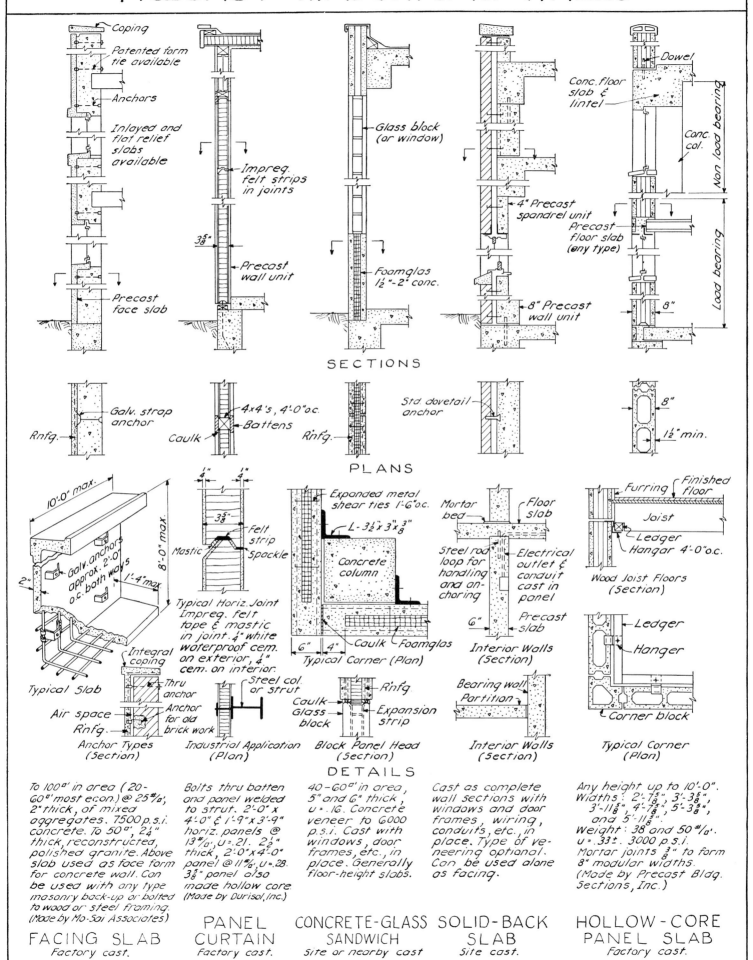

SECTIONS

PLANS

DETAILS

FACING SLAB
Factory cast.

PANEL CURTAIN
Factory cast.

CONCRETE-GLASS SANDWICH
site or nearby cast

SOLID-BACK SLAB
Site cast.

HOLLOW-CORE PANEL SLAB
Factory cast.

CONCRETE TILE

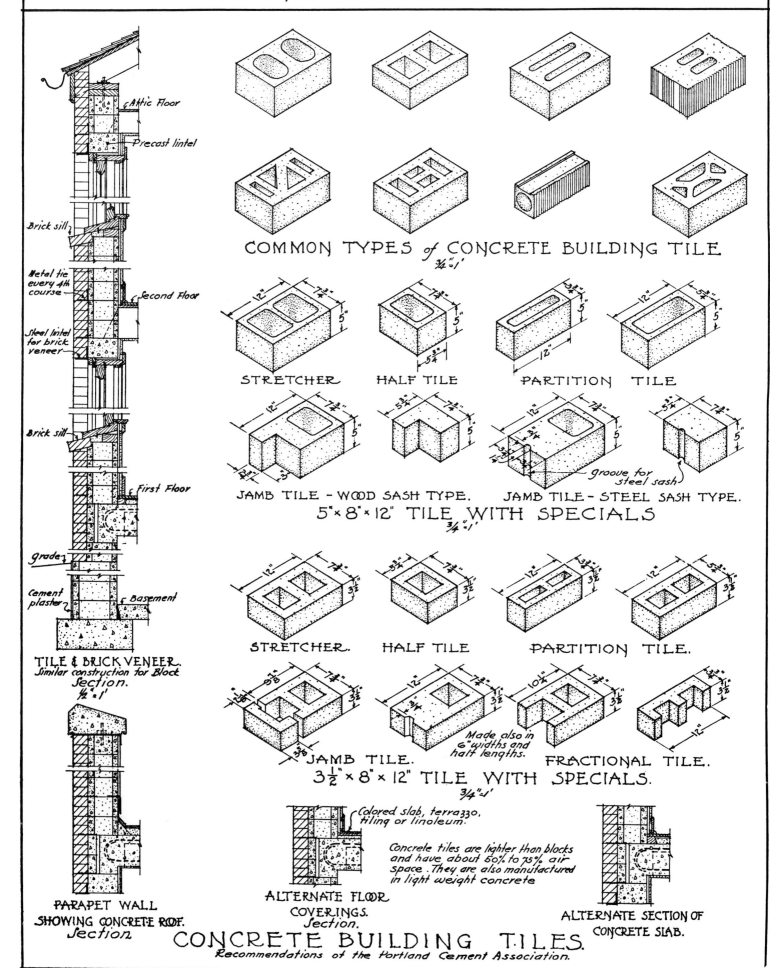

COMMON TYPES of CONCRETE BUILDING TILE
¾"=1'

STRETCHER   HALF TILE   PARTITION   TILE

JAMB TILE - WOOD SASH TYPE.   JAMB TILE - STEEL SASH TYPE.

groove for steel sash

5" × 8" × 12" TILE WITH SPECIALS
¾"=1'

STRETCHER.   HALF TILE   PARTITION   TILE.

JAMB TILE.   FRACTIONAL TILE.

Made also in 6" widths and half lengths.

3½" × 8" × 12" TILE WITH SPECIALS.
¾"=1'

Attic Floor
Precast lintel
Brick sill
Metal tie every 4th course
Second Floor
Steel lintel for brick veneer
Brick sill
First Floor
grade
Cement plaster
Basement

TILE & BRICK VENEER.
Similar construction for Block
Section.
½"=1'

PARAPET WALL
SHOWING CONCRETE ROOF.
Section

Colored slab, terrazzo, tiling or linoleum.

Concrete tiles are lighter than blocks and have about 50% to 75% air space. They are also manufactured in light weight concrete

ALTERNATE FLOOR
COVERINGS.
Section.

ALTERNATE SECTION OF
CONCRETE SLAB.

CONCRETE BUILDING TILES.
Recommendations of the Portland Cement Association.

4

METALS

COMPARATIVE GAUGES

GAUGE NO. These run from #0,000,000 to #40	GRAPHIC SIZES Based on U.S.Gauge		U.S.STANDARD Generally used for Steel,Iron, Stainless Steel, Monel, plates and sheets ~ Fractions used instead of gauge for 3/16" and over.		WASHBURN & MOEN, ROEBLING AMERICAN STEEL & WIRE CO. Used for Steel Wire		BROWN AND SHARPE Known as B&S Gauge Used generally for Copper Wire & Nickel Silver		CIRCULAR MILLS Gauge based on Area. Used for Copper Wire in place of B&S	GRAPHIC SIZES Based on B.S.Gauge		GAUGE NO. These run from #0,000,000 to #40
			Decimal	Fract?	Decimal	Fract?	Decimal	Fract?	C.M.			
000			.3750"	3/8	.3625"	23/64	.4096"	13/32+	167,800			000
00			.3437"	11/32	.3310"	21/64+	.3648"	23/64+	133,100			00
0			.3125"	5/16	.3065"	5/16-	.3249"	21/64-	105,500			0
1			.2812"	9/32	.2830"	9/32+	.2893"	19/64-	83,690			1
2			.2656"	17/64	.2625"	17/64-	.2576"	1/4+	66,370			2
3			.2500"	1/4"	.2437"	1/4-	.2294"	15/64-	52,630			3
4			.2344"	15/64	.2253"	7/32+	.2043"	13/64+	41,740			4
5			.2187"	7/32	.2070"	13/64+	.1819"	3/16-	33,100			5
6			.2031"	13/64	.1920"	3/16+	.1620	5/32+	26,250			6
7			.1875"	3/16	.1770"	11/64+	.1443"	9/64+	—			7
8			.1719"	11/64	.1620"	5/32+	.1285"	1/8+	16,510			8
9			.1562"	5/32	.1483"	9/64+	.1144"	7/64+	—			9
10			.1406"	9/64	.1350"	9/64-	.1019"	7/64-	10,380			10
11			.1250"	1/8	.1205"	1/8-	.0907"	3/32-	—			11
12			.1094"	7/64	.1055"	7/64-	.0808"	5/64+	6,530			12
13			.0934"	3/32	.0915"	3/32-	.0719"	5/64-	—			13
14			.0781"	5/64	.0800"	5/64+	.0640"	1/16+	4,107			14
15			.0703"	5/64-	.0720"	5/64-	.0571"	1/16-	—			15
16			.0625"	1/16	.0625"	1/16	.0508"	3/64+	2583			16
17			.0562"	1/16-	.0540"	3/64+	.0452"	3/64-	—			17
18			.0500"	3/64+	.0475"	3/64+	.0403"	3/64-	1624			18
19			.0437"	3/64-	.0410"	3/64-	.0359"	1/32+	—			19
20			.0375".	1/32+	.0348"	1/32+	.0320"	1/32+	—			20
21			.0344"	1/32+	.0317"	1/32+	.0285"	1/32+	—			21
22			.0312"	1/32	.0286"	1/32-	.0253"	1/32-	—			22
23			.0281"	1/32-	.0258"	1/32-	.0226"	1/64+	—			23
24			.0250"	1/32-	.0230"	1/64+	.0201"	1/64+	—			24
25			.0219"	1/64+	.0204"	1/64+	.0179"	1/64+	—			25
26			.0187"	1/64+	.0181"	1/64+	.0159"	1/64+	—			26
27			.0172"	1/64+	.0173"	1/64+	.0142"	1/64-	—			27
28			.0156"	1/64	.0162"	1/64+	.0126"	1/64-	—			28
29			.0141"	1/64-	.0150"	1/64-	.0112"	1/64-	-			29
30			.0125"	1/64-	.0140"	1/64-	.0100"	1/64-	—			30

LALLY COLUMNS

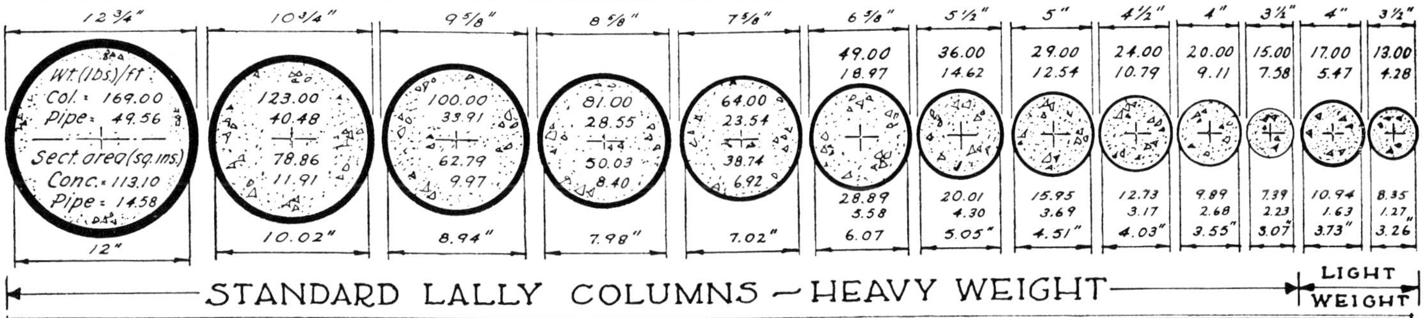
12 3/4"
Wt.(lbs)/ft
Col. = 169.00
Pipe = 49.56
Sect. area(sq. ins.)
Conc. = 113.10
Pipe = 14.58
12"
10 3/4"
123.00
40.48
78.86
11.91
10.02"
9 5/8"
100.00
33.91
62.79
9.97
8.94"
8 5/8"
81.00
28.55
50.03
8.40
7.98"
7 5/8"
64.00
23.54
38.74
6.92
7.02"
6 5/8"
49.00
18.97
28.89
5.58
6.07
5 1/2"
36.00
14.62
20.01
4.30
5.05"
5"
29.00
12.54
15.95
3.69
4.51"
4 1/2"
24.00
10.79
12.73
3.17
4.03"
4"
20.00
9.11
9.89
2.68
3.55"
3 1/2"
15.00
7.58
7.39
2.23
3.07"
4"
17.00
5.47
10.94
1.63
3.73"
3 1/2"
13.00
4.28
8.35
1.27
3.26"
STANDARD LALLY COLUMNS — HEAVY WEIGHT
LIGHT WEIGHT

EXAMPLE OF LALLY COLUMN DESIGN WITH ECCENTRIC LOADS

Given:
9'-0" unbraced hgt of column.
Concentric load = 80 Kips.
One eccentric load = 10 Kips & one = 5 Kips.

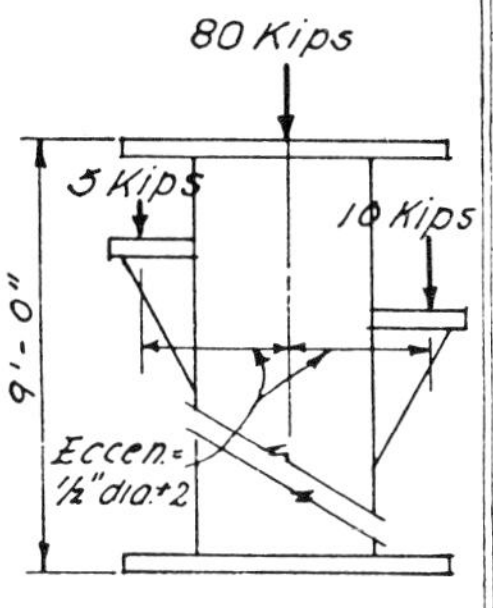
80 Kips
5 Kips
10 Kips
9'-0"
Eccen. = 1/2" dia. + 2

Find:
Required size of column.

Solution:

1. Assume a column 6 5/8" diameter.
2. Direct load = 80 + 10 + 5 = 95 Kips.
3. Resultant eccentric load = 10 - 5 = 5 K.
4. Bending Moment = $5\left(\frac{6\frac{5}{8}}{2}+2\right)$ = 26,500"/lbs.
5. From "Safe Loads" table for a 6 5/8" dia. col. the equivalent direct load = $\frac{26{,}500}{10{,}000} \times 7.4$ = 19.5 Kips.
6. Equivalent Total load = 95 + 19.5 = 114.5 K.
7. From "Safe Loads" table, a 6 5/8" dia. col. with 9'-0" unbr. hgt. is good for 116 K.

Elwyn E. Seelye, Consulting Eng'r.

SAFE LOADS (IN THOUSANDS OF POUNDS)

Dia. of Col. (inches)	Max. Length (feet)	Unbraced Length of Column (feet) 6	7	8	9	10	11	12	13	14	15	16	17	18	19	20	*Eccentric Loads
3 1/2	9.0	26.1	24.2	22.2	20.3												
4	9.0	35.6	33.4	31.2	29.0												
3 1/2	11.64	37.9	35.1	32.3	29.4	26.7	24.0										13.3
4	13.37	49.2	46.1	43.1	40.1	37.0	33.9	30.9	27.9								11.9
4 1/2	15.10	61.8	58.5	55.3	52.0	48.8	45.5	42.3	39.0	35.8	32.5						10.8
5	16.83	75.6	72.0	68.6	65.2	61.7	58.2	54.7	51.3	47.8	44.3	40.9	37.4				9.8
5 1/2	18.78	92.1	88.3	84.6	80.8	77.1	73.3	69.6	65.8	62.1	58.3	54.6	50.8	47.1	43.3		8.7
6 5/8	22.45	128.3	124.2	120.0	115.8	111.7	107.5	103.4	99.2	95.0	90.9	86.7	82.6	78.4	74.2	70.1	7.4
7 5/8	25.92	166.0	161.4	156.9	152.3	147.8	143.2	138.6	134.1	129.7	125.0	120.5	115.9	111.4	106.8	102.3	6.7
8 5/8	29.38	211.1	206.1	201.1	196.1	191.0	186.0	181.0	175.9	170.9	165.9	160.8	155.8	150.8	145.8	140.7	5.8
9 5/8	32.84	259.2	253.8	248.3	242.8	237.4	231.9	226.5	221.0	215.6	210.1	204.6	199.2	193.7	188.3	182.8	5.4
10 3/4	36.74	319.1	313.1	307.2	301.3	295.4	289.4	283.5	277.6	271.6	265.7	259.7	253.8	247.9	241.9	236.0	4.9
12 3/4	43.77	421.9	415.4	408.8	402.3	395.8	389.2	382.8	376.2	369.7	363.2	356.7	350.1	343.6	337.1	330.6	4.2

* For each 10,000 in. lbs. unbalanced moment on the col. add the no. of Kips as shown to the sum of all vertical loads. Safe Load Formula: $P = (A_c + 12A_s)(1600 - 24\,L/d)$. P = Safe carrying capacity in lbs., A_c = Area of concrete in sq. in., A_s = Area of steel in sq. in., L = Length of col. in inches, d = Diameter of column in inches.

STANDARD BASE PLATES & CAPS

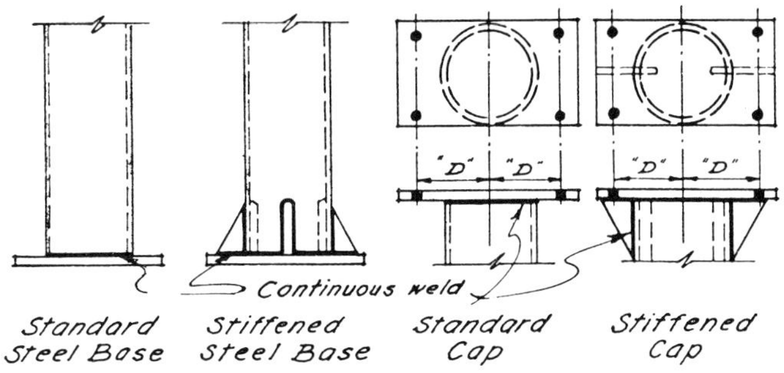
"D"
"D"
"D"
"D"
Continuous weld
Standard Steel Base
Stiffened Steel Base
Standard Cap
Stiffened Cap

Base Plates* Col. dia.	Size of Base	Safe Load in Kips	Thickness of Base: Standard	Thickness of Base: Stiffened	Caps: Distance "D" Standard	Caps: Distance "D" Stiffened	Thickness of Cap
3 1/2	8 x 8	32.0	5/8	1/2	3 1/4	4 1/4	1/2
4	9 x 9	40.5	3/4	1/2	3 1/2	4 1/2	1/2
4 1/2	10 x 10	50.0	7/8	1/2	3 3/4	4 3/4	1/2
5	12 x 12	72.0	1	1/2	4	5	5/8
5 1/2	14 x 14	98.0	1 1/4	3/4	4 1/2	5 1/4	5/8
6 5/8	16 x 16	128.0	1 3/8	3/4	4 3/4	6 1/4	3/4
7 5/8	18 x 18	162.0	1 5/8	3/4	5	6 3/4	3/4
8 5/8	20 x 20	200.0	1 3/4	3/4	5 3/4	7 1/4	3/4
9 5/8	22 x 22	242.0	1 7/8	3/4	6 1/4	7 3/4	3/4
10 3/4	24 x 24	288.0	2	7/8	7	8 1/4	3/4
12 3/4	28 x 28	392.0	2 1/4	7/8	8	9	3/4

* Assumed bearing of Bases = 500 lbs. per sq. inch.

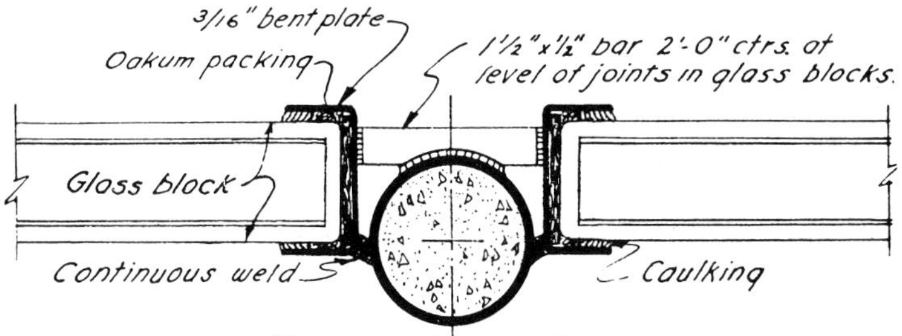
3/16" bent plate
Oakum packing
1 1/2" x 1/2" bar 2'-0" ctrs. at level of joints in glass blocks.
Glass block
Continuous weld
Caulking

Using Glass Block

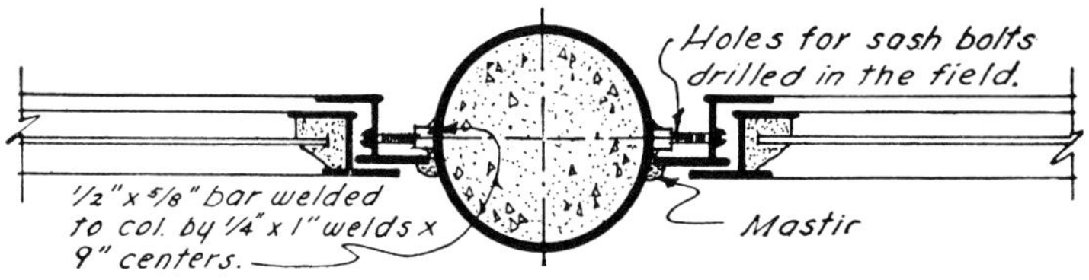
Holes for sash bolts drilled in the field.
1/2" x 5/8" bar welded to col. by 1/4" x 1" welds x 9" centers.
Mastic

With Steel Sash

TYPICAL DETAILS
Scale 1 1/2" = 1'-0"

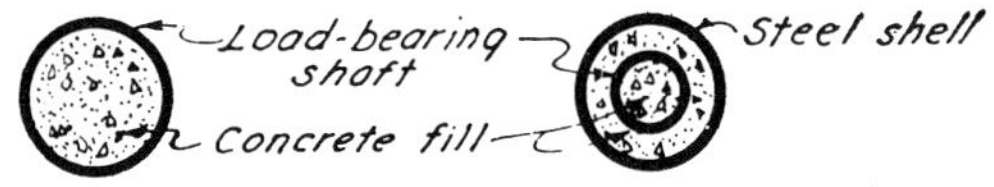
Load-bearing shaft
Steel shell
Concrete fill

Standard Lally   Fireproofed Lally
Scale: 1" = 1'-0"

Data furnished by Lally Col. Co.

NAIL USES

USE (All wood sizes are nominal)	SIZE PENNY	INCHES	TYPE, MATERIAL & FINISH NOTES ETC.
CARPENTRY-WOOD-ROUGH			
1" Thick stock	8d	2½"	Common nails
2" Thick stock	16d to 20d	3½" or 4"	Common nails
3" Thick stock	40d to 60d	6"	Common nails or spikes
Concrete Forms	variable		Common or double headed nails
Framing generally—Sizes to fit conditions	10d,16d 20d,60d	3", 3½", 4", 6"	Common nails or spikes for large members
Toe nailing studs etc.	16d	3½"	Common nails
Spiking usual plates & sills	20d	4"	Common nails
Toe nailing studs	16d	3½"	Common nails
Sheathing & roofers Rough flooring	8d	2½"	Common nails, may be zinc coated
CARPENTRY-WOOD-FINISHING			
Moldings—Size as required		⅞",1",1⅛",1¼"	Molding nails (brads)
Carpet strips, shoes, door & window stops and members ¼" to ½" thick	4d	1½"	Finishing or casing nails
Ceiling, trim, casing, picture mold, base balusters and members ½" to ¾" thick	6d	2"	Finishing or casing nails
Ceiling, trim, casing, base, jambs, trim and members ¾" to 1" thick	8d	2½"	Finishing or casing nails
Door & window trim boards and other members 1" to 1¼" thick	10d	3	Finishing or casing nails
Drop siding, 1" thick	*7d or □8d	*2¼" or □2½	*Siding nails —□Casing nails
Bevel siding, ½" thick	*6d or □7d	*2" or 2¼	*Finishing ——□Siding
FLOORING WOOD	See wood flooring sheet for sizes & types recommended		Cut steel, wire, finishing, wire casing, flooring brads, parquet, flooring nails
LATHING			
Wood lath	3d	1¼"	Blued lath nail
Gypsum lath	3d	1¼"	Blued common
Fiber lath			
Metal lath, interior		1"	Blued lath nails, staples or offset head nails
Metal lath, exterior	*3d	*1¼"	Self furring nails (double heads). Staples or cement coated
INSULATION (Excluding wall board)			
Fiber board ½" thick	2d		
Fiber board 1" thick	4d to 5d		
Cork		3" to 10"	Cork insulation nails, zinc coated
Felts			
Quilting			
Mineral wool, paper backed			
ROOFING & SHEET METAL			
Asbestos, corrugated or sheets	Depends on thickness		Leak proof roofing nails (available with lead heads)
Asbestos shingles		1" to 2"	See "Asbestos, Asphalt & Metal Shingles" sheet
Asphalt shingles			
Copper cleats & flashing to wood			Copper wire or cut slating nails
" " " to prevent joints			Barbed copper nails
Clay tile	4d to 6d	1½" to 2"	See clay tile Roofing Sheets. Use copper
Prepared felt roofing		1" to 1¼	Roofing nails or large head roofing nails; barbed preferred—Heads may be reinforced. Zinc
Shingles, wood	3d to 4d usual 4d to 8d for heavy butts		See "Roofing Finish" sheet for sizes. Zinc coated, copper wire shingle, copper clad shingle, cut iron or cut steel
Slate	Use nails 1" larger than thickness of slate		Copper wire slating nail (large head) In dry climates zinc coated or copper clad nails may be used
Tin roofing			Zinc coated nails—Roofing or slating
Zinc roofing			" " " " "
Nailing to sheet metal			Self tapping screws, helical drive-screws
NAILING TO CONCRETE & CEMENT MORTAR			Concrete or cement nails (hardened) or helical drive nails or drive bolts

75

NAILS

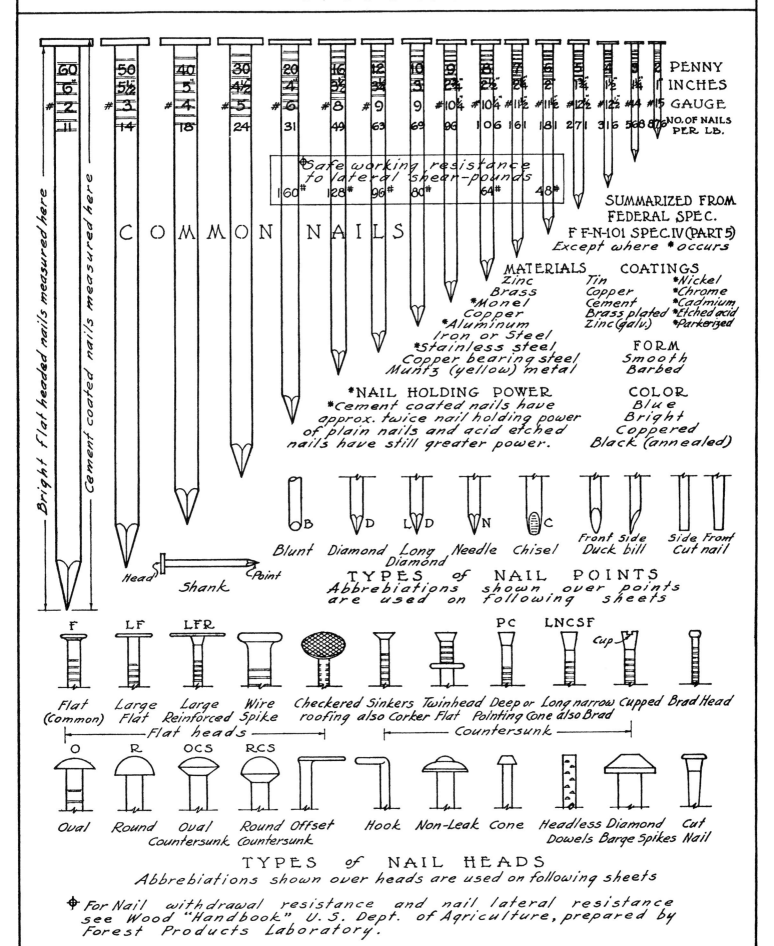

COMMON NAILS

| PENNY | INCHES | GAUGE | NO. OF NAILS PER LB. |

⊕ Safe working resistance to lateral shear-pounds
160# 128# 96# 80# 64# 48#

SUMMARIZED FROM FEDERAL SPEC.
F F-N-101 SPEC.IV (PART 5)
*Except where * occurs*

MATERIALS
Zinc
Brass
*Monel
Copper
*Aluminum
Iron or Steel
*Stainless steel
Copper bearing steel
Muntz (yellow) metal

COATINGS
Tin   *Nickel
Copper   *Chrome
Cement   *Cadmium
Brass plated *Etched acid
Zinc (galv.) *Parkerized

FORM
Smooth
Barbed

*NAIL HOLDING POWER
*Cement coated nails have approx. twice nail holding power of plain nails and acid etched nails have still greater power.

COLOR
Blue
Bright
Coppered
Black (annealed)

Bright flat headed nails measured here
Cement coated nails measured here

Blunt Diamond Long Diamond Needle Chisel Front Side Duck bill Side Front Cut nail

Head Shank Point

TYPES of NAIL POINTS
Abbrebiations shown over points are used on following sheets

F LF LFR PC LNCSF Cup

Flat (Common) Large Flat Large Reinforced Wire Spike Checkered roofing also Corker Sinkers also Flat Twinhead Pointing Deep or Cone Long narrow also Brad Cupped Brad Head

— Flat heads — — Countersunk —

O R OCS RCS

Oval Round Oval Countersunk Round Countersunk Offset Hook Non-Leak Cone Headless Dowels Diamond Barge Spikes Cut Nail

TYPES of NAIL HEADS
Abbrebiations shown over heads are used on following sheets

⊕ For Nail withdrawal resistance and nail lateral resistance see Wood "Handbook" U.S. Dept. of Agriculture, prepared by Forest Products Laboratory.

NAILS

Sizes and types are taken from U.S. Federal Specification IV FF-N-101 (Part 5) unless marked *
For abbreviation for heads and points see other "Nails" sheet

NAIL TYPE	Shown 4d (1½") unless noted otherwise	SIZES	SPECIFICATION
F; #14 gauge; D	Barbed nails	¼" to 1½"	Cement coated, brass, steel
L C.S.N #14 gauge D	Casing nails	2d to 40d	Bright & cement coated *Cupped heads available
O 1" Long #8 gauge D *Also flat head CS.	Cement nails also called concrete nails & hardened nails	½", ⅝", ¾", ⅞", 1"	Smooth, bright *Oil quenched
L.N.F. Light gauge #16 gauge Med. " #14 " Heavy. " #12½, 13	Common brad: Light gauge Medium gauge Heavy " Heavy "	⅜" to 2½" ½" to 2 " ¾" to 6 " 1" to 60d	Bright " — may be secured with cupped head " Cement coated {ussually made in heavy gauges
F	Cut common	2d to 60d	Steel or Iron Plain & zinc coated
Slightly smaller gauge than bright common	Copper-clad common nails	2d to 60d	Also used for shingle nails
F; D Light gauge .095" or .083" Heavy .120"	Common brass wire nails: Light gauge Heavy "	*½", 1" to 3½" ¾ to 6"	Brass
F; D .109 (about 12 gauge)	Common copper wire nails	⅝" to 6"	Also used for shingle nails
	Standard cut nails (non-ferrous)	⅝" to 6"	Copper, muntz metal, or zinc
F; 2" Long; D #11½ gauge	Double headed	*1¾, 2, *2¼, 2½, *2¾, 3, 3½, *4, *4½"	Bright & cement coated made in several designs
Made in 4 diameters D Cupped head available	Dowel Pins	½" to 2"	Barbed — *may have cupped head
O Made in 3 gauges D	Escutcheon Pins	½" to 2"	Bright steel, brass plated, brass *also nickel-silver & copper
F; 6d – 2"; D #10 gauge	Fence nails	5d to 20d	Smooth; bright & cement coated (Gauge are heavier than common)
LNF #15 gauge D	Finishing nail, wire	2d to 20d	Smooth; *Cupped heads available (Smaller gauge than usual common brads)
	Finishing nails Cut iron & steel	Standard — 3d to 20d Fine — 6d to 10d	
*; 3d – 1⅛" #15 & 16 gauge	*Fine nails	*2d & 2d Ex. Fine *3d & 3d Ex. Fine	*Bright — Smaller gauge & heads than common nails
P.C. #14 gauge B	Flooring nails (Also with D point)	*3d to *20d 6d to 9d	*Bright & cement coated (different gauge) *Cupped heads available
6d – 2" L.N.C.S. #11 gauge; D or Blunt D	Flooring brad	6d to 20d	Smooth; bright & cement coated Cupped heads available
1⅛" Long N.C.S.F. #15 gauge N	Parquet flooring nail or brad	1", 1⅛", 1¼"	Smooth or barbed
2"	Flooring nails Cut iron or steel	4d to 8d	Iron or steel
Oval ¼" Heavy chisel — also CS. head	Hinge nails: Heavy — ¼ to ⅜ dia. Light — 3/16 to ¼ dia.	1½" to 4" Long	Smooth; bright or annealed
Oval 3/16" Light Long D	Hinge nails: Heavy — ¼" dia. Light — 3/16 dia.	1½" to 3" also to *4"	Smooth; bright or annealed
3d – 1⅛" F #15 gauge D	Lath nails (wood)	2d, 2d Light, 3d 3d Light, 3d heavy, 4d	Bright, (not recommended) blued or cement coated
Hook 1⅛" #12 gauge	Lath nails (Metal lath) Staples #14, 15 gauge	1⅛" Staples 1" to ½"	Bright, blued, zinc coated
*Offset F #10 gauge D	*Lath offset head nails (For self furring metal lath)	*1¼ to *1¾"	Bright, zinc coated

NAILS

Sizes and types are taken from U.S. Federal Specification IV FF-N-101 (Part 5) unless marked *
For abbreviation for heads and points see other "Nails" sheet

NAIL TYPE	Shown 4d (1½") unless noted otherwise	SIZES	SPECIFICATION
 N.C.S.F. #14 gauge — needle	Molding nails (brads)	7/8" to 1¼"	Smooth; bright or cement coated
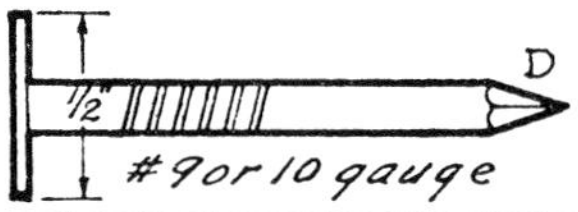 ½" #9 or 10 gauge — D	Plaster-board nails Used also for wall board	1" to 1¾"	Smooth; bright or cement coated Available in wood
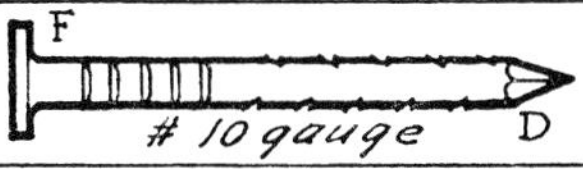 F #10 gauge D	Roofing nails (standard)	¾" to 2"	Bright, cement coated, zinc coated Barbed
F 3/8" to ½" Checkered D	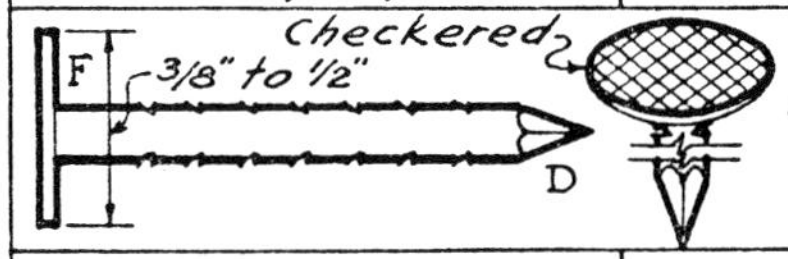 Roofing nails Large head	¾" to 1¾" also *2" made in #12 to #8 gauge	Barbed; bright or zinc coated Checkered available
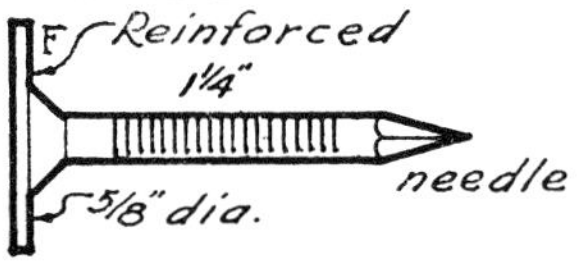 F Reinforced 1¼" 5/8" dia. needle	Roofing nails for prepared roofing	¾" to 1¼" #11 to #12g *also #10 gauge	Bright or zinc coated
	Sheathing nails Cut copper or muntz M.	¾" to 3"	Copper or muntz metal
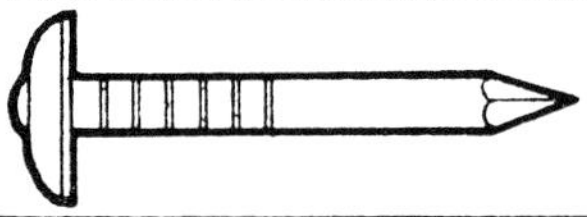	*Non-leaking roofing nails	*1½" to 2"	*Zinc coated—also with lead heads
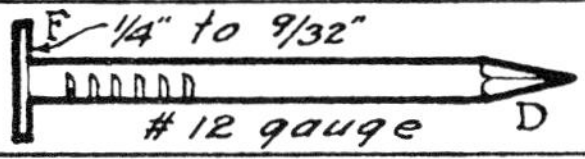 F ¼" to 9/32" #12 gauge D	Shingle nails Large headed also available 5/16 dia.	3d to 6d	Smooth; bright or zinc coated, cement coated, light & heavy
	Shingle nails Cut iron or steel	2d to 6d	Plain or zinc coated

Shingle nails, copper wire are the same as common copper wire nails
Shingle nails, copper clad, are the same as copper clad common wire nails

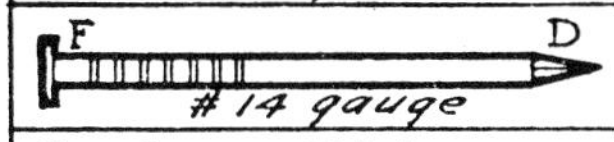 F D #14 gauge	Siding nails	2d to 4d	Smooth; bright or cement coated Smaller diameter than common nails
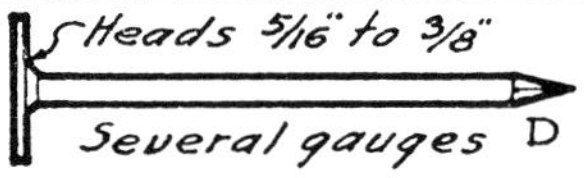 Heads 5/16 to 3/8 Several gauges D	Slating nails—3/8" head 1" to 2" Slating nails—small heads 1" to 2" Slating nails—copper wire 1" to 2"		Zinc coated Bright; cement coated and copper clad, copper
	Cut slating nails non-ferrous	1¼" to 2"	Copper or muntz metal or zinc

Oval, square or *round heads — Chisel

BARGE SPIKES, SQUARE
¼" to 5/8" sq. 3" to 12" long, *also 16"

Square or diamond heads

BOAT SPIKES, SQUARE
¼" to 5/8" sq. 3" to 12" long heads from 7/32" to 1⅛"

These spikes are usually used for hard wood, made plain and zinc coated

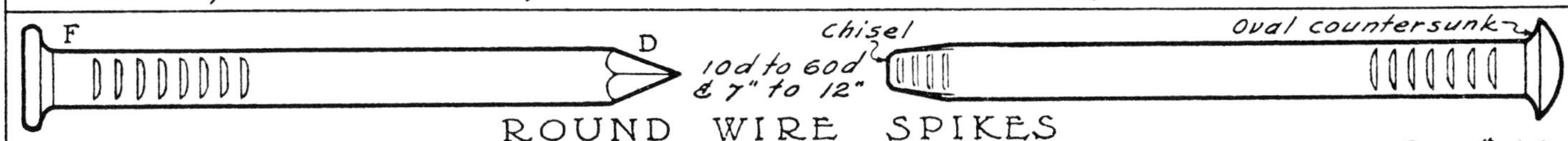

F D Chisel 10d to 60d & 7" to 12" Oval countersunk

ROUND WIRE SPIKES
*May be secured up to 16" long. Smooth; bright or zinc coated. Gauges vary from #6 to 3/8"

Gutter Spikes — 5½" to 10½", ¼" dia. oval head; chisel point; or flat head diamond point. Bright or zinc coated

Common cut iron or steel spikes — 20d to 100d (4" to 8") Plain or zinc coated

"Stronghold-One-Way-Nails" | Spirally grooved (helical)

METAL STUD ANCHORAGE & ERECTION

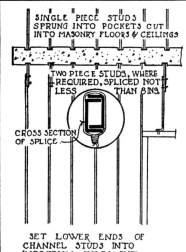

SINGLE PIECE STUDS SPRUNG INTO POCKETS CUT INTO MASONRY FLOORS & CEILINGS

TWO PIECE STUDS, WHERE REQUIRED, SPLICED NOT LESS THAN 8 INS.

CROSS SECTION OF SPLICE.

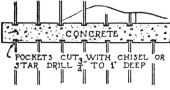

SET LOWER ENDS OF CHANNEL STUDS INTO INDIVIDUAL HOLES CUT INTO CONCRETE.

CONCRETE

POCKETS CUT WITH CHISEL OR STAR DRILL 3/4" TO 1" DEEP

Anchorage in flat slab concrete floors and ceilings using notching method.

Whenever Masonry Nails are specified, Expansion Drive Bolts or equivalent attachments may be used.

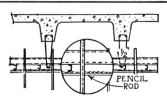

ALTERNATE METHOD FOR SUSPENDED CEILINGS. 3/4" OR 1/4" PENCIL ROD WIRED TO UNDERSIDE OF METAL LATH AND USED FOR ALIGNMENT. CHANNEL STUDS PUSHED THRU METAL LATH CEILING AND WIRED TO ALIGNMENT CHANNEL OR ROD

PENCIL ROD

TYPICAL BAR JOIST CONSTRUCTION. METHOD OF SECURING CHANNELS TO FLOOR SIMILAR TO OTHERS SHOWN OR USE:

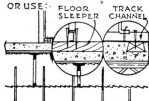

FLOOR SLEEPER   TRACK CHANNEL

(ABOVE) Upper ends of studs pushed through holes in ceiling lath and tied to alignment channel.

(BELOW) Attachment of lower ends of studs to wood floor runners on masonry slab.

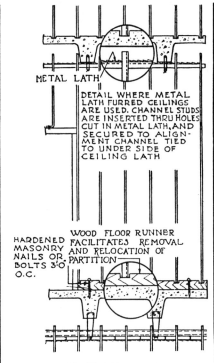

METAL LATH

DETAIL WHERE METAL LATH FURRED CEILINGS ARE USED. CHANNEL STUDS ARE INSERTED THRU HOLES CUT IN METAL LATH, AND SECURED TO ALIGNMENT CHANNEL TIED TO UNDER SIDE OF CEILING LATH

HARDENED MASONRY NAILS OR BOLTS 3'-0 O.C.

WOOD FLOOR RUNNER FACILITATES REMOVAL AND RELOCATION OF PARTITION

(ABOVE) Upper ends of studs secured to furred Metal Lath Ceiling under concrete joists.

(BELOW) Lower stud ends secured to wood floor runner for attachment of wood base.

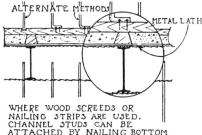

ALTERNATE METHOD   METAL LATH

WHERE WOOD SCREEDS OR NAILING STRIPS ARE USED, CHANNEL STUDS CAN BE ATTACHED BY NAILING BOTTOM ENDS DIRECT TO SCREEDS, OR TO FLOOR RUNNER ATTACHED TO SCREEDS

ANCHOR STUDS TO TOP OF CONCRETE SLAB IN STEEL JOIST FLOOR CONSTRUCTION SIMILAR TO REINFORCED CONCRETE CONSTRUCTION OR AS SHOWN

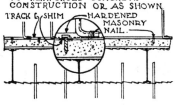

TRACK & SHIM   HARDENED MASONRY NAIL

(ABOVE) Studs pushed through holes cut in ceiling lath; alignment channel omitted.

(BELOW) Lower ends of studs attached to track channels nailed to concrete floor.

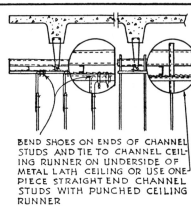

BEND SHOES ON ENDS OF CHANNEL STUDS AND TIE TO CHANNEL CEILING RUNNER ON UNDERSIDE OF METAL LATH CEILING OR USE ONE-PIECE STRAIGHT END CHANNEL STUDS WITH PUNCHED CEILING RUNNER

LOWER END OF CHANNEL STUDS TIED TO OR INSERTED IN FLOOR RUNNER SECURED TO MASONRY WITH HARDENED MASONRY NAILS 4'-0" O.C.

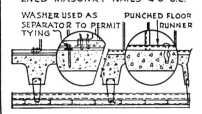

WASHER USED AS SEPARATOR TO PERMIT TYING   PUNCHED FLOOR RUNNER

(ABOVE) Upper ends of studs secured to suspended Metal Lath Ceiling; masonry floor.

(BELOW) Lower ends secured to metal channel floor runner on masonry floor.

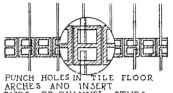

PUNCH HOLES IN TILE FLOOR ARCHES AND INSERT ENDS OF CHANNEL STUDS. ALL CHANNELS MAY BE CUT TO SAME LENGTH

Top and bottom ends of studs secured to structural tile floor without use of runners.

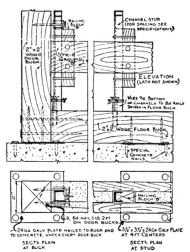

NAILING BLOCK

CHANNEL STUD (FOR SPACING SEE SPECIFICATIONS)

2"x2" WOOD DOOR BUCK

STRIP GROUND

ELEVATION (LATH NOT SHOWN)

WIRE TIE BOTTOM OF CHANNELS TO 8d NAILS DRIVEN IN FLOOR BUCK

2"x WOOD FLOOR BUCK

SPECIAL CONCRETE NAILS

NAILING BLOCK

2, 8d NAILS @ 2 FT ON DOOR BUCKS

24 GA GALV PLATE NAILED TO BUCK AND TO CONCRETE, UNDER EVERY DOOR BUCK

3/8" x 3 1/2" x 24 GA GALV PLATE AT 4 FT CENTERS

SECT. PLAN AT BUCK

SECT. PLAN AT STUD

Studs secured to wood floor buck nailed to concrete floor. Wood buck facilitates movability; provides grounds.

From "Partition Handbook" published by Metal Lath Mfrs. Association

METAL POSTS, BALUSTERS, RAILINGS,—ATTACHMENT, ETC

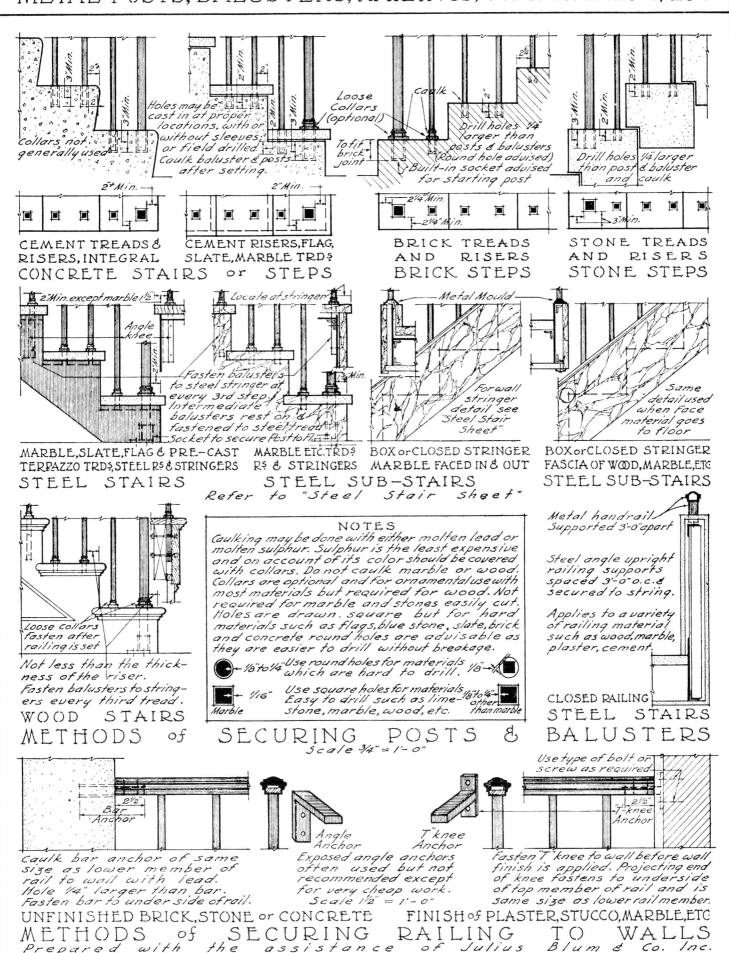

CONCRETE STAIRS or STEPS — CEMENT TREADS & RISERS, INTEGRAL / CEMENT RISERS, FLAG, SLATE, MARBLE TRDS

BRICK STEPS — BRICK TREADS AND RISERS

STONE STEPS — STONE TREADS AND RISERS

Collars not generally used.

Holes may be cast in at proper locations, with or without sleeves; or field drilled. Caulk baluster & posts after setting.

Loose Collars (optional) To fit brick joint. Caulk. Drill holes ¼ larger than posts & balusters (Round hole advised) Built-in socket advised for starting post.

Drill holes ¼ larger than post & baluster and caulk.

STEEL STAIRS — MARBLE, SLATE, FLAG & PRE-CAST TERRAZZO TRDS, STEEL RS & STRINGERS

STEEL SUB-STAIRS — MARBLE ETC. TRDS RS & STRINGERS / BOX or CLOSED STRINGER MARBLE FACED IN & OUT
Refer to "Steel Stair sheet"

STEEL SUB-STAIRS — BOX or CLOSED STRINGER FASCIA OF WOOD, MARBLE, ETC

Angle knee. Fasten balusters to steel stringer at every 3rd step. Intermediate balusters rest on & fastened to steel tread. Socket to secure Post to Fl.

Metal Mould. For wall stringer detail see "Steel Stair Sheet". Same detail used when face material goes to floor.

WOOD STAIRS
Loose Collars fasten after railing is set. Not less than the thickness of the riser. Fasten balusters to stringers every third tread.

METHODS of SECURING POSTS & BALUSTERS
NOTES
Caulking may be done with either molten lead or molten sulphur. Sulphur is the least expensive and on account of its color should be covered with collars. Do not caulk marble or wood. Collars are optional and for ornamental use with most materials but required for wood. Not required for marble and stones easily cut. Holes are drawn square but for hard materials such as flags, blue stone, slate, brick and concrete round holes are advisable as they are easier to drill without breakage.
⅛ to ¼ Use round holes for materials which are hard to drill.
1/16" Use square holes for materials Easy to drill such as lime-stone, marble, wood, etc.
Scale ¾" = 1'-0"

STEEL STAIRS
Metal handrail Supported 3'-0 apart. Steel angle upright railing supports spaced 3'-0" o.c. & secured to string. Applies to a variety of railing material such as wood, marble, plaster, cement.
CLOSED RAILING

METHODS of SECURING RAILING TO WALLS
UNFINISHED BRICK, STONE or CONCRETE
Caulk bar anchor of same size as lower member of rail to wall with lead. Hole ¼" larger than bar. Fasten bar to under side of rail.
Bar Anchor. Angle Anchor. Exposed angle anchors often used but not recommended except for very cheap work. Scale 1½" = 1'-0". T'knee Anchor.
FINISH of PLASTER, STUCCO, MARBLE, ETC
Use type of bolt or screw as required. T-knee Anchor. Fasten T'knee to wall before wall finish is applied. Projecting end of knee fastens to underside of top member of rail and is same size as lower rail member.

Prepared with the assistance of Julius Blum & Co. Inc.

SPIRAL STAIRS & PIPE RAILINGS

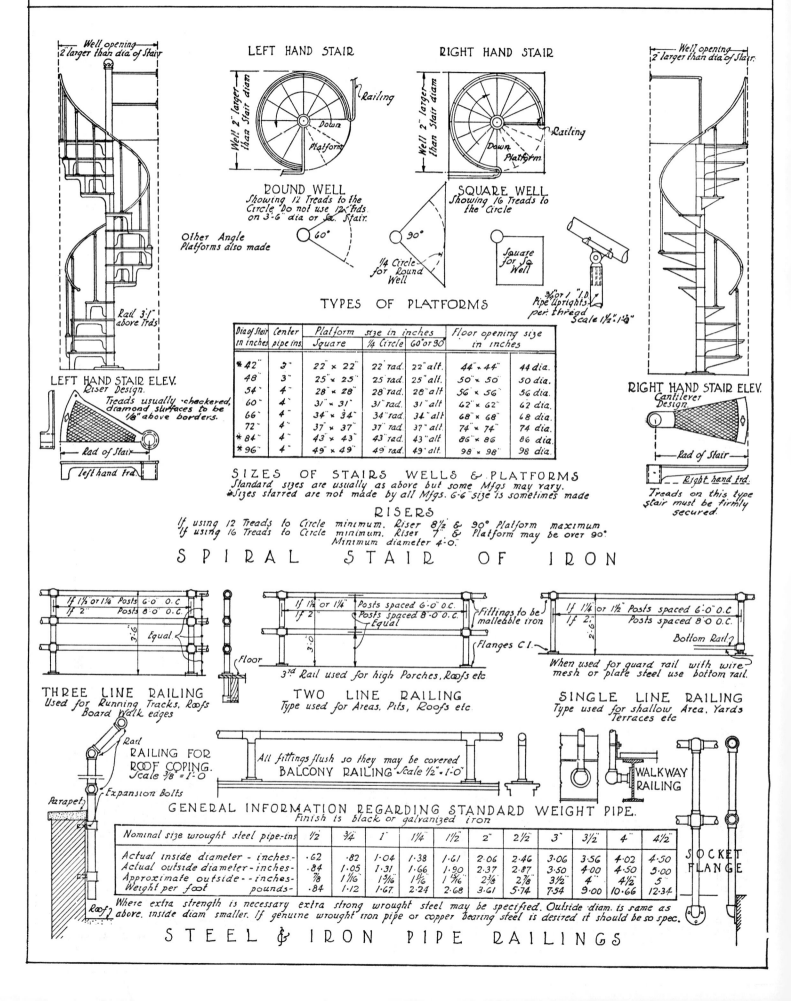

LEFT HAND STAIR

ROUND WELL
Showing 12 Treads to the Circle Do not use 12 Trds. on 3'-6" dia or Sq. Stair.

Other Angle Platforms also made

RIGHT HAND STAIR

SQUARE WELL
Showing 16 Treads to the Circle

Well opening 2" larger than dia of Stair
Well 2" larger than Stair diam

TYPES OF PLATFORMS

Railing

Down / Platform

1/4 Circle for Round Well

Square for Sq. Well

3/4" or 1" I.D. Pipe Uprights per thread. Scale 1 1/2" : 1'-0"

Well opening 2" larger than dia of Stair

LEFT HAND STAIR ELEV.
Rail 3'-1" above Trds.
Riser Design.
Treads usually checkered, diamond surfaces to be 1/8" above borders.
Rad of Stair
left hand trd.

RIGHT HAND STAIR ELEV.
Cantilever Design
Rad of Stair
Right hand trd.
Treads on this type stair must be firmly secured.

Dia of Stair in inches	Center pipe ins.	Platform size in inches			Floor opening size in inches	
		Square	1/4 Circle	60 or 90		
*42"	3"	22" x 22"	22" rad.	22" alt.	44" x 44"	44 dia.
48"	3"	25" x 25"	25" rad.	25" alt.	50" x 50"	50 dia.
54"	4"	28" x 28"	28" rad.	28" alt.	56" x 56"	56 dia.
60"	4"	31" x 31"	31" rad.	31" alt.	62" x 62"	62 dia.
66"	4"	34" x 34"	34" rad.	34" alt.	68" x 68"	68 dia.
72"	4"	37" x 37"	37" rad.	37" alt.	74" x 74"	74 dia.
*84"	4"	43" x 43"	43" rad.	43" alt.	86" x 86"	86 dia.
*96"	4"	49" x 49"	49" rad.	49" alt.	98" x 98"	98 dia.

SIZES OF STAIRS WELLS & PLATFORMS
Standard sizes are usually as above but some Mfgs may vary.
*Sizes starred are not made by all Mfgs. 6'-6" size is sometimes made

RISERS
If using 12 Treads to Circle minimum. Riser 8 1/2 & 90° Platform maximum
If using 16 Treads to Circle minimum. Riser 7 & Platform may be over 90°
Minimum diameter 4'-0"

SPIRAL STAIR OF IRON

THREE LINE RAILING
Used for Running Tracks, Roofs Board Walk edges
If 1 1/2 or 1 1/4 Posts 6'-0" O.C.
If 2" Posts 8'-0" O.C.
3'-6" Equal
Floor

TWO LINE RAILING
Type used for Areas, Pits, Roofs etc.
If 1 1/2 or 1 1/4 Posts spaced 6'-0" O.C.
If 2" Posts spaced 8'-0" O.C. Equal
3'-0"
3rd Rail used for high Porches, Roofs etc.
Fittings to be malleable iron
Flanges C.I.

SINGLE LINE RAILING
Type used for shallow Area, Yards Terraces etc.
If 1 1/4 or 1 1/2 Posts spaced 6'-0" O.C.
If 2" Posts spaced 8'-0" O.C.
2'-6"
Bottom Rail
When used for guard rail with wire mesh or plate steel use bottom rail.

RAILING FOR ROOF COPING.
Scale 3/8" = 1'-0"
Rail
Expansion Bolts
Parapet
Roof

BALCONY RAILING Scale 1/2" = 1'-0"
All fittings flush so they may be covered

WALKWAY RAILING

SOCKET FLANGE

GENERAL INFORMATION REGARDING STANDARD WEIGHT PIPE.
Finish is black or galvanized iron

Nominal size wrought steel pipe-ins	1/2	3/4	1"	1 1/4	1 1/2	2"	2 1/2	3"	3 1/2	4"	4 1/2
Actual inside diameter - inches	.62	.82	1.04	1.38	1.61	2.06	2.46	3.06	3.56	4.02	4.50
Actual outside diameter - inches	.84	1.05	1.31	1.66	1.90	2.37	2.87	3.50	4.00	4.50	5.00
Approximate outside - inches	7/8	1 1/16	1 5/16	1 4/6	1 9/16	2 3/8	2 7/8	3 1/2	4	4 1/2	5
Weight per foot - pounds	.84	1.12	1.67	2.24	2.68	3.61	5.74	7.54	9.00	10.66	12.34

Where extra strength is necessary extra strong wrought steel may be specified. Outside diam. is same as above. inside diam smaller. If genuine wrought iron pipe or copper bearing steel is desired it should be so spec.

STEEL & IRON PIPE RAILINGS

STEEL STAIRS

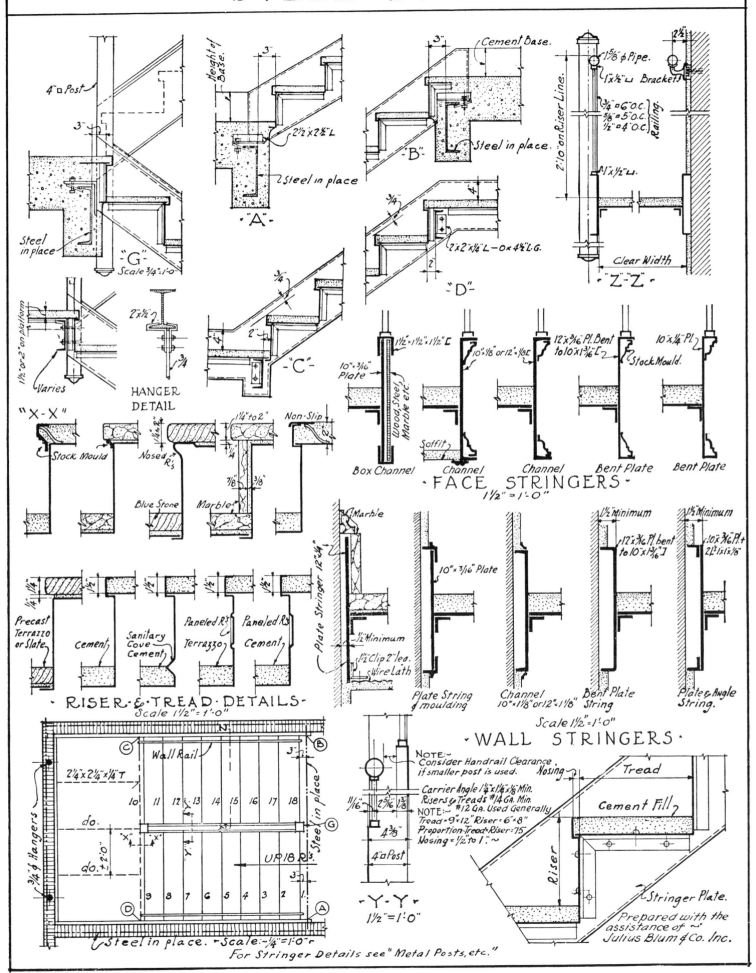

"G" Scale 3/4"=1'-0"

Steel in place

4"□ Post

3"

Height of Base.

2½ x 2½ L

Steel in place

"A"

Cement Base.

3"

3/4"

Steel in place

"B"

3/4"

2" x 2" x 1/4" L - or 4½" L.G.

2'

"D"

1⅝"φ Pipe.

1"x½"□ Brackets

¾"= 6' O.C.
⅝"= 5' O.C.
½"= 4' O.C.

Railing.

2'-0" on Riser Line.

1"x½" Li.

Clear Width

"Z-Z"

2"x½"

1 3/4"

HANGER DETAIL

1½" or 2" on platform

Varies

"X - X"

Stock Mould

Nosed R's

Blue Stone

1¼" to 2"

¼" to 2"

¼"

Non-Slip

7/8" 3/8"

Marble

1½"x 1½"x 1½" L

10"x 3/16" Plate

Wood, Steel, Marble etc.

Soffit

Box Channel

10"x 1/8" or 12"x 1/8" L

Channel

12"x 3/16" Pl. Bent to 10"x 1 3/16" L

Channel

Stock Mould.

Bent Plate

10"x 1/4" Pl.

Bent Plate

FACE STRINGERS
1½" = 1'-0"

1¼" ½" ½" ½" ½" ½"

Precast Terrazzo or Slate

Cement

Sanitary Cove Cement

Paneled R's
Terrazzo

Paneled R's
Cement

RISER & TREAD DETAILS
Scale 1½" = 1'-0"

Plate Stringer 12"x 4"

Marble

½" Minimum

1½" Clip 2" leg.
Wire lath

Plate String & moulding

10"x 3/16" Plate

Channel
10"x 1/8" or 12"x 1 1/8"

1½" Minimum

12"x 3/16" Pl. bent to 10"x 1 3/16" L

Bent Plate String

1½" Minimum

10"x 3/16" Pl. +
2 L's 1 1/2"x 1 1/2"x 1/8"

Plate & Angle String.

WALL STRINGERS
Scale 1½" = 1'-0"

Wall Rail

2¼" x 2¼" x 1/4" T

¾"φ Hangers

Steel in place

10 11 12 13 14 15 16 17 18

do.

do.

"X" "X"

"Y"

UP 18 R

9 8 7 6 5 4 3 2 1

Steel in place. Scale 1/4" = 1'-0"

For Stringer Details see "Metal Posts, etc."

NOTE:- Consider Handrail Clearance if smaller post is used.

Carrier Angle 1¼"x 1¼"x 1/8" Min.
Risers & Treads #14 Ga. Min.
#12 Ga. Used Generally
NOTE:- Tread = 9"x 12" Riser = 6"x 8"
Proportion Tread x Riser = 75
Nosing = ½" to 1"

11/16" 2 5/16" 1 3/8"

4 3/8"

4"□ Post

"Y-Y"
1½" = 1'-0"

Nosing

Tread

Cement Fill

Riser

Stringer Plate.

Prepared with the assistance of
Julius Blum & Co. Inc.

FACINGS and CURTAIN WALL PANELS

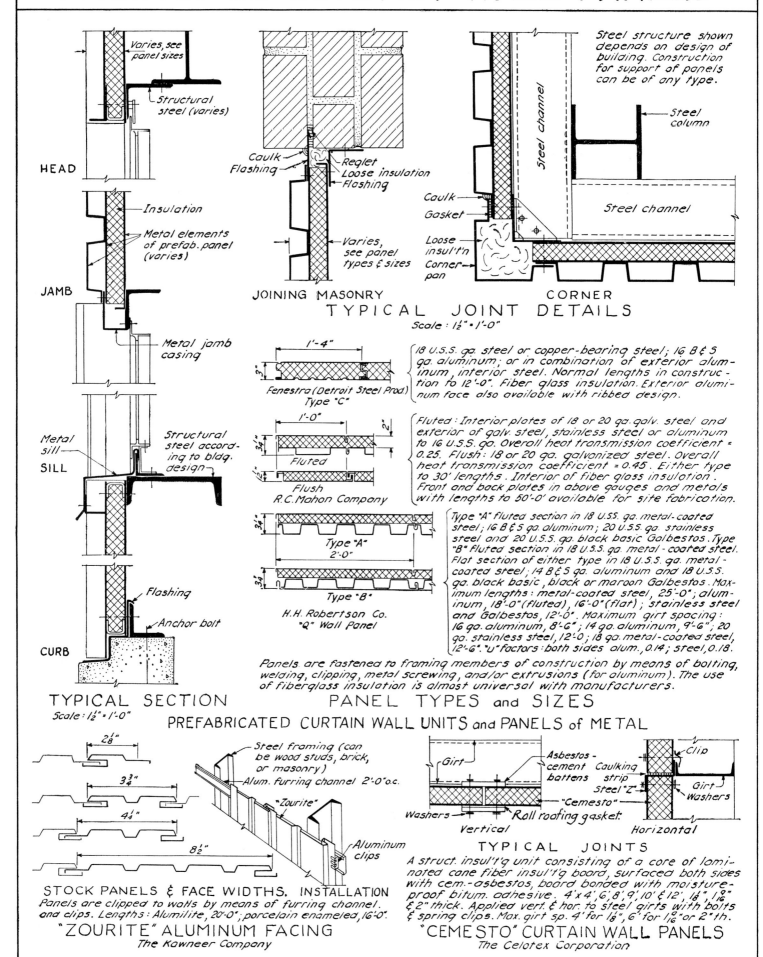

HEAD

Varies, see panel sizes

Structural steel (varies)

JAMB

Insulation

Metal elements of prefab. panel (varies)

Metal jamb casing

SILL

Metal sill

Structural steel according to bldg. design

CURB

Flashing

Anchor bolt

TYPICAL SECTION
Scale: 1½" = 1'-0"

JOINING MASONRY

Caulk Flashing

Reglet
Loose insulation
Flashing

Varies, see panel types & sizes

CORNER

Steel structure shown depends on design of building. Construction for support of panels can be of any type.

Steel channel

Steel column

Steel channel

Caulk

Gasket

Loose insul't'n

Corner pan

TYPICAL JOINT DETAILS
Scale: 1½" = 1'-0"

1'-4"
3"
Fenestra (Detroit Steel Prod.) Type "C"

18 U.S.S. ga. steel or copper-bearing steel; 16 B & 5 ga. aluminum; or in combination of exterior aluminum, interior steel. Normal lengths in construction to 12'-0". Fiber glass insulation. Exterior aluminum face also available with ribbed design.

1'-0"
2"
2¾"
2"
Fluted
Flush
R.C. Mahon Company

Fluted: Interior plates of 18 or 20 ga. galv. steel and exterior of galv. steel, stainless steel or aluminum to 16 U.S.S. ga. Overall heat transmission coefficient = 0.25. Flush: 18 or 20 ga. galvanized steel. Overall heat transmission coefficient = 0.45. Either type to 30' lengths. Interior of fiber glass insulation. Front and back plates in above gauges and metals with lengths to 50'-0' available for site fabrication.

2¾"
Type "A"
2'-0"
3"
Type "B"
H.H. Robertson Co. "Q" Wall Panel

Type "A" fluted section in 18 U.S.S. ga. metal-coated steel; 16 B & 5 ga. aluminum; 20 U.S.S. ga. stainless steel and 20 U.S.S. ga. black basic Galbestos. Type "B" fluted section in 18 U.S.S. ga. metal-coated steel. Flat section of either type in 18 U.S.S. ga. metal-coated steel; 14 B & 5 ga. aluminum and 18 U.S.S. ga. black basic, black or maroon Galbestos. Maximum lengths: metal-coated steel, 25'-0"; aluminum, 18'-0" (fluted), 16'-0" (flat); stainless steel and Galbestos, 12'-0". Maximum girt spacing: 16 ga. aluminum, 8'-6"; 14 ga. aluminum, 9'-6"; 20 ga. stainless steel, 12'-0; 18 ga. metal-coated steel, 12'-6". "u" factors: both sides alum., 0.14; steel, 0.18.

Panels are fastened to framing members of construction by means of bolting, welding, clipping, metal screwing, and/or extrusions (for aluminum). The use of fiberglass insulation is almost universal with manufacturers.

PANEL TYPES and SIZES
PREFABRICATED CURTAIN WALL UNITS and PANELS of METAL

2⅛"
3¾"
4¼"
8½"

STOCK PANELS & FACE WIDTHS.
Panels are clipped to walls by means of furring channel and clips. Lengths: Alumilite, 20'-0"; porcelain enameled, 16'-0".

"ZOURITE" ALUMINUM FACING
The Kawneer Company

Steel framing (can be wood studs, brick, or masonry)
Alum. furring channel 2'-0" o.c.
"Zourite"
Aluminum clips

INSTALLATION

Girt
Washers
Vertical

Asbestos-cement battens
Caulking strip
Steel "Z"
"Cemesto"
Roll roofing gasket
Horizontal

Clip
Girt
Washers

TYPICAL JOINTS
A struct. insul't'g unit consisting of a core of laminated cane fiber insul't'g board, surfaced both sides with cem-asbestos. board bonded with moisture-proof bitum. adhesive. 4'x4', 6', 8', 9', 10' & 12', 1⅛", 1⁹⁄₁₆" & 2" thick. Applied vert. & hor. to steel girts with bolts & spring clips. Max. girt sp. 4' for 1⅛", 6' for 1⁹⁄₁₆" or 2" th.

"CEMESTO" CURTAIN WALL PANELS
The Celotex Corporation

5

CARPENTRY

LUMBER SIZES & GRADING

AMERICAN STANDARD LUMBER SIZES for SOFTWOODS
THICKNESSES APPLY TO ALL WIDTHS & WIDTHS TO ALL THICKNESSES

LUMBER ITEM	SIZE BOARD MEASURE		DRESSED DIMENSIONS	
	THICKNESS	WIDTH	STANDARD THICKNESS	STANDARD WIDTH
Finish	Less than 1 inch	3"	5/16"	2 5/8"
	Less than 1 inch	4"	7/16"	3 1/2"
	Less than 1 inch	5"	9/16"	4 1/2"
	Less than 1 inch	6"	11/16"	5 1/2"
	1"	7"	25/32"	6 1/2"
	1 1/4"	8"	1 5/16"	7 1/4"
	1 1/2"	9"	1 5/16"	8 1/4"
	1 3/4"	10"	1 7/16"	9 1/4"
	2"	11"	1 5/8"	10 1/4"
	2 1/2"	12"	2 1/8"	11 1/4"
	3"		2 5/8"	
Common Boards and strips	1"	3"		2 5/8"
		4"		3 5/8"
		5"	25/32"	4 5/8"
		6"		5 5/8"
	1 1/4"	7"	1 1/16"	6 5/8"
		8"		7 1/2"
	1 1/2"	9"	1-5/16"	8 1/2"
		10"		9 1/2"
		11"		10 1/2"
		12"		11 1/2"
Dimension and Heavy Joists	2"	2	1 5/8"	1 5/8"
	2 1/2"	4	2 1/8"	3 5/8"
	3"	6	2 5/8"	5 5/8"
	4"	8	3 5/8"	7 1/2"
		10		9 1/2"
		12		11 1/2"
Bevel Siding		4"	3/16" - 7/16"	3 1/2"
		5"	3/16" - 5/8"	4 1/2"
		6"		5 1/2"
		8"	3/16" - 7/16"	7 1/4"
		10"	3/16" - 9/16"	9 1/4"
		12"	3/16" - 11/16"	11 1/4"
Flooring (excluding Hardwood Flooring)	1"	2"	5/16"	1 1/2"
		3"	7/16"	2 3/8"
		4"	9/16"	3 1/4"
	1 1/4"	5"	25/32"	4 1/4"
	1 1/2"	6"	1-1/16"	5 3/16"
			1-5/16"	
Dressed and Matched	1"	4"	25/32"	3 1/4"
	1 1/4"	6"	1 1/16"	5 1/4"
	1 1/2"	8"	1 5/16"	7 1/4"
		10"		9 1/4"
		12"		11 1/4"

BASIC GRADE CLASSIFICATION FOR YARD LUMBER

Total products of a typical log arranged in series according to quality as determined by appearance.

SELECT — Lumber of good appearance & finishing qualities.

Suitable for natural finishes
- Grade A — Practically free from defects.
- Grade B — Allows a few small defects or blemishes

Suitable for paint finishes
- Grade C — Allows a limited number of small defects or blemishes that can be covered with paint.
- Grade D — Allows any number of defects or blemishes which do not detract from a finish appearance, especially when painted.

COMMON — Lumber containing defects or blemishes which detract from a finish appearance but which is suitable for general utility and construction purposes.

Lumber suitable for use without waste
- #1 Common — Sound and tight knotted stock. Size of defects and blemishes limited. May be considered water-tight lumber.
- #2 Common — Allows large and course defects. May be considered grain-tight lumber.

Lumber permitting waste
- #3 Common — Allows larger and courser defects than No. 2, and occassional knot holes.
- #4 Common — Low quality lumber admitting the coarsest defect, such as decay and holes.
- #5 Common — Must hold together under ordinary handling.

Data supplied by National Lumber Manufacturers' Association

WOOD JOIST SIZES

MAXIMUM SPANS FOR FLOOR JOISTS   NO 1 COMMON

LIVE LOAD OF 60# PER SQ. FT. UNIFORMLY DISTRIBUTED WITH PLASTERED CEILING

AMERICAN STANDARD LUMBER SIZES		DIST. ON CENTER	SO. PINE & DOUGLAS FIR		WESTERN HEMLOCK		SPRUCE	
NOMINAL	NET		UNPLAST'D	PLASTERED	UNPLAST'D	PLASTERED	UNPLAST'D	PLASTERED
3" x 6"	2 5/8" x 5 5/8"	12"	11'-10"	10'-6"	11'-4"	10'-1"	10'-10"	9'-7"
		16"	10'-4"	9'-7"	9'-10"	9'-3"	9'-5"	8'-9"
2" x 8"	1 5/8" x 7 1/2"	12"	12'-5"	12'-0"	11'-11"	11'-6"	11'-4"	10'-11"
		16"	10'-10"	11'-0"	10'-4"	10'-6"	9'-11"	9'-11"
3" x 8"	2 5/8" x 7 1/2"	12"	15'-7"	14'-0"	14'-11"	13'-4"	14'-3"	12'-9"
		16"	13'-7"	12'-10"	13'-0"	12'-3"	12'-5"	11'-7"
2" x 10"	1 5/8" x 9 1/2"	12"	15'-8"	15'-2"	15'-0"	14'-6"	14'-4"	13'-9"
		16"	13'-8"	13'-10"	13'-1"	13'-3"	12'-6"	12'-7"
4" x 8"	3 5/8" x 7 1/2"	12"	18'-1"	15'-5"	17'-5"	14'-10"	16'-7"	14'-0"
		16"	15'-11"	14'-1"	15'-3"	13'-6"	14'-6"	12'-11"
3" x 10"	2 5/8" x 9 1/2"	12"	19'-7"	17'-7"	18'-10"	16'-10"	17'-11"	15'-11"
		16"	17'-1"	16'-1"	16'-5"	15'-5"	15'-9"	14'-7"
2" x 12"	1 5/8" x 11 1/2"	12"	18'-11"	18'-3"	18'-1"	17'-6"	17'-3"	16'-8"
		16"	16'-6"	16'-8"	15'-9"	16'-0"	15'-1"	15'-2"
3" x 12"	2 5/8" x 11 1/2"	12"	23'-6"	21'-1"	22'-6"	20'-3"	21'-5"	19'-3"
		16"	20'-7"	19'-4"	19'-9"	18'-6"	18'-10"	17'-7"
3" x 14"	2 5/8" x 13 1/2"	12"	27'-4"	24'-7"	26'-3"	23'-7"	25'-0"	22'-5"
		16"	24'-0"	22'-7"	23'-0"	21'-7"	21'-11"	20'-6"

*Note:- Deflection limited to 1/360 th. of the span.
Dead load figured to include weight of joists, lath, and plaster ceiling (10 lbs.) and sub-floor and finish floor.

MAXIMUM SPANS FOR FLOOR JOISTS   NO 1 COMMON

LIVE LOAD OF 75# PER SQ. FT. UNIFORMLY DISTRIBUTED WITH PLASTERED CEILING.

AMERICAN STANDARD LUMBER SIZES		DIST. ON CENTER	SO. PINE & DOUGLAS FIR		WESTERN HEMLOCK		SPRUCE	
NOMINAL	NET		UNPLAST'D	PLASTERED	UNPLAST'D	PLASTERED	UNPLAST'D	PLASTERED
2" x 8"	1 5/8" x 7 1/2"	12"	11'-5"	11'-4"	11'-1"	10'-10"	10'-5"	10'-3"
		16"	9'-11"	10'-4"	9'-6"	9'-10"	9'-1"	9'-5"
3" x 8"	2 5/8" x 7 1/2"	12"	14'-5"	13'-2"	13'-9"	12'-8"	13'-2"	12'-1"
		16"	12'-6"	12'-1"	12'-1"	11'-7"	11'-5"	11'-0"
2" x 10"	1 5/8" x 9 1/2"	12"	14'-5"	14'-3"	13'-10"	13'-8"	13'-2"	12'-11"
		16"	12'-6"	13'-0"	12'-0"	12'-5"	11'-5"	11'-10"
4" x 8"	3 5/8" x 7 1/2"	12"	16'-9"	14'-7"	16'-0"	14'-0"	15'-4"	13'-3"
		16"	14'-8"	13'-4"	14'-0"	12'-9"	13'-3"	12'-2"
3" x 10"	2 5/8" x 9 1/2"	12"	18'-1"	16'-8"	17'-4"	15'-11"	16'-6"	15'-2"
		16"	15'-10"	15'-2"	15'-2"	14'-7"	14'-5"	13'-9"
2" x 12"	1 5/8" x 11 1/2"	12"	17'-4"	17'-2"	16'-6"	16'-5"	15'-11"	15'-8"
		16"	15'-1"	15'-9"	14'-6"	15'-1"	13'-10"	14'-3"
4" x 10"	3 5/8" x 9 1/2"	12"	21'-0"	18'-4"	20'-1"	17'-7"	19'-1"	16'-2"
		16"	18'-5"	16'-10"	17'-7"	16'-2"	16'-10"	15'-3"
3" x 12"	2 5/8" x 11 1/2"	12"	21'-8"	20'-1"	20'-10"	19'-2"	19'-10"	18'-2"
		16"	19'-0"	18'-4"	18'-3"	17'-7"	17'-5"	16'-8"
3" x 14"	2 5/8" x 13 1/2"	12"	25'-3"	23'-5"	24'-3"	22'-3"	23'-1"	21'-3"
		16"	22'-2"	21'-6"	21'-3"	20'-6"	20'-3"	19'-6"

*Note:- Deflection limited to 1/360 th. of the span.
Dead load figured to include weight of joists, lath, and plaster ceiling (10 lbs.) and sub-floor and finish floor.

Data supplied by National Lumber Manufacturers Association.

WOOD JOIST & RAFTER SIZES

MAXIMUM SPANS FOR FLOOR JOISTS Nº 1 COMMON

LIVE LOAD FOR RESIDENTIAL USE OF 40# PER SQ. FOOT UNIFORMLY DISTRIBUTED WITH PLASTERED CEILING

AMERICAN STANDARD LUMBER SIZES		DIST. ON CENTER	MAXIMUM CLEAR SPAN BETWEEN SUPPORTS					
			SO. PINE & DOUGLAS FIR		WESTERN HEMLOCK		SPRUCE	
NOMINAL	NET		UNPLAST'D	PLASTERED*	UNPLAST'D	PLASTERED*	UNPLAST'D	PLASTERED*
2" x 6"	1·5/8" x 5·5/8"	12"	10'-11"	10'-0"	10'-5"	9'-6"	10'-0"	9'-1"
		16"	9'-6"	9'-1"	9'-1"	8'-8"	8'-8"	8'-3"
3" x 6"	2·5/8" x 5·5/8"	12"	13'-8"	11'-8"	13'-1"	11'-2"	12'-5"	10'-6"
		16"	11'-5"	10'-8"	11'-5"	10'-2"	10'-11"	9'-8"
2" x 8"	1·5/8" x 7·1/2"	12"	14'-5"	13'-3"	13'-10"	12'-8"	13'-2"	12'-0"
		16"	12'-7"	12'-1"	12'-0"	11'-7"	11'-6"	11'-0"
3" x 8"	2·5/8" x 7·1/2"	12"	18'-0"	15'-4"	17'-3"	14'-8"	16'-5"	13'-11"
		16"	15'-9"	14'-0"	15'-1"	13'-5"	14'-5"	12'-9"
2" x 10"	1·5/8" x 9·1/2"	12"	18'-2"	16'-8"	17'-4"	16'-0"	16'-7"	15'-2"
		16"	15'-10"	15'-3"	15'-2"	14'-7"	14'-6"	13'-10"
3" x 10"	2·5/8" x 9·1/2"	12"	22'-6"	19'-3"	21'-7"	18'-5"	20'-7"	17'-6"
		16"	19'-9"	17'-8"	18'-11"	16'-11"	18'-1"	16'-1"
2" x 12"	1·5/8" x 11·1/2"	12"	21'-11"	20'-1"	20'-11"	19'-3"	19'-11"	18'-3"
		16"	19'-1"	18'-5"	18'-3"	17'-7"	17'-5"	16'-9"
3" x 12"	2·5/8" x 11·1/2"	12"	26'-11"	23'-1"	25'-9"	22'-1"	24'-7"	20'-11"
		16"	23'-9"	21'-3"	22'-9"	20'-4"	21'-8"	19'-4"
2" x 14"	1·5/8" x 13·1/2"	12"	25'-4"	23'-5"	24'-3"	22'-6"	23'-2"	21'-2"
		16"	22'-3"	21'-5"	21'-3"	20'-6"	20'-3"	19'-6"
3" x 14"	2·5/8" x 13·1/2"	12"	—	26'-11"	30'-0"	25'-9"	28'-6"	24'-5"
		16"	27'-7"	24'-10"	26'-5"	23'-9"	25'-2"	22'-6"

*Note:- Deflection limited to 1/360 th. of the span.
Dead load figured to include weight of joists, lath and plaster ceiling (10 lbs.) and sub-floor and finish floor.

MAXIMUM SPANS FOR RAFTERS Nº 1 COMMON

ROOF LOAD OF 30# PER SQ. FT. UNIFORMLY DISTRIBUTED FOR SLOPES OF 20° OR MORE

AMERICAN STANDARD LUMBER SIZES		DIST ON CENTER	MAXIMUM CLEAR SPAN - PLATE TO RIDGE.					
			SO. PINE & DOUGLAS FIR		WESTERN HEMLOCK		SPRUCE	
NOMINAL	NET		UNPLAST'D	PLASTERED*	UNPLAST'D	PLASTERED*	UNPLAST'D	PLASTERED*
2" x 4"	1·5/8" x 3·5/8"	16"	7'-8"	6'-10"	7'-4"	6'-6"	7'-0"	6'-2"
		24"	6'-3"	6'-0"	6'-0"	5'-8"	5'-9"	5'-5"
2" x 6"	1·5/8" x 5·5/8"	16"	11'-9"	10'-6"	11'-3"	10'-1"	10'-9"	9'-7"
		24"	9'-8"	9'-3"	9'-3"	8'-10"	8'-10"	8'-5"
3" x 6"	2·5/8" x 5·5/8"	16"	14'-10"	12'-3"	14'-1"	11'-9"	13'-6"	11'-1"
		24"	12'-3"	10'-10"	11'-9"	10'-4"	11'-1"	9'-10"
2" x 8"	1·5/8" x 7·1/2"	16"	15'-7"	14'-0"	15'-3"	13'-4"	14'-3"	12'-9"
		24"	12'-10"	12'-3"	12'-4"	11'-9"	11'-9"	11'-2"
3" x 8"	2·5/8" x 7·1/2"	16"	19'-5"	16'-1"	18'-7"	15'-5"	17'-9"	14'-7"
		24"	16'-1"	14'-3"	15'-5"	13'-7"	14'-9"	12'-11"
2" x 10"	1·5/8" x 9·1/2"	16"	19'-7"	17'-6"	18'-9"	16'-10"	17'-11"	15'-11"
		24"	16'-3"	15'-6"	15'-6"	14'-10"	14'-10"	14'-0"
2" x 12"	1·5/8" x 11·1/2"	16"	23'-6"	21'-2"	22'-6"	19'-4"	21'-6"	19'-3"
		24"	19'-6"	18'-8"	18'-8"	17'-1"	17'-10"	17'-0"

*Note:- Deflection limited to 1/360 th of the span.
Dead load figured to include weight of rafters, roof sheathing, and 2.5 lbs. for wood shingle or 3-ply ready-made roofing. For heavier roof finishes use rafter next size larger
Data supplied by National Lumber Manufacturers Association

WOOD DOUBLE-HUNG WINDOWS

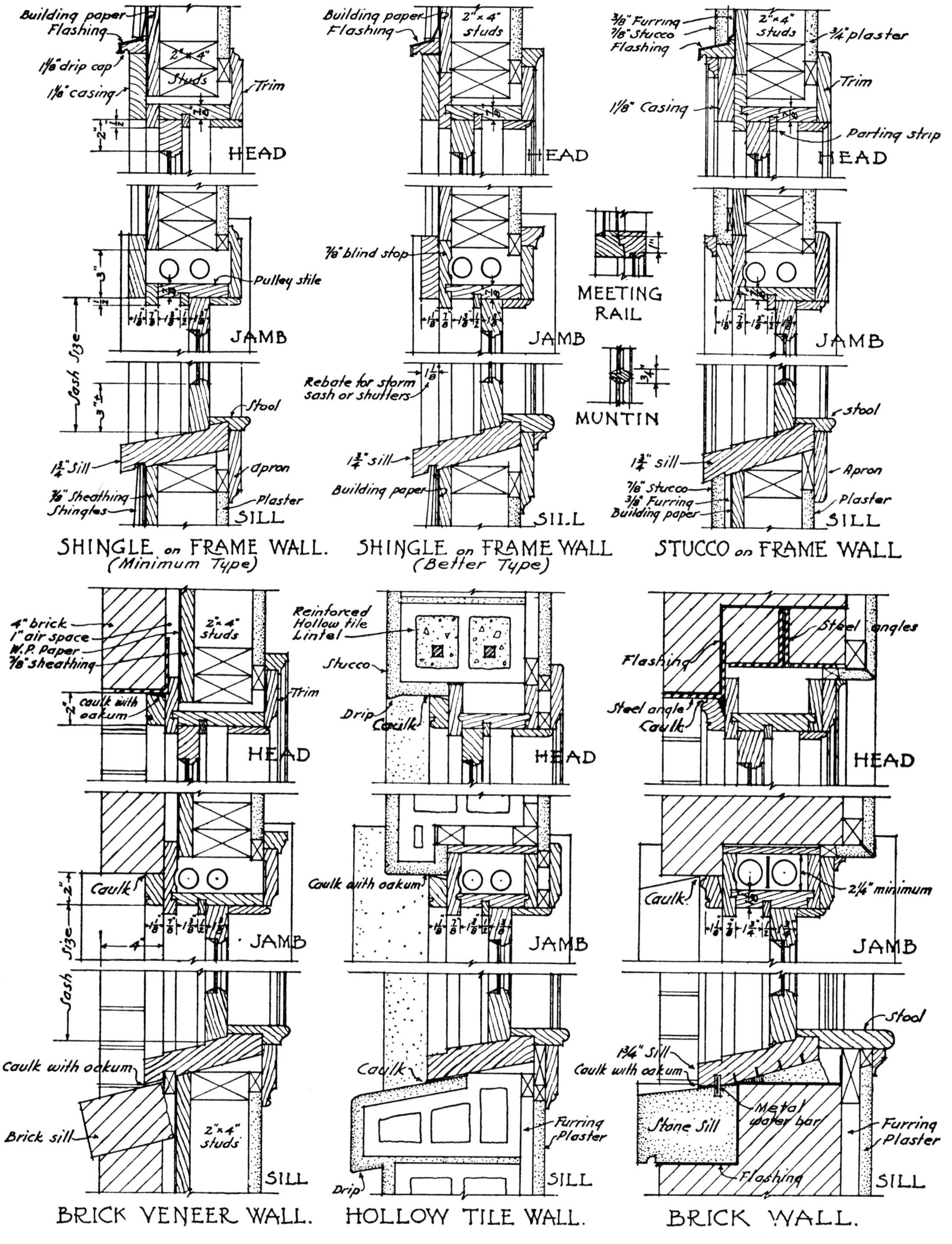

1½" = 1'-0"

STANDARD MILL CONSTRUCTION

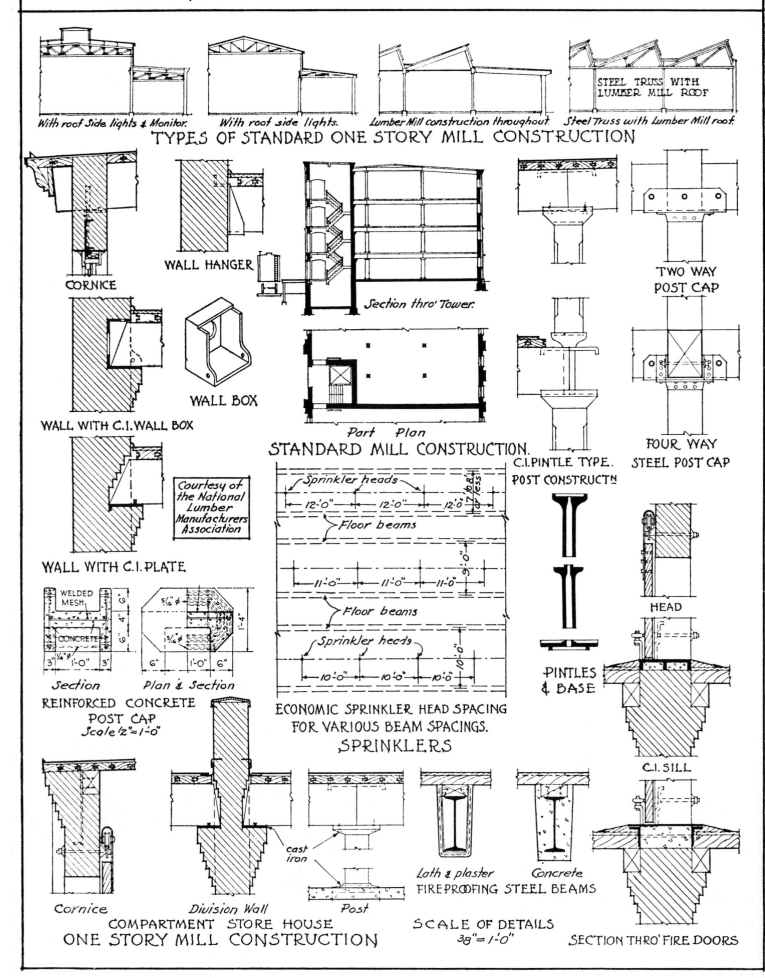

With roof Side lights & Monitor.   With roof side lights.   Lumber Mill construction throughout.   Steel Truss with Lumber Mill roof.

TYPES OF STANDARD ONE STORY MILL CONSTRUCTION

STEEL TRUSS WITH LUMBER MILL ROOF

CORNICE

WALL HANGER

WALL BOX

WALL WITH C.I. WALL BOX

Section thro' Tower.

TWO WAY POST CAP

FOUR WAY STEEL POST CAP

WALL WITH C.I. PLATE

Courtesy of the National Lumber Manufacturers Association

Part Plan

STANDARD MILL CONSTRUCTION.

C.I. PINTLE TYPE. POST CONSTRUCT'N

WELDED MESH

CONCRETE

Section   Plan & Section

REINFORCED CONCRETE POST CAP
Scale 1½"=1'-0"

Sprinkler heads
12'-0"   12'-0"   12'-0"
Floor beams
11'-0"   11'-0"   11'-0"
Floor beams
Sprinkler heads
10'-0"   10'-0"   10'-0"

ECONOMIC SPRINKLER HEAD SPACING FOR VARIOUS BEAM SPACINGS.

SPRINKLERS

PINTLES & BASE

HEAD

C.I. SILL

Cornice   Division Wall

cast iron

Post

Lath & plaster   Concrete
FIREPROOFING STEEL BEAMS

COMPARTMENT STORE HOUSE

ONE STORY MILL CONSTRUCTION

SCALE OF DETAILS
3⁄8"=1'-0"

SECTION THRO' FIRE DOORS

STANDARD MILL CONSTRUCTION

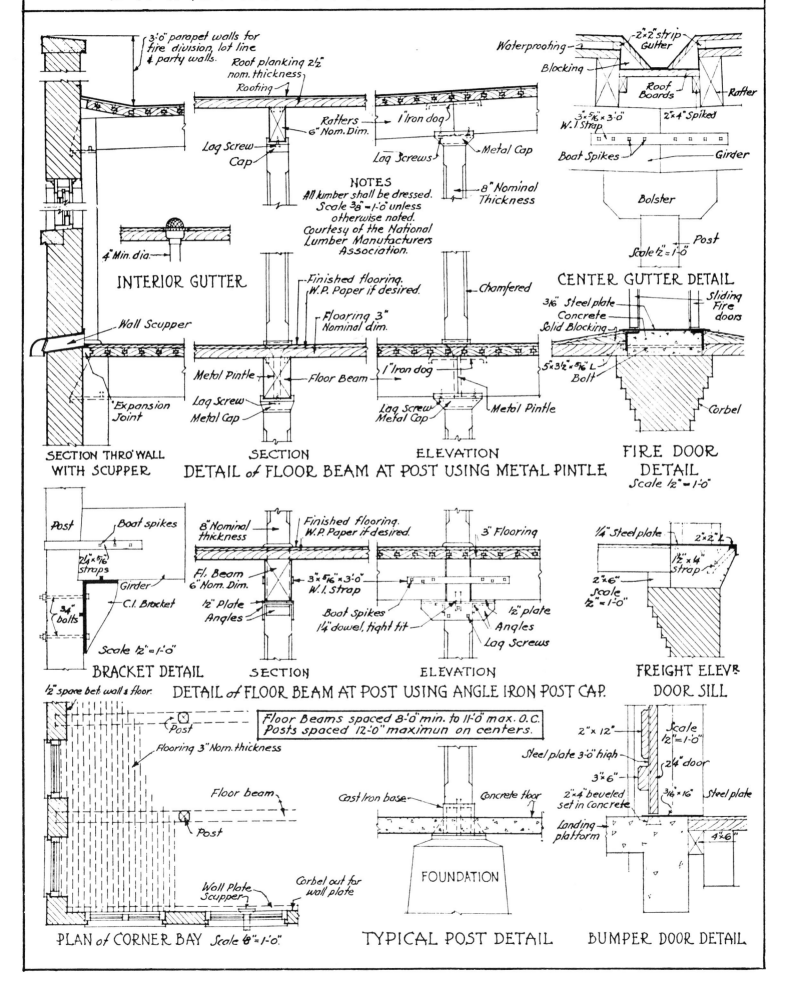

3'-0" parapet walls for fire division, lot line & party walls.

Root planking 2½" nom. thickness

Roofing

Rafters 6" Nom. Dim.

Lag Screw Cap

4" Min. dia.

INTERIOR GUTTER

1" Iron dog

Lag Screws

Metal Cap

8" Nominal Thickness

NOTES
All lumber shall be dressed. Scale ⅜" = 1'-0" unless otherwise noted. Courtesy of the National Lumber Manufacturers Association.

Waterproofing

2" × 2" strip Gutter

Blocking

Roof Boards

Rafter

3" × 5/16 × 3'-0" W.I. Strap

2" × 4" Spiked

Boat Spikes

Girder

Bolster

Post

Scale ½" = 1'-0"

CENTER GUTTER DETAIL

Wall Scupper

Finished flooring. W.P. Paper if desired.

Flooring 3" Nominal dim.

Chamfered

Metal Pintle

Lag Screw Metal Cap

Floor Beam

1" Iron dog

Lag Screw Metal Cap

Metal Pintle

3/16" Steel plate
Concrete
Solid Blocking

Sliding Fire doors

5" × 3½" × 5/16" L Bolt

Corbel

Expansion Joint

SECTION THRO' WALL WITH SCUPPER

SECTION

ELEVATION

DETAIL of FLOOR BEAM AT POST USING METAL PINTLE

FIRE DOOR DETAIL
Scale ½" = 1'-0"

Post

Boat spikes

2¼ × 5/16" straps

Girder

C.I. Bracket

¾" bolts

Scale ½" = 1'-0"

BRACKET DETAIL

8" Nominal thickness

Fl. Beam 6" Nom. Dim.

½" Plate Angles

Finished flooring. W.P. Paper if desired.

3" × 5/16 × 3'-0" W.I. Strap

Boat Spikes

1¼" dowel, tight fit

3" Flooring

½" plate Angles

Lag Screws

SECTION

ELEVATION

DETAIL of FLOOR BEAM AT POST USING ANGLE IRON POST CAP.

¼" Steel plate

2" × 2" L

1½" × 4" Strap

2" × 6"

Scale ½" = 1'-0"

FREIGHT ELEVR. DOOR SILL

½" space bet. wall & floor.

Flooring 3" Nom. thickness

Post

Floor Beams spaced 8'-0" min. to 11'-0" max. O.C. Posts spaced 12'-0" maximum on centers.

Floor beam

Post

Wall Plate Scupper

Corbel out for wall plate

Cast Iron base

Concrete floor

FOUNDATION

2" × 12"

Steel plate 3'-0" high

3" × 6"

2" × 4" beveled set in Concrete

Landing platform

Scale ½" = 1'-0"

2¼" door

3/16" × 16" Steel plate

4" × 6"

PLAN of CORNER BAY Scale ⅜" = 1'-0"

TYPICAL POST DETAIL

BUMPER DOOR DETAIL

LAMINATED MILL CONSTRUCTION

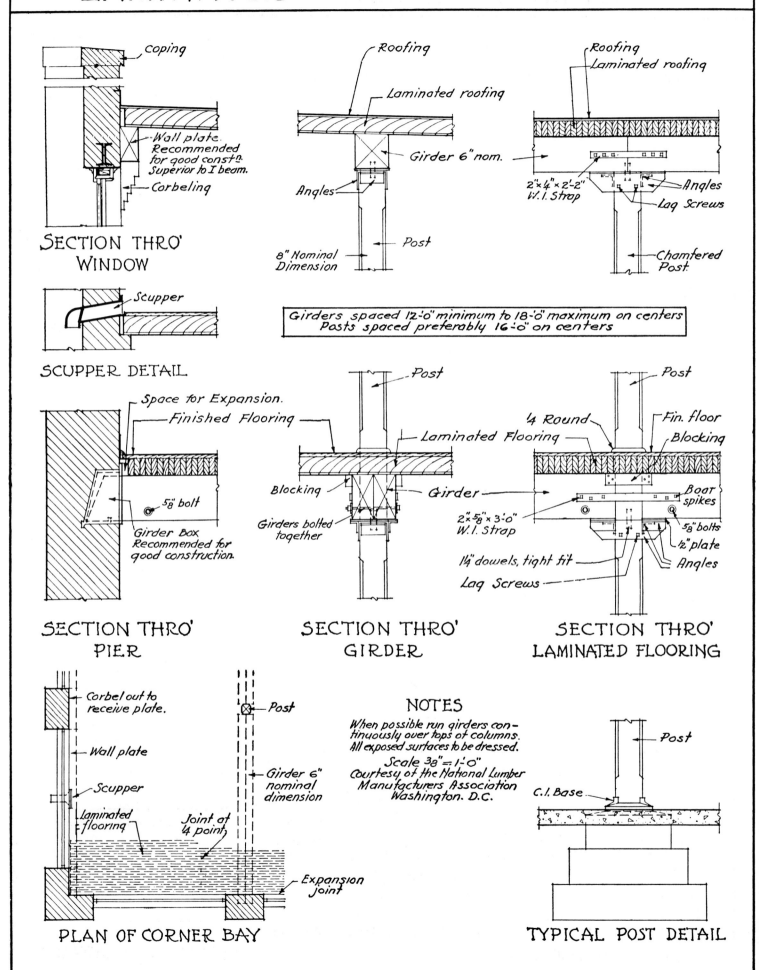

SECTION THRO' WINDOW

- Coping
- Wall plate. Recommended for good const⁰. Superior to I beam.
- Corbeling

SCUPPER DETAIL

- Scupper

- Roofing
- Laminated roofing
- Girder 6" nom.
- Angles
- Post
- 8" Nominal Dimension

- Roofing
- Laminated roofing
- 2"x 4"x 2'-2" W.I. Strap
- Angles
- Lag Screws
- Chamfered Post

Girders spaced 12'-0" minimum to 18'-0" maximum on centers
Posts spaced preferably 16'-0" on centers

SECTION THRO' PIER

- Space for Expansion.
- Finished Flooring
- 5⁄8" bolt
- Girder Box Recommended for good construction.

SECTION THRO' GIRDER

- Post
- Laminated Flooring
- Blocking
- Girder
- Girders bolted together

SECTION THRO' LAMINATED FLOORING

- Post
- ¼ Round
- Fin. floor
- Blocking
- Boat spikes
- 2"x 5⁄8"x 3'-0" W.I. Strap
- 5⁄8" bolts
- ½" plate
- Angles
- 1¼" dowels, tight fit
- Lag Screws

PLAN OF CORNER BAY

- Corbel out to receive plate.
- Wall plate
- Scupper
- Laminated flooring
- Post
- Girder 6" nominal dimension
- Joint at ¼ point.
- Expansion joint

NOTES

When possible run girders continuously over tops of columns.
All exposed surfaces to be dressed.

Scale 3⁄8" = 1'-0"
Courtesy of the National Lumber
Manufacturers Association
Washington. D.C.

TYPICAL POST DETAIL

- Post
- C.I. Base

SEMI-MILL CONSTRUCTION

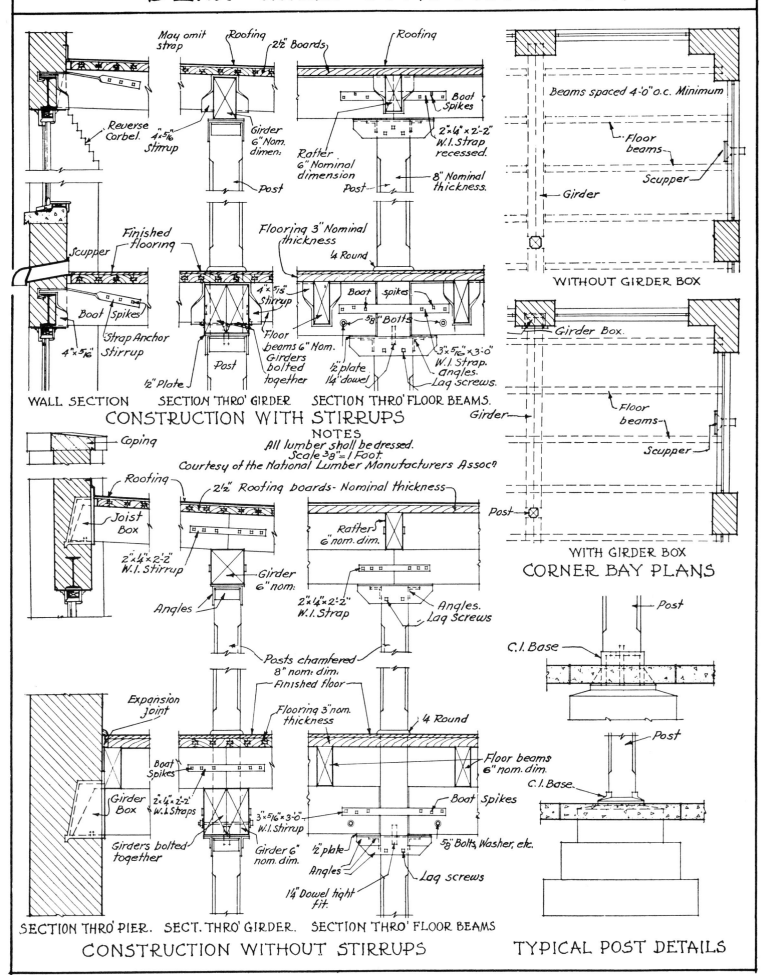

May omit strap

Roofing

2½" Boards

Roofing

Reverse Corbel.

4"×5/16" Stirrup

Girder 6" Nom. dimen:

Rafter 6" Nominal dimension

Post

Boat Spikes

2"×4"×2'-2" W.I. Strap recessed.

8" Nominal thickness.

Post

Finished flooring

Flooring 3" Nominal thickness

4 Round

Scupper

4"×5/16" Stirrup

Boat Spikes

Boat spikes

⅝" Bolts

Strap Anchor Stirrup

4"×5/16"

½" Plate

Post

Floor beams 6" Nom. Girders bolted together

½" plate

1¼" dowel

3"×5/16"×3'-0" W.I. Strap. Angles. Lag screws.

WALL SECTION   SECTION THRO' GIRDER   SECTION THRO' FLOOR BEAMS.

CONSTRUCTION WITH STIRRUPS

NOTES
All lumber shall be dressed.
Scale ⅜" = 1 Foot.
Courtesy of the National Lumber Manufacturers Assoc'n.

Coping

Roofing

2½" Roofing boards- Nominal thickness

Joist Box

2"×4"×2'-2" W.I. Stirrup

Rafter 6" nom. dim.

Girder 6" nom:

2"×4"×2'-2" W.I. Strap.

Angles. Lag Screws

Angles

Posts chamfered 8" nom: dim.

Finished floor

Expansion Joint

Flooring 3" nom. thickness

4 Round

Boat Spikes

Floor beams 6" nom. dim.

Girder Box

2"×4"×2'-2" W.I. Straps

3"×5/16"×3'-0" W.I. stirrup

Boat Spikes

Girders bolted together

Girder 6" nom. dim.

½" plate

Angles

⅝" Bolts, Washer, etc.

1¼" Dowel tight fit.

Lag screws

SECTION THRO' PIER.   SECT. THRO' GIRDER.   SECTION THRO' FLOOR BEAMS

CONSTRUCTION WITHOUT STIRRUPS

Beams spaced 4'-0"o.c. Minimum

Floor beams

Scupper

Girder

WITHOUT GIRDER BOX

Girder Box.

Floor beams

Girder

Scupper

Post

WITH GIRDER BOX

CORNER BAY PLANS

Post

C.I. Base

Post

C.I. Base.

TYPICAL POST DETAILS

COMPARATIVE FRAMING

	* A screeded Cement finish is assumed as basic where marked	Base Price per Square Ft. Details are below	Adaptability for Cement finish or Terrazzo	Suitability for Winter Construction	Fireproof value and Insurance	Do special Building Laws bar this type	How foolpr is this construction
1	OPEN WEB STEEL JOISTS	66.4	*Basic	O.K.	Handicapped	Handicapped	O.K.
2	TWO WAY CONCRETE SLAB	61.9	O.K.	Handicapped	O.K	No	Inspection req
3	METAL TILE & CONCRETE SLAB	63.3	O.K	Handicapped	O.K.	No	Inspection req
4	GYPSUM PLANK	68.3	O.K.	O.K.	Handicapped	Handicapped	O.K.
5	GRITCRETE	62.6	O.K.	O.K.	O.K.	No	O.K.
6	STEEL & CINDER CONCRETE ARCHES	73.2	O.K.	Fair	O.K.	No	O.K.
7	REINFORCED CONCRETE BEAM & SLAB	68.0	O.K.	Handicapped	O.K.	No	Inspection req
8	TWO-WAY TILE - SCHUSTER	71.7	O.K.	Handicapped	O.K.	No	Inspection req
9	TWO-WAY SLAG BLOK-REPUBLIC	71.7	O.K.	Handicapped	O.K.	No	Inspection req
10	NASSAU	63.6	O.K.	Handicapped	O.K.	No	Inspection req
11	WOOD OPEN JOIST-NON-FIREPROOF	37.8	No	O.K.	Not Fireproof	No	Inspection req
12	AEROCRETE	69.9	O.K.	Fair	O.K.	No	O.K.
13	ROBERTSON, KEYSTONE STEEL						
14							

The first column shows the basic cost, where such are modified by suitability it is indicated in the other columns. For instance, a high basic first cost may be neutralized by the economy obtained because of the light weight of the system as it affects the supporting columns and girders etc.
* A screeded intregal cement finish is assumed basic.

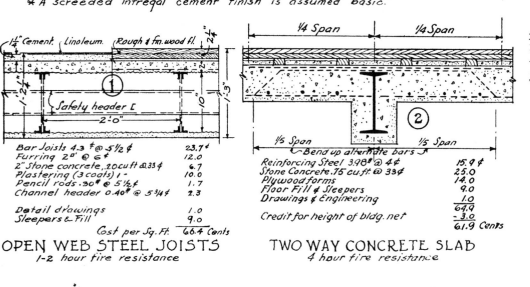

OPEN WEB STEEL JOISTS
1-2 hour fire resistance

Bar Joists 4.3# @ 5½#	23.7¢
Furring 2″ @ 6¢	12.0
2″ Stone concrete .20 cu.ft @ .33¢	6.7
Plastering (3 coats)	10.0
Pencil rods .30# @ 5½¢	1.7
Channel header 0.40# @ 5¾¢	2.3
Detail drawings	1.0
Sleepers & Fill	9.0
Cost per Sq.Ft.	66.4 Cents

TWO WAY CONCRETE SLAB
4 hour fire resistance

Reinforcing Steel 3.98# @ 4¢	15.9¢
Stone Concrete .75 cu.ft. @ .33¢	25.0
Plywood forms	14.0
Floor Fill & Sleepers	9.0
Drawings & Engineering	1.0
	64.9
Credit for height of bldg. net	-3.0
	61.9 Cents

METAL TILE & CONCRETE SLAB
4 hour fire resistance
* Increase to 20¢ if small job. Decreas to 12¢ for large job with 3 reuses of pa
~ Arch. Rib System Comparable ~

Arch. Rib uses Trussed Joist to reduce forms. Also narrow

Reinforcing steel .2# @ 4¢	8.0¢
Concrete .40 cu.ft. @ .33¢	13.3
Lath	6.0
Metal Tile	5.0*
Forms	10.0*
Plaster	10.0
Drawing and Engineering	2.0
Fill and sleepers	9.0
Cost per Sq. Ft.	63.3¢

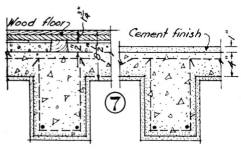

REINFORCED CONC. BEAM & SLAB
4 hour fire resistance
if plastered

Reinforcing steel 3.0# @ 4¢	12.0¢
Stone concrete .42 cu.ft @ 3¢	13.9
*Forms 1□′ (including beams)	17.7
Plaster (bond & 2 coats) incl. beams	14.4
Floor fill and sleepers	9.0
Drawing & engineering	1.0
Cost per Sq. ft.	68.0 Cents

* If plywood forms are used and 3 coats of paint in place of plaster cost =59.9

SCHUSTER 2-WAY TILE SYSTEM
4 hour fire resistance
(9) REPUBLIC SYSTEM COMPARABLE

Semi-continuous each WL/15

Reinforcing steel 2.3# @ 4¢	9.2¢
Concrete .24 cu.ft. @ 33¢	8.0
Tile 1□′ 7″	11.0
Forms 1□′	19.0
Plaster (3 coats)	10.0
Drawings & Engineering	1.0
Soffit blocks	1.6
Floor fill and sleepers	9.0
*Fireproofing I beam	2.0
*Steel for one side beam	6.9
Cost per sq. ft.	74.7¢
Credit for reduced ht. of bldg.	3.7
	71.7¢

* Omit for skeleton design or 4way bearing

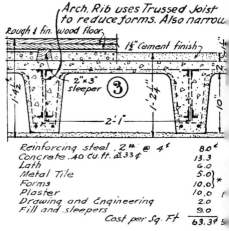

LONGITUDINAL & CROSS SECTION

NASSAU SYSTEM
4 hour resistant

Reinf. Steel 1.7# @ .04	6.8¢	Plaster (3 coats)	
Conc. .24 cu.ft. @ 33¢	8.0	Fill & Sleepers	
Tile per sq.ft. 8″ Tile	14.0	D'wgs. & Eng.	
Soffit Blocks	0.8		
Forms 1 Sq.ft	14.0		

The authors do not vouch for the accuracy of costs or statements herein as these are merely unbiased opinions base on the results of their experience. The conditions governing these are continually changing, and all use of the da should include allowance for such changes. This data in several instances does not agree with claims of the Manufacturers. Due to limitations of space many types of floor construction have been omitted.

Elwyn E. Seelye an

YSTEMS FOR FLOORS

is cost of orting struct-steel affected	Absence of local suitable cinders affects	Base for rubber tile, lineoleum etc.	Suitability to form flat ceiling	Ruggedness for concentrated and moving loads	Is fill required to take Conduits	Sound Transmission properties	Permanency	
Credit	No	Basic	O. K.	Barred	No Fill	Questionable	Fair	1
Basic	No	No	Debit 9¢	O. K.	No Fill	O. K.	O. K.	2
Basic	No	Basic	O. K.	Handicapped	No Fill	O. K	O. K	3
Credit			Debit 10¢	Barred	No Fill	{ Sound O.K } Vibration possible	Fair	4
Basic	No	Use without finish. Basic	Debit 9¢	O K	Fill required		O.K	5
Basic	Debit	Debit 12¢	Debit 9¢	Handicapped	Fill required	O. K	O. K	6
Basic	No	No	Debit 9¢	O. K.	No Fill	O. K.	O. K.	7
Basic	No	Debit 12¢	O. K.	O. K.	Fill required	O. K	O. K.	8
Basic	No	Debit 12¢	O. K.	O. K.	Fill required	O. K.	O. K.	9
Debit	No	Basic	O. K.	O. K.	No Fill	O. K.	O. K.	10
Credit	No	Debit 12¢	O. K.	O. K.	No Fill	Bad	Fair	11
Basic	No	Basic	O. K.	O. K.	No Fill.	O. K.	O. K.	12
								13
								14

he break down of costs in first column is shown below. The prices used are for New York City and vicinity –1941 other costs nay be substituted to get total for other localities so that a correct comparison may be made. Prices are for material in floor panel 20' × 25'; 60 lbs. live load; 18,000 lbs. stress in steel; bar joist stressed in accordance with Steel Joist Institute. educed by the factor 8/9; J. and L. beams stressed at 16,000 lbs; semi-continuous conditions for those systems where con-nuity is utilized; and no account taken for supporting beams and columns. Finish and rough flooring not included.

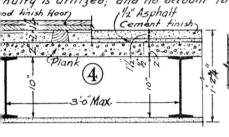

```
teel Bar Joist 4# @ 5½¢      22.0¢
unior Plank                  18.0
aster                        10.0
ill and sleepers              9.0
rawings                       1.0
hannel Header                 2.3
urring                        6.0
          Cost per Sq.Ft.    68.3¢
```

GYPSUM PLANK
1-2 hour fire resistance
Cinder Plank comparable
add 4¢ per Square Foot

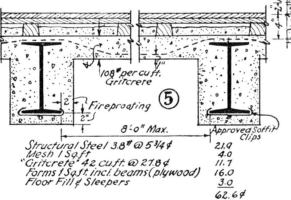

```
Structural Steel 3.8# @ 5¾¢   21.9
Mesh 1 Sq.ft                    4.0
"Gritcrete" .42 cu.ft @ 27.8¢  11.7
Forms 1 Sq.ft. incl. beams (plywood)  16.0
Floor Fill & Sleepers           3.0
                               62.6¢
```

GRITCRETE
4 hour fire resistance (Plaster omitted)

```
Structural steel 3.8# @ 5¼¢   21.9¢
Mesh 1 sq. ft.                  3.5
Cinder concrete .42 cu.ft @ 25¢  10.5
Forms 1 sq. Ft. (including beam)  14.0 *
Plaster (bond & 2 coats)¼ includ'g beam 13.3
Floor fill and sleepers         10.0
          Cost per Sq. ft    73.2 ¢
```

STEEL & CINDER CONCRETE
4 hour fire resistance
× Add 3¢ per. sq. ft. outside New York City

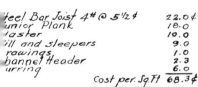

```
mber   2 F.B.M   2oo¢
th                 6.1
aster             11.7
  Cost per Sq. Ft.   37.8 ¢
```

OOD OPEN JOISTS
Not Fireproof

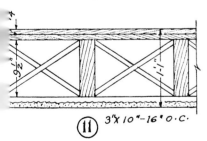

```
Steel joist 4# @ 5½¢    22.0¢
Aerocrete 0.5 cu.ft @ 27¢  13.5
Stone concrete .21 cu.ft @ 33¢  6.9
Forms hung from steel    8.0
Pencil rod reinforcement  3.5
Fill and sleepers         9.0
Plastering              10.0
          Cost per Sq. Ft.   72.9
Credit for height of building  3.0
                          69.9 ¢
```

AEROCRETE
4 hour fire resistance
plaster bond questionable

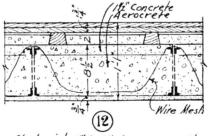

Finish floor in mastic on concrete fill

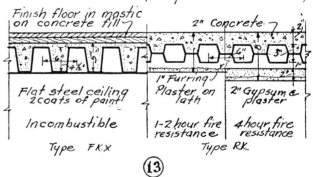

Flat steel ceiling 2 coats of paint

Incombustible

Type FKX

1" Furring Plaster on lath

1-2 hour fire resistance

2" Gypsum & plaster

4 hour fire resistance

Type RK

KEYSTONE STEEL FLOOR
ROBERTSON

Permits use of cells as wire raceways for rubber insulated wires. Maximum spans vary depending on thickness of sheet steel used. Sizes obtainable, FKX 1½/16-20'0", RK 1½/16-10'0"

ere cement finish is indicated 1¼" or 1½" thick a monolithic finish is not assumed. If finish is monolithic th slab 1" may be used instead. Fill is only shown when it is required for conduits in usual construction; if is required for heating pipes increase it to 4"; in some work it may be decreased to 2" for conduits.

lting Engineers.

BALLOON FRAMING

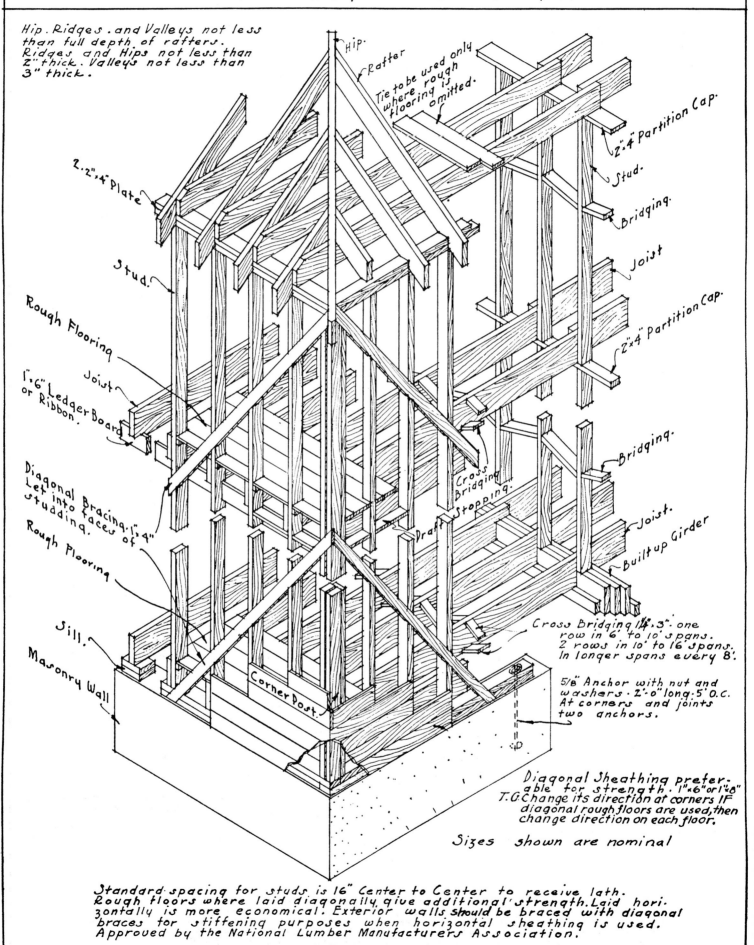

Hip. Ridges. and Valleys not less than full depth of rafters. Ridges and Hips not less than 2" thick. Valleys not less than 3" thick.

Hip.

Rafter

Tie to be used only where rough flooring is omitted.

2".4" Partition Cap.

Stud.

Bridging.

2.2",4" Plate

Joist

Stud.

2"x4" Partition Cap.

Rough Flooring

Joist.

1".6" Ledger Board or Ribbon.

Bridging.

Diagonal Bracing 1".4" Let into faces of studding.

Cross Bridging.

Joist.

Rough Flooring

Draft Stopping.

Built up Girder

Sill.

Masonry Wall

Corner Post.

Cross Bridging 1".3". one row in 6' to 10' spans. 2 rows in 10' to 16' spans. In longer spans every 8'.

5/8" Anchor with nut and washers. 2'-0" long. 5' O.C. At corners and joints two anchors.

Diagonal Sheathing preferable for strength. 1"x6" or 1"x8" T.G. Change its direction at corners IF diagonal rough floors are used, then change direction on each floor.

Sizes shown are nominal

Standard spacing for studs is 16" Center to Center to receive lath. Rough floors where laid diagonally give additional strength. Laid horizontally is more economical. Exterior walls should be braced with diagonal braces for stiffening purposes when horizontal sheathing is used. Approved by the National Lumber Manufacturers Association.

BRACED FRAMING

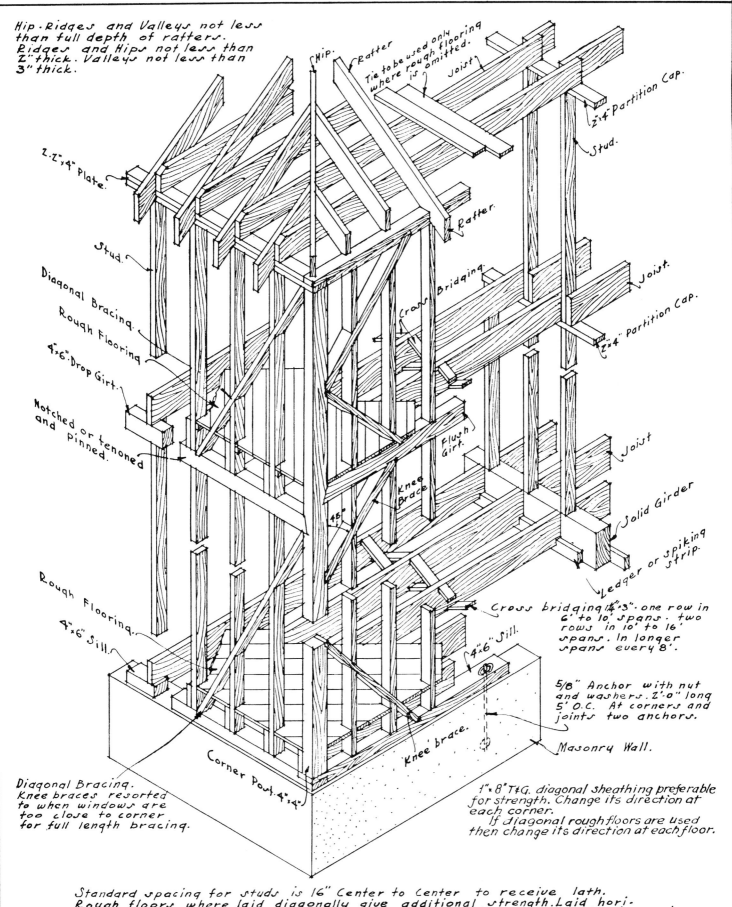

Hip·Ridges and Valleys not less than full depth of rafters. Ridges and Hips not less than 2" thick. Valleys not less than 3" thick.

Hip.

Rafter.

Tie to be used only where rough flooring is omitted.

Joist.

2"×4" Partition Cap.

Stud.

2.2",4" Plate.

Rafter.

Stud.

Diagonal Bracing.

Rough Flooring.

Cross Bridging.

Joist.

4"×6" Drop Girt.

2"×4" Partition Cap.

Notched or tenoned and pinned.

Flush Girt.

Joist

Knee Brace.

Solid Girder

45°

Ledger or spiking strip.

Rough Flooring.

Cross bridging 2"×3". one row in 6' to 10' spans. two rows in 10' to 16' spans. In longer spans every 8'.

4"×6" Sill.

4"×6" Sill.

5/8" Anchor with nut and washers. 2'-0" long 5' O.C. At corners and joints two anchors.

Knee brace.

Masonry Wall.

Corner Post. 4"×4".

Diagonal Bracing. Knee braces resorted to when windows are too close to corner for full length bracing.

1"×8" T&G. diagonal sheathing preferable for strength. Change its direction at each corner.
If diagonal rough floors are used then change its direction at each floor.

Standard spacing for studs is 16" Center to Center to receive lath. Rough floors where laid diagonally give additional strength. Laid horizontally is more economical. Exterior walls may be braced with diagonal braces for stiffening purposes where horizontal sheathing is used. Approved by the National Lumber Manufacturers Association.

WESTERN FRAMING

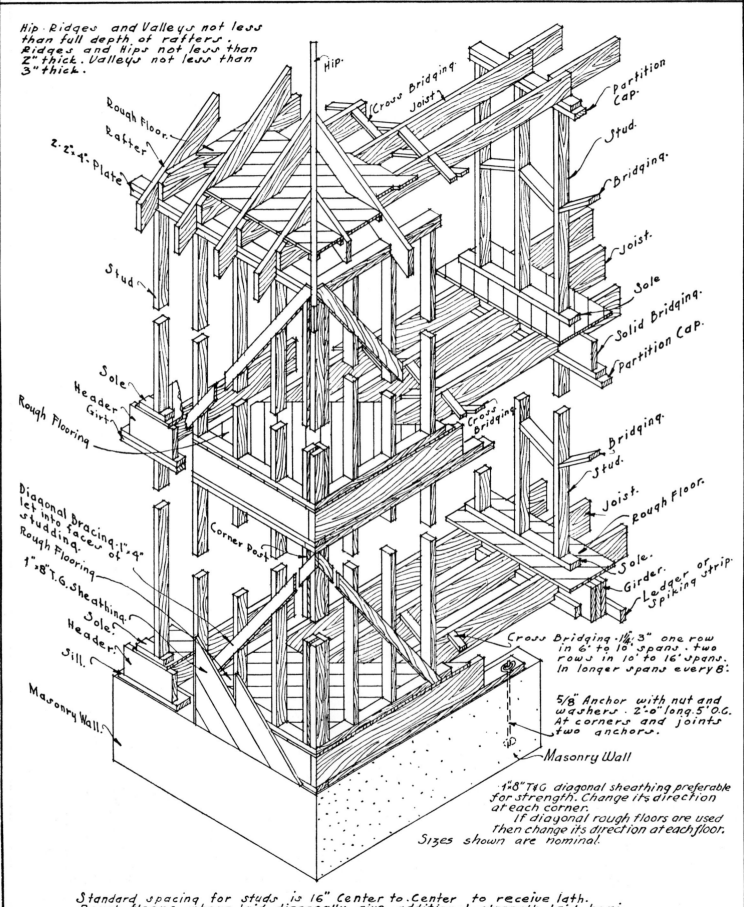

Hip·Ridges and Valleys not less
than full depth of rafters.
Ridges and Hips not less than
2" thick. Valleys not less than
3" thick.

Rough Floor.

Rafter.

2.2"x4".Plate.

Stud.

Sole.

Header
Girt.

Rough Flooring

Diagonal Bracing·1"x4"
let into faces of
studding.
Rough Flooring

1"x8"T.G.Sheathing.

Sole.

Header.

Sill.

Masonry Wall.

Corner Post.

Hip.

(Cross Bridging.
Joist.)

Cross
Bridging.

Partition
Cap.

Stud.

Bridging.

Joist.

Sole

Solid Bridging.

Partition Cap.

Bridging.

Stud.

Joist.

Rough Floor.

Sole.

Girder.

Ledger or
Spiking strip.

Cross Bridging·1¼x3" one row
in 6' to 10' spans. two
rows in 10' to 16' spans.
In longer spans every 8'.

5/8" Anchor with nut and
washers· 2'-0" long. 5'O.C.
At corners and joints
two anchors.

Masonry Wall

1"x8"T&G diagonal sheathing preferable
for strength. Change its direction
at each corner.
    If diagonal rough floors are used
then change its direction at each floor.
Sizes shown are nominal.

Standard spacing for studs is 16" Center to Center to receive lath.
Rough floors where laid diagonally give additional strength. Laid horizontally is more economical. Exterior walls may be braced with diagonal
braces for stiffening purposes when horizontal sheathing is used.
Approved by the National Lumber Manufacturers Association.

MODERN BRACED FRAMING

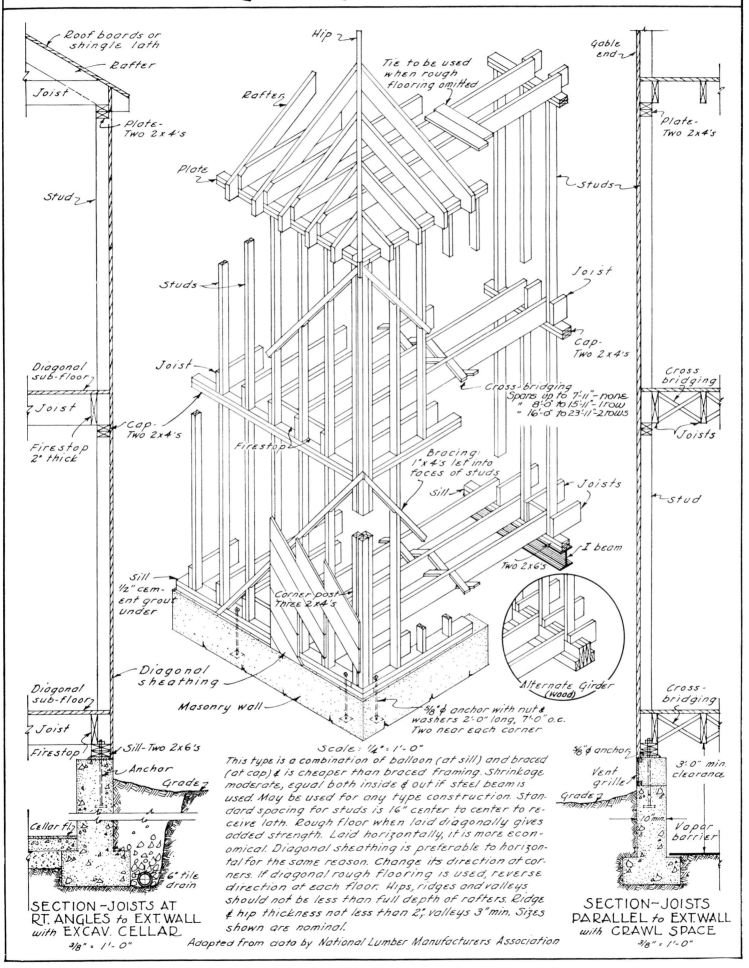

Roof boards or shingle lath

Rafter

Joist

Plate-Two 2x4's

Stud

Diagonal sub-floor

Joist

Cap. Two 2x4's

Firestop 2" thick

Diagonal sub-floor

Joist

Firestop

Sill-Two 2x6's

Anchor

Grade

Cellar fl.

6" tile drain

Hip

Tie to be used when rough flooring omitted

Rafter

Plate

Studs

Joist

Studs

Joist

Cap- Two 2x4's

Cross-bridging
Spans up to 7'-11"-none
" 8'-0 to 15'-11"-1 row
" 16'-0 to 23'-11"-2 rows

Firestop

Bracing: 1"x 4's let into faces of studs

Sill

Joists

I beam

Two 2x6's

Corner post-Three 2x4's

Sill 1/2" cement grout under

Diagonal sheathing

Masonry wall

5/8"ø anchor with nut & washers 2'-0" long, 7'-0" o.c. Two near each corner

Alternate Girder (wood)

Gable end

Plate-Two 2x4's

Studs

Cross bridging

Joists

Stud

Cross-bridging

5/8"ø anchor

Vent grille

Grade

3'-0" min. clearance

10"min.

Vapor barrier

Scale: 1/4" = 1'-0"

This type is a combination of balloon (at sill) and braced (at cap) & is cheaper than braced framing. Shrinkage moderate, equal both inside & out if steel beam is used. May be used for any type construction. Standard spacing for studs is 16" center to center to receive lath. Rough floor when laid diagonally gives added strength. Laid horizontally, it is more economical. Diagonal sheathing is preferable to horizontal for the same reason. Change its direction at corners. If diagonal rough flooring is used, reverse direction at each floor. Hips, ridges and valleys should not be less than full depth of rafters. Ridge & hip thickness not less than 2"; valleys 3" min. Sizes shown are nominal.

SECTION-JOISTS AT RT. ANGLES to EXT. WALL with EXCAV. CELLAR
3/8" = 1'-0"

SECTION-JOISTS PARALLEL to EXT.WALL with CRAWL SPACE
3/8" = 1'-0"

Adapted from data by National Lumber Manufacturers Association

WOOD FRAMING

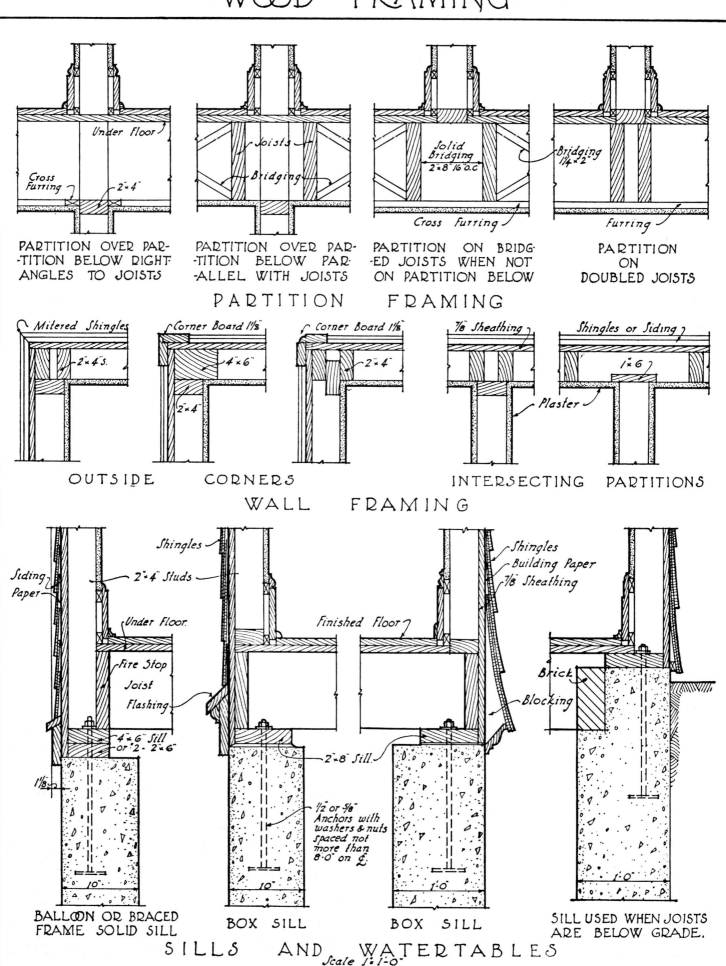

PARTITION OVER PAR-
-TITION BELOW RIGHT
ANGLES TO JOISTS

PARTITION OVER PAR-
-TITION BELOW PAR-
-ALLEL WITH JOISTS

PARTITION ON BRIDG-
-ED JOISTS WHEN NOT
ON PARTITION BELOW

PARTITION
ON
DOUBLED JOISTS

PARTITION   FRAMING

OUTSIDE   CORNERS   INTERSECTING   PARTITIONS

WALL   FRAMING

BALLOON OR BRACED
FRAME SOLID SILL

BOX SILL

BOX SILL

SILL USED WHEN JOISTS
ARE BELOW GRADE.

SILLS   AND   WATERTABLES

Scale 1:1-0"

LIGHT WOOD FRAMING DETAILS

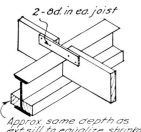

2-8d. in ea. joist

Approx. same depth as ext. sill to equalize shrinkage.

ON WOOD BLOCKING

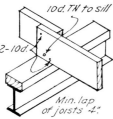

10d. TN to sill

2-10d.

Min. lap of joists 4".

LAPPED OVER WOOD SILL

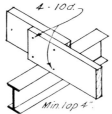

4-10d.

Min. lap 4".

LAPPED OVER GIRDER

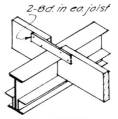

2-8d. in ea. joist

ON STEEL ANGLES

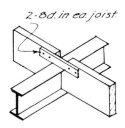

2-8d. in ea. joist

ON LOWER FLANGE

WOOD JOISTS SUPPORTED on STEEL GIRDERS

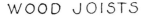

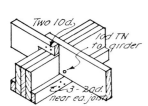

Two 10d.

10d TN to girder

3-20d. near ea. joist.

OVERLAPPING JOISTS NOTCHED over GIRDER
Bearing only on ledger, not on top of girder.

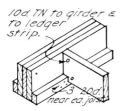

10d TN to girder & to ledger strip.

3-20d. near ea. joist.

JOIST NOTCHED OVER LEDGER STRIP
Notching over bearing not recommend.

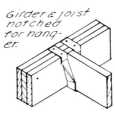

Girder & joist notched for hanger.

JOIST IN BRIDLE IRON
Also called joist hanger or stirrup

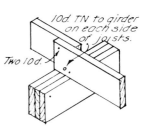

10d. TN to girder on each side of joists.

Two 10d.

JOISTS BEARING on GIRDER
Min. lap 4 inches

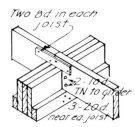

Two 8d. in each joist

2-10d. TN to girder

3-20d. near ea. joist.

JOISTS NOTCHED OVER GIRDER
Bearing only on ledger, not on top of girder.

WOOD JOISTS SUPPORTED on WOOD GIRDERS

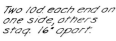

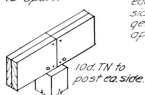

Two 10d. each end on one side, others stag. 16" apart.

10d. TN to post ea. side.

TWO PIECE GIRDER
Girder joints only at supports.

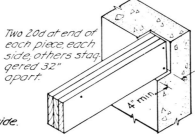

Two 20d at end of each piece, each side, others staggered 32" apart.

4" min.

THREE PIECE GIRDER
Four piece girder: add 1 pc. nailed with 20d to three pc.

GIRDERS

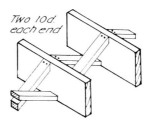

Two 10d. each end

1"x3" CROSS BR'G. 2"x3" REC'D.
Lower ends not nailed until flooring laid.

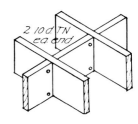

2-10d TN ea end

SOLID BRIDGING
Used for heavy loading, under partitions

BRIDGING

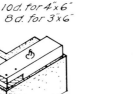

10d. Toenails

Bolt

2"x6" SILL

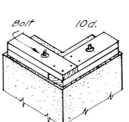

10d. for 4"x6"
8d. for 3"x6"

Bolt

3"x6, 4"x6" SILL
Halved at corners

Bolt   10d.

4"x6" DOUBLE SILL
Nails staggered along sill 24" on centers.

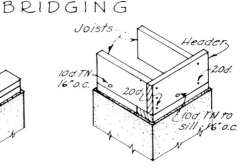

Joists

Header

10d. TN 16" o.c.

20d

20d

10d. TN to sill 16" o.c.

PLATFORM FRAMING
Toenail to sill not required if diagonal sheathing used.

SILL DETAILS

3/8" = 1'-0"

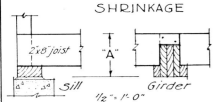

SHRINKAGE

2"x8" joist

"A"

Sill   Girder

1/2" = 1'-0"

Select joist-girder detail which has the approx. same shrinkage "A" as the sill detail used.

Steel Girders: Provide steel bearing plate on outside wall.
Anchor Bolts: 1/2" to 3/4" dia. 1'-6" to 2'-0" long, 6' to 8' o.c. Two at each corner (see Sill Details), two at each joint.
Sills: 3" thickness or more affords more nailing surface for sheathing & a better lap splice. Impregnate or creosote for long life. Lay on 1/2" cement mortar grout.
Wood Posts: Rest on C.I. plates or cement footing & keep at least 3" above floor to prevent rotting & termites.
All dimensions nominal. TN=toenail, d=penny(nail size), stag.=staggered.

LIGHT WOOD FRAMING DETAILS

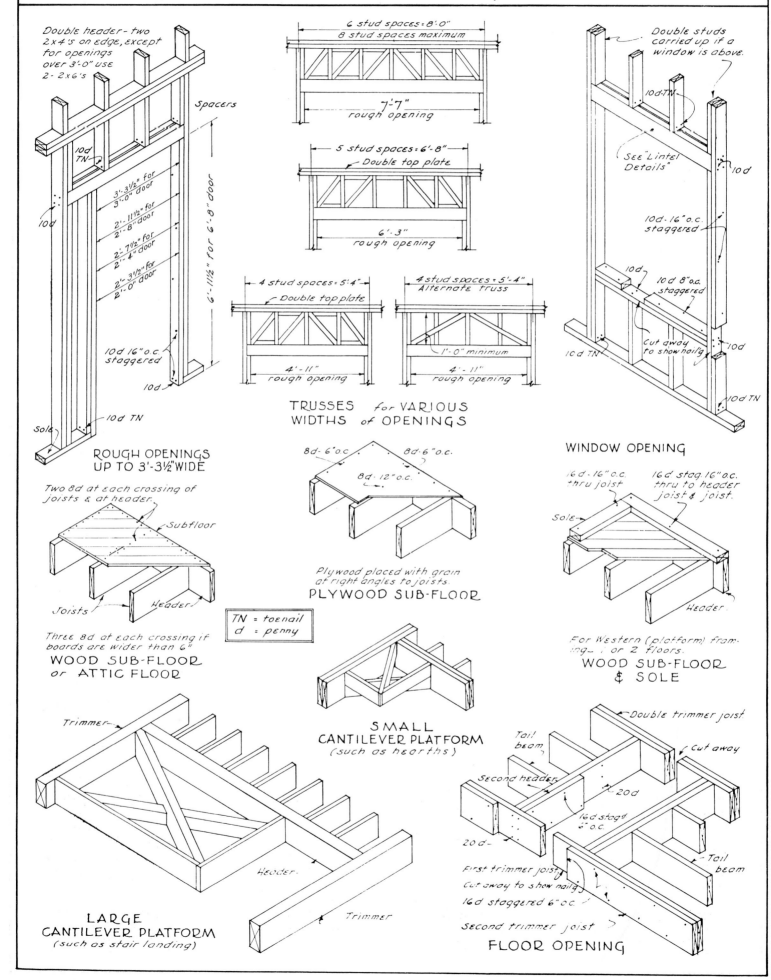

LIGHT WOOD FRAMING DETAILS

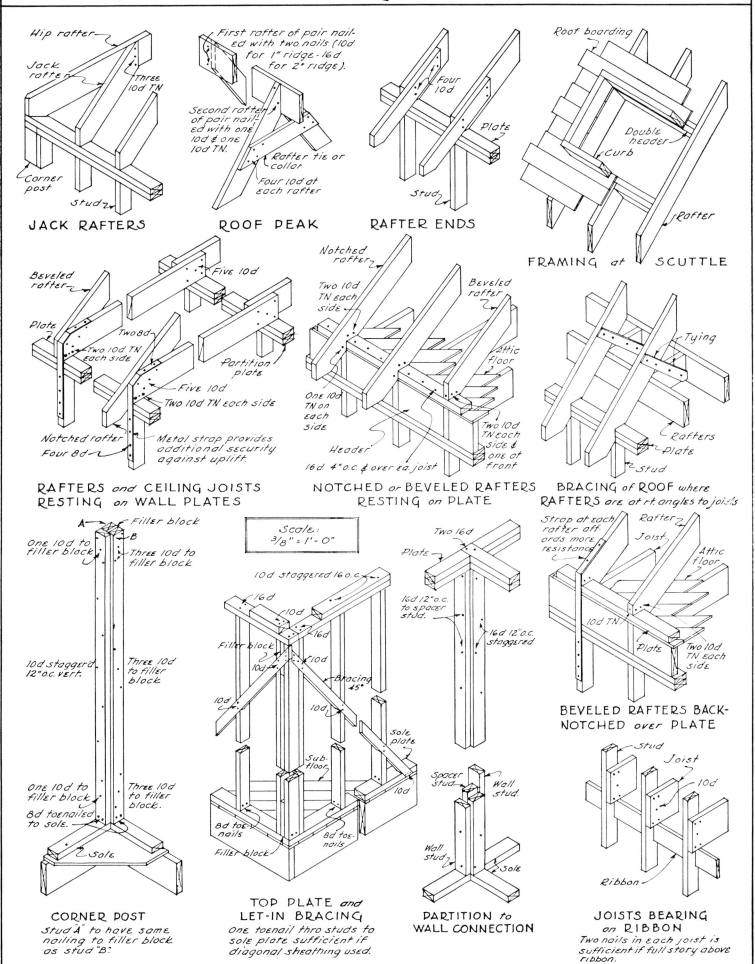

JACK RAFTERS

Hip rafter
Jack rafter
Three 10d TN
Corner post
Stud

ROOF PEAK

First rafter of pair nailed with two nails (10d for 1" ridge - 16d for 2" ridge).
Second rafter of pair nailed with one 10d & one 10d TN.
Rafter tie or collar
Four 10d at each rafter

RAFTER ENDS

Four 10d
Plate
Stud

FRAMING at SCUTTLE

Roof boarding
Double header
Curb
Rafter

RAFTERS and CEILING JOISTS RESTING on WALL PLATES

Beveled rafter
Plate
Five 10d
Two 8d
Two 10d TN each side
Five 10d
Two 10d TN each side
Partition plate
Notched rafter
Four 8d
Metal strap provides additional security against uplift.

NOTCHED or BEVELED RAFTERS RESTING on PLATE

Notched rafter
Two 10d TN each side
Beveled rafter
Attic floor
One 10d TN on each side
Two 10d TN each side & one at front
Header
16d 4" o.c. & over ea. joist

BRACING of ROOF where RAFTERS are at rt. angles to joists

Tying
Rafters
Plate
Stud

CORNER POST

A
Filler block
B
One 10d to filler block
Three 10d to filler block
10d stagger'd 12" o.c. vert.
Three 10d to filler block
One 10d to filler block
Three 10d to filler block
8d toenailed to sole.
Sole

Stud "A" to have same nailing to filler block as stud "B".

TOP PLATE and LET-IN BRACING

Scale: 3/8" = 1'-0"

10d staggered 16 o.c.
16d
10d
16d
Filler block
10d
10d
10d
Bracing 45°
10d
Sub-floor
Sole plate
10d
8d toe nails
8d toe nails
Filler block

One toenail thro studs to sole plate sufficient if diagonal sheathing used.

PARTITION to WALL CONNECTION

Two 16d
Plate
16d 12" o.c. to spacer stud.
16d 12" o.c. staggered
Spacer stud
Wall stud.
Wall stud
Sole

BEVELED RAFTERS BACK-NOTCHED over PLATE

Strap at each rafter affords more resistance
Rafter
Joist
Attic floor
10d TN
Plate
Two 10d TN each side

JOISTS BEARING on RIBBON

Stud
Joist
10d
Ribbon

Two nails in each joist is sufficient if full story above ribbon.

LIGHT WOOD FRAMING DETAILS

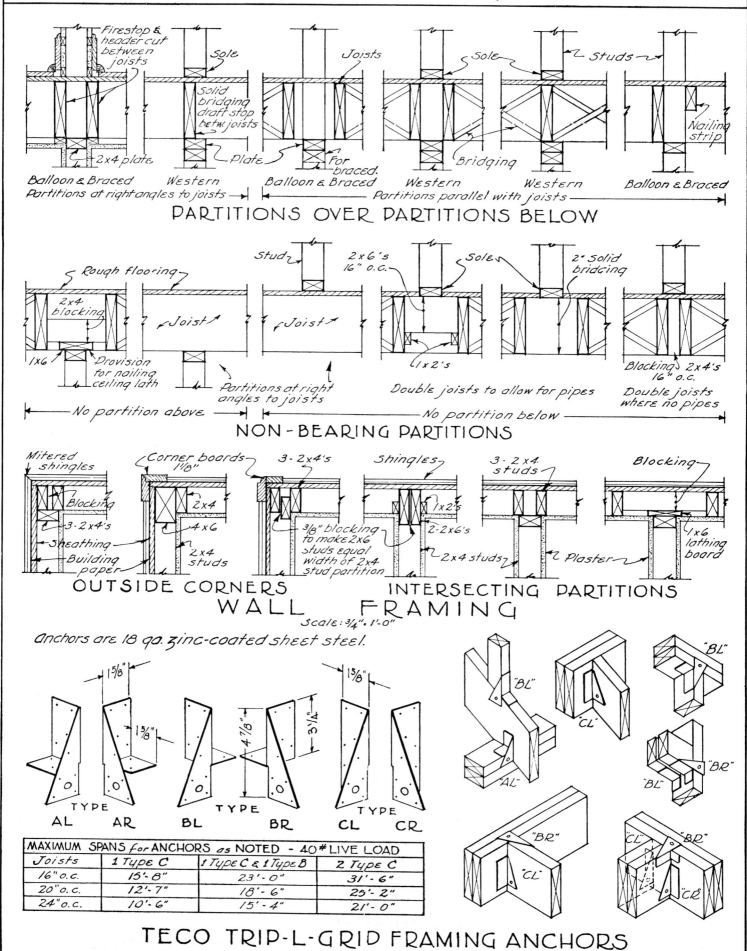

PARTITIONS OVER PARTITIONS BELOW

Balloon & Braced Partitions at right angles to joists — Western — Balloon & Braced — Western — Western — Balloon & Braced — Partitions parallel with joists

Firestop & header cut between joists — Sole — Joists — Sole — Studs — Solid bridging draft stop betw joists — Bridging — Nailing strip — 2x4 plate — Plate — For braced

NON-BEARING PARTITIONS

No partition above — No partition below — Double joists where no pipes

Rough flooring — Stud — 2x6's 16" o.c. — Sole — 2" solid bridging — 2x4 blocking — Joist — Joist — 1x6 — Provision for nailing ceiling lath — Partitions at right angles to joists — 1x2's — Double joists to allow for pipes — Blocking 2x4's 16" o.c.

OUTSIDE CORNERS — **INTERSECTING PARTITIONS**

WALL FRAMING
Scale: 3/4" = 1'-0"

Mitered shingles — Corner boards 1 1/8" — 3-2x4's — Shingles — 3-2x4 studs — Blocking — Blocking — 2x4 — 3-2x4's — 4x6 — Sheathing — 2x4 studs — 3/8" blocking to make 2x6 studs equal width of 2x4 stud partition — 2-2x6's — 1x2's — 2x4 studs — Plaster — 1x6 lathing board — Building paper

Anchors are 18 ga. zinc-coated sheet steel.

TYPE AL AR — TYPE BL BR — TYPE CL CR

"BL" "CL" "BR" "AL" "BL" "BR" "CL" "CR"

MAXIMUM SPANS for ANCHORS as NOTED - 40# LIVE LOAD			
Joists	1 Type C	1 Type C & 1 Type B	2 Type C
16" o.c.	15'-8"	23'-0"	31'-6"
20" o.c.	12'-7"	18'-6"	25'-2"
24" o.c.	10'-6"	15'-4"	21'-0"

TECO TRIP-L-GRID FRAMING ANCHORS

LIGHT WOOD FRAMING DETAILS

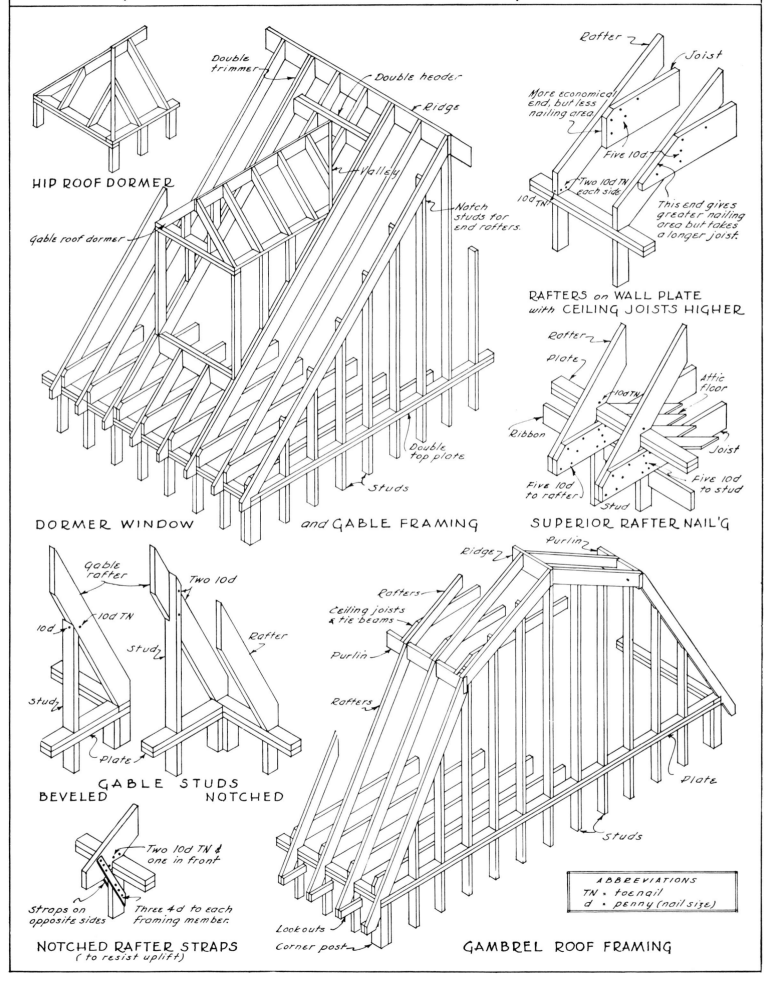

HIP ROOF DORMER

Double trimmer

Double header

Ridge

Valley

Notch studs for end rafters.

Gable roof dormer

Double top plate

Studs

DORMER WINDOW   and GABLE FRAMING

Rafter

Joist

More economical end, but less nailing area.

Five 10d.

Two 10d TN each side

10d TN

This end gives greater nailing area but takes a longer joist.

RAFTERS on WALL PLATE
with CEILING JOISTS HIGHER

Rafter

Plate

10d TN

Attic floor

Ribbon

Joist

Five 10d to rafter

Five 10d to stud

Stud

SUPERIOR RAFTER NAIL'G

Gable rafter

Two 10d

10d TN

10d

Stud

Rafter

Stud

Plate

GABLE STUDS
BEVELED   NOTCHED

Ridge

Purlin

Rafters

Ceiling joists & tie beams

Purlin

Rafters

Plate

Studs

Two 10d TN & one in front

Straps on opposite sides

Three 4d to each framing member.

NOTCHED RAFTER STRAPS
(to resist uplift)

Lookouts

Corner post

GAMBREL ROOF FRAMING

ABBREVIATIONS
TN = toenail
d = penny (nail size)

EAVES

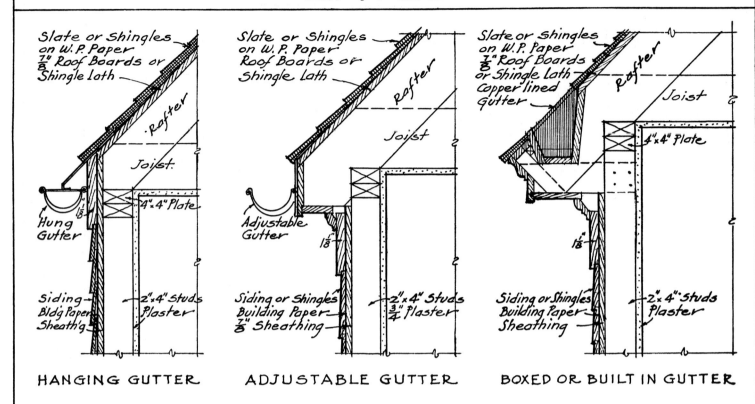

Top row, left (HANGING GUTTER):

Slate or Shingles on W.P. Paper
7/8" Roof Boards or Shingle Lath

Rafter

Joist

4"x4" Plate

1 3/8"

Hung Gutter

Siding
Bld'g Paper
Sheath'g

2"x4" Studs
Plaster

HANGING GUTTER

Top row, center (ADJUSTABLE GUTTER):

Slate or Shingles on W.P. Paper
Roof Boards or Shingle Lath

Rafter

Joist

Adjustable Gutter

1 3/8"

Siding or Shingles
Building Paper
7/8" Sheathing

2"x4" Studs
3/4" Plaster

ADJUSTABLE GUTTER

Top row, right (BOXED OR BUILT IN GUTTER):

Slate or Shingles on W.P. Paper
7/8" Roof Boards or Shingle Lath
Copper lined Gutter

Rafter

Joist

4"x4" Plate

1 3/8"

Siding or Shingles
Building Paper
Sheathing

2"x4" Studs
Plaster

BOXED OR BUILT IN GUTTER

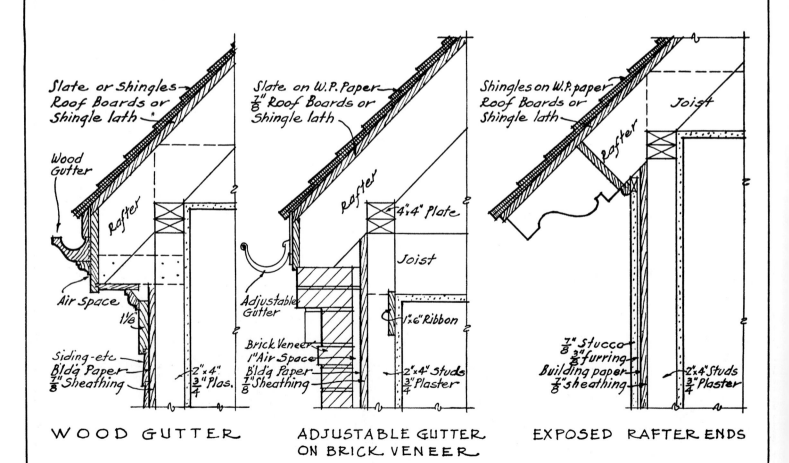

Bottom row, left (WOOD GUTTER):

Slate or Shingles
Roof Boards or Shingle lath

Wood Gutter

Rafter

Air Space

1 1/8"

Siding-etc
Bld'g Paper
7/8" Sheathing

2"x4"
3/4" Plas.

WOOD GUTTER

Bottom row, center (ADJUSTABLE GUTTER ON BRICK VENEER):

Slate on W.P. Paper
7/8" Roof Boards or Shingle lath

Rafter

4"x4" Plate

Joist

Adjustable Gutter

1"x6" Ribbon

Brick Veneer
1" Air Space
Bld'g Paper
7/8" Sheathing

2"x4" Studs
3/4" Plaster

ADJUSTABLE GUTTER ON BRICK VENEER

Bottom row, right (EXPOSED RAFTER ENDS):

Shingles on W.P. paper
Roof Boards or Shingle lath

Rafter

Joist

7/8" Stucco
3/8" furring
Building paper
7/8" sheathing

2"x4" Studs
3/4" Plaster

EXPOSED RAFTER ENDS

1" = 1'-0"

WOOD STAIRS

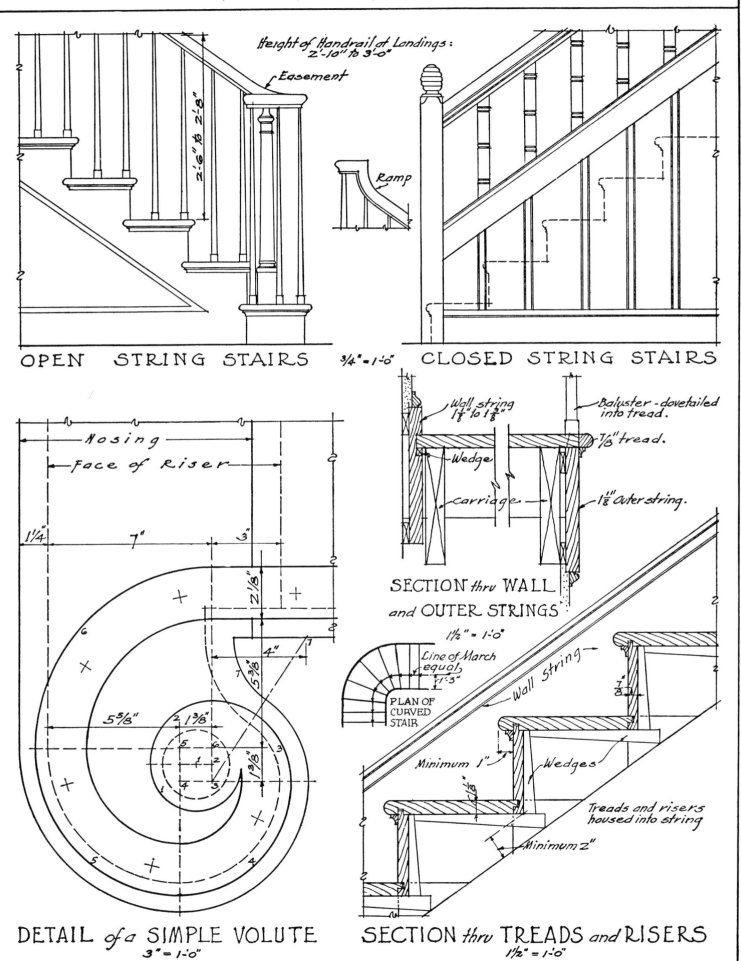

Height of Handrail at Landings:
2'-10" to 3'-0"

Easement

2'-6" to 2'-8"

Ramp

OPEN STRING STAIRS   3/4"=1'-0"   **CLOSED STRING STAIRS**

Wall string 1⅛" to 1⅞"

Baluster - dovetailed into tread.

7⅞" tread.

Wedge

1⅛" Outer string.

carriage

SECTION thru WALL and OUTER STRINGS

1½" = 1'-0"

Nosing

Face of Riser

1¼"   7"   3"

2⅛"

4"

5⅜"

5⅝"   1⅜"

1⅜"

Line of March equal 1'-3"

PLAN OF CURVED STAIR

Wall String

7/8"

Minimum 1"

Wedges

Treads and risers housed into string

Minimum 2"

DETAIL of a SIMPLE VOLUTE   3"=1'-0"   **SECTION thru TREADS and RISERS**   1½"=1'-0"

JOINTS in WOODWORK ~ PANELLING

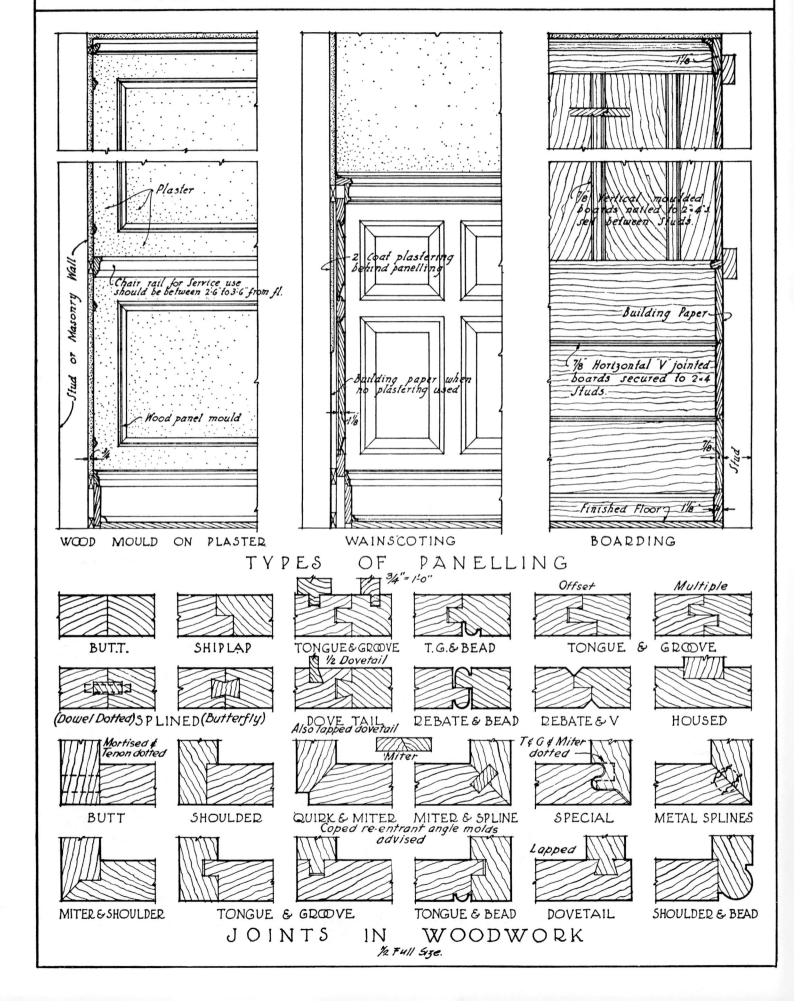

WOOD MOULD ON PLASTER WAINSCOTING BOARDING

TYPES OF PANELLING

3/4" = 1'-0"

BUTT.   SHIPLAP   TONGUE & GROOVE   T.G. & BEAD   Offset TONGUE & GROOVE   Multiple

1/2 Dovetail

(Dowel Dotted) SPLINED (Butterfly)   DOVE TAIL Also lapped dovetail   REBATE & BEAD   REBATE & V   HOUSED

Mortised & Tenon dotted   Miter   T & G & Miter dotted

BUTT   SHOULDER   QUIRK & MITER Coped re-entrant angle molds advised   MITER & SPLINE   SPECIAL   METAL SPLINES

Lapped

MITER & SHOULDER   TONGUE & GROOVE   TONGUE & BEAD   DOVETAIL   SHOULDER & BEAD

JOINTS IN WOODWORK
1/2 Full Size.

Labels within the drawings: Plaster; Stud or Masonry Wall; Chair rail for Service use should be between 2'-6 to 3'-6 from fl.; Wood panel mould; 3/4; 2 Coat plastering behind panelling; Building paper when no plastering used; 1⅛; 7/8 Vertical moulded boards nailed to 2·4 s set between Studs.; Building Paper; 7/8 Horizontal 'V' jointed boards secured to 2·4 Studs.; 1⅛; Stud; 7/8; Finished Floor; 1⅛

WOOD BOOK SHELVES

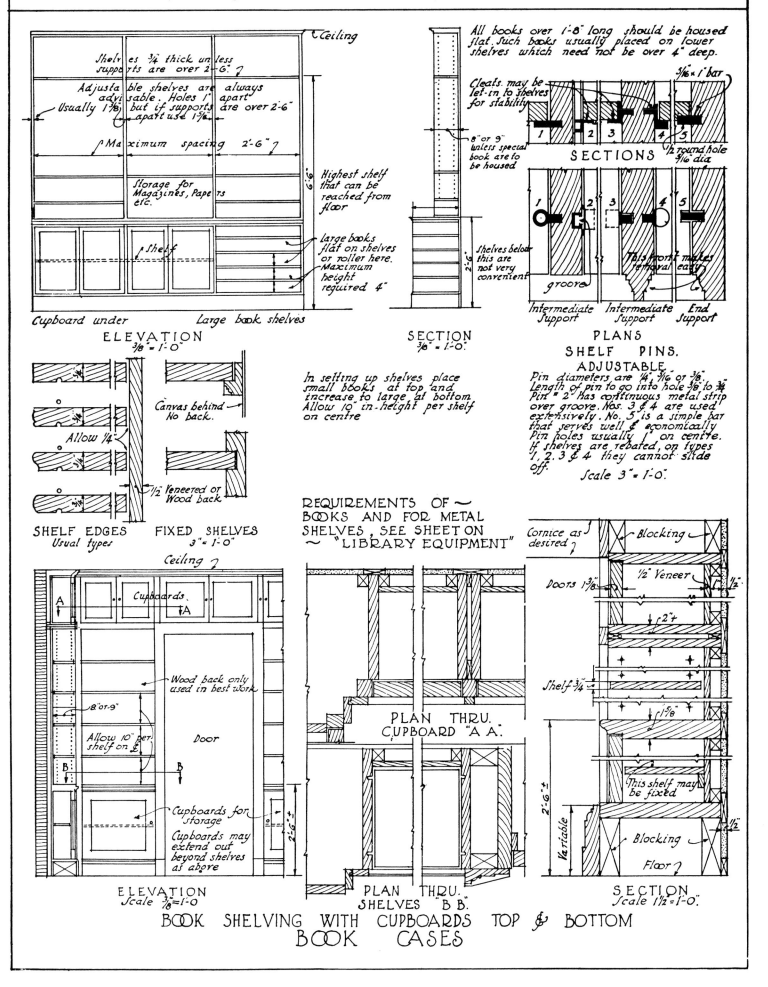

Ceiling

Shelves 3/4 thick unless supports are over 2'-6".

Adjustable shelves are always advisable. Holes 1" apart
Usually 1 1/8" but if supports are over 2'-6" apart use 1 5/8"

Maximum spacing 2'-6"

Storage for Magazines, Papers etc.

Shelf

Cupboard under

Large book shelves

Highest shelf that can be reached from floor

Large books flat on shelves or roller here.
Maximum height required 4"

ELEVATION
3/8" = 1'-0"

All books over 1'-8" long should be housed flat. Such books usually placed on lower shelves which need not be over 4" deep.

Cleats may be let-in to shelves for stability

8" or 9" unless special book are to be housed

5/16" x 1" bar

SECTIONS

1/2 round hole 5/16 dia.

Shelves below this are not very convenient

groove

This front makes removal easy

Intermediate Support   Intermediate Support   End Support

PLANS
SHELF PINS.
ADJUSTABLE.

Pin diameters are 1/4, 5/16 or 3/8.
Length of pin to go into hole 3/8" to 3/4"
Pin # 2 has continuous metal strip over groove. Nos. 3 & 4 are used extensively. No. 5 is a simple bar that serves well & economically
Pin holes usually 1" on centre.
If shelves are rebated, on types 1, 2, 3 & 4 they cannot slide off.

Scale 3" = 1'-0".

SECTION
3/8" = 1'-0".

In setting up shelves place small books at top and increase to large at bottom
Allow 10" in height per shelf on centre

SHELF EDGES
Usual types

Canvas behind No back.

Allow 1/4"

1/2" Veneered or Wood back

FIXED SHELVES
3" = 1'-0"

REQUIREMENTS OF ~
BOOKS AND FOR METAL
SHELVES, SEE SHEET ON
~ "LIBRARY EQUIPMENT"

Ceiling

Cupboards.

A   A

Wood back only used in best work

8" or 9"

Allow 10" per shelf on C.

B   B

Cupboards for storage

Cupboards may extend out beyond shelves as above

Door

ELEVATION
Scale 3/8" = 1'-0"

PLAN THRU.
CUPBOARD "A A".

PLAN THRU.
SHELVES "B B".

Cornice as desired

Blocking

Doors 1 3/8"

1/2" Veneer

2"+

Shelf 3/4"

1 5/8"

This shelf may be fixed

Variable

2'-6"±

Blocking

Floor

SECTION
Scale 1 1/2" = 1'-0".

BOOK SHELVING WITH CUPBOARDS TOP & BOTTOM
BOOK CASES

WOOD FLOORING

OAK STRIP FLOORING

FLOORING SIZES							NAILING			QUANTITIES	
Type	Thickness nom!	Thickness act!	Widths (face)			Nailing	Sizes (nominal)	O.C.	Nail Size	Increase fl. areas by	Counted as
	13/16"	25/32"	1½"	2"	2¼"	Blind	13/16"×2¼"	10"	8d cut steel	33⅓%	1"×3"
	* ½"	15/32"	1½"	2"		Blind	13/16"×2"	10"	8d " "	37½%	1"×2¾"
	* 3/8"	11/32"	1½"	2"		Blind	13/16"×1½"	12"	8d " "	50%	1"×2¼"
	* 5/16"	10/32"	1½"	2"		Surface	½"×2"	10"	6d wire fin.	25%	1"×2½"
							½"×1½"	10"	6d " "	33½%	1"×2"
							3/8"×2"	8"	4d wire casing	25%	1"×2½"
							3/8"×1½"	8"	4d " "	33⅓%	1"×2"
							5/16"×2"	7(2)	1/8" barbed wire	—	1"×2"
							5/16"×1½"	7(2)	Floor brad #16	—	1"×1½"

*These should always be used over sub-flooring. Narrow widths cost more laid.

For irregularities add 5% more for waste

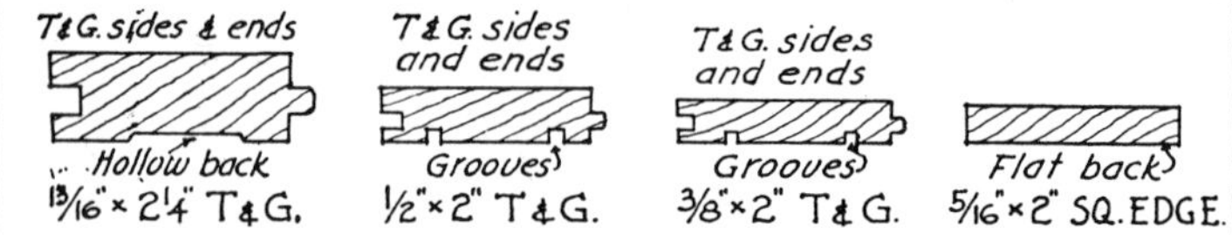

T&G. sides & ends
T&G. sides and ends
T&G. sides and ends
Hollow back
Grooves
Grooves
Flat back
13/16"×2¼" T&G.
½"×2" T&G.
3/8"×2" T&G.
5/16"×2" SQ. EDGE.

STANDARD GRADES

Grade	Allowed Defects	Bundle Lengths	Uses
Clear Quartered or Plain Sawed.	Face practically free from defects except 3/8" bright sap.	2'-0" & up. Max. of 20% under 4'-0". Aver. 5'-0"	Fine domestic work, clubs, hotels, also churches, schools.
Sap Clear Quartered	Face practically free from defects except unlimited bright sap.	ditto.	Fine domestic work, clubs, hotels etc.
Select Quartered or Plain Sawed.	Sap, pin worm holes, streaks, slight working imperfections, small tight knots - 1 to every 3'-0".	2'-0" and up average 4'-0"	Medium domestic work, schools, offices, stores & institutions.
#1 Common Plain Sawed	Shall be of such nature as will make and lay a sound floor without cutting.	2'-0" and up average 3'-0"	cheap apartments, schools, stores, high class lofts & factories.
#2 Common Plain Sawed.	May contain defects of all types. Will lay a serviceable floor.	1'-3" and up average 2'-6"	Cheap apartments, lofts and factories.

Grades; do not consider the question of color.

Recommendations & Grading rules of the National Oak Flooring Association. 830 Dermon Building. Memphis. Tennessee.

NORTHERN HARD MAPLE, BEECH and BIRCH FLOORING (STRIP & BLOCK)

FLOORING SIZES-STRIP									
Type	Thickness nom!	Thickness act!	Widths (face)						
Standard	13/16"	25/32"	1½"	2"	2¼"	3¼"	*2½"	*3½"
Special	1 11/16"	53/32"		2"	2¼"	3¼"		
Special	1 5/16"	41/32"		2"	2¼"	3¼"		
Special	1 1/16"	33/32"		2"	2¼"	3¼"	*2½"	*3½"
Special	5/8"	5/8"	1½"	2"	2¼"			
Special	½"	½"	1½"	2"	2¼"			
Special	3/8"	11/32"	1½"	2"	2¼"			

*Square edged (jointed) only; other sizes T & G sides and ends.

NAILING		
Sizes (nominal)	O.C.	Nail Size
1"	12" to 16"	7d cut steel
13/16"	16"	6d or 7d cut steel
3/8"	9"	4d cut steel or 3d wire fin.

STANDARD MEASUREMT

½" & thicker, all widths, are measured ¾" waste for matching. 3/8", all widths, is measured ½" waste for matching. Jointed flooring all widths and thicknesses; measured ½" waste.

QUANTITIES		
Width	½"-5/8"-13/16" incr. fl. area by	3/8" incr. fl. area by
1½"	50%	33⅓%
2"	37½%	25%
2¼"	33⅓%	22½%
3¼"	24%	
2½"	* 20%	
3½"	* 15%	

For thicker flooring determine number of feet for 25/32" as above and add as follows:
33/32" " — 25%
41/32" " — 50%
53/32" " — 100%
For wastage add 5% to above

widths 1½", 2", 2¼", 3¼"
13/16
STANDARD.
SPECIALS
widths 2½" & 3½" square edge, for industrial floors

STANDARD GRADES

Grade	Uses
1st Grade. Length 2' to 16', 25% 2' to 3½'	Highest standard made, fine houses, apar'mts, churches, public bldgs, clubs, dance fls, gyms, hotels, offices, skating rinks, schools.
2nd Grade. Length 1½' to 16', 40% 1½' to 3½'	Slight imperfections permitted, same use as above but where imperfections are not objectionable or when colored finish desired.
3rd Grade. Length 1' to 16', 60% 1' to 3½'	Serviceable for factories, warehouses, workshops, farms, industrial buildings.
Special Grades	White Clear Northern Hard Maple, selected for color uniformity. Brown Clear Northern Hard Maple, selected for color uniformity. "Birdseye Figured" Clear Northern Hard Maple - Special selected. Red Clear Northern Beech. Red Clear Northern Birch, especially selected for color.

Marked color variations not a defect except in special grades

Northern Hard Maple is botanically "Acer Saccharum."

Recommendations and Grading Rules of the Maple Flooring Manufacturers Association 332 S. Michigan Ave; Chicago; Ill. Trade Mark "MFMA"

FLOORING BLOCKS

For Patterns, Squares or Herringbone

Single Piece Blocks:
25/32" & 33/32" - Face widths of 1½", 2", 2¼", 3¼",
Face lengths from 6¾" to 15¾" long } T & G on wood or concrete

FABRICATED BLOCKS-SQUARES & RECTANGLES on wood or concrete.

Material	1½" strips	2" strips	2¼" Strips	3¼" strips
Maple 25/32" thick	6¾" sq. to 11¼ sq. 6"×12"	6¾" sq. to 11¼" sq, 6¾"×13½"	6¾" sq. to 11¼" sq.	6½"×13"
Maple 33/32" thick	6¾" sq to 11¼" sq.	6¾" sq. to 11¼" square	6¾" sq. to 11¼" sq.	—
Beech 25/32" thick	6¾" sq. to 11¼" sq. 6"×12".	— —	6¾" sq. to 11¼" sq.	—

SOFTWOOD STRIP FLOORING

THICK	WIDTH (FACE)	GRADE		QUALITY. all grades come in flat & edge grain	USE
5/16"	1½", 2⅜", 3¼", 4¼", 5 3/16"	A-Select	also B & Better	Practically clear of defects, except slight.	Best type house work for light stain.
7/16"	" " " " "	B-Select		Unnoticeable defects & imperfections.	High class work for stain.
9/16"	" " " " "	C-Select		Medium size defects & imperfections.	Med: class work, with dark stain or paint.
25/32"	" " " " "	D-Select		Defects not to cause waste nor mar paint finish.	When defects not objectionable, for paint.
1 1/16"	" " " " "	No. 1 Common		No waste, tight knotted, sound stock.	Utility for paint; unfinished spaces.
1 5/16"	" " " " "	No. 2 Common		No waste, some loose knots, discolorations.	Used chiefly for sub-floors.
1⅝", 2⅛", 2⅝", 3⅝"	for shiplap 3", 5", 7", 9", 11"; for T&G 3⅛", 5⅛", 7⅛", 9⅛", 11⅛"; for spline 3½", 5½", 7½", 9⅛", 11½"	No. 3 Common		Some knot holes, decay, wane, some waste.	Chiefly for temporary construction.

QUANTITIES for ESTIMATING

Size-Add to floor area as follows:

Size	Add
25/32" × 2⅜"	27%
" × 3¼"	23%
" × 5 3/16"	15%
1 1/16" × 2⅜"	58%
" × 3¼"	54%
" × 5 3/16"	43%
1 5/16" × 2⅜"	90%
" × 3¼"	85%
" × 5 3/16"	72%

Also add 3% to 5% to these for waste.

WOOD SPECIES AND GRADES AVAILABLE

SPECIES	FLAT-GRAIN		EDGE-GRN	SPECIES	FLAT-GRAIN		EDGE-GRN
Cedar; Incense and Western.	B & Better, C.	#1, #2, #3 Common	Incense only	Pine; Southern Yellow	A, B, C, D.	#1, #2, #3 Common	A, B, C, D. #1, #2 Com.
Cypress; Red	A (all heart) B, C, D	Ext. use mostly		Pine; Northern White & Norway	D	#1, #2 #3	
Douglas Fir; Coast Type	B & Better, C, D		Clear all heart	Pine; Sugar	B & Better, C, D		B & Better, C, D
Douglas Fir; Inland Empire & California	B & Better, C, D	#1, #2, #3 Common	B & Better, C.	Redwood; California	Clear Heart, A, B	Ext. use mostly	Clear Heart, A, B
Hemlock; Eastern and Northern	D & Better	#1, #2, #3 Common		Spruce; Eastern	D	#1, #2, #3 Common	
Hemlock; West Coast	B & Better		A, B, C, D	Spruce; Sitka	B & Better		B & Better
Larch Western - Ponderosa - White Idaho	C & Better, D	#1, #2, #3 Common	C & Better, D	Tamarack; (Fir and Larch)	D & Better, D	#1, #2, #3 Common	

Data checked by National Lumber Manufacturers Association, 1337 Connecticut Ave. Wash. D.C.

OTHER MATERIALS

Oak, Teak, Walnut, Mahogany planks (laminated or veneer) and Pine and Oak solid planks.
Sizes not standard but usually available:-
33/32" thick, 4" to 8" wide, 4" to 12" in plain Oak and Teak.
25/32" thick, 4" to 8" wide, 4" to 12" in plain Oak and Teak.
Planks, screwed as well as nailed, plugged or butterflied.
These materials available for parquetry, in blocks (see Maple sizes).

Fin. ¼" min.
chestnut core

PLANK

DETAILS

W.P. Paper.
Sub Floor.
Finish Floor
Sleepers 2"×3" or 3"×3" bev.
sleepers 1'-4" o.c.
sleepers 1'-0" o.c.
Base
Shoe Mold
Fin. Fl.
Sub. Fl.

SLEEPER SPACING (MAXIMUM).

FLOOR AT BASE.

WOOD COLUMNS or POSTS

WOOD COLUMNS for LIGHT CONSTRUCTION — MAX. LOAD IN LBS.

SECTION	SIZE	COMPRESSIVE STRENGTH in lbs/sq.in.	6'-0"	7'-0"	8'-0"	9'-0"	10'-0"	11'-0"	12'-0"
3⅝" × 3⅝" 4×4 *A=13.1	4×4 *A=13.1	1150 to 1400	13,460	12,170	10,280	7,700	5,670	4,340	4,340
		1400 to 1750	15,370	13,060					
		1750	17,000	13,130					
5⅝" × 5⅝" 6×6 *A=30.3	6×6 *A=30.3	1150 to 1400	33,800		32,800	31,500	27,800	23,500	23,500
		1400 to 1750	40,800		38,700	35,300	30,000		
		1750	49,700		45,850	39,000	30,500		
7½" × 7½" 8×8 *A=56.3	8×8 *A=56.3	1150 to 1400	64,740		63,000	60,910	60,910	60,910	57,420
		1400 to 1750	78,820		75,670	71,950	71,950	71,950	65,590
		1750	98,520		92,330	84,960	84,960	84,960	72,510
9½" × 9½" 10×10 *A=90.3	10×10 *A=90.3	1150 to 1400	103,840				101,050	101,050	97,700
		1400 to 1750	126,420				121,360	121,360	115,450
		1750	158,020				148,090	148,090	136,250
11½" × 11½" 12×12 *A=132	12×12 *A=132	1150 to 1400	152,140					148,040	148,040
		1400 to 1750	185,220					177,810	177,810
		1750	231,520					217,970	217,970

*Area of Sections

COMPRESSIVE STRENGTHS of VARIOUS TYPES of WOOD used for COLUMNS

COMPRESSIVE STRENGTH in lbs./sq.in.	WOOD	TYPE	GRADE
1150	Pine	Southern Long Leaf	#1 Structural Long Leaf
		Southern	Dense #1 Structural
1200	Douglas Fir	Coast Region	#1
	Oak	Red & White	1200 C - Grade
1250	Douglas Fir	Inland Region	Common Structural
1300	Pine	Southern	Dense Structural S.E. & S.
		Southern Long Leaf	Merchantable Structural Long Leaf
			Structural S.E. & S. Long Leaf
1325	Oak	Red & White	1325 C - Grade
1400	Douglas Fir	Coast Region	Dense #1
		Inland Region	Structural
	Pine	Southern	Dense Structural
		Southern Long Leaf	Prime Structural Long Leaf
1450	Douglas Fir	Coast Region	Select Structural
	Redwood		Dense Structural
1550	Douglas Fir	Coast Region	Dense Select Structural
1750	Douglas Fir	Inland Region	Select Structural
	Pine	Southern	Select Structural
		Southern Long Leaf	Select Structural Long Leaf

Data by Seelye, Stevenson & Value, Consulting Engineers

WOOD LINTELS and BEAMS

STRESSES of VARIOUS GRADES of WOOD

TYPE of WOOD	GRADE	f Unit Stress(#/□")	V Horizontal Shear(#/□")	E Modulus of Elast.(#/□")
Douglas Fir, Coast Region	Dense Select Structural	2150	145	
	Select Structural	1900	120	
	1700f Dense #1	1700	145	1,600,000
	1450f - #1	1450	120	
	1100f - #2	1100	110	
Douglas Fir, Inland Region	Select Structural	2150	145	1,600,000
	Structural	1900	100	1,500,000
	Common Structural	1450	95	
Hemlock, Eastern	Select Structural	1300	85	
	Prime Structural	1200	60	1,100,000
	Common Structural	1100		
Hemlock, West Coast	1600f - Select Structural	1600	100	
	1450f #1	1450		1,400,000
	1100f - #2	1100	90	
Pine, Southern	Dense Select Structural	2400		
	Dense Structural	2000		
	Dense Structural S.E.&S.	1800	120	
	Dense #1 Structural	1600		
	#1 Dense	1700	150	1,600,000
	#1	1450	125	
	#2 Dense	1250	100	
	#2	1100	85	
Pine, Southern Long Leaf	Select Structural Long Leaf	2400		
	Prime Structural Long Leaf	2000		
	Merchantable Structural Long Leaf	1800	120	
	Structural S.E.&S. Long Leaf			1,600,000
	#1 Structural Long Leaf	1600		
	#1 Long Leaf	1700	150	
	#2 Long Leaf	1250	100	
Redwood	Dense Structural	1700	110	
	Heart Structural	1300	95	1,200,000
Spruce, Eastern	1450f - Structural Grade	1450	110	
	1300f - Structural Grade	1300		1,200,000
	1200f - Structural Grade	1200	95	

WOOD LINTELS & BEAMS—MAX LOAD in lbs.

SPAN (c.c. of supports)		6"	8"	10"	12"	14"
6'-0"	M	561	1310	1667	2450	3400
	D	568	1800	2910	5200	8400
7'-0"	M	482	1060	1425	2090	2900
	D	417	1320	2140	3800	6160
8'-0"	M	422	985	1250	1840	2540
	D	318	1020	1680	3000	4850
9'-0"	M	375	870	1111	1630	2260
	D	252	805	1310	2340	3780
10'-0"	M	337	784	1000	1462	2030
	D	204	650	1050	1870	3040
11'-0"	M	307	710	910	1340	1850
	D	168	536	870	1550	2503
12'-0"	M	280	651	833	1220	1690
	D	141	458	745	1330	2150
13'-0"	M	260	600	770	1130	1562
	D	120	383	620	1051	1700
14'-0"	M	241	560	715	1050	1450
	D	103	330	535	955	1550
15'-0"	M	225	521	667	980	1355
	D	90	289	470	840	1360
16'-0"	M	210	490	625	920	1272
	D	80	254	410	730	1180
Horizontal Shear	V	880	1200	1520	1840	2080

Loads given are uniform loads _per inch of finished width_ of member & are based on f = 1000 #/□"
M = total safe load in bending measured in #(lbs)
V = total safe load in shear (120 #/□")   E = 1,000,000 #/□"
D = total safe load in deflection (1/360)

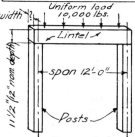

Example #1

USING THE ABOVE TABLE

Given: Conditions of example #1
Find: Required width of lintel
Solution
In table above, loads M = 1220
D = 1330 and V = 1840
$$\frac{Uniform\ load}{Lowest\ of\ 3\ loads} = \frac{10,000}{1220} = 8.2''$$

Answer: 8.2" is width required. Lintel can be made up of two 2 x 12's & two 3 x 12's which gives a total width of 8 ⅜", closest above that required. See "Lumber Grades & Sizes" for finished dimensions (2 x 12's etc)

USING THE TABLE FOR STRONGER WOODS

The following formulae are used with the above table to determine new values for the three loads M, D & V in case a wood of greater strength than that which the table is based on is used. For example #1 Southern Pine (see "Stresses of Various Grades of Woods" table on left): f = 1450, E = 1,600,000 and V = 125.

New M Load = $\frac{new\ f \times M\ load\ in\ table}{f\ of\ table} = \frac{1450 \times 1220}{1000} = 1769$

New D Load = $\frac{new\ E \times D\ load\ in\ table}{E\ of\ table} = \frac{1,600,000 \times 1330}{1,000,000} = 2128$

New V Load = $\frac{new\ V \times V\ load\ in\ table}{V\ of\ table} = \frac{125 \times 1840}{120} = 1917$

The three new values replace those in table for Example #1 and the width of lintel required is then obtained similarly. (The width required would be 5.6")

Data by Seelye, Stevenson & Value, Consulting Engineers

STANDARD WOOD MOULDINGS

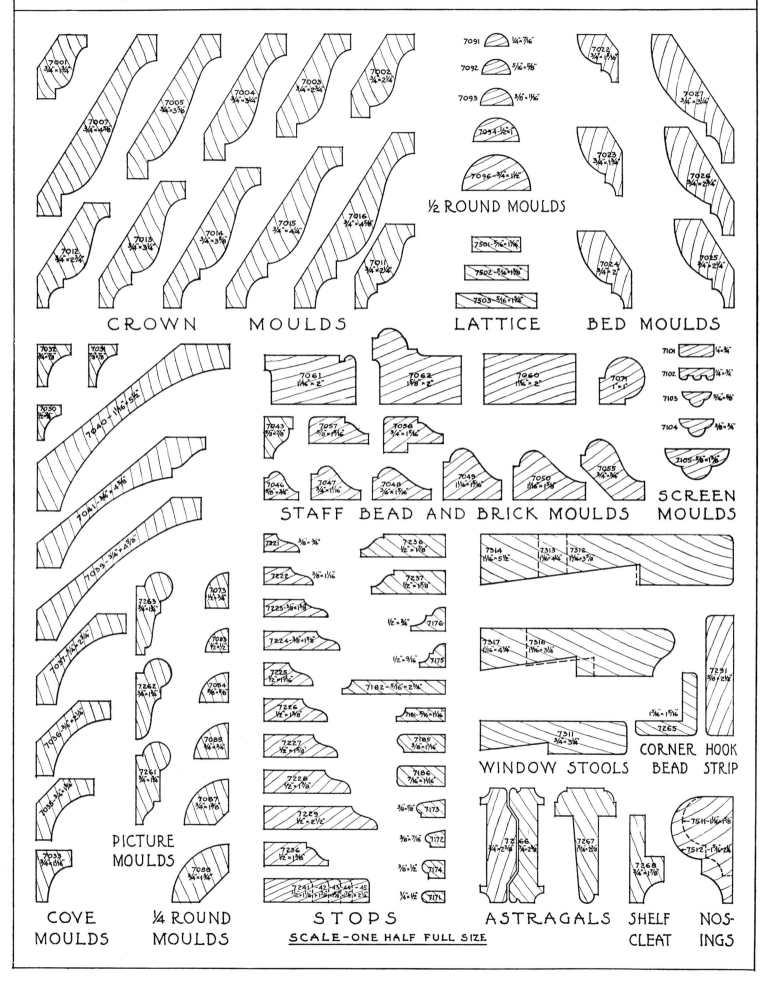

CROWN MOULDS

½ ROUND MOULDS

LATTICE

BED MOULDS

STAFF BEAD AND BRICK MOULDS

SCREEN MOULDS

PICTURE MOULDS

STOPS

WINDOW STOOLS

CORNER BEAD

HOOK STRIP

COVE MOULDS

¼ ROUND MOULDS

ASTRAGALS

SHELF CLEAT

NOSINGS

SCALE—ONE HALF FULL SIZE

WOOD MOULDINGS - 7000 SERIES

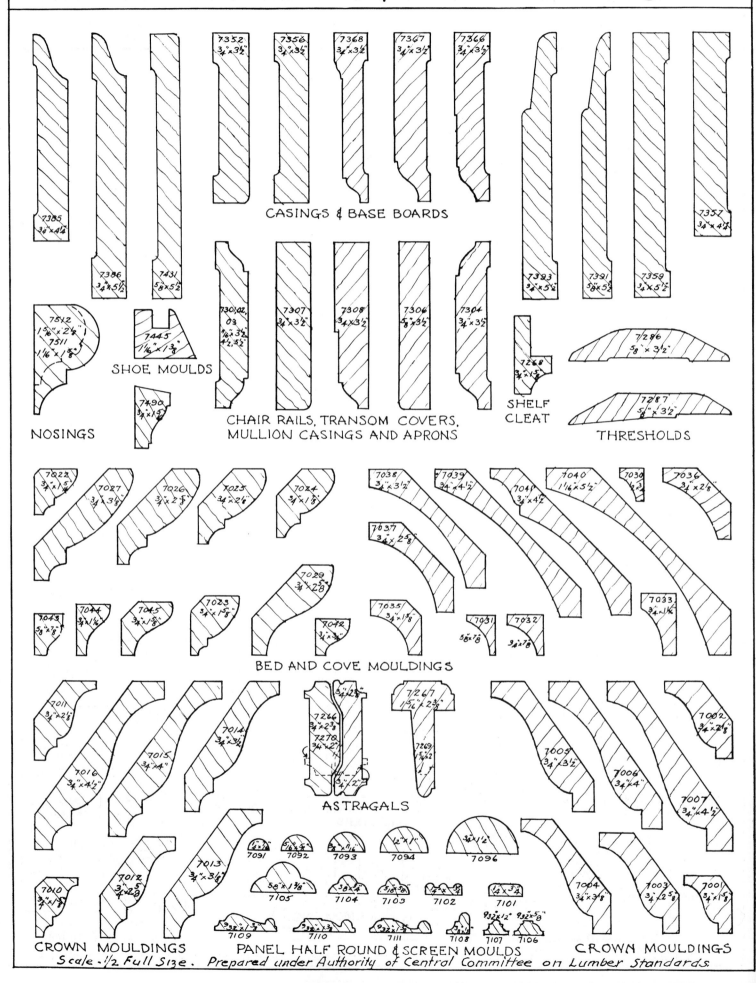

CASINGS & BASE BOARDS

SHOE MOULDS

NOSINGS

CHAIR RAILS, TRANSOM COVERS, MULLION CASINGS AND APRONS

SHELF CLEAT

THRESHOLDS

BED AND COVE MOULDINGS

ASTRAGALS

CROWN MOULDINGS

PANEL HALF ROUND & SCREEN MOULDS

CROWN MOULDINGS

Scale - ½ Full Size.   Prepared under Authority of Central Committee on Lumber Standards.

WOOD MOULDINGS — 7000 SERIES

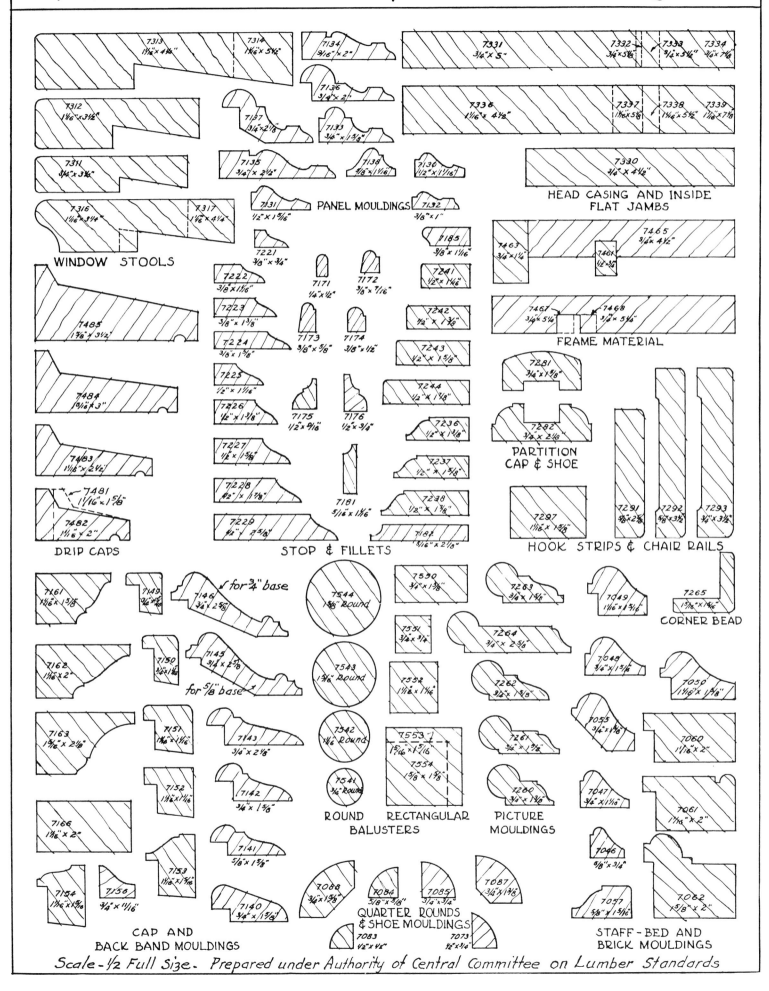

Scale — 1/2 Full Size. Prepared under Authority of Central Committee on Lumber Standards

WOOD MOULDINGS - 8000 SERIES

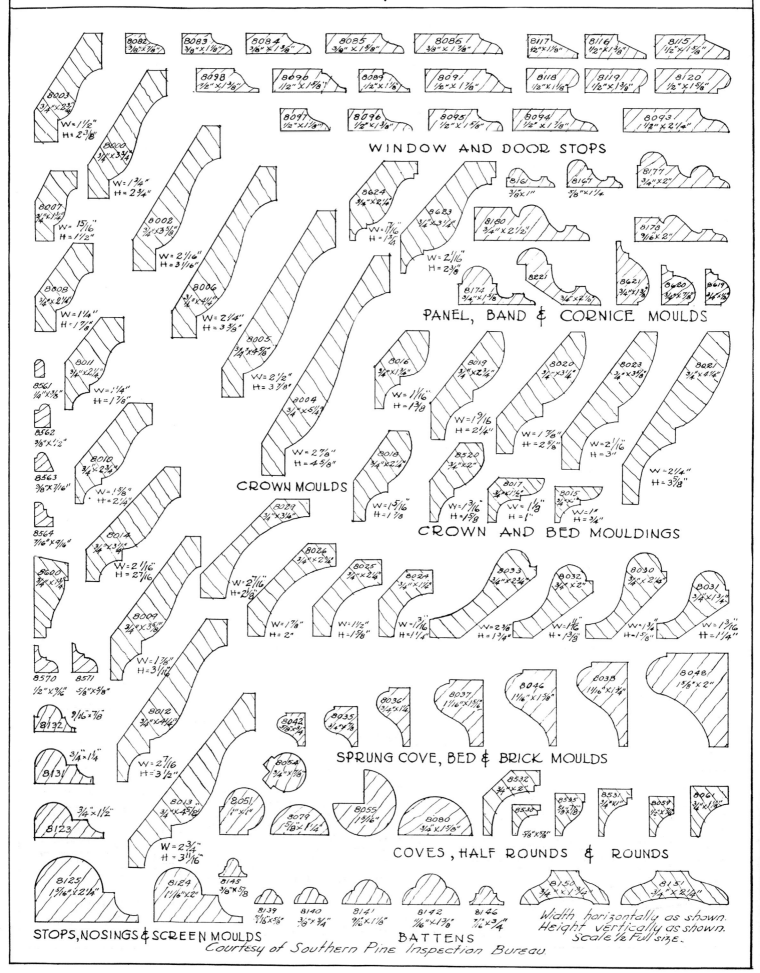

WINDOW AND DOOR STOPS

PANEL, BAND & CORNICE MOULDS

CROWN MOULDS

CROWN AND BED MOULDINGS

SPRUNG COVE, BED & BRICK MOULDS

COVES, HALF ROUNDS & ROUNDS

STOPS, NOSINGS & SCREEN MOULDS

BATTENS

Width horizontally as shown.
Height vertically as shown.
Scale ½ Full size.

Courtesy of Southern Pine Inspection Bureau.

WOOD MOULDINGS ~ 8000 SERIES

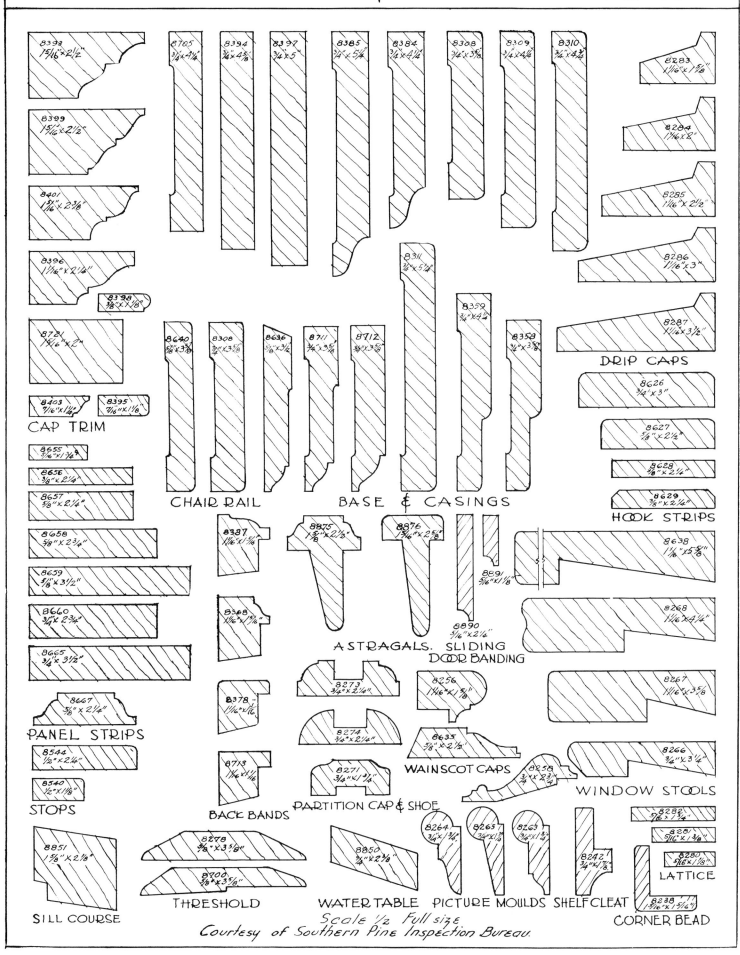

Scale ½ Full Size
Courtesy of Southern Pine Inspection Bureau.

116

WOOD SIDING

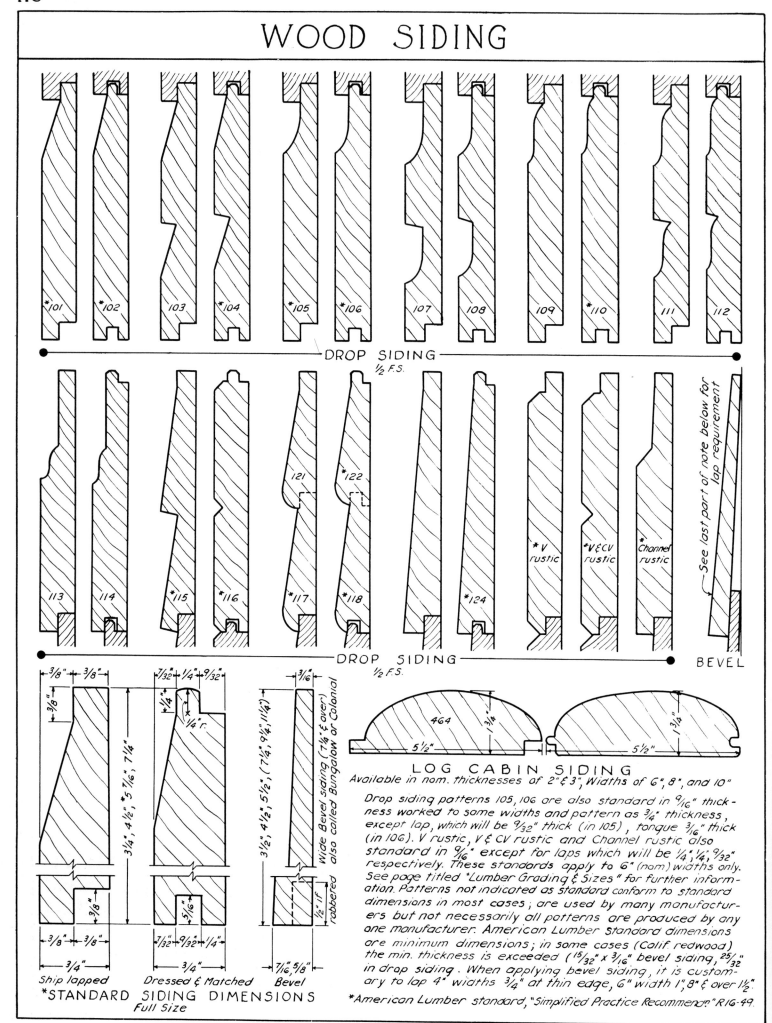

DROP SIDING
½ F.S.

*101 *102 103 *104 *105 *106 107 108 109 *110 111 112

DROP SIDING
½ F.S.

113 114 *115 *116 *117 *118 *124 *V rustic *V & CV rustic *Channel rustic

121 *122

See last part of note below for lap requirement

BEVEL

3/8" 3/8" 7/32" 1/4" 9/32" 3/16"
3/8" 1/4" 1/4" r.

3/4", 4½", 5 5/16", 7¼"

Wide Bevel siding (7½" & over) also called Bungalow or Colonial

3½", 4½", 5½", (7¼", 9¼", 11¼")

3/8" 5/16" ½" if rabbeted

3/8" 3/8" 7/32" 9/32" 1/4" 7/16", 5/8"
3/4" 3/4"

Ship lapped   Dressed & Matched   Bevel

*STANDARD SIDING DIMENSIONS
Full Size

464   1¾"   1¾"
5½"   5½"

LOG CABIN SIDING
Available in nom. thicknesses of 2" & 3", Widths of 6", 8", and 10"

Drop siding patterns 105,106 are also standard in 9/16" thickness worked to same widths and pattern as 3/4" thickness, except lap, which will be 9/32" thick (in 105), tongue 3/16" thick (in 106). V rustic, V & CV rustic and Channel rustic also standard in 9/16" except for laps which will be 1/4", 1/4", 9/32" respectively. These standards apply to 6" (nom) widths only. See page titled "Lumber Grading & Sizes" for further information. Patterns not indicated as standard conform to standard dimensions in most cases; are used by many manufacturers but not necessarily all patterns are produced by any one manufacturer. American Lumber standard dimensions are minimum dimensions; in some cases (Calif. redwood) the min. thickness is exceeded (15/32" x 3/16" bevel siding, 25/32" in drop siding. When applying bevel siding, it is customary to lap 4" widths 3/4" at thin edge, 6" width 1", 8" & over 1½".

*American Lumber standard, "Simplified Practice Recommend." R16-49.

6

THERMAL AND MOISTURE PROTECTION

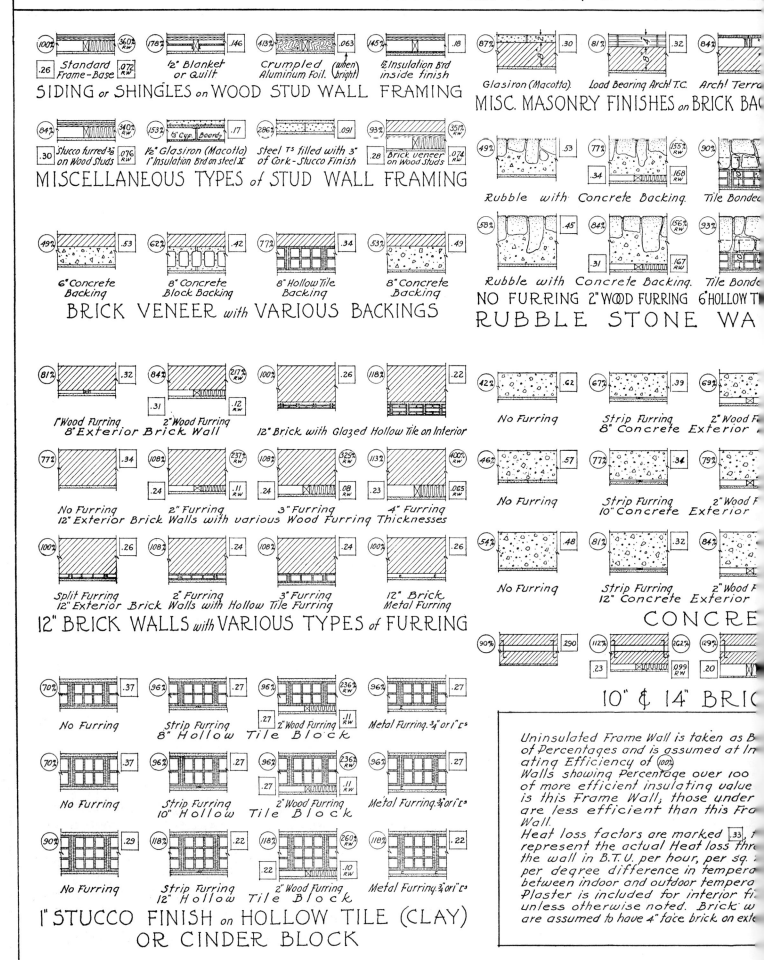

SIDING or SHINGLES on WOOD STUD WALL FRAMING

(100%) .26 Standard Frame-Base .072 RW 360% RW

(178%) ½" Blanket or Quilt .146

(41%) Crumpled Aluminum Foil (when bright) .063

(145%) ½" Insulation B'rd inside finish .18

MISCELLANEOUS TYPES of STUD WALL FRAMING

(84%) .30 Stucco furred 3½" on Wood Studs .076 RW 340% RW

(153%) ½" Glasiron (Macotta) 1" Insulation B'rd on steel II .17

(286%) Steel T's filled with 3" of Cork-Stucco Finish .091

(93%) .28 Brick veneer on Wood Studs 35½% RW .074 RW

BRICK VENEER with VARIOUS BACKINGS

(49%) 6" Concrete Backing .53

(62%) 8" Concrete Block Backing .42

(77%) 8" Hollow Tile Backing .34

(53%) 8" Concrete Backing .49

8" EXTERIOR BRICK WALL

(81%) 1" Wood Furring .32

(84%) 2" Wood Furring .31 .12 RW 21½% RW

12" Brick with Glazed Hollow Tile on Interior

(100%) .26

(118%) .22

12" Exterior Brick Walls with various Wood Furring Thicknesses

(77%) No Furring .34

(108%) 2" Furring .24 .11 RW 237% RW

(108%) 3" Furring .24 .08 RW 325% RW

(113%) 4" Furring .23 .065 RW 400% RW

12" BRICK WALLS with VARIOUS TYPES of FURRING

(100%) Split Furring .26

(108%) 2" Furring .24

(108%) 3" Furring .24

(100%) 12" Brick Metal Furring .26

12" Exterior Brick Walls with Hollow Tile Furring

1" STUCCO FINISH on HOLLOW TILE (CLAY) OR CINDER BLOCK

8" Hollow Tile Block

(70%) No Furring .37

(96%) Strip Furring .27

(96%) 2" Wood Furring .27 .11 RW 236% RW

(96%) Metal Furring ¾" or 1" L's .27

10" Hollow Tile Block

(70%) No Furring .37

(96%) Strip Furring .27

(96%) 2" Wood Furring .27 .11 RW 236% RW

(96%) Metal Furring ¾" or 1" L's .27

12" Hollow Tile Block

(90%) No Furring .29

(118%) Strip Furring .22

(118%) 2" Wood Furring .22 .10 RW 260% RW

(118%) Metal Furring ¾" or 1" L's .22

MISC. MASONRY FINISHES on BRICK BAC...

(87%) Glasiron (Macotta) .30

(81%) Load Bearing Arch'l T.C. .32

(84%) Arch'l Terra...

RUBBLE STONE WA...

(49%) Rubble with Concrete Backing .53 .34 168 RW

(77%) .53 155% RW

(90%)

(58%) Rubble with Concrete Backing .45 .31 167 RW 156% RW

(84%) Tile Bonded...

(93%)

NO FURRING   2" WOOD FURRING   6" HOLLOW T...

8" Concrete Exterior...

(42%) No Furring .62

(67%) Strip Furring .39

(69%) 2" Wood F...

10" Concrete Exterior...

(46%) No Furring .57

(77%) Strip Furring .34

(79%) 2" Wood F...

12" Concrete Exterior...

(54%) No Furring .48

(81%) Strip Furring .32

(84%) 2" Wood F...

CONCRE...

10" & 14" BRIC...

(90%) .290

(112%) .23

(262%) .099 RW

(129%) .20

F EXTERIOR WALLS

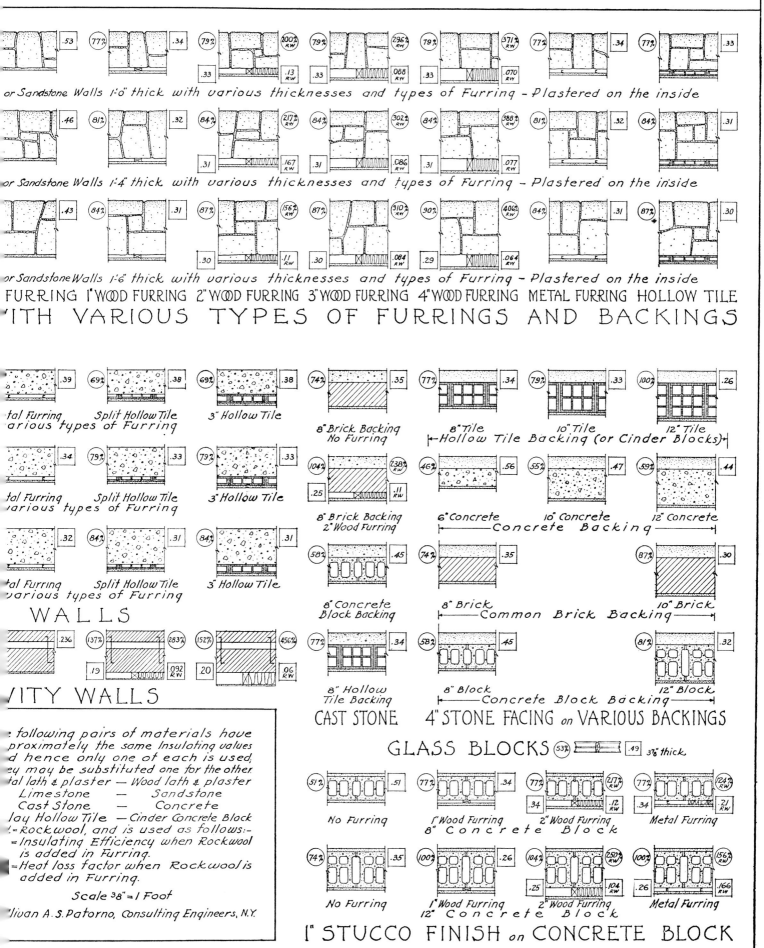

or Sandstone Walls 1'-0" thick with various thicknesses and types of Furring - Plastered on the inside

or Sandstone Walls 1'-4" thick with various thicknesses and types of Furring - Plastered on the inside

or Sandstone Walls 1'-6" thick with various thicknesses and types of Furring - Plastered on the inside

FURRING   1" WOOD FURRING   2" WOOD FURRING   3" WOOD FURRING   4" WOOD FURRING   METAL FURRING   HOLLOW TILE

ITH VARIOUS TYPES OF FURRINGS AND BACKINGS

tal Furring   Split Hollow Tile   3" Hollow Tile
arious types of Furring

tal Furring   Split Hollow Tile   3" Hollow Tile
arious types of Furring

tal Furring   Split Hollow Tile   3" Hollow Tile
arious types of Furring

WALLS

ITY WALLS

e following pairs of materials have
proximately the same Insulating values
d hence only one of each is used,
ey may be substituted one for the other
tal lath & plaster — Wood lath & plaster
  Limestone   —   Sandstone
  Cast Stone   —   Concrete
lay Hollow Tile — Cinder Concrete Block
d = Rockwool, and is used as follows:-
= Insulating Efficiency when Rockwool
  is added in Furring.
= Heat loss factor when Rockwool is
  added in Furring.

Scale ³⁄₈" = 1 Foot

llivan A.S. Patorno, Consulting Engineers, N.Y.

8" Brick Backing   8" Tile   10" Tile   12" Tile
No Furring |—Hollow Tile Backing (or Cinder Blocks)—|

8" Brick Backing   6" Concrete   10" Concrete   12" Concrete
2" Wood Furring   Concrete Backing

8" Concrete   8" Brick   10" Brick
Block Backing   Common Brick Backing

8" Hollow   8" Block   12" Block
Tile Backing   Concrete Block Backing

CAST STONE   4" STONE FACING on VARIOUS BACKINGS

GLASS BLOCKS   .49   3⅞ thick

No Furring   1" Wood Furring   2" Wood Furring   Metal Furring
8" Concrete Block

No Furring   1" Wood Furring   2" Wood Furring   Metal Furring
12" Concrete Block

1" STUCCO FINISH on CONCRETE BLOCK

WATERPROOFING

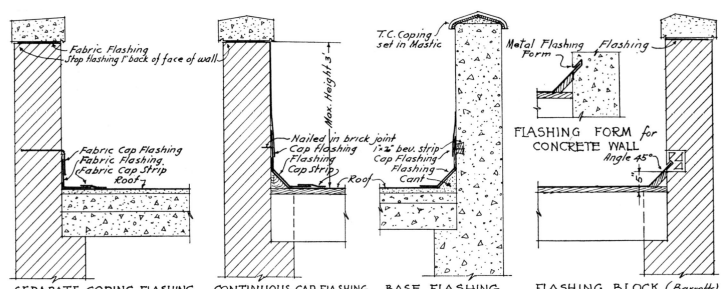

SEPARATE COPING FLASHING & CAP FLASHING THRO' WALL Concrete Roof

CONTINUOUS CAP FLASHING UP TO ℄ UNDER COPING Wood Roof

BASE FLASHING NAILED TO STRIP Concrete Roof and Wall

FLASHING BLOCK (Barretts) TO RECEIVE ROOFING Brick Wall

FLASHING FORM for CONCRETE WALL Angle 45°

WATERPROOFING of COPINGS with MEMBRANE and MASTIC MATERIALS
See Manufacturers Catalogues for exact sizes, materials & installations.

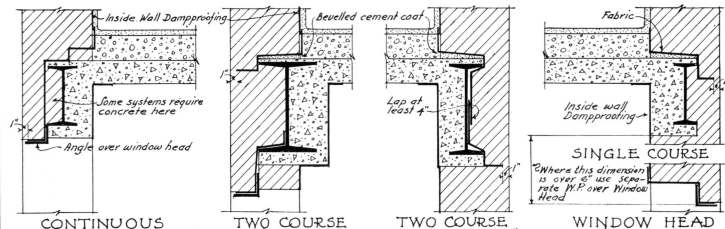

CONTINUOUS For short spandrel beams under 15."

TWO COURSE For deep spandrels 15" or over.

TWO COURSE Deep spandrels & narrow flanges.

WINDOW HEAD Extend 8" beyond jambs & tar up.

SINGLE COURSE

SPANDREL WATERPROOFING with MEMBRANE and MASTIC
¾"=1'

All joints to lap minimum of 3". Flash up at all columns 6" minimum and up all chases, cutouts etc.
Bevelled cement finish on slab over flanges of spandrel beams.
Trowel coat of mastic on cement and on all steel that fabric is to rest on or against.
Apply impregnated felt or cloth as system calls for.
Some systems call for a second coat of mastic on horizontal surfaces.
Apply mastic at all joints where fabric laps, and at all pipes, ducts etc.
Apply mastic to both sides of turned up, inside ends of fabric.
See Manufacturers Catalogues for Material and application.

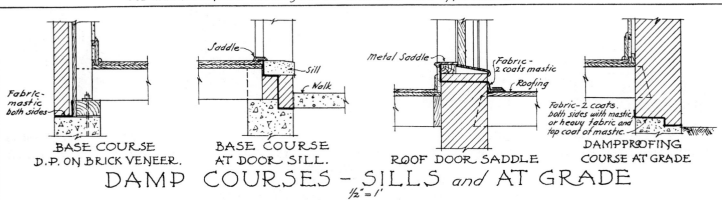

BASE COURSE D.P. ON BRICK VENEER.

BASE COURSE AT DOOR SILL.

ROOF DOOR SADDLE

DAMPPROOFING COURSE AT GRADE

DAMP COURSES - SILLS and AT GRADE
½"=1'

CLAY TILE ROOFING

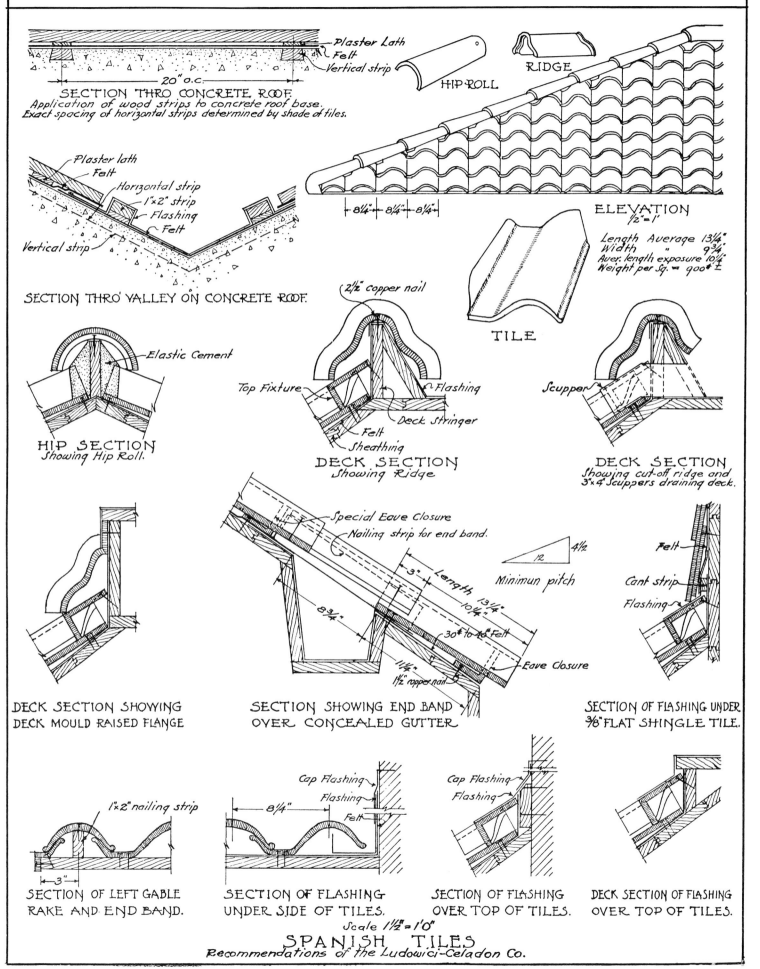

SECTION THRO CONCRETE ROOF.
Application of wood strips to concrete roof base.
Exact spacing of horizontal strips determined by shade of tiles.

Plaster Lath
Felt
Vertical strip
20" o.c.

HIP ROLL
RIDGE

Plaster lath
Felt
Horizontal strip
1"x2" strip
Flashing
Felt
Vertical strip

SECTION THRO' VALLEY ON CONCRETE ROOF.

ELEVATION
½"=1'

Length Average 13¼"
Width " 9¾"
Aver. length exposure 10¼"
Weight per Sq. = 900# ±

8¼" 8¼" 8¼"

TILE

Elastic Cement

HIP SECTION
Showing Hip Roll.

2½" copper nail
Top Fixture
Flashing
Deck Stringer
Felt
Sheathing

DECK SECTION
Showing Ridge

Scupper

DECK SECTION
Showing cut-off ridge and
3"x4" Scuppers draining deck.

**DECK SECTION SHOWING
DECK MOULD RAISED FLANGE**

Special Eave Closure
Nailing strip for end band.
3"
8¾"
Length 13¼"
10¼"
30# to 45# Felt
11¼"
1½" copper nail
Eave Closure
4½
12
Minimum pitch

**SECTION SHOWING END BAND
OVER CONCEALED GUTTER**

Felt
Cant strip
Flashing

**SECTION OF FLASHING UNDER
⅜" FLAT SHINGLE TILE.**

1"x2" nailing strip
3"

**SECTION OF LEFT GABLE
RAKE AND END BAND.**

Cap Flashing
Flashing
Felt
8¼"

**SECTION OF FLASHING
UNDER SIDE OF TILES.**

Cap Flashing
Flashing

**SECTION OF FLASHING
OVER TOP OF TILES.**

**DECK SECTION OF FLASHING
OVER TOP OF TILES.**

Scale 1½"=1'0"

SPANISH TILES
Recommendations of the Ludowici-Celadon Co.

CLAY TILE ROOFING

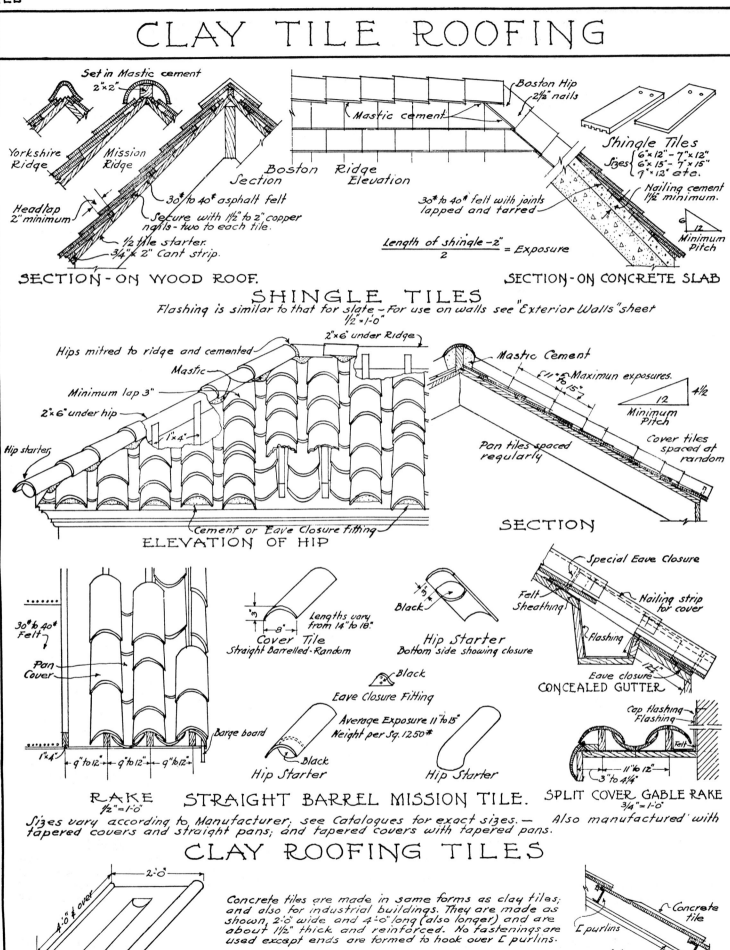

Set in Mastic cement
2"x2"

Yorkshire Ridge   Mission Ridge

Boston Section

Headlap 2" minimum

30# to 40# asphalt felt

Secure with 1½" to 2" copper nails - two to each tile.

½ tile starter.

¾"x 2" Cant strip.

SECTION - ON WOOD ROOF.

Boston Ridge Elevation

Mastic cement

Boston Hip 2½" nails

30# to 40# felt with joints lapped and tarred

$$\frac{Length\ of\ shingle - 2"}{2} = Exposure$$

Shingle Tiles
Sizes 6"x12" - 7"x12"
6"x15" - 7"x15"
7"x12" etc.

Nailing cement 1½" minimum.

Minimum Pitch 6 / 12

SECTION - ON CONCRETE SLAB

SHINGLE TILES
Flashing is similar to that for slate - For use on walls see "Exterior Walls" sheet
½"=1'-0"

Hips mitred to ridge and cemented

2"x6" under Ridge

Mastic

Minimum lap 3"

2"x6" under hip

1"x4"

Hip starter

Cement or Eave Closure fitting

ELEVATION OF HIP

Mastic Cement

11" to 15" Maximum exposures.

Minimum Pitch 12 / 4½

Pan tiles spaced regularly

Cover tiles spaced at random

SECTION

30# to 40# Felt

Pan Cover

Barge board

1"x4"   9" to 12"   9" to 12"   9" to 12"

RAKE
½"=1'-0"

3" 8"
Cover Tile
Straight Barrelled - Random
Lengths vary from 14" to 18"

Black
Hip Starter
Bottom side showing closure

Black
Eave Closure Fitting

Average Exposure 11" to 15"
Weight per Sq. 1250#

Black
Hip Starter

Hip Starter

STRAIGHT BARREL MISSION TILE.

Special Eave Closure

Felt Sheathing

Nailing strip for cover

Flashing

Eave closure

CONCEALED GUTTER

Cap flashing
Flashing

Felt

11" to 12"
3" to 4¼"

SPLIT COVER GABLE RAKE
¾"=1'-0"

Sizes vary according to Manufacturer; see Catalogues for exact sizes. — Also manufactured with tapered covers and straight pans; and tapered covers with tapered pans.

CLAY ROOFING TILES

2'-0"
4'-0" & over

Concrete tiles are made in same forms as clay tiles; and also for industrial buildings. They are made as shown, 2'-0" wide and 4'-0" long (also longer) and are about 1½" thick and reinforced. No fastenings are used except ends are formed to hook over L purlins.

Concrete tile

L purlins

Top of truss

CONCRETE ROOFING TILES

CLAY TILE ROOFING

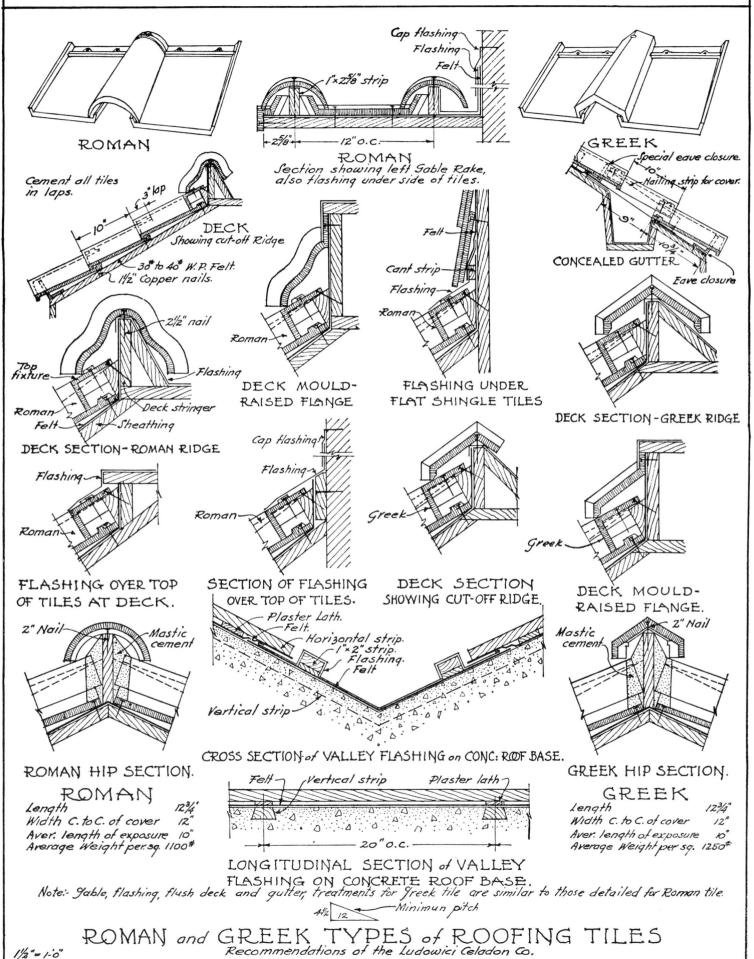

ROMAN

ROMAN
Section showing left Gable Rake,
also flashing under side of tiles.

GREEK

Cap flashing
Flashing
Felt
1"x2⅝" strip
2⅝"
12" O.C.

Cement all tiles in laps.
3" lap
10"
DECK
Showing cut-off Ridge
30# to 40# W.P. Felt.
1½" Copper nails.

Special eave closure.
Nailing strip for cover.
9"
CONCEALED GUTTER
Eave closure

2½" nail
Top fixture
Roman
Felt
Deck stringer
Sheathing
Flashing
DECK SECTION-ROMAN RIDGE

Roman
DECK MOULD-RAISED FLANGE

Felt
Cant strip
Flashing
Roman
FLASHING UNDER FLAT SHINGLE TILES

DECK SECTION-GREEK RIDGE

Flashing
Roman
FLASHING OVER TOP OF TILES AT DECK.

Cap flashing
Flashing
Roman
SECTION OF FLASHING OVER TOP OF TILES.

Greek
DECK SECTION SHOWING CUT-OFF RIDGE.

Greek
DECK MOULD-RAISED FLANGE.

2" Nail
Mastic cement
ROMAN HIP SECTION.

Plaster Lath.
Felt
Horizontal strip.
1"x2" strip.
Flashing.
Felt
Vertical strip
CROSS SECTION of VALLEY FLASHING on CONC. ROOF BASE.

Mastic cement
2" Nail
GREEK HIP SECTION.

ROMAN
Length	12¾"
Width C. to C. of cover	12"
Aver. length of exposure	10"
Average Weight per sq.	1100#

Felt
Vertical strip
Plaster lath
20" O.C.
LONGITUDINAL SECTION of VALLEY FLASHING ON CONCRETE ROOF BASE.

GREEK
Length	12¾"
Width C. to C. of cover	12"
Aver. length of exposure	10"
Average Weight per sq.	1250#

Note:- Gable, flashing, flush deck and gutter, treatments for Greek tile are similar to those detailed for Roman tile.

4½ / 12 Minimum pitch

ROMAN and GREEK TYPES of ROOFING TILES
Recommendations of the Ludowici Celadon Co.

1½" = 1-0"

CLAY TILE ROOFING

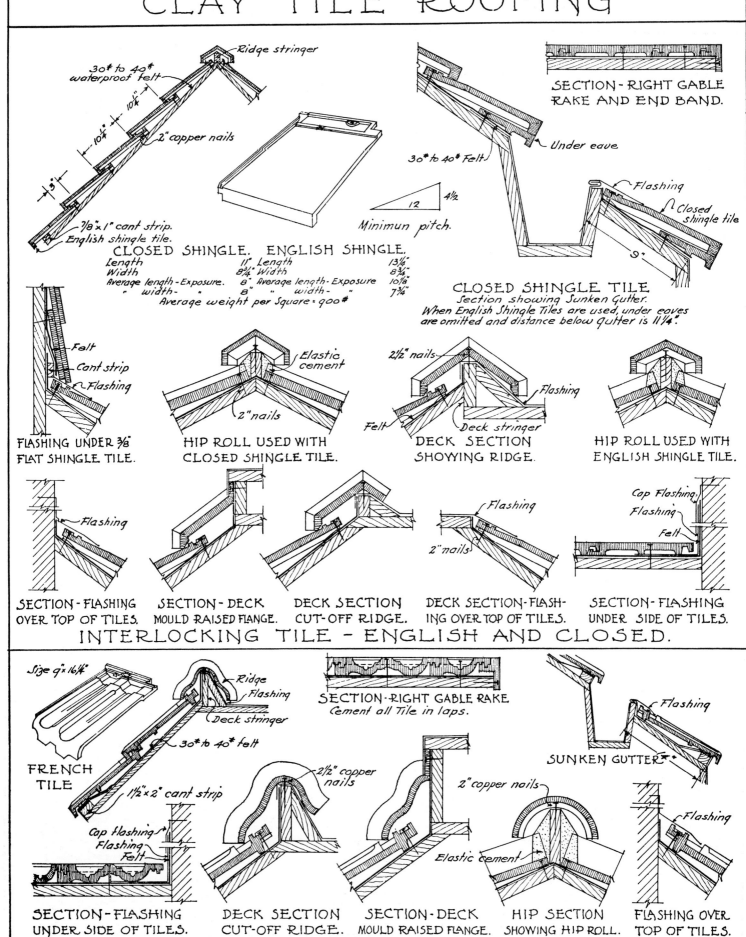

Ridge stringer

30# to 40# waterproof felt

10½"

10½"

10½"

5"

2" copper nails

⅞"x1" cant strip.
English shingle tile.

SECTION-RIGHT GABLE
RAKE AND END BAND.

30# to 40# Felt

Under eave

12   4½
Minimun pitch.

Flashing

Closed
shingle tile

9"

CLOSED SHINGLE.   ENGLISH SHINGLE.

Length	11"	Length	13⅛"
Width	8¼"	Width	8¾"
Average length - Exposure	8"	Average length - Exposure	10⅛"
" width - "	8"	" width - "	7¾"

Average weight per Square = 900#

CLOSED SHINGLE TILE
Section showing Sunken Gutter.
When English Shingle Tiles are used, under eaves
are omitted and distance below gutter is 11¼".

Felt
Cant strip
Flashing

**FLASHING UNDER ⅜"
FLAT SHINGLE TILE.**

Elastic cement
2" nails

**HIP ROLL USED WITH
CLOSED SHINGLE TILE.**

2½" nails
Flashing
Felt
Deck stringer

**DECK SECTION
SHOWING RIDGE.**

**HIP ROLL USED WITH
ENGLISH SHINGLE TILE.**

Flashing

**SECTION-FLASHING
OVER TOP OF TILES.**

**SECTION-DECK
MOULD RAISED FLANGE.**

**DECK SECTION
CUT-OFF RIDGE.**

Flashing
2" nails

**DECK SECTION-FLASH-
ING OVER TOP OF TILES.**

Cap Flashing
Flashing
Felt

**SECTION-FLASHING
UNDER SIDE OF TILES.**

INTERLOCKING TILE - ENGLISH AND CLOSED.

Size 9"x16¼"

Ridge
Flashing
Deck stringer
30# to 40# felt

**FRENCH
TILE**

1½"x2" cant strip

Cap flashing
Flashing
Felt

**SECTION-FLASHING
UNDER SIDE OF TILES.**

2½" copper
nails

**DECK SECTION
CUT-OFF RIDGE.**

**SECTION-DECK
MOULD RAISED FLANGE.**

SECTION-RIGHT GABLE RAKE
Cement all Tile in laps.

Flashing

SUNKEN GUTTER

2" copper nails
Elastic cement

**HIP SECTION
SHOWING HIP ROLL.**

Flashing

**FLASHING OVER
TOP OF TILES.**

FRENCH TILES
Recommendations of the Ludowici-Celadon Co.

COPPER ROOFING

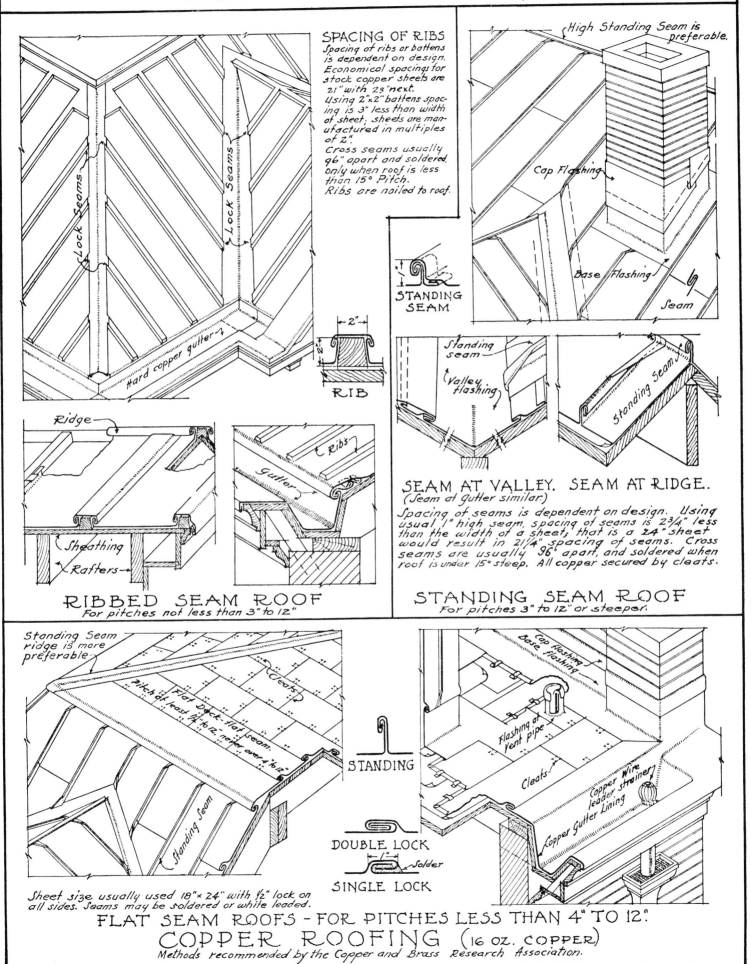

SPACING OF RIBS
Spacing of ribs or battens is dependent on design. Economical spacings for stock copper sheets are 21" with 23" next.
Using 2"x2" battens spacing is 3" less than width of sheet; sheets are manufactured in multiples of 2".
Cross seams usually 96" apart and soldered, only when roof is less than 15° Pitch.
Ribs are nailed to roof.

STANDING SEAM

RIB

RIBBED SEAM ROOF
For pitches not less than 3" to 12"

SEAM AT VALLEY. SEAM AT RIDGE.
(Seam at Gutter similar.)
Spacing of seams is dependent on design. Using usual 1" high seam, spacing of seams is 2¾" less than the width of a sheet; that is a 24" sheet would result in 21¼" spacing of seams. Cross seams are usually 96" apart, and soldered when roof is under 15° steep. All copper secured by cleats.

STANDING SEAM ROOF
For pitches 3" to 12" or steeper.

STANDING
DOUBLE LOCK
SINGLE LOCK

Sheet size usually used 18"x 24" with ½" lock on all sides. Seams may be soldered or white leaded.

FLAT SEAM ROOFS - FOR PITCHES LESS THAN 4" TO 12".

COPPER ROOFING (16 OZ. COPPER)
Methods recommended by the Copper and Brass Research Association.

GALVANIZED IRON ROOFING

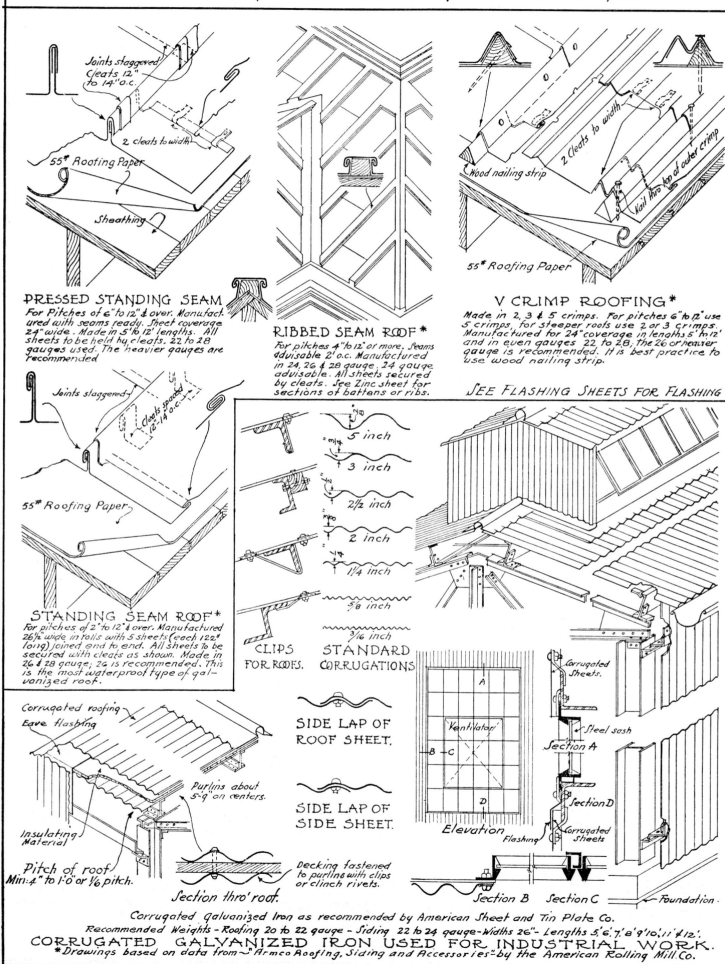

PRESSED STANDING SEAM
For Pitches of 6" to 12" & over. Manufactured with seams ready. Sheet coverage 24" wide. Made in 5' to 12' lengths. All sheets to be held by cleats. 22 to 28 gauges used. The heavier gauges are recommended

RIBBED SEAM ROOF *
For pitches 4" to 12" or more. Seams advisable 2' o.c. Manufactured in 24, 26 & 28 gauge. 24 gauge advisable. All sheets secured by cleats. See Zinc sheet for sections of battens or ribs.

V CRIMP ROOFING *
Made in 2, 3 & 5 crimps. For pitches 6" to 12" use 5 crimps, for steeper roofs use 2 or 3 crimps. Manufactured for 24" coverage in lengths 5' to 12' and in even gauges 22 to 28; the 26 or heavier gauge is recommended. It is best practice to use wood nailing strip.

SEE FLASHING SHEETS FOR FLASHING

STANDING SEAM ROOF *
For pitches of 2" to 12" & over. Manufactured 26½" wide in rolls with 5 sheets (each 122" long) joined end to end. All sheets to be secured with cleats as shown. Made in 26 & 28 gauge; 26 is recommended. This is the most waterproof type of galvanized roof.

CLIPS FOR ROOFS.

STANDARD CORRUGATIONS
5 inch
3 inch
2½ inch
2 inch
1¼ inch
5/8 inch
3/16 inch

SIDE LAP OF ROOF SHEET.

SIDE LAP OF SIDE SHEET.

Section thro' roof.

Corrugated roofing
Eave flashing
Purlins about 5'-9" on centers.
Insulating Material
Pitch of roof Min: 4" to 1'-0" or 1/6 pitch.
Decking fastened to purlins with clips or clinch rivets.

Ventilator
A
B C
D
Elevation

Corrugated Sheets.
Steel sash
Section A
Section D
Corrugated sheets
Flashing
Section B   Section C   Foundation

Corrugated Galvanized Iron as recommended by American Sheet and Tin Plate Co.
Recommended Weights - Roofing 20 to 22 gauge - Siding 22 to 24 gauge - Widths 26" - Lengths 5', 6', 7', 8', 9', 10', 11' & 12'.

CORRUGATED GALVANIZED IRON USED FOR INDUSTRIAL WORK.
*Drawings based on data from "Armco Roofing, Siding and Accessories" by the American Rolling Mill Co.

LEAD & CANVAS ROOFING

Weight per □'	Thickness in inches	Use for which it is recommended	Lengths
2½#	1/24	Cap flashing, batten roofing if less than 24"o.c.	For Cap flashing, batten caps, gutter lining: 8'-0"
3#	3/64	Other roofing, cornice, base flashing, gutter lining.	For all other purposes: 4'-0"
4#	1/16	Special conditions of roofing.	Widths
6#	3/32	Scolloped edgings. Ornaments.	Stock widths are rolled 24," 30" & 36" wide.
8#	1/8	" " " " & Shower pans.	Do not use steel near lead.

For Flashing and method of forming ribs etc. see other Roofing Sheets.

Notes.

Never nail lead, but secure with lead or copper cleats which are nailed to roof boards with two hard copper wire nails. Secure lead to masonry with brass screws into lead shields. All cleats to be approximately 10"on centers. On steep roots run cleats continuously in horizontal plane and secure them every 12." Hem all lead edges ½" for stiffness.. All joints should be lock seams, not soldered. Lap all vertical joints not less than 3. inches. Vertical surfaces over 18" high to have seams 18" apart. Lead expands but does not contract. Maximum expansion is .0187per ft. Lead coated copper is very permanent & should be used as copper. 12 lbs of lead per square is usual.

LEAD (HARD) ROOFING

Also see "Flashing" and "Leaders & Gutters" sheets

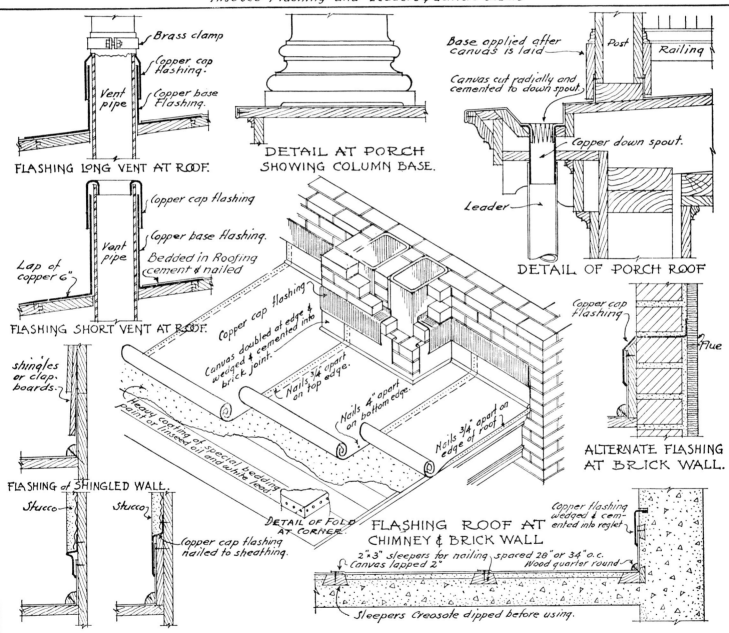

FLASHING LONG VENT AT ROOF.

DETAIL AT PORCH SHOWING COLUMN BASE.

DETAIL OF PORCH ROOF

FLASHING SHORT VENT AT ROOF.

FLASHING of SHINGLED WALL.

DETAIL OF FOLD AT CORNER

FLASHING ROOF AT CHIMNEY & BRICK WALL

ALTERNATE FLASHING AT BRICK WALL.

TWO METHODS OF FLASHING ROOF at STUCCO WALL.

METHOD OF LAYING & FLASHING ON CONCRETE WALL.

The use of treated Canvas is advisable to insure against mildew and damage from oil in paints. Canvas to be nailed with ¾" copper tacks. Lay in heavy bed of white lead then paint 2 coats of lead and oil. Repaint every two or three years.

Widths { Material made in two widths: 30" and 36".

Weights { Light weight for roots with little traffic. Medium for Porches & Roofs with medium traffic. Heavy weight for Porches and Roots with severe traffic.

CANVAS ROOFING

Methods recommended by William L. Barrell Co. Inc. N.Y.C.

SLATE ROOFING

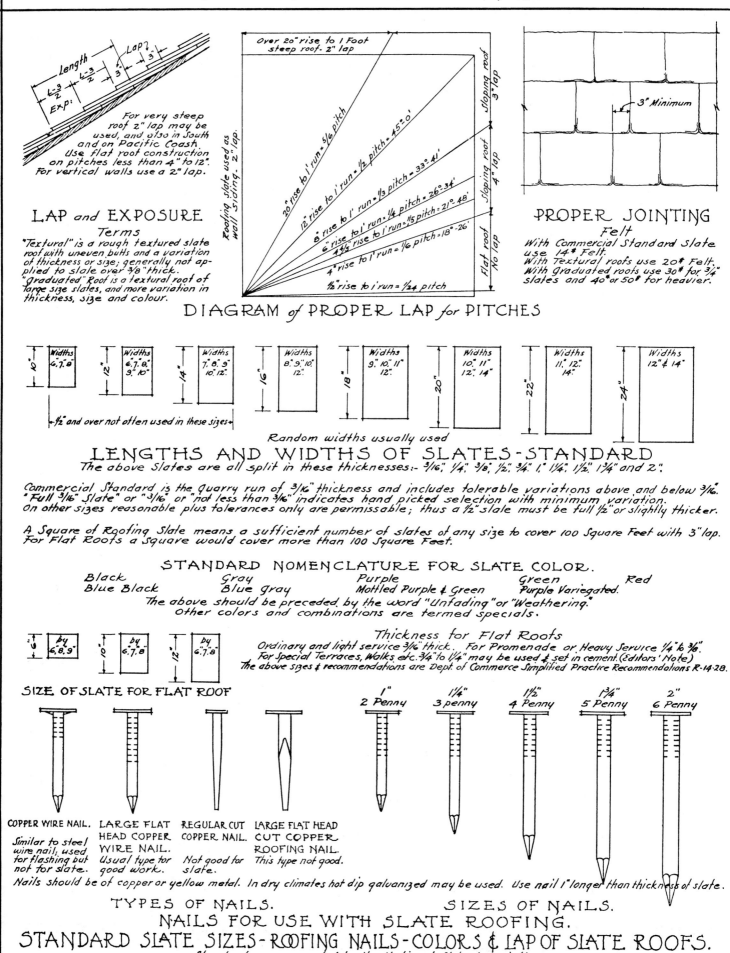

For very steep roof 2" lap may be used, and also in South and on Pacific Coast. Use flat roof construction on pitches less than 4" to 12". For vertical walls use a 2" lap.

LAP and EXPOSURE
Terms

"Textural" is a rough textured slate roof with uneven butts and a variation of thickness or size; generally not applied to slate over 3/8" thick. "Graduated" Roof is a textural roof of large size slates, and more variation in thickness, size and colour.

DIAGRAM of PROPER LAP for PITCHES

Over 20" rise to 1 Foot steep roof - 2" lap

Roofing slate used as wall siding - 2" lap.

20" rise to 1' run = 5/6 pitch
12" rise to 1' run = 1/2 pitch = 45°-0'
8" rise to 1' run = 1/3 pitch = 33°-41'
6" rise to 1' run = 1/4 pitch = 26°-34'
4 4/5" rise to 1' run = 1/5 pitch = 21°-48'
4" rise to 1' run = 1/6 pitch = 18°-26'
1/2" rise to 1'run = 1/24 pitch

Sloping roof 3" lap
Sloping roof 4" lap
Flat roof No lap

PROPER JOINTING
Felt

3" Minimum

With Commercial Standard Slate use 14# Felt. With Textural roofs use 20# Felt. With Graduated roofs use 30# for 3/4 slates and 40# or 50# for heavier.

LENGTHS AND WIDTHS OF SLATES-STANDARD

	Widths
10"	6, 7, 8
12"	6, 7, 8, 9, 10
14"	7, 8, 9, 10, 12
16"	8, 9, 10, 12
18"	9, 10, 11, 12
20"	10, 11, 12, 14
22"	11, 12, 14
24"	12 & 14

1/2" and over not often used in these sizes

Random widths usually used

The above Slates are all split in these thicknesses:- 3/16", 1/4", 3/8", 1/2", 3/4", 1", 1/4", 1/2", 1/4" and 2".

Commercial Standard is the Quarry run of 3/16" thickness and includes tolerable variations above and below 3/16". "Full 3/16" Slate" or "3/16" or "not less than 3/16" indicates hand picked selection with minimum variation. On other sizes reasonable plus tolerances only are permissable; thus a 1/2" slate must be full 1/2" or slightly thicker.

A Square of Roofing Slate means a sufficient number of slates of any size to cover 100 Square Feet with 3" lap. For Flat Roofs a Square would cover more than 100 Square Feet.

STANDARD NOMENCLATURE FOR SLATE COLOR.

Black	Gray	Purple	Green	Red
Blue Black	Blue Gray	Mottled Purple & Green	Purple Variegated	

The above should be preceded by the word "Unfading" or "Weathering." Other colors and combinations are termed specials.

Thickness for Flat Roofs

Ordinary and light service 3/16" thick. For Promenade or Heavy Service 1/4" to 3/8". For Special Terraces, Walks etc. 3/4" to 1/4" may be used & set in cement. (Editors' Note) The above sizes & recommendations are Dept. of Commerce Simplified Practice Recommendations R-14-28.

SIZE OF SLATE FOR FLAT ROOF

	by
8"	6, 8, 9
10"	6, 7, 8
12"	6, 7, 8

NAILS FOR USE WITH SLATE ROOFING.

COPPER WIRE NAIL.
Similar to steel wire nail, used for flashing but not for slate.

LARGE FLAT HEAD COPPER WIRE NAIL.
Usual type for good work.

REGULAR CUT COPPER NAIL.
Not good for slate.

LARGE FLAT HEAD CUT COPPER ROOFING NAIL.
This type not good.

1" 2 Penny
1/4" 3 penny
1/2" 4 Penny
1/4" 5 Penny
2" 6 Penny

Nails should be of copper or yellow metal. In dry climates hot dip galvanized may be used. Use nail 1" longer than thickness of slate.

TYPES OF NAILS.   SIZES OF NAILS.

STANDARD SLATE SIZES-ROOFING NAILS-COLORS & LAP OF SLATE ROOFS.
Standards recommended by the National Slate Association.

SLATE ROOFING

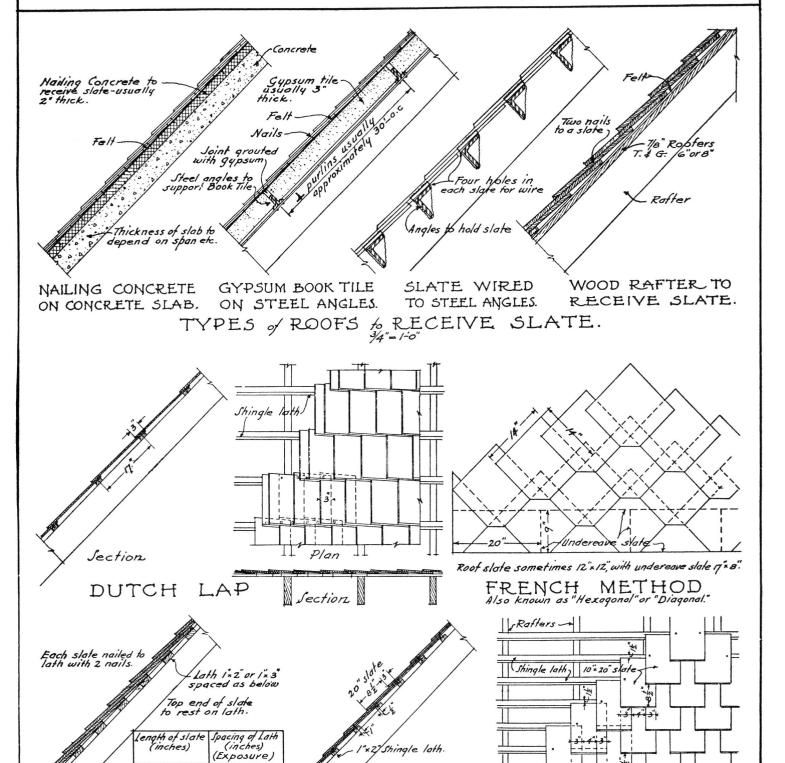

NAILING CONCRETE ON CONCRETE SLAB.

Nailing Concrete to receive slate—usually 2" thick.

Felt

Thickness of slab to depend on span etc.

GYPSUM BOOK TILE ON STEEL ANGLES.

Concrete

Gypsum tile usually 3" thick.

Felt

Nails

Joint grouted with gypsum

Steel angles to support Book Tile

Purlins usually approximately 3′-0″ o.c.

SLATE WIRED TO STEEL ANGLES.

Four holes in each slate for wire

Angles to hold slate

WOOD RAFTER TO RECEIVE SLATE.

Felt

Two nails to a slate

7/8″ Roofers T. & G. 6″ or 8″

Rafter

TYPES of ROOFS to RECEIVE SLATE.
3/4″ = 1′-0″

DUTCH LAP

Section

Shingle lath

Plan

Section

FRENCH METHOD
Also known as "Hexagonal" or "Diagonal."

Undereave slate

Roof slate sometimes 12″ × 12″, with undereave slate 17″ × 8″.

LAYING on WOOD LATH

Each slate nailed to lath with 2 nails.

Lath 1″×2″ or 1″×3″ spaced as below

Top end of slate to rest on lath.

Section

Length of slate (inches)	Spacing of Lath (inches) (Exposure)
24	10½
22	9½
20	8½
18	7½
16	6½
14	5½
12	4½

OPEN SLATING
For use where ventilation is desired

20″ slate 8½ + 3

1″×2″ Shingle lath.

Section

Rafters

Shingle lath

10″ × 20″ slate

Plan

VARIOUS METHODS OF LAYING SLATE.
1/2″ = 1′-0″

TYPES of ROOFS to RECEIVE SLATE and LAYING SLATE ROOFS.
Methods recommended by the National Slate Association in "Slate Roofs."

SLATE ROOFING

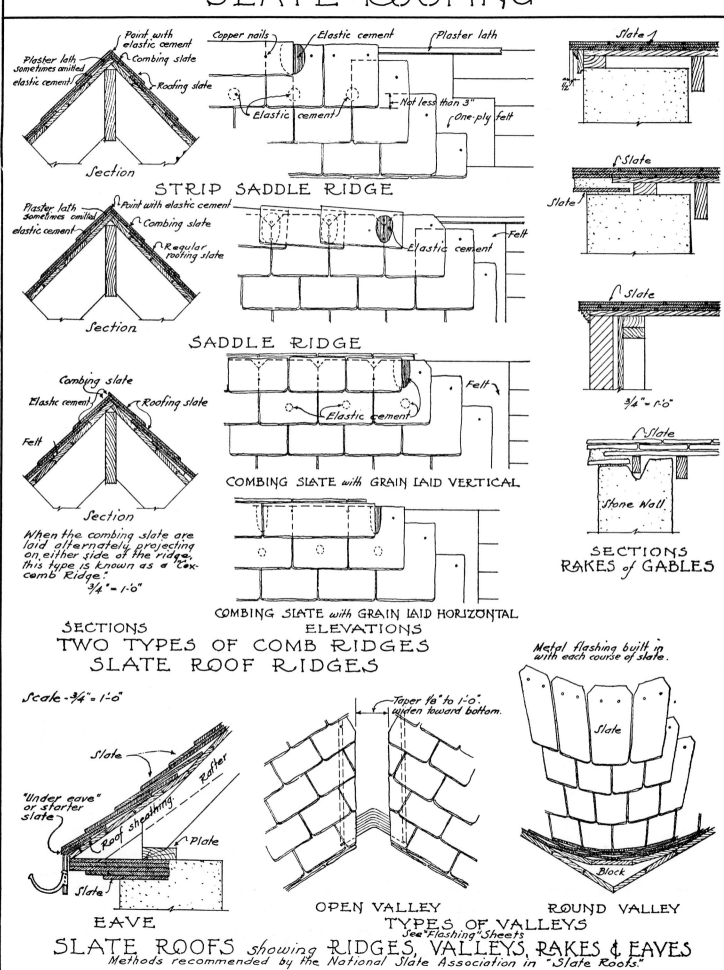

STRIP SADDLE RIDGE

SADDLE RIDGE

COMBING SLATE with GRAIN LAID VERTICAL

COMBING SLATE with GRAIN LAID HORIZONTAL
ELEVATIONS

SECTIONS
TWO TYPES OF COMB RIDGES
SLATE ROOF RIDGES

When the combing slate are laid alternately projecting on either side of the ridge, this type is known as a "Coxcomb Ridge."
3/4" = 1'-0"

SECTIONS
RAKES of GABLES

Scale - 3/4" = 1'-0"

EAVE

OPEN VALLEY
TYPES OF VALLEYS
See "Flashing" Sheets

ROUND VALLEY

SLATE ROOFS showing RIDGES, VALLEYS, RAKES & EAVES
Methods recommended by the National Slate Association in "Slate Roofs."

SLATE ROOFING

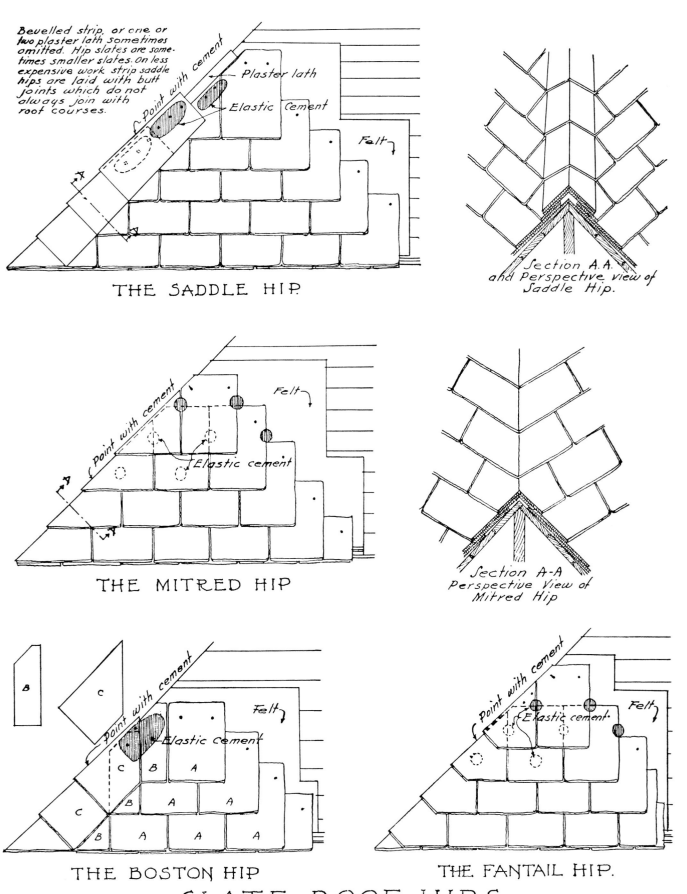

Bevelled strip, or one or two plaster lath sometimes omitted. Hip slates are sometimes smaller slates. On less expensive work strip saddle hips are laid with butt joints which do not always join with roof courses.

Point with cement

Plaster lath

Elastic Cement

Felt

THE SADDLE HIP.

Section A.A. and Perspective view of Saddle Hip.

Point with cement

Elastic cement

Felt

THE MITRED HIP

Section A-A Perspective View of Mitred Hip

Point with cement

Elastic Cement

Felt

THE BOSTON HIP

Point with cement

Elastic cement

Felt

THE FANTAIL HIP.

SLATE ROOF HIPS

Methods recommended by the National Slate Association in "Slate Roofs."

ZINC ROOFING

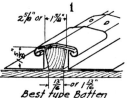

1

2⁵/₈" or 1⁷/₈"

¹³/₁₆" or 1¹³/₁₆"

Best type Batten
For pitch of 3" to 12" & over.
1⁵/₈ x 1⁵/₈ is standard size.

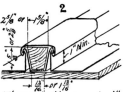

2

2⁵/₈" or 1⁷/₈"

¹³/₁₆" or 1¹³/₁₆"

1" Min.

These Battens used with clips to hold sheet. For pitches 3" to 12" up to 6" to 12" but not over.

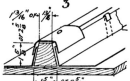

3

1³/₁₆" or ⁷/₈"

1⁵/₈" or 2⁵/₈"

This type not as good as 1st and 2nd. type.

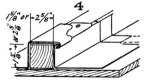

4

1⁵/₈" or 2⁵/₈"

Used for same pitch as 2nd. type.

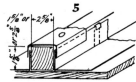

5

1⁵/₈" or 2⁵/₈"

For small roof only. Must be most carefully installed.

SPACING OF BATTENS AND WEIGHT OF ZINC.

Standard battens (1⁵/₈"x1⁵/₈") take spacing 2¼" less than width of sheet.   When battens are not over 18" apart use #11 or #12 guage Zinc.
Large battens (2⁵/₈"x2⁵/₈")   "   "   3"   "   "   "   "   "   "   "   30"   "   12 " 13   "
Stock sheet = 20", 30", 36" and 40" wide.   *Lengths 84"and 96".*   "   "   "   "   40"   "   13 " 14   "
   "   "   "   over 40" apart   "   14 " 15   "

Battens over 40" apart not recommended

On slopes less than 4" to 12" solder end joints. If more than 3 sheets (over 21'-0") are used provide step for expansion. Ends of sheets are secured by cleats. Actual coverage is 5" less than length of sheet.

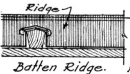

Ridge

2⁷/₈" for standard batten
3⁷/₈" for large batten

Batten Ridge.   *Ridge without battens.*

ELEVATION of RIDGES

Roof slope

Solder

SOLDERED JOINT for BATTEN ROOF LESS than 4" to 12" PITCH.

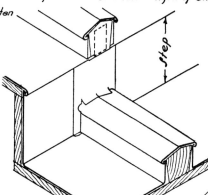

step

STEP in PITCHES 4" to 12" or LESS if LENGTH RUN is 21'
Used both in batten & standing seam.

Nailed clip

7/8"

3"

1"

LOCK SEAM USED in STANDING SEAM ROOF FOR RUNS over 21' and OVER 4" to 12" PITCH.

BATTEN ROOFING

NOTES ON ZINC ROOFING

gauge #	9	10	11	12	13	14	15	16
Thickness	.018	.02	.024	.028	.032	.036	.04	.045
Lbs per ▢'	.67	.75	.9	1.05	1.2	1.35	1.5	1.68

Zinc should never be used in contact with copper, steel, iron because of electrolosis. Nor should it be used where acid fumes occur, nor with oak, redwood or red cedar. Zinc expands about 2½"per 100' in temperature change from 0° to 120°. Copper expands about ½ this amount. Always use hot dipped galvanized nails with Zinc. Always use glassy, saturated and coated paper under. For "Flashing" and "Leaders & Gutters" see sheets of those titles. Zinc should not be painted unless weathered for 2 months or especially prepared. Use Zinc paint.
Methods shown are recommended by the American Zinc Institute, New York City.

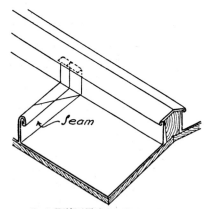

Seam

BATTEN RIDGE

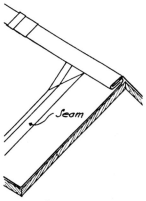

Seam

LOCK SEAM

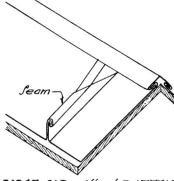

Seam

RIDGE CAP without BATTEN

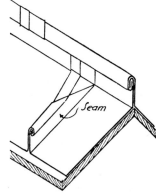

Seam

STANDING SEAM

TYPES OF RIDGES

Minimum pitch for this type 2" to 12" and when much snow occurs increase to 3" to 12". Use #10 Zinc. Standard width of sheets is 20" and lengths 84" or 96". Seams 17½" o.c. It is recommended that crimped metal not be used.   Lengths should not exceed 21' without expansion joint. If the pitch is 4" to 12" or less use steps for expansion; if greater use lock seam. All sheets are secured by clips 1"x 3" long nailed to roof 8" to 10" on centers.

STANDING SEAM ROOFS
See Copper Roofing as methods are similar

FLAT ROOF { Flat roofs are to be avoided except on small areas of 200 square feet; for such usage use #10 guage Zinc, and pieces not over 14"x 20" maximum. These held by clips.

ROOFING FINISHES

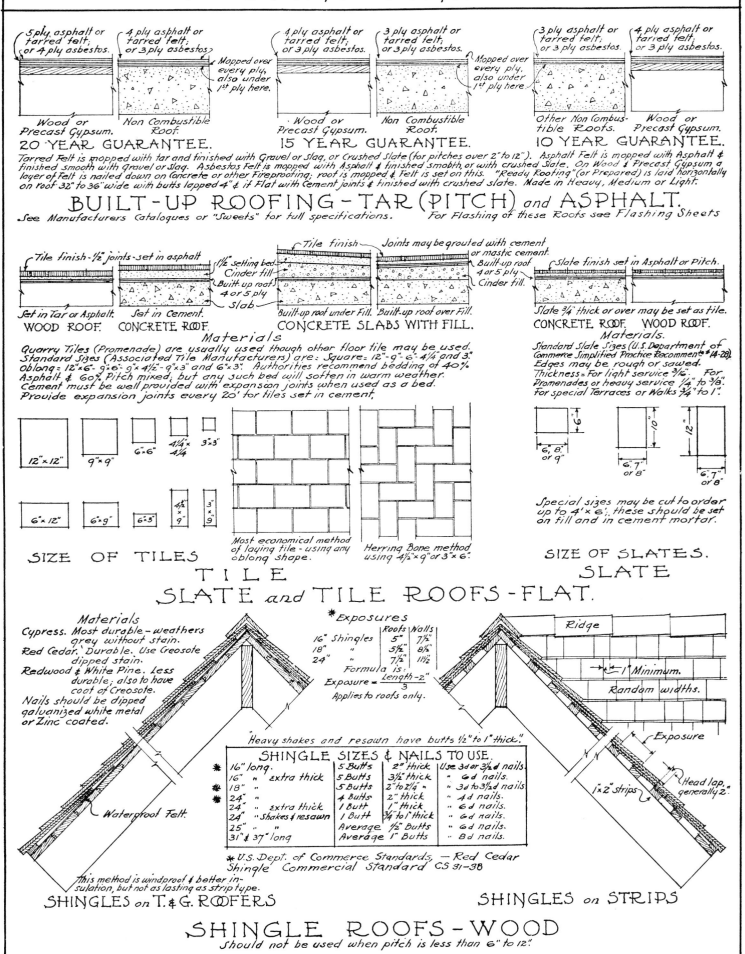

5 ply. asphalt or tarred felt; or 4 ply asbestos. 4 ply asphalt or tarred felt; or 3 ply asbestos. Mopped over every ply, also under 1st ply here.

Wood or Precast Gypsum. Non Combustible Roof.

20 YEAR GUARANTEE.

4 ply asphalt or tarred felt; or 3 ply asbestos. 3 ply asphalt or tarred felt; or 3 ply asbestos. Mopped over every ply, also under 1st ply here.

Wood or Precast Gypsum. Non Combustible Roof.

15 YEAR GUARANTEE.

3 ply asphalt or tarred felt; or 3 ply asbestos. 4 ply asphalt or tarred felt; or 3 ply asbestos.

Other Non Combustible Roofs. Wood or Precast Gypsum.

10 YEAR GUARANTEE.

Tarred Felt is mopped with tar and finished with Gravel or Slag, or Crushed Slate (for pitches over 2" to 12"). Asphalt Felt is mopped with Asphalt & finished smooth with Gravel or Slag. Asbestos Felt is mopped with Asphalt & finished smooth, or with crushed Slate. On Wood & Precast Gypsum a layer of Felt is nailed down on Concrete or other Fireproofing; roof is mopped & Felt is set on this. "Ready Roofing" (or Prepared) is laid horizontally on roof 32" to 36" wide with butts lapped 4" & if Flat with Cement joints & finished with crushed slate. Made in Heavy, Medium or Light.

BUILT-UP ROOFING – TAR (PITCH) and ASPHALT.

See Manufacturers Catalogues or "Sweets" for full specifications.   For Flashing of these Roofs see Flashing Sheets

Materials

Quarry Tiles (Promenade) are usually used though other floor tile may be used. Standard Sizes (Associated Tile Manufacturers) are: Square= 12"-9"-6"-4¼" and 3". Oblong= 12"x6"- 9"x6"- 9"x4½"-9"x3" and 6"x3". Authorities recommend bedding of 40% Asphalt & 60% Pitch mixed; but any such bed will soften in warm weather. Cement must be well provided with expansion joints when used as a bed. Provide expansion joints every 20' for tiles set in cement.

Materials

Standard Slate Sizes (U.S. Department of Commerce Simplified Practice Recommend.* 14-28). Edges may be rough or sawed. Thickness= For light service 3/16". For Promenades or heavy service ¼" to 3/8". For special Terraces or Walks ¾" to 1".

Special sizes may be cut to order up to 4'x6'; these should be set on fill and in cement mortar.

SIZE OF TILES   **SIZE OF SLATES.**

TILE   **SLATE**

SLATE and TILE ROOFS – FLAT.

Materials
Cypress. Most durable – weathers grey without stain.
Red Cedar. Durable. Use Creosote dipped stain.
Redwood & White Pine. Less durable; also to have coat of Creosote.
Nails should be dipped galvanized white metal or Zinc coated.

Exposures

	Roofs	Walls
16" Shingles	5"	7½"
18" "	5½"	8½"
24" "	7½"	11½"

Formula is:
$$Exposure = \frac{Length - 2"}{3}$$
Applies to roofs only.

Ridge — 1" Minimum. — Random widths. — Exposure — Head lap, generally 2". — 1"x2" strips.

"Heavy shakes and resawn have butts ½" to 1" thick."

SHINGLE SIZES & NAILS TO USE.			
16" long.	5 Butts	2" thick	Use 3d or 3½d nails.
16" " extra thick	5 Butts	3½" thick	" 6d nails.
18" "	5 Butts	2" to 2¼"	" 3d to 3½d nails
24" "	4 Butts	2" thick	" 4d nails.
24" " extra thick	1 Butt	1" thick	" 6d nails.
24" "Shakes & resawn	1 Butt	¾" to 1" thick	" 6d nails.
25" "	Average ½" Butts		" 6d nails.
31" & 37" long	Average 1" Butts		" 8d nails.

*U.S. Dept. of Commerce Standards, – Red Cedar Shingle Commercial Standard CS 31-38

Waterproof Felt.

This method is windproof & better insulation, but not as lasting as strip type.

SHINGLES on T. & G. ROOFERS   **SHINGLES on STRIPS**

SHINGLE ROOFS – WOOD
Should not be used when pitch is less than 6" to 12".

SKYLIGHTS

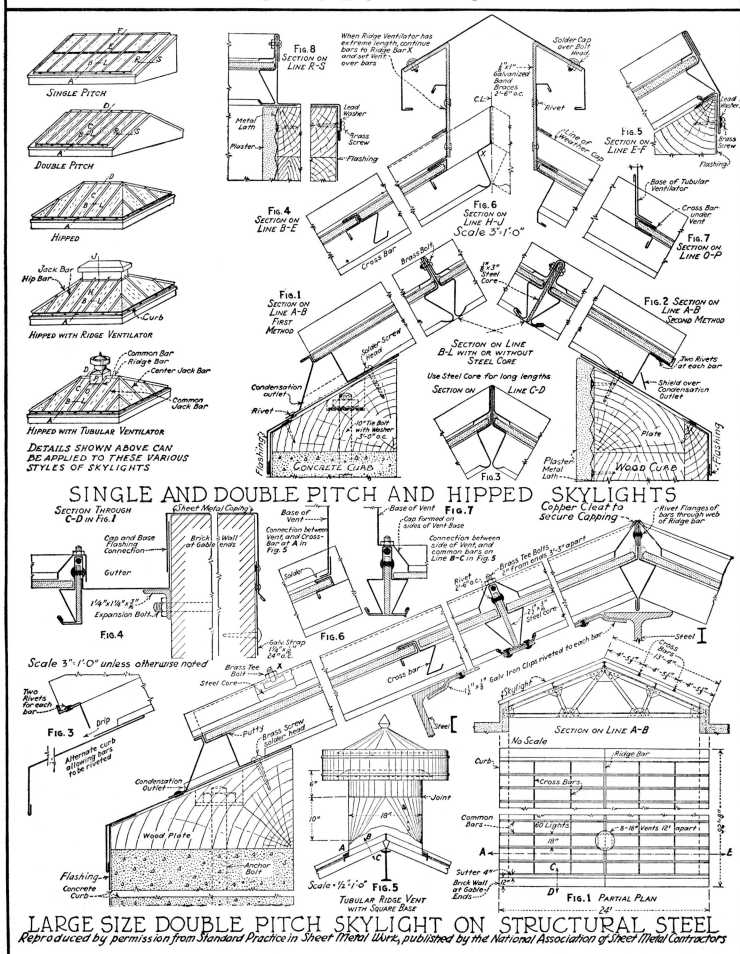

SINGLE PITCH

DOUBLE PITCH

HIPPED

HIPPED WITH RIDGE VENTILATOR

HIPPED WITH TUBULAR VENTILATOR

DETAILS SHOWN ABOVE CAN BE APPLIED TO THESE VARIOUS STYLES OF SKYLIGHTS

FIG.8 SECTION ON LINE R-S

FIG.4 SECTION ON LINE B-E

FIG.6 SECTION ON LINE H-J Scale 3":1'0"

FIG.5 SECTION ON LINE E-F

FIG.7 SECTION ON LINE O-P

FIG.1 SECTION ON LINE A-B FIRST METHOD

SECTION ON LINE B-L WITH OR WITHOUT STEEL CORE

Use Steel Core for long lengths

SECTION ON LINE C-D

FIG.2 SECTION ON LINE A-B SECOND METHOD

FIG.3

CONCRETE CURB

WOOD CURB

SINGLE AND DOUBLE PITCH AND HIPPED SKYLIGHTS

SECTION THROUGH C-D IN FIG.1

FIG.4

Scale 3":1'0" unless otherwise noted

FIG.3

FIG.6

FIG.7

Copper Cleat to Secure Capping

FIG.5 TUBULAR RIDGE VENT WITH SQUARE BASE

Scale 1/2":1'0"

SECTION ON LINE A-B No Scale

FIG.1 PARTIAL PLAN

LARGE SIZE DOUBLE PITCH SKYLIGHT ON STRUCTURAL STEEL

Reproduced by permission from Standard Practice in Sheet Metal Work, published by the National Association of Sheet Metal Contractors

SKYLIGHTS

FLAT SKYLIGHT OVER ELEVATOR AND STAIR SHAFTS
Scale 3"=1'0" unless otherwise noted

FIG. 3 SECTION AT E

Cap Flashing to extend 4" in Wall

Skylight Cap

Concrete leveled to proper pitch

Offset

Wall

FIG. 4 SECTION ON LINE H-J IN FIG.1 SHOWING GUTTER AND HALF BAR AT SIDE WALLS

Stepped Cap-Flashing

Side Wall

2"x2"x3/16"

Expansion Bolt

FIG. 5 SECTION ON LINE F-G
Scale 3/4"=1'-0"

Cap Flashing

Elevation of Collar and Flashing

1 1/2"

Collar 1 1/2"x1"

Vent hood over 1 1/2"x 3/16"

Strap

Solder

Side Elevation of Vent

Expansion bolt

Wall

PLAN VIEW OF STRAP

SIZES OF STEEL CORES FOR SKYLIGHT BARS

SPAN	CORE
6'-6" or less	2 1/2" x 3/16"
6'-7" to 7'-6"	3" x 3/16"
7'-7" to 8'-6"	3 1/2" x 3/16"
8'-7" to 9'-6"	4" x 3/16"
9'-7" to 11'-0"	4 1/2" x 3/16"
11'-1" to 12'-6"	5" x 3/16"
Over 12'-6" use Center Purlin

Spacing of Bars not to exceed 1'-6" o.c.

FIG. 2 SECTION AT C IN FIG.1

3/8" Steel Rod

1"x1/16" Strap

Leader

Solder Strap all around

Washer

Wood Plate

1/2" Anchor Bolt 8" Long 2'-6" o.c.

Wall

Brass Bolts 2' o.c.

Cross Bar Drip

Two Rivets at each bar

SECTION AT D IN FIG.1

Steel Core 4"-3/16" for 9' span

Solder Brass Screw Head

Condensation Outlet

Shield

Not less than 3" Pitch to 1'0"

Damper and Chain or Movable Register can be installed

SECTION ON LINE A-B

FIG.1 PARTIAL PLAN OF TYPICAL FLAT SKYLIGHT MINUS STEEL FRAMING — No Scale

Curb, Cross Bar, Common Bar, Eaves Gutter, 16" 15 Divisions 1/4" Glass, 3" Gutter, Outlet, Vents 8 ft.

CURBLESS FLAT SKYLIGHT ON PITCHED ROOF
Scale 3"=1'0" unless otherwise noted

FIG.1 PARTIAL FRONT ELEVATION Scale 3/4"=1'-0"

Metal, Roofing, Glass

NOTE: Imbed all Glass in White Lead Putty

SECTIONAL VIEW SHOWING CONSTRUCTION OF TOP AND BOTTOM CURBS

Slide this weather cap under lock from bottom

FIG.4 SECTION ON LINE E-F IN FIG.1 SHOWING PROFILE OF SIDE BAR AT LOWER CURB-A IN THE SECTIONAL VIEW

Metal-Roofing

FIG. 2 SECTION AT A IN FIG.1

Lead Washers, Brass Bolt 3' o.c., Two Rivets at each Bar, Solder head, Condensation Outlet, Shield

SECTION ON LINE C-D IN FIG.1

Steel Core, Brass Bolt

Flat Seam, Standing Seam, or Batten Roof

PROFILE OF SIDE BAR AT UPPER CURB-B IN SECTIONAL VIEW IN FIG.1

Roofing

FIG.5

FIG. 3 SECTION AT B IN FIG.1

Lead Washers, Drip, Common Bar, Cross Bar for long lights, Metal-Roofing

Reproduced by permission from Standard Practice in Sheet Metal Work, published by the National Association of Sheet Metal Contractors

FLASHING

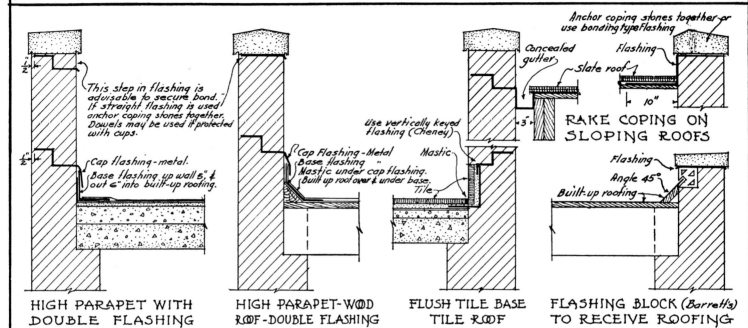

PARAPET WALL and COPING FLASHING

HIGH PARAPET WITH DOUBLE FLASHING

HIGH PARAPET-WOOD ROOF-DOUBLE FLASHING

FLUSH TILE BASE TILE ROOF

FLASHING BLOCK (Barrett's) TO RECEIVE ROOFING

RAKE COPING ON SLOPING ROOFS

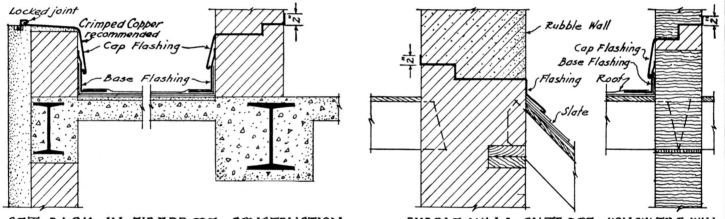

SET-BACK IN FIREPROOF CONSTRUCTION

RUBBLE WALL-SLATE ROOF.

HOLLOW TILE WALL

FLASHING AT THE INTERSECTION OF WALLS AND ROOFS
3/4"=1'

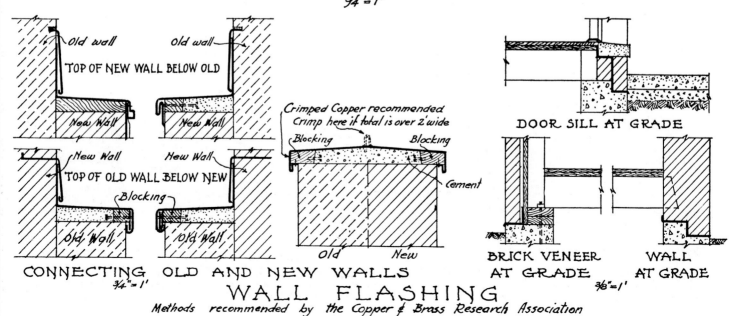

CONNECTING OLD AND NEW WALLS
3/4"=1'

DOOR SILL AT GRADE

BRICK VENEER AT GRADE

WALL AT GRADE
3/8"=1'

WALL FLASHING
Methods recommended by the Copper & Brass Research Association

FLASHING

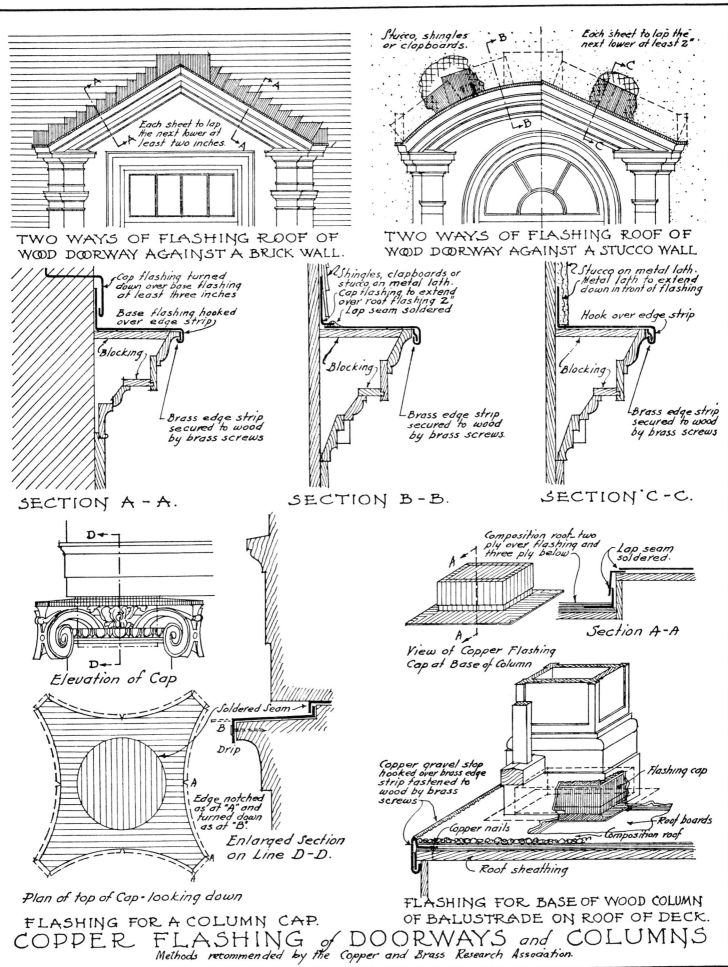

TWO WAYS OF FLASHING ROOF OF WOOD DOORWAY AGAINST A BRICK WALL.

Each sheet to lap the next lower at least two inches.

TWO WAYS OF FLASHING ROOF OF WOOD DOORWAY AGAINST A STUCCO WALL

Stucco, shingles or clapboards.
Each sheet to lap the next lower at least 2"

SECTION A-A.

Cap flashing turned down over base flashing at least three inches
Base flashing hooked over edge strip
Blocking
Brass edge strip secured to wood by brass screws

SECTION B-B.

Shingles, clapboards or stucco on metal lath.
Cap flashing to extend over roof flashing 2"
Lap seam soldered
Blocking
Brass edge strip secured to wood by brass screws.

SECTION C-C.

Stucco on metal lath.
Metal lath to extend down in front of flashing
Hook over edge strip
Blocking
Brass edge strip secured to wood by brass screws

Elevation of Cap

Enlarged Section on Line D-D.
Soldered Seam
Drip
Edge notched as at "A" and turned down as at "B".

Plan of top of Cap-looking down

FLASHING FOR A COLUMN CAP.

Composition roof two ply over flashing and three ply below
Lap seam soldered.
Section A-A

View of Copper Flashing Cap at Base of Column

Copper gravel stop hooked over brass edge strip fastened to wood by brass screws
Flashing cap
Copper nails
Roof boards
Composition roof
Roof sheathing

FLASHING FOR BASE OF WOOD COLUMN OF BALUSTRADE ON ROOF OF DECK.

COPPER FLASHING of DOORWAYS and COLUMNS

Methods recommended by the Copper and Brass Research Association.

FLASHING

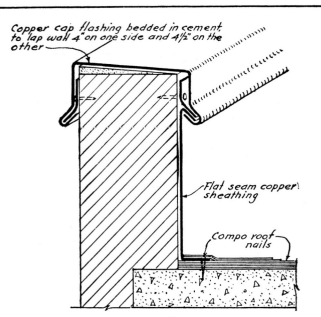

Copper cap flashing bedded in cement to lap wall 4" on one side and 4½" on the other

Flat seam copper sheathing

Compo roof nails

FLASHING FOR BRICK WALL LESS THAN TWO FEET HIGH

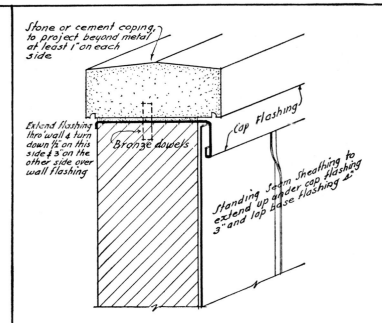

Stone or cement coping, to project beyond metal at least 1" on each side

Extend flashing thro' wall & turn down ½ on this side & 3" on the other side over wall flashing

Bronze dowels

Cap Flashing

Standing Seam Sheathing to extend up under cap flashing 3" and lap base flashing 4"

FLASHING FOR BRICK WALL MORE THAN ONE FOOT ABOVE COUNTER FLASHING

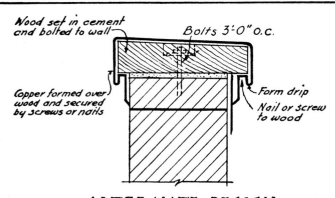

Wood set in cement and bolted to wall

Bolts 3'-0" o.c.

Copper formed over wood and secured by screws or nails

Form drip

Nail or screw to wood

ALTERNATE DESIGN FOR A COPPER COPING

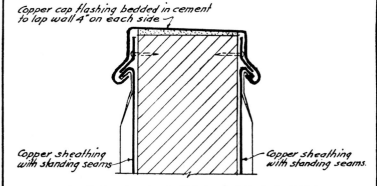

Copper cap flashing bedded in cement to lap wall 4" on each side

Copper sheathing with standing seams

Copper sheathing with standing seams.

COPPER COPING & FLASHING FOR THE TOP OF A BRICK WALL

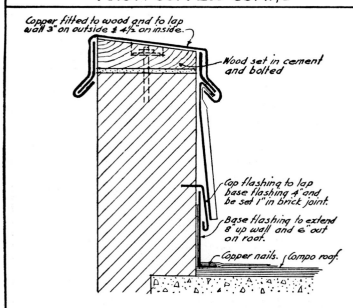

Copper fitted to wood and to lap wall 3" on outside & 4½" on inside.

Wood set in cement and bolted

Cap flashing to lap base flashing 4" and be set 1" in brick joint.

Base flashing to extend 8" up wall and 6" out on roof.

Copper nails. Compo roof.

FLASHING FOR A BRICK WALL MORE THAN TWO FEET HIGH

Stone Coping

If this dimension is over 5'-0" place flashing here also

Stone facing

Preferred Method

Copper cap flashing to extend thro brickwork and lap stone 1"

Copper base flashing turned up 5" on wall and 6" on roof

Compo roof

FLASHING FOR A BRICK PARAPET WALL FACED WITH STONE

Methods as recommended by The Copper & Brass Research Association

FLASHING

139

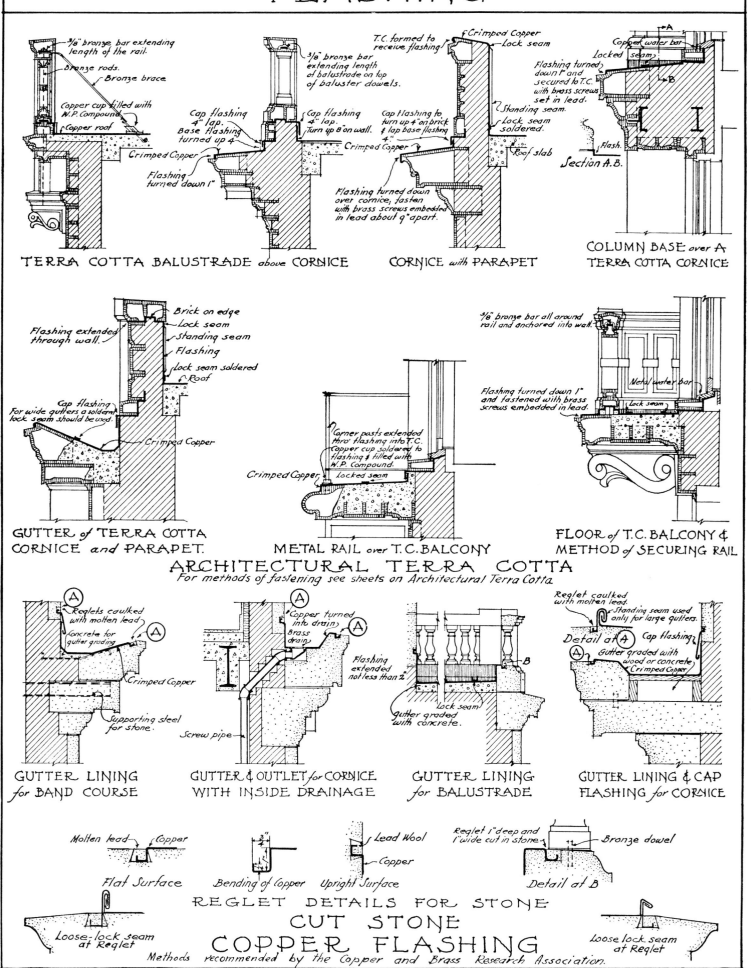

TERRA COTTA BALUSTRADE *above* **CORNICE**   **CORNICE** *with* **PARAPET**   **COLUMN BASE** *over A* **TERRA COTTA CORNICE**

GUTTER *of* **TERRA COTTA CORNICE** *and* **PARAPET.**   **METAL RAIL** *over* **T.C. BALCONY**   **FLOOR** *of* **T.C. BALCONY** & **METHOD** *of* **SECURING RAIL**

ARCHITECTURAL TERRA COTTA
For methods of fastening see sheets on Architectural Terra Cotta

GUTTER LINING *for* **BAND COURSE**   **GUTTER & OUTLET** *for* **CORNICE** **WITH INSIDE DRAINAGE**   **GUTTER LINING** *for* **BALUSTRADE**   **GUTTER LINING** & **CAP FLASHING** *for* **CORNICE**

Flat Surface   *Bending of Copper*   *Upright Surface*   *Detail at B*

REGLET DETAILS FOR STONE
CUT STONE
COPPER FLASHING
Methods recommended by the Copper and Brass Research Association.

FLASHING

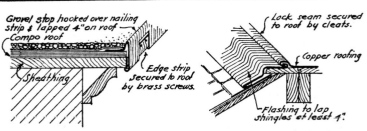

GRAVEL STOP for FLAT COMPOSITION ROOF on WOOD.

EDGE of COPPER DECK ROOF ABOVE a SLOPING SHINGLE ROOF.

EDGE of COMPOSITION DECK ROOF above a SLOPING SHINGLE ROOF.

COPPER GRAVEL STOP for FLAT COMPOSITION ROOF on CONCRETE.

ROOF EDGES (Crimped Copper recommended)

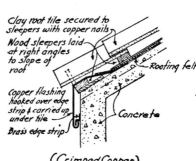
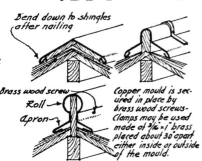
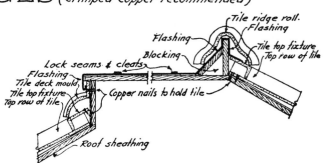

(Crimped Copper) FLASHING of EAVES for a SLOPING TILE ROOF ON CONCRETE.

THREE TYPES of HIP or RIDGE FLASHING for a SHINGLE ROOF.

TWO WAYS OF FLASHING THE EDGE of a FLAT DECK above SLOPING TILE ROOF.

RIDGES

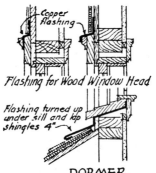
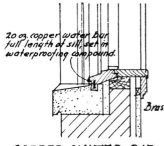
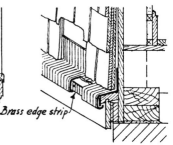
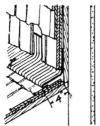
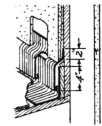

DORMER WINDOW SILL.

COPPER WATER BAR for STONE WINDOWS.

FLASHING for WOOD WATERTABLE.

SHINGLE ROOF AGAINST SHINGLE or CLAPBOARD WALL.

STUCCO WALL on WOOD ABOVE COMPO ROOF.

WINDOWS. WATERTABLES and WALLS.

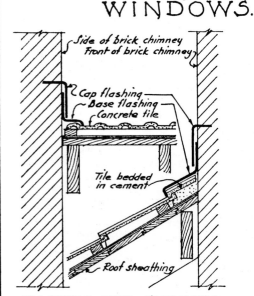
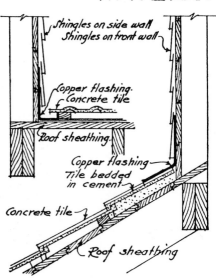
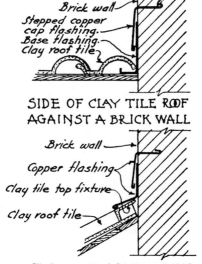

FLASHING FOR CHIMNEY THRO' CONCRETE TILE ROOF.

FLASHING FOR VERTICAL WALL OVER CONCRETE TILE ROOF.

SIDE OF CLAY TILE ROOF AGAINST A BRICK WALL

TOP OF CLAY TILE ROOF AGAINST A BRICK WALL

COPPER FLASHING for ROOF EDGES, RIDGES, EAVES & at WALLS, WINDOWS & WATERTABLES.

Methods recommended by the Copper and Brass Research Association

FLASHING

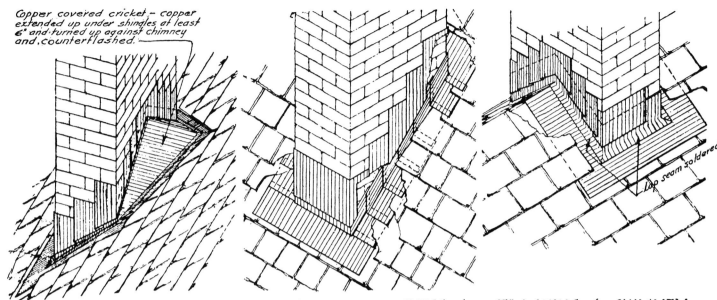

CHIMNEY·FLASHING ON SLOPE of SHINGLE ROOF.

BUILT IN BASE FLASHING for CHIMNEY on SLOPE of SHINGLE ROOF.

FLASHING for CHIMNEY on RIDGE of SHINGLE ROOF.

All cap flashing to lap base flashing 4" minimum. All cap flashing to lap itself - vertical seams - 2" minimum. Shingles to lap copper 4" minimum. In best construction chimney flashing is carried entirely through chimney, up flues to first joint, through same and up ½" inside. All joints to be soldered within chimney.

CHIMNEY FLASHING

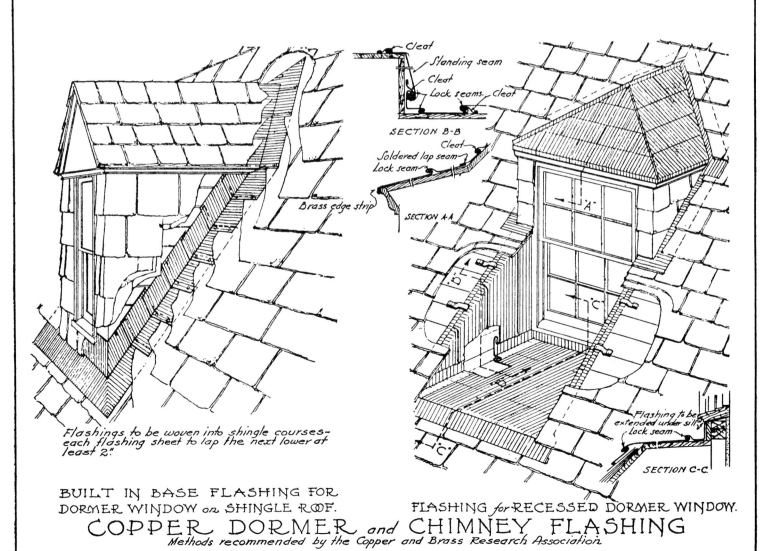

Flashings to be woven into shingle courses- each flashing sheet to lap the next lower at least 2".

BUILT IN BASE FLASHING FOR DORMER WINDOW on SHINGLE ROOF.

FLASHING for RECESSED DORMER WINDOW.

COPPER DORMER and CHIMNEY FLASHING
Methods recommended by the Copper and Brass Research Association.

FLASHING

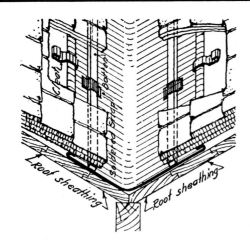

When roof slopes do not have the same pitch, or when one roof discharges more water than the other the crimp is placed in the valley to break the force of the descending water and prevent the water from one roof being forced above the top of the flashing on the opposite slope.

OPEN VALLEY FLASHING SECURED BY CLEATS.

CRIMP USED in OPEN VALLEYS

"FOLD OVER" VALLEY FLASHING

Notes
Distance from edge of shingles to bottom of Valley should be not less than 2" at narrow part with ½" in 8' increase toward gutter. Flashing to be secured by soft copper cleats 1½" wide and 3" long - each fastened to roof with two copper nails and ends turned over nail heads. Cleats spaced 8" to 10" on center and locked to sheets by ½" flat lock.

OPEN VALLEY FLASHING

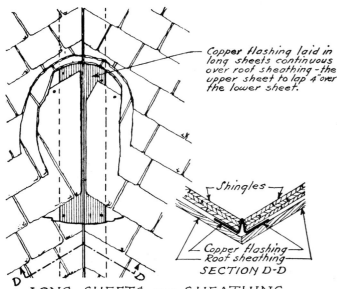

Copper flashing laid in long sheets continuous over roof sheathing - the upper sheet to lap 4" over the lower sheet.

LONG SHEETS over SHEATHING

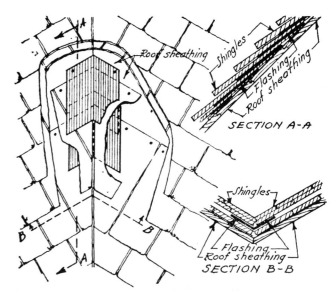

SHORT SHEETS INTERWOVEN with SHINGLES

CLOSED VALLEY FLASHING

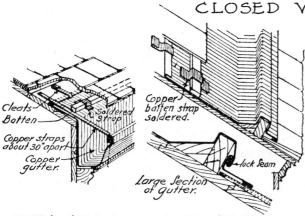

HUNG GUTTER

POLE GUTTER

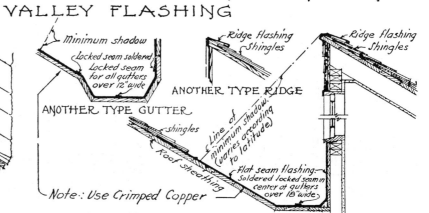

METHOD of FORMING & FLASHING GUTTER of SAW TOOTH ROOF

GUTTERS

COPPER GUTTER and VALLEY FLASHING

Methods recommended by the Copper & Brass Research Association.

FLASHING

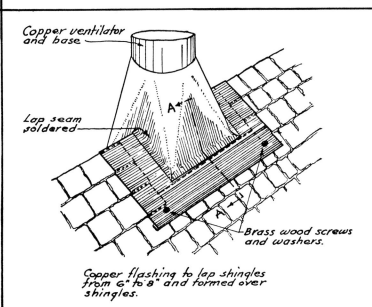

Copper ventilator and base

Lap seam soldered

Copper flashing to lap shingles from 6" to 8" and formed over shingles.

Brass wood screws and washers.

VENTILATOR ON RIDGE OF SHINGLE ROOF.

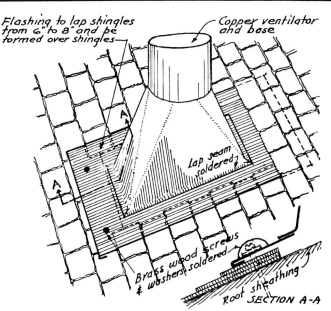

Flashing to lap shingles from 6" to 8" and be formed over shingles

Copper ventilator and base

Lap seam soldered

Brass wood screws & washers soldered

Root sheathing

SECTION A-A

VENTILATOR ON SLOPE OF SHINGLE ROOF.

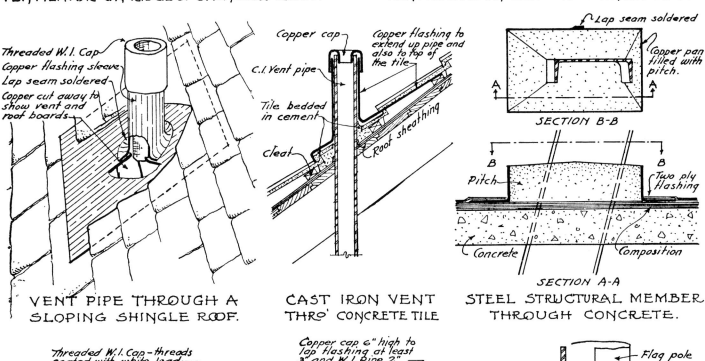

Threaded W.I. Cap
Copper flashing sleeve
Lap seam soldered
Copper cut away to show vent and roof boards

VENT PIPE THROUGH A SLOPING SHINGLE ROOF.

Copper cap
C.I. Vent pipe

Copper flashing to extend up pipe and also to top of the tile

Tile bedded in cement

Cleat

Root sheathing

CAST IRON VENT THRO' CONCRETE TILE

Lap seam soldered
Copper pan filled with pitch.

A   A

SECTION B-B

B   B

Pitch

Two ply flashing

Concrete

Composition

SECTION A-A

STEEL STRUCTURAL MEMBER THROUGH CONCRETE.

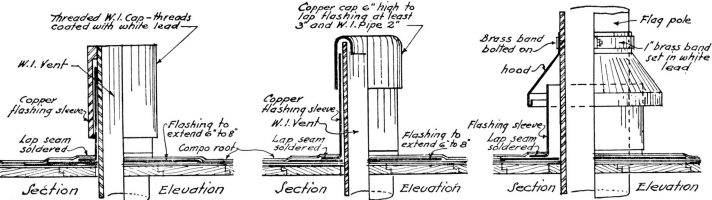

Threaded W.I. Cap—threads coated with white lead

W.I. Vent

Copper flashing sleeve

Lap seam soldered

Flashing to extend 6" to 8"

Compo roof

Section   Elevation

FLASHING FOR IRON VENT with SCREW CAP

Copper cap 6" high to lap flashing at least 3" and W.I. Pipe 2"

Copper flashing sleeve
W.I. Vent

Lap seam soldered

Flashing to extend 6" to 8"

Section   Elevation

FLASHING FOR IRON VENT with COPPER CAP

Flag pole
Brass band bolted on
hood
1" brass band set in white lead

Flashing sleeve
Lap seam soldered

Section   Elevation

FLASHING for FLAG POLE

COPPER FLASHING for ROOF VENTS, VENTILATORS, FLAG POLES ETC.
Methods recommended by the Copper and Brass Research Association.

FLASHING

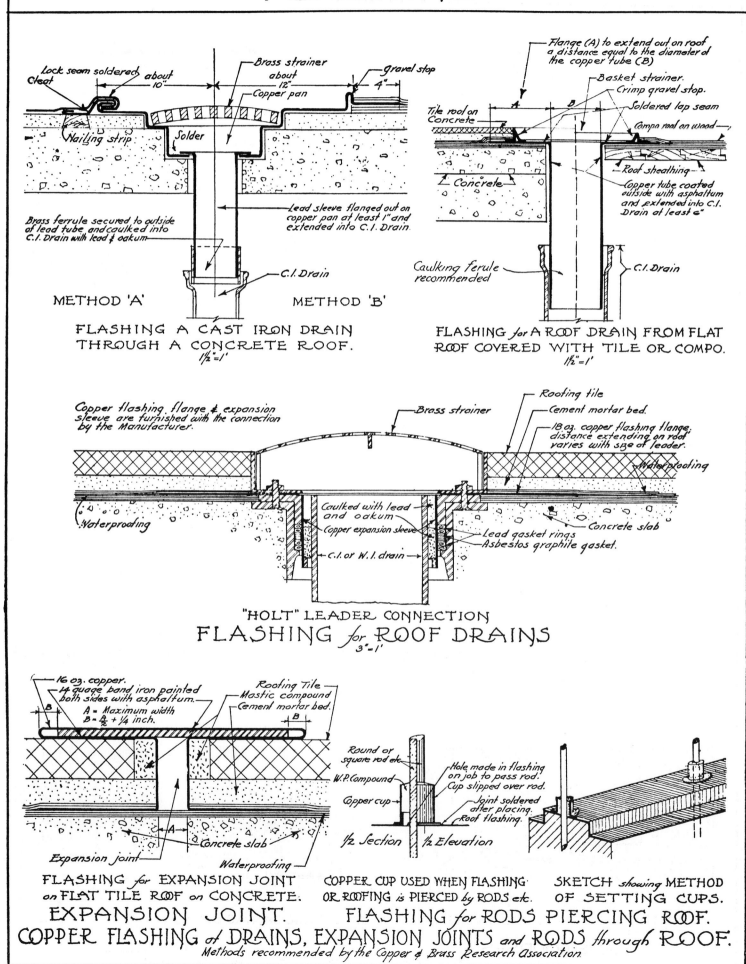

Lock seam soldered
Cleat — about 10"
Nailing strip
Brass ferrule secured to outside of lead tube and caulked into C.I. Drain with lead & oakum
Brass strainer about 12"
Copper pan
Solder
gravel stop — 4"
Lead sleeve flanged out on copper pan at least 1" and extended into C.I. Drain
C.I. Drain

METHOD 'A'   METHOD 'B'

FLASHING A CAST IRON DRAIN THROUGH A CONCRETE ROOF.
1½"=1'

Flange (A) to extend out on roof a distance equal to the diameter of the copper tube (B)
Basket strainer.
Crimp gravel stop.
Soldered lap seam
Compo. roof on wood
Tile roof on Concrete
Concrete
Root sheathing
Copper tube coated outside with asphaltum and extended into C.I. Drain at least 6"
Caulking ferule recommended
C.I. Drain

FLASHING for A ROOF DRAIN FROM FLAT ROOF COVERED WITH TILE OR COMPO.
1½"=1'

Copper flashing flange & expansion sleeve are furnished with the connection by the Manufacturer.
Waterproofing
Brass strainer
Caulked with lead and oakum
Copper expansion sleeve
C.I. or W.I. drain
Rooting tile
Cement mortar bed.
18 oz. copper flashing flange, distance extending on roof varies with size of leader.
Waterproofing
Lead gasket rings
Asbestos graphite gasket.
Concrete slab

"HOLT" LEADER CONNECTION
FLASHING for ROOF DRAINS
3"=1'

16 oz. copper.
14 gauge band iron painted both sides with asphaltum.
A = Maximum width
B = A/2 + ¼ inch.
Rooting Tile
Mastic compound
Cement mortar bed
Concrete slab
Expansion joint
Waterproofing

FLASHING for EXPANSION JOINT on FLAT TILE ROOF on CONCRETE.
EXPANSION JOINT.

Round or square rod etc.
W.P. Compound
Copper cup
Hole made in flashing on job to pass rod. Cup slipped over rod.
Joint soldered after placing.
Roof flashing.
½ Section   ½ Elevation

COPPER CUP USED WHEN FLASHING OR ROOFING is PIERCED by RODS etc.
FLASHING for RODS PIERCING ROOF.

SKETCH showing METHOD OF SETTING CUPS.

COPPER FLASHING of DRAINS, EXPANSION JOINTS and RODS through ROOF.
Methods recommended by the Copper & Brass Research Association.

FLASHING

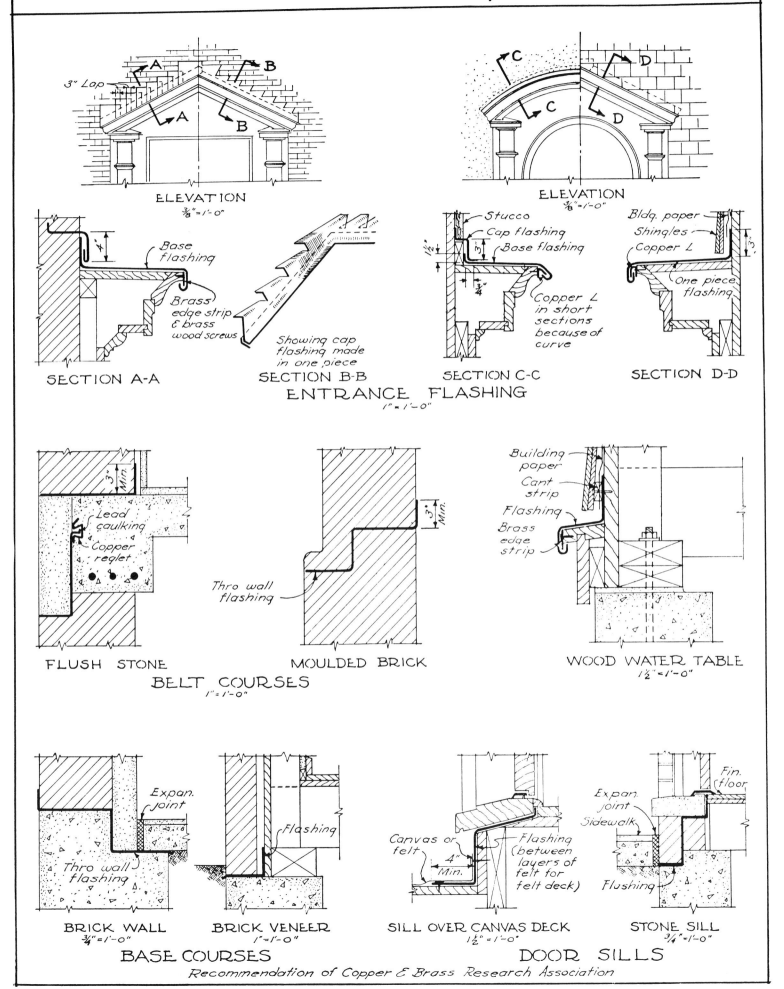

145

ELEVATION
3/8" = 1'-0"

ELEVATION
3/8" = 1'-0"

3" Lap

Base flashing

Brass edge strip & brass wood screws

Showing cap flashing made in one piece

SECTION A-A

SECTION B-B

Stucco
Cap flashing
Base flashing

Copper L in short sections because of curve

SECTION C-C

Bldg. paper
Shingles
Copper L

One piece flashing

SECTION D-D

ENTRANCE FLASHING
1" = 1'-0"

Lead caulking
Copper reglet

FLUSH STONE

Thro wall flashing

MOULDED BRICK

BELT COURSES
1" = 1'-0"

Building paper
Cant strip
Flashing
Brass edge strip

WOOD WATER TABLE
1½" = 1'-0"

Expan. joint

Thro wall flashing

BRICK WALL
3/4" = 1'-0"

Flashing

BRICK VENEER
1" = 1'-0"

BASE COURSES

Canvas or felt

Flashing (between layers of felt for felt deck)

4" Min.

SILL OVER CANVAS DECK
1½" = 1'-0"

Expan. joint
Sidewalk
Fin. floor
Flashing

STONE SILL
3/4" = 1'-0"

DOOR SILLS

Recommendation of Copper & Brass Research Association

FLASHING

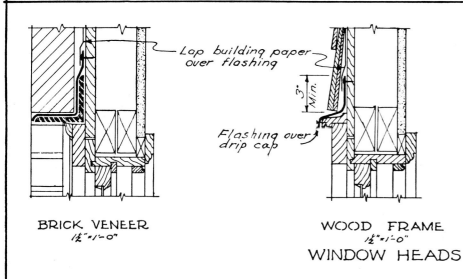
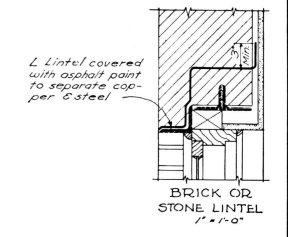

Lap building paper over flashing

3" Min.

Flashing over drip cap

L Lintel covered with asphalt paint to separate copper & steel

3" Min.

BRICK VENEER
1½"=1'-0"

WOOD FRAME
1½"=1'-0"

WINDOW HEADS

BRICK OR STONE LINTEL
1"=1'-0"

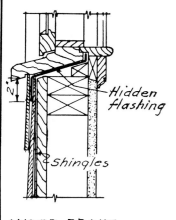
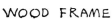
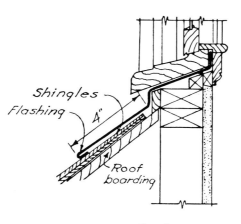
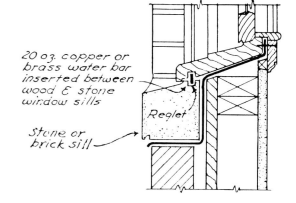

2"

Hidden Flashing

Shingles

Shingles
Flashing
4"

Roof boarding

20 oz. copper or brass water bar inserted between wood & stone window sills

Reglet

Stone or brick sill

WOOD FRAME

DORMER WINDOW SILLS
1½"=1'-0"

BRICK VENEER

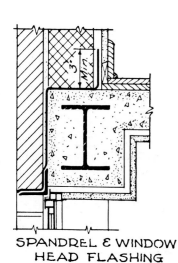
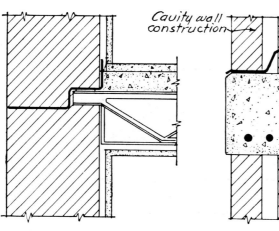
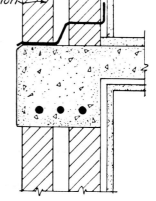
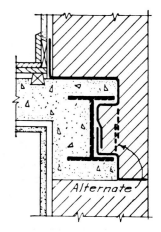

3" Min.

Cavity wall construction

Alternate

SPANDREL & WINDOW HEAD FLASHING

OPEN WEB JOIST

SPANDREL BEAM

OPEN WEB SPANDREL

SPANDRELS
1"=1'-0"

Recommendation of Copper & Brass Research Association.

FLASHING

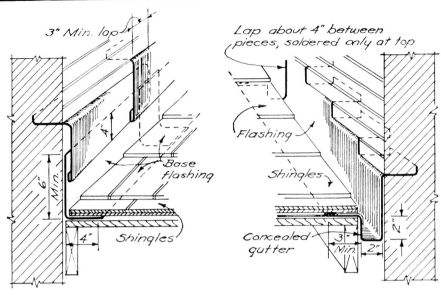
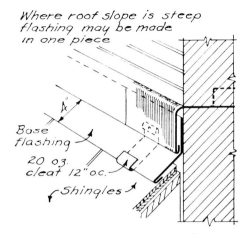

STEPPED FLASHING   STEPPED ONE PIECE FLASHING   TOP OF ROOF FLASHING

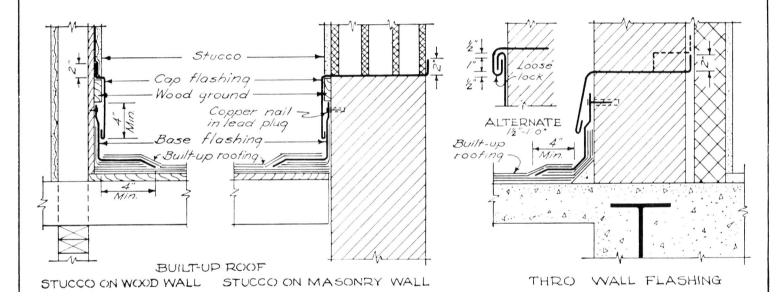

STUCCO ON WOOD WALL   STUCCO ON MASONRY WALL   THRO WALL FLASHING

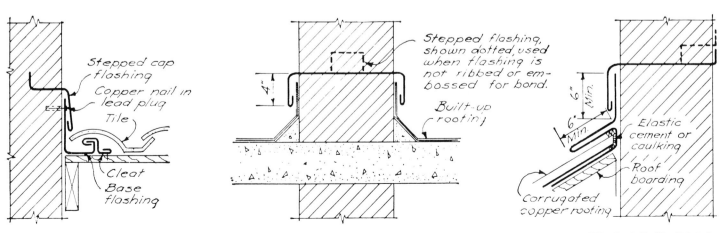

TILE ROOF   FIREWALL FLASHING   CORRUGATED COPPER ROOF

FLASHING AT JUNCTURES OF ROOFS & WALLS

1" = 1'-0"

Recommendation of Copper & Brass Research Association

FLASHING

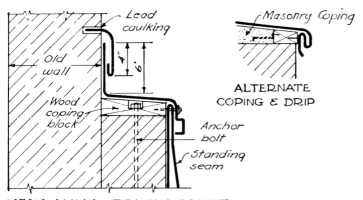

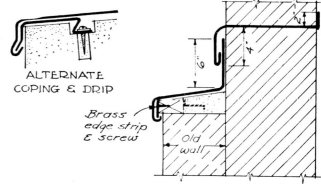

NEW WALL BELOW EXISTING WALL

NEW WALL ABOVE EXISTING WALL

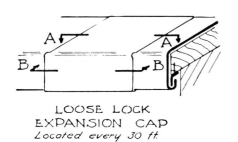

**LOOSE LOCK
EXPANSION CAP**
Located every 30 ft.

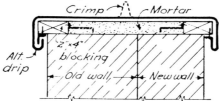

Copper sheet with flat locked seams soldered. If width exceeds 24" crimp or standing seam is provided for movement.

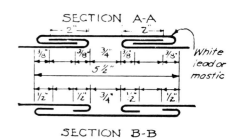

SECTION A-A

SECTION B-B

NEW WALL LEVEL WITH EXISTING WALL

FLASHING BETWEEN OLD & NEW WALLS
1" = 1'-0"

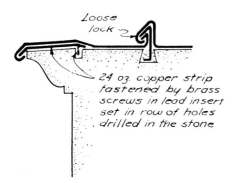

24 oz. copper strip fastened by brass screws in lead insert set in row of holes drilled in the stone

Large sheets are not caulked directly into reglets as movement from temperature changes will tear them. Use auxiliary strips set in reglets.

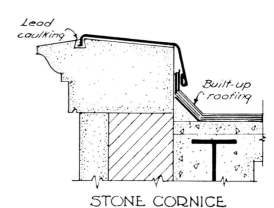

STONE CORNICE
1" = 1'-0"

STONE CORNICE
1" = 1'-0"

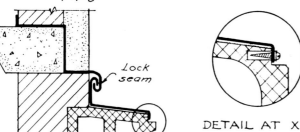

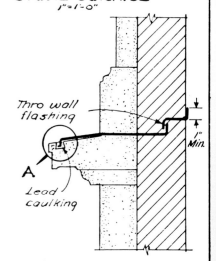

TERRA COTTA CORNICE
3/4" = 1'-0"

DETAIL AT X

**ALTERNATE
DRIP A**

STONE CORNICE
3/4" = 1'-0"

CORNICE FLASHING
Recommendation of Copper & Brass Research Association.

FLASHING

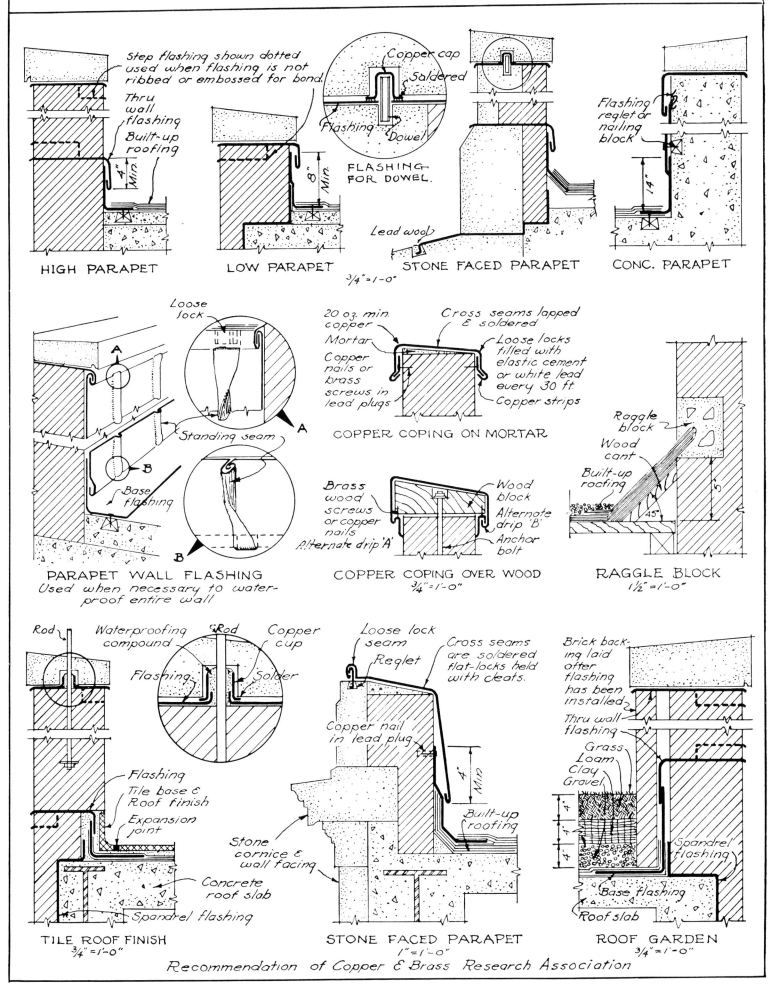

Step flashing shown dotted used when flashing is not ribbed or embossed for bond.
Thru wall flashing
Built-up roofing
4" Min

HIGH PARAPET

8" Min

LOW PARAPET

Copper cap
Soldered
Flashing
Dowel
FLASHING FOR DOWEL.

Lead wool
STONE FACED PARAPET
3/4"=1'-0"

Flashing reglet or nailing block
14"
CONC. PARAPET

Loose lock
Standing seam
Base flashing
PARAPET WALL FLASHING
Used when necessary to water-proof entire wall

20 oz. min. copper
Mortar
Copper nails or brass screws in lead plugs
Cross seams lapped & soldered
Loose locks filled with elastic cement or white lead every 30 ft.
Copper strips
COPPER COPING ON MORTAR

Brass wood screws or copper nails
Alternate drip 'A'
Wood block
Alternate drip 'B'
Anchor bolt
COPPER COPING OVER WOOD
3/4"=1'-0"

Raggle block
Wood cant
Built-up roofing
45°
5
RAGGLE BLOCK
1½"=1'-0"

Rod
Waterproofing compound
Flashing
Flashing
Tile base & Roof finish
Expansion joint
Concrete roof slab
Spandrel flashing
Rod
Copper cup
Solder
TILE ROOF FINISH
3/4"=1'-0"

Loose lock seam
Reglet
Cross seams are soldered flat-locks held with cleats.
Copper nail in lead plug
4" Min
Built-up roofing
Stone cornice & wall facing
STONE FACED PARAPET
1"=1'-0"

Brick backing laid after flashing has been installed
Thru wall flashing
Grass Loam Clay Gravel
4" 4" 4"
Spandrel flashing
Base flashing
Roof slab
ROOF GARDEN
3/4"=1'-0"

Recommendation of Copper & Brass Research Association

FLASHING

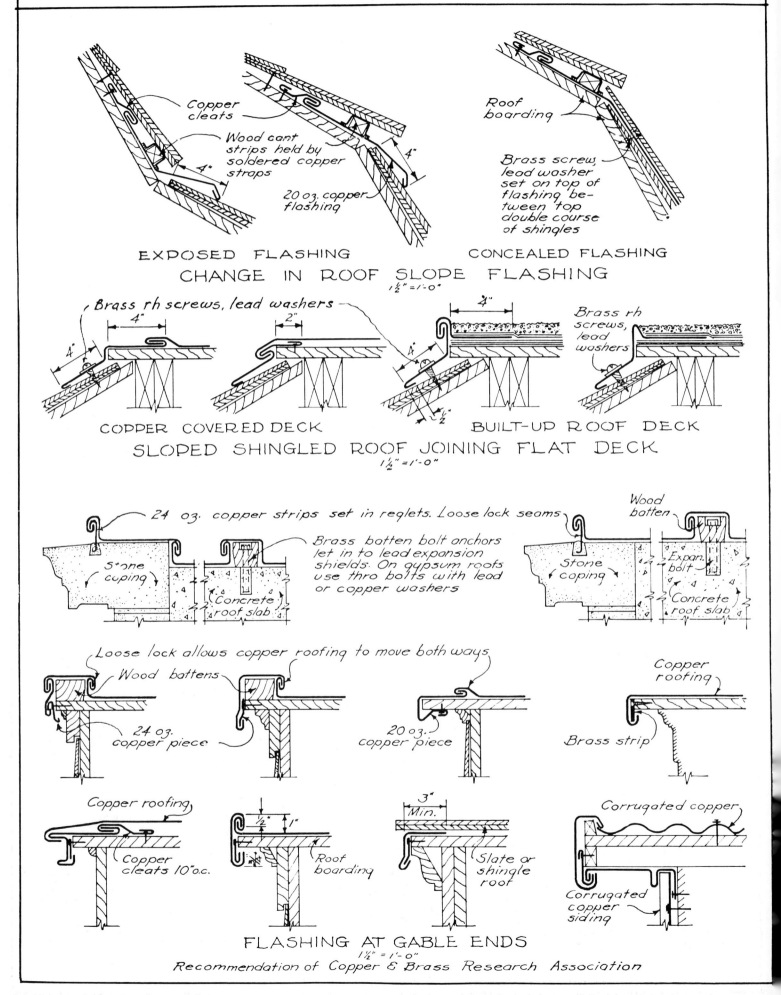

Copper cleats

Wood cant strips held by soldered copper straps

4"

20 oz. copper flashing

4"

Roof boarding

Brass screw, lead washer set on top of flashing between top double course of shingles

EXPOSED FLASHING   CONCEALED FLASHING

CHANGE IN ROOF SLOPE FLASHING
$1\frac{1}{2}" = 1'-0"$

Brass rh screws, lead washers

4"

4"

2"

4"

A

Brass rh screws, lead washers

COPPER COVERED DECK   BUILT-UP ROOF DECK

SLOPED SHINGLED ROOF JOINING FLAT DECK
$1\frac{1}{2}" = 1'-0"$

24 oz. copper strips set in reglets. Loose lock seams

Brass batten bolt anchors let in to lead expansion shields. On gypsum roofs use thro bolts with lead or copper washers

Stone coping

Concrete roof slab

Wood batten

Stone coping

Expan. bolt

Concrete roof slab

Loose lock allows copper roofing to move both ways

Wood battens

24 oz. copper piece

20 oz. copper piece

Copper roofing

Brass strip

Copper roofing

Copper cleats 10" o.c.

$\frac{1}{2}"$ 1"

Roof boarding

3" Min.

Slate or shingle roof

Corrugated copper

Corrugated copper siding

FLASHING AT GABLE ENDS
$1\frac{1}{2}" = 1'-0"$

Recommendation of Copper & Brass Research Association

FLASHING

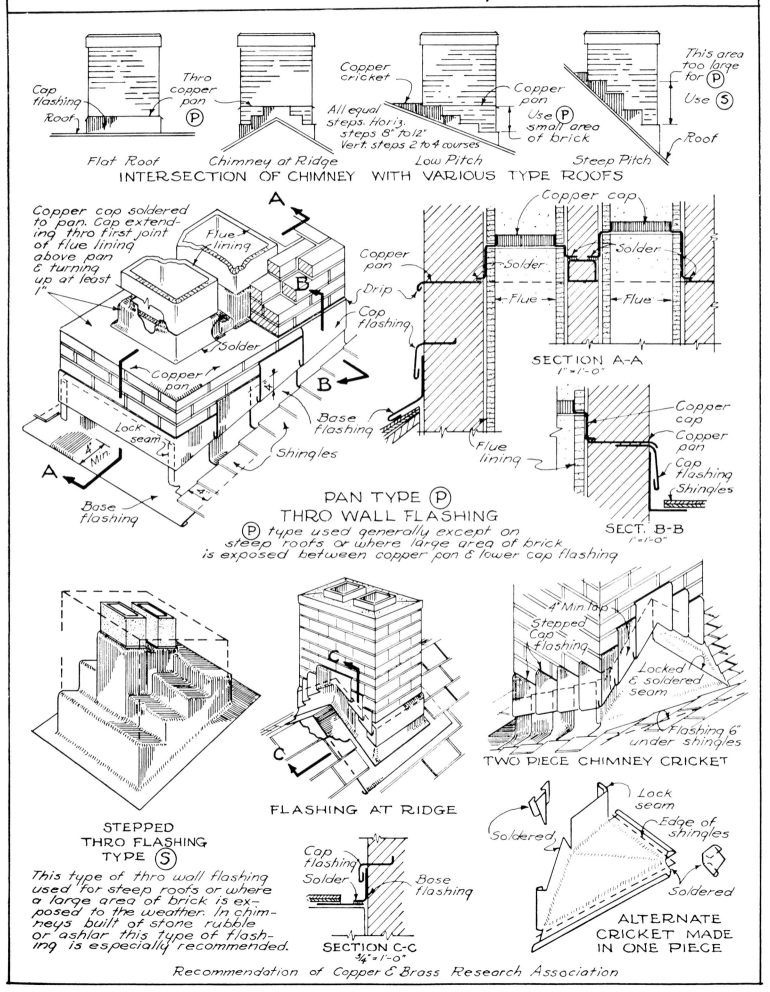

INTERSECTION OF CHIMNEY WITH VARIOUS TYPE ROOFS

Flat Roof — Cap flashing, Roof, Thro copper pan (P)

Chimney at Ridge — Copper cricket, All equal steps. Horiz. steps 8" to 12" Vert. steps 2 to 4 courses

Low Pitch — Copper pan (P), Use small area of brick

Steep Pitch — This area too large for (P) Use (S), Roof

Copper cap soldered to pan. Cap extending thro first joint of flue lining above pan & turning up at least 1"

Flue lining, Copper pan, Drip, Cap flashing, Solder, Copper pan, Base flashing, Shingles, Lock seam, 4" Min., Base flashing

PAN TYPE (P) THRO WALL FLASHING

(P) type used generally except on steep roofs or where large area of brick is exposed between copper pan & lower cap flashing

SECTION A-A
1" = 1'-0"

Copper cap, Solder, Flue, Flue

SECT. B-B
1" = 1'-0"

Copper cap, Copper pan, Cap flashing, Shingles, Flue lining

STEPPED THRO FLASHING TYPE (S)

This type of thro wall flashing used for steep roofs or where a large area of brick is exposed to the weather. In chimneys built of stone rubble or ashlar this type of flashing is especially recommended.

FLASHING AT RIDGE

SECTION C-C
3/4" = 1'-0"

Cap flashing, Solder, Base flashing

TWO PIECE CHIMNEY CRICKET

4" Min. lap, Stepped Cap flashing, Locked & soldered seam, Flashing 6" under shingles

ALTERNATE CRICKET MADE IN ONE PIECE

Soldered, Lock seam, Edge of shingles, Soldered

Recommendation of Copper & Brass Research Association

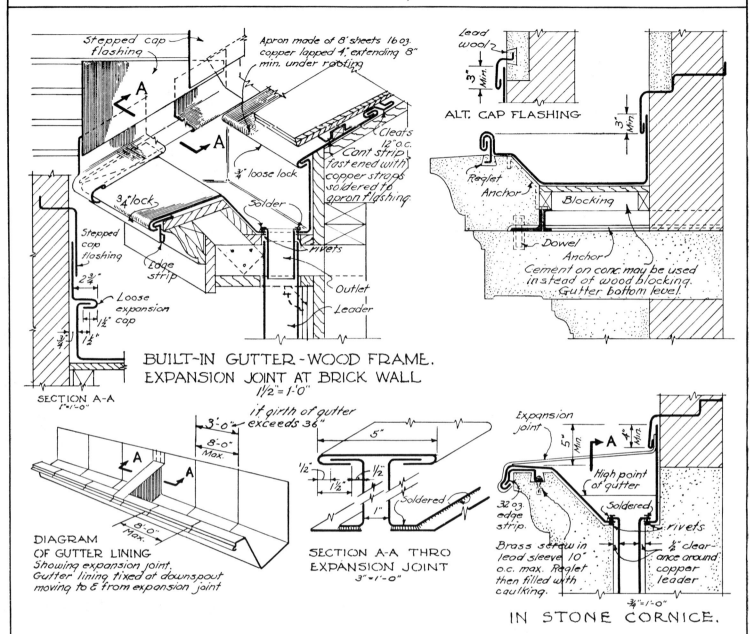

BUILT-IN GUTTERS

Stepped cap flashing

Apron made of 8' sheets 16 oz. copper lapped 4", extending 8" min. under roofing

Cleats 12" o.c.

Cont. strip fastened with copper straps soldered to apron flashing.

3/4" loose lock

3/4" lock

Solder

Stepped cap flashing

2 3/4"

Edge strip

rivets

Outlet

Leader

Loose expansion cap

1 1/2"

3/4" 1 1/2"

BUILT-IN GUTTER - WOOD FRAME.
EXPANSION JOINT AT BRICK WALL
1 1/2" = 1'-0"

SECTION A-A
1" = 1'-0"

Lead wool

3" Min.

ALT. CAP FLASHING

3" Min.

Reglet Anchor

Blocking

Dowel

Anchor

Cement on conc. may be used instead of wood blocking. Gutter bottom level.

DIAGRAM OF GUTTER LINING
Showing expansion joint. Gutter lining fixed at downspout moving to & from expansion joint

if girth of gutter exceeds 36"

3'-0"

8'-0" Max.

8'-0" Max.

5"

1/2" 1/2"

1 1/2"

1"

Soldered

SECTION A-A THRO EXPANSION JOINT
3" = 1'-0"

Expansion joint

5" Min.

4" Min.

High point of gutter

32 oz. edge strip

Soldered

Brass screw in lead sleeve 10' o.c. max. Reglet then filled with caulking.

1/2" clearance around copper leader

rivets

IN STONE CORNICE.
3/4" = 1'-0"

*DETERMINATION OF GAUGE and EXPANSION JOINT LOCATION for COPPER GUTTER LININGS

min angle 45° Max angle Width of Gutter Bottom

Exp Joint — Downspout — Exp Joint — Max Safe Distance see table — Max Safe Distance see table

Wall or fixed end — Downspout — Exp Joint — Max Safe Distance see table

Weight of Cold Rolled Copper in Ounces	Width of Gutter Bottom	Max. distance between Exp. Joint & Downspout, in ft. Angle of Gutter Sides					Weight of Cold Rolled Copper in Ounces	Width of Gutter Bottom	Max. distance between Exp. Joint & Downspout, in ft. Angle of Gutter Sides				
		90°/45°	90°/60°	90°/90°	60°/60°	45°/45°			90°/45°	90°/60°	90°/90°	60°/60°	45°/45°
16	6	18'-6"	19'-6"	21'-6"	17'-6"	15'-0"	20	6	24'-0"	26'-0"	29'-0"	23'-0"	20'-0"
	8	16'-0"	17'-6"	19'-0"	15'-0"	13'-0"		8	20'-6"	22'-0"	24'-6"	19'-6"	17'-0"
	10	14'-0"	15'-0"	16'-6"	13'-0"	11'-0"		10	18'-0"	19'-6"	21'-6"	17'-0"	15'-0"
24	8	26'-0"	28'-0"	31'-0"	25'-0"	22'-0"	32	10	40'-6"	43'-6"	47'-6"	39'-0"	34'-6"
	10	23'-0"	25'-0"	27'-0"	22'-0"	19'-6"		12	37'-6"	39'-6"	43'-0"	35'-6"	31'-6"
	12	21'-0"	22'-6"	24'-6"	20'-0"	17'-6"		14	34'-6"	36'-6"	40'-0"	32'-6"	29'-0"

Gutter linings must be unrestrained, except at downspouts. Built-in gutters are lined with cold rolled Copper. Sheets of 16 & 20 oz. are joined by 3/4" wide locked & soldered seams. Sheets of 24 & 32 oz. are joined by 1 1/2" wide lapped, riveted & soldered seams. Rivets are copper 3/16" dia. with burrs under peened heads. Rivets spaced 3" o.c., two rows staggered.

BUILT-IN GUTTERS
Recommendation of Copper & Brass Research Association
*Data recommendation of Revere Copper & Brass Incorporated

GUTTERS & LEADERS

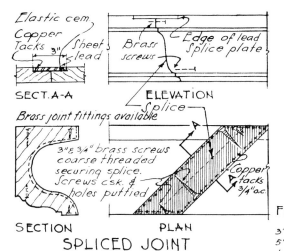

SECT. A-A

ELEVATION
Splice

Brass joint fittings available

3"& 3/4" brass screws
coarse threaded
securing splice.
Screws csk. &
holes puttied

SECTION

PLAN

SPLICED JOINT
1 1/2" = 1'-0"

REDWOOD GUTTERS
Sizes
3" x 4"
4" x 4"
4" x 6"

GUTTERS
Sizes
3" x 4"
4" x 4"

FIR GUTTER
Sizes
3"x5", 4"x5", 4"x6",
5"x7", 6"x8".
Length up to 40'

FIR LEADER
Sizes
2 1/4" x 3 1/8 inside
with 5/8" walls &
3"x 4" inside with 3/4"
walls. Lengths: 6' to 20'

open between
blocking

1/4" x 1 1/4" block-
ing 24" o.c. vertically
3" brass
screws

TYPICAL GUTTER CONNECTION
1 1/2" = 1'-0"

WOOD GUTTERS & LEADERS
Long Fir Gutter Co.

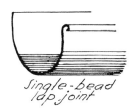
Single-bead lap joint

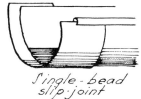
Single-bead slip joint

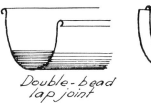
Double-bead lap joint

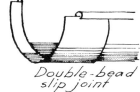
Double-bead slip joint

HALF ROUND GUTTERS
Copper: All above types in 4" to 10" diam.
Stainless Steel: Single bead in 4" to 10" diam.
Aluminum: Single bead lap joint in 5" diam.
Galv. Iron: All above types in 3 1/2" to 8" diam.
Lengths 10'. Double bead is stiffer
than single bead and permits wider
hanger spacing. But is more difficult to
line inside bead against roof. With con-
siderable slope lengths may be lapped
3" and left unsoldered.

SLIP JOINT CONNECTION
Set 30' apart to pro-
vide for expansion &
contraction in long runs
of lap gutters.
Joints between are lap-
ped & soldered. Slip
joint not soldered.

GUTTER DESIGN for SMALL RESIDENTIAL WORK
Avoid gutters under 4" wide.
Min. slope 1/16" per ft. required.
Min. depth equal to 1/2 & max.
depth not over 3/4 of width.
If leader spacing is less than
20' use a gutter same size
as leader. If leader spacing
is over 20' add 1" to leader dia.
for every add'l 30' on peak roofs,
1" for every add'l 40' on flat.

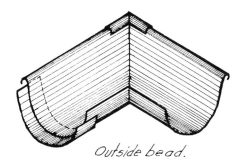
Outside bead.

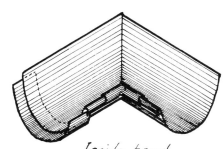
Inside bead.

GUTTER MITRES-SINGLE BEAD
Available without slip joint connection & in double bead or box gutter
type

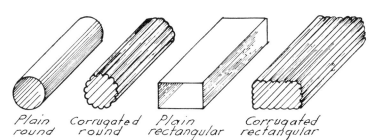
Plain round / Corrugated round / Plain rectangular / Corrugated rectangular

METAL LEADERS (downspouts)
Copper: See Leader Dimension Table on other page
Galvanized Iron: Same sizes as Copper.
Stainless Steel: 2" to 6" round & 2" to 5" rect. plain & corrug.
Aluminum: 3" round & 2 3/8" x 3 1/4" rect. plain & corrug.
Lengths 10'. General rule: 1 sq. in. of leader to 100 sq. ft.
of roof area drained. Corrugated resists bursting
from freezing best.

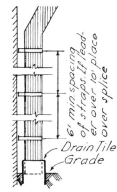
6' min. spacing of straps. If lead-
er over 10' place over splice
Drain Tile Grade

LEADER WITH TILE SHOE

WEIGHTS of SHEET METAL
Metal	for Leader	for Gutter
Aluminum	23 ga.	25 ga.
Zinc	11-13 ga.	12-13 ga.
Galv. Iron	24-26 ga.	24-26 ga.
Tin on Steel	1 x	1 x
Lead, hard	4-8 lbs.	4-8 lbs.
Stain. Steel	28 ga.	28 ga.
Copper	16 oz.	16 oz.
Monel	26 ga.	25-26 ga.

The above metals are ar-
ranged in order of galvanic
activity.
Do not place metal far apart on this table in contact with each other.

GUTTER & LEADER ACCESSORIES

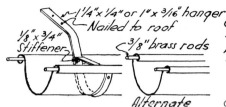

FIXED STRAP HANGER OF BRASS – SPECIAL
(For the best class of residence) Space hangers 3'-0"o.c. for 1"x3/16" hanger and 3'-6" o.c. for 1¼"x¼" hanger.

- 1¼"x¼" or 1"x3/16" hanger
- Nailed to roof
- 1/8"x3/4" Stiffener
- 3/8" brass rods
- Alternate

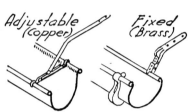

STOCK STRAP HANGERS COPPER & BRASS
Spaced not over 2'-6" o.c. Blocking between bldg. & gutter essential to provide for overflow.

Adjustable (copper)   Fixed (Brass)

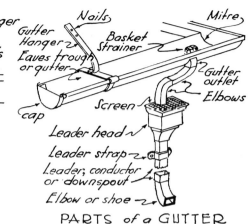

PARTS of a GUTTER

- Nails
- Mitre
- Gutter Hanger
- Basket Strainer
- Eaves trough or gutter
- Screen
- cap
- Gutter outlet
- Elbows
- Leader head
- Leader strap
- Leader, conductor or downspout
- Elbow or shoe

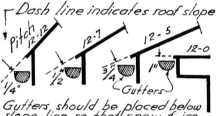

Dash line indicates roof slope
Pitch 12-12   12-7   12-5   12-0
1/4   1/2   3/4   1"
Gutters

PLACING of GUTTERS
Gutters should be placed below slope line so that snow & ice can slide clear. Steeper pitch requires less clearance.

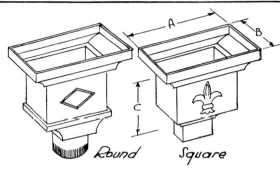

Round   Square

STOCK LEADER HEADS

SIZE	OUTLET Square	OUTLET Round	A	B	C
Small	2"x3"	3"	9"	5½"	7½"
	3"x4"	4"	10"	6"	7½"
Large	2"x3"	3"	10"	6"	9"
	3"x4"	4"	11"	6½"	9"

Wired

BRONZE LEADER STRAPS
Set 6'-0" apart min.

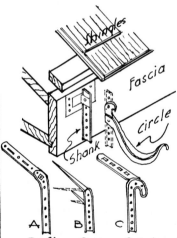

- Shingles
- Fascia
- circle
- Shank
- A B C

Rafter Spike Subshingle
BRONZE HANGERS
A Nailed to side of rafter
B Spiked into rafter or fascia
C Adjustable, nailed under shingles. Others available

Copper Wire   Cast Bronze
BASKET STRAINERS
Copper wire type also made in square form to fit standard gutter outlets. Cast Bronze made 3,4,5,6, 7,8, in. round. 2"x3"; 3"x4" sq.

COPPER ELBOWS and SHOES

① 45°   ② 60°   ③ 75°   ④ 90°
Side Views

			Dia. or Size			
Elbows	Round	Plain & corrugated #1,2,3,4	2"	3"	5"	6"
	Square	" " "	2"	3"	5"	
Shoes	Round	" " #3	2"	3"	5"	6"
	Square	Corrugated only #3	2"	3"	5"	

CAST IRON DOWNSPOUT SHOES

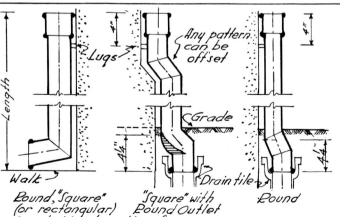

- Length
- 2 Lugs
- Any pattern can be offset
- Grade
- Drain tile
- Walk

Round, "Square" (or rectangular)   "Square" with Round Outlet   Round

Available lengths from 12" to 72" in increments of 6 inches; Plain, fluted or panel designs.

SQUARE & RECTANGULAR								ROUND			
Spout size	2½x2"	2"x3"	3"x3"	3"x4"	4"x4"	4"x5"	4"x6"	Spout dia.	3"	4"	5"
Outlet dia.	3"	3"	4"	4"	4"	4"	5"	Outlet dia.	3"	4"	5"

Contractor's Foundry, Inc.
Data by Coppers Brass Research Association

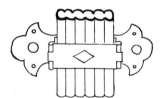

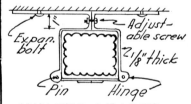

- Expan. bolt
- Adjustable screw
- 2 1/8" thick
- Pin   Hinge

HINGED LEADER STRAP – BRONZE.
Loose pin in left side permits removal of leader without taking strap off wall. Also made for round leaders.

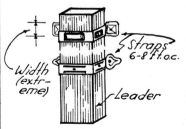

- Straps 6-8 ft. o.c.
- Width (extreme)
- Leader

COPPER LEADER STRAPS
Variety of ornamentation available. Lengths 13" to 20". Widths 1½"-4 3/8"

LEADER & GUTTER ~ SIZE REQUIREMENTS

WIDTHS of RECTANGULAR GUTTERS *(For level gutters. If slope exceeds 2%, gutter is narrowed & deepened.)*

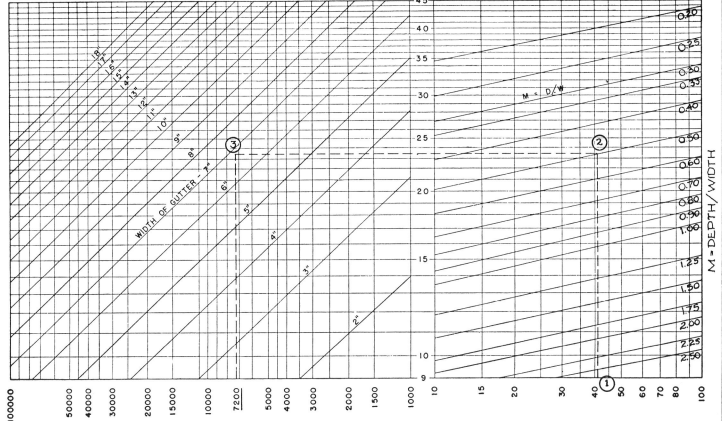

IA = RAINFALL INTENSITY × AREA   L = LENGTH OF GUTTER IN FEET

EXAMPLE: To design rectangular gutter in Atlanta. Roof 20'×40'. Gutter assumed width is ½ depth (M = 0.5). From Rainfall Table Intensity I = 9"/hr. Area drained A = 800 sq.ft. IA = 7200. Start at ① on Rect. Gutter Graph using L = 40' for Gutter length & follow vertically to intersection ② with oblique line M=0.5. Follow horiz. to intersection ③ with vert. line IA=7200. Point of intersection occurs between gutter widths of 6" & 7". Required width is 7" & depth is 3½".

EXAMPLE: To design semi-circular gutter in Buffalo. Roof Area = 800 sq.ft. From Rainfall table Intensity =10"/hr. Using Semi-Circ. Gutter graph find intersection of 800 sq.ft. & 10"/hr. to be 8" which is required gutter width.

EXAMPLE: To design leader in Knoxville. Roof Area drained per leader = 3000 sq. in. From Rainfall Table 1 sq. in. of leader serves 200 sq. ft. of roof area. Therefore 15 sq. in. is required. From Leader Dimensions Table select either 5" round, octagonal or square or 4"×5" rectangular. (NOTE: Gutter design is for large Buildings.)

RAINFALL DATA & DRAINAGE FACTORS

CITIES	MAXIMUM RECORD STORMS Intensity in In./Hr. lasting for 5 minutes	Sq.ft. of roof drained per sq. in. of leader area.	CITIES	MAXIMUM RECORD STORMS Intensity in In./Hr. lasting for 5 minutes	Sq. ft. of roof drained per sq. in. of leader area.
NOTE: Roof drainage data based on assumption that for intensity of 8"/Hr. 1 sq.in. of leader drains 150 sq.ft.					
Albany, N.Y.	7	175	New Orleans, La.	8	150
Atlanta, Ga.	9	130	New York, N.Y.	9	130
Boston, Mass.	7	175	Norfolk, Va.	8	150
Buffalo, N.Y.	10	120	Philadelphia, Pa.	8	150
Chicago, Ill.	7	175	Pittsburg, Pa.	7	175
Detroit, Mich.	7	175	St. Louis, Mo.	11	110
Duluth, Minn.	7	175	St. Paul, Minn.	8	150
Kansas City, Mo.	10	120	San Francisco, Cal.	3	400
Knoxville, Tenn.	6	200	Savannah, Ga.	8	150
Louisville, Ky.	8	150	Seattle, Wash.	2	600
Memphis, Tenn.	10	120	Washington, D.C.	8	150
Montgomery, Ala.	7	175			

DIMENSIONS of LEADERS

TYPE	AREA sq.in	NOM. SIZE
Plain Round	7.07	3"
	12.57	4"
	19.63	5"
	28.27	6"
Corrugated Round	5.94	3"
	11.04	4"
	17.72	5"
	25.97	6"
Polygon Octagonal	6.36	3"
	11.30	4"
	17.65	5"
	25.40	6"
Square Corrugated	3.80	2"
	7.73	3"
	11.70	4"
	18.75	5"
Plain Rectangular	3.94	1¾"×2¼"
	6.00	2"×3"
	8.00	2"×4"
	12.00	3"×4"
	20.00	4"×5"
	24.00	4"×6"

WIDTHS of SEMI-CIRC. GUTTERS

RAINFALL INTENSITY IN./HR.

Recommendation of Copper & Brass Research Assn.

STOCK METAL GUTTERS

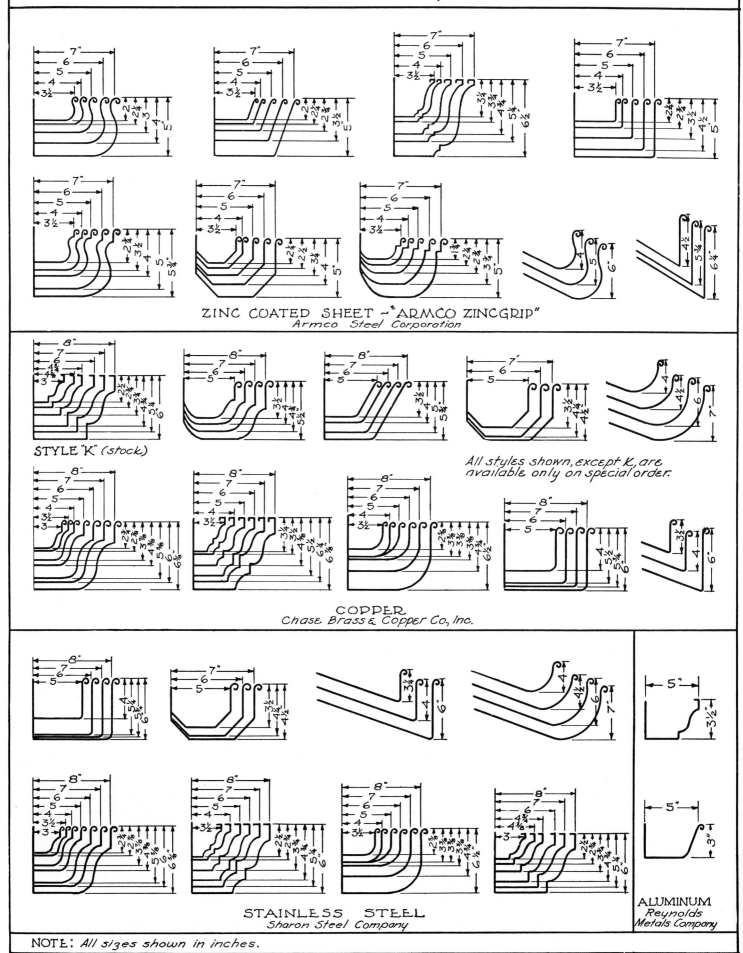

ZINC COATED SHEET ~ "ARMCO ZINCGRIP"
Armco Steel Corporation

STYLE "K" (stock)

All styles shown, except K, are
available only on special order.

COPPER
Chase Brass & Copper Co., Inc.

STAINLESS STEEL
Sharon Steel Company

ALUMINUM
Reynolds
Metals Company

NOTE: All sizes shown in inches.

EAVES and OVERHANGS

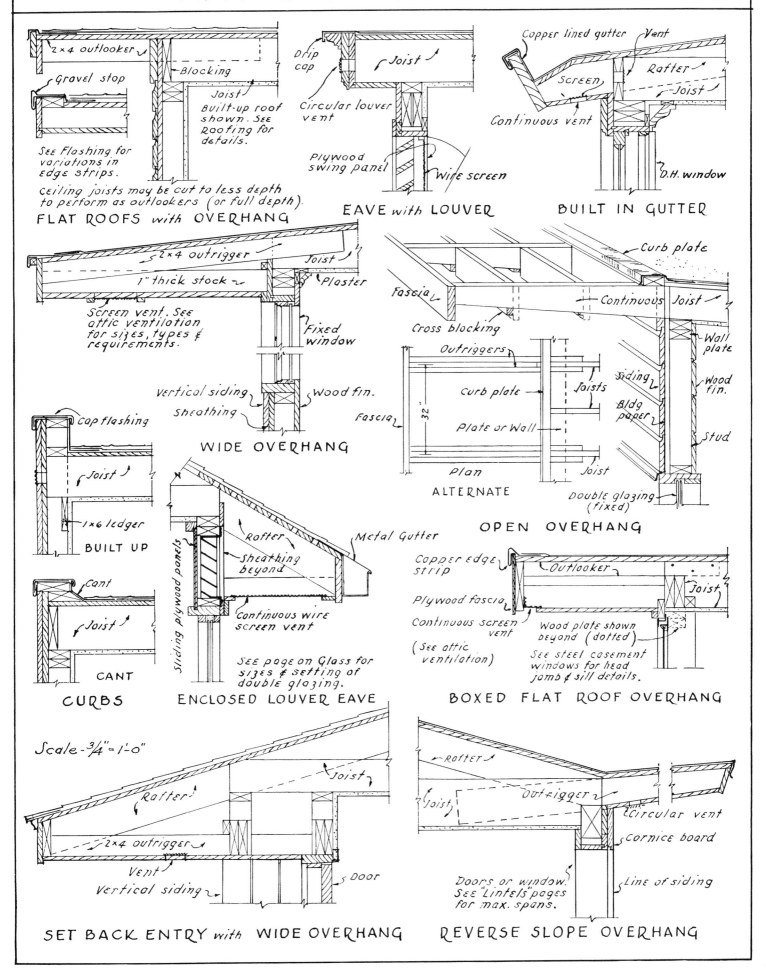

FLAT ROOFS with OVERHANG

2×4 outlooker
Gravel stop
Blocking
Joist
Built-up roof shown. See Roofing for details.
See Flashing for variations in edge strips.
Ceiling joists may be cut to less depth to perform as outlookers (or full depth).

EAVE with LOUVER

Drip cap
Joist
Circular louver vent
Plywood swing panel
Wire screen

BUILT IN GUTTER

Copper lined gutter
Vent
Rafter
Screen
Joist
Continuous vent
D.H. window

WIDE OVERHANG

2×4 outrigger
Joist
1" thick stock
Plaster
Screen vent. See attic ventilation for sizes, types & requirements.
Fixed window
Vertical siding
Sheathing
Wood fin.

ALTERNATE

Outriggers
Curb plate
Fascia
Plate or Wall
32"
Plan
Joist

OPEN OVERHANG

Curb plate
Fascia
Continuous Joist
Cross blocking
Wall plate
siding
Bldg paper
Wood fin.
Stud
Double glazing (fixed)

CURBS
BUILT UP
Cap flashing
Joist
1×6 ledger
CANT
Cant
Joist

ENCLOSED LOUVER EAVE

Rafter
Sheathing beyond
Metal Gutter
Sliding plywood panels
Continuous wire screen vent
See page on Glass for sizes & setting of double glazing.

BOXED FLAT ROOF OVERHANG

Copper edge strip
Outlooker
Joist
Plywood fascia
Continuous screen vent
(See attic ventilation)
Wood plate shown beyond (dotted)
See steel casement windows for head jamb & sill details.

SET BACK ENTRY with WIDE OVERHANG

Scale-¾"=1'-0"
Rafter
Joist
2×4 outrigger
Vent
Vertical siding
Door

REVERSE SLOPE OVERHANG

Rafter
Joist
Outrigger
Circular vent
Cornice board
Doors or window. See "Lintels" pages for max. spans.
Line of siding

EAVES and WATERTABLES

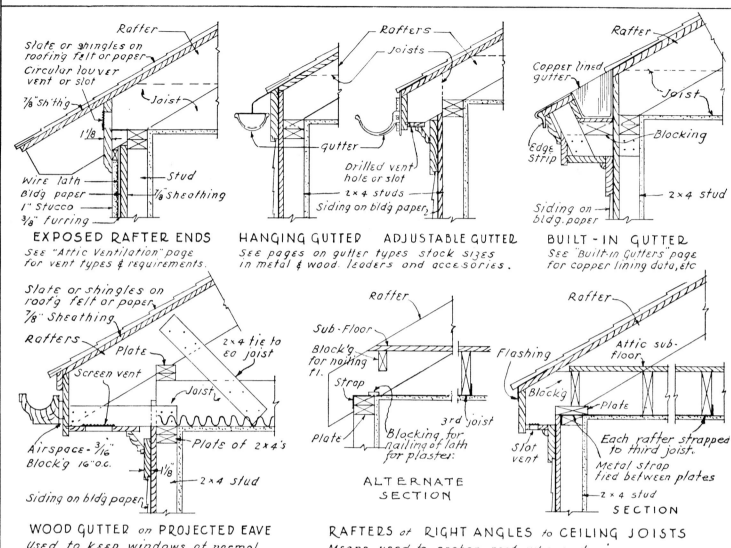

EXPOSED RAFTER ENDS
See "Attic Ventilation" page for vent types & requirements.

HANGING GUTTER   ADJUSTABLE GUTTER
See pages on gutter types stock sizes in metal & wood. leaders and accesories.

BUILT-IN GUTTER
See "Built-in Gutters" page for copper lining data, etc

WOOD GUTTER on PROJECTED EAVE
Used to keep windows at normal elevation when overhang is large.

ALTERNATE SECTION

RAFTERS at RIGHT ANGLES to CEILING JOISTS
Means used to anchor roof where design necessitates construction of this type. (Infrequently encountered)

EAVE DETAILS for PITCHED ROOFS

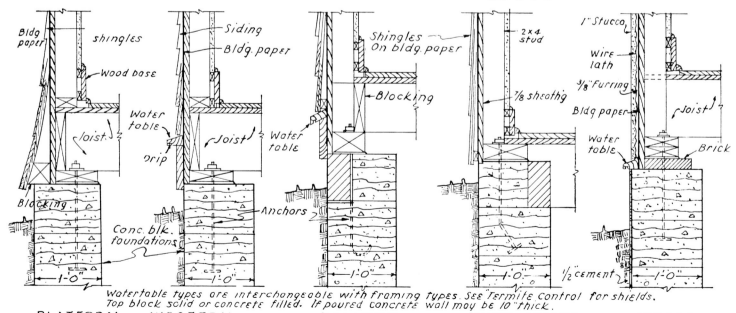

Watertable types are interchangeable with framing types. See Termite Control for shields. Top block solid or concrete filled. If poured concrete wall may be 10" thick.

PLATFORM or WESTERN FRAMING   **BALLOON or BRACED**   **WITH JOISTS BELOW GRADE**   **STUCCO FINISH**

SILLS and WATERTABLES
Scale 3/4" = 1'0"

7

DOORS, WINDOWS, AND GLASS

DORMER WINDOWS - CASEMENT

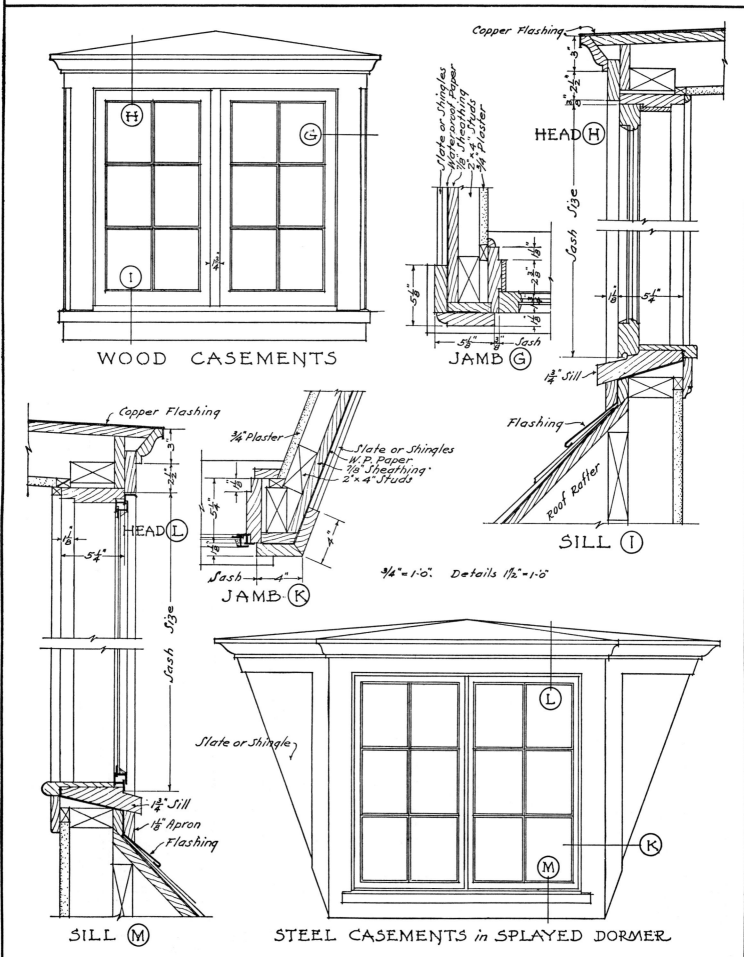

WOOD CASEMENTS

Slate or Shingles
Waterproof Paper
⅞" Sheathing
2" × 4" Studs
¾" Plaster

JAMB G

HEAD H

Copper Flashing

Sash Size

1¾" Sill

Flashing

Roof Rafter

SILL I

Copper Flashing

HEAD L

¾" Plaster

Slate or Shingles
W.P. Paper
⅞" Sheathing
2" × 4" Studs

Sash

JAMB K

¾" = 1'-0".   Details 1½" = 1'-0"

Sash Size

1¾" Sill
1½" Apron
Flashing

SILL M

Slate or Shingle

STEEL CASEMENTS in SPLAYED DORMER

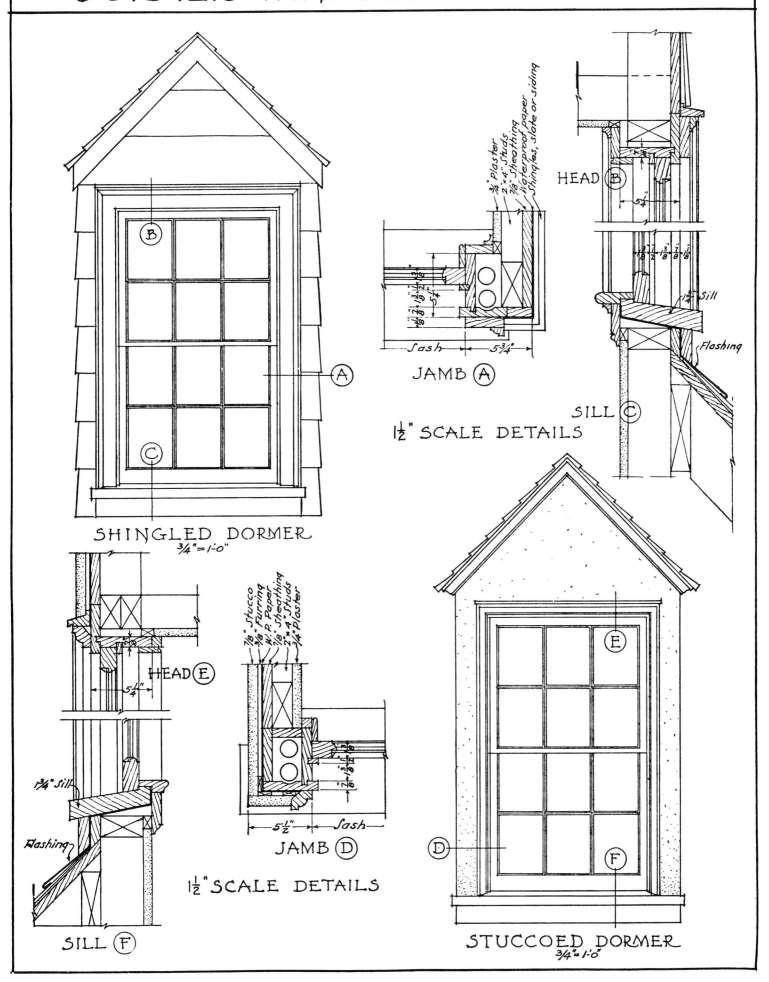

DORMER WINDOWS - DOUBLE HUNG

JAMB (A)

¾" Plaster
2"×4" Studs
⅞" Sheathing
Waterproof paper
Shingles, slate or siding

Sash   5¾"

1½" SCALE DETAILS

HEAD (B)

5¼"

1¾" Sill

Flashing

SILL (C)

SHINGLED DORMER
¾"=1'-0"

HEAD (E)

5¼"

1¾" Sill

Flashing

SILL (F)

JAMB (D)

⅞" Stucco
⅜" Furring
W. P. Paper
⅞" Sheathing
2"×4" Studs
¾" Plaster

5½"   Sash

1½" SCALE DETAILS

STUCCOED DORMER
¾"=1'-0"

RESIDENTIAL STEEL CASEMENT WINDOWS, SHINGLES on FRAME

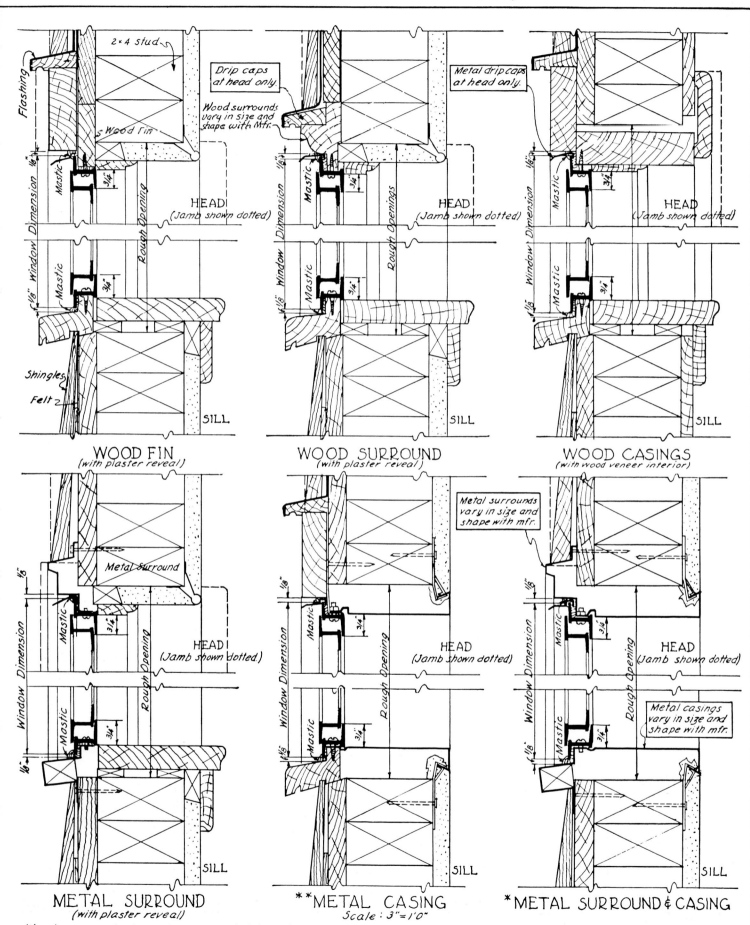

WOOD FIN
(with plaster reveal)

WOOD SURROUND
(with plaster reveal)

WOOD CASINGS
(with wood veneer interior)

METAL SURROUND
(with plaster reveal)

**METAL CASING
Scale: 3" = 1'0"

*METAL SURROUND & CASING

Wood surrounds & wood fins supplied by window manufacturers only when specified. Flashing, building paper, structural lintels, blocking, woodstops, stools, aprons, inside trim, etc., are not generally supplied by window mfr. *Metal surrounds may also be used with wood casings. ** Metal casings may also be used with wood surrounds.

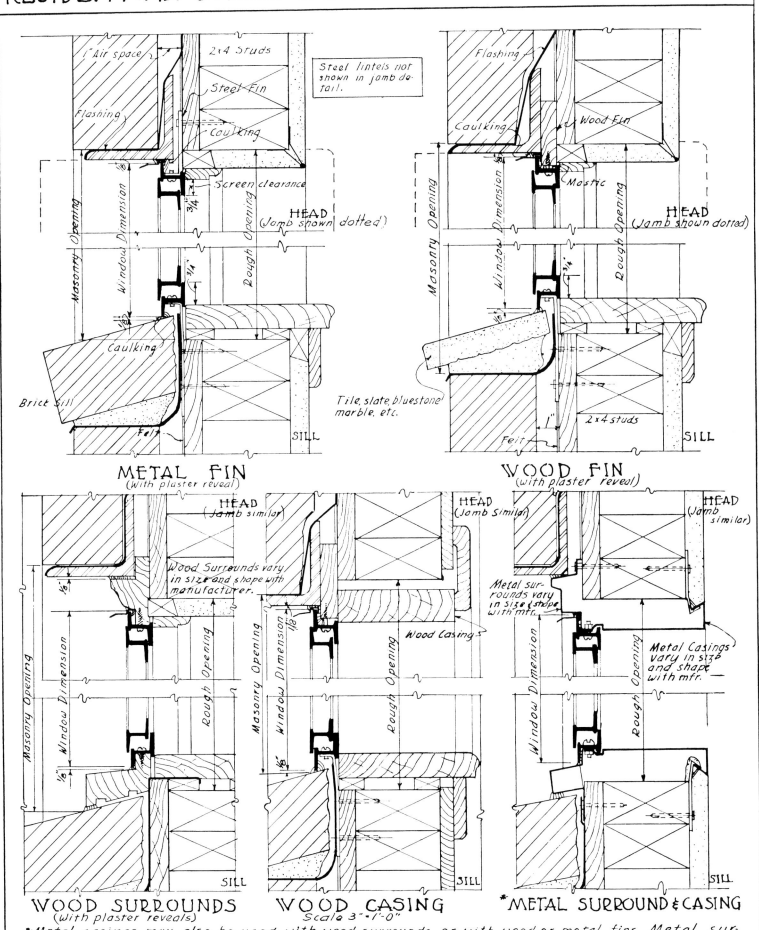

RESIDENTIAL STEEL CASEMENT WINDOWS, BRICK VENEER

Steel lintels not shown in jamb detail.

METAL FIN
(With plaster reveal)

WOOD FIN
(with plaster reveal)

WOOD SURROUNDS
(with plaster reveals)

WOOD CASING
Scale 3"=1'-0"

*METAL SURROUND & CASING

*Metal casings may also be used with wood surrounds or with wood or metal fins. Metal surrounds may also be used with plaster or wood casings. For note on supplies furnished by Window Manufacturers see page on Steel Casement Details (Wood-Frame-shingle).

RESIDENTIAL STEEL CASEMENT WINDOWS, STUCCO on BLOCK and FRAME

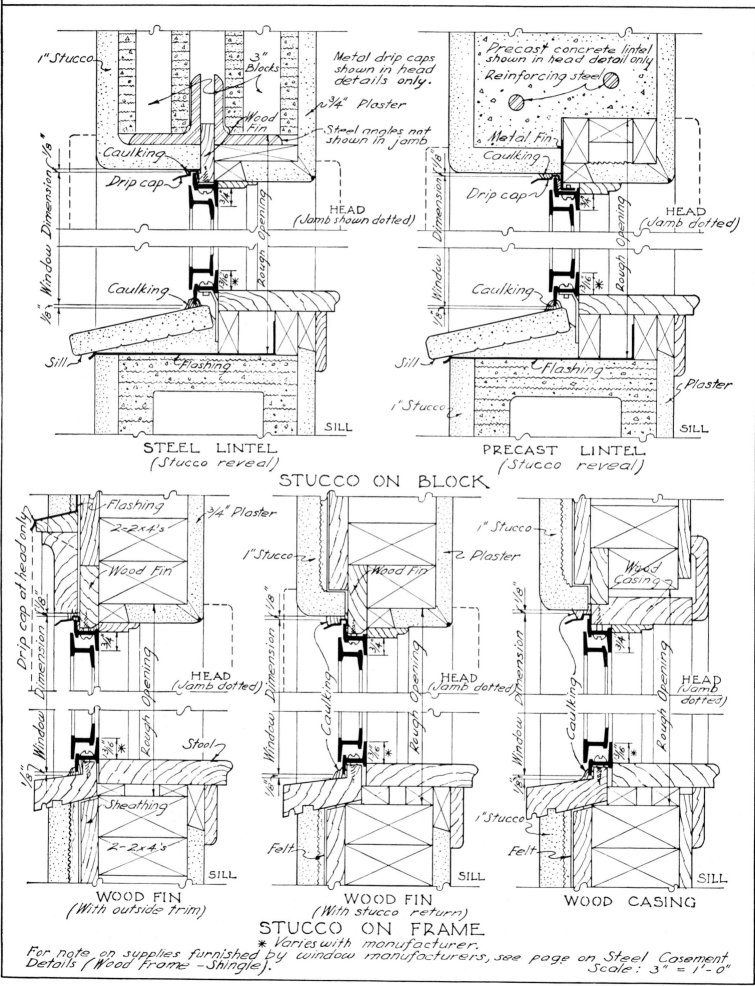

1" Stucco

3" Blocks

Metal drip caps shown in head details only.

3/4" Plaster

Wood Fin

Steel angles not shown in jamb

Caulking

Drip cap

Window Dimension 1/8"

1/8"

Rough Opening

3/4"

HEAD
(Jamb shown dotted)

Caulking

Sill

Flashing

SILL

STEEL LINTEL
(Stucco reveal)

Precast concrete lintel shown in head detail only

Reinforcing steel

Metal Fin

Caulking

Drip cap

Window Dimension 1/8"

1/8"

Rough Opening

3/4"

HEAD
(Jamb dotted)

Caulking

Sill

Flashing

1" Stucco

Plaster

SILL

PRECAST LINTEL
(Stucco reveal)

STUCCO ON BLOCK

Flashing

3/4" Plaster

2-2x4's

Wood Fin

Drip cap at head only 1/8"

3/4"

Window Dimension 1/8"

1/8"

Rough Opening

HEAD
(Jamb dotted)

Stool

Sheathing

2-2x4's

SILL

WOOD FIN
(With outside trim)

1" Stucco

Wood Fin

Plaster

Caulking

3/4"

Window Dimension

1/8"

Rough Opening

HEAD
(Jamb dotted)

Felt

SILL

WOOD FIN
(With stucco return)

1" Stucco

Wood Casing

Caulking

3/4"

Window Dimension 1/8"

1/8"

Rough Opening

HEAD
(Jamb dotted)

1" Stucco

Felt

SILL

WOOD CASING

STUCCO ON FRAME

* Varies with manufacturer.

For note on supplies furnished by window manufacturers, see page on Steel Casement Details (Wood Frame - Shingle).

Scale: 3" = 1'- 0"

RESIDENTIAL STEEL CASEMENT WINDOWS, SOLID BRICK WALLS

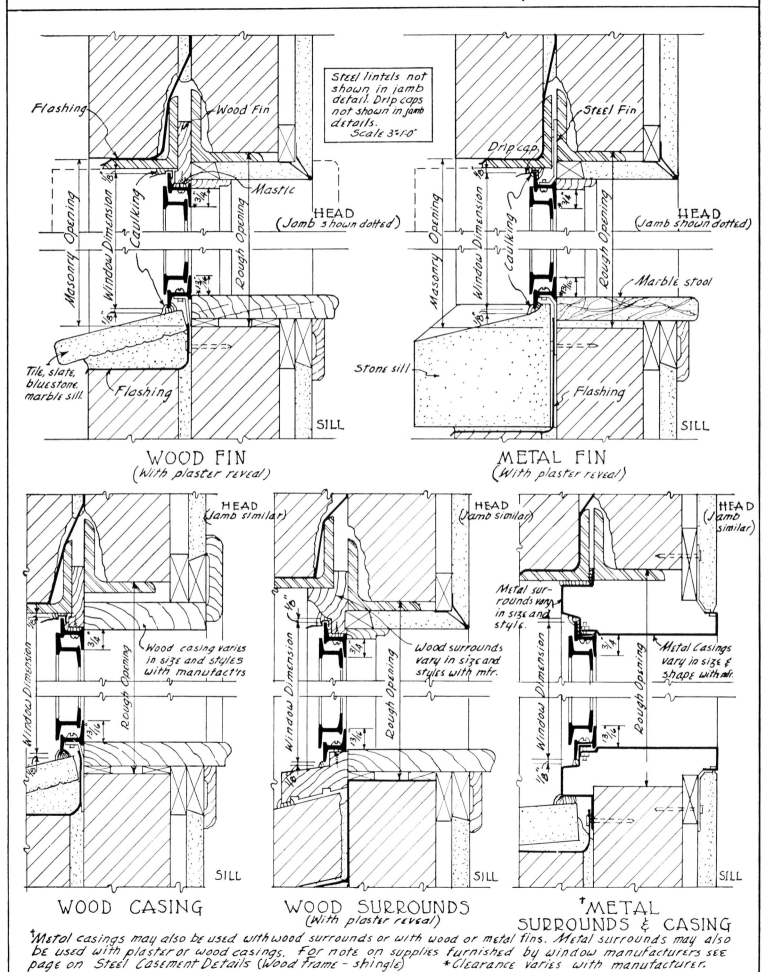

Steel lintels not shown in jamb detail. Drip caps not shown in jamb details. Scale 3"=1'-0"

WOOD FIN (With plaster reveal)

Flashing — Wood Fin — Mastic
HEAD (Jamb shown dotted)
Caulking — Window Dimension
Tile, slate, bluestone, marble sill. — Flashing
SILL

METAL FIN (With plaster reveal)

Steel Fin — Drip cap
HEAD (Jamb shown dotted)
Caulking — Marble stool
Stone sill — Flashing
SILL

WOOD CASING

HEAD (Jamb similar)
Wood casing varies in size and styles with manufact'rs
SILL

WOOD SURROUNDS (With plaster reveal)

HEAD (Jamb similar)
Wood surrounds vary in size and styles with mfr.
SILL

†METAL SURROUNDS & CASING

HEAD (Jamb similar)
Metal surrounds vary in size and styles.
Metal Casings vary in size & shape with mfr.
SILL

†Metal casings may also be used with wood surrounds or with wood or metal fins. Metal surrounds may also be used with plaster or wood casings. For note on supplies furnished by window manufacturers see page on Steel Casement Details (Wood frame - shingle)   *Clearance varies with manufacturer.

RESIDENTIAL STEEL CASEMENT WINDOWS, MASONRY WALLS

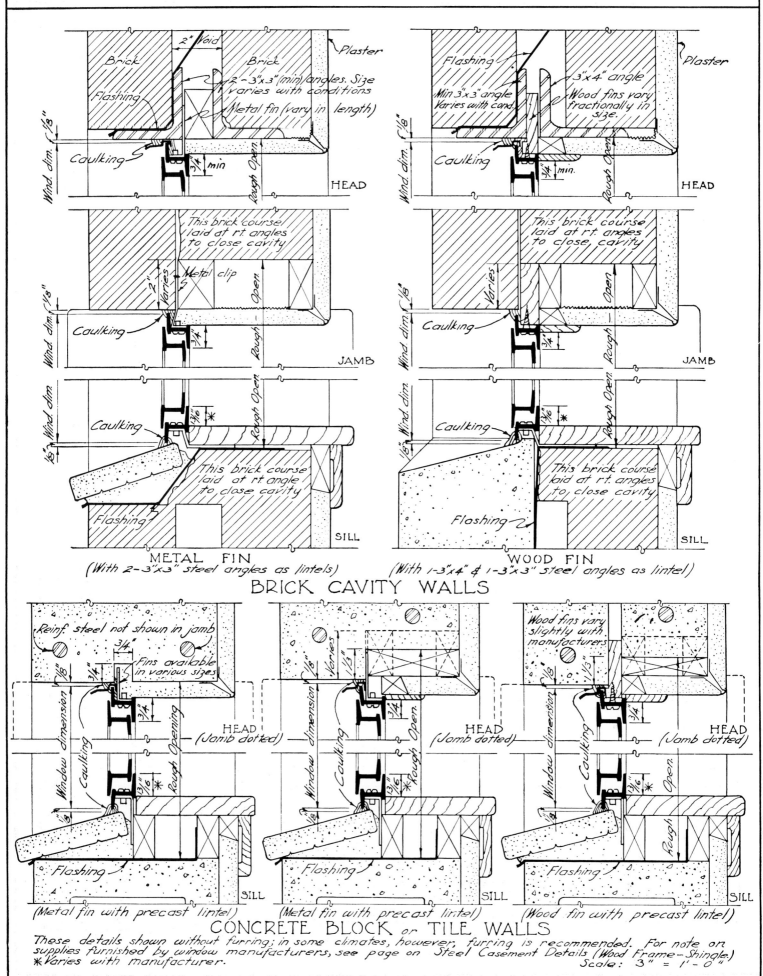

HEAD — 2" Void, Brick, Plaster, Flashing, 2-3"x3"(min)angles. Size varies with conditions, Metal fin (vary in length), Caulking, 3/4" min, Rough Open, Wind. dim. 1/8"

HEAD — Flashing, Plaster, Min 3"x3" angle Varies with cond., 3"x4" angle, Wood fins vary fractionally in size, Caulking, 3/4" min., Rough Open, Wind. dim. 1/8"

JAMB — This brick course laid at rt. angles to close cavity, Metal clip, Caulking, Varies, 2", 3/4", Rough Open, Wind dim. 1/8"

JAMB — This brick course laid at rt. angles to close cavity, Caulking, Varies, 3/4", Rough Open, Wind. dim. 1/8"

SILL — Caulking, 13/16", This brick course laid at rt. angle to close cavity, Flashing, Rough Open, Wind. dim. 1/8"

SILL — Caulking, 13/16", This brick course laid at rt. angle to close cavity, Flashing, Rough Open, Wind. dim. 1/8"

METAL FIN
(With 2-3"x3" steel angles as lintels)

WOOD FIN
(With 1-3"x4" & 1-3"x3" steel angles as lintel)

BRICK CAVITY WALLS

HEAD (Jamb dotted) — Reinf. steel not shown in jamb, 3/4", Fins available in various sizes, 3/4", Caulking, 13/16", Window dimension, Rough Opening, 1/8"

HEAD (Jamb dotted) — Varies, 1/8", 1/3", 3/4", Caulking, 13/16", Window dimension, Rough Open., 1/8"

HEAD (Jamb dotted) — Wood fins vary slightly with manufacturers, 1/8", 1/3", 3/4", Caulking, 13/16", Window dimension, Rough Open., 1/8"

SILL — Flashing (×3)

(Metal fin with precast lintel)   (Metal fin with precast lintel)   (Wood fin with precast lintel)

CONCRETE BLOCK or TILE WALLS

These details shown without furring; in some climates, however, furring is recommended. For note on supplies furnished by window manufacturers, see page on Steel Casement Details (Wood Frame–Shingle).
* Varies with manufacturer.   Scale: 3" = 1'-0"

RESIDENTIAL STEEL CASEMENT, BAY WINDOWS

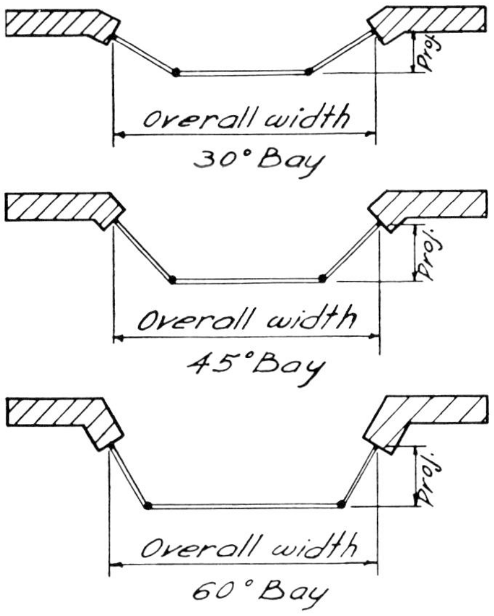

SPLAYED

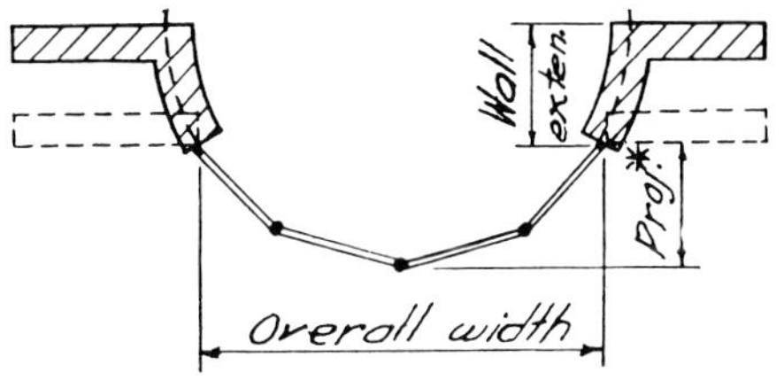

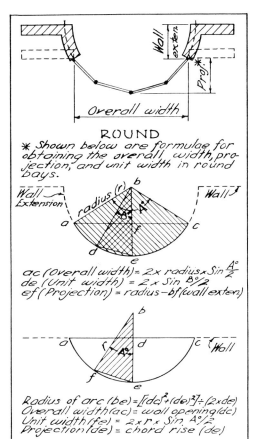

ROUND

∗ Shown below are formulae for obtaining the overall width, projection, and unit width in round bays.

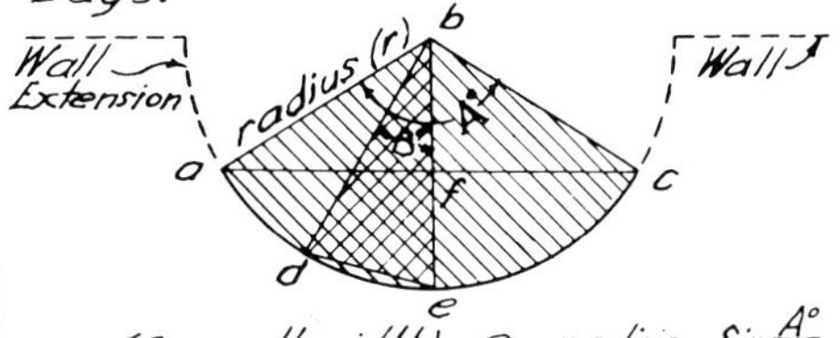

ac (Overall width) = 2 × radius × Sin $\frac{A°}{2}$
de (Unit width) = 2 × Sin B°/2
ef (Projection) = radius − bf (wall exten)

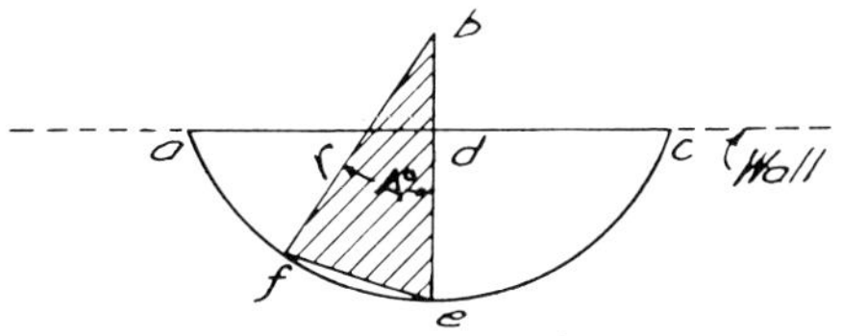

Radius of arc (be) = $[(dc)^2+(de)^2] \div (2 \times de)$
Overall width (ac) = wall opening (dc)
Unit width (fe) = 2 × r × Sin A°/2
Projection (de) = chord rise (de)

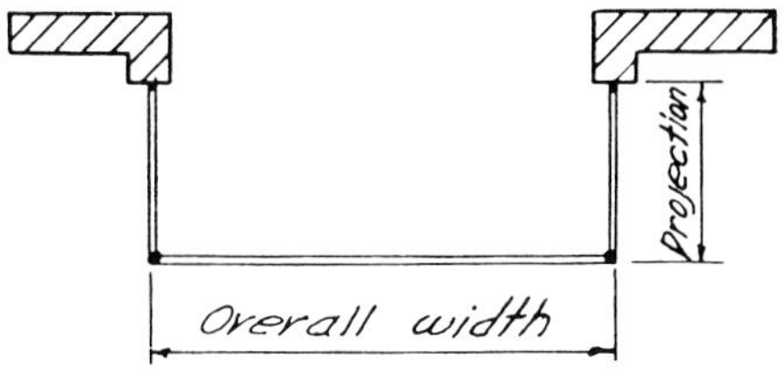

SQUARE

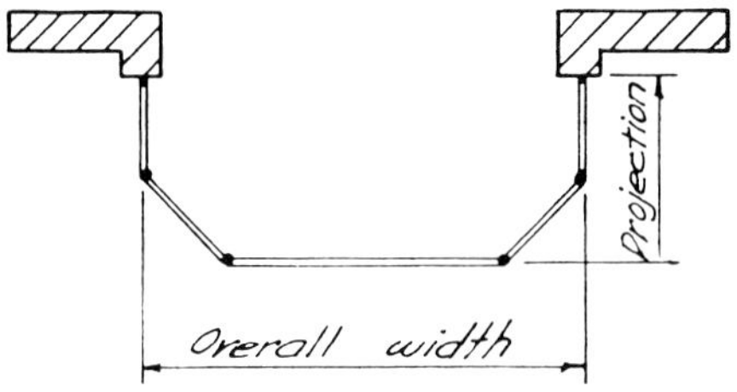

SQUARE-SPLAYED

ANGLE of BAY	Lights in Return	OVERALL WIDTH Lights in Front Section ∗2	3	4	PROJECTION
30°	1	6'-1 1/8"	7'-5 1/4"	8'-9 1/2"	10"
	2	8'-8 1/8"	10'-0 1/4"	11'-4 1/2"	1'-6 7/8"
45°	1	5'-7 1/4"	6'-11 3/8"	8'-3 5/8"	1'-2 1/4"
	2	7'-8 1/2"	9'-0 5/8"	10'-4 7/8"	2'-2 7/8"
60°	1	4'-11 1/4"	6'-3 3/8"	7'-7 5/8"	1'-5 1/2"
	2	6'-5 1/8"	7'-9 1/4"	9'-1 1/2"	2'-9"

ANGLE of BAY	Lights in return	OVERALL WIDTH Lights in Front Section ∗2	3	4	PROJECTION
SQUARE	1	3'-4"	4'-8 1/8"	6'-0 3/8"	1'-8 3/4"
	2	3'-4"	4'-8 1/8"	6'-0 3/8"	3'-2 5/8"
SQUARE SPLAYED	1	5'-8 1/4"	7'-0 3/8"	8'-4 5/8"	2'-10 7/8"
	2	7'-9 1/2"	9'-1 5/8"	10'-5 7/8"	5'-5 3/8"

∗ Dimensions based on single vent in returns & double (2) vented units in front.

Residence casements may be combined to form bay windows as suggested above. Such combinations require the use of bearing or non-bearing mullions. T-bar mullions cannot be used. Standard non-bearing mullions are generally supplied by the window manufacturer. These mullions are not designed to support any building construction. Structural angle shown below is only bearing mullion shown.

STANDARD BAY COMBINATIONS

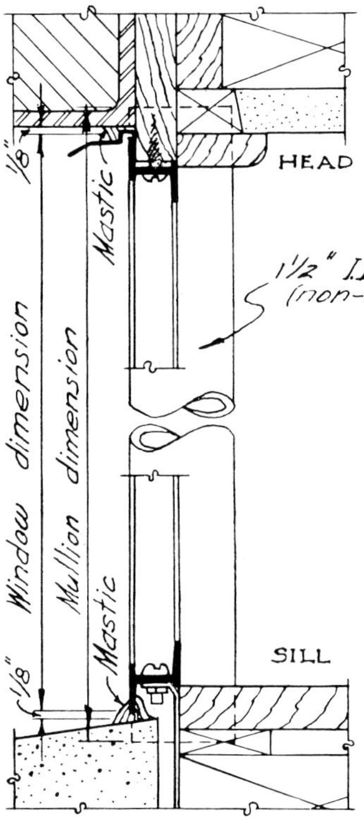

VERTICAL SECTION

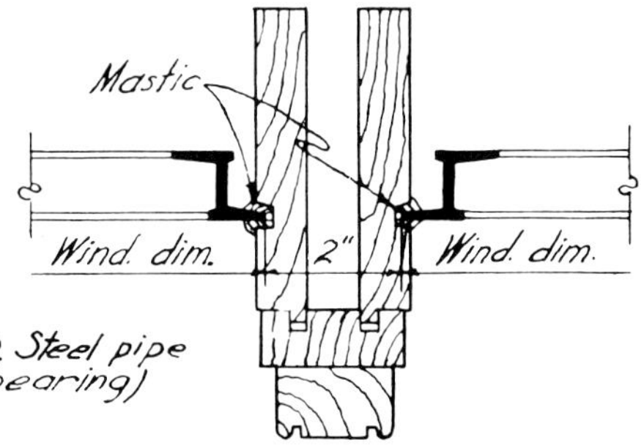

WOOD CASING

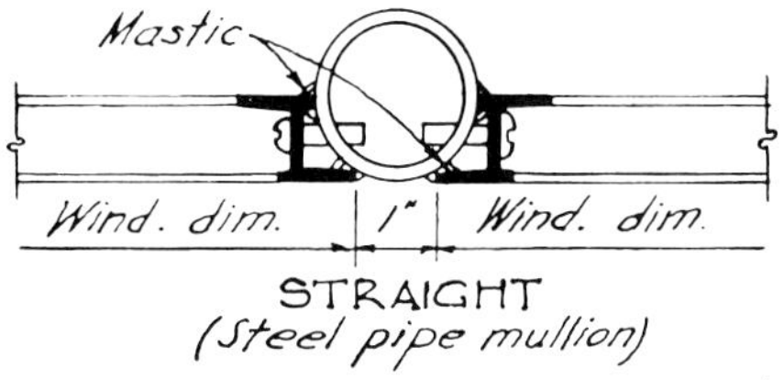

STRAIGHT (Steel pipe mullion)

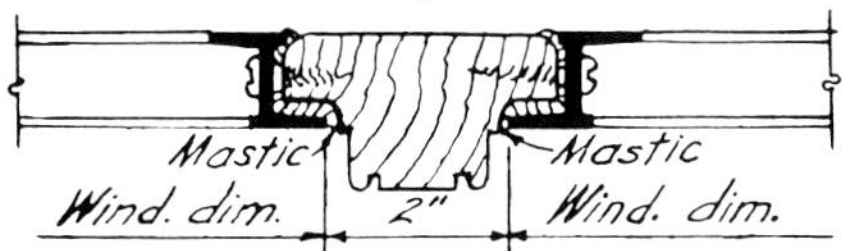

WOOD SURROUND

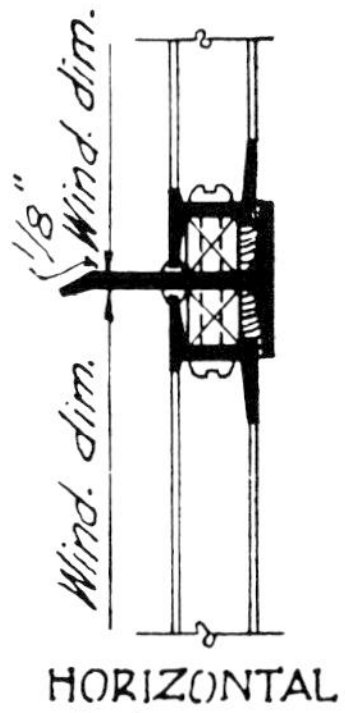

HORIZONTAL "T"-BAR

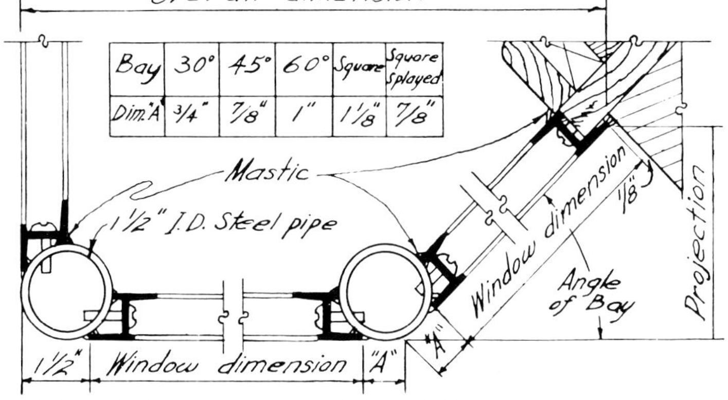

Bay	30°	45°	60°	Square	Square Splayed
Dim."A"	3/4"	7/8"	1"	1 1/8"	7/8"

SQUARE BAY SPLAYED BAY

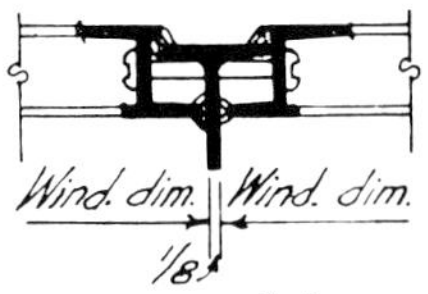

VERTICAL "T"-BAR

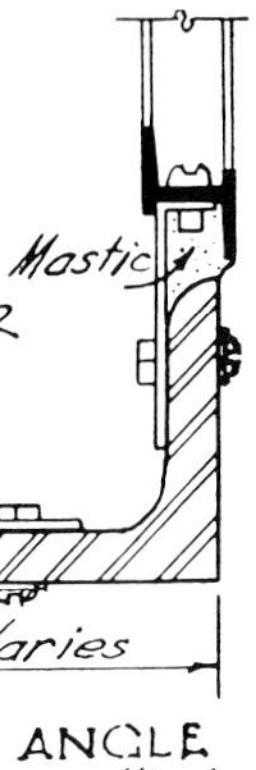

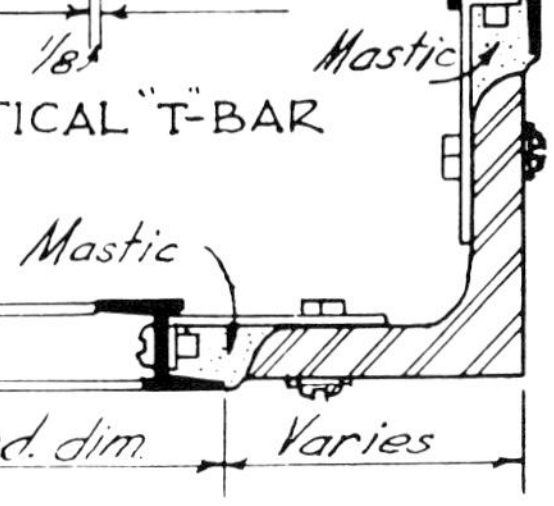

STRUCTURAL ANGLE (This is bearing mullion)

MULLION DETAILS

Scale: 3" = 1'-0"

168

SCREENS *for* METAL WINDOWS & PORCHES

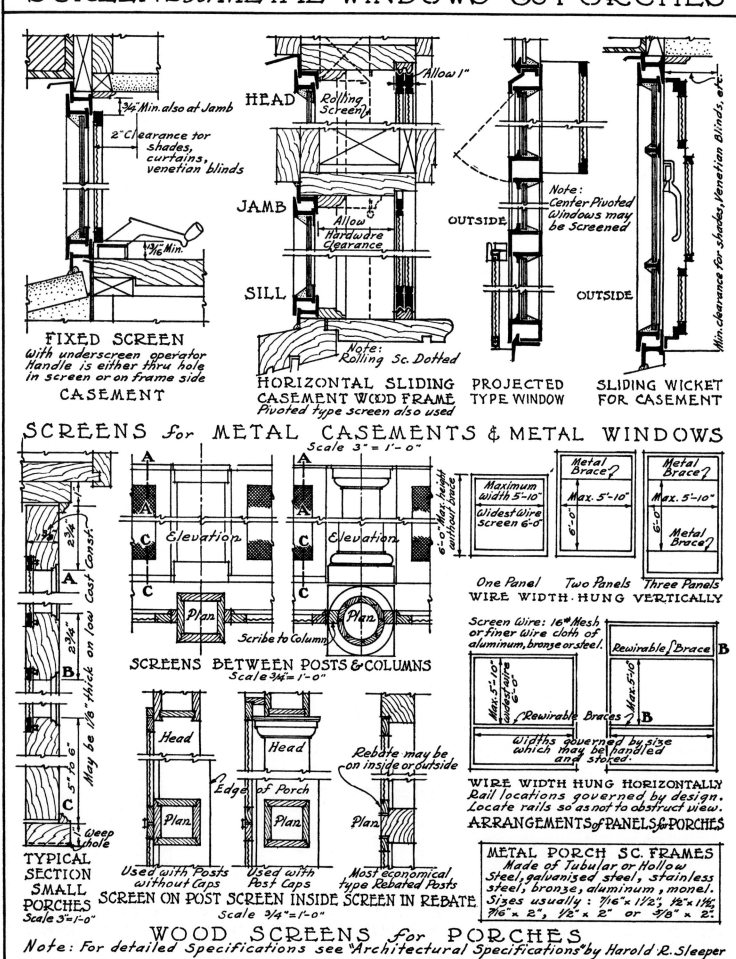

FIXED SCREEN
With underscreen operator
Handle is either thru hole
in screen or on frame side
CASEMENT

¾" Min. also at Jamb
2" Clearance for shades, curtains, venetian blinds
1 3/16" Min.

HEAD
Rolling Screen
Allow 1"
JAMB
Allow Hardware Clearance
SILL
Note: Rolling Sc. Dotted

HORIZONTAL SLIDING CASEMENT WOOD FRAME
Pivoted type screen also used

OUTSIDE
Note: Center Pivoted Windows may be Screened
PROJECTED TYPE WINDOW

OUTSIDE
Min. clearance for shades, Venetian Blinds, etc.
SLIDING WICKET FOR CASEMENT

SCREENS *for* METAL CASEMENTS & METAL WINDOWS

Scale 3" = 1'-0"

A A
Elevation Elevation
C C
Plan Plan
Scribe to Column
SCREENS BETWEEN POSTS & COLUMNS
Scale ¾" = 1'-0"

6'-0" Max. height without brace

Maximum width 5'-10"
Widest Wire Screen 6'-0"
One Panel

Metal Brace?
Max. 5'-10"
6'-0"
Two Panels

Metal Brace?
Max. 5'-10"
6'-0"
Metal Brace?
Three Panels
WIRE WIDTH HUNG VERTICALLY

Screen Wire: 16# Mesh or finer Wire cloth of aluminum, bronze or steel.

Max. 5'-10" widest wire 6'-0"
Rewirable Braces?
Rewirable Brace B
Max. 5'-10"
B
Widths governed by size which may be handled and stored.
WIRE WIDTH HUNG HORIZONTALLY
Rail locations governed by design.
Locate rails so as not to obstruct view.
ARRANGEMENTS of PANELS for PORCHES

3¾
2¾
A
2¾
B
5' to 6'
May be 1/8" thick on low cost Const.
C
Weep hole
TYPICAL SECTION SMALL PORCHES
Scale 3"=1'-0"

Head
Plan
Used with Posts without Caps
Head
Plan
Used with Post Caps
Rebate may be on inside or outside
Edge of Porch
Plan
Most economical type Rebated Posts
SCREEN ON POST SCREEN INSIDE SCREEN IN REBATE
Scale ¾"=1'-0"

METAL PORCH SC. FRAMES
Made of Tubular or Hollow Steel, galvanized steel, stainless steel, bronze, aluminum, monel.
Sizes usually: 7/16"x1½", ½"x1½", 7/16"x 2", ½"x 2" or 5/8"x 2".

WOOD SCREENS *for* PORCHES
Note: For detailed Specifications see "Architectural Specifications" by Harold R. Sleeper

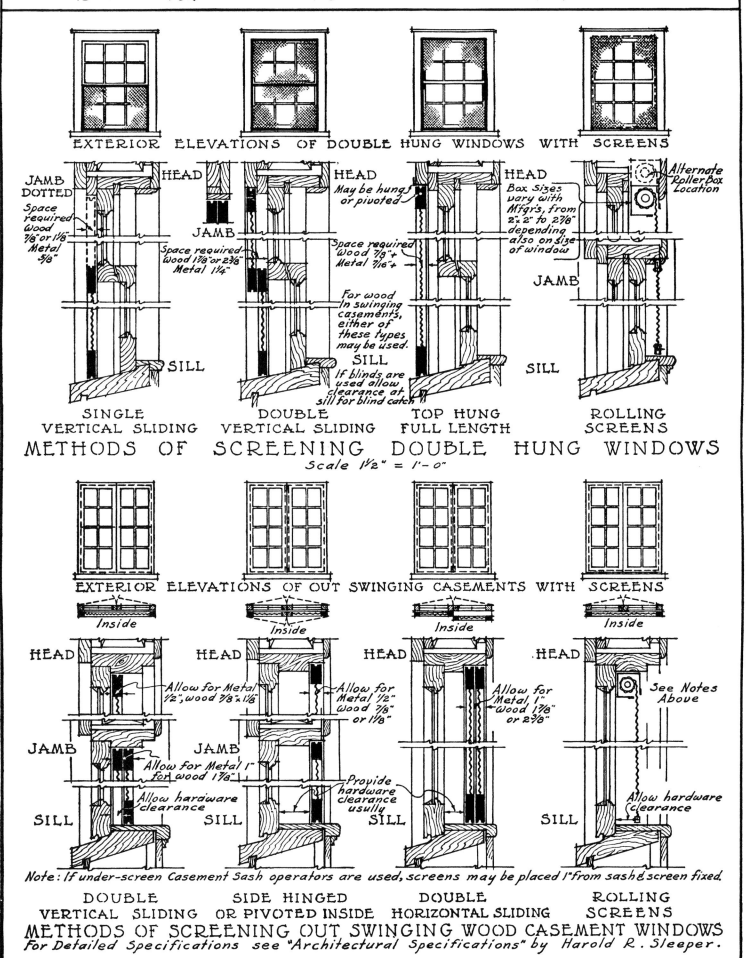

SCREENS FOR WOOD WINDOWS

EXTERIOR ELEVATIONS OF DOUBLE HUNG WINDOWS WITH SCREENS

SINGLE VERTICAL SLIDING · DOUBLE VERTICAL SLIDING · TOP HUNG FULL LENGTH · ROLLING SCREENS

METHODS OF SCREENING DOUBLE HUNG WINDOWS

Scale 1½" = 1'-0"

EXTERIOR ELEVATIONS OF OUT SWINGING CASEMENTS WITH SCREENS

DOUBLE VERTICAL SLIDING · SIDE HINGED OR PIVOTED INSIDE · DOUBLE HORIZONTAL SLIDING · ROLLING SCREENS

METHODS OF SCREENING OUT SWINGING WOOD CASEMENT WINDOWS

For Detailed Specifications see "Architectural Specifications" by Harold R. Sleeper.

WOOD WINDOW & DOOR DETAILS

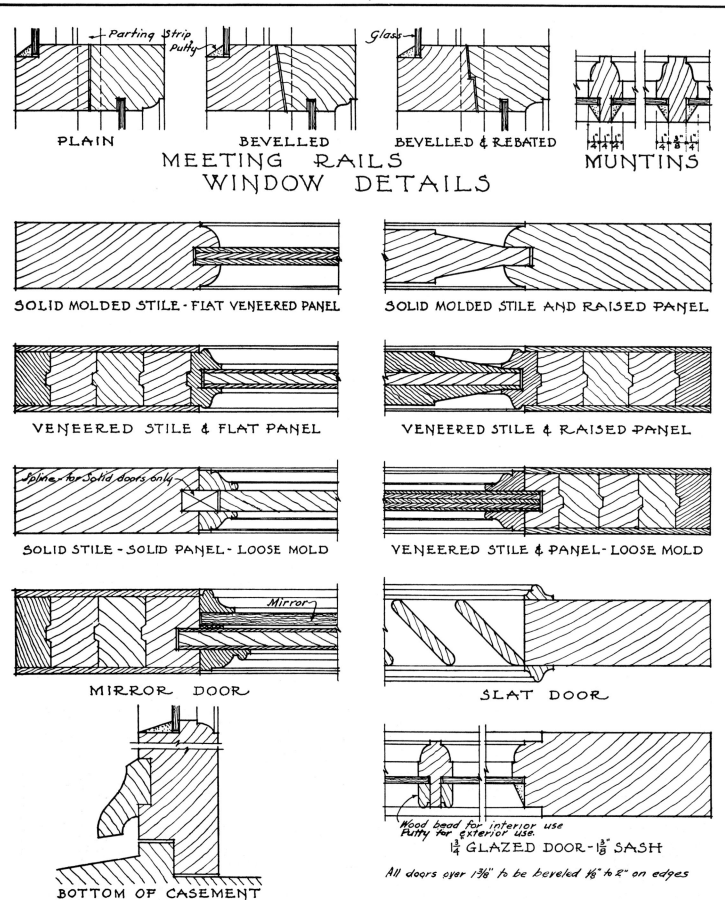

Parting Strip
Putty
Glass

PLAIN   BEVELLED   BEVELLED & REBATED   MUNTINS

MEETING RAILS
WINDOW DETAILS

SOLID MOLDED STILE - FLAT VENEERED PANEL   SOLID MOLDED STILE AND RAISED PANEL

VENEERED STILE & FLAT PANEL   VENEERED STILE & RAISED PANEL

Spline for Solid doors only

SOLID STILE - SOLID PANEL - LOOSE MOLD   VENEERED STILE & PANEL - LOOSE MOLD

Mirror

MIRROR DOOR   SLAT DOOR

Wood bead for interior use
Putty for exterior use.
1¾" GLAZED DOOR - 1⅜" SASH

All doors over 1⅜" to be beveled ⅛" to 2" on edges

BOTTOM OF CASEMENT
WINDOW OR DOOR-OPENING IN

DOOR DETAILS
Scale. ½ Full Size

WEATHERSTRIPS~EXTERIOR SADDLES, INTERIOR STRIPS

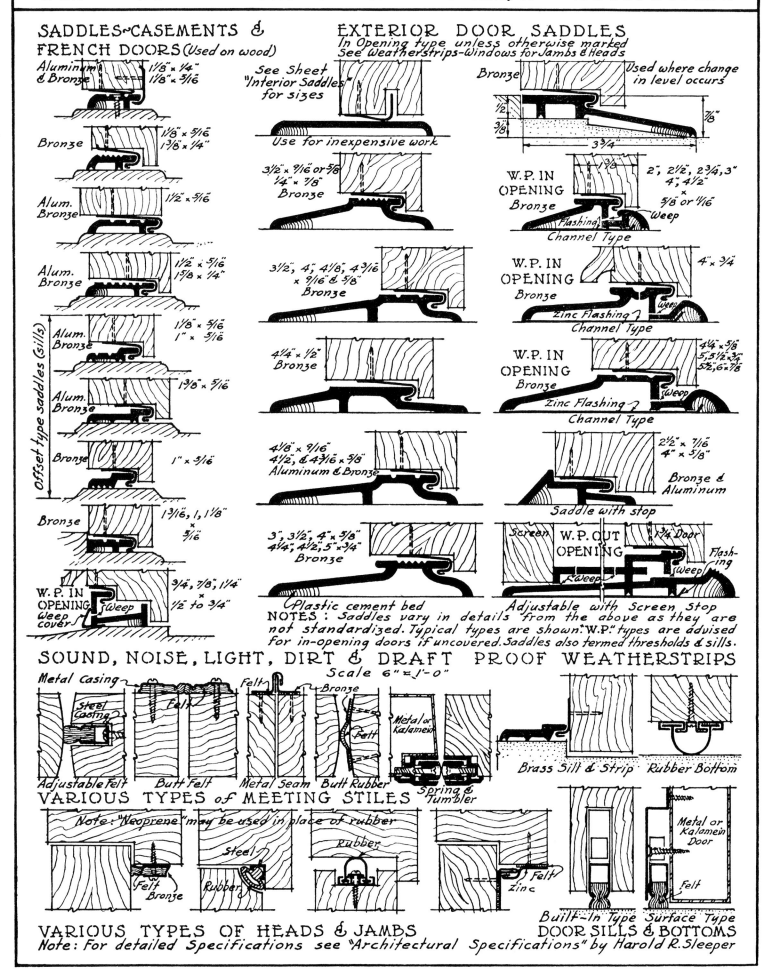

SADDLES~CASEMENTS & FRENCH DOORS (Used on wood)

Aluminum & Bronze · 1⅛" × ¼" · 1⅛" × 5/16"

Bronze · 1⅛" × 5/16" · 1⅜" × ¼"

Alum. Bronze · 1½" × 5/16"

Alum. Bronze · 1½" × 5/16" · 1⅝" × ¼"

Alum. Bronze · 1⅛" × 5/16" · 1" × 5/16"

Alum. Bronze · 1⅜" × 5/16"

Bronze · 1" × 5/16"

Bronze · 1 3/16", 1, 1⅛" × 5/16"

Offset type saddles (sills)

W.P. IN OPENING Weep cover · ¾", ⅞", 1¼" × ½ to ¾"

EXTERIOR DOOR SADDLES
In Opening type unless otherwise marked
See Weatherstrips~Windows for Jambs & Heads

See Sheet "Interior Saddles" for sizes

Use for inexpensive work

3½" × 9/16 or ⅝ · ¼" × ⅞" · Bronze

3½", 4", 4⅛", 4 3/16" × 9/16 & ⅝" · Bronze

4¼" × ½" · Bronze

4⅛" × 9/16 · 4½", & 4 3/16" × ⅝" · Aluminum & Bronze

3", 3½", 4" × ⅝" · 4¼", 4½", 5" × ¾" · Bronze

Plastic cement bed

Bronze · Used where change in level occurs · ½" · ⅜" · ⅞" · 3¾"

W.P. IN OPENING Bronze · Flashing · Weep · Channel Type · 1⅜" · 2", 2½", 2¾", 3", 4", 4½" × ⅝ or 11/16"

W.P. IN OPENING Bronze · Zinc Flashing · Weep · Channel Type · 4" × ¾"

W.P. IN OPENING Bronze · Zinc Flashing · Weep · Channel Type · 4¼" × ⅝ · 5, 5½" × ¾ · 5½", 6" × ⅞

Bronze & Aluminum · Saddle with stop · 2½" × 7/16" · 4" × ⅝"

W.P. OUT OPENING · Screen · ¾" Door · Weep · Flashing sweep · Adjustable with Screen Stop

NOTES: Saddles vary in details from the above as they are not standardized. Typical types are shown. "W.P." types are advised for in-opening doors if uncovered. Saddles also termed thresholds & sills.

SOUND, NOISE, LIGHT, DIRT & DRAFT PROOF WEATHERSTRIPS
Scale 6" = 1'-0"

Metal Casing · Steel Casing · Felt · Adjustable Felt

Felt · Butt Felt

Bronze · Felt · Metal Seam

Felt · Metal or Kalamein · Butt Rubber · Spring & Tumbler

Brass Sill & Strip

Rubber Bottom

VARIOUS TYPES of MEETING STILES
Note: "Neoprene" may be used in place of rubber

Felt · Bronze

Steel · Rubber

Rubber

Felt · Zinc

Metal or Kalamein Door · Felt · Built-In Type · Surface Type · DOOR SILLS & BOTTOMS

VARIOUS TYPES of HEADS & JAMBS
Note: For detailed Specifications see "Architectural Specifications" by Harold R. Sleeper

WEATHERSTRIPS ~ WINDOWS

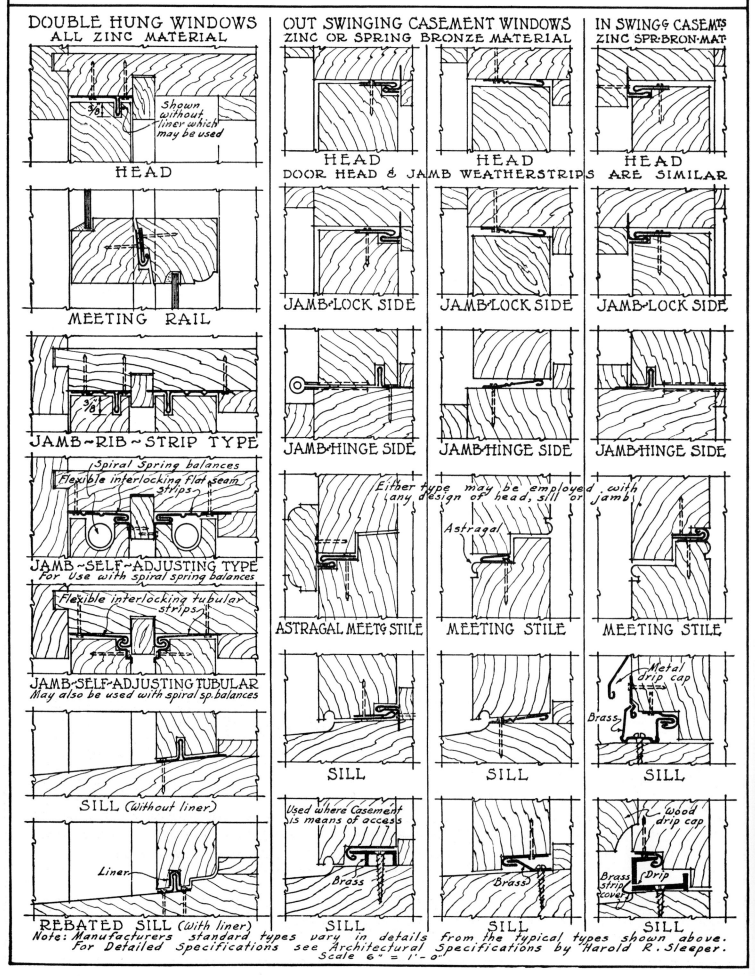

DOUBLE HUNG WINDOWS
ALL ZINC MATERIAL

Shown without liner which may be used

⅜

HEAD

MEETING RAIL

⅜

JAMB~RIB~STRIP TYPE

Spiral Spring balances
Flexible interlocking flat seam strips

JAMB~SELF~ADJUSTING TYPE
For use with spiral spring balances

Flexible interlocking tubular strips

JAMB~SELF~ADJUSTING TUBULAR
May also be used with spiral sp. balances

SILL (Without liner)

Liner

REBATED SILL (With liner)

OUT SWINGING CASEMENT WINDOWS
ZINC OR SPRING BRONZE MATERIAL

HEAD
DOOR HEAD & JAMB WEATHERSTRIPS ARE SIMILAR

HEAD

JAMB·LOCK SIDE

JAMB·LOCK SIDE

JAMB·HINGE SIDE

JAMB·HINGE SIDE

Either type may be employed with any design of head, sill or jamb

Astragal

ASTRAGAL MEETG STILE

MEETING STILE

SILL

SILL

Used where Casement is means of access

Brass

SILL

Brass

SILL

IN SWING CASEMTS
ZINC SPR·BRON·MAT

HEAD

JAMB·LOCK SIDE

JAMB·HINGE SIDE

MEETING STILE

Metal drip cap

Brass

SILL

Wood drip cap

Brass strip cover

Drip

SILL

Note: Manufacturers standard types vary in details from the typical types shown above.
For Detailed Specifications see Architectural Specifications by Harold R. Sleeper.
Scale 6" = 1'-0"

SADDLES, THRESHOLDS~INTERIOR

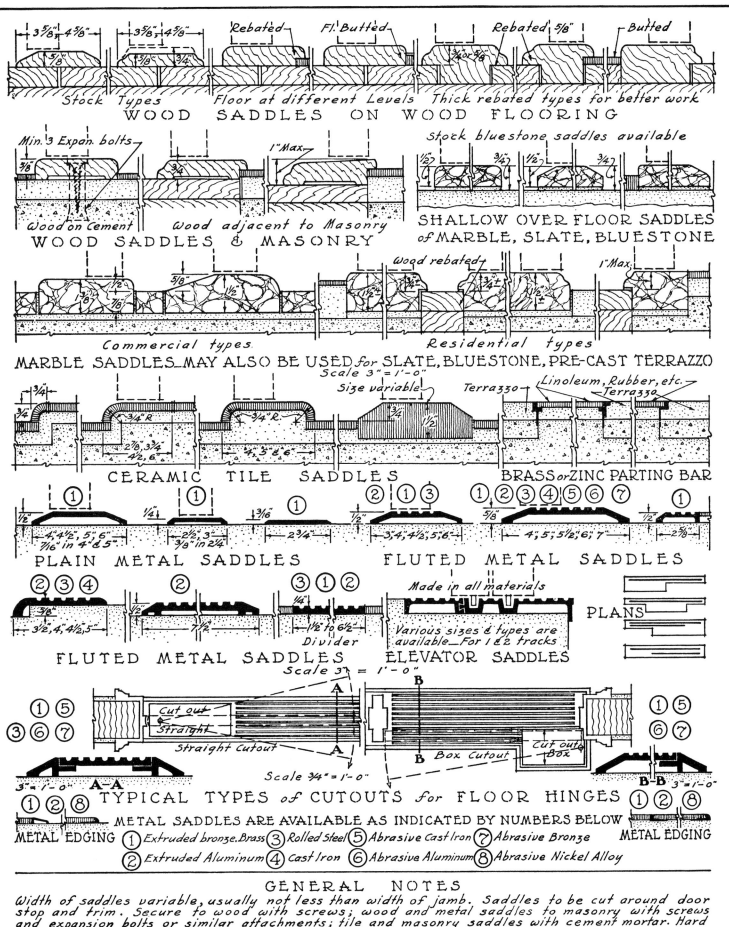

WOOD SADDLES ON WOOD FLOORING

Stock Types · Floor at different Levels · Thick rebated types for better work

Rebated · Fl. Butted · Rebated · Butted

3⁵/₈" · 4⁵/₈" · 3⁵/₈" · 4⁵/₈" · ⁵/₈" · ³/₄" · ³/₄ or ⁵/₈" · 5/8"

WOOD SADDLES & MASONRY

Min. 3 Expan. bolts · 1" Max.

Wood on Cement · Wood adjacent to Masonry

Stock bluestone saddles available

SHALLOW OVER FLOOR SADDLES of MARBLE, SLATE, BLUESTONE

MARBLE SADDLES MAY ALSO BE USED for SLATE, BLUESTONE, PRE-CAST TERRAZZO

Commercial types · Residential types · Wood rebated · 1" Max.

CERAMIC TILE SADDLES

Scale 3" = 1'-0" · Size variable · ³/₄"R. · ³/₄"R.

BRASS or ZINC PARTING BAR

Terrazzo · Linoleum, Rubber, etc. · Terrazzo

PLAIN METAL SADDLES

FLUTED METAL SADDLES

FLUTED METAL SADDLES · Divider

ELEVATOR SADDLES

Made in all materials

Various sizes & types are available—For 1 & 2 tracks

PLANS

TYPICAL TYPES of CUTOUTS for FLOOR HINGES

Scale 3" = 1'-0"

Cut out Straight · Straight Cutout

Box Cutout · Cut out Box

Scale ³/₄" = 1'-0"

A-A · 3"=1'-0" · B-B 3"=1'-0"

METAL EDGING · METAL EDGING

METAL SADDLES ARE AVAILABLE AS INDICATED BY NUMBERS BELOW

① Extruded bronze, Brass ③ Rolled Steel ⑤ Abrasive Cast Iron ⑦ Abrasive Bronze
② Extruded Aluminum ④ Cast Iron ⑥ Abrasive Aluminum ⑧ Abrasive Nickel Alloy

GENERAL NOTES

Width of saddles variable, usually not less than width of jamb. Saddles to be cut around door stop and trim. Secure to wood with screws; wood and metal saddles to masonry with screws and expansion bolts or similar attachments; tile and masonry saddles with cement mortar. Hard flooring may butt against or under saddle (not asphalt tile). Rebates recommended for soft floors.

Scale 3" = 1'-0" Except where noted

HARDWARE

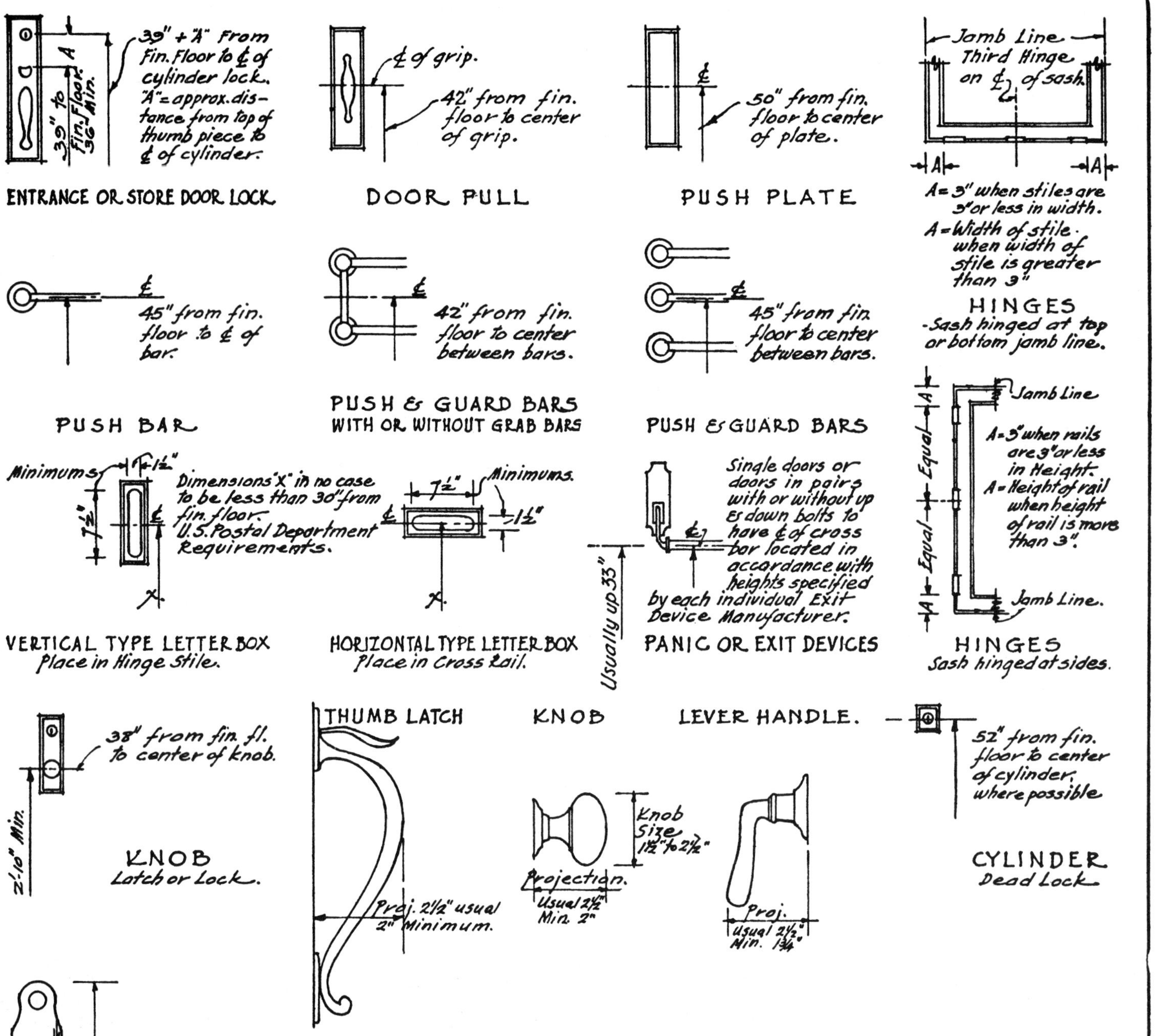

39" + "A" From Fin. Floor to ℄ of cylinder lock. "A" = approx. distance from top of thumb piece to ℄ of cylinder.
39" to A
Fin. Floor 36" Min.
ENTRANCE OR STORE DOOR LOCK
℄ of grip.
42" from fin. floor to center of grip.
DOOR PULL
℄
50" from fin. floor to center of plate.
PUSH PLATE
Jamb Line
Third Hinge on ℄ of sash.
A
A = 3" when stiles are 3" or less in width.
A = Width of stile when width of stile is greater than 3"
HINGES
Sash hinged at top or bottom jamb line.
℄
45" from fin. floor to ℄ of bar.
PUSH BAR
42" from fin. floor to center between bars.
PUSH & GUARD BARS
WITH OR WITHOUT GRAB BARS
45" from fin. floor to center between bars.
PUSH & GUARD BARS
Jamb Line
A = 3" when rails are 3" or less in Height.
A = Height of rail when height of rail is more than 3".
Equal
Equal
Jamb Line.
HINGES
Sash hinged at sides.
Minimums
1½"
7½"
Dimensions "X" in no case to be less than 30" from fin. floor. U.S. Postal Department Requirements.
X
VERTICAL TYPE LETTER BOX
Place in Hinge Stile.
7½"
Minimums.
1½"
X
HORIZONTAL TYPE LETTER BOX
Place in Cross Rail.
Usually up 33"
Single doors or doors in pairs with or without up & down bolts to have ℄ of cross bar located in accordance with heights specified by each individual Exit Device Manufacturer.
PANIC OR EXIT DEVICES
38" from fin. fl. to center of knob.
2'-10" Min.
KNOB
Latch or Lock.
THUMB LATCH
Proj. 2½" usual 2" Minimum.
KNOB
Knob Size 1½" to 2½"
Projection.
Usual 2½" Min. 2"
LEVER HANDLE.
Proj.
Usual 2½" Min. 1¾"
52" from fin. floor to center of cylinder, where possible
CYLINDER
Dead Lock

CLEARANCE FOR KNOBS, LEVER HANDLES & THUMB LATCHES.

The above projections govern Rebate widths for storm doors, screen doors, screens, louvre doors, etc.

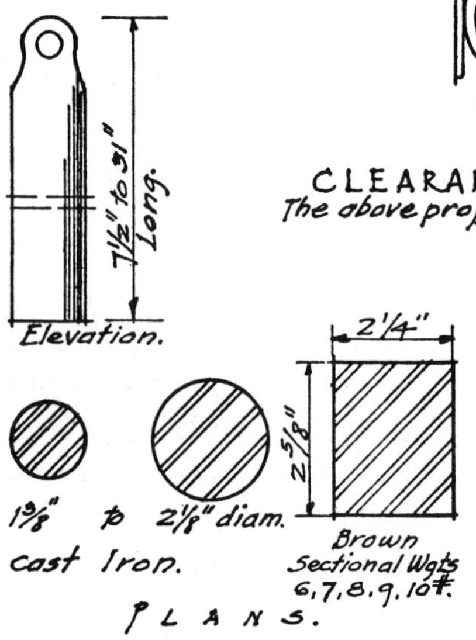

7½" to 31" Long.
Elevation.
2¼"
2⅝"
1⅜" to 2⅛" diam.
Cast Iron.
Brown Sectional Wgts 6, 7, 8, 9, 10#.
PLANS.

SASH WEIGHTS

Pocket for sash weights generally 2¼" for Residential work.

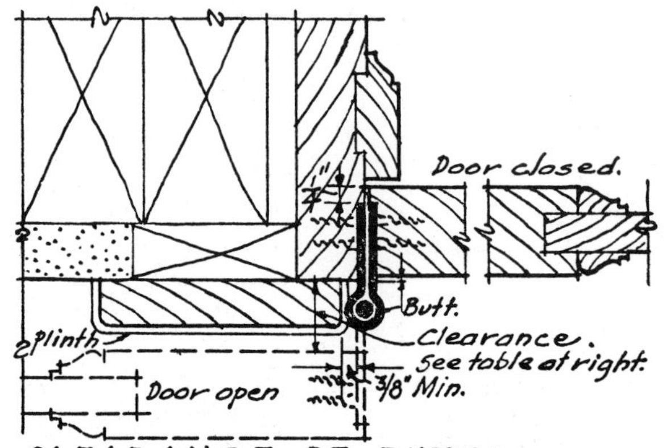

Door closed.
2"
Butt.
Clearance.
See table at right.
Plinth
Door open
3/8" Min.

CLEARANCE OF BUTTS.

Data checked by Ostrander & Eshleman. N.Y.C.

CLEARANCE OF STOCK SIZE BUTTS

Thickness of door	Size of Butt.	Maximum clearance
1⅜"	3" × 3" 3½" × 3½" 4" × 4"	3/4" 7/8" 1⅝"
1¾"	4" × 4" 4½" × 4½" 5" × 5"	1" 1⅜" 2"
2"	4½" × 4½" 5" × 5" 6" × 6"	1¼" 1¾" 2¾"
2¼"	5" × 5" 6" × 6" 6" × 7" 6" × 8"	1¼" 2¼" 3¼" 4¼"

DOOR HARDWARE REQUIREMENTS

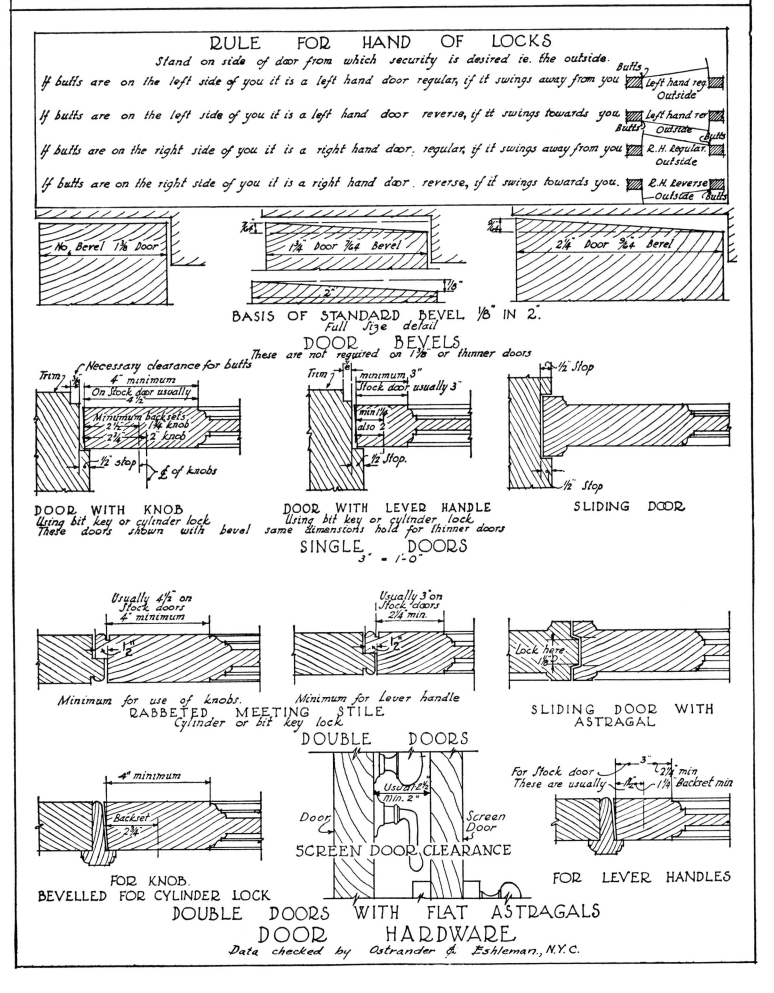

RULE FOR HAND OF LOCKS

Stand on side of door from which security is desired ie. the outside.

If butts are on the left side of you it is a left hand door regular, if it swings away from you

If butts are on the left side of you it is a left hand door reverse, if it swings towards you

If butts are on the right side of you it is a right hand door. regular, if it swings away from you

If butts are on the right side of you it is a right hand door. reverse, if it swings towards you

Butts — Left hand reg. Outside
Left hand rev. Outside — Butts
Butts — R.H. Regular. Outside
R.H. Reverse Outside — Butts

No Bevel 1⅜ Door — 1¾ Door 7/64 Bevel — 2¼ Door 9/64 Bevel

BASIS OF STANDARD BEVEL ⅛" IN 2".
Full size detail

DOOR BEVELS
These are not required on 1⅜ or thinner doors

DOOR WITH KNOB
Using bit key or cylinder lock
These doors shown with bevel

DOOR WITH LEVER HANDLE
Using bit key or cylinder lock
same dimensions hold for thinner doors

SLIDING DOOR

SINGLE DOORS
3" = 1'-0"

Minimum for use of knobs.
RABBETED MEETING STILE
Cylinder or bit key lock

Minimum for Lever handle

SLIDING DOOR WITH ASTRAGAL

DOUBLE DOORS

FOR KNOB.
BEVELLED FOR CYLINDER LOCK

SCREEN DOOR CLEARANCE

FOR LEVER HANDLES

DOUBLE DOORS WITH FLAT ASTRAGALS

DOOR HARDWARE
Data checked by Ostrander & Eshleman., N.Y.C.

WINDOW HARDWARE REQUIREMENTS

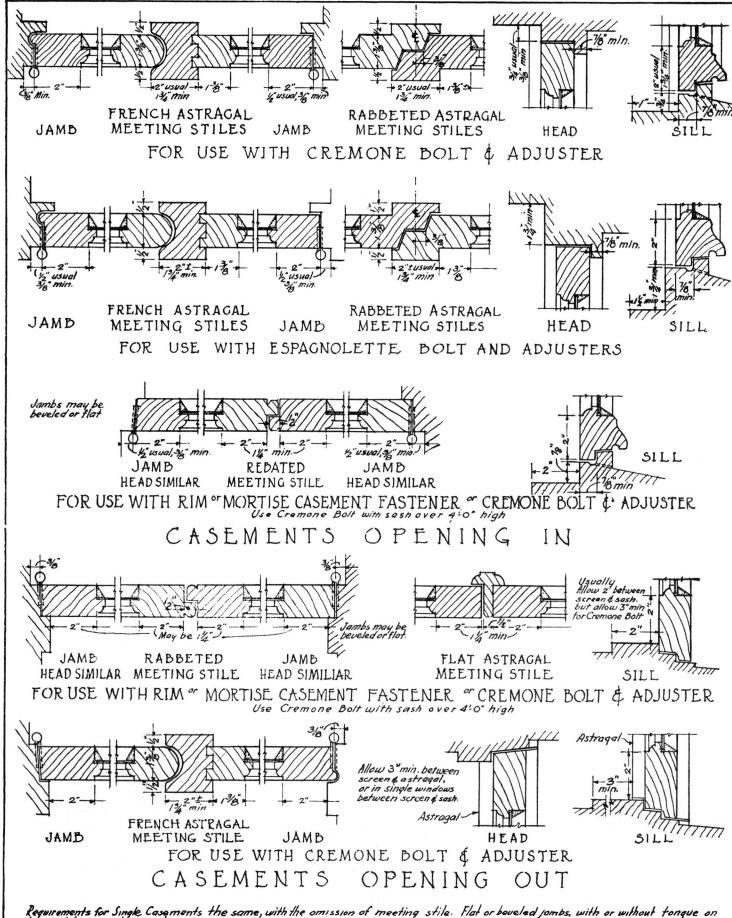

JAMB FRENCH ASTRAGAL MEETING STILES JAMB RABBETED ASTRAGAL MEETING STILES HEAD SILL

FOR USE WITH CREMONE BOLT & ADJUSTER

JAMB FRENCH ASTRAGAL MEETING STILES JAMB RABBETED ASTRAGAL MEETING STILES HEAD SILL

FOR USE WITH ESPAGNOLETTE BOLT AND ADJUSTERS

Jambs may be beveled or flat

JAMB HEAD SIMILAR REBATED MEETING STILE JAMB HEAD SIMILAR SILL

FOR USE WITH RIM or MORTISE CASEMENT FASTENER or CREMONE BOLT & ADJUSTER
Use Cremone Bolt with sash over 4'-0" high

CASEMENTS OPENING IN

JAMB HEAD SIMILAR RABBETED MEETING STILE JAMB HEAD SIMILIAR FLAT ASTRAGAL MEETING STILE SILL

Jambs may be beveled or flat.

Usually Allow 2" between screen & sash, but allow 3" min for Cremone Bolt

FOR USE WITH RIM or MORTISE CASEMENT FASTENER or CREMONE BOLT & ADJUSTER
Use Cremone Bolt with sash over 4'-0" high

JAMB FRENCH ASTRAGAL MEETING STILE JAMB

Allow 3" min. between screen & astragal, or in single windows between screen & sash.

Astragal Astragal HEAD SILL

FOR USE WITH CREMONE BOLT & ADJUSTER

CASEMENTS OPENING OUT

Requirements for Single Casements the same, with the omission of meeting stile. Flat or beveled jambs, with or without tongue on hinge side, may be used.

Data checked by "Ostrander and Eshleman" N.Y.C.

3" = 1'-0"

BUCKS & PLASTER PARTITIONS

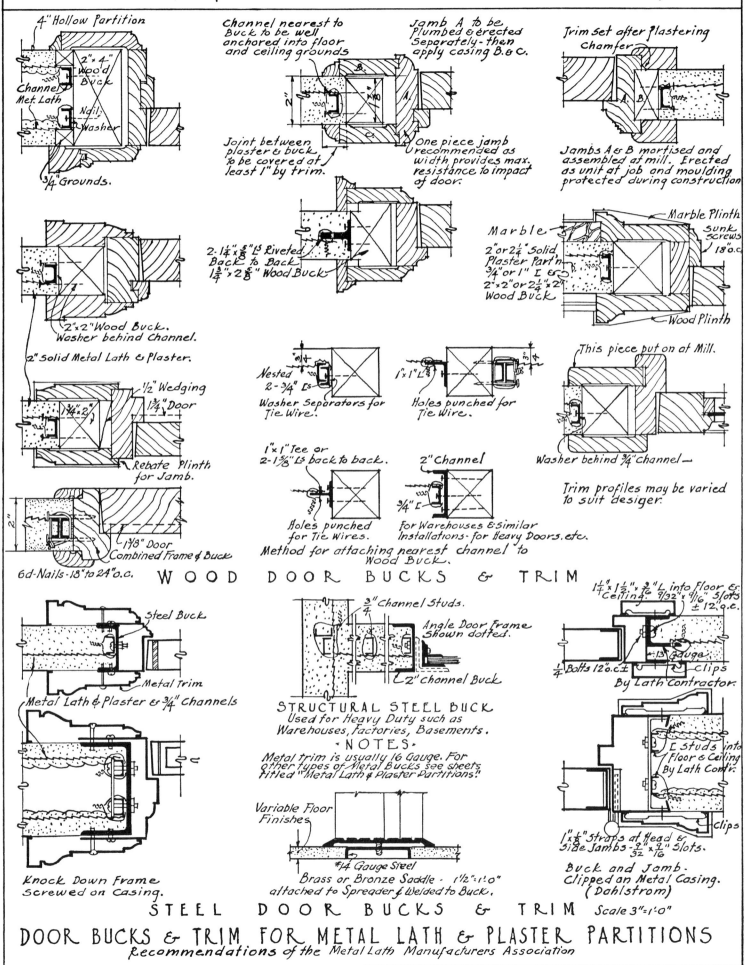

4" Hollow Partition

2"x4" Wood Buck

Channel
Met. Lath

Nail
Washer

¾" Grounds.

Channel nearest to Buck to be well anchored into floor and ceiling grounds

Joint between plaster & buck to be covered at least 1" by trim.

Jamb A to be plumbed & erected separately—then apply casing B. & C.

One piece jamb recommended as width provides max. resistance to impact of door.

Trim set after plastering Chamfer

Jambs A & B mortised and assembled at mill. Erected as unit at job and moulding protected during construction

2"x2" Wood Buck. Washer behind Channel.

2" Solid Metal Lath & Plaster.

½" Wedging
1¾" Door
¾"x2"

Rebate Plinth for Jamb.

2"
1⅜" Door
Combined Frame & Buck

6d-Nails-18" to 24"o.c.

2·1¼"x⅝"L's Riveted Back to Back
1¾"x2⅝" Wood Buck

Nested 2 - ¾" L's
Washer Separators for Tie Wire.

1"x1" L's
Holes punched for Tie Wire.

1"x1" Tee or 2-1⅝" L's back to back.
Holes punched for Tie Wires.

2" Channel
¾" L
for Warehouses & Similar Installations - for Heavy Doors, etc.

Method for attaching nearest channel to Wood Buck.

Marble
2" or 2¼" Solid Plaster Part'n
¾" or 1" L &c
2"x2" or 2¼"x2" Wood Buck

Marble Plinth
sunk screws 18"o.c.

Wood Plinth

This piece put on at Mill.

Washer behind ¾" channel

Trim profiles may be varied to suit desiger.

W O O D   D O O R   B U C K S   &   T R I M

Steel Buck
Metal Trim
Metal Lath & Plaster & ¾" Channels

Knock Down Frame Screwed on Casing.

¾" Channel Studs.
Angle Door Frame shown dotted.
2" channel Buck

STRUCTURAL STEEL BUCK
Used for Heavy Duty such as Warehouses, Factories, Basements.

·NOTES·
Metal trim is usually 16 Gauge. For other types of Metal Bucks see sheets titled "Metal Lath & Plaster Partitions"

Variable Floor Finishes

#14 Gauge Steel
Brass or Bronze Saddle - 1½"=1'·0"
attached to Spreader & Welded to Buck.

1¼"x1½"x¾"L into Floor & Ceiling· 9/32"x9/16" slots ± 12"o.c.
¼" Bolts 12"o.c.±
13 Gauge
Clips
By Lath Contractor.

L Studs into Floor & Ceiling By Lath Contr.
Clips

1"x⅛" Straps at Head & Side Jambs -9/32"x9/16" Slots.

Buck and Jamb. Clipped an Metal Casing. (Dahlstrom)

S T E E L   D O O R   B U C K S   &   T R I M   Scale 3"=1'·0"

DOOR BUCKS & TRIM FOR METAL LATH & PLASTER PARTITIONS
Recommendations of the Metal Lath Manufacturers Association

BUCKS & PLASTER PARTITIONS

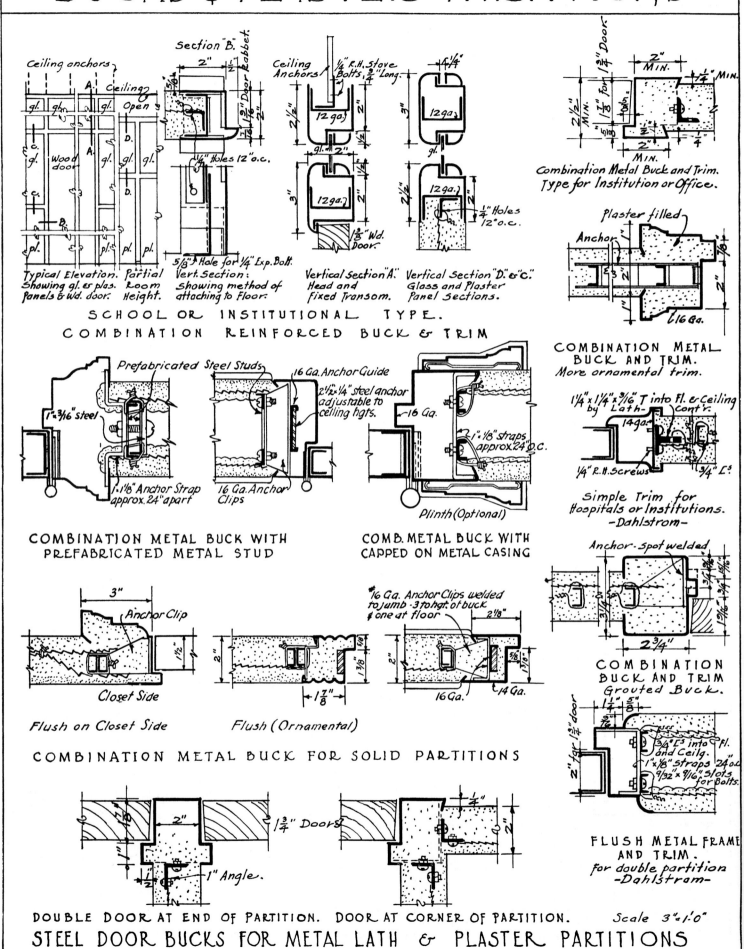

Section "B."

Ceiling anchors

Ceiling Anchors

¼" R.H.Stove Bolts ¾" Long.

gl. gl. Ceiling Open

Wood door

2" MIN.

Combination Metal Buck and Trim. Type for Institution or Office.

Typical Elevation. Showing gl. & plas. panels & Wd. door.

Partial Room Height.

Vert. Section: Showing method of attaching to Floor. 5/8" Hole for ¼" Exp. Bolt.

Vertical Section "A." Head and fixed Transom.

Vertical Section "D." & "C." Glass and Plaster Panel Sections.

Plaster filled

Anchor

16 Ga.

COMBINATION METAL BUCK AND TRIM. More ornamental trim.

SCHOOL OR INSTITUTIONAL TYPE.
COMBINATION REINFORCED BUCK & TRIM

Prefabricated Steel Studs

16 Ga. Anchor Guide

2½" x ¼" steel anchor adjustable to ceiling hgts.

1" x 3/16" steel

16 Ga.

2 - 1" x 1/8" straps approx. 24" O.C.

1 - 1 1/8" Anchor Strap approx. 24" apart

16 Ga. Anchor Clips

Plinth (Optional)

1¼" x 1¼" x 3/16" T into Fl. & Ceiling by Lath. Cont'r.

14 Ga.

¼" R.H.Screws   ¾" L's

Simple Trim for Hospitals or Institutions. —Dahlstrom—

COMBINATION METAL BUCK WITH PREFABRICATED METAL STUD

COMB. METAL BUCK WITH CAPPED ON METAL CASING

Anchor spot welded

2¾"

COMBINATION BUCK AND TRIM. Grouted Buck.

3"

Anchor Clip

Closet Side

16 Ga. Anchor Clips welded to jamb - 3 to hgt. of buck & one at floor

2 1/8"

16 Ga.   14 Ga.

Flush on Closet Side   Flush (Ornamental)

¾" L's into fl. and Ceilg. 1" x 1/8" straps 24" o.c. 9/32" x 9/16" Slots for Bolts.

COMBINATION METAL BUCK FOR SOLID PARTITIONS

FLUSH METAL FRAME AND TRIM. for double partition —Dahlstrom—

2"   1¾" Doors

1" Angle.

DOUBLE DOOR AT END OF PARTITION.   DOOR AT CORNER OF PARTITION.   Scale 3"=1'0"

STEEL DOOR BUCKS FOR METAL LATH & PLASTER PARTITIONS

METAL BUCKS- 2" PARTITION-HOUSING TYPE

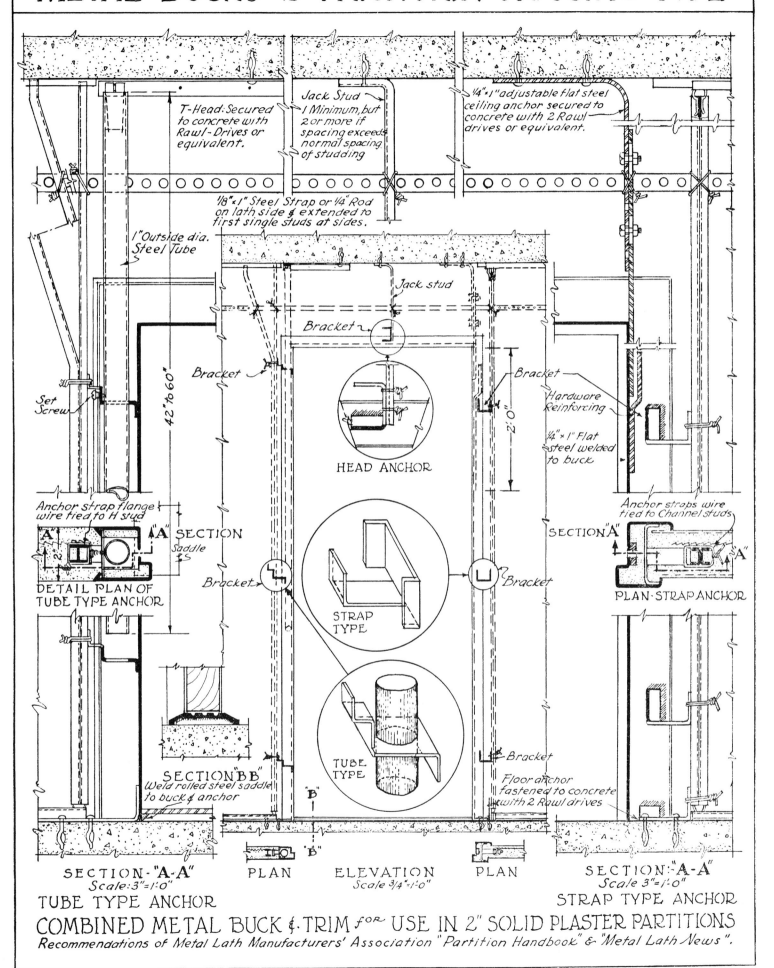

T-Head: Secured to concrete with Rawl-Drives or equivalent.

Jack Stud 1 Minimum, but 2 or more if spacing exceeds normal spacing of studding

¼"×1" adjustable flat steel ceiling anchor secured to concrete with 2 Rawl drives or equivalent.

⅛"×1" Steel Strap or ¼" Rod on lath side & extended to first single studs at sides.

1" Outside dia. Steel Tube

Jack stud

Bracket

Bracket

Bracket

Hardware Reinforcing

HEAD ANCHOR

¼"×1" Flat steel welded to buck

42" to 60"

2'-0"

Set Screw

Anchor strap flange wire tied to H stud

Anchor straps wire tied to Channel studs

SECTION "A"

Bracket

A" SECTION Saddle

STRAP TYPE

Bracket

PLAN-STRAP ANCHOR

DETAIL PLAN OF TUBE TYPE ANCHOR

TUBE TYPE

SECTION "BB" Weld rolled steel saddle to buck & anchor

Bracket

Floor anchor fastened to concrete with 2 Rawl drives

SECTION-"A-A" Scale: 3"=1'-0"

PLAN

ELEVATION Scale 3/4"=1'-0"

PLAN

SECTION-"A-A" Scale 3"=1'-0"

TUBE TYPE ANCHOR

STRAP TYPE ANCHOR

COMBINED METAL BUCK & TRIM for USE IN 2" SOLID PLASTER PARTITIONS

Recommendations of Metal Lath Manufacturers' Association "Partition Handbook" & "Metal Lath News".

LIGHT STEEL CASEMENTS & DOORS

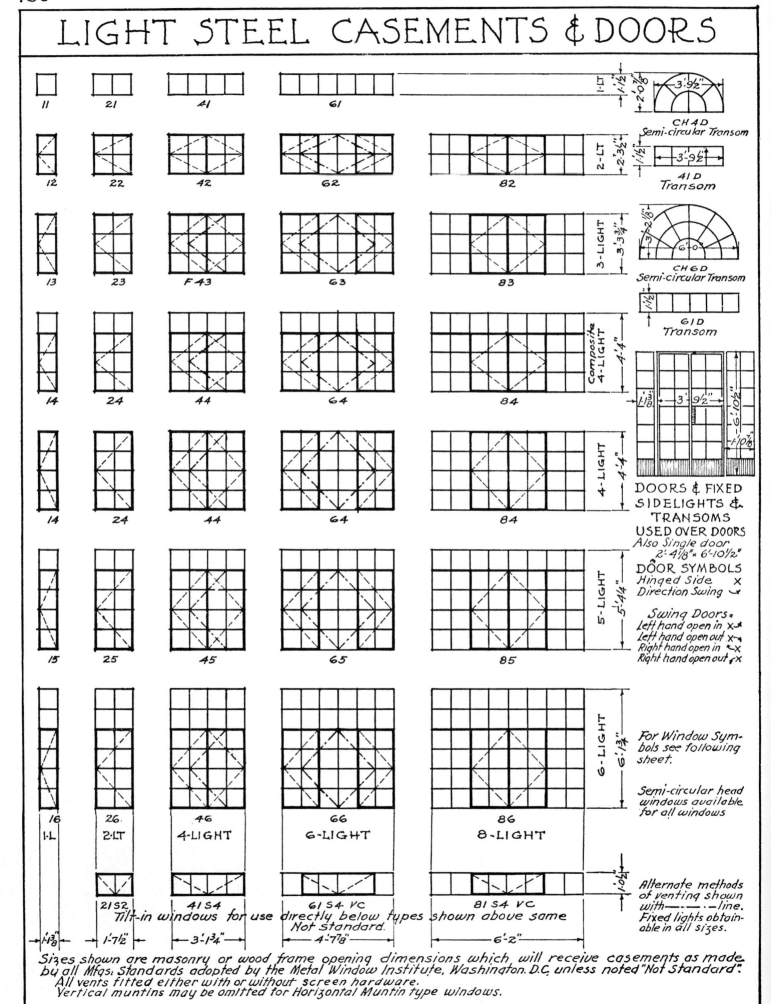

CH 4D
Semi-circular Transom

41 D
Transom

CH 6D
Semi-circular Transom

61 D
Transom

DOORS & FIXED
SIDELIGHTS &
TRANSOMS
USED OVER DOORS
Also Single door
2'-4⅛" x 6'-10½"
DOOR SYMBOLS
Hinged Side   X
Direction Swing   ↳

Swing Doors:
Left hand open in   X↲
Left hand open out X↳
Right hand open in ↳X
Right hand open out ↲X

For Window Symbols see following sheet.

Semi-circular head windows available for all windows.

Alternate methods of venting shown with —·—·— line. Fixed lights obtainable in all sizes.

Tilt-in windows for use directly below types shown above same Not standard.

Sizes shown are masonry or wood frame opening dimensions which will receive casements as made by all Mfgs. Standards adopted by the Metal Window Institute, Washington. D.C. unless noted "Not Standard".
All vents fitted either with or without screen hardware.
Vertical muntins may be omitted for Horizontal Muntin type windows.

181

LIGHT STEEL CASEMENT DETAILS

OUTWARD SWINGING

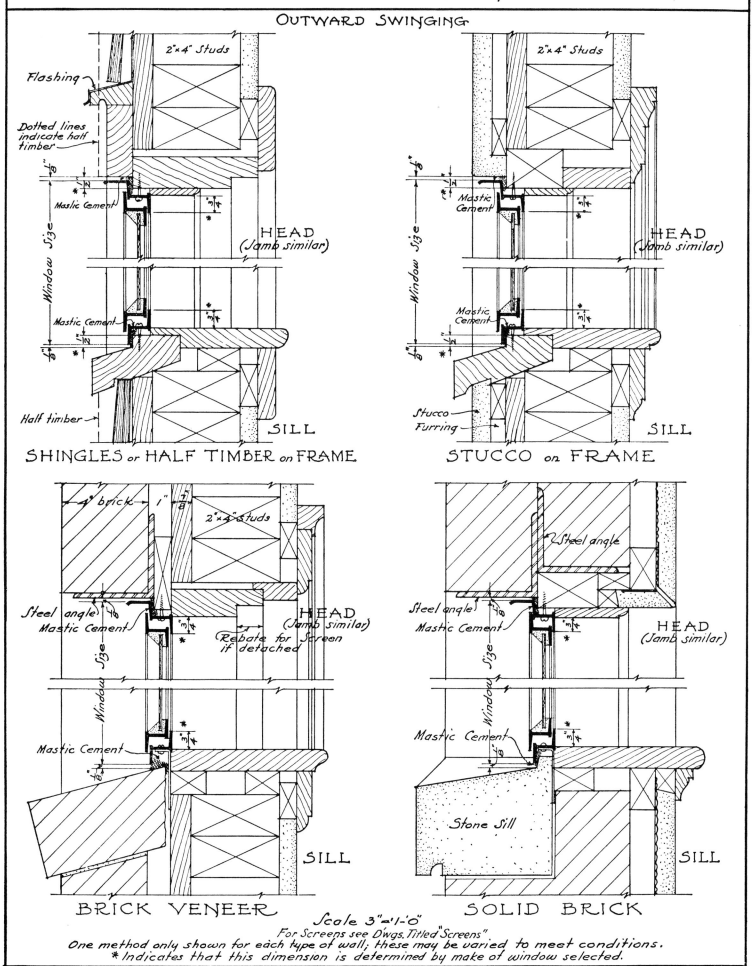

SHINGLES or HALF TIMBER on FRAME

STUCCO on FRAME

BRICK VENEER

SOLID BRICK

Scale 3"=1'-0"
For Screens see Dwgs. Titled "Screens"
One method only shown for each type of wall; these may be varied to meet conditions.
* Indicates that this dimension is determined by make of window selected.

REVOLVING DOORS

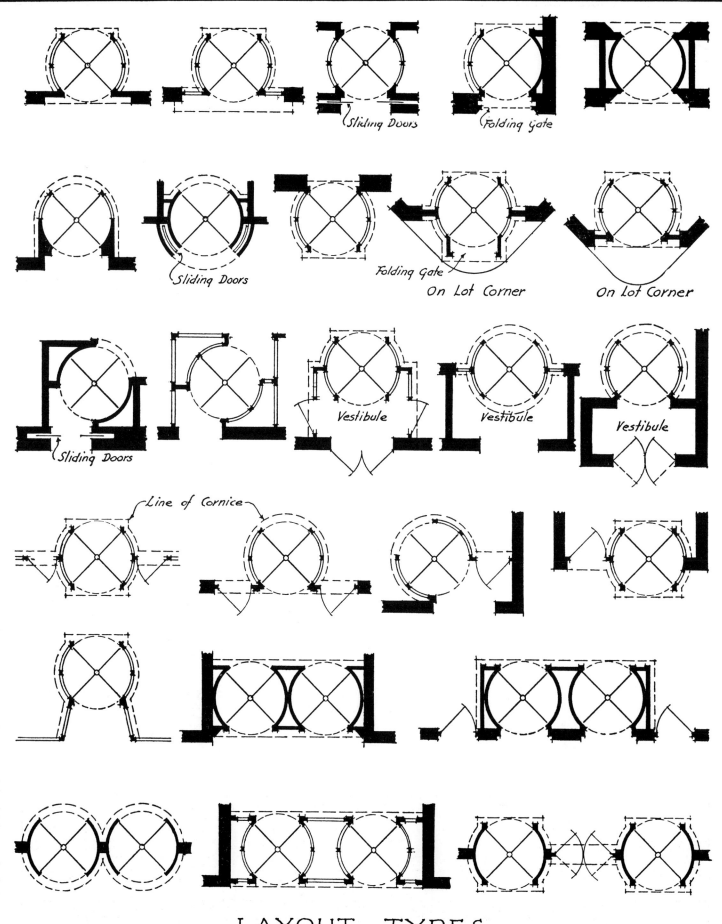

Sliding Doors

Folding Gate

Sliding Doors

Folding Gate
On Lot Corner

On Lot Corner

Sliding Doors

Vestibule

Vestibule

Vestibule

Line of Cornice

LAYOUT TYPES

REVOLVING DOORS

Locked

Central Open

Full Open.

Panic Collapsed

Full Open with wings collapsed.
Hinged walls may be flexed for added space as shown by dotted lines.

4 Wings   WING POSITIONS for ALL TYPES of DOORS.   1/8" = 1'-0".

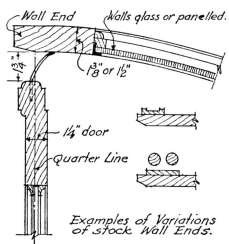

Wall End   Walls glass or panelled.
1 3/4"
1 3/8" or 1 1/2"
1 1/4" door
Quarter Line

Examples of Variations of stock Wall Ends.

ELEVATION

Overhead thrust Bearing   Lock Plate, Overhead Trolley
Trolley Track
Top Felt   Top Hanger
Push Bars
Push Plate
Pivot Litter
Bottom Disc   Kick Plate
Tension Release   Bottom Hang.
Floor Socket & Pivot   Floor Bracket
Vertical Rubber & Felt

Cornice may be stock or special.
Cornice may be less than 10", then use box covering to conceal mechanism.
Vestibule ceilings may be of wood, metal, marble or Formica. Provide slot in ceiling for mechanism.
Vestibule walls may be of glass, wood, metal, marble or Formica.
Wings-: Wood, metal, Formica. All tempered glass. Tempered plate glass & metal trim.
Speed control mechanism & photo-electric cell controlling equipment available.

MARBLE WALLS

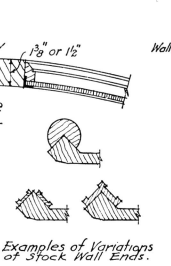

3"   2 3/4"
1 1/2"   1 1/8"
1 3/8" or 1 1/2"
7"   1 1/8"

Examples of Variations of Stock Wall Ends.

STOCK WALL ENDS
(and Variations)

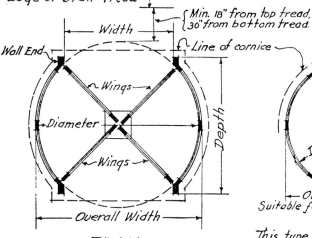

Edge of stair tread
Width
Min. 18" from top tread, 30" from bottom tread.
Line of cornice
Wall End
Wings
Diameter   Depth
Wings
Overall Width

PLAN
4 WING TYPE
Special types are available for use with screen doors, when open.
1/4" = 1'-0"

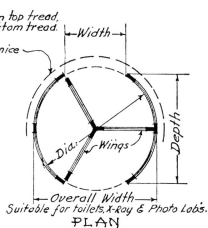

Width
Dia.   Wings
Depth
Overall Width
Suitable for toilets, X-Ray & Photo Labs.

PLAN
3 WING TYPE
(Rarely used)
This type used only when space saving is necessary. Capacity is less.

| | STOCK SIZES GENERALLY MANUFACTURED | | | | | | | | HEIGHTS of VESTIBULE |
	3 Wing Type				4 Wing Type				6'-9" to 8'-0". 7'-0" Average.
Diameter	4'-8"	4'-10"	5'-0"	5'-2"	5'-6"	6'-0"	6'-6"	7'-0"	7'-6"
Width	2'-1 3/4"	2'-2 3/4"	2'-3 3/4"	2'-4 3/4"	3'-9"	4'-1"	4'-5 1/4"	4'-9 1/2"	5'-1 1/2"
Depth	4'-4 1/2"	4'-6 1/4"	4'-8"	4'-9 3/4"	4'-4 1/4"	4'-8 1/2"	5'-0 3/4"	5'-5"	5'-9 1/4"
Overall Width	4'-10 3/4"	5'-0 3/4"	5'-2 3/4"	5'-4 3/4"	5'-8 3/4"	6'-2 3/4"	6'-8 3/4"	7'-2 3/4"	7'-9"

For Diameter: Above sizes may vary from 1" to 2" according to Manufacturer.

For 4 Wing Type: Above sizes may vary 1" according to Manufacturer. Sizes between the above are also made by some Manufr's.

For general use, use 6'-0" to 7'-0" diameter.
For Hotels use 7'-0" to 8'-0" dia. to accommodate luggage.

Capacity per hour both ways for 4 wings, tests show over 1000 persons.

FLOORING ON CONCRETE OVER EARTH

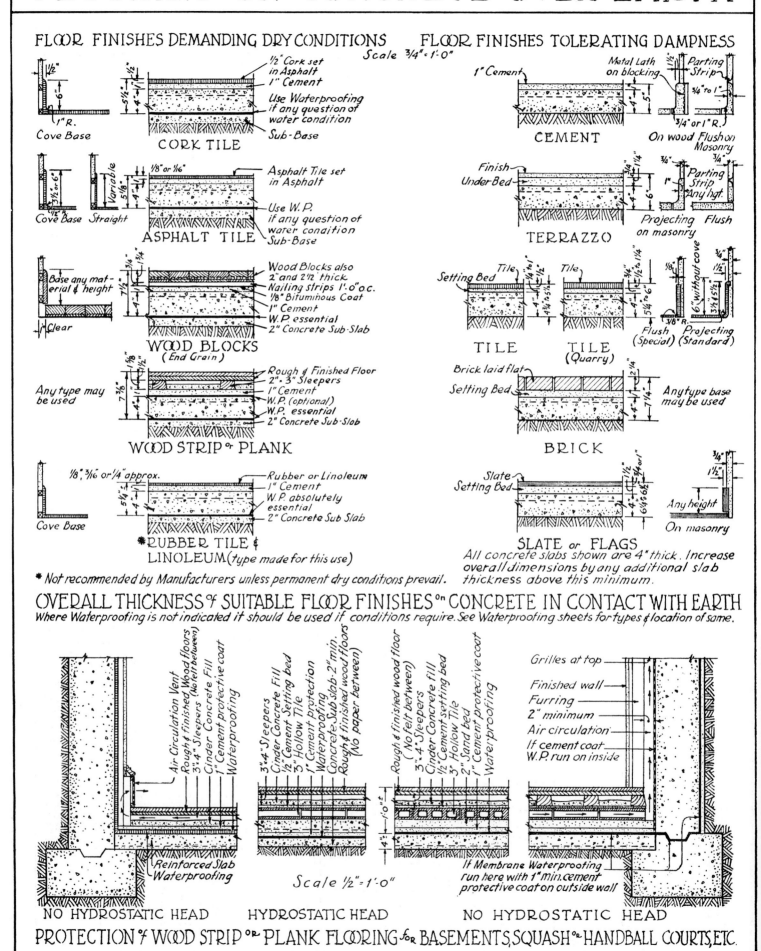

FLOOR FINISHES DEMANDING DRY CONDITIONS

Scale 3/4"=1'-0"

CORK TILE

1/2"
6"
1"R.
Cove Base
5 1/2"
4"
1/2"
1/2" Cork set in Asphalt
1" Cement
Use Waterproofing if any question of water condition
Sub-Base

ASPHALT TILE

3 1/2" or 6"
1/4"
Cove Base
Straight
Variable
5 5/8"
4"
1/2"
1/8" or 1/16"
Asphalt Tile set in Asphalt
Use W.P. if any question of water condition
Sub-Base

WOOD BLOCKS (End Grain)

Base any material & height
Clear
7 1/2"
4"
1"
3/4" 3/4"
Wood Blocks also 2" and 2 1/2" thick
Nailing strips 1'-0" o.c.
1/8" Bituminous Coat
1" Cement
W.P. essential
2" Concrete Sub-Slab

WOOD STRIP or PLANK

Any type may be used
7 3/8"
4"
1"
1 5/8"
1/2"
Rough & Finished Floor
2"-3" Sleepers
1" Cement
W.P. (optional)
W.P. essential
2" Concrete Sub-Slab

✷ RUBBER TILE & LINOLEUM (type made for this use)

Cove Base
5 1/4"
4"
1/8", 3/16" or 1/4" approx.
Rubber or Linoleum
1" Cement
W.P. absolutely essential
2" Concrete Sub Slab

FLOOR FINISHES TOLERATING DAMPNESS

CEMENT

On wood
Flush on Masonry
1" Cement
4"
5"
Metal Lath on blocking
1 1/2"
Parting Strip
3/4" to 1"
3/4" or 1"R.

TERRAZZO

Projecting on masonry
Flush
Finish
Under Bed
3/4" 1/4"
4"
6"
3/4"
3/4"
Parting Strip Any hgt.
1"

TILE   **TILE** (Quarry)

Setting Bed
Tile
Tile
1/4 to 1
1/4" 1/2"
4 1/4" 5 1/4"
4"
3/4" 1/2" to 1
1/4" 1/2" to 1
5 1/4" 6"
4"
Flush (Special)
Projecting (Standard)
6" without cove
3 1/4" 5 1/4"
1/8"
3/8"R.
1 1/2"
3/4"

BRICK

Brick laid flat
Setting Bed
2 1/4"
7 1/4"
4"
Any type base may be used

SLATE or FLAGS

Slate
Setting Bed
On masonry
Any height
1/2"
6 1/2" 6 1/2"
4"
3/4" or 1"
3/4"
1 1/2"

All concrete slabs shown are 4" thick. Increase overall dimensions by any additional slab thickness above this minimum.

✷ *Not recommended by Manufacturers unless permanent dry conditions prevail.*

OVERALL THICKNESS of SUITABLE FLOOR FINISHES on CONCRETE IN CONTACT WITH EARTH

Where Waterproofing is not indicated it should be used if conditions require. See Waterproofing sheets for types & location of same.

NO HYDROSTATIC HEAD

Air Circulation Vent
Rough & finished Wood Floors (No felt between)
3"-4" Sleepers
Cinder Concrete Fill
1" Cement protective coat
Waterproofing
Reinforced Slab
Waterproofing

HYDROSTATIC HEAD

3"x4" Sleepers
Cinder Concrete Fill
1/2" cement Setting bed
5" Hollow Tile
1" Cement protection
Waterproofing
Concrete Sub-slab-2" min.
Rough & finished wood floors (No paper between)

Scale 1/2"=1'-0"

NO HYDROSTATIC HEAD

Rough & finished wood floor (No felt between)
3"-4" Sleepers
Cinder Concrete fill
1/2" Cement setting bed
5" Hollow Tile
2" Sand bed
1" Cement protective coat
Waterproofing

Grilles at top
Finished wall
Furring
2" minimum
Air circulation
If cement coat W.P. run on inside

If Membrane Waterproofing run here with 1" min. cement protective coat on outside wall

PROTECTION of WOOD STRIP or PLANK FLOORING for BASEMENTS, SQUASH or HANDBALL COURTS, ETC.

GLASS BLOCKS

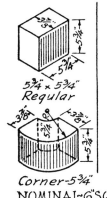

5¾" × 5¾"
Regular

Corner-5¾"
NOMINAL-6"SQ

Radial type
Regular
8½"
7¾" × 8½"
Corner-7¾"
NOMINAL-8" SQ.

Blocks weigh approx. 20 lbs. per sq. ft.
11¾"
NOMINAL-12"SQ.

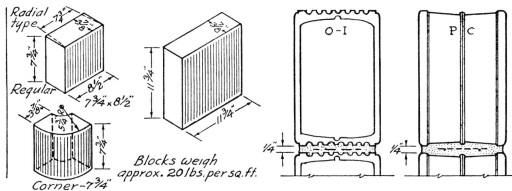

O-I   P C
¼"   ¼"
OWENS-ILLINOIS PITTSBURGH
CORNING
BLOCK & JOINTS
Scale 3"=1'-0"

BLOCK SIZES ~ ALL MADE BY O-I & P C
Scale ¾"=1'-0"

Block Sizes	Reserved for New Shapes		O-I, PC 5¾" × 5¾"	O-I, PC 7¾" × 7¾"	O-I, PC 11¾" × 11¾"
No. of Units	Height	Width	Height or Width	Height or Width	Height or Width
	¼" joints	¼" joints	¼" joints	¼" joints	¼" joints
1				6"	8"	1'-0"
2			1'-0"	1'-4"	2'-0"
3			1'-6"	2'-0"	3'-0"
4			2'-0"	2'-8"	4'-0"
5			2'-6"	3'-4"	5'-0"
6			3'-0"	4'-0"	6'-0"
7			3'-6"	4'-8"	7'-0"
8			4'-0"	5'-4"	8'-0"
9			4'-6"	6'-0"	9'-0"
10			5'-0"	6'-8"	10'-0"
11			5'-6"	7'-4"	11'-0"
12			6'-0"	8'-0"	12'-0"
13			6'-6"	8'-8"	13'-0"
14			7'-0"	9'-4"	14'-0"
15			7'-6"	10'-0"	15'-0"
16			8'-0"	10'-8"	16'-0"
17			8'-6"	11'-4"	17'-0"
18			9'-0"	12'-0"	18'-0"
19			9'-6"	12'-8"	19'-0"
20			10'-0"	13'-4"	20'-0"
21			10'-6"	14'-0"	21'-0"
22			11'-0"	14'-8"	22'-0"
23			11'-6"	15'-4"	23'-0"
24			12'-0"	16'-0"	24'-0"
25			12'-6"	16'-8"	25'-0"
26			13'-0"	17'-4"	26'-0"
27			13'-6"	18'-0"	27'-0"
28			14'-0"	18'-8"	28'-0"
29			14'-6"	19'-4"	29'-0"
30			15'-0"	20'-0"	30'-0"
31			15'-6"	20'-8"	31'-0"
32			16'-0"	21'-4"	32'-0"
33			16'-6"	22'-0"	33'-0"
34			17'-0"	22'-8"	34'-0"

WALL TIES

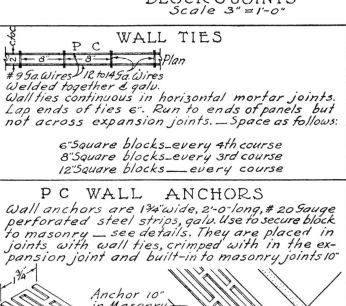

PC   Plan.
#9 Ga. Wires 12 to 14 Ga. Wires
Welded together & galv.
Wall ties continuous in horizontal mortar joints.
Lap ends of ties 6". Run to ends of panels but not across expansion joints.—Space as follows:

6" Square blocks—every 4th course
8" Square blocks—every 3rd course
12" Square blocks——every course

P C WALL ANCHORS

Wall anchors are 1¾" wide, 2'-0" long, #20 Gauge perforated steel strips, galv. Use to secure block to masonry — see details. They are placed in joints with wall ties, crimped with in the expansion joint and built-in to masonry joints 10"

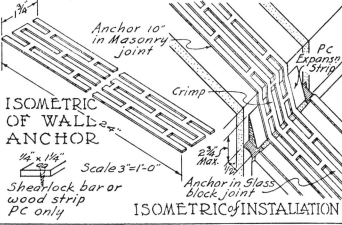

Anchor 10" in Masonry joint
PC Expans'n Strip
Crimp
ISOMETRIC OF WALL ANCHOR
Shearlock bar or wood strip PC only
¼" × 1¼"
Scale 3"=1'-0"
2¾" Max.
Anchor in Glass block joint
ISOMETRIC of INSTALLATION

EXPANSION STRIPS

Expansion strips made of cork fiber or glass wool ½" thick, 4" or 4⅛" wide, 25" or 36" long; adhered to surfaces with asphalt emulsion; used at all heads & jambs.

CURVED PANEL RADII LIMITS —To outside

Block size	Mfgs.	Reg. Block Min. Radii	Joints Ext.	Joints Inter.	Radial block Min. Radii	Joints Ext.	Joints Inter.
6" square	P C	4'-4½"	⅝"	⅛" ⅛"	2'-5" *	⅝"	⅛"
8" square	P C	5'-9"	⅝"	⅛" ⅛"	2'-6"	⁷⁄₁₆"	⁷⁄₁₆"
12" square	P C	8'-6	⅝"	⅛" ⅛"	(*Max. Rad. 6'-6½")		

Abbreviations used: P C for Pittsburgh Corning Corp.—O-I for Owens Illinois Glass Co.
For Specifications see Glass Block Div., "Architectural Spec." Harold R. Sleeper

GLASS BLOCK ~ EXTERIOR

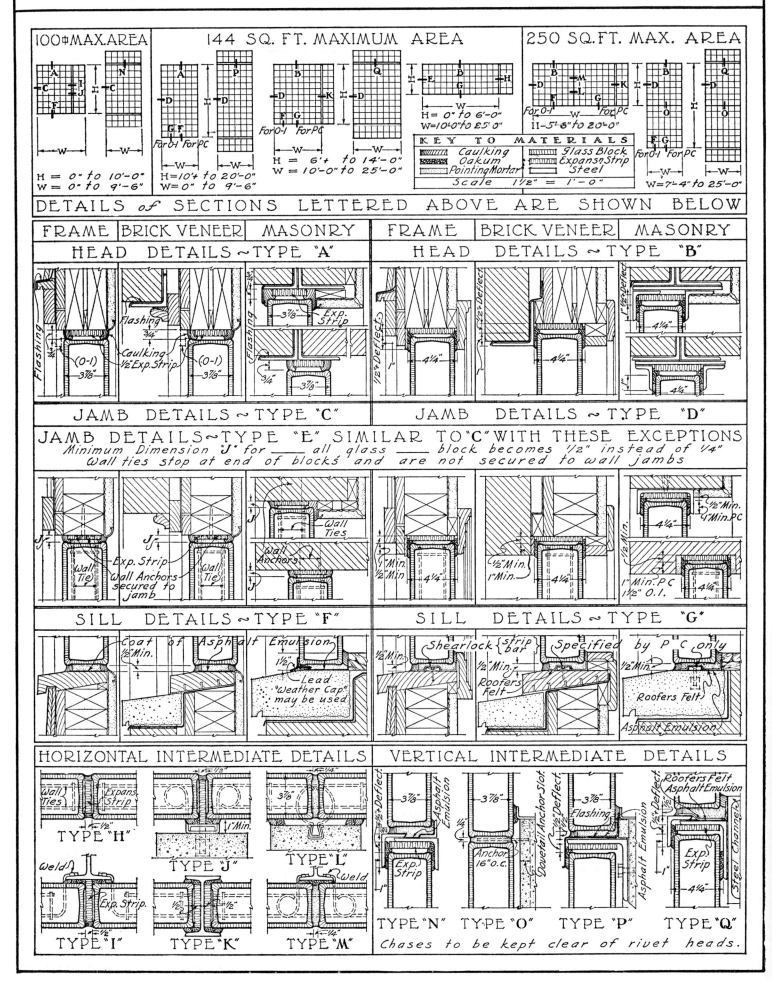

GLASS BLOCKS WITH METAL FRAMES

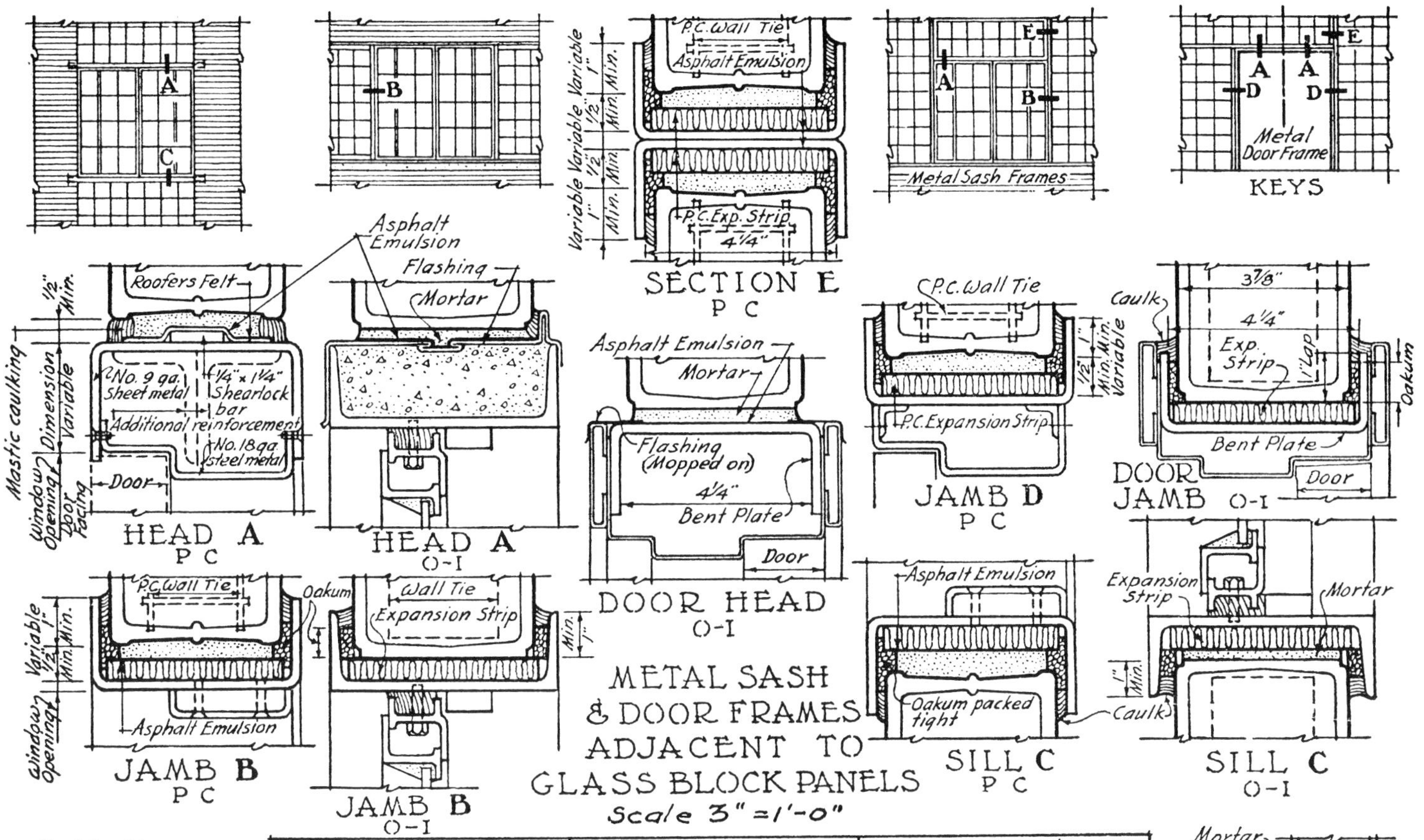

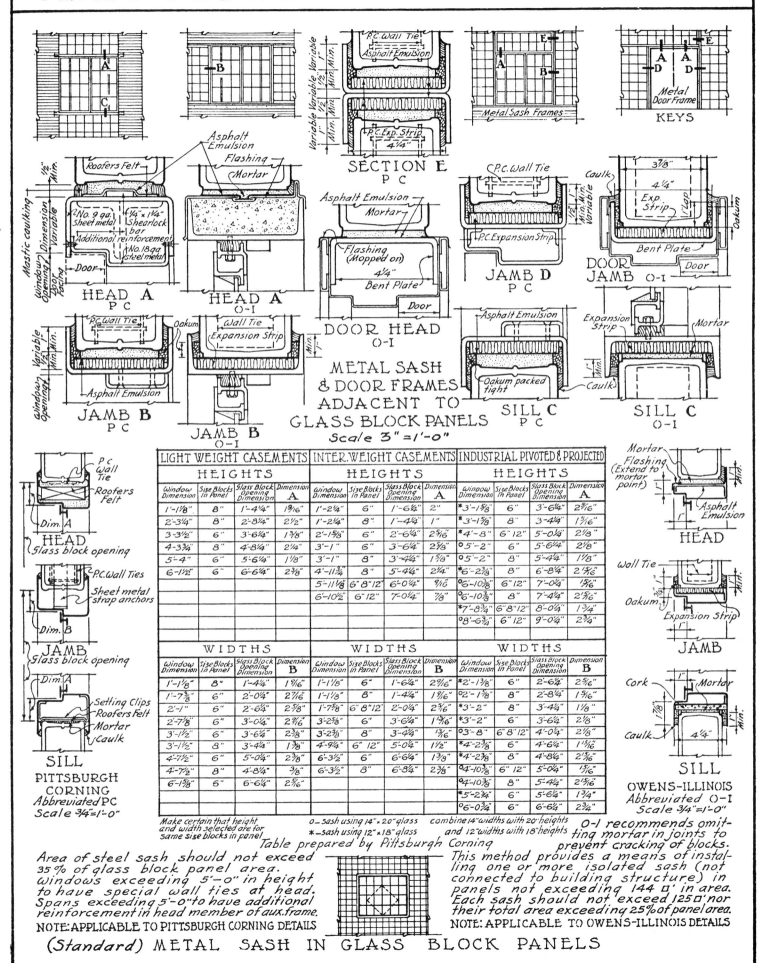

Metal Sash Frames
Metal Door Frame
KEYS
P.C. Wall Tie
Asphalt Emulsion
P.C. Exp. Strip
4¼"
SECTION E
P C
Roofers Felt
Flashing
Mortar
No. 9 ga. Sheet metal
¼" x 1¼" Shearlock bar
Additional reinforcement
No. 18 ga. steel metal
Door
Mastic caulking
Window Opening / Door Facing
Dimension Variable
HEAD A
P C
HEAD A
O-I
Flashing (Mopped on)
4¼"
Bent Plate
Door
DOOR HEAD
O-I
P.C. Expansion Strip
JAMB D
P C
Caulk
3⅞"
Exp. Strip
Oakum
DOOR JAMB O-I
P.C. Wall Tie
Wall Tie
Expansion Strip
Oakum
JAMB B
P C
JAMB B
O-I
Oakum packed tight
Caulk
SILL C
P C
Expansion Strip
Mortar
SILL C
O-I

METAL SASH & DOOR FRAMES ADJACENT TO GLASS BLOCK PANELS

Scale 3" = 1'-0"

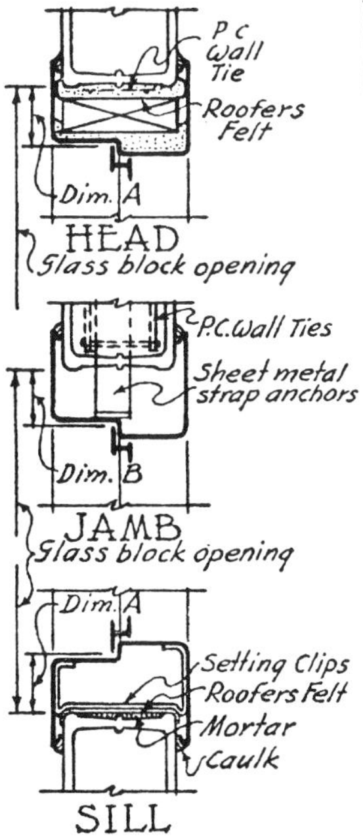

P C Wall Tie
Roofers Felt
Dim. A
HEAD
Glass block opening
P.C. Wall Ties
Sheet metal strap anchors
Dim. B
JAMB
Glass block opening
Dim. A
Setting Clips
Roofers Felt
Mortar
Caulk
SILL

PITTSBURGH CORNING
Abbreviated PC
Scale ¾" = 1'-0"

LIGHT WEIGHT CASEMENTS				INTER. WEIGHT CASEMENTS				INDUSTRIAL PIVOTED & PROJECTED			
HEIGHTS				HEIGHTS				HEIGHTS			
Window Dimension	Size Blocks in Panel	Glass Block Opening Dimension	Dimension A	Window Dimension	Size Blocks in Panel	Glass Block Opening Dimension	Dimension A	Window Dimension	Size Blocks in Panel	Glass Block Opening Dimension	Dimension A
1'-1⅛"	8"	1'-4¼"	1 9/16"	1'-2¼"	6"	1'-6¼"	2"	*3'-1⅝"	6"	3'-6¼"	2 5/16"
2-3¼"	8"	2-8¼"	2½"	1'-2¼"	8"	1'-4¼"	1"	*3'-1⅝"	8"	3-4¼"	1 5/16"
3-3½"	6"	3-6¼"	1⅜"	2'-1⅝"	6"	2-6¼"	2 5/16"	*4'-8"	6" 12"	5'-0¼"	2⅛"
4-3¾"	8"	4-8¼"	2¼"	3'-1"	6"	3-6¼"	2⅝"	°5'-2"	6"	5-6¼"	2⅛"
5-4"	6"	5-6¼"	1⅛"	3'-1"	8"	3'-4¼"	1⅝"	°5'-2"	8"	5-4¼"	1⅛"
6-1½"	6"	6-6¼"	2⅜"	4'-11¾"	8"	5'-4¼"	2¼"	*6'-2⅜"	8"	6'-8¼"	2 15/16"
				5'-11⅛"	6" 8" 12"	6'-0¼"	9/16"	°6'-10⅜"	6" 12"	7'-0¼"	15/16"
				6'-10½"	6" 12"	7'-0¼"	⅞"	°6'-10⅜"	8"	7'-4¼"	2 5/16"
								*7'-8¾"	6" 8" 12"	8'-0¼"	1¾"
								°8'-6¾"	6" 12"	9'-0¼"	2¾"
WIDTHS				WIDTHS				WIDTHS			
Window Dimension	Size Blocks in Panel	Glass Block Opening Dimension	Dimension B	Window Dimension	Size Blocks in Panel	Glass Block Opening Dimension	Dimension B	Window Dimension	Size Blocks in Panel	Glass Block Opening Dimension	Dimension B
1'-1⅛"	8"	1'-4¼"	1 9/16"	1'-1⅛"	6"	1'-6¼"	2 9/16"	*2'-1⅜"	6"	2'-6¼"	2 5/16"
1'-7⅜"	6"	2'-0¼"	2 7/16"	1'-1⅛"	8"	1'-4¼"	1 9/16"	°2'-1⅝"	8"	2'-8¼"	1 5/16"
2'-1"	6"	2'-6¼"	2⅝"	1'-7⅝"	6" 8" 12"	2'-0¼"	2 5/16"	*3'-2"	8"	3'-4¼"	1⅛"
2'-7⅛"	6"	3'-0¼"	2 9/16"	3'-2⅝"	6"	3'-6¼"	1 13/16"	*3'-2"	6"	3'-6¼"	2⅛"
3'-1½"	6"	3'-6¼"	2⅜"	3'-2⅝"	8"	3'-4¼"	13/16"	°3'-8"	6" 8" 12"	4'-0¼"	2⅛"
3'-1½"	8"	3'-4¼"	1⅜"	4'-9¼"	6" 12"	5'-0¼"	1½"	*4'-2⅜"	6"	4'-6¼"	1 15/16"
4'-7½"	6"	5'-0¼"	2⅜"	6'-3½"	6"	6'-6¼"	1⅜"	*4'-2⅜"	8"	4'-8¼"	2 15/16"
4'-7½"	8"	4'-8¼"	⅜"	6'-3½"	8"	6'-8¼"	2⅜"	°4'-10⅜"	6" 12"	5'-0¼"	15/16"
6'-1⅝"	6"	6'-6¼"	2 5/16"					°4'-10⅜"	8"	5'-4¼"	2 15/16"
								*5'-2¾"	6"	5'-6¼"	1¾"
								°6'-0¾"	6"	6'-6¼"	2¾"

Make certain that height and width selected are for same size blocks in panel

o – sash using 14" × 20" glass
** – sash using 12" × 18" glass*

combine 14" widths with 20" heights and 12" widths with 18" heights

Table prepared by Pittsburgh Corning

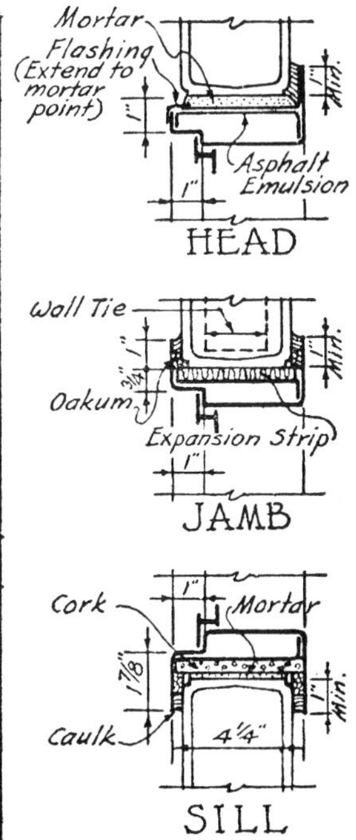

Mortar
Flashing (Extend to mortar point)
Asphalt Emulsion
HEAD
Wall Tie
Oakum
Expansion Strip
JAMB
Cork
Mortar
Caulk
4¼"
SILL

OWENS-ILLINOIS
Abbreviated O-I
Scale ¾" = 1'-0"

O-I recommends omitting mortar in joints to prevent cracking of blocks.

Area of steel sash should not exceed 35% of glass block panel area. Windows exceeding 5'-0" in height to have special wall ties at head. Spans exceeding 5'-0" to have additional reinforcement in head member of aux. frame.

NOTE: APPLICABLE TO PITTSBURGH CORNING DETAILS

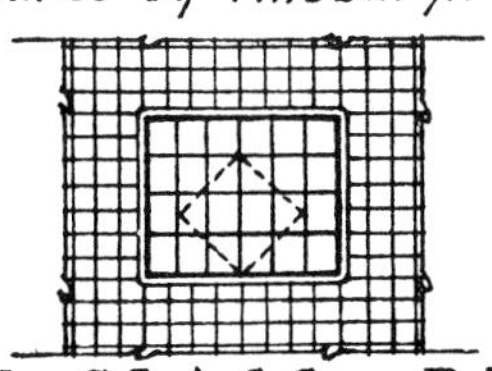

This method provides a means of installing one or more isolated sash (not connected to building structure) in panels not exceeding 144 □' in area. Each sash should not exceed 125 □' nor their total area exceeding 25% of panel area.

NOTE: APPLICABLE TO OWENS-ILLINOIS DETAILS

(Standard) METAL SASH IN GLASS BLOCK PANELS

GLASS BLOCKS: WOOD FRAMES-INTERIOR PANELS

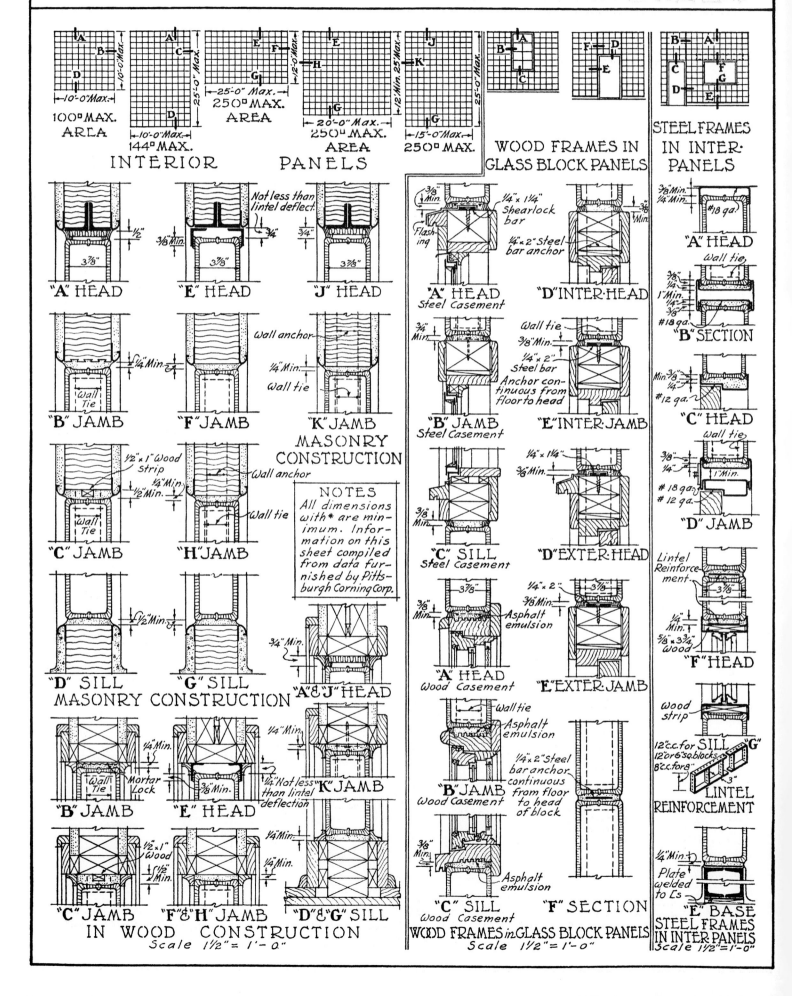

INTERIOR PANELS

100□ MAX. AREA
144□ MAX.
250□ MAX. AREA
250□ MAX. AREA
250□ MAX.

WOOD FRAMES IN GLASS BLOCK PANELS

STEEL FRAMES IN INTER-PANELS

"A" HEAD   "E" HEAD   "J" HEAD

"B" JAMB   "F" JAMB   "K" JAMB
MASONRY CONSTRUCTION

"C" JAMB   "H" JAMB

NOTES
All dimensions with * are minimum. Information on this sheet compiled from data furnished by Pittsburgh Corning Corp.

"D" SILL   "G" SILL
MASONRY CONSTRUCTION

"A" HEAD — Steel Casement
"D" INTER-HEAD
"B" JAMB — Steel Casement
"E" INTER-JAMB
"C" SILL — Steel Casement
"D" EXTER-HEAD
"A" HEAD — Wood Casement
"E" EXTER-JAMB
"B" JAMB — Wood Casement
"C" SILL — Wood Casement
"F" SECTION

"A" & "J" HEAD
"K" JAMB

"B" JAMB   "E" HEAD

"C" JAMB   "F" & "H" JAMB   "D" & "G" SILL
IN WOOD CONSTRUCTION
Scale 1½" = 1'-0"

WOOD FRAMES in GLASS BLOCK PANELS
Scale 1½" = 1'-0"

"A" HEAD
"B" SECTION
"C" HEAD
"D" JAMB
"F" HEAD
"G" SILL
LINTEL REINFORCEMENT
"E" BASE
STEEL FRAMES IN INTER PANELS
Scale 1½" = 1'-0"

VENTS—WALL, PARTITION and DOOR

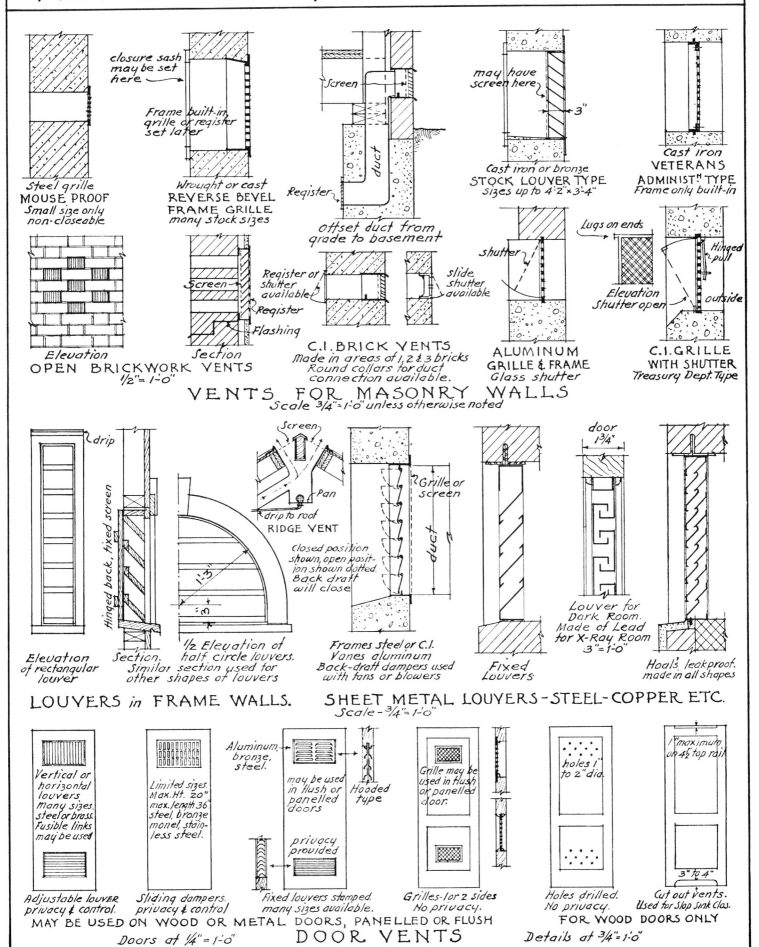

closure sash may be set here→

Frame built-in, grille or register set later

Steel grille MOUSE PROOF Small size only non-closeable

Wrought or cast REVERSE BEVEL FRAME GRILLE many stock sizes

Screen

duct

Register

offset duct from grade to basement

may have screen here→ 3"

Cast iron or bronze STOCK LOUVER TYPE sizes up to 4'2"×3'4"

Cast iron VETERANS ADMINIST⁵ TYPE Frame only built-in

Elevation
OPEN BRICKWORK VENTS ½"=1'-0"

Screen
Register
Flashing
Section

Register or shutter available.
C.I. BRICK VENTS Made in areas of 1, 2 & 3 bricks. Round collars for duct connection available.

slide shutter available

shutter
ALUMINUM GRILLE & FRAME Glass shutter

Lugs on ends
Hinged pull
outside
Elevation Shutter open
C.I. GRILLE WITH SHUTTER Treasury Dept. Type

VENTS FOR MASONRY WALLS
Scale ¾"=1'-0" unless otherwise noted

drip

Elevation of rectangular louver

Hinged back, fixed screen

Section.

½ Elevation of half circle louvers. Similar section used for other shapes of louvers

Screen
Pan
drip to roof
RIDGE VENT

Grille or screen
duct
Closed position shown, open position shown dotted. Back draft will close
Frames steel or C.I. Vanes aluminum Back-draft dampers used with fans or blowers

Fixed Louvers

door 1¾"
Louver for Dark Room. Made of Lead for X-Ray Room 3"=1'-0"

Hoals leakproof. made in all shapes

LOUVERS in FRAME WALLS.

SHEET METAL LOUVERS—STEEL—COPPER ETC.
Scale—¾"=1'-0"

Vertical or horizontal louvers many sizes. steel or brass. Fusible links may be used.
Adjustable louver privacy & control.

Limited sizes. Max. Ht. 20" max. length 36 steel, bronze, monel, stainless steel.
Sliding dampers. privacy & control

Aluminum, bronze, steel.
may be used in flush or panelled doors
privacy provided
Hooded type
Fixed louvers stamped. many sizes available.

Grille may be used in flush or panelled door.
Grilles—for 2 sides No privacy.

holes 1" to 2" dia.
Holes drilled. No privacy.
FOR WOOD DOORS ONLY

1" maximum on 4½" top rail
3" to 4"
Cut out vents. Used for Slop Sink Clos.

MAY BE USED ON WOOD OR METAL DOORS, PANELLED OR FLUSH
DOOR VENTS
Doors at ¼"=1'-0"   Details at ¾"=1'-0"

ALUMINUM WINDOWS

Without Muntins   With Muntins

ELEVATION DOUBLE HUNG

MUNTIN

JAMB

Furring

Window Opening

HEAD

Removable Spring Balances

Catch

MEETING RAIL

Pull

SILL

Lift

DOUBLE HUNG · SERIES H-2 *Scale Details 6"=1'-0"*

Without Muntins   With Muntins

ELEVATION CASEMENT

MULLION

Window Opening

JAMB

CASEMENT · SERIES K-1

"PERMATITE"· GENERAL BRONZE CORP

HEAD

TRANSOM

MUNTIN

SILL

Window Opening

Without Muntins   With Muntins

ELEVATION DOUBLE HUNG

Sliding Anchor

This channel used when height exceeds 5'6"

JAMB   MULLION

Window Opening

4" Minimum Clearance

Sash Balances

Access to Balances thru removable plg.

HEAD

Screen

MUNTIN

Catch

MEETING RAIL

Lift

SILL

Window Opening

DOUBLE HUNG · SERIES - 120 *Scale Details: 3"=1'-0"*

Without Muntins   With Muntins

ELEVATION CASEMENT

MULLION

JAMB

Masonry Opening
Frame Opening

CASEMENT · SERIES - 420

HEAD

TRANSOM

MUNTIN

SILL

Frame Opening
Masonry Opening

"SEALAIR"· THE KAWNEER CO.

8

FINISH MATERIALS

METAL LATHING

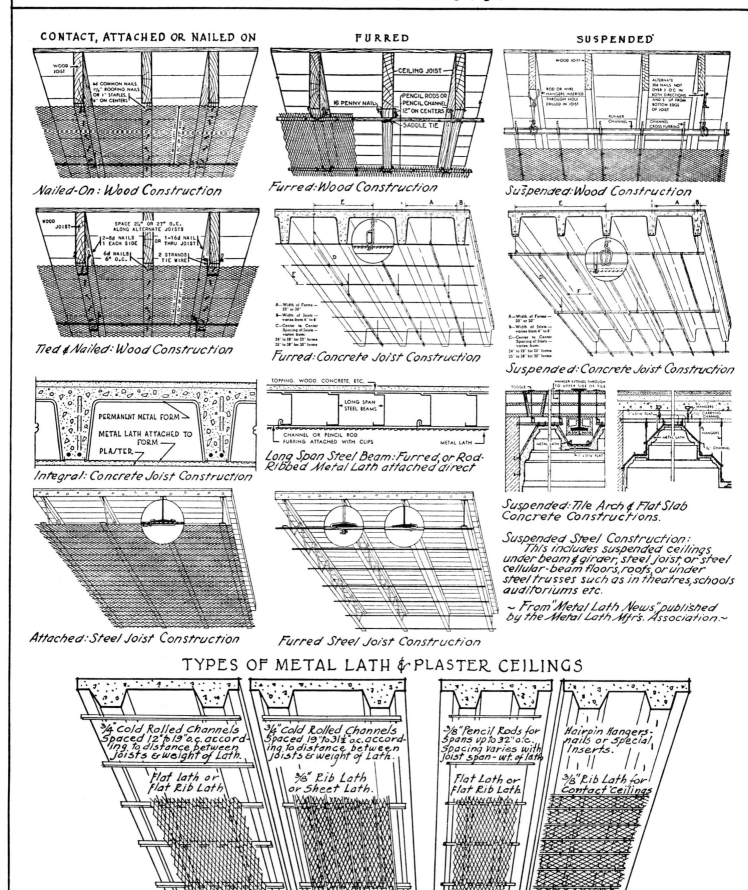

CONTACT, ATTACHED OR NAILED ON

Nailed-On: Wood Construction

Tied & Nailed: Wood Construction

Integral: Concrete Joist Construction

Attached: Steel Joist Construction

FURRED

Furred: Wood Construction

Furred: Concrete Joist Construction

Long Span Steel Beam: Furred, or Rod-Ribbed Metal Lath attached direct

Furred Steel Joist Construction

SUSPENDED

Suspended: Wood Construction

Suspended: Concrete Joist Construction

Suspended: Tile Arch & Flat Slab Concrete Constructions.

Suspended Steel Construction:
This includes suspended ceilings under beam & girder, steel joist or steel cellular-beam floors, roofs, or under steel trusses such as in theatres, schools auditoriums etc.

~ From "Metal Lath News" published by the Metal Lath Mfr's. Association.~

TYPES OF METAL LATH & PLASTER CEILINGS

3/4" Cold Rolled Channels Spaced 12" to 19" o.c. according to distance between joists & weight of Lath.

Flat lath or Flat Rib Lath

3/4" Cold Rolled Channels Spaced 19" to 31½" o.c. according to distance between joists & weight of Lath.

3/8" Rib Lath or Sheet Lath.

3/8" Pencil Rods for Spans up to 32" o.c. Spacing varies with joist span – wt. of lath

Flat Lath or Flat Rib Lath

Hairpin Hangers, nails or Special Inserts.

3/8" Rib Lath for Contact Ceilings

A   B   C   D

CONTACT & FURRED CEILING ON REINF. CONCRETE SLAB

METAL LATH & PLASTER

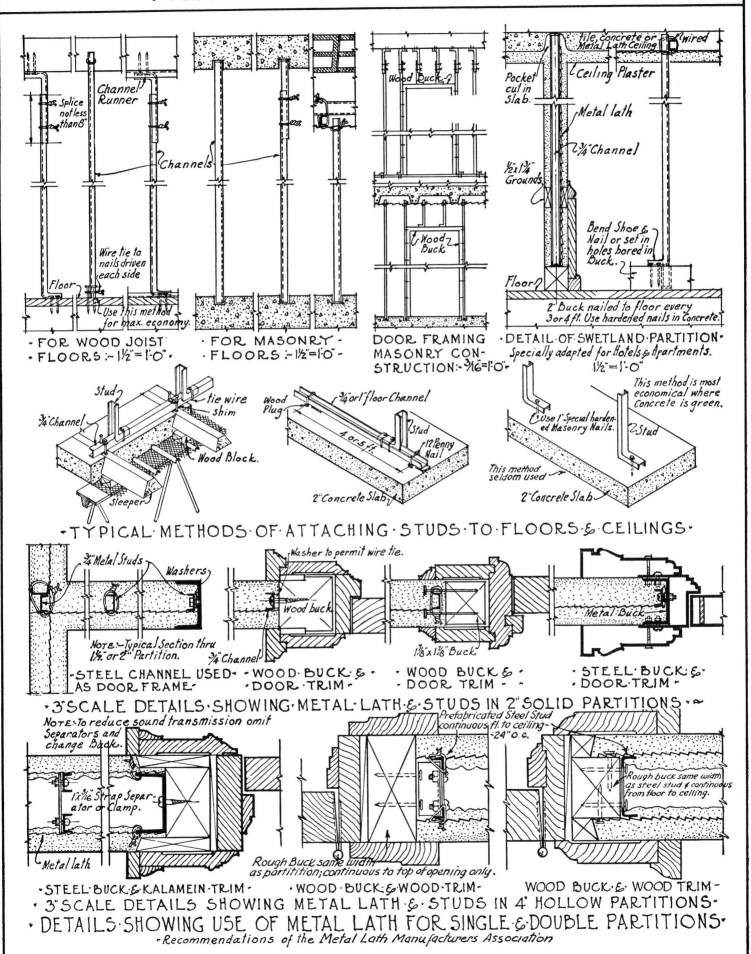

·FOR WOOD JOIST· ·FLOORS· ~1½"=1'·0'·

·FOR MASONRY· ·FLOORS· ~1½"=1'·0'·

DOOR FRAMING MASONRY CON- STRUCTION ~3/16"=1'·0'·

·DETAIL·OF·SWETLAND·PARTITION· Specially adapted for Hotels & Apartments. 1½"=1'-0"

·TYPICAL·METHODS·OF·ATTACHING·STUDS·TO·FLOORS·&·CEILINGS·

·STEEL·CHANNEL·USED· AS·DOOR·FRAME·

·WOOD·BUCK·&· ·DOOR·TRIM·

·WOOD·BUCK·&· ·DOOR·TRIM·

·STEEL·BUCK·&· ·DOOR·TRIM·

·3"·SCALE·DETAILS·SHOWING·METAL·LATH·&·STUDS·IN·2"·SOLID·PARTITIONS·~

·STEEL·BUCK·&·KALAMEIN·TRIM·

·WOOD·BUCK·&·WOOD·TRIM·

WOOD·BUCK·&·WOOD·TRIM·

·3"·SCALE·DETAILS·SHOWING·METAL·LATH·&·STUDS·IN·4"·HOLLOW·PARTITIONS·

·DETAILS·SHOWING·USE·OF·METAL·LATH·FOR·SINGLE·&·DOUBLE·PARTITIONS·

·Recommendations of the Metal Lath Manufacturers Association·

METAL LATH & PLASTER
SPECIAL & PATENTED TYPES OF STUD ANCHORAGE

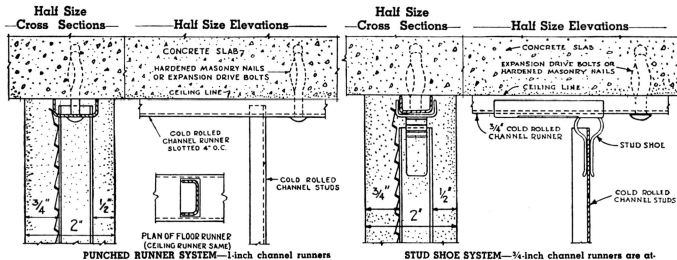

PUNCHED RUNNER SYSTEM—1-inch channel runners are attached to floor and ceiling with masonry nails or other anchors. Runners have slots punched every 4 inches to receive channel studs, spacing of studs depending on type and weight of Metal Lath used. Studs are dropped into slot in floor runner and slipped into slot in ceiling runner.

STUD SHOE SYSTEM—¾-inch channel runners are attached to floor and ceiling with Rawl Drives. Special stud shoes clamp with a driving fit onto runners, and are placed to correspond with stud spacing. Studs are slipped into floor shoes or clips and top end then sprung into position in ceiling clips.

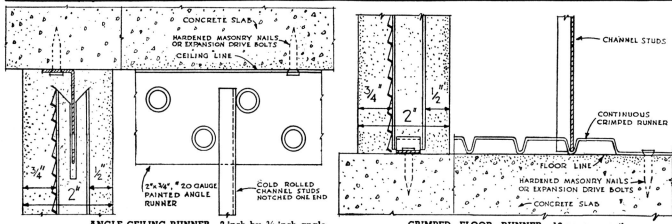

ANGLE CEILING RUNNER—2-inch by ¾-inch angle runners are attached to ceiling with masonry nails or equivalent anchors. Channel studs are notched and slotted at one end. Studs are placed by slipping slotted end upward onto downstanding leg of angle runner and dropping down into crimped floor runner as in Fig. at right. Burrs on holes prevent tipping of channels.

CRIMPED FLOOR RUNNER—18-gauge continuous crimped runners are attached to floor with masonry nails or equivalent anchors. Grooves in runner provide slot into which ¾-inch channel studs are dropped. Top ends are secured as shown in Fig. at left.

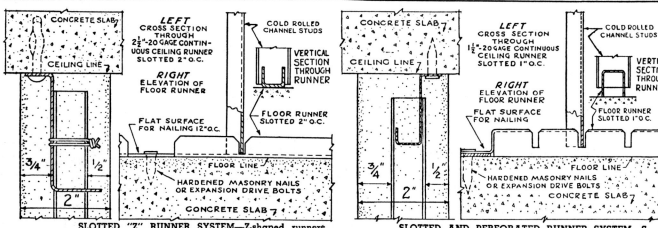

SLOTTED "Z" RUNNER SYSTEM—Z-shaped runners for ceiling have ½-inch nailing flange and 1⅛-inch horizontal flange with openings punched for channel studs. Floor runners are channel-shaped, with upstanding flanges slotted. Studs are first slipped into ceiling runner, and then dropped into floor runner.

SLOTTED AND PERFORATED RUNNER SYSTEM—S-shaped runners for ceiling have ½-inch nailing flange and ½-inch horizontal flange with upturned edge both slotted for channel studs. Floor runners are U-shaped with flanges down and web and flanges slotted. Studs are first slipped into ceiling runner and then dropped into floor runner.

From "Partition Handbook," published by Metal Lath Mfrs. Association.

METAL LATH & PLASTER

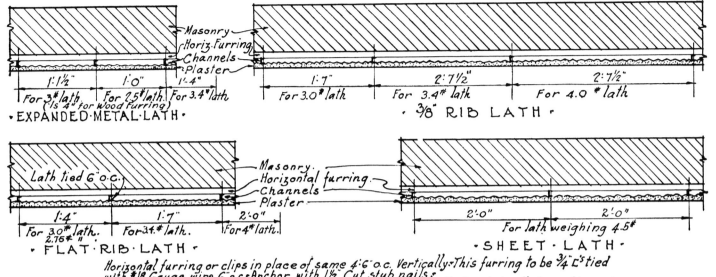

· EXPANDED · METAL · LATH ·

For 3# lath (Is 4" for Wood furring) For 2.5# lath For 3.4# lath
1'·1½" 1'·0" 1'·4"

· ⅜" RIB LATH ·
For 3.0# lath For 3.4# lath For 4.0 # lath
1'·7" 2'·7½" 2'·7½"

Masonry
Horiz. Furring
Channels
Plaster

· FLAT · RIB · LATH ·
Lath tied 6" o.c.
For 3.0# lath. 2.75# " For 3.4# lath. For 4# lath.
1'·4" 1'·7" 2'·0"

· SHEET · LATH ·
Masonry.
Horizontal furring.
Channels.
Plaster.
For lath weighing 4.5#
2'·0" 2'·0"

Horizontal furring or clips in place of same 4'·6" o.c. Vertically. This furring to be ¾" L's tied with #18 Gauge wire 6" o.c. Anchor with 1½" Cut stub nails.
Vertical furring to be ¾" L's minimum. Standard or box cold rolled or hot rolled, weighing not less than 276# per thousand lineal feet. LATH WEIGHTS SAME AS FOR HOLLOW PARTITION.
· STANDING · FURRING · SHALL · BE · SAME · DESIGN · AS · SOLID · PLASTER · PARTITION ·

· METAL · LATH · & · PLASTER · FURRING · MINIMUM · REQUIREMENTS ·
¾" = 1'·0"

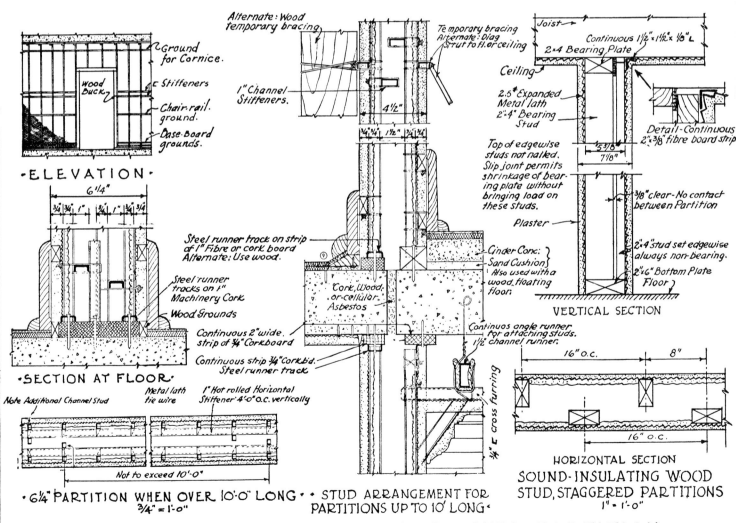

· SOUND · RESISTIVE · METAL · LATH · & · PLASTER · PARTITION ·
· Recommended by the · Metal Lath Manufacturers Association ·

METAL LATH & PLASTER CEILINGS

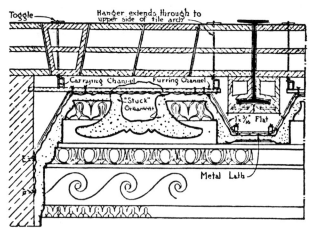

ORNAMENTAL CORNICE, CEILING & BEAM FURRING
SUSPENDED FROM STRUCTURAL CLAY TILE ARCH

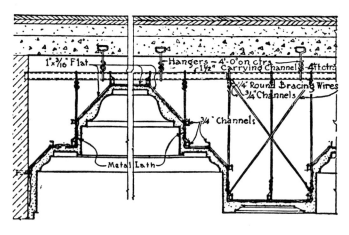

TYPICAL CORNICE AND FALSE BEAM
SUSPENDED FROM CONCRETE SLAB

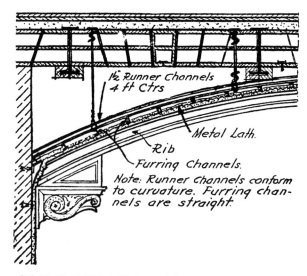

SCALE DETAILS OF VAULTED CEILING
HUNG FROM TERRA COTTA ARCH

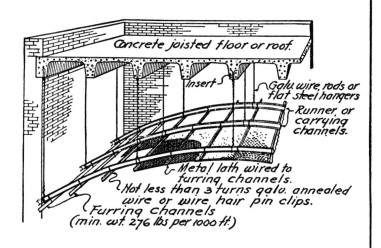

DETAILS OF SUSPENDED CEILING HUNG
FROM CONCRETE JOISTED FLOOR OR ROOF

SPACING of SUPPORTS for CEILINGS and OTHER HORIZONTAL SURFACES

TYPE OF LATH	Weight Sq. Yard	SPACING OF SUPPORTS						
		12"	Over 12" Incl. 13½"	Over 13½" Incl. 16"	Over 16" Incl. 19½"	Over 19½" Incl. 23½"	Over 23½" Incl. 31½"	Over 31½" Incl. 33½"
Flat Expanded Lath	3.0	*	o					
	3.4	**	*	o				
Flat Rib	3.0	**	**	**	o			
	3.4	**	**	**	**			
	4.0	*	**	**	**			
3⁄8" Rib or Lath of Equal Rigidity	3.4	*	**	*	*	**	**	●
	4.0	**	**	**	**	**	**	●
Sheet Lath +	4.5	*	*	*	o			

* Permissible for all purposes.
o Permissible only for nailed on work (to wood joists,
● Permissible only under concrete joists, etc.)
+ Recommended spacings for other weights of Sheet Lath may be obtained from manufacturers.

Note: Min. weight of metal lath for ceiling construction shall be 2.75 lbs per sq. yd., excl. of paper or other backing.

SUSPENDED CEILING DETAILS
Recommendations of the Metal Lath Manufacturers Association.

WALL FURRING & METHODS of ATTACHMENT

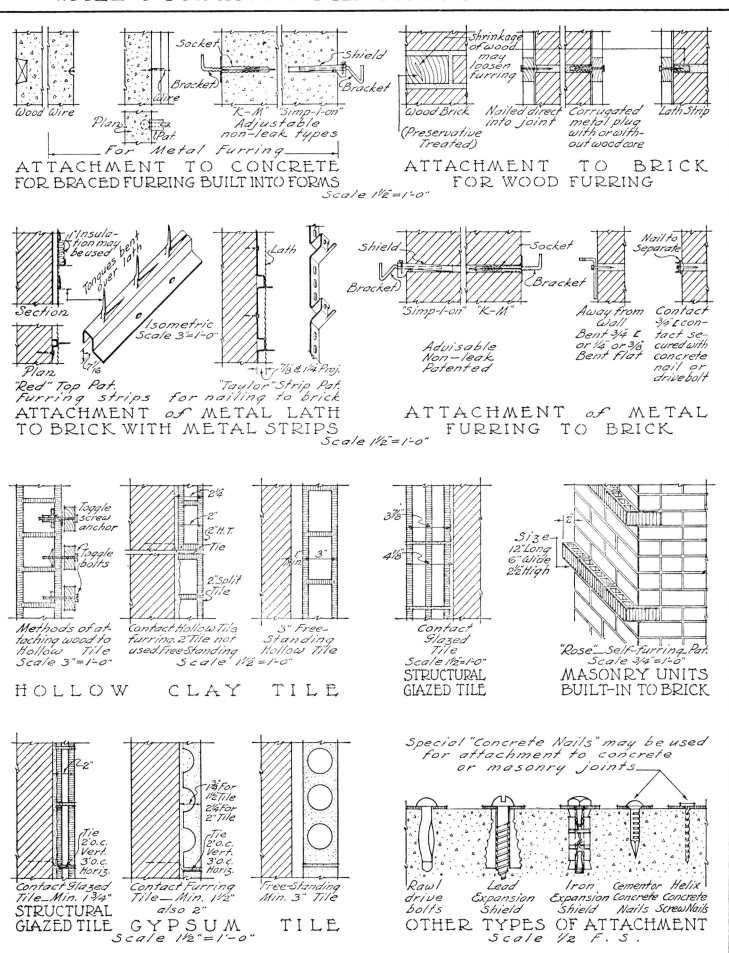

ATTACHMENT TO CONCRETE
FOR BRACED FURRING BUILT INTO FORMS

Wood Wire — Plan — Pat. — For Metal Furring —
Socket — Bracket — Wire — "K-M" "Simp-l-on" Adjustable non-leak types — Shield — Bracket

Scale 1½"=1'-0"

ATTACHMENT TO BRICK
FOR WOOD FURRING

shrinkage of wood may loosen furring — Wood Brick (Preservative Treated) — Nailed direct into joint — Corrugated metal plug with or without wood core — Lath Strip

ATTACHMENT of METAL LATH
TO BRICK WITH METAL STRIPS

1" Insulation may be used — Section — Tongues bent over lath — Plan — "7/16" — "Red" Top Pat. Furring strips for nailing to brick — Isometric Scale 3"=1'-0" — Lath — 7/8 & 1/4 Proj. — "Taylor" Strip Pat.

Scale 1½"=1'-0"

ATTACHMENT of METAL FURRING TO BRICK

Shield — Bracket — "Simp-l-on" — Socket — Bracket — "K-M" — Advisable Non-leak Patented — Nail to Separate — Away from Wall Bent 3/4 L or 1/4 or 3/8 Bent flat — Contact 3/4 L contact secured with concrete nail or drive bolt

HOLLOW CLAY TILE

Toggle screw anchor — Toggle bolts — Methods of attaching wood to Hollow Tile Scale 3"=1'-0" — 2¼" — 2" — 2" H.T. Tie — 2" Split Tile — Contact Hollow Tile furring. 2" Tile not used. Free-Standing Scale 1½"=1'-0" — 1" Min. — 3" — 3" Free-Standing Hollow Tile

STRUCTURAL GLAZED TILE

3⅞" — 4⅛" — Contact Glazed Tile Scale 1½"=1'-0"

MASONRY UNITS BUILT-IN TO BRICK

2" — Size 12" Long 6" Wide 2½" High — "Rose" Self-furring Pat. Scale 3/4"=1'-0"

STRUCTURAL GLAZED TILE

2" — Tie 2' o.c. Vert. 3' o.c. Horiz. — Contact Glazed Tile - Min. 1¾"

GYPSUM TILE

1¾" For 1½" Tile 2¼" For 2" Tile — Tie 2' o.c. Vert. 3' o.c. Horiz. — Contact Furring Tile - Min. 1½" also 2" — Free-Standing Min. 3" Tile

Scale 1½"=1'-0"

OTHER TYPES OF ATTACHMENT

Special "Concrete Nails" may be used for attachment to concrete or masonry joints — Rawl drive bolts — Lead Expansion Shield — Iron Expansion Shield — Cement or Concrete Nails — Helix Concrete Screw Nails

Scale ½ F.S.

GYPSUM

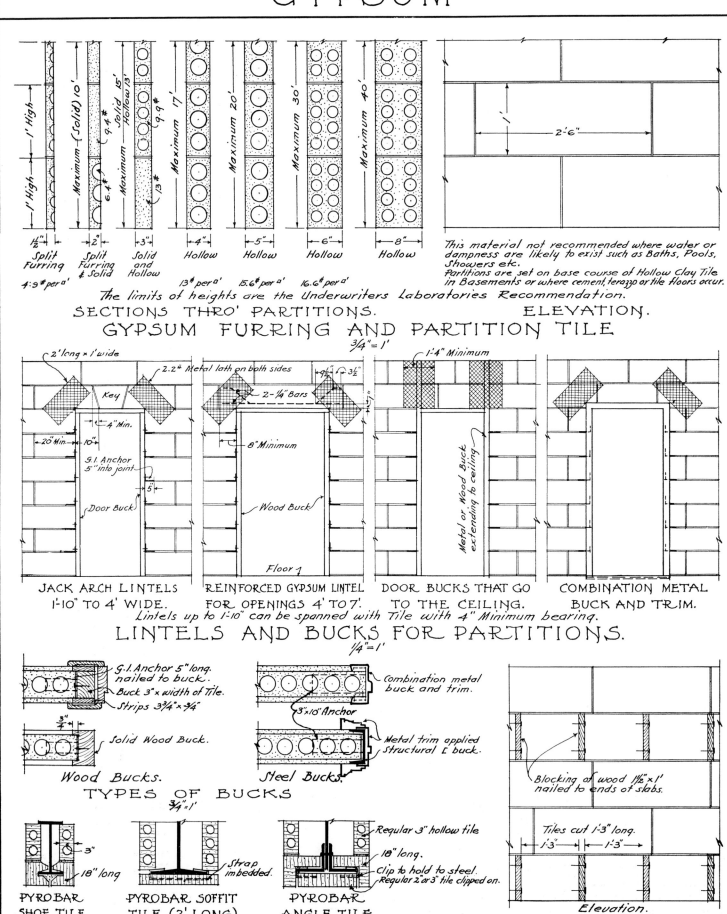

SECTIONS THRO' PARTITIONS.

Split Furring · Split Furring & Solid · Solid and Hollow · Hollow · Hollow · Hollow · Hollow

This material not recommended where water or dampness are likely to exist such as Baths, Pools, Showers etc.
Partitions are set on base course of Hollow Clay Tile in Basements or where cement, terazzo or tile floors occur.

ELEVATION.

The limits of heights are the Underwriters Laboratories Recommendation.

GYPSUM FURRING AND PARTITION TILE
3/4" = 1'

JACK ARCH LINTELS 1'-10" TO 4' WIDE.

REINFORCED GYPSUM LINTEL FOR OPENINGS 4' TO 7'.

DOOR BUCKS THAT GO TO THE CEILING.

COMBINATION METAL BUCK AND TRIM.

Lintels up to 1'-10" can be spanned with Tile with 4" Minimum bearing.

LINTELS AND BUCKS FOR PARTITIONS.
1/4" = 1'

Wood Bucks. · Steel Bucks.

TYPES OF BUCKS
3/4" = 1'

PYROBAR SHOE TILE For flange under 9"

PYROBAR SOFFIT TILE (2' LONG). When beam is not over 3' deep and flange is 9" wide & over.

PYROBAR ANGLE TILE For large Sections

GYPSUM BEAM and GIRDER FIREPROOFING
3/4" = 1'

Elevation.

METHOD OF PROVIDING NAILING FOR HEAVY FIXTURES. Such as Blackboards etc.
1/2" = 1'

CERAMIC TILE

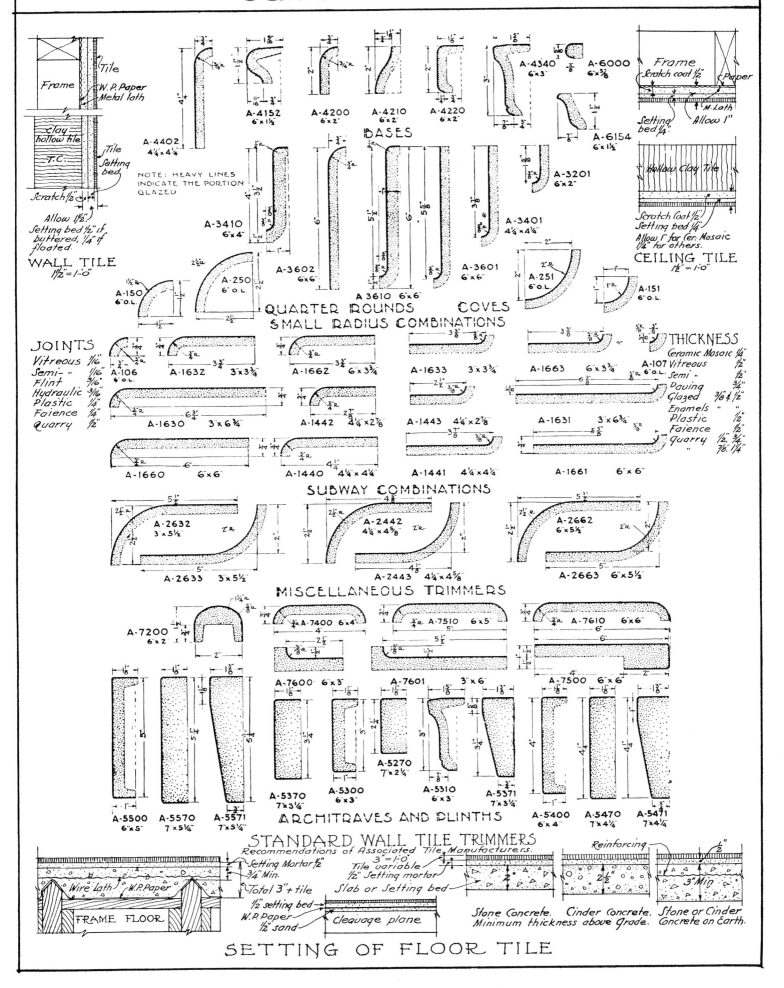

SETTING OF FLOOR TILE

MARBLE FLOORS, WALLS & WAINSCOTS

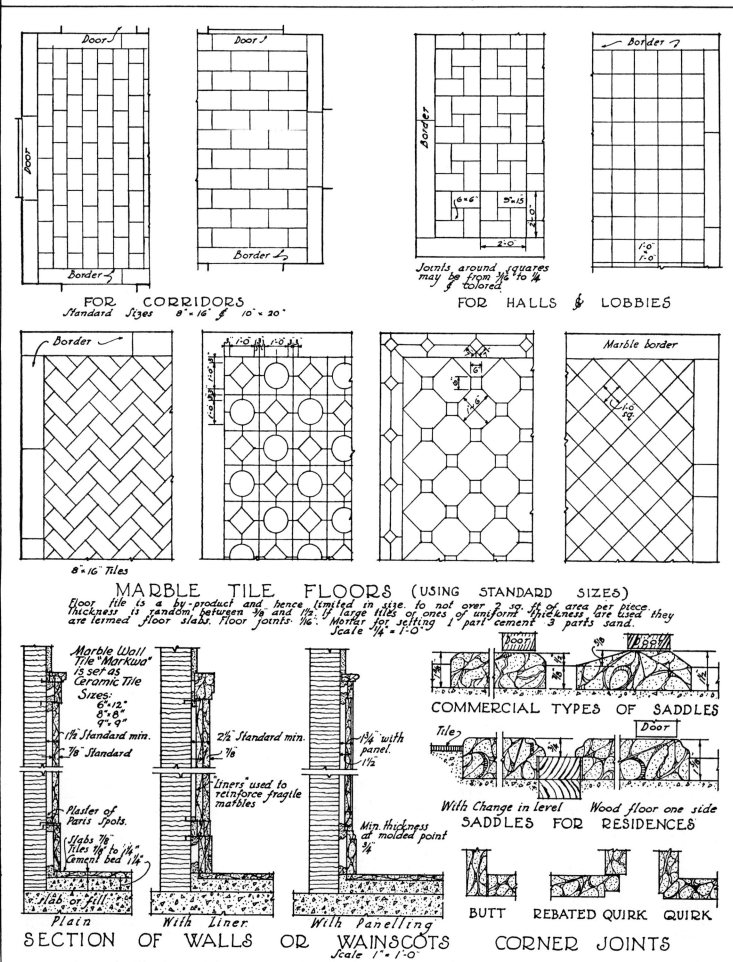

FOR CORRIDORS
Standard Sizes 8"×16" & 10"×20"

FOR HALLS & LOBBIES

Joints around squares may be from 3/16 to 1/4 & colored.

6"×6" 5"×15"

MARBLE TILE FLOORS (USING STANDARD SIZES)

8"×16" Tiles

Floor tile is a by-product and hence limited in size to not over 2 sq. ft of area per piece. Thickness is random between 3/8 and 1½". If large tiles or ones of uniform thickness are used they are termed floor slabs. Floor joints 1/16". Mortar for setting 1 part cement 3 parts sand.
Scale ¼" = 1'-0"

Marble Wall Tile "Markwa" is set as Ceramic Tile
Sizes:
6"×12"
8"×8"
9"×9"
1½ Standard min.
7/8" Standard

Plaster of Paris Spots.
Slabs 7/8"
Tiles 7/8 to 1¼"
Cement bed 1¼"
Slab or fill

Plain

2½" Standard min.
7/8"
"Liners" used to reinforce fragile marbles

With Liner.

1¾" with panel.
1½"

Min. thickness at molded point ¾"

With Panelling

SECTION OF WALLS OR WAINSCOTS
Scale 1" = 1'-0"

COMMERCIAL TYPES OF SADDLES

With Change in level   Wood floor one side
SADDLES FOR RESIDENCES

BUTT   REBATED QUIRK   QUIRK
CORNER JOINTS

FINISHED FLOORING THICKNESS

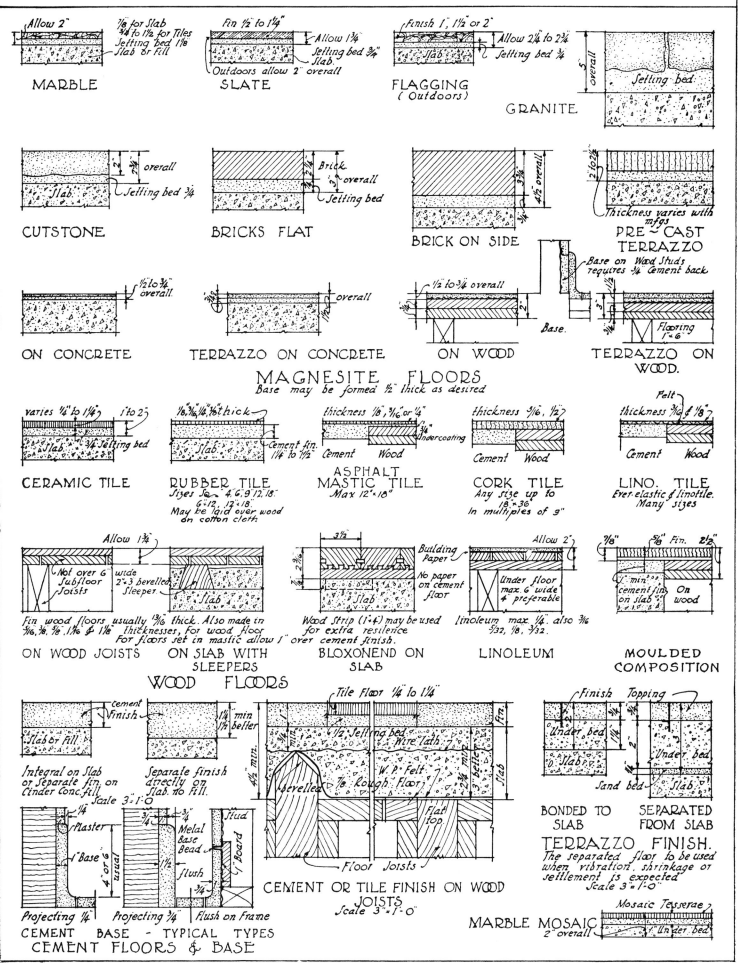

MARBLE

SLATE

FLAGGING
(Outdoors)

GRANITE

CUTSTONE

BRICKS FLAT

BRICK ON SIDE

PRE~CAST TERRAZZO

ON CONCRETE

TERRAZZO ON CONCRETE

ON WOOD

TERRAZZO ON WOOD.

MAGNESITE FLOORS
Base may be formed ½" thick as desired

CERAMIC TILE

RUBBER TILE
Sizes Sq. 4, 6, 9, 12, 18.
6·12, 12·18.
May be laid over wood
on cotton cloth

ASPHALT
MASTIC TILE
Max 12"×18"

CORK TILE
Any size up to
18·36
In multiples of 3"

LINO. TILE
Ever-elastic & linotile.
Many sizes

ON WOOD JOISTS

ON SLAB WITH SLEEPERS

Fin wood floors usually ¹³⁄₁₆ thick. Also made in
⁵⁄₁₆, ⅜, ⅞, 1¹⁄₁₆ & 1⅛ thicknesses, for wood floor
For floors set in mastic allow 1" over cement finish

BLOXONEND ON SLAB
Wood Strip (1·4) may be used
for extra resilience

LINOLEUM
linoleum max. ¼. also ³⁄₁₆
⁵⁄₃₂, ⅛, ³⁄₃₂.

MOULDED COMPOSITION

WOOD FLOORS

Integral on Slab
or Separate fin. on
Cinder Conc.fill.

Separate finish
directly on
Slab. no fill.
Scale 3"=1'-0

CEMENT OR TILE FINISH ON WOOD
JOISTS
Scale 3"=1'-0

BONDED TO SLAB   SEPARATED FROM SLAB
TERRAZZO FINISH.
The separated floor to be used
when vibration, shrinkage or
settlement is expected
Scale 3"=1'-0

Projecting ¼   Projecting ¾   Flush on Frame
CEMENT BASE - TYPICAL TYPES
CEMENT FLOORS & BASE

MARBLE MOSAIC
2" overall

FLOOR CONSTRUCTION

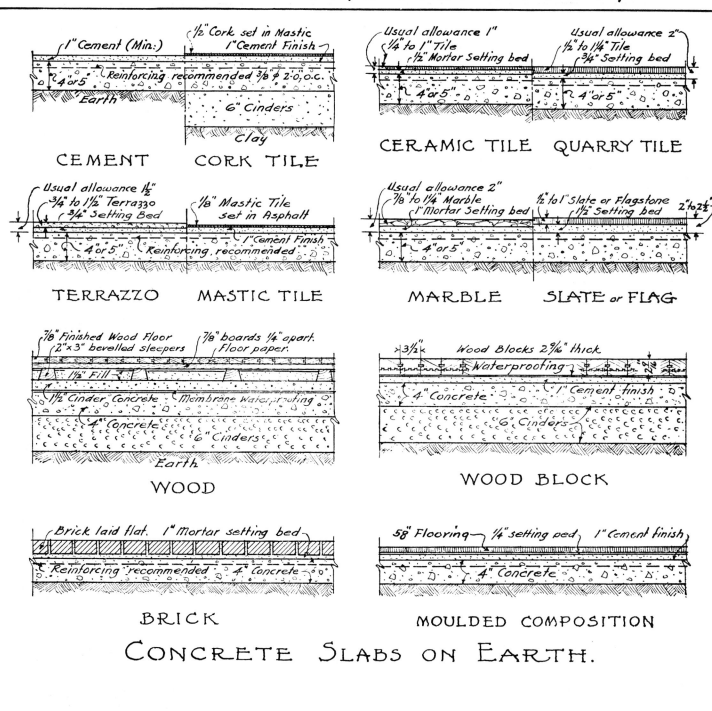

CEMENT   **CORK TILE**   **CERAMIC TILE   QUARRY TILE**

TERRAZZO   MASTIC TILE   **MARBLE   SLATE or FLAG**

WOOD   **WOOD BLOCK**

BRICK   **MOULDED COMPOSITION**

CONCRETE SLABS ON EARTH.

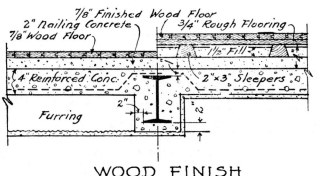

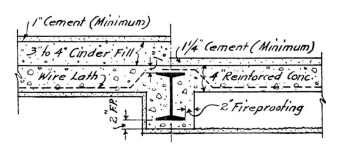

WOOD FINISH
ON FILL   ON SLEEPERS   **CEMENT FINISH**
ON FILL   ON SLAB

REINFORCED CINDER CONCRETE ARCHES.

Scale 3/4" = 1'-0"

FLOORING ON CONCRETE OVER EARTH

FLOOR FINISHES DEMANDING DRY CONDITIONS   **FLOOR FINISHES TOLERATING DAMPNESS**

Scale 3/4"= 1'·0"

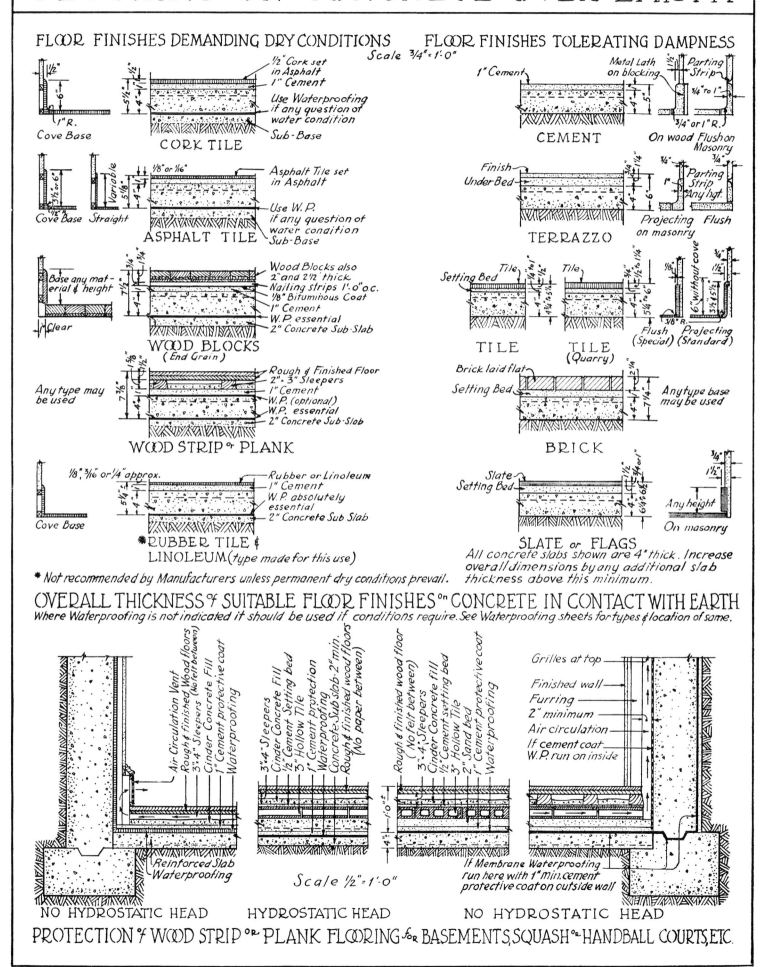

CORK TILE
- ½" Cork set in Asphalt
- 1" Cement
- Use Waterproofing if any question of water condition
- Sub-Base

Cove Base — 1" R.

CEMENT
- 1" Cement
- Metal Lath on blocking
- Parting Strip — ¾" to 1"
- 3/4" or 1" R.
- On wood Flush on Masonry

ASPHALT TILE
- Asphalt Tile set in Asphalt
- Use W.P. if any question of water condition
- Sub-Base

Cove Base   Straight   Variable

TERRAZZO
- Finish
- Under Bed
- Parting Strip Any hgt.
- Projecting on masonry   Flush

WOOD BLOCKS (End Grain)
- Wood Blocks also 2" and 2½" thick
- Nailing strips 1'·0" o.c.
- ⅛" Bituminous Coat
- 1" Cement
- W.P. essential
- 2" Concrete Sub-Slab

Base any material & height — 1" Clear

TILE   TILE (Quarry)
- Tile
- Setting Bed
- 6" without cove
- Flush (Special)   Projecting (Standard)

WOOD STRIP or PLANK
- Rough & Finished Floor
- 2"-3" Sleepers
- 1" Cement
- W.P. (optional)
- W.P. essential
- 2" Concrete Sub-Slab

Any type may be used

BRICK
- Brick laid flat
- Setting Bed
- Any type base may be used

RUBBER TILE & LINOLEUM (type made for this use)
- Rubber or Linoleum
- 1" Cement
- W.P. absolutely essential
- 2" Concrete Sub Slab
- ⅛", 3/16" or ¼" approx.

Cove Base

SLATE or FLAGS
- Slate
- Setting Bed
- Any height
- On masonry

All concrete slabs shown are 4" thick. Increase overall dimensions by any additional slab thickness above this minimum.

* Not recommended by Manufacturers unless permanent dry conditions prevail.

OVERALL THICKNESS of SUITABLE FLOOR FINISHES on CONCRETE IN CONTACT WITH EARTH

Where Waterproofing is not indicated it should be used if conditions require. See Waterproofing sheets for types & location of same.

NO HYDROSTATIC HEAD
- Air Circulation Vent
- Rough & finished Wood Floors (No felt between)
- 3"-4" Sleepers
- Cinder Concrete Fill
- 1" Cement protective coat
- Waterproofing
- Reinforced Slab
- Waterproofing

HYDROSTATIC HEAD
- 3"-4" Sleepers
- Cinder Concrete Fill
- ½" Cement Setting bed
- 5" Hollow Tile
- 1" Cement protection
- Waterproofing
- Concrete Sub-slab 2" min.
- Rough & finished wood floors (No paper between)

Scale ½"= 1'·0"

NO HYDROSTATIC HEAD
- Rough & finished wood floor (No felt between)
- 3"-4" Sleepers
- Cinder Concrete Fill
- ½" Cement setting bed
- 3" Hollow Tile
- 2" Sand bed
- 1" Cement protective coat
- Waterproofing

NO HYDROSTATIC HEAD
- Grilles at top
- Finished wall
- Furring
- 2" minimum
- Air circulation
- If cement coat W.P. run on inside
- If Membrane Waterproofing run here with 1" min. cement protective coat on outside wall

PROTECTION of WOOD STRIP or PLANK FLOORING for BASEMENTS, SQUASH or HANDBALL COURTS, ETC.

LINOLEUM — METAL WALL MOULDS

FULL SIZE SECTION	BATTLESHIP		PLAIN		JASPE		INLAY		MARBLEIZED		BORDER	
	NAME	GAUGE	NAME	GAUGE	NAME	GAUGE	NAME	GAUGE	NAME	GAUGE	NAME	GAUGE
	6 MM	.236"	—	—	—	—	—	—	—	—	—	—
	3/16"	.188"	—	—	3/16"	.188"	—	—	—	—	—	—
	1/8"	.125"	1/8" heavy	.125"	1/8"	.125"	Heavy	.125"	Heavy	.125"	Heavy	.125"
	—	—	Medium	.095"	Medium	.095"	Medium	.095"	Medium	.095"	Medium	.095"
	—	—	Standard	.075"	—	—	Standard	.075"	Standard	.075"	Standard	.075"
Data from the Linoleum and Felt base Manufacturing Association.												
Width 2 Yards			Cork Carpet 4" thick			Wall Linoleums no standard thickness, usually .05"						

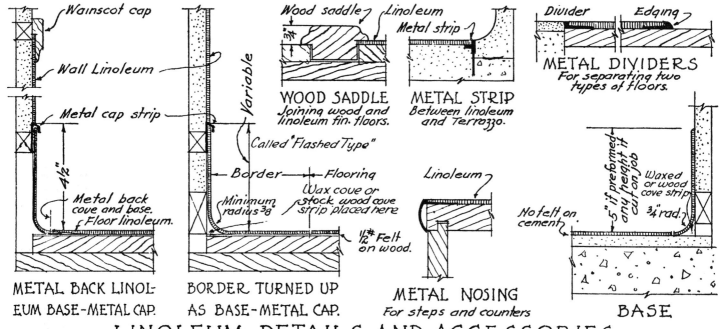

METAL BACK LINOLEUM BASE-METAL CAP.

BORDER TURNED UP AS BASE-METAL CAP.

WOOD SADDLE
Joining wood and linoleum fin. floors.

METAL STRIP
Between linoleum and Terrazzo.

METAL DIVIDERS
For separating two types of floors.

METAL NOSING
For steps and counters

BASE

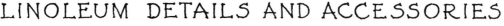

LINOLEUM DETAILS AND ACCESSORIES

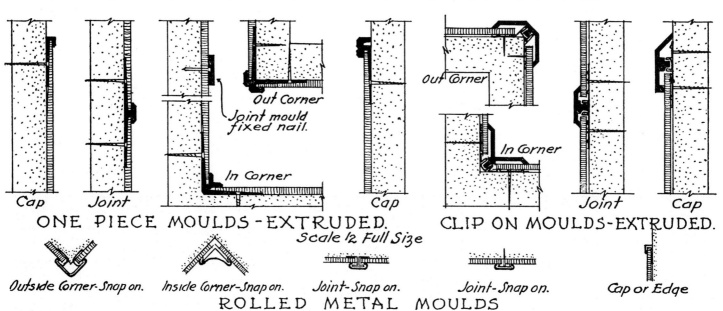

Cap   Joint

ONE PIECE MOULDS - EXTRUDED.
Scale ½ Full Size

Cap

CLIP ON MOULDS - EXTRUDED.

Joint   Cap

Outside Corner - Snap on.   Inside Corner - Snap on.   Joint - Snap on.   Joint - Snap on.   Cap or Edge

ROLLED METAL MOULDS

METAL MOULDS for LINOLEUM, RUBBER, WALL B'RDS, ASBESTOS ETC.

STRUCTURAL GLASS—GENERAL & EXTER·DETAILS

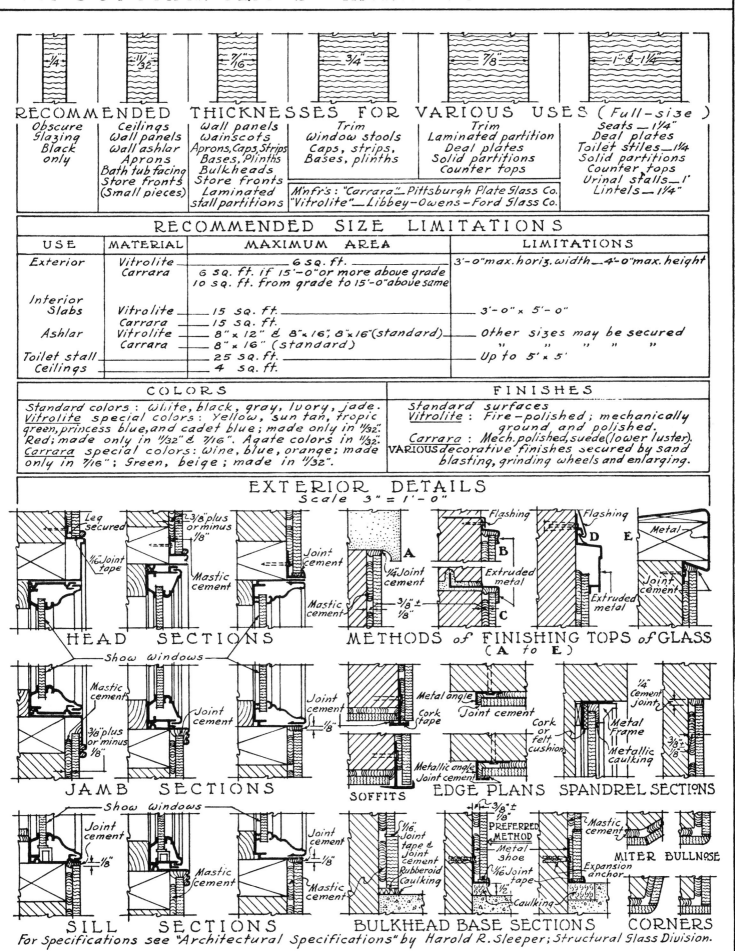

RECOMMENDED THICKNESSES FOR VARIOUS USES (Full-size)

1/4"	11/32"	7/16"	3/4"	7/8"	1" & 1 1/4"
Obscure Glazing Black only	Ceilings Wall panels Wall ashlar Aprons Bath tub facing Store fronts (Small pieces)	Wall panels Wainscots Aprons, Caps, Strips Bases, Plinths Bulkheads Store fronts Laminated stall partitions	Trim Window stools Caps, strips, Bases, plinths	Trim Laminated partition Deal plates Solid partitions Counter tops	Seats — 1 1/4" Deal plates Toilet stiles — 1 1/4" Solid partitions Counter tops Urinal stalls — 1" Lintels — 1 1/4"

M'nfr's: "Carrara"—Pittsburgh Plate Glass Co. "Vitrolite"—Libbey-Owens-Ford Glass Co.

RECOMMENDED SIZE LIMITATIONS

USE	MATERIAL	MAXIMUM AREA	LIMITATIONS
Exterior	Vitrolite	6 sq. ft.	3'-0" max. horiz. width — 4'-0" max. height
	Carrara	6 sq. ft. if 15'-0" or more above grade / 10 sq. ft. from grade to 15'-0" above same	
Interior Slabs	Vitrolite	15 sq. ft.	3'-0" x 5'-0"
	Carrara	15 sq. ft.	
Ashlar	Vitrolite	8"x12" & 8"x16", 8"x16" (standard)	Other sizes may be secured
	Carrara	8" x 16" (standard)	" " " " "
Toilet stall		25 sq. ft.	Up to 5' x 5'
Ceilings		4 sq. ft.	

COLORS

Standard colors: White, black, gray, ivory, jade.
Vitrolite special colors: Yellow, sun tan, tropic green, princess blue, and cadet blue; made only in 11/32". Red; made only in 11/32" & 7/16". Agate colors in 11/32".
Carrara special colors: Wine, blue, orange; made only in 7/16"; Green, beige; made in 11/32".

FINISHES

Standard surfaces
Vitrolite: Fire-polished; mechanically ground and polished.
Carrara: Mech. polished, suede (lower luster).
VARIOUS decorative finishes secured by sand blasting, grinding wheels and enlarging.

EXTERIOR DETAILS
Scale 3" = 1'-0"

HEAD SECTIONS   METHODS of FINISHING TOPS of GLASS (A to E)

JAMB SECTIONS   SOFFITS   EDGE PLANS   SPANDREL SECTIONS

SILL SECTIONS   BULKHEAD BASE SECTIONS   CORNERS

For Specifications see "Architectural Specifications" by Harold R. Sleeper; Structural Glass Division.

STRUCTURAL GLASS—INTERIOR

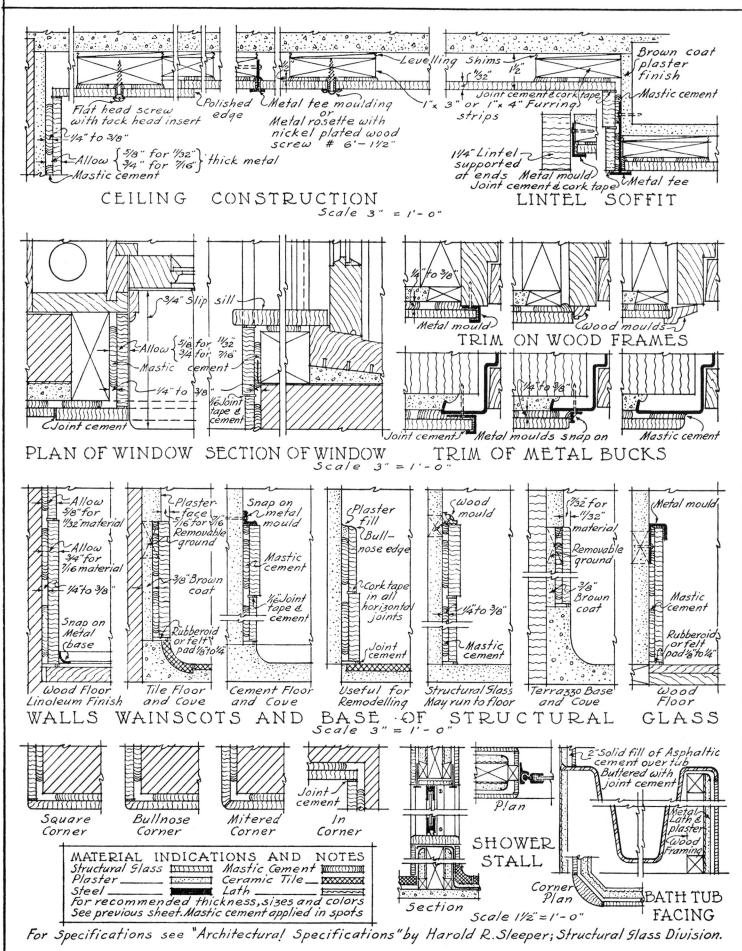

CEILING CONSTRUCTION
Scale 3" = 1'-0"

LINTEL SOFFIT

PLAN OF WINDOW   SECTION OF WINDOW   TRIM OF METAL BUCKS
Scale 3" = 1'-0"

TRIM ON WOOD FRAMES

WALLS WAINSCOTS AND BASE OF STRUCTURAL GLASS
Scale 3" = 1'-0"

Square Corner   Bullnose Corner   Mitered Corner   In Corner

SHOWER STALL

BATH TUB FACING

MATERIAL INDICATIONS AND NOTES
Structural Glass   Mastic Cement
Plaster   Ceramic Tile
Steel   Lath
For recommended thickness, sizes and colors
See previous sheet. Mastic cement applied in spots

Section   Scale 1½" = 1'-0"

For Specifications see "Architectural Specifications" by Harold R. Sleeper; Structural Glass Division.

PORCELAIN ENAMEL *on* STEEL

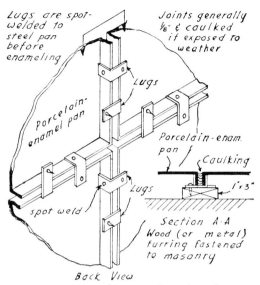

Lugs are spot-welded to steel pan before enameling

Joints generally ⅛" & caulked if exposed to weather

Porcelain-enamel pan

Lugs

Porcelain-enam. pan

Caulking

Lugs

spot weld

1"x3"

Section A-A
Wood (or metal) furring fastened to masonry

Back View

Pans can be fastened to furring on two adjacent sides. Lugs from the remaining 2 sides are forced under previously fastened panels.
NOTE: METHODS VARY. CONSULT MFR.

PAN & LUG METHOD OF FASTENING

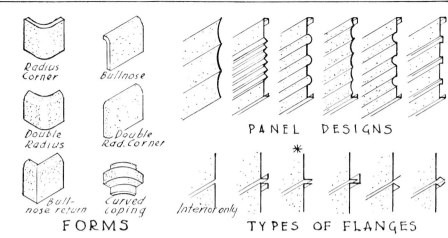

Radius Corner

Bullnose

Double Radius

Double Rad. Corner

Bullnose return

Curved coping

FORMS

PANEL DESIGNS

Interior only

TYPES OF FLANGES

Any shape which can be made in sheet metal by rolling, braking, spinning or cutting & welding can be porcelain enameled. Die stamped shapes are easier to enamel than welded. The max. panel area for practical use is 10 to 12 sq. ft. Plywood or insulating board may be used to deaden metallic ring when struck, increase rigidity and reduce heat loss. Some mfrs. laminate backing to panels; or spray on a ⅛" backing. In most cases, backing is optional. Cutting or drilling holes in porcelain-enameled units is not recommended. Min radius of edges should be no less than 3/16" radius. Gauges of metal #20 to #16, determined by design.

* Type of panel shown in details

PORCELAIN-ENAMEL FASTENING & BASIC DESIGN DATA

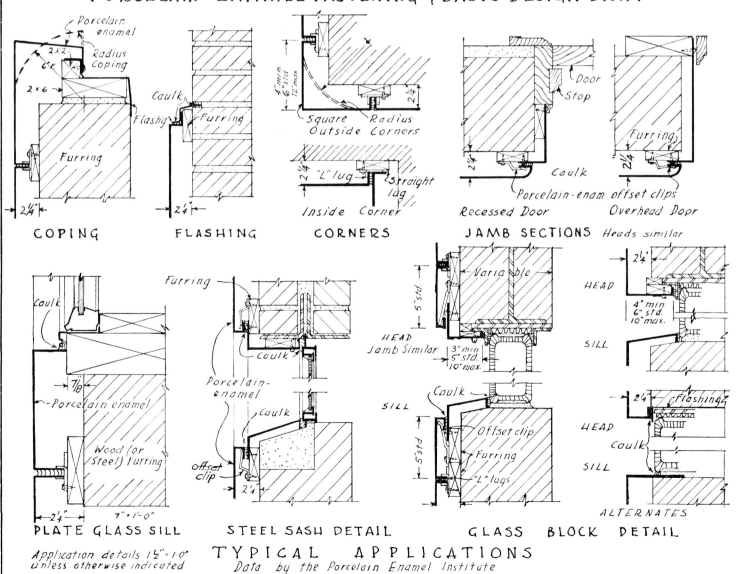

COPING   **FLASHING**   **CORNERS**   **JAMB SECTIONS** *Heads similar*

PLATE GLASS SILL   **STEEL SASH DETAIL**   **GLASS BLOCK DETAIL**

Application details 1½"=1'-0" unless otherwise indicated

TYPICAL APPLICATIONS
Data by the Porcelain Enamel Institute

GRILLES

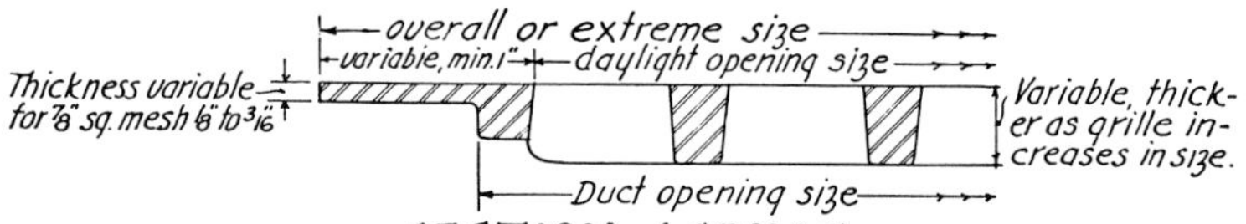
overall or extreme size
variable, min. 1"
daylight opening size
Thickness variable for 7/8" sq. mesh 1/8" to 3/16"
Variable, thicker as grille increases in size.
Duct opening size

SECTION of GRILLE

MATERIALS	STANDARD SQ. MESH OR LATTICE			
	Sq. holes	Bars	Free area	Margin
Iron, Brass, Bronze, Monel, Aluminum	1/2"	1/4"	44%	Margin is variable from 1" to 2"+
	3/4"	1/4" ±	56%	
	7/8"	1/4" ±	61%	

All details are 1/2 Full Size. "Finish" as herein used refers to finishing material adjacent to grille frame.

CAST GRILLES

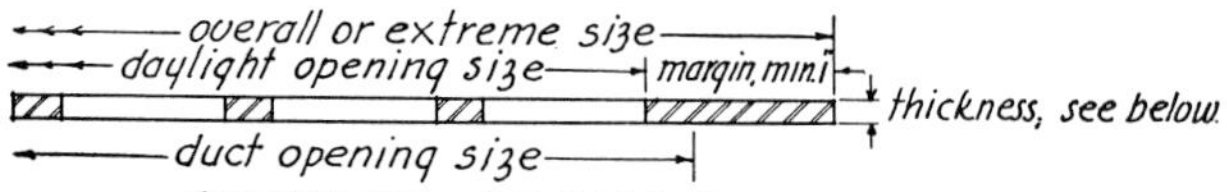
overall or extreme size
daylight opening size
margin, min. 1"
thickness, see below.
duct opening size

SECTION of GRILLE

MATERIALS	STANDARD SQ. MESH			DIAGONAL MESH		
	Sq. holes	Bars	Free area	Sq. holes	Bars	Free area
B&S. Gauge:- Brass, bronze, aluminum, nickel silver.	1/2"	3/16"-1/4"	48%, 45%	1/2"	1/4"	43%
U.S.S. Gauge:- Steel, monel, and stainless steel.	5/8"	*1/4"-3/8"	*51%	3/4"	1/4"	56%
Gauges #16 to #3, #12 most	3/4"	1/4"	57%	1"	1/4"	62%
common; large grilles #10,	7/8"	1/4"	60%			
small grilles #12 or #14	1"	1/4"	65%			

STAMPED GRILLES

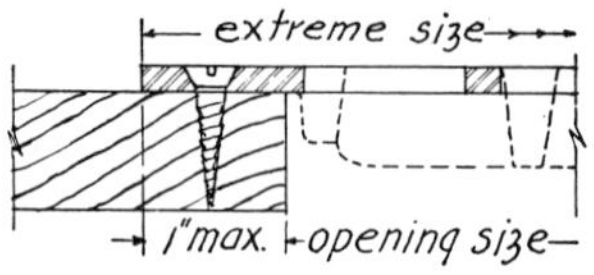
extreme size
1" max.
opening size

Over Wood Frame.

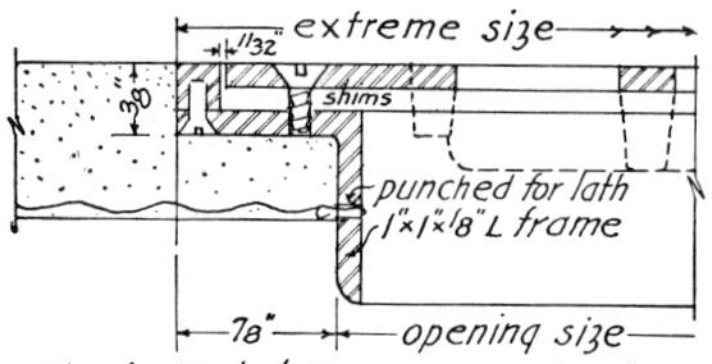
extreme size
11/32"
shims
punched for lath
1"×1"×1/8" L frame
7/8"
opening size

Flush Metal Frame in Plaster.

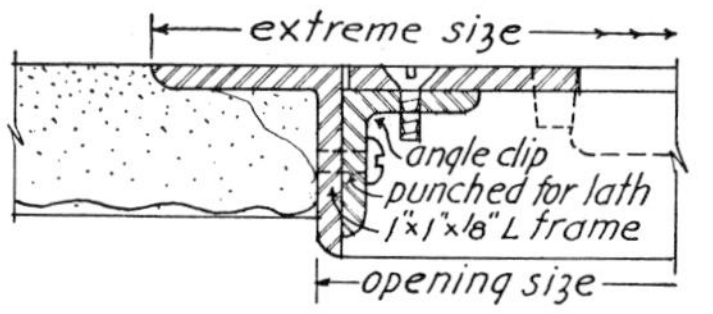
extreme size
angle clip
punched for lath
1"×1"×1/8" L frame
opening size

In Plaster with Angle Frame.

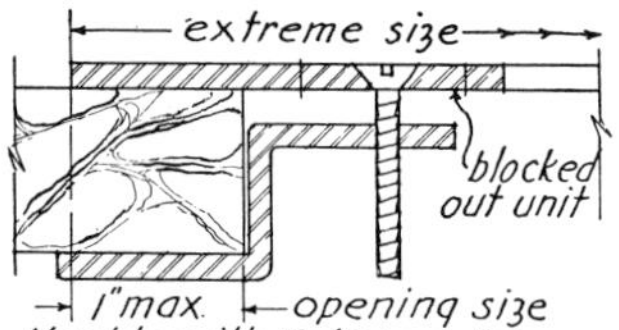
extreme size
blocked out unit
1" max.
opening size

Marble with Z Lugs & Screws through Blocked Out Unit.

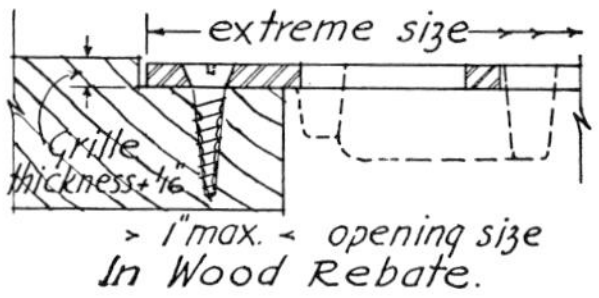
extreme size
Grille thickness + 1/16
1" max.
opening size

In Wood Rebate.

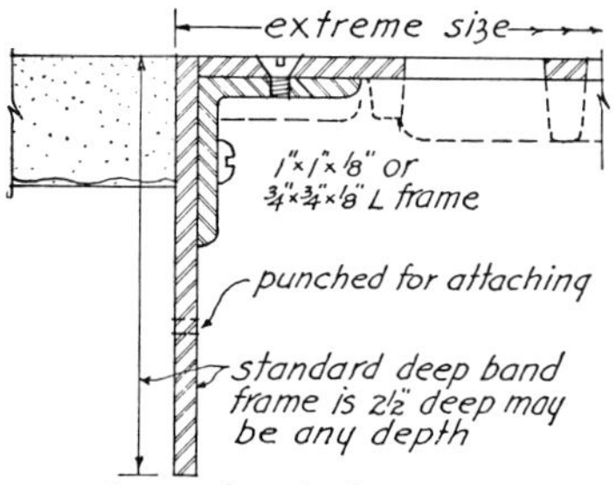
extreme size
1"×1"×1/8" or 3/4"×3/4"×1/8" L frame
punched for attaching
standard deep band frame is 2 1/2" deep may be any depth

Shown in Plaster, may be used with any finish when narrow exposed steel frame is desired.

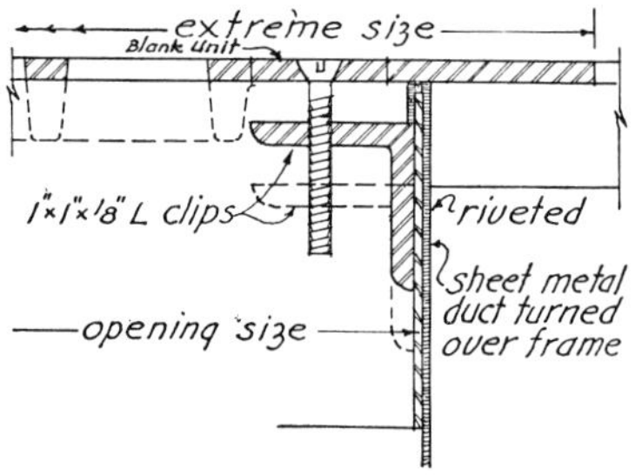
extreme size
Blank Unit
1"×1"×1/8" L clips
riveted
sheet metal duct turned over frame
opening size

Attached to Steel Band Frame, may also be used with other finishes.

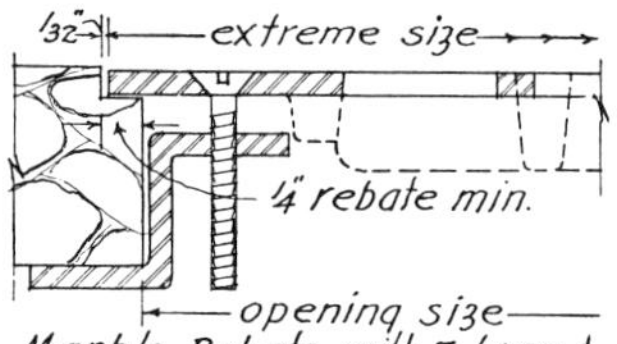
1/32"
extreme size
1/4" rebate min.
opening size

Marble Rebate with Z Lugs & screws through rim.

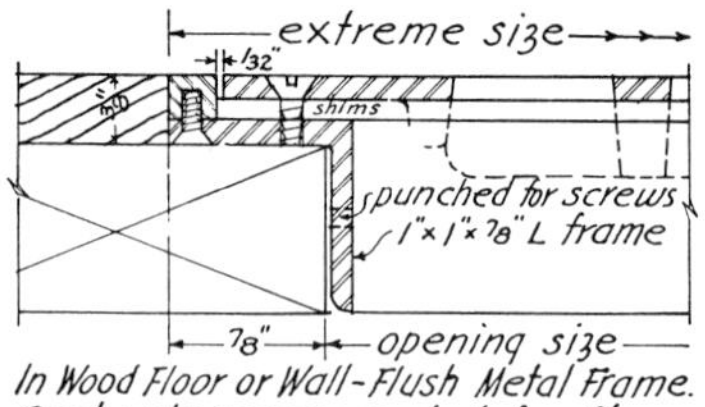
extreme size
1/32"
shims
punched for screws
1"×1"×7/8" L frame
7/8"
opening size

In Wood Floor or Wall-Flush Metal Frame. Cast only recommended for floor.

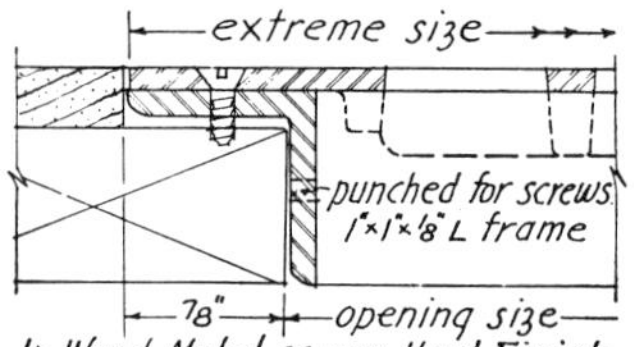
extreme size
punched for screws
1"×1"×1/8" L frame
7/8"
opening size

In Wood, Metal or any Hard Finish. Angle frame on back.

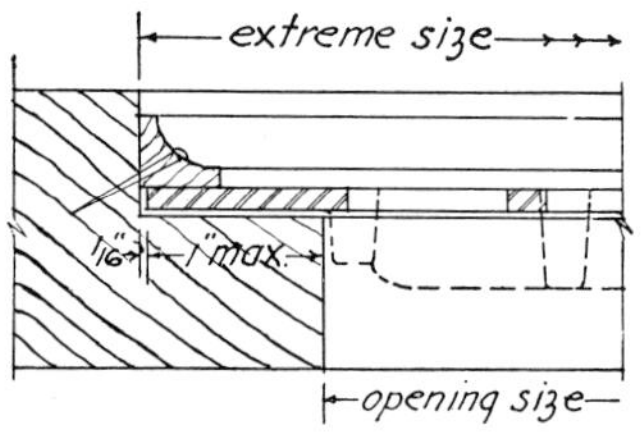
extreme size
1/16"
1" max.
opening size

In Wood Rebate with Mould.

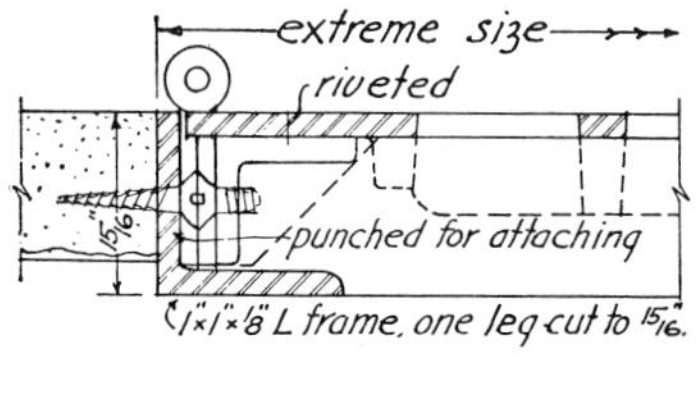
extreme size
riveted
15/16"
punched for attaching
1"×1"×1/8" L frame, one leg cut to 15/16.

For any Finish where Narrow Frame is desired. With Reverse Angle Frame on back. Hinged with Exposed Butt.

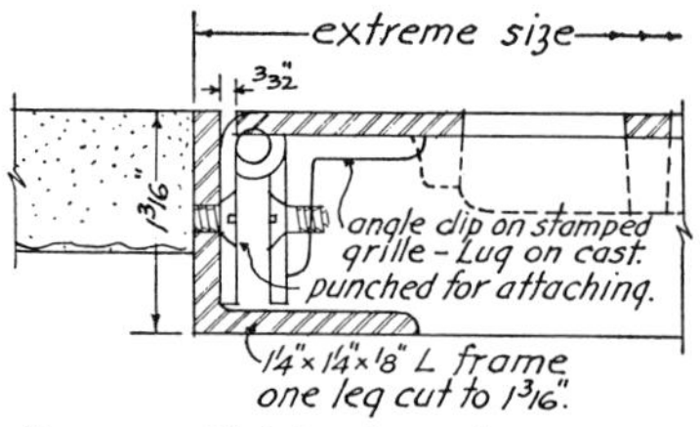
extreme size
3/32"
1 3/16"
angle clip on stamped grille - Lug on cast. punched for attaching.
1 1/4"×1 1/4"×1/8" L frame one leg cut to 1 3/16".

For any Finish where Narrow Frame is desired. Reversed Angle Frame. Hinged with Recessed Butt.

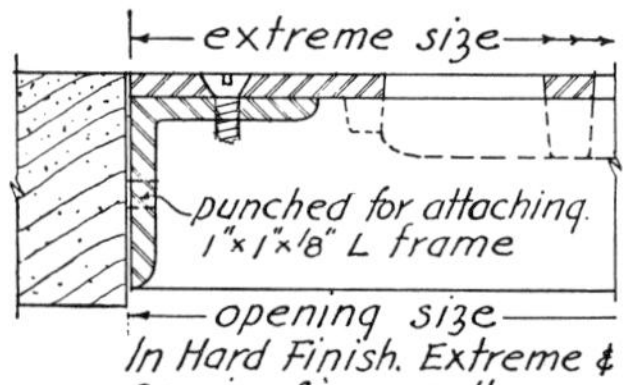
extreme size
punched for attaching.
1"×1"×1/8" L frame
opening size

In Hard Finish. Extreme & Opening Sizes are the same. Reversed Angle Frame on Back.

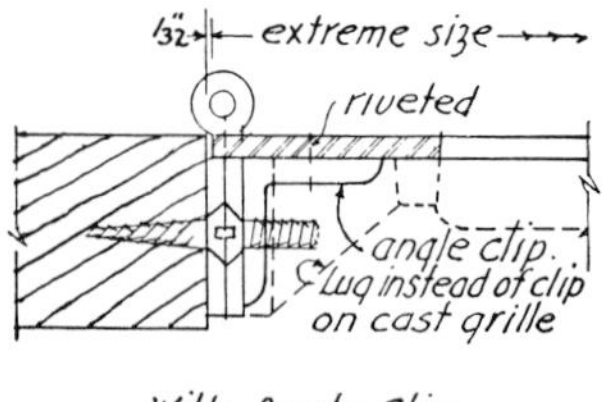
1/32"
extreme size
riveted
angle clip.
Lug instead of clip on cast grille

With Angle Clip Hinged with Exposed Butt.

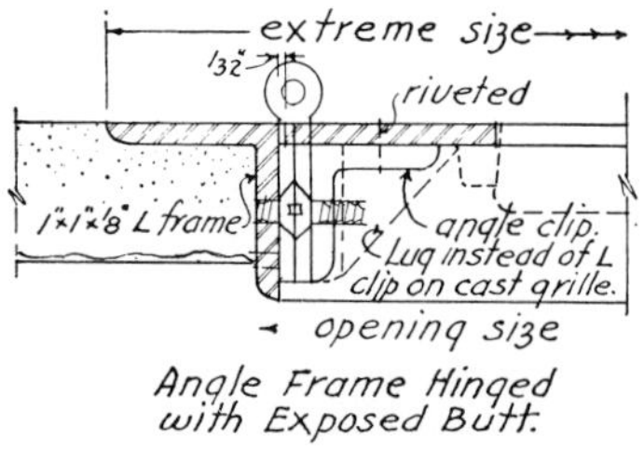
extreme size
1/32"
riveted
1"×1"×1/8" L frame
angle clip.
Lug instead of L clip on cast grille.
opening size

Angle Frame Hinged with Exposed Butt.

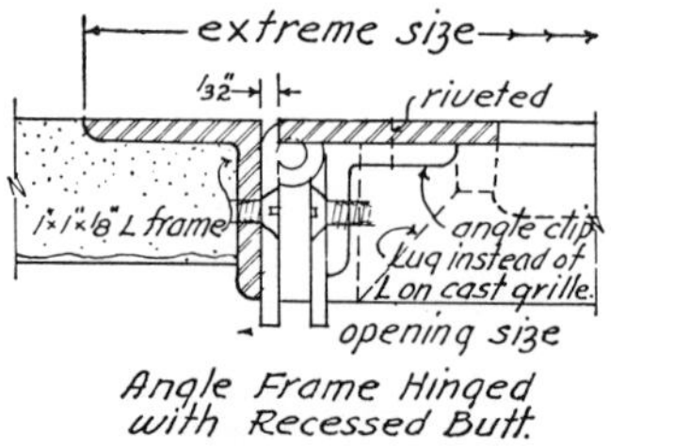
extreme size
1/32"
riveted
1"×1"×1/8" L frame
angle clip
Lug instead of L on cast grille.
opening size

Angle Frame Hinged with Recessed Butt.

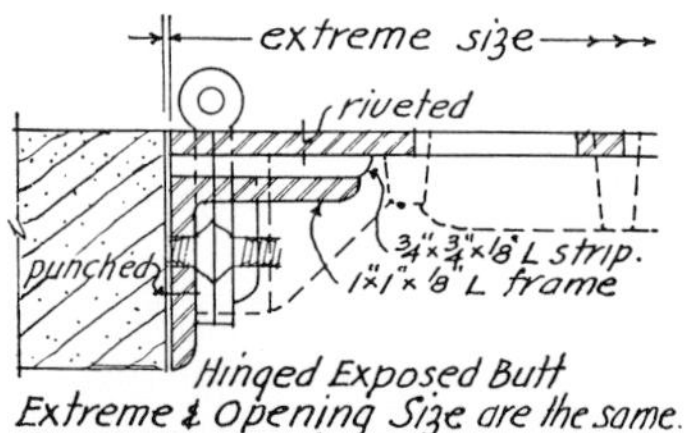
extreme size
riveted
punched
3/4"×3/4"×1/8" L strip.
1"×1"×1/8" L frame

Hinged Exposed Butt. Extreme & Opening Size are the same. Reverse Angle Frame on Back.

IN WOOD FRAME — IN PLASTER FINISH — IN MARBLE & HARD TYPE FINISH

STAMPED or CAST GRILLES (cast are shown dotted)

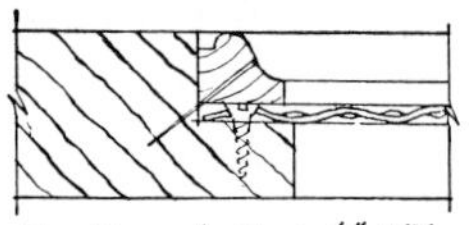

For Panels Max. 1-2' Wide.

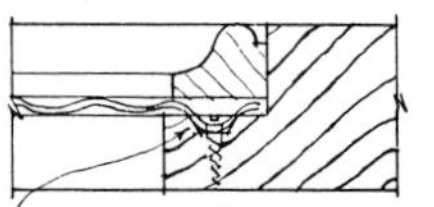

Groove to Tighten Mesh.

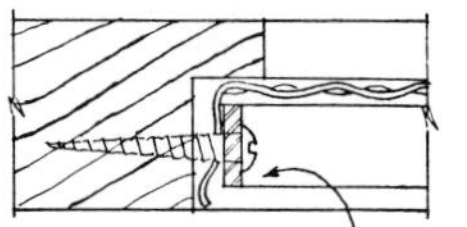

Steel Strip

SECURED IN WOOD

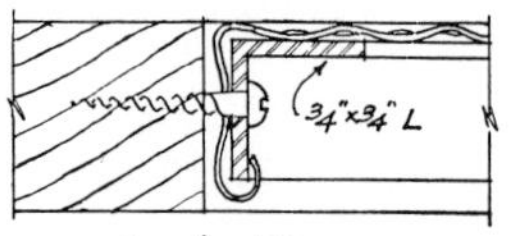
3/4"×3/4" L

Angle Frame

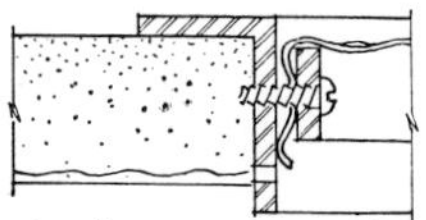

Angle Frame & Strip.

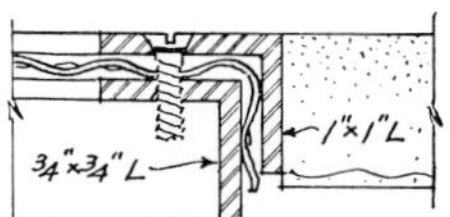
1"×1" L
3/4"×3/4" L

2 Angles and Screws

IN PLASTER

WOVEN WIRE MESH

9

SPECIALTIES AND EQUIPMENT

CHIMNEYS

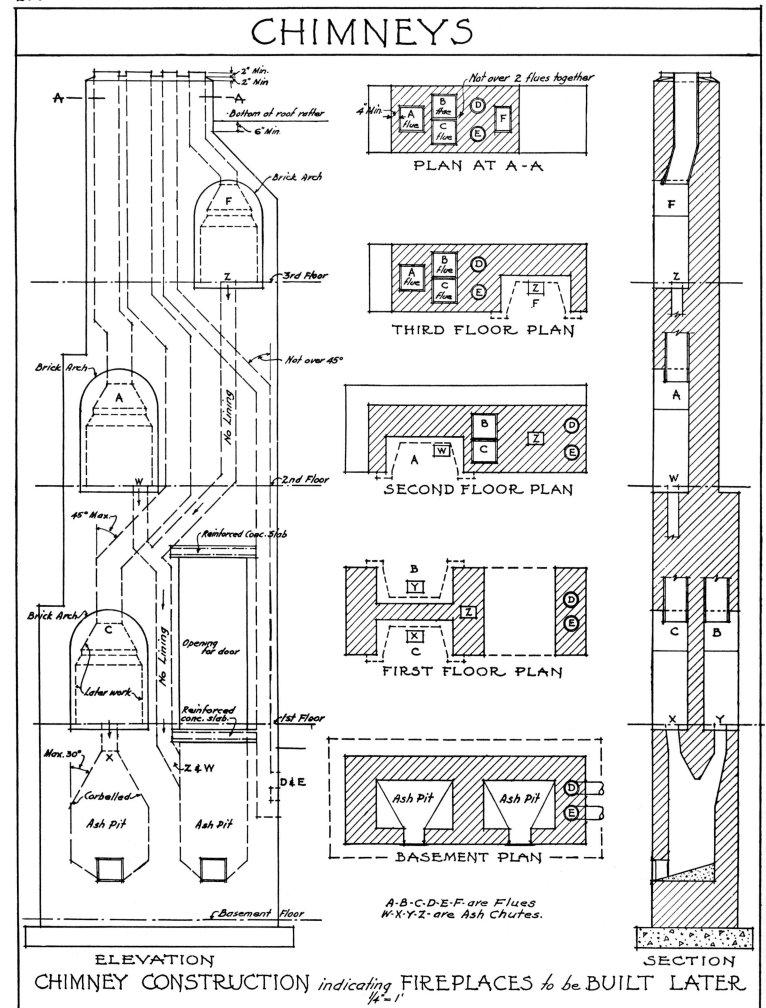

2" Min.
2" Min.
Bottom of roof rafter
6" Min.

A——A

Brick Arch

F

3rd Floor

Not over 45°

No Lining

Brick Arch

A

2nd Floor

W

45° Max.

Reinforced Conc. Slab

Brick Arch

C

Opening for door

No Lining

Later work

Reinforced conc. slab.

1st Floor

Max. 30°

X

Z & W

D & E

Corbelled

Ash Pit

Ash Pit

Basement Floor

ELEVATION

Not over 2 flues together

4" Min.

A flue | B flue | D
C flue | F
E

PLAN AT A-A

A flue | B flue | D
C flue | E
Z
F

THIRD FLOOR PLAN

B | D
C | Z
E
A | W

SECOND FLOOR PLAN

B
Y
Z
X
C
D
E

FIRST FLOOR PLAN

Ash Pit | Ash Pit
D
E

BASEMENT PLAN

A·B·C·D·E·F· are Flues
W·X·Y·Z· are Ash Chutes.

F

Z

A

W

C | B

X | Y

SECTION

CHIMNEY CONSTRUCTION *indicating* FIREPLACES *to be* BUILT LATER

1/4" = 1'

CHIMNEYS

Top of Chimney Pots to be equal to Flue diameter.

Wash

2' Minimum above pitched Roof peak or 3' above Flat Roof

Roof Line

Corbel not over 30°

Recommended Corbel projection not over 3/8 width of chimney below

Attic Floor

Flue above top of chimney 4" Minimum

2"

2" Wash

Maximum Corbel projection 3/8 width of chimney

4" Minimum with Lining
8" " without "

Flue Lining

Throat

Damper

Fireplace

2nd Floor

Ash Chute

Offsets never greater than 45°

Flue Lining

Throat

Damper

Fireplace

1st Floor

Ash Chute

Fire Stop

Cleanout door

Ash Pit

Cleanout door

2' up to Empty into Ash Can.

Basement

Elevation

4" Min

Plan at A-A

Ash drop

Plan at Second Floor

Ash drop

Plan at First Floor

Ash Pit

Cleanout

Plan at Basement.

1/4" = 1'-0"

Cleanout door

Section

DRAWING showing CHIMNEY when FIREPLACES are FINISHED with ROUGH MASONRY
See other sheet for type of Chimney that omits Fireplace during Rough Construction.

CHIMNEYS

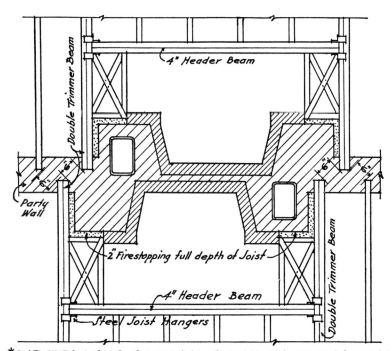

*FIREPLACES BACK TO BACK IN PARTY WALL
SHOWING SPACING BETWEEN JOISTS
3/8"=1'-0"

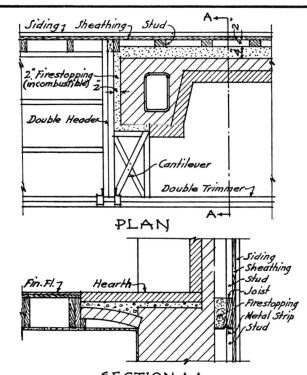

PLAN

SECTION A·A
**FIREPLACE IN EXTERIOR FRAME
WALL- BRICKWORK CONCEALED
3/8"=1'-0"

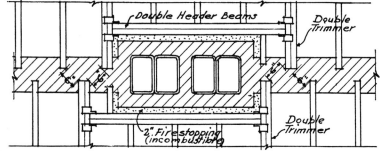

*CHIMNEY IN PARTY WALL SHOWING SPACING
BETWEEN JOISTS AND FIRESTOPPING
3/8"=1'-0"

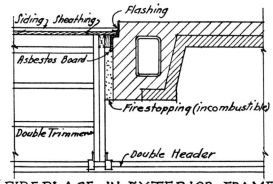

**FIREPLACE IN EXTERIOR FRAME
WALL – BRICKWORK EXPOSED.
3/8"=1'-0"

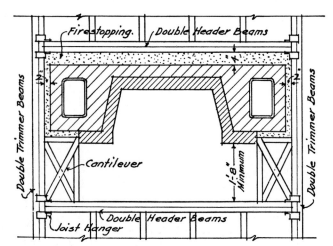

*FIREPLACE FRAMING & FIRESTOPPING
3/8"=1'-0"

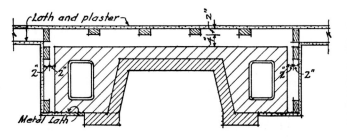

*FIREPLACE IN FRAME PARTITION
3/8"=1'-0"

CHIMNEYS & FIREPLACES showing FRAMING & FIRESTOPPING in WOOD CONST.ᴺ
* Recommendations of the National Board of Fire Underwriters.
** Recommendations of National Lumber Manufacturers Association.

DAMPERS

Rotary	Damper Number	Front width of Fireplace opeing in Inches	Base open'g of Throat not including Flange A	B	C	Shipping Weight in Pounds	FLUE: Proper Flue Lining Exterior Dimensions	FLUE: Equivalent Round Flue Inside Diameter
	OLD STYLE DAMPER SERIES "A"							
	224	24	24	24	12	26	8½ × 8½	8
	230	30	30	30	12	36	8½ × 13	10
	232	32	32	32	12	40	8½ × 13	10
	236	36	36	36	12	46	8½ × 13	10
	242	42	42	42	12	56	13 × 13	12
	248	48	48	48	12	66	13 × 13	12
	254	54	54	54	12	80	13 × 18	15
	260	60	60	60	12	97	13 × 18	15
	272	72	72	72	12	110	18 × 18	20
	OLD STYLE DAMPER SERIES "B"							
	36½	36	36	36	16	85	8½ × 13	10
	42½	42	42	42	16	93	13 × 13	12
	48½	48	48	48	16	105	13 × 13	12
	54½	54	54	54	16	120	13 × 18	15
	60½	60	60	60	16	130	13 × 18	15
	72½	72	72	72	16	176	18 × 18	20
	84½	84	84	84	16	210	20 × 24	22
	OLD STYLE DAMPER SERIES "C"							
	30	30	30	24	10	36	8½ × 13	10
	36	36	36	30	10	46	8½ × 13	10
	42	42	42	36	10	56	13 × 13	12
	48	48	48	42	10	66	13 × 13	12
ROTARY	**OLD STYLE DAMPER SERIES "F"**							
624	724	24	24	18	9	25	8½ × 8½	8
630	730	30	30	24	9	30	8½ × 13	10
632	732	32	32	26	9	32	8½ × 13	10
636	736	36	36	30	9	35	8½ × 13	10
642	742	42	42	36	9	40	13 × 13	12
648	748	48	48	42	9	43	13 × 13	12

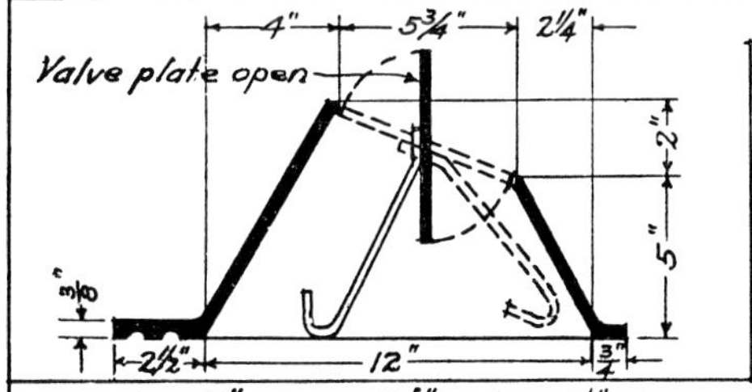

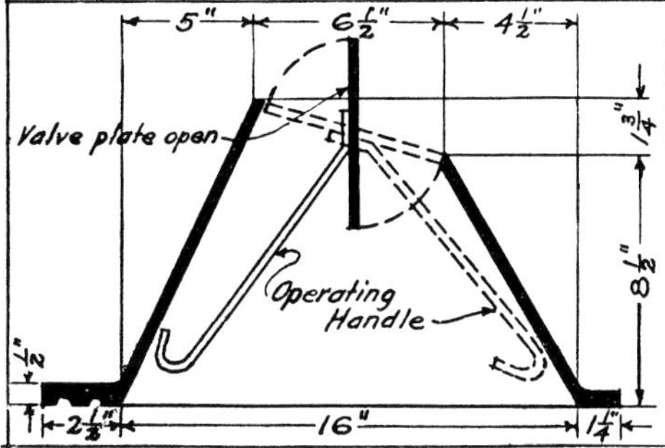

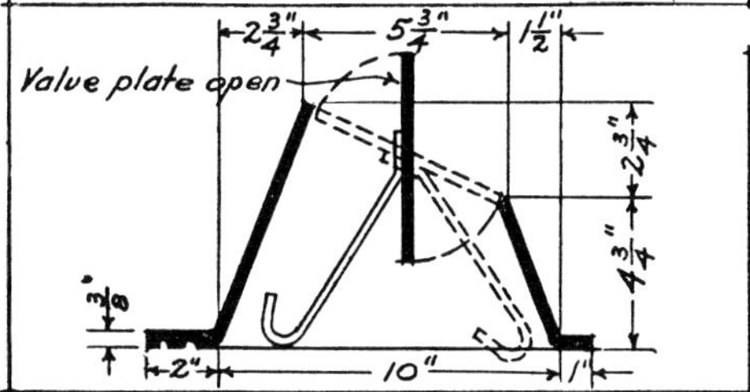

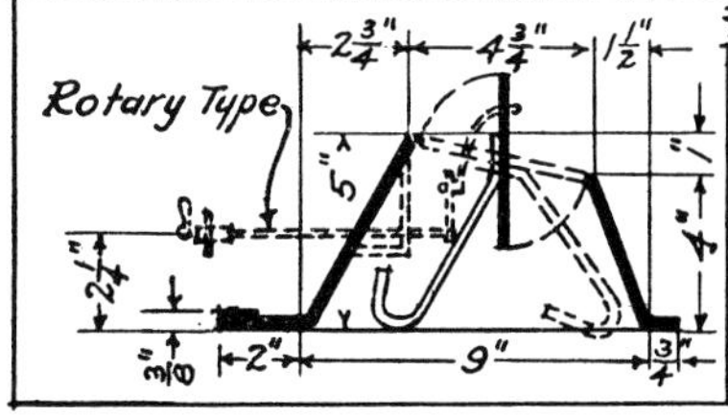

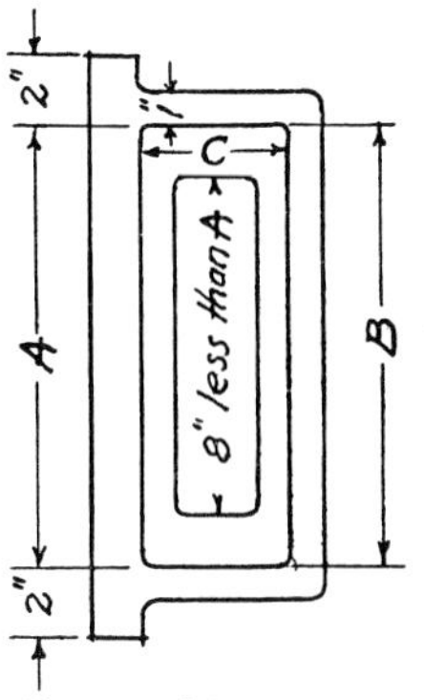

KEY PLAN OF SERIES 'A' & 'B'

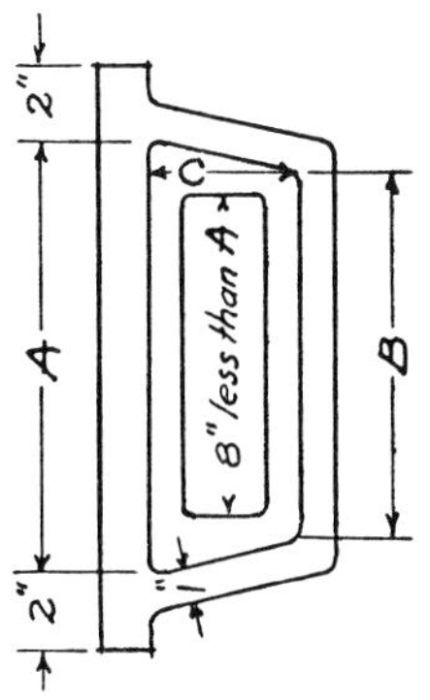

KEY PLAN OF SERIES 'C' & 'F'

COVERT OLD STYLE THROAT and DAMPER

Has high dome operated by poker or chain pulls. May be fixed in three positions except type "F" which has only two.

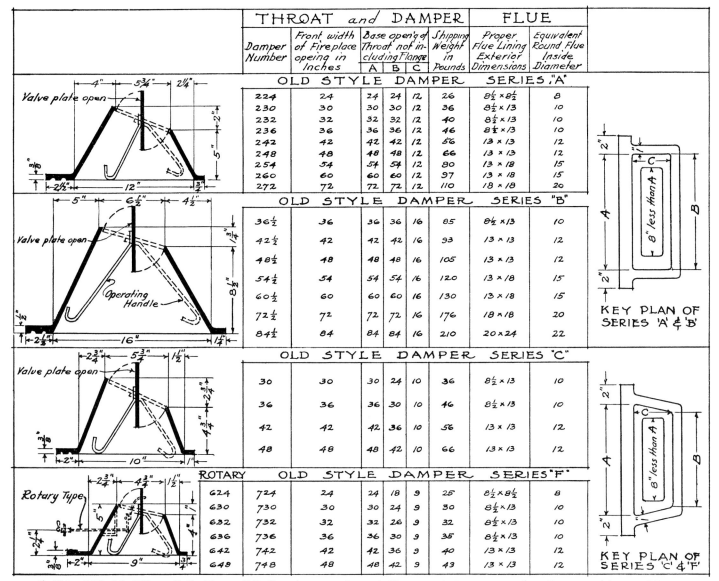

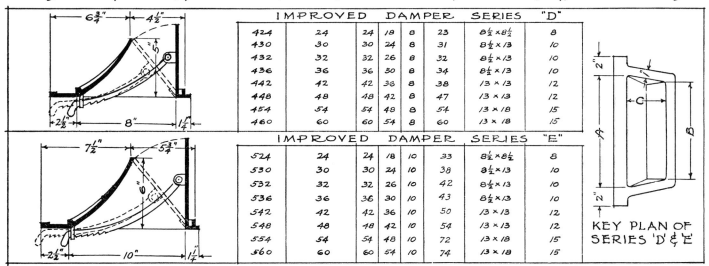

Damper Number	Front width of Fireplace opeing in Inches	A	B	C	Shipping Weight in Pounds	Proper Flue Lining Exterior Dimensions	Equivalent Round Flue Inside Diameter
IMPROVED DAMPER SERIES "D"							
424	24	24	18	8	23	8½ × 8½	8
430	30	30	24	8	31	8½ × 13	10
432	32	32	26	8	32	8½ × 13	10
436	36	36	30	8	34	8½ × 13	10
442	42	42	36	8	38	13 × 13	12
448	48	48	42	8	47	13 × 13	12
454	54	54	48	8	54	13 × 18	15
460	60	60	54	8	60	13 × 18	15
IMPROVED DAMPER SERIES "E"							
524	24	24	18	10	33	8½ × 8½	8
530	30	30	24	10	38	8½ × 13	10
532	32	32	26	10	42	8½ × 13	10
536	36	36	30	10	43	8½ × 13	10
542	42	42	36	10	50	13 × 13	12
548	48	48	42	10	54	13 × 13	12
554	54	54	48	10	72	13 × 18	15
560	60	60	54	10	74	13 × 18	15

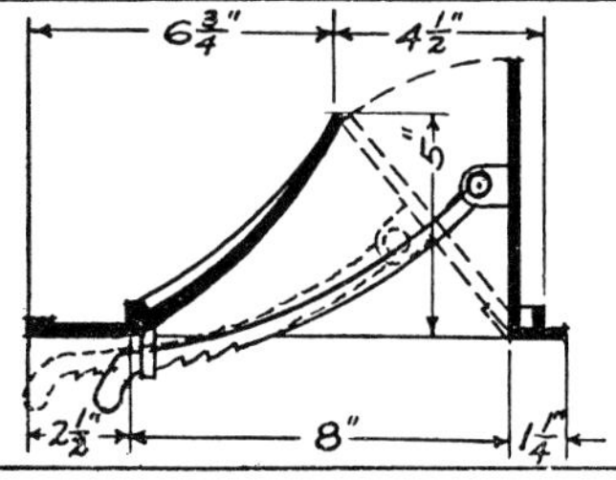

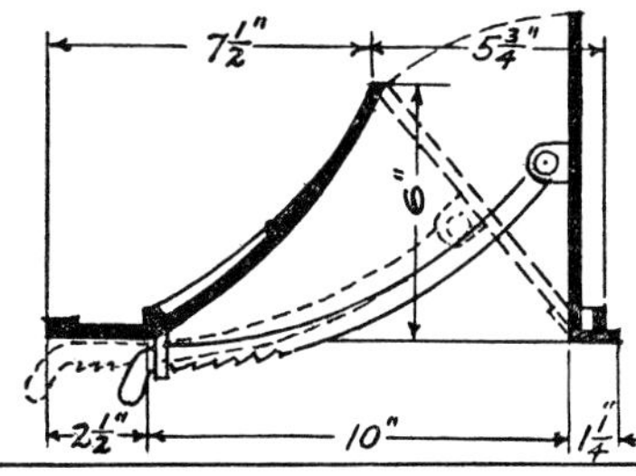

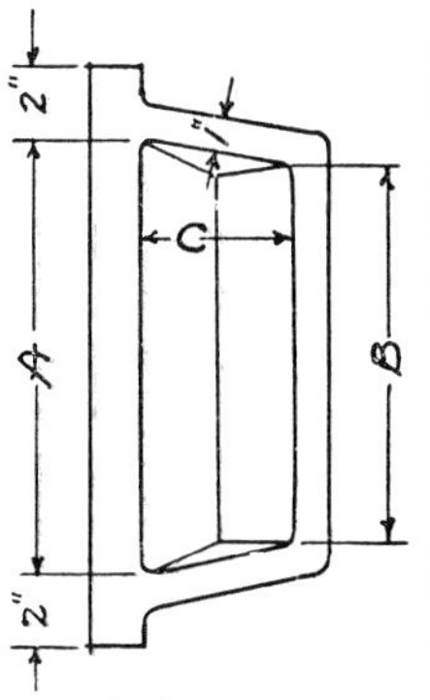

KEY PLAN OF SERIES 'D' & 'E'

COVERT IMPROVED THROAT and DAMPER

All flue sizes to be calculated from Sheets Preceeding

DAMPERS

Poker Control No.	Rotary Control No.	Throat Bot. T	Throat Top A	Throat Opng O	Overall Length L	Overall Back B	Overall Width W	Width A	Height B	Depth C	Back D	Vert. Back E	Slope Back F	Throat G	Width H	Depth I	Smoke Chamb. J	Slope Sm.ch. K	Rectangular Flue Lining L×M	Round Fl. Lin. ø	Rotary No.	Poker No.
224	324	24	17 5/16	4 1/4	28 1/2	21	9 7/8	26	24	16	13	14	14	8 3/4	39	20	24	15	8 1/2 × 8 1/2	10	330	230
230	330	30	23 5/16	4 1/4	34 1/2	27	9 7/8	28	28	16	15	14	18	8 3/4	42	20	25	14 1/2	8 1/2 × 13	10	330	230
233	333	33	26 5/16	4 1/4	37 1/2	30	9 7/8	30	30	16	17	14	20	8 3/4	42	20	25	14 1/2	8 1/2 × 13	10	330	230
236	336	36	29 5/16	4 1/4	40 1/2	33	9 7/8	32	28	16	19	14	20	8 3/4	44	20	26	15 1/2	8 1/2 × 13	10	333	233
242	342	42	35 5/16	4 1/4	46 1/2	34	4 7/8	34	30	16	21	14	20	8 3/4	46	20	28	16 1/2	8 1/2 × 13	12	336	236
248	348	48	41 5/16	4 1/4	52 1/2	45	9 7/8	36	30	16	23	14	20	8 3/4	46	20	28	16 1/2	13 × 13	12	336	236
254	354	54	42 1/2	7	58 1/2	46	14 5/8	40	30	16	27	14	20	8 3/4	50	20	32	18 1/2	13 × 13	12	342	242
260	360	60	49 1/2	7	64 1/2	53	14 5/8	42	30	16	29	14	20	8 3/4	54	20	35	20 1/2	13 × 13	12	342	242
272	372	72	60 1/2	7	76 1/2	64	14 5/8	48	33	18	33	14	23	8 3/4	59	22	40	23	13 × 13	15	348	248
*284	*384	*84	73 1/2	7	88 1/2	77	14 5/8	54	36	20	37	14	26	13	67	24	42	24 1/2	13 × 18	15	354	254
*296	*396	*96	85 3/4	7	100 1/2	89	14 5/8	60	39	22	42	14	29	13	71	26	45	26 1/2	18 × 18	18	360	260
*Two Value Plates								72	40	22	54	14	30	13	83	26	56	32 1/2	18 × 18	18	372	272

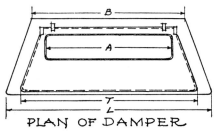

PLAN OF DAMPER

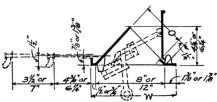

SECTION OF DAMPER

Where two dimensions are shown the smaller applies to Dampers 248-348 and under, the larger to 254-354 & over. Both operating devices are shown.

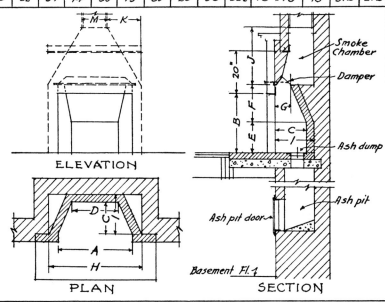

ELEVATION

PLAN

SECTION

DONLEY THROAT and DAMPER

No.	L	WD	D	F	H	B	R	O	C	K	E	Rect. Flue Lining outside	Round Flue Lining Inside
124-W	30"	24"	13 1/8"	10"	6 1/4"	21 1/8"	20"	16 1/8"	2 1/4"	4 3/4"	4 1/4"	8 1/2" × 8 1/2"	8"
128-W	34"	28"	"	"	"	25 1/4"	24"	20 1/4"	"	"	"	8 1/2" × 13"	10"
130-W	36"	30"	"	"	"	27 1/4"	26"	22 1/4"	"	"	"	8 1/2" × 13"	10"
132-W	38"	32"	"	"	"	29 1/4"	28"	24 5/8"	"	"	"	8 1/2" × 13"	10"
134-W	40"	34"	"	"	"	31 1/4"	30"	26 1/8"	"	"	"	8 1/2" × 13"	10"
136-W	42"	36"	"	"	"	33 1/4"	32"	28 5/8"	"	"	"	13" × 13"	12"
139-W	45"	39"	"	"	"	36 1/4"	35"	31 1/2"	"	"	"	13" × 13"	12"
142-W	48"	42"	"	"	"	39 1/4"	38"	34 1/2"	"	"	"	13" × 13"	12"
146-W	52"	46"	"	"	"	43 1/4"	41 1/2"	38 1/8"	"	"	"	13" × 13"	12"
148-W	54"	48"	"	"	"	45 1/4"	43 5/8"	40 1/4"	"	"	"	13" × 18"	15"
154-W	60"	54"	"	"	"	52 3/8"	50"	47 1/8"	"	"	"	13" × 18"	15"
160-W	66"	60"	"	"	"	58 1/2"	56"	53 1/8"	"	"	"	18" × 18"	18"
166-W	72"	66"	"	"	"	64 1/2"	62"	59"	"	"	"	18" × 18"	18"
172-W	78"	72"	"	"	"	70 1/2"	68"	65"	"	"	"	18" × 18"	18"

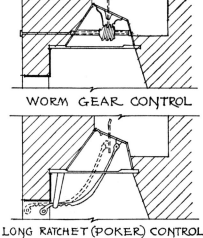

WORM GEAR CONTROL

LONG RATCHET (POKER) CONTROL

SHORT RATCHET (POKER) CONTROL

"SUTTON" DOME DAMPERS

SPECIFICATIONS OF "SUTTON" DOME DAMPERS

Select damper in which WD = Fireplace opening. If Fireplace opening is between two WD sizes always select WD that is next larger. Example: Fireplace width = 40", use 142 Damper.

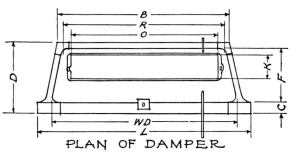

PLAN OF DAMPER

SUTTON THROAT and DAMPER

DAMPERS

Number	Fireplace Width	Extreme of Damper Flange Front	Back	Depth
24	24"	28"	20"	12"
30	30"	34"	25"	12"
32	32"	36"	27"	12"
36	36"	40"	31"	12"
42	42"	46"	37"	12"
48	48"	52"	43"	15"
54	54"	58"	50"	15"
60	60"	64"	58"	19"
*72	72"	76"	70"	19"
*84	84"	88"	82"	19"

*Sizes not made in Rotary Control

DAMPER SIZES & NUMBERS FOR PUSH CONTROL & ROTARY CONTROL

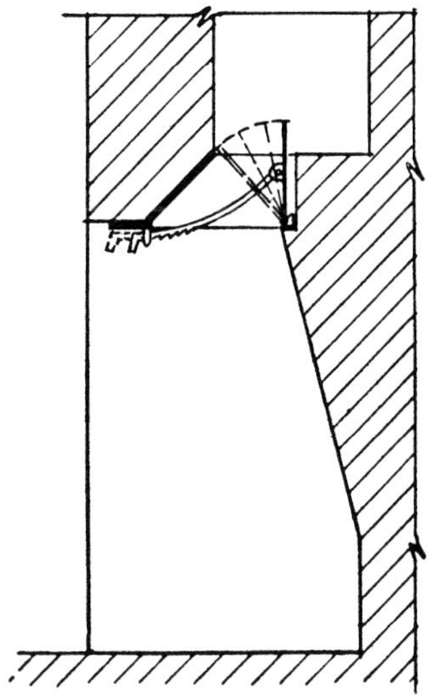

PUSH DAMPER

Throat	Fireplace Width	Damper Sizes Front	Back	Depth
No. x 36x	36"	40"	40"	20½"
No. x 42x	42"	46"	46"	20½"
No. x 48x	48"	52"	52"	20½"
No. x 54x	54"	58"	58"	20½"
No. x 60x	60"	64"	64"	22"
No. x 66x	66"	70"	70"	22"
No. x 72x	72"	76"	76"	24"
No. x 78x	78"	84"	84"	24"
No. x 84x	84"	88"	88"	26"
No. x 96x	96"	100"	100"	26"
No. x 108x	108"	112"	112"	28"
No. x 120x	120"	124"	124"	28"

EXTRA DEEP THROAT DAMPER

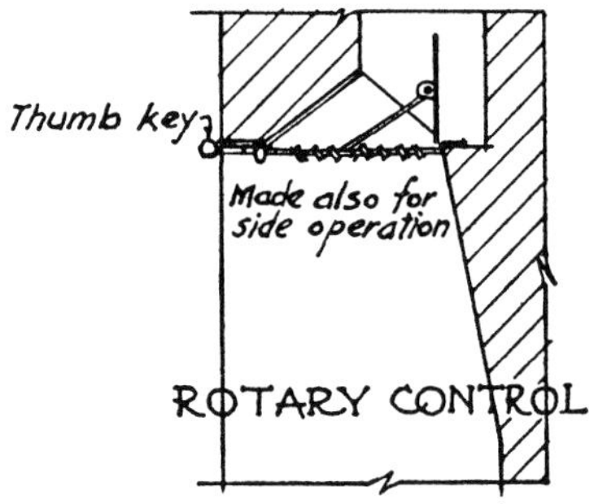
Thumb key
Made also for side operation

ROTARY CONTROL

JAXON THROATS AND DAMPERS.

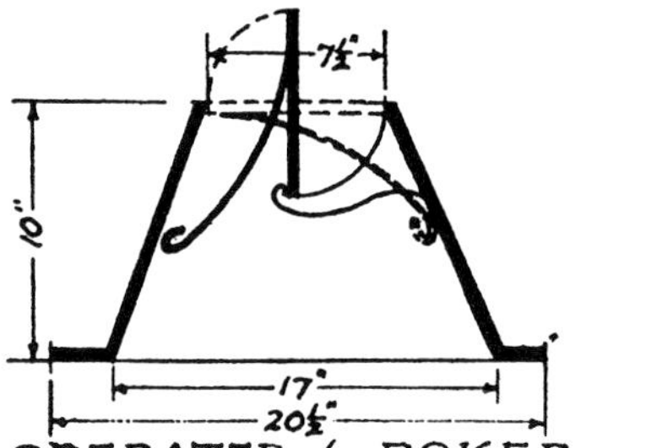
7½"
10"
17"
20½"

OPERATED by POKER
For fireplaces 22" deep or deeper

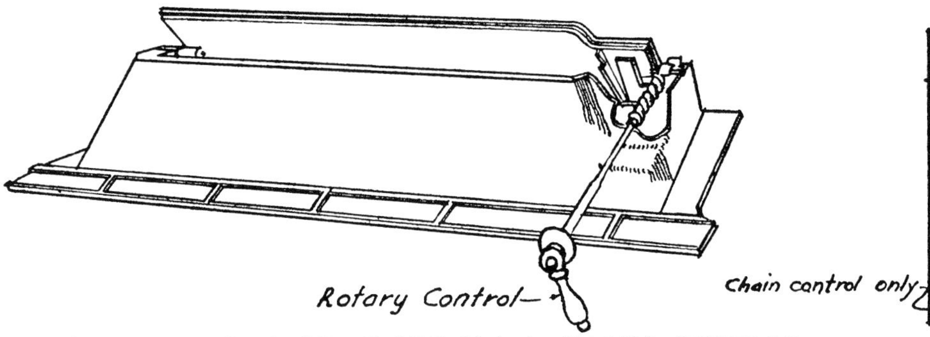
Rotary Control

MADE IN POKER, ROTARY & CHAIN CONTROL

Number	Fireplace Width	Overall Length	Overall Depth	Crated Weight
B 24	24"	28"	13¾"	36#
B 28	28"	32"	13¾"	39#
B 30	30"	34"	13¾"	43#
B 33	33"	37"	13¾"	46#
B 36	36"	40"	13¾"	50#
B 42	42"	46"	13¾"	55#
B 48	48"	52"	13¾"	64#
B 54	54"	58½"	15¼"	90#
B 60	60"	64"	16½"	100#
B 68	68"	72"	19¼"	200#

Chain control only → B 68

SCHEDULE OF SIZES

PEERLESS THROATS and DAMPERS

Damper No.	24-26	28-30		32-34		36-38		40-42		44-46		48-50		52-54		58-60	
A, in.	28¾	32¾		36¾		40¾		44¾		48¾		52¾		56¾		62¾	
B, in.	25¾	29¾		33¾		37¾		41¾		45¾		49¾		53¾		59¾	
C, in.	20	24		28		32		36		40		44		48		54	
D, in.	24	28		32		36		40		44		48		52		58	
Finished Opening: Width, in.	24-26	28	30	32	34	36	38	40	42	44	46	48	50	52	54	58	60
Height, in.	28	29	30	30	30	31	31	31	31	32	32	32	32	32	32	32	32
Firebox depth, in.	16	16	17	17	18	18	19	19	20	20	21	21	22	22	23	23	24
Flue Size, in.	8×8	8×12				12×12						12×16			12×18	12×18	

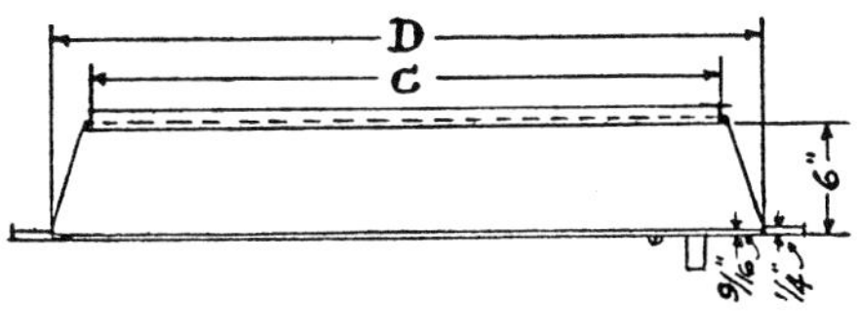
D
C
6"
9/16"
1/4"

ELEVATION

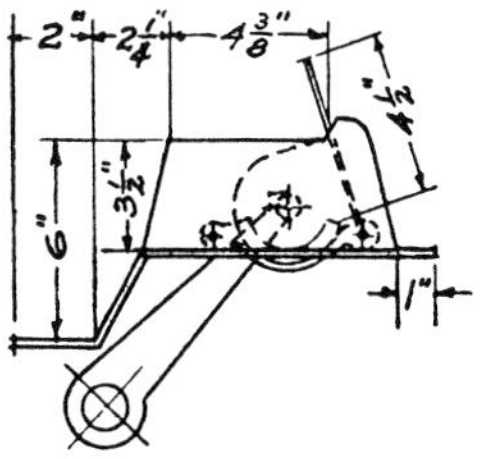
2"
2¼"
4⅜"
4½"
6"
3½"
1"

DETAIL

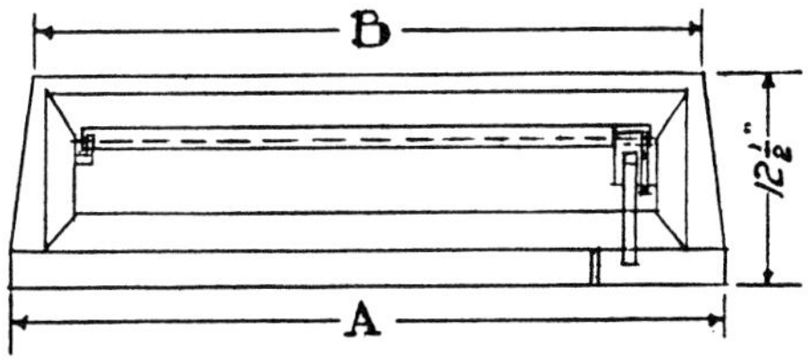
B
A
12½"

PLAN

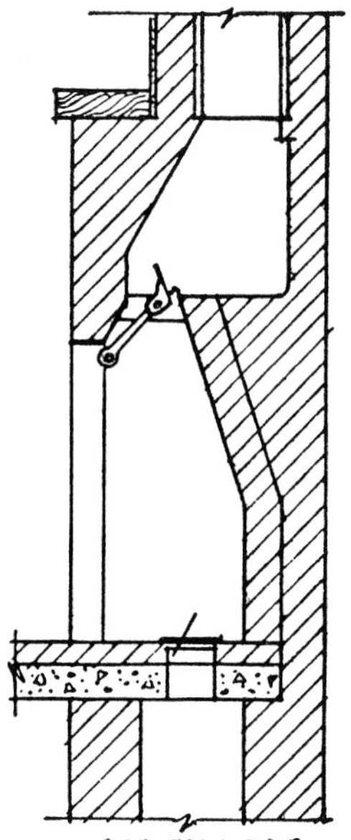

SECTION

MAJESTIC THROATS and DAMPERS

FLUES

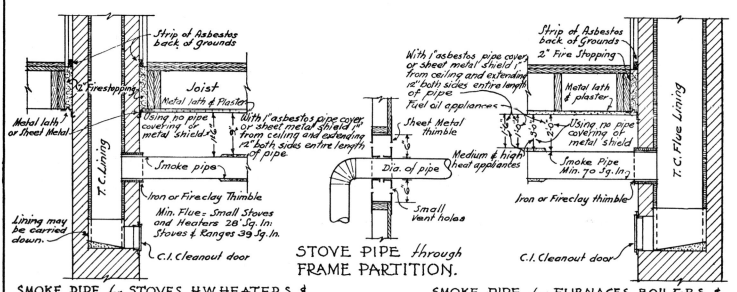

STOVE PIPE *through* FRAME PARTITION.

SMOKE PIPE *for* STOVES, H.W. HEATERS & SMALL RANGES—CONNECTIONS & CLEARANCES.

SMOKE PIPE *for* FURNACES, BOILERS & LARGE RANGES—CONNECTIONS & CLEARANCES.

SMOKE PIPE CONNECTIONS *and* CLEARANCES

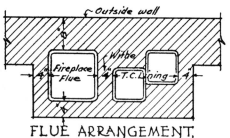

FLUE ARRANGEMENT, OUTSIDE BRICK WALL

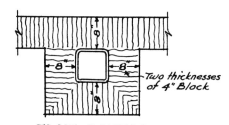

FLUE LINING IN OUTSIDE T.C. WALL
Not to be used except in connection with T.C. Wall.

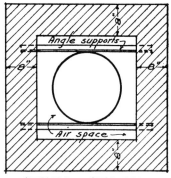

STEEL STACK SURROUNDED *with* BRICK
Used for large Boilers

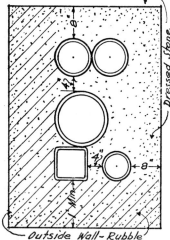

FLUE ARRANGEMENTS IN STONE CHIMNEY

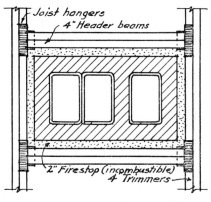

FRAMING (WOOD) AROUND CHIMNEY

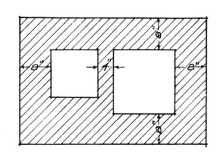

REQUIRED PROTECTION AROUND UNLINED FLUES

Sheet Metal Min.#24 Ga.

Where run to outer air does not exceed 15'-0". Clearances thru combustible material as for smoke pipe.

½" Asbestos

Air tight metal flue with ½" asbestos covering

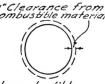

1" Clearance from combustible material

Incombustible non-corrible material, to insulate adjacent combustible material to 160°F.

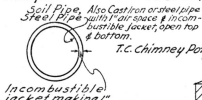

Soil Pipe, Steel Pipe Also Cast Iron or steel pipe with 1" air space & incombustible jacket, open top & bottom.

Incombustible jacket making 1" continuous air space

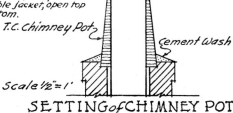

T.C. Chimney Pot

Cement Wash

Scale ½"=1'

FLUE FROM GAS BURNING EQUIPMENT
May be without masonry

SETTING *of* CHIMNEY POT

Recommendations of the National Board of Fire Underwriters.

FLUES

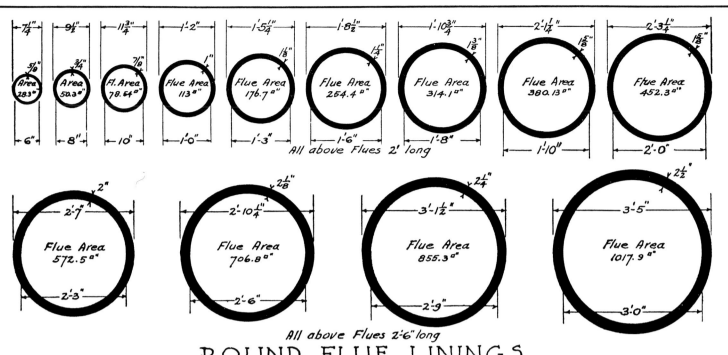

All above Flues 2' long

All above Flues 2'-6" long

ROUND FLUE LININGS
Nominal Flue Sizes for Round Flues is interior diameter

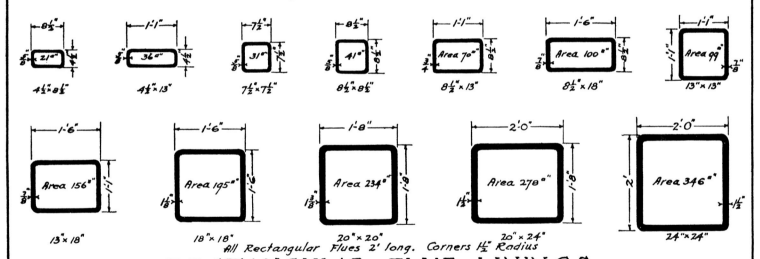

All Rectangular Flues 2' long. Corners 1½ Radius

RECTANGULAR FLUE LININGS
Nominal Flue size for Rectangular Flues is Exterior Dimension – Effective Areas only are shown.

1. Round Flue Lined.
   Entire Area is Effective

4. Square Flue Unlined. Area of Circle whose diameter is 2" less than an Inscribed Circle.

2. Round Flue Unlined, Cast or Moulded Units.
   Deduct 2" from Diameter.

5. Lined Rectangular Flue.
   Entire Area Effective except Corners.

3. Square Flue Lined.
   Area of Inscribed Circle is Effective

6. Unlined Rectangular Flue.
   Less 1" all around than effective Area of No.5.

EFFECTIVE AREAS of CHIMNEY FLUES
Hatched Area is effective

Fireplace Flue Sizes:- 1/10 Area of Fireplace opening recommended. Absolute minimum size:- 1/12 area of Fireplace opening. Flues should never be less than 70 square inches effective area.
Flues for Stoves and Ranges and Room Heaters:- 39 Sq. In. minimum using Rectangular flue, or 6" dia. (inside) using Round Flue.
Flues for Gas Furnaces, Boilers and Automatic Water Heaters to be same size as for Coal.
Vents for other Gas fired equipment may be smaller, but should never be less than 10 square inches.

Fire Clay Flue Linings Standardized by the Eastern Clay Products Association.

FLUES

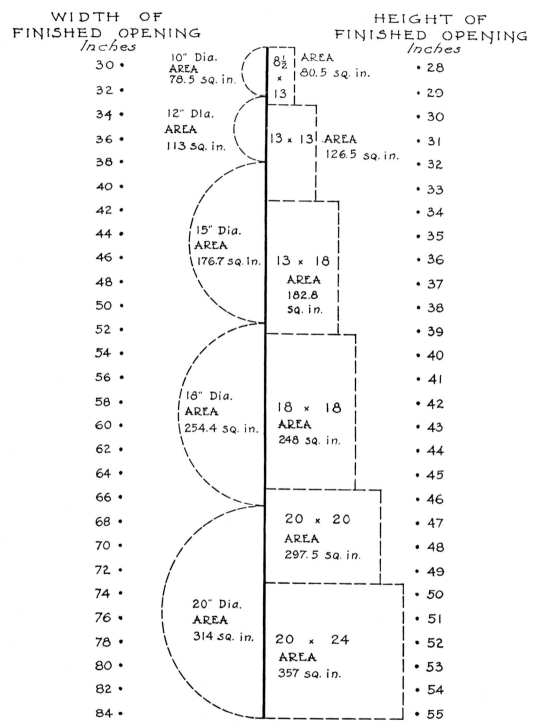

WIDTH OF
FINISHED OPENING
Inches

HEIGHT OF
FINISHED OPENING
Inches

30 •
32 •
34 •
36 •
38 •
40 •
42 •
44 •
46 •
48 •
50 •
52 •
54 •
56 •
58 •
60 •
62 •
64 •
66 •
68 •
70 •
72 •
74 •
76 •
78 •
80 •
82 •
84 •

• 28
• 29
• 30
• 31
• 32
• 33
• 34
• 35
• 36
• 37
• 38
• 39
• 40
• 41
• 42
• 43
• 44
• 45
• 46
• 47
• 48
• 49
• 50
• 51
• 52
• 53
• 54
• 55

10" Dia. AREA 78.5 sq. in.

12" Dia. AREA 113 sq. in.

15" Dia. AREA 176.7 sq. in.

18" Dia. AREA 254.4 sq. in.

20" Dia. AREA 314 sq. in.

8½ × 13 AREA 80.5 sq. in.

13 × 13 AREA 126.5 sq. in.

13 × 18 AREA 182.8 sq. in.

18 × 18 AREA 248 sq. in.

20 × 20 AREA 297.5 sq. in.

20 × 24 AREA 357 sq. in.

CHART *for* DETERMINING PROPER FLUE SIZES FOR OPEN FIREPLACES

Directions for use

Lay straight edge through dots at numbers indicating width and height
of fireplace opening. Proper flue size will be shown at intersection
with center line.   When straight edge comes between two flue sizes
it is advisable to use the larger. Flue sizes are standard, the rectangular being outside dimensions and the round inside diameter.
If the flue is 20 feet or less in height it is advisable to use the next
larger size flue than that indicated in the table.

Designed by W. Covert Co. New York

FIREPLACES

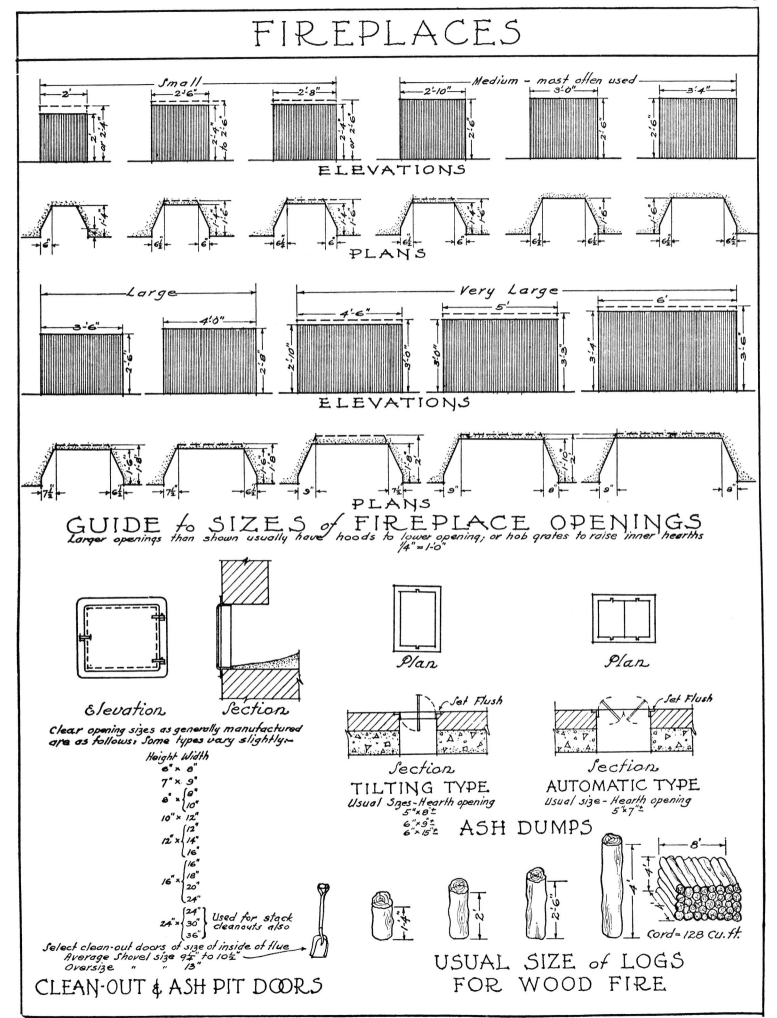

ELEVATIONS

PLANS

ELEVATIONS

PLANS

GUIDE to SIZES of FIREPLACE OPENINGS
Larger openings than shown usually have hoods to lower opening; or hob grates to raise inner hearths
1/4" = 1'-0"

Elevation

Section

Clear opening sizes as generally manufactured are as follows: Some types vary slightly:-

Height Width
6" × 8"
7" × 9"
8" × {8", 10"}
10" × 12"
12" × {12", 14", 16"}
16" × {16", 18", 20", 24"}
24" × {24", 30", 36"} Used for stack cleanouts also

Select clean-out doors of size of inside of flue
Average Shovel size 9½" to 10½"
Oversize " " 13"

CLEAN-OUT & ASH PIT DOORS

Plan

Plan

Section — TILTING TYPE
Usual Sizes - Hearth opening
5"×8"±
6"×9"±
6"×15"±

Section — AUTOMATIC TYPE
Usual size - Hearth opening
5"×7"±

ASH DUMPS

Cord = 128 cu. ft.

USUAL SIZE of LOGS FOR WOOD FIRE

FIREPLACES

Effective Flue size 1/10 to 1/12 area of Fireplace opening. See sheet titled "Flues".

Minimum Flues:- * Round 8", Rectangular 8½" x 13". Effective Area 50.3 ☐"

May set back to 4" Minimum

Flue should center over Fireplace

Fire Clay Flue Lining

Angle 30° or

Steel Smoke chamber shown

Throat area always more than Flue area

4" Min. 5½" Max.

If brick is used cut bricks flush.

4" Min. 5½" Max.

Wood trim to be kept away from opening - Minimum

Lintel

Allow 2" for soapstone set in Cement.

Fireplace opening. For heights generally used see Sheet Preceding

Not over 30

1'-4" Min. 2' Max. except for special conditions.

Approx. 8", never over ½ height of opening

See Sheet Preceding

ELEVATION

SECTION
Fireplace without Damper

Ash chute

SECTION
Fireplace with Damper

Fire stop here with incombustible material

8" Minimum 12" if exterior wall

* 4" to wood studs or joists

* 4" Minimum

* 2" to wood studs or joists

* 4" Minimum. 8" if no flue lining is used

Fire clay Flue Lining

Fire clay Flue Lining

* 4" Minimum; 8" if no Flue lining is used.

6"x9 Cast Iron Ash Dump & Frame. or 6"x15"

* 2" to wood studs or joists

Back hearth of Brick, Soapstone, cement or Briquettes

Minimum Linings:- Firebrick 4" Briquettes & cem: backing 2" Soapstone " " 2"

Usually 4", may be less

* Limit for wood trim

Splay

1'-0" Width of opening 2' to 7'. See Sheet Preceding

About 4½" to Foot of depth

1'-8"

Front Hearth of Marble, Tile, Soapstone, Stone, Brick, Cement or Briquettes.

PLAN

* National Board of Fire Underwriters recommendation

¾" = 1'

FIREPLACES

Patent Damper

May set back to

Allow 4" for Brick

Allow 3" for Brick

Concrete Fill

4" Brick Arch

PATENT DAMPER-STRAIGHT TYPE
Placed high – Brick Trimmer Arch

May set back to

Depends on Damper used

Allow 4" for Firebrick set in Fireclay

PATENT DAMPER–CURVED TYPE

Allow 2" for Soapstone

4" to 6" Slab ½" bars 6" o.c.

T.C. Flue lining

May set back to

Min. 4"
Max. 5½"

No damper

Lintel

Allow 2" for Briquettes

Allow 2" for soap-stone set in cement

FIREPLACE without DAMPER
SLAB TRIMMER ARCH, ASHPIT

Relieving L placed high

Facing placed later

Cement Fill

TYPE of ROUGH WORK FINISHED FIRST
Angle supports rough work. Damper and Fireplace finished later.

Flue

Dash line indicates future work

½ PLAN · ELEVATION

TYPE SHOWING ROUGH WORK FINISHED FIRST
Circular Arch and Jamb made large enough to take Fireplace built later.
3/4" = 1'

4" Min.
8" if Ashpit is wide

ASH PIT

Angle Lintel

Cement

2' above floor

Damper set forward

Flat irons

PROJECTING MANTEL
3/8" = 1'

AVERAGE DIMENSIONS of BATH ROOM FIXTURES

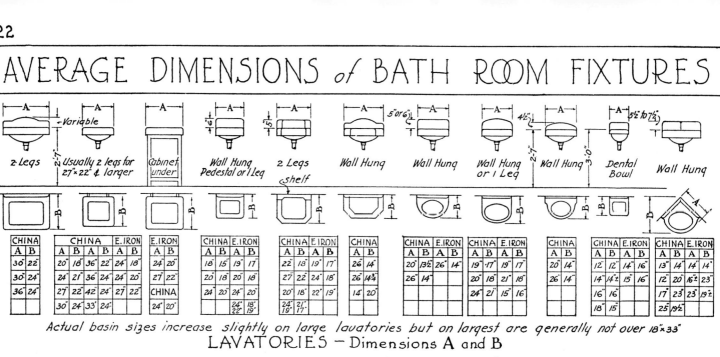

Actual basin sizes increase slightly on large lavatories but on largest are generally not over 18"×33"

LAVATORIES – Dimensions A and B

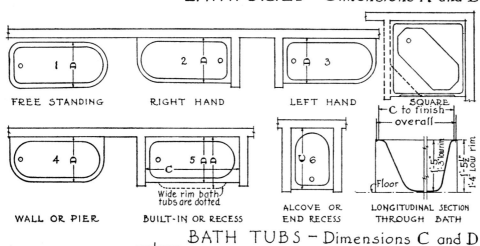

FREE STANDING — RIGHT HAND — LEFT HAND — SQUARE

WALL OR PIER — BUILT-IN OR RECESS — ALCOVE OR END RECESS — LONGITUDINAL SECTION THROUGH BATH

Wide rim bath tubs are dotted

C to finish overall

BATH TUBS – Dimensions C and D

NOMINAL SIZE	OVERALL (THESE ARE MAXIMUM REQUIRED BY ANY M'F'R)	C	D (SEE CAT. FOR EXACT SIZE)
* 3'-6"	3'-7"	3'-5½"	Wide rim
* 4'-0"	4'-0"	3'-10½"	tub 2'-9"
4'-6"	4'-7"	4'-5¼"	2'-4 to 2'-6½"
5'-0"	5'-1"	4'-10½"	2'-9, 3'-0¼"
5'-6"	5'-6"	5'-4½"	Square tub
6'-0"	6'-1"	5'-10½"	allow 4'-2

NOTES
Baths usually build in ¾" or ⅞" except tile faced baths build in 1½.
Fittings may be at either end and are designated as left or right hand.

Always indicate bath tub outlet.

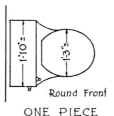

8½" Maximum

3'-5" Maximum

SYPHON-JET WITH FLUSH VALVE — LOW FLUSH TANK — ONE PIECE — Round Front

Extended front round front dotted

WATER CLOSETS – Dimension E

TYPE OF FRONT	FLUSH VALVES EXTENDED	FLUSH VALVES ROUND	LOW TANKS EXTENDED	LOW TANKS ROUND
SYPHON JET	2'-4 to 2'-7	2'-2±	2'-6½±	2'-4±
REVERSE TRAP	2'-4±	2'-2±	2'-6±	2'-4±
WASH DOWN	2'-3½	2'-1½±	2'-6±	2'-4±
ONE PIECE	—	—	2'-3½-2'-5£	2'-2±
WALL BLOW OUT	2'-0"±	—	—	—
WALL SYPHON JET	2'-2½±	—	—	—
JUNIOR (13" HIGH)	—	2'-1¾	—	—
BABY (10" HIGH)	2'-3¾"	2'-0-2'-2½	2'-5"	2'-1"

DIMENSION "E" FOR WATER CLOSETS

THE ABOVE ARE AVERAGES–NOT STANDARDS

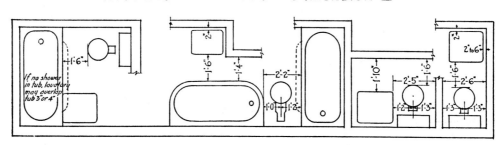

If no shower in tub, lavatory may overlap tub 3" or 4"

MINIMUM DESIRABLE FIXTURE CLEARANCES

Wide rim bath tubs are indicated by dotted lines.

BATHROOM EQUIPMENT & FIXTURES

TYPES	MIRROR SIZE WIDTH	MIRROR SIZE HEIGHT	USES	
CURVED HEAD (Venetian)			This type is most expensive	Mirrors may be had with or without frames
Large	1-8"	2-6"	Luxury type Bathrooms	
Medium	1-6"	2-2" or 2-4"	Master's Bathrooms	
Small	1-4"	1-10" or 2-0"	Guest's Bathrooms. Toilets	
FULL MIRROR FRONT OR NARROW FRAME			High quality, less costly type	No Frame With Frames 6" to 10" Frames usually chrome, but may be enamelled
Large	1-8"	2-4"	Master's & Utility Bathrooms.	
Medium	1-6"	2-0"	Master's & Guest Bathrooms.	
Medium	1-4"	1-10"	Guest or Childrens Bathrooms.	
Small	1-1" or 1-3"	1-7"	Guest's Bathrooms; Toilets	
MIRROR ON DOOR	For over all size add 2" to 4" to Mirror.		Less expensive; Used where appearance is unimportant.	Frames usually enamelled. Mirror sizes are standard but over-all sizes are not
Large	1-4"	1-10"	Master's or Utility Bathr'ms.	
Medium	1-2"	1-6"	Guest or Children's Bathrms.	
Small	1-0"	1-4"		
OPEN BOTTOM SHELF	For over-all size add 3½" to 5" to width & 9" to 11" to height of Mirror		Low cost (no other shelf required)	Lights may be placed on sides. Frames usually enamelled. Mirror sizes standard, but over-all are not.
Large	1-4"	1-8"	Servant's Bathrooms.	
Medium	1-2"	1-6"	Servant's or Childrens Bath.	
Small	1-0"	1-4"	Children's Bathrooms	

No definite standards accepted, but Mirror sizes are generally as above. Depths vary slightly, but all are made to build into 4" stud partitions.

MEDICINE CABINETS WITH MIRRORS

Width	1-6" or 1-8"	1-6" or 1-8"	1-6" or 1-8"	1-6" or 1-8"	1-6" or 1-8"	These are made as stock by some Manufacturers. Doors may be all steel or may have Mirror panel. Locate bottom approximately 1-0" above floor.
Height	5-0"	5-0"	5-0"	5-0"	5-0"	
Depth	4½"	6"	8"	10"	1-0"	

SUPPLY CABINETS — STEEL

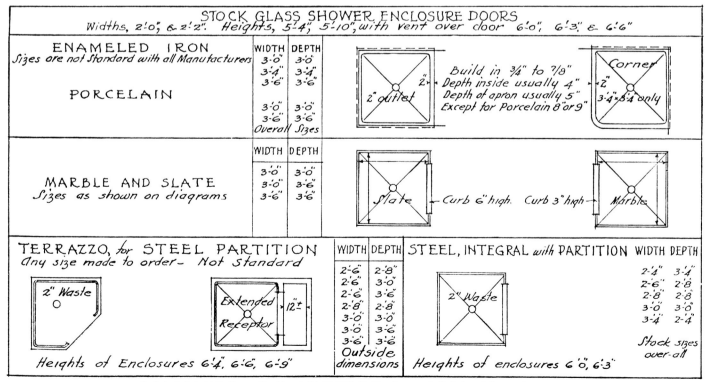

STOCK GLASS SHOWER ENCLOSURE DOORS
Widths, 2-0", & 2-2". Heights, 5-4", 5-10", with vent over door 6-0", 6-3" & 6-6"

ENAMELED IRON
Sizes are not Standard with all Manufacturers

PORCELAIN

WIDTH	DEPTH
3-0"	3-0"
3-4"	3-4"
3-6"	3-6"
3-0"	3-0"
3-6"	3-6"
Overall Sizes	

2" outlet

Build in ¾" to ⅞"
Depth inside usually 4"
Depth of apron usually 5"
Except for Porcelain 8" or 9"

Corner 3-4" x 3-4" only

MARBLE AND SLATE
Sizes as shown on diagrams

WIDTH	DEPTH
3-0"	3-0"
3-0"	3-6"
3-6"	3-6"

Slate — Curb 6" high. Curb 3" high — Marble

TERRAZZO, for STEEL PARTITION
Any size made to order - Not Standard

2" Waste

Extended Receptor 12"±

Heights of Enclosures 6-4", 6-6", 6-9"

WIDTH	DEPTH
2-6"	2-8"
2-6"	3-0"
2-6"	3-6"
2-8"	2-8"
3-0"	3-0"
3-0"	3-6"
3-6"	3-6"
Outside dimensions	

STEEL, INTEGRAL with PARTITION

2" Waste

WIDTH	DEPTH
2-4"	3-4"
2-6"	2-8"
2-8"	2-8"
3-0"	3-0"
3-4"	2-4"
Stock sizes over-all	

Heights of enclosures 6-0", 6-3"

SHOWER RECEPTORS — STOCK SIZES

BATH ROOM FIXTURES & ACCESSORIES (MISCELLANEOUS)

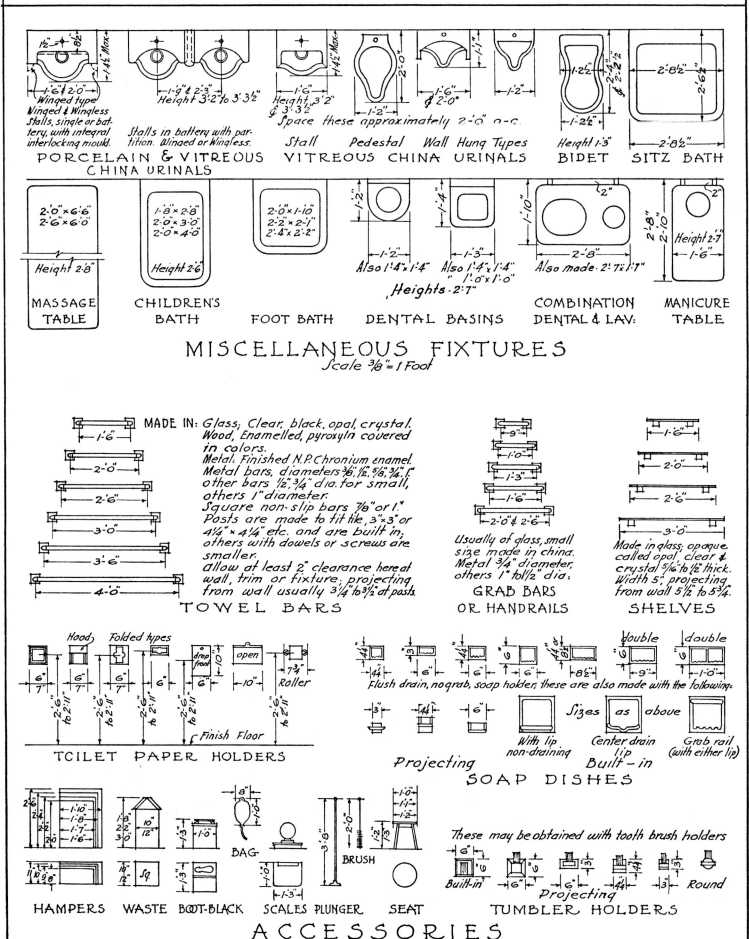

PORCELAIN & VITREOUS CHINA URINALS

Winged type. Winged & Wingless Stalls, single or battery, with integral interlocking mould.

Stalls in battery with partition. Winged or Wingless.

VITREOUS CHINA URINALS — Stall, Pedestal, Wall Hung Types. Space these approximately 2'-0" o-c.

Height 3'-2" to 3'-3½"   Height 3'-2" & 3'-3½"

BIDET — Height 1'-3"

SITZ BATH

MASSAGE TABLE — 2'-0" × 6'-6", 2'-6" × 6'-0", Height 2'-8"

CHILDREN'S BATH — 1'-8" × 2'-8", 2'-0" × 3'-0", 2'-0" × 4'-0", Height 2'-6"

FOOT BATH — 2'-0" × 1'-10", 2'-2" × 2'-1", 2'-4" × 2'-2"

DENTAL BASINS — Also 1'-4" × 1'-4", 1'-0" × 1'-0". Heights 2'-7"

COMBINATION DENTAL & LAV. — Also made 2'-7" × 1'-7"

MANICURE TABLE — Height 2'-7"

MISCELLANEOUS FIXTURES
Scale 3/8" = 1 Foot

TOWEL BARS — 1'-6", 2'-0", 2'-6", 3'-0", 3'-6", 4'-0"

MADE IN: Glass; Clear, black, opal, crystal. Wood, Enamelled, pyroxyln covered in colors. Metal: Finished N.P. Chronium enamel. Metal bars, diameters 3/8", 1/2", 5/8", 3/4", 1". Other bars 1/2", 3/4" dia. for small, others 1" diameter. Square non-slip bars 7/8" or 1". Posts are made to fit tile, 3"×3" or 4¼"×4¼" etc. and are built in; others with dowels or screws are smaller. Allow at least 2" clearance here at wall, trim or fixture; projecting from wall usually 3¾" to 3½" at posts.

GRAB BARS OR HANDRAILS — 9", 1'-0", 1'-3", 1'-6", 2'-0" & 2'-6". Usually of glass, small size made in china. Metal 3/4" diameter, others 1" to 1½" dia.

SHELVES — 1'-6", 2'-0", 2'-6", 3'-0". Made in glass; opaque called opal, clear & crystal 5/16" to 1/2" thick. Width 5", projecting from wall 5½" to 5¾".

TOILET PAPER HOLDERS — Hood, Folded types, drop front, open, Roller. 6", 7", 10", 7¾". 2'-6" to 2'-11". Finish Floor

SOAP DISHES — Projecting, Built-in. Flush drain, no grab, soap holder; these are also made with the following: With lip non-draining, Center drain lip, Grab rail (with either lip). Sizes as above. Double, double.

ACCESSORIES

HAMPERS — 2'-6", 2'-4", 2'-2", 1'-10", 1'-8", 1'-7", 1'-6", 11", 10", 9", 8"

WASTE — 8", 9", 10", 12", sq.

BOOT-BLACK — 1'-3"

BAG — 8"

SCALES — 1'-3"

PLUNGER — 3'-8", 2'-0"

SEAT — 1'-0", 1'-1", 1'-2", 1'-2", 1'-3"

TUMBLER HOLDERS — These may be obtained with tooth brush holders. Built-in, Projecting, Round. 6"

LOCATION of BATH ROOM ACCESSORIES

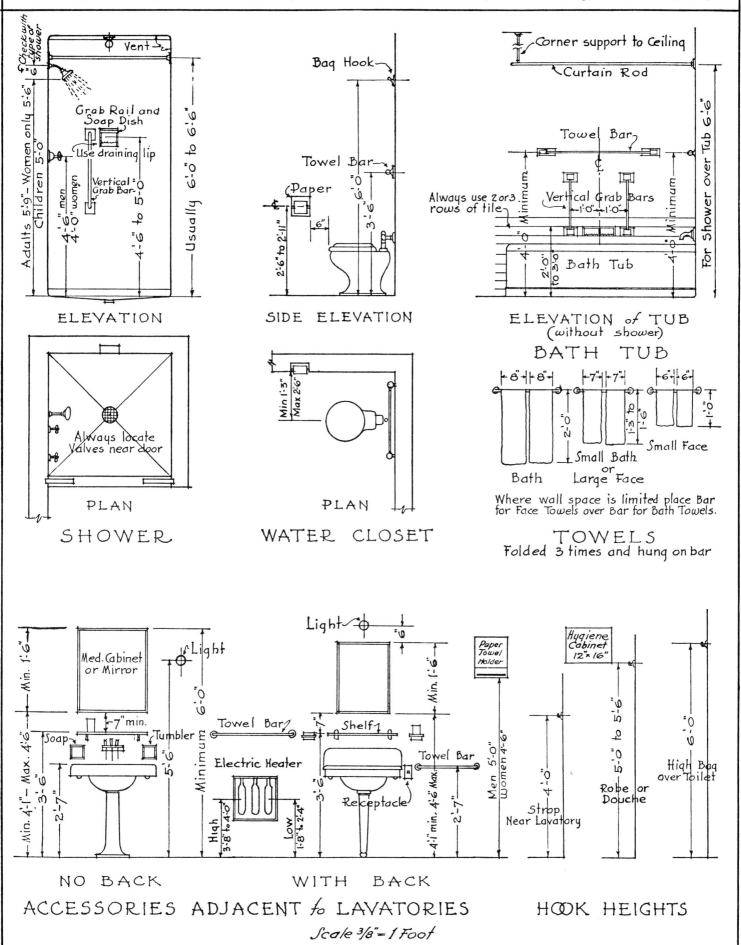

ELEVATION

SIDE ELEVATION

ELEVATION of TUB
(without shower)

BATH TUB

SHOWER

WATER CLOSET

TOWELS
Folded 3 times and hung on bar

Where wall space is limited place Bar
for Face Towels over Bar for Bath Towels.

NO BACK

WITH BACK

ACCESSORIES ADJACENT to LAVATORIES

HOOK HEIGHTS

Scale 3/8"= 1 Foot

CLOSETS

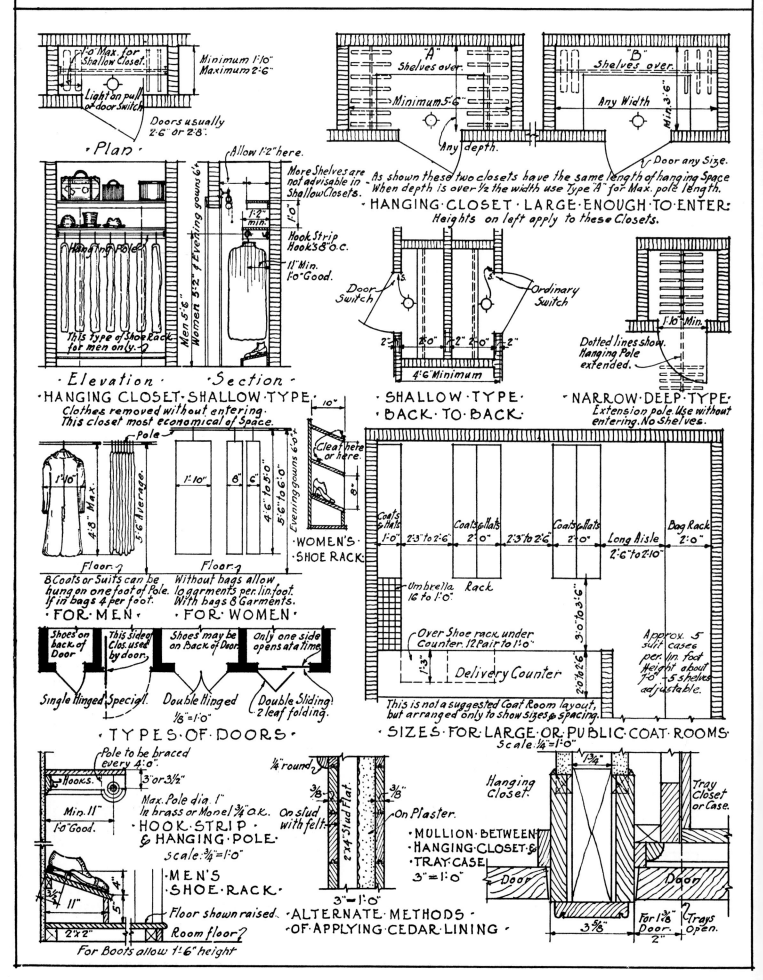

· Plan ·

Minimum 1'-10"
Maximum 2'-6"
1'-0" Max. for Shallow Closet.
Light on pull of door Switch.
Doors usually 2'-6" or 2'-8".

"A" Shelves over.
Minimum 5'-6"
Any depth.

"B" Shelves over.
Any Width
Min. 3'-6"
Door any Size.

As shown these two closets have the same length of hanging Space. When depth is over ½ the width use Type "A" for Max. pole length.

· HANGING · CLOSET · LARGE · ENOUGH · TO · ENTER ·
Heights on left apply to these Closets.

More Shelves are not advisable in Shallow Closets.
Allow 1'-2" here.
Men's 5'-6" Women 5'-2" Evening gowns 6'.
1'-2" min.
1'-0"
Hook Strip Hooks 8" O.C.
11" Min. 1'-0" Good.
Hanging Pole.
This type of Shoe Rack for men only.

· Elevation · · Section ·

· HANGING · CLOSET · SHALLOW · TYPE ·
Clothes removed without entering. This closet most economical of Space.

Door Switch
Ordinary Switch
2" 2'-0" 2" 2'-0" 2"
4'-6" Minimum

· SHALLOW · TYPE · BACK · TO · BACK ·

· NARROW · DEEP · TYPE ·
Extension pole. Use without entering. No shelves.
1'-10" Min.
Dotted lines show Hanging Pole extended.

Pole
1'-10"
4'-8" Max.
5'-6" Average
Floor
1'-10" 8" 6'
4'-6" to 5'-0"
5'-6" to 6'-0"
Floor

10"
Cleat here or here.
8"
· WOMEN'S · SHOE · RACK ·
Evening gowns 6'-0"

8 Coats or Suits can be hung on one foot of Pole. If in bags 4 per foot.
· FOR · MEN ·

Without bags allow 10 garments per lin. foot. With bags 8 Garments.
· FOR · WOMEN ·

Shoes on back of Door
This side of Clos. used by door.
Single Hinged Special.

Shoes may be on Back of Door
Double Hinged
⅛"=1'-0"

Only one side opens at a time.
Double Sliding 2 leaf folding.

· TYPES · OF · DOORS ·

Coats & Hats 1'-0"
2'-3" to 2'-6"
Coats & Hats 2'-0"
2'-3" to 2'-6"
Coats & Hats 2'-0"
Long Aisle 2'-6" to 2'-10"
Bag Rack 2'-0"
3'-0" to 3'-6"
Umbrella Rack 16 to 1'-0"
Over Shoe rack under Counter. 12 Pair to 1'-0"
1'-3"
2'-0" to 2'-6"
Delivery Counter
Approx. 5 suit cases per lin. foot. Height about 1'-0". 5 shelves adjustable.

This is not a suggested Coat Room layout, but arranged only to show sizes & spacing.

· SIZES · FOR · LARGE · OR · PUBLIC · COAT · ROOMS ·
Scale ¼"=1'-0"

Pole to be braced every 4'-0".
Hooks.
Min. 11"
1'-0" Good.
3" or 3½"
Max. Pole dia. 1" In brass or Monel ¾" O.K.

· HOOK · STRIP · & · HANGING · POLE ·
scale ¾"=1'-0"

· MEN'S · SHOE · RACK ·
Floor shown raised.
Room floor?
3½" 4" 5" 11" 2"x2"
For Boots allow 1'-6" height

¼ round
⅜ ⅜
On stud with felt.
2"x4" Stud Flat.
On Plaster.
· MULLION · BETWEEN · HANGING · CLOSET · & · TRAY · CASE ·
3"=1'-0"
3"=1'-0"

· ALTERNATE · METHODS · OF · APPLYING · CEDAR · LINING ·

Hanging Closet.
1¾"
Tray Closet or Case.
Door
Door
3⅝"
For 1¾" Door.
Trays open.
2"
⅝"

LAUNDRY, WASTE and MAIL CHUTES

plan *plan* *plan* *plan*

Inside diameters

1'-0" — HOUSEHOLD
1'-6" — MEDIUM (1'-2" may be obtained)
1'-8" — LARGE (2'-4" may be obtained)
2'-0"

USUAL STOCK SIZES of LAUNDRY CHUTES
Scale ½"=1'-0"

13" or 14" square
22" or 23" Sq.
27" or 28" Square

These sizes may vary slightly according to Company
Scale ½"=1'-0"

These may also be obtained in same round sizes as laundry chutes, & in large square size as 34" or 46". Any special sizes square or rectangular may be made to order.

3" Vent by others
¾" Water supply.
Connecting flushing ring furnished by others.
2" block for F.P. buildings
door
Variable
Rough opening 4" larger than chute
INTAKES
Usually secured to floor with angles
Variable
Outlet
Variable
Both are recommended by manufacturers.
Floor
May be open or with fire door.
4'-0"
90° OUTLET
2" drain by others
STRAIGHT END OUTLET

MATERIALS
Best: Aluminum 16 gauge B&S. Glass enameled Steel 16 or 18 gauge.
Can also be made in other water resisting metals such as monel, allegany, tinned copper or galvanized Armco or Toncan iron. All joints flanged and rivetted watertight.

LAUNDRY or CLOTHES CHUTES
Scale ¼"=1'-0"

MATERIALS
Usually made of 14 or 16 gauge (U.S.) steel, flanged and bolted, or may be of aluminum or other sheet metal.

3" Vent by others
Sprinkler by others

INTAKE or INLET
These are made flush & 45° when closed
Door
Hopper shown open, second door closing when Hopper door is opened

¼" steel
Sprinkler by others
12 gauge
OUTLET (or discharge hopper) may also be straight end
3" block for F.P. buildings
Support

WASTE & RUBBISH CHUTES
Scale ¼"=1'-0"

10½"
2"x2" angles
4½"
3½"
chute
Rough opening 7"x12"- by others
Floor thimble
Plan

Floor thimble
Rough opening 7"x12" for single chute, and 7"x21" for double chute.
Design of box variable. Size shown is usual.
Box must be within 11'-9" of main entrance.
Chute of 20 gauge cold rolled steel.
May be used in public buildings, hotels, and R.R. Stations 5 stories or over, in business and office buildings 4 stories and over, apartment houses of 40 families or over, with the permission of P.O. Dept.

LETTERS
LETTER BOX
US MAIL
37"
35 to floor
19"
21½"
10"

Angle Chute
Floor thimble
Floor line
Rough opening
Ceiling collar
Ceiling connection
Chute

Preliminary Work. Chute in place
Scale 1½"=1'-0"
Side

MAIL CHUTE & BOX
Courtesy of Cutler Mail Chute Co.

TELEPHONES

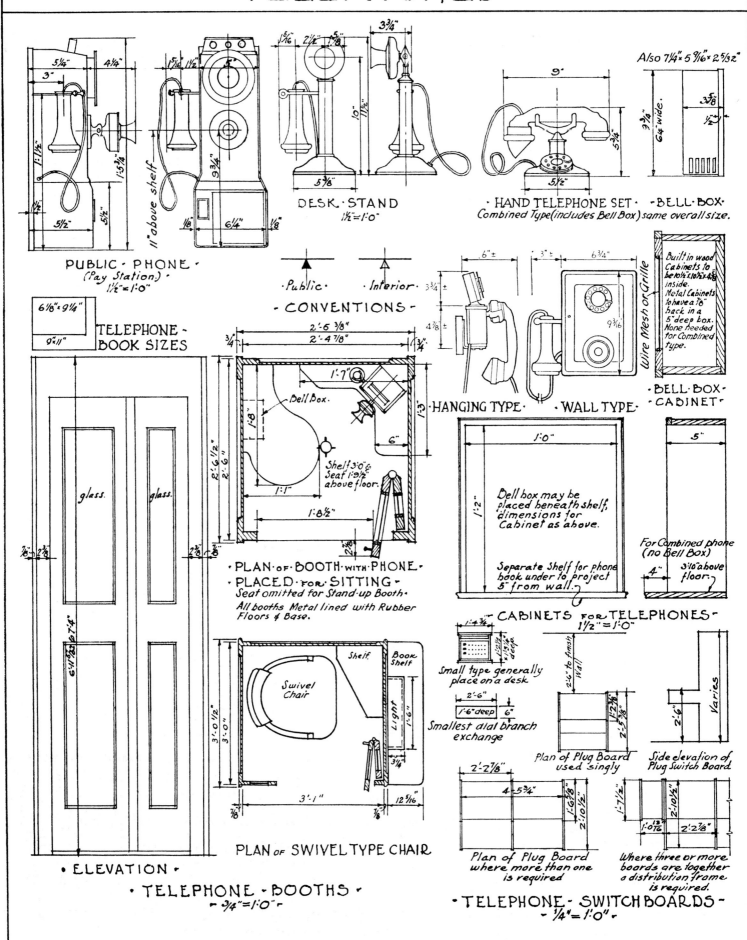

5¼" 4¼"
3"
1:1½" 1:5¾"
1½" 5½"
5½"
PUBLIC · PHONE ·
(Pay Station.)
1½" = 1'·0"

15/16" 1½"
5"
9¾"
11" above shelf
1⅛" 6¼" 1⅛"

3¾"
5/16" 2½" 5/8"
10" 11½"
5⅛"
DESK · STAND
1½" = 1'·0"

9'
3¾"
6¼" wide.
3⅝"
5½"
5¾"
½"
Also 7¼" × 5 9/16" × 2 5/32"
· HAND TELEPHONE SET · · BELL · BOX ·
Combined Type (includes Bell Box) same overall size.

6⅛" × 9¼"
9" × 11"
· TELEPHONE ·
BOOK SIZES

· CONVENTIONS ·
· Public ·   · Interior ·

3¾" ±
4⅞" ±
6" ±   3" ±   6¾"
9 3/16"
Wire Mesh or Grille
· HANGING TYPE · · WALL TYPE ·

Built in wood Cabinets to be 10½" × 10½" × 4⅞" inside. Metal Cabinets to have a ⅞" back in a 5" deep box. None needed for Combined Type.
· BELL · BOX ·
· CABINET ·

2'·5⅜"
2'·4⅞"
¾"   ¾"
2'·6½" 2'·6"
1:7"
Bell Box
1:8"
1:1"
1:3"
6"
Shelf 3'·0" & Seat 1'·9½" above floor.
1'·8½"
· PLAN · of · BOOTH · with · PHONE ·
· PLACED · for · SITTING ·
Seat omitted for Stand-up Booth.
All booths Metal lined with Rubber Floors & Base.

1'·0"
1:2"
5"
Bell box may be placed beneath shelf, dimensions for Cabinet as above.
Separate Shelf for phone book under to project 5" from wall.
For Combined phone (no Bell Box)
4"   3'·0" above floor.
· CABINETS · for · TELEPHONES ·
1½" = 1'·0"

glass.   glass.
⅞" 2⅜"   2⅜" ⅞"
6'·4½"×3'·7¼"
· ELEVATION ·

3'·0½" 3'·0"
Swivel Chair
Shelf.
Book Shelf
Light
1'·6"
3¼"
3'·1"   12 5/16"
⅞"   ⅞"
· PLAN · of · SWIVEL · TYPE · CHAIR ·

· TELEPHONE · BOOTHS ·
· ¾" = 1'·0" ·

1'·4¾"
Small type generally place on a desk
2'·6"
1'·6" deep   6"
Smallest dial branch exchange

2'·6" to finish Wall
1:2⅜"
2:5⅝"
Plan of Plug Board used singly

Varies
2'·6"
Side elevation of Plug Switch Board

2'·2⅞"
4·5¾"
1:6⅞"
1:6⅝"
2'·10½"
Plan of Plug Board where more than one is required

1:7½"
2'·10½"
1'·0 13/16"   2'·2⅞"
Where three or more boards are together a distribution frame is required.

· TELEPHONE · SWITCHBOARDS ·
· ¼" = 1'·0" ·

GREENHOUSES

Rafters Approx. 8:3" on Centers.
8:3"± 8:3"± 8:3"± 8:3"±

Bench | Aisle | Bench

Bench | Aisle | Bench | Aisle | Bench

Bench | Aisle | Bench | Aisle | Bench | Aisle | Bench

10:0" or 11:0"

18:0"
15:0" widths also made.

25:0"
Certain Co's also make 21:0" or 23:0" Size.

15°
N
Good

15°
N
Best

Orientation & Location of Greenhouses.

Twice height of house etc.

height

Desirable location from houses, trees etc.

Wider Houses are made but are not Standard.

· PLANS ·
· Scale: 1/8" = 1:0" ·

Width of Benches and aisles vary with Mfg. But sizes drawn are approx. average.
When cross partitions are required these must occur under Rafters.

Alternate Straight Eaves.

Alternate Straight Eaves.

(Approx. 30° Pitch)

24"R.

24"R.

24"R.

Vents in Wall under bench, also made for all sizes of Houses.

9:6"±   2:10"±
2:6"±
2"   8
3:0"±

8

8

8

8

12:0"±

14:0"±

10:0" or 11:0"

18:0"
15:0" widths also made.

25:0"

Certain Co's also make 21:0" or 23:0" Size.

· SECTIONS ·

Glass usually 1:8"

Grade

· END · ELEVATIONS ·
Scale: 1/8" = 1:0"

Nearly all Mfg. furnish 2:0" wide glass. Some use 1:8" glass.

· SIDE · ELEVATIONS ·

4"±   8:3"±   8:3"±

8:3"±

Grade

8:3"±   8:3"±   4"±

MISCELLANEOUS DATA

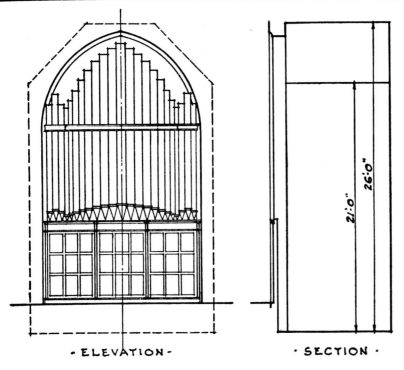

· ELEVATION ·

· SECTION ·

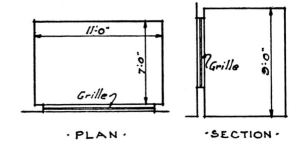

· PLAN ·

· SECTION ·

· RESIDENCE · ORGAN ·
· Minimum · Size ·

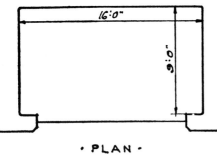

· PLAN ·

· CHURCH ORGAN ·
Minimum Size

· Organ Chamber should be thoroughly
· watertight and have walls and ceilings
· of Keene's Cement and floors of Concrete if
· possible, painted with two coats of deck paint.

All corners of Organ Chamber should be rounded with 2" radius. —
N° windows in Organ Chamber, nor should any heating or plumbing
Pipes pass through same. Grilles should be as large as or larger than open-
ing to Organ Chamber
Opening to Organ Chamber should be approximately 5% to 7% of Cubic
Capacity of Organ Chamber.
Provide Space for Motor etc. below or adjacent to Organ Chamber.

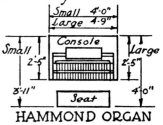

Tone Cabinet, Max. Sizes
One for small rooms —
Several for Large rooms —
Churches etc.
Locate remote from Organ
and Audience

HAMMOND ORGAN

· ORGAN · CHAMBERS ·
· Scale:— 1/8" = 1'-0" ·

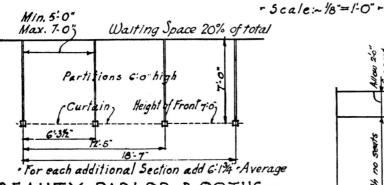

· For each additional Section add 6'-1¾" Average

· BEAUTY · PARLOR · BOOTHS ·

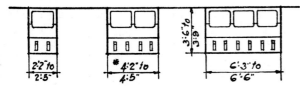

· SHOE · SHINING · STANDS ·

*For more ample sizes use 5'-0" or 6'-0"

Scale - 1/8" = 1'-0"

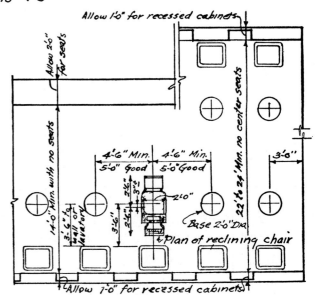

& Plan of reclining chair

BARBER SHOPS

TOWER CLOCKS and BELLS

Arabic Numbers

Roman Numbers

DIAL TYPES

Skeleton Dial

No Numbers

DIAL TYPES

anchor

dial may be any size cast iron or brass

anchor

dials may be of sectional glass or wood 3'-6 to 15'-0 dia.

4" minimum

SKELETON METAL DIAL
outstanding from face
SURFACE DIAL *shown* DOTTED
numerals on wall

FLUSH DIAL
in masonry

SECTIONS thro' DIALS

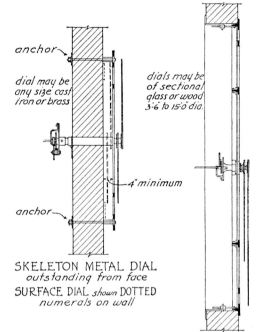

HEIGHT ABOVE GROUND OR STREET

DIA = HEIGHT / 10

SIZE of CLOCK RELATIVE TO HEIGHT ABOVE GRADE

dials may be of wood or sectional glass, any diameter from 3'-6 to 15'-0. Glass ⅜" thick. Structural Glass 5/16" thick. Wood ⅞" thick-2 ply-4" wide maximum

glass dial max⁰ size one piece 4'-0 diamᵗʳ Wood dial any diamᵗʳ

DIAL REBATED
in frame

DIAL REBATED
in masonry

SECTIONS thro' DIALS

Standard dials made up to 15'-0 dia. and specials up to 50'-0 *Standard dials made in multiples of 6"*

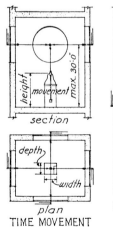

height — movement — max. 30'-0

section

depth

width

plan

TIME MOVEMENT

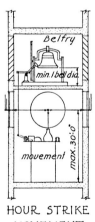

Belfry
min. 1 bell dia.
movement
max. 30'-0

HOUR STRIKE MOVEMENT

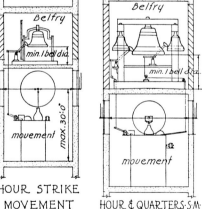

Belfry
min. 1 bell dia.
movement

HOUR & QUARTERS-S·M·

Types of clocks =
1. Time movement
2. Time & strike movement. 3. Time-strike & quarter-strike movemt Belfry= Place over movement if practical Make openings max. size. Head of opening near ceiling & sill near floor See Mfrs. Cat for exact movement sizes, which vary according to number of dials, size of dials, and type of clock. Movements: Many horizontal locations possible; directly behind dial is preferable Electric movement indicated & now largely used

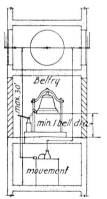

max. 30'
Belfry
min. 1 bell dia.
movement

BELFRY BETWEEN DIAL & MOVEMENT

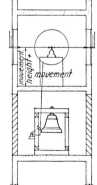

movement height + movement

CLOCK OVER BELFRY

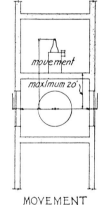

movement
maximum 20'

MOVEMENT ABOVE CLOCK

DIAGRAMMATIC ARRANGEMENTS and RECOMMENDATIONS - CLOCK TOWER ELEMENTS

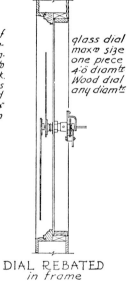

CHURCH BELL DATA					
Medium Tone	Weight lbs	Size Diameter	Height	Mounting Outside Frame	Dia Wheel
D	400 lbs	2'-3"	1'-10"	3'-5" × 3'-8"	4'-4"
C sharp	450 lbs	2'-4"	2'-0"	3'-5" × 3'-8"	4'-4"
C	500 lbs	2'-5"	2'-0"	3'-5" × 3'-8"	4'-4"
B	600 lbs	2'-7"	2'-1"	3'-8" × 3'-11"	4'-9"
B	700 lbs	2'-9"	2'-3"	3'-11" × 4'-2"	4'-9"
B flat	800 lbs	2'-10"	2'-4"	3'-11" × 4'-2"	5'-6"
A	900 lbs	3'-0"	2'-5"	4'-2" × 4'-6"	5'-9"
A	1000 lbs	3'-1"	2'-7"	4'-2" × 4'-6"	5'-9"
A flat	1200 lbs	3'-3"	2'-9"	4'-8" × 4'-9"	6'-3"
G	1500 lbs	3'-6"	3'-0"	4'-10" × 4'-10"	6'-6"

CHURCH BELL DATA					
Medium Tone	Weight lbs	Size Diameter	Height	Mounting Outside Frame	Dia Wheel
F sharp	1800 lbs	3'-9"	3'-1"	5'-5" × 5'-7"	7'-0"
F	2000 lbs	3'-10"	3'-3"	5'-5" × 5'-7"	7'-0"
E	2500 lbs	4'-2"	3'-5"	5'-9" × 6'-0"	7'-0"
E flat	3000 lbs	4'-5"	3'-7"	6'-4" × 6'-8"	7'-8"
D	3500 lbs	4'-8"	3'-9"	6'-4" × 6'-8"	7'-8"
C sharp	4000 lbs	4'-10"	3'-11"	7'-4" × 7'-2"	8'-6"
C	4500 lbs	5'-1"	4'-1"	7'-4" × 7'-2"	8'-6"
C	5000 lbs	5'-3"	4'-2"	7'-4" × 7'-2"	8'-6"
B	6000 lbs	5'-7"	4'-5"	7'-4" × 7'-2"	8'-6"
B flat	7000 lbs	5'-9"	4'-8"	8'-11" × 9'-2"	9'-6"

DISAPPEARING STAIRS

THE BESSLER DISAPPEARING STAIRWAY Co. AKRON, OHIO.

A Height from floor to floor. B Width of finished opening between jambs. C Length of finished opening between jambs. D Dimensions from upper end of stringer to P. E Distance from front edge of stair stringer to fin. jamb. *97- Two drums

Model 29 Panel independant of stairs, hinged at side. Model 39 similar but B always 2'-6"

A	B	C	D	E
7'-7"	2'-0"	5'-6"	4'-8"	5'-6"
8'-1"	2'-0"	5'-6"	5'-0"	5'-10"
8'-7"	2'-0"	5'-6"	5'-4"	6'-2"
9'-1"	2'-0"	6'-0"	5'-7"	6'-6"
9'-7"	2'-0"	6'-0"	6'-0"	6'-10"

Model #45 & 60 — Models 35 & 50 (see B below). Model 75 (see C & D below).

A	B	C	D	E
7'-7"	2'-6" Model	5'-6"	4'-10" / 4'-6	5'-6"
8'-1"	2'-6" #35	5'-6" Model	5'-3" / 4'-11	5'-10"
8'-7"	Model 2'-6" / 2'-0"	5'-6" #75	5'-7" / 5'-3	6'-2"
9'-1"	*50 2'-6"	5'-6" / 5'-10"	5'-11" Model / 5'-6	6'-6"
9'-7"	2'-0" 2'-6"	6'-0"	6'-6" #75 / 6'-4	6'-10"
10'-1"	2'-6"	6'-0"	6'-10" / 6'-6	7'-2"
10'-7"	2'-6"	6'-0"	7'-1" / 7'-0	7'-6"

Model #97 and All Steel Model #300. (see D below).

A (Model 89)	B (Model 89)	C (Model 89)	D (Model 89)	E (Model 89)
7'-7"	2'-6"	5'-10"	4'-4"	6'-5"
8'-1"	2'-6"	5'-10"	4'-11"	6'-10"
8'-7"	2'-6"	5'-10"	5'-7"	7'-3"
9'-1"	2'-6"	6'-0"	6'-2"	7'-7"
9'-7"	2'-6"	6'-4"	6'-4"	8'-0"
10'-1"	2'-6"	6'-8"	6'-8"	8'-4"
10'-7"	2'-6"	6'-11"	7'-1"	8'-9"
11'-1"	2'-6"	7'-3"	7'-6"	9'-2"
11'-7"	2'-6"	7'-6"	7'-9"	9'-6"
12'-1"	2'-6"	7'-9"	8'-1"	9'-10"
12'-7"	2'-6"	8'-1"	8'-5"	10'-3"
13'-1"	2'-6"	8'-4"	8'-9"	10'-8"
13'-7"	2'-6"	8'-8"	9'-1"	11'-0"
14'-1"	2'-6"	9'-0"	9'-5"	11'-5"
14'-7"	2'-6"	9'-3"	9'-8"	11'-9"
15'-1"	2'-6"	9'-6"	10'-3"	12'-3"
15'-7"	2'-6"	9'-9"	10'-9"	12'-10"
16'-1"	2'-6"	10'-1"	11'-1"	13'-1"
16'-7"	2'-6"	10'-5"	11'-7"	13'-1"

(For Model #300 add 4". For Model 300 add 5".)

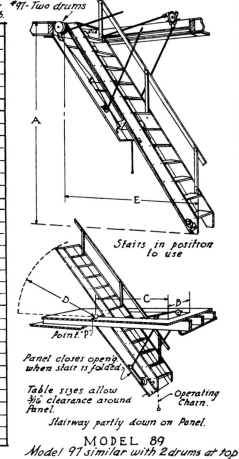

Stairs in position to use

Panel closes opening when stair is folded.
Operating Chain.
Table sizes allow 3/16 clearance around Panel.
Point P.
Stairway partly down on Panel.

MODEL 89
Model 97 similar with 2 drums at top

FRAZIER STAIR COMPANY INC.

Floor to floor height.	Model No.	Rough opening space. in	Run down stair A to B	Operating rad. A to C
7'-10 to 8'-2"	0	2'-2½ x 4'-0½	4'-9"	5'-8"
8'-2 to 8'-7"	1	2'-2½ x 4'-2½	4'-11"	5'-10
8'-7 to 8'-11	2	2'-2½ x 4'-2½	5'-1"	6'-1"
8'-11 to 9'-2	3	2'-2½ x 4'-4½	5'-3"	6'-4"
9'-2 to 9'-7	4	2'-2½ x 4'-4½	5'-5"	6'-6"
9'-7 to 10'-0	5	2'-2½ x 4'-9½	5'-6"	7'-0"

In ordering give joist size & floor to floor height. This stair is self balanced

These stairs are also made in a "Jumbo" series requiring a 4" wider rough opening.

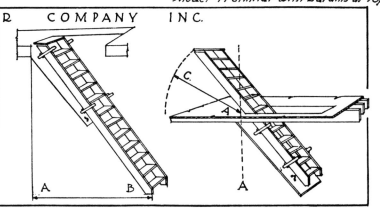

FARLEY & LOETSCHER MFG. CO.
Dubuque, Iowa.

Ceiling Height C.	Run D	Run B	Finished Opening A
The Presto			
7'-6 to 7'-11	7'-2	4'-11	2'-6 x 6'-3
8'-0 to 9'-0	7'-6	5'-8	2'-6 x 6'-3
9'-1 to 10'-0	8'-1	6'-3	2'-6 x 6'-11
10'-1 to 10'-11	8'-10	6'-11	2'-6 x 7'-3
11'-0	9'-1	7'-5	2'-6 x 7'-6
The Victor			
7'-4	5'-0	4'-6	2'-4 x 4'-6
7'-6	5'-3	5'-3	2'-4 x 4'-6
8'-0	5'-7	5'-9	2'-4 x 4-6
8'-6	5'-10	6'-6	2'-4 x 4-6
9'-0	5'-10	6'-6	2'-4 x 4-6

Key to measurements.

Presto operated by drums & cables. Victor rolls on brackets.

THE MARSCHKE COMPANY.
St. Paul. Minnesota.

Sizes and opening dimensions

No.	Model	Clg. height maximum	Rough Opening Width	Length	Finished Opening Width	Length
24	Telefold	10'-3"	2'-2"	4'-4"	2'-0"	4'-4"
36	Junior	9'-1½"	2'-2"	4'-6"	2'-2"	4'-6"
48	Standard	10'-1½"	2'-6"	5'-2"	2'-4"	5'-10"
66	Standard	13'-0"	2'-6"	6'-0"	2'-4"	5'-10"

These stairs fold within the size of the ceiling opening when closed & require no rafter clearance.
No jambs are furnished with the Junior Model.
* 24 slides on itself then folds, no springs, 2 sections. Other models are counterbalanced by springs & fold in 3 sections

for further details see Sweet's.

10

FURNISHINGS

FURNITURE

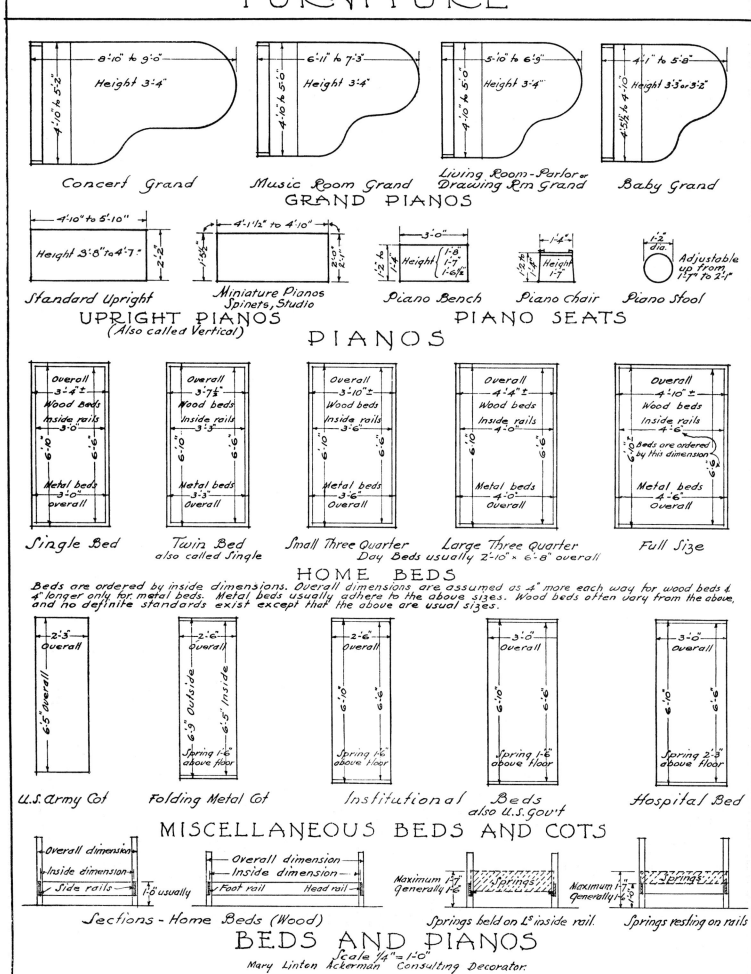

Concert Grand — 8'-10" to 9'-0" — Height 3'-4" — 4'-10" to 5'-2"

Music Room Grand — 6'-11" to 7'-3" — Height 3'-4" — 4'-10" to 5'-0"

Living Room–Parlor or Drawing Rm Grand — 5'-10" to 6'-9" — Height 3'-4" — 4'-10" to 5'-0"

Baby Grand — 4'-1" to 5'-8" — Height 3'-3 or 3'-2" — 4'-5½" to 4'-10"

GRAND PIANOS

Standard Upright — 4'-10" to 5'-10" — Height 3'-8" to 4'-7" — 2'-2"

Miniature Pianos Spinets, Studio — 4'-1½" to 4'-10" — 1'-5½" — 2'-0" 2'-1"

Piano Bench — 3'-0" — Height {1'-8" 1'-7" 1'-6½"} — 1'-2" to 1'-4"

Piano Chair — 1'-4" — Height 1'-7" — 1'-2" to 1'-4"

Piano Stool — 1'-2" dia. — Adjustable up from 1'-7" to 2'-1"

UPRIGHT PIANOS
(Also called Vertical)

PIANO SEATS

PIANOS

Single Bed — Overall 3'-4"± — Wood Beds — Inside rails 3'-0" — 6'-10" 6'-6" — Metal beds 3'-0" overall

Twin Bed also called Single — Overall 3'-7½" — Wood beds — Inside rails 3'-3" — 6'-10" 6'-6" — Metal beds 3'-3" Overall

Small Three Quarter — Overall 3'-10"± — Wood beds — Inside rails 3'-6" — 6'-10" 6'-6" — Metal beds 3'-6" Overall

Large Three Quarter — Overall 4'-4"± — Wood beds — Inside rails 4'-0" — 6'-10" 6'-6" — Metal beds 4'-0" Overall

Full Size — Overall 4'-10"± — Wood beds — Inside rails 4'-6" — 6'-10" 6'-6" — Beds are ordered by this dimension — Metal beds 4'-6" Overall

Day Beds usually 2'-10" × 6'-8" overall

HOME BEDS

Beds are ordered by inside dimensions. Overall dimensions are assumed as 4" more each way for wood beds & 4" longer only for metal beds. Metal beds usually adhere to the above sizes. Wood beds often vary from the above, and no definite standards exist except that the above are usual sizes.

U.S. Army Cot — 2'-3" Overall — 6'-5" overall

Folding Metal Cot — 2'-6" Overall — 6'-9" Outside — 6'-5" Inside — Spring 1'-6" above floor

Institutional — 2'-6" Overall — 6'-10" 6'-6" — Spring 1'-6" above floor

Beds also U.S. Gov't — 3'-0" Overall — 6'-10" 6'-6" — Spring 1'-6" above floor

Hospital Bed — 3'-0" Overall — 6'-10" 6'-6" — Spring 2'-3" above floor

MISCELLANEOUS BEDS AND COTS

Sections - Home Beds (Wood) — Overall dimension — Inside dimension — Side rails — 1'-0" usually — Overall dimension — Inside dimension — Foot rail — Head rail

Springs held on L's inside rail. — Maximum 1'-7" Generally 1'-6" — Springs

Springs resting on rails — Maximum 1'-7" Generally 1'-6" — Springs

BEDS AND PIANOS
Scale ¼"=1'-0"
Mary Linton Ackerman   Consulting Decorator.

FURNITURE

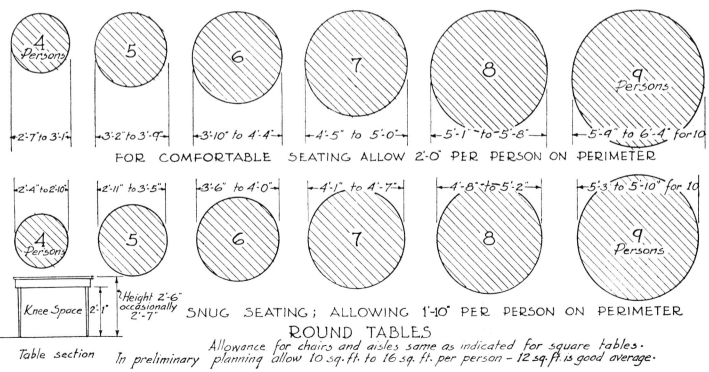

SQUARE TABLES

2 Persons — 2'-0"×2'-6" — 3'-8" to 3'-10" to wall for service

3 or 4 Persons — 2'-6" & 3'-0" square — 1'-4" · 2'-4" to 2'-6" · 1'-4" — 5'-0" to 5'-2" table to table

6 to 8 Persons — 4'-0" sq.

6 Persons — 3'-6" × 5'-0"

RECTANGULAR TABLES
Allowance for chairs & aisles as above.

Very Narrow — Used for service — 2'-3" · 5'-0" · 6'-0"

Narrow — 2'-6" · 3'-6" 4'-0" 5'-0" 6'-0" 8'-0"

Medium — 2'-9" · 6'-0" 7'-0" 8'-0"

Ample — 3'-0" · 6'-0" 8'-0"

Wide — 3'-6" and 4'-0" · 5'-0" 6'-0" · 6'-6" 7'-0" 8'-0"

— These are often termed refectory tables —

FOR COMFORTABLE SEATING ALLOW 2'-0" FOR EACH PERSON — MINIMUM IS 1'-10" PER P.
Tables accomodate same number if seats are placed at ends except on wide table where two extra are cared for.
Numbers marked are 2'-0" spacings.
Table sizes are not standard but are sizes that are generally manufactured — many other sizes are available.

4 Persons — 2'-7" to 3'-1"
5 — 3'-2" to 3'-9"
6 — 3'-10" to 4'-4"
7 — 4'-5" to 5'-0"
8 — 5'-1" to 5'-8"
9 Persons — 5'-9" to 6'-4" for 10

FOR COMFORTABLE SEATING ALLOW 2'-0" PER PERSON ON PERIMETER

4 Persons — 2'-4" to 2'-10"
5 — 2'-11" to 3'-5"
6 — 3'-6" to 4'-0"
7 — 4'-1" to 4'-7"
8 — 4'-8" to 5'-2"
9 Persons — 5'-3" to 5'-10" for 10

SNUG SEATING; ALLOWING 1'-10" PER PERSON ON PERIMETER

ROUND TABLES
Allowance for chairs and aisles same as indicated for square tables.
In preliminary planning allow 10 sq. ft. to 16 sq. ft. per person — 12 sq. ft. is good average.

Table section — Knee Space 2'-1" — Height 2'-6" occasionally 2'-7"

1/4" = 1'-0"

TABLES
Mary Linton Ackerman Consulting Decorator.

FURNITURE

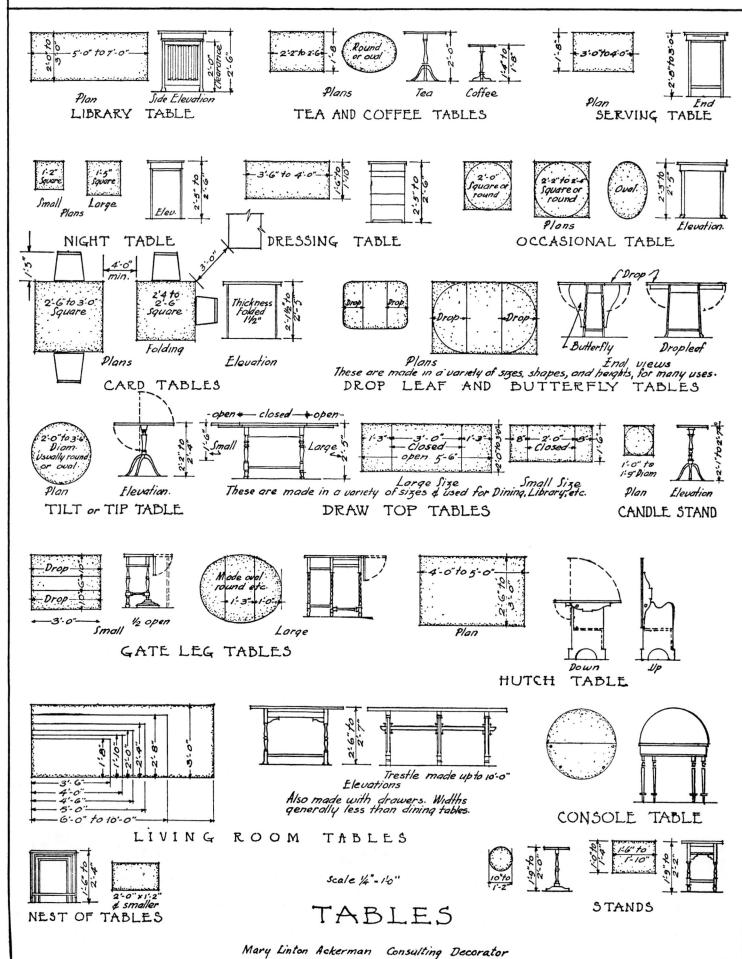

Scale ¼" = 1'-0"

TABLES

Mary Linton Ackerman   Consulting Decorator

FURNITURE

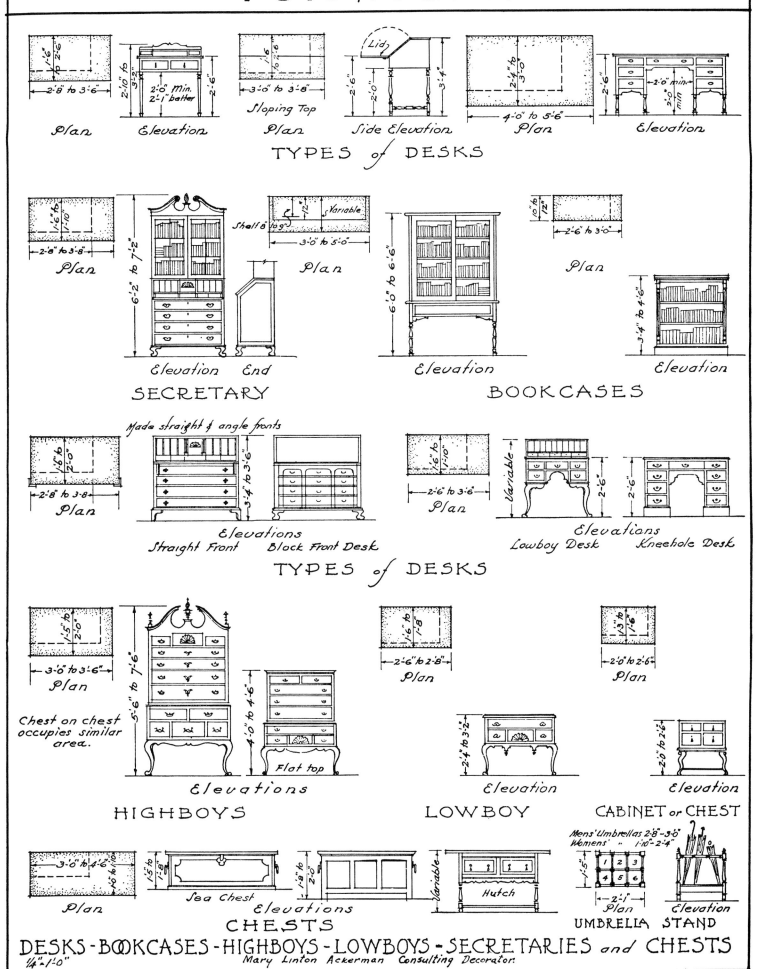

Plan — Elevation — Plan — Side Elevation — Plan — Elevation

TYPES of DESKS

SECRETARY

BOOKCASES

Made straight & angle fronts

TYPES of DESKS

Straight Front — Block Front Desk — Lowboy Desk — Kneehole Desk

HIGHBOYS — LOWBOY — CABINET or CHEST

Chest on chest occupies similar area.

Flat top

Sea Chest — Hutch — Umbrella Stand

CHESTS

Mens' Umbrellas 2'-8"-3'-0"
Womens' " 1'-10"-2'-4"

DESKS-BOOKCASES-HIGHBOYS-LOWBOYS-SECRETARIES and CHESTS

¼"=1'-0"   Mary Linton Ackerman Consulting Decorator.

FURNITURE

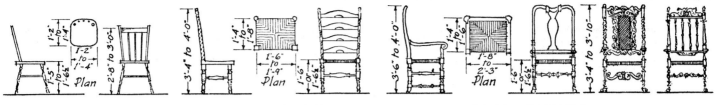

KITCHEN CHAIR   SIDE CHAIR   ARM CHAIRS

UNUPHOLSTERED CHAIRS

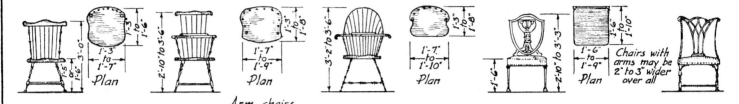

Arm chairs

WINDSOR CHAIRS   DINING ROOM CHAIRS

Chairs with arms may be 2" to 3" wider over all

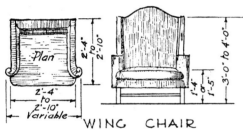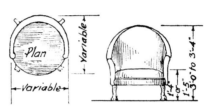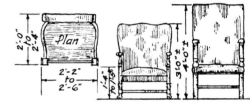

WING CHAIR   BARREL CHAIR   ARM CHAIRS

UPHOLSTERED CHAIRS

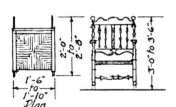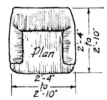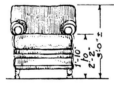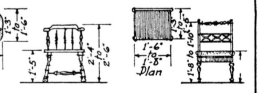

ROCKING CHAIR   CLUB CHAIR   TAVERN CHAIR   SIDE CHAIR

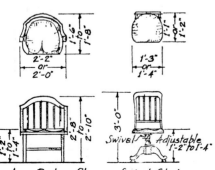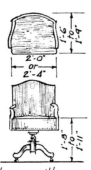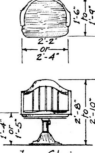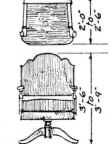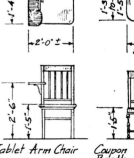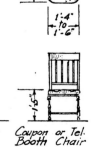

Arm Posture Chair   Swivel Chair   Large - with arms   Jury Chair   Judge's Chair   Tablet Arm Chair   Coupon or Tel. Booth Chair

OFFICE CHAIRS   SPECIAL CHAIRS

CHAIRS
Mary Linton Ackerman Consulting Decorator.

1/4" = 1'-0"

FURNITURE

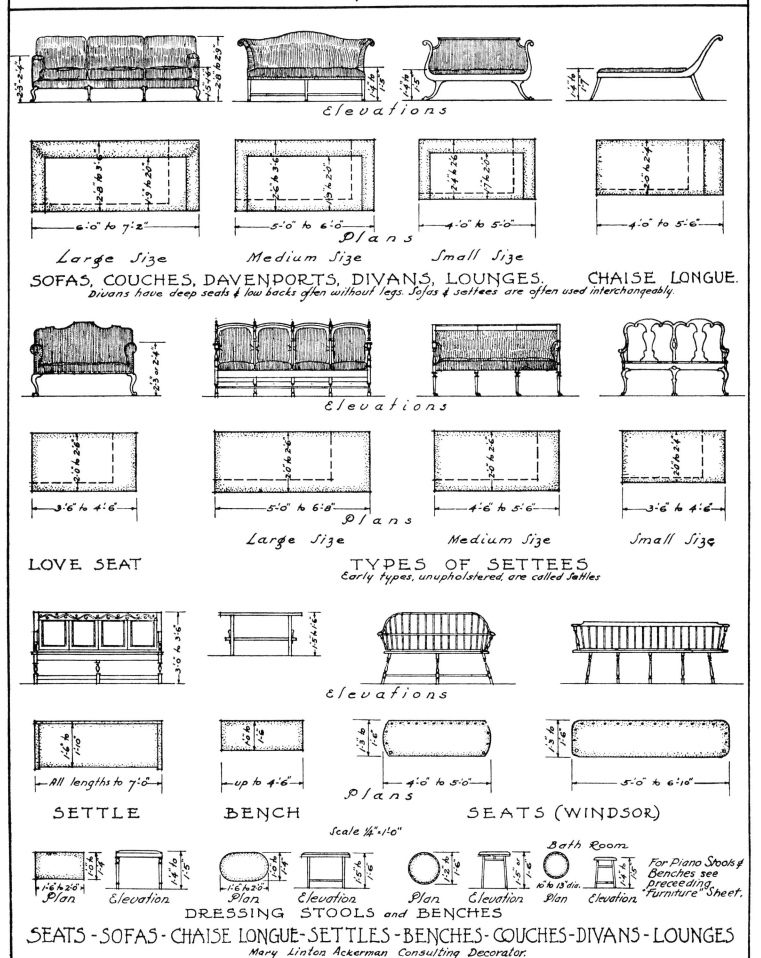

Elevations

Plans

Large Size   Medium Size   Small Size

SOFAS, COUCHES, DAVENPORTS, DIVANS, LOUNGES.   CHAISE LONGUE.
Divans have deep seats & low backs often without legs. Sofas & settees are often used interchangeably.

Elevations

Plans

Large Size   Medium Size   Small Size

LOVE SEAT   TYPES OF SETTEES
Early types, unupholstered, are called Settles

Elevations

Plans

All lengths to 7:0   up to 4:6   4:0 to 5:0   5:0 to 6:10

SETTLE   BENCH   SEATS (WINDSOR)
Scale ¼"=1:0"

Plan   Elevation   Plan   Elevation   Plan   Elevation   Plan   Elevation

Bath Room

For Piano Stools & Benches see preceeding "Furniture" Sheet.

DRESSING STOOLS and BENCHES

SEATS - SOFAS - CHAISE LONGUE - SETTLES - BENCHES - COUCHES - DIVANS - LOUNGES
Mary Linton Ackerman Consulting Decorator.

FURNITURE

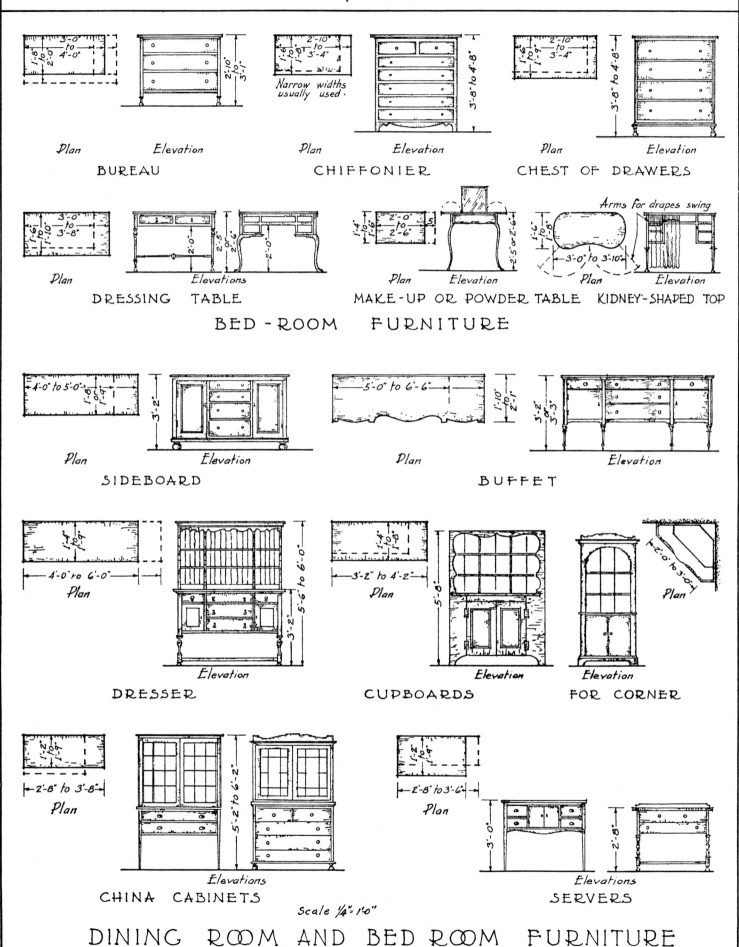

Plan — Elevation
BUREAU

Narrow widths usually used.
Plan — Elevation
CHIFFONIER

Plan — Elevation
CHEST OF DRAWERS

Plan — Elevations
DRESSING TABLE

Plan — Elevation
MAKE-UP OR POWDER TABLE

Arms for drapes swing
Plan — Elevation
KIDNEY-SHAPED TOP

BED-ROOM FURNITURE

Plan — Elevation
SIDEBOARD

Plan — Elevation
BUFFET

Plan — Elevation
DRESSER

Plan — Elevation
CUPBOARDS

Plan — Elevation
FOR CORNER

Plan — Elevations
CHINA CABINETS

Plan — Elevations
SERVERS

Scale ¼"=1'0"

DINING ROOM AND BED ROOM FURNITURE

Mary Linton Ackerman   Consulting Decorator.

FURNITURE

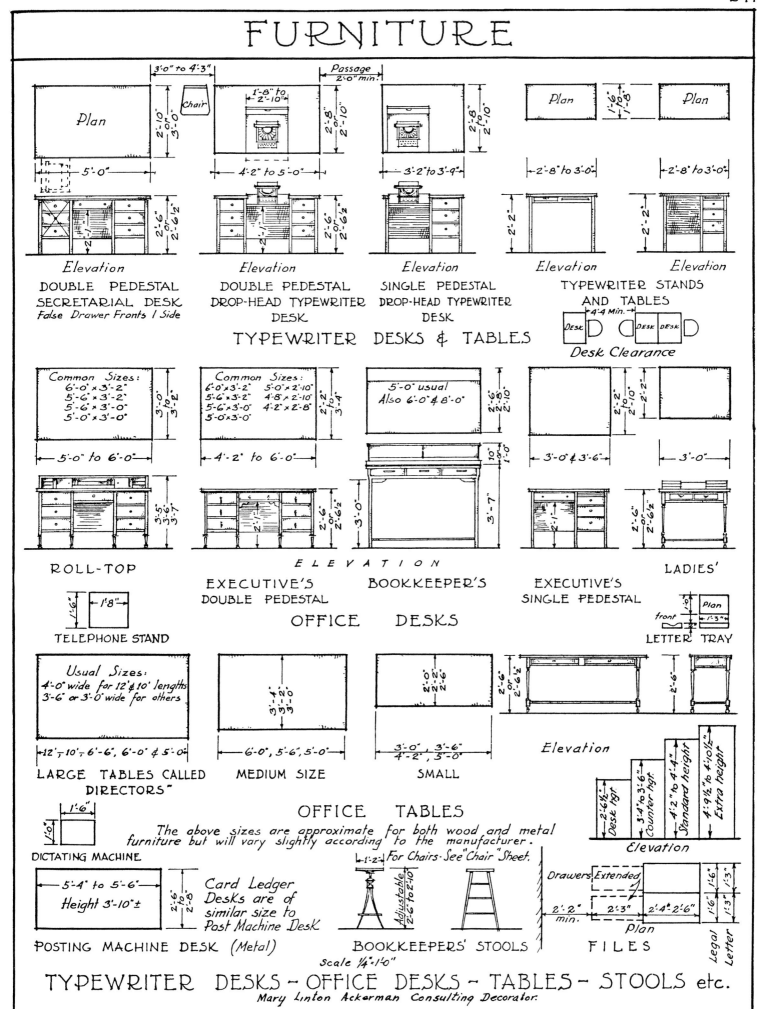

TYPEWRITER DESKS & TABLES

DOUBLE PEDESTAL SECRETARIAL DESK
False Drawer Fronts 1 Side

DOUBLE PEDESTAL DROP-HEAD TYPEWRITER DESK

SINGLE PEDESTAL DROP-HEAD TYPEWRITER DESK

TYPEWRITER STANDS AND TABLES

Desk Clearance

OFFICE DESKS

ROLL-TOP

EXECUTIVE'S DOUBLE PEDESTAL

BOOKKEEPER'S

EXECUTIVE'S SINGLE PEDESTAL

LADIES'

TELEPHONE STAND

LETTER TRAY

OFFICE TABLES

LARGE TABLES CALLED DIRECTORS"

MEDIUM SIZE

SMALL

The above sizes are approximate for both wood and metal furniture but will vary slightly according to the manufacturer.

For Chairs- See "Chair" Sheet.

DICTATING MACHINE

POSTING MACHINE DESK (Metal)

Card Ledger Desks are of similar size to Post Machine Desk

BOOKKEEPERS' STOOLS

Scale ¼"=1'0"

FILES

TYPEWRITER DESKS ~ OFFICE DESKS ~ TABLES ~ STOOLS etc.

Mary Linton Ackerman Consulting Decorator.

FURNITURE

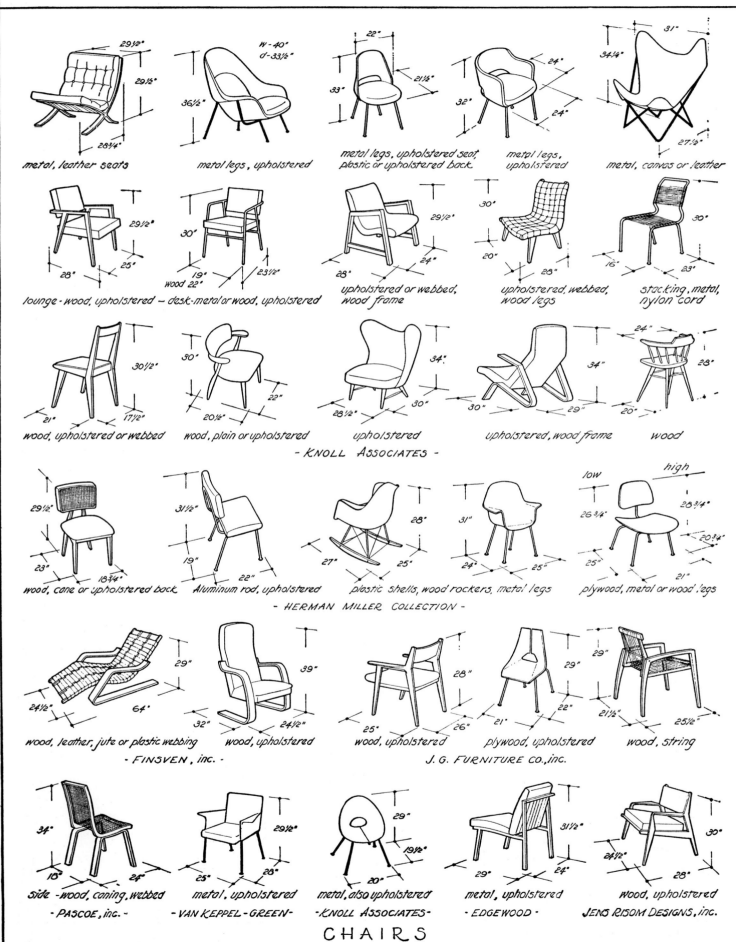

metal, leather seats

metal legs, upholstered

metal legs, upholstered seat, plastic or upholstered back

metal legs, upholstered

metal, canvas or leather

lounge-wood, upholstered – desk-metal or wood, upholstered

upholstered or webbed, wood frame

upholstered, webbed, wood legs

stacking, metal, nylon cord

wood, upholstered or webbed

wood, plain or upholstered

upholstered

upholstered, wood frame

wood

- KNOLL ASSOCIATES -

wood, cane or upholstered back

Aluminum rod, upholstered

plastic shells, wood rockers, metal legs

low   high

plywood, metal or wood legs

- HERMAN MILLER COLLECTION -

wood, leather, jute or plastic webbing

wood, upholstered

wood, upholstered

plywood, upholstered

wood, string

- FINSVEN, inc. -

J. G. FURNITURE CO., inc.

side - wood, caning, webbed

metal, upholstered

metal, also upholstered

metal, upholstered

wood, upholstered

- PASCOE, inc. -

- VAN KEPPEL-GREEN -

-KNOLL ASSOCIATES-

- EDGEWOOD -

JENS RISOM DESIGNS, inc.

CHAIRS

BEACH EQUIPMENT

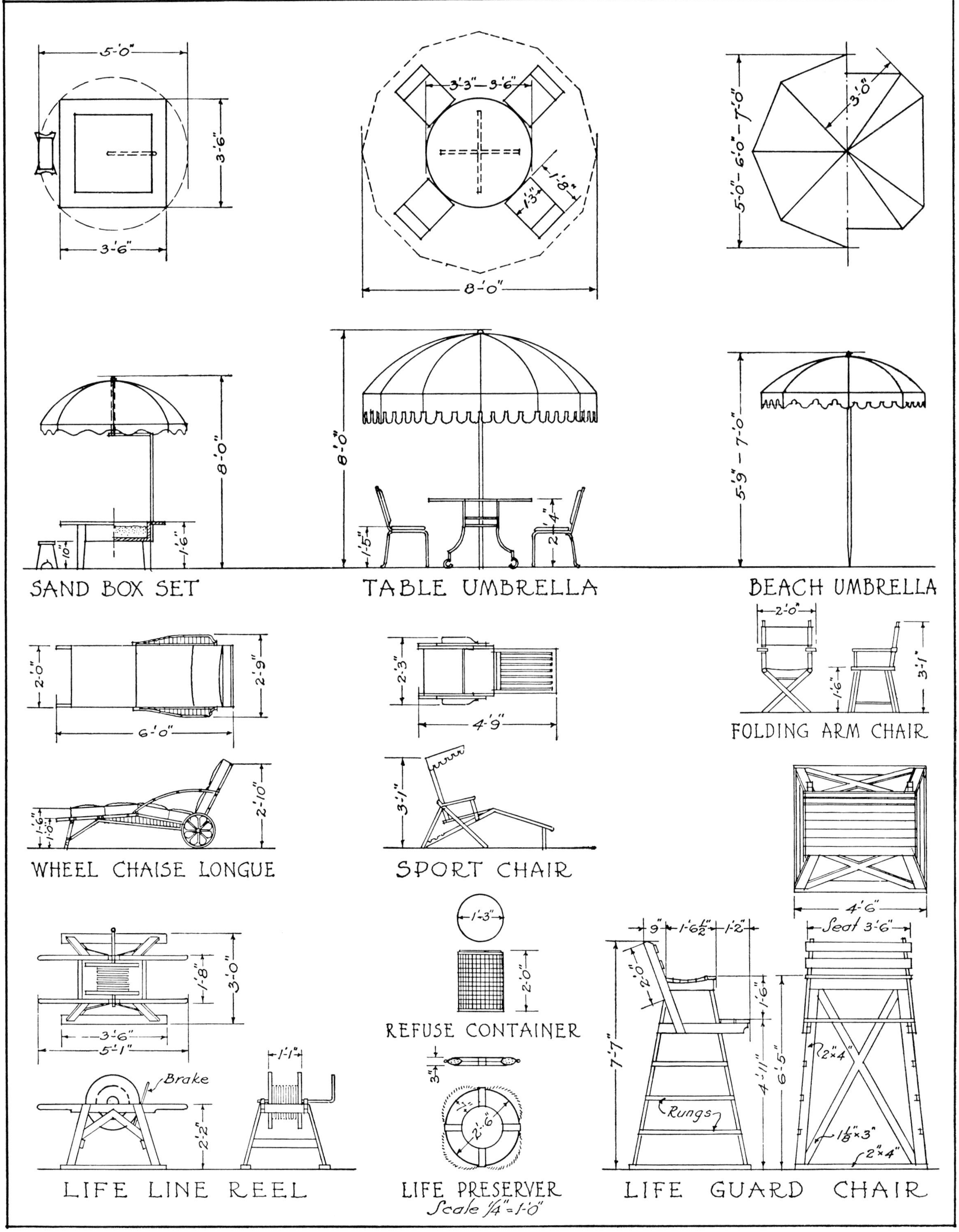

5'-0"
3'-6"
3'-6"

3'3" - 3'-6"
1'-3"
1'-8"
8'-0"

3'-0"
5'-0" - 6'-0" - 7'-0"

SAND BOX SET

8'-0"
1'-6"
1'-0"

TABLE UMBRELLA

8'-0"
1'-5"
2'-4"

BEACH UMBRELLA

5'-9" - 7'-0"

2'-0"
1'-6"
3'-1"

FOLDING ARM CHAIR

2'-0"
2'-9"
6'-0"
1'-6"
1'-0"
2'-10"

WHEEL CHAISE LONGUE

2'-3"
4'-9"
3'-1"

SPORT CHAIR

4'-6"
Seat 3'-6"

1'-3"
2'-0"

REFUSE CONTAINER

3'-0"
1'-8"
3'-6"
5'-1"

9" 1'-6½" 1'-2"
2'-0"
1'-6"
7'-7"
4'-11"
6'-5"
2"×4"
1½"×3"
2"×4"
Rungs

LIFE LINE REEL

Brake
1'-1"
2'-2"

LIFE PRESERVER

3"
2'-6"

Scale ¼"=1'-0"

LIFE GUARD CHAIR

GLASS, WALL PAPER, VENETIAN BLINDS

GLASS for GLAZING

CLEAR FLAT WINDOW GLASS

	Picture Glass 16 oz.	Single Strength 18.5 oz.	Double Strength 26 oz.	Crystal Sheet or heavy window gl. 39 oz.	Crystal Sheet or heavy window gl. 45 oz.
Lights per 1"	13 to 13½	10½ to 12	8 to 9	5+	4 to 5
Thickness Average	5/64" (.077)	3/32 (.09)	1/8" (.125)	3/16 (.193)	7/32 (.218)
Full Size Sections					
A.A Quality Max. sizes	40"×40"	40"×44"	60"×80"	76"×120"	76"×120"
A Quality " "	40"×40"	40"×44"	60"×80"	76"×120"	76"×120"
B Quality " "	40"×40"	40"×44"	60"×80"	76"×120"	76"×120"
Greenhouse Quality			{16"×18" & ×20, 18"×20"}		
Steel Sash Quality			12"×18 & 14"×20"		
Relation of Heat Transmission		100%	50%		

PLATE GLASS

Thickness 1/8"	3/16"	1/4"	3/8"	1/2", 5/8", 3/4", 1", 1¼"
Weight in lbs. per Sq. Foot				Colored Plate
1.6	2.45	3.15	5.50	
Full Size Sections				13/64" & 7/32" For sizes see catalogues

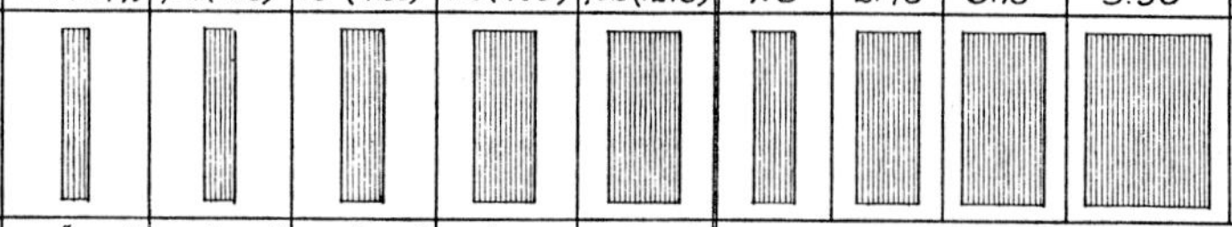

POLISHED PLATE max. sizes

72" to 123"	123" to 216"	150"×252" 160"×216"		Sizes vary with M'frs. see catalogues.

Qualities:- * 2nd Silvering; Only for high class glazing, not over 20 square feet area. ** Glazing:- Usual selection for large sizes

FIGURED PLATE max. sizes 1/4"

48"×144"	48" & 60" ×144"	48" & 60" ×144"	60"×144"	sizes vary with M'f'rs

½" to 1" SAFETY GLASS

1/4" For shock vibration & slight impact.
1½" For low powered pistols and guns.
2" For high powered rifles.
Sizes 46"×80" (variable).

X-RAY GLASS

Sizes 5 to 7 mm, 40"×72" max.

Double Glazing THERMOPANE Libby-Owens-Ford Scale 6" = 1'-0"

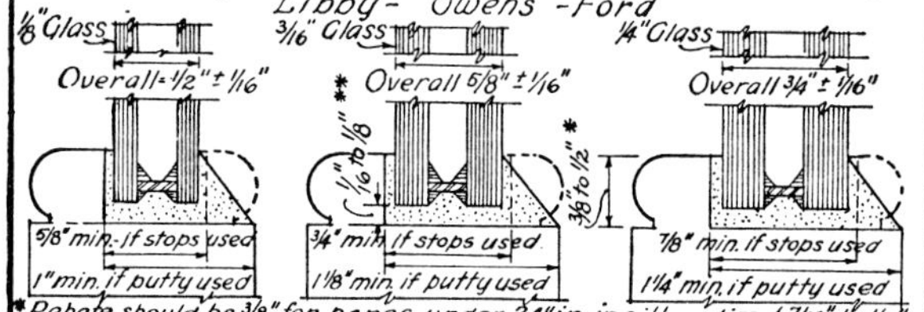

1/8" Glass
Overall = 1/2" ± 1/16"
5/8" min. if stops used
1" min. if putty used
3/16" Glass
Overall 5/8" ± 1/16"
**
1/16" to 1/8"
3/4" min. if stops used
1 1/8" min. if putty used
*
3/8" to 1/2"
1/4" Glass
Overall 3/4" ± 1/16"
7/8" min. if stops used
1¼" min. if putty used

*Rebate should be 3/8" for panes under 24" in. in either dim. & 7/16" to 1/2" for panes over 24". **Allow 1/16" under 30" & 3/32" to 1/8" for over 30".

PLATE GLASS MIRRORS

Thickness - 3/16" to 5/16". If specific thickness is ordered allowable tolerance of 1/32" is allowed

Maximum size 72" × 120"

Qualities

A.A - Free of major defects as possible.
A - Center free of major defects.
#1 Quality
#2 Quality
#3 Quality - May contain all defects

Commercial Standard C.S. 27-30

WIRE GLASS

Thickness, {1/4", 3/8", 1/2", 5/8" & 3/4"}. Max sizes 48 & 60"×144"
For Floors 3/4" thick Max. sizes 30"×72" & 48"×144"

CORRUGATED WIRE GLASS

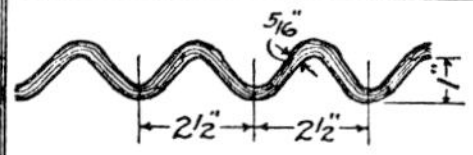

5/16"
2½"
2½"

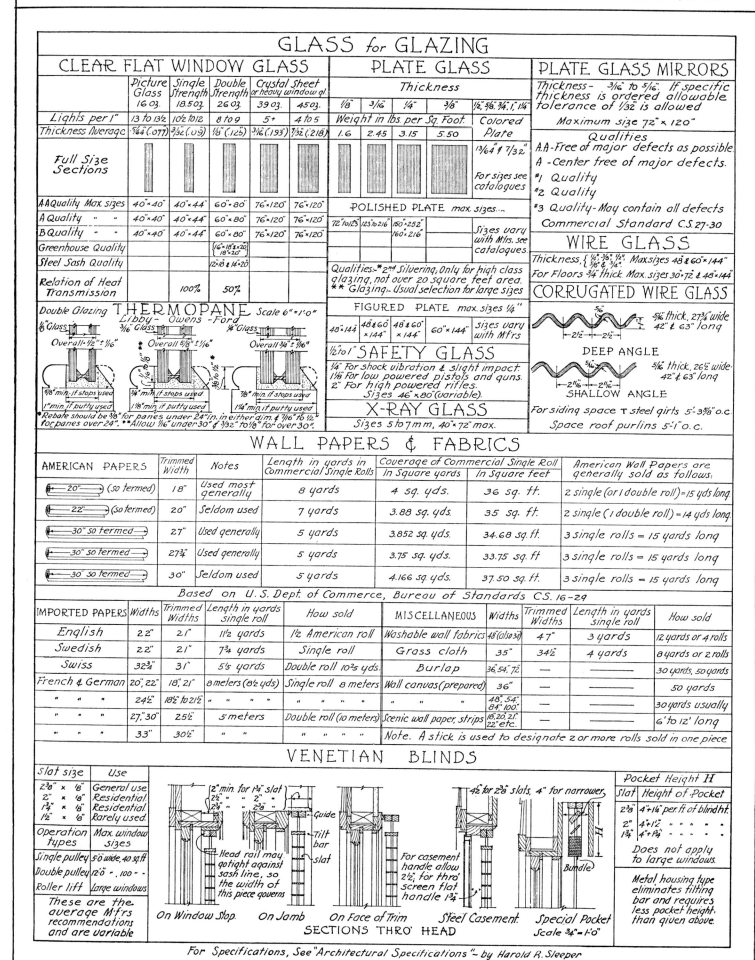

5/16" thick, 27¾" wide 42" & 63" long

DEEP ANGLE

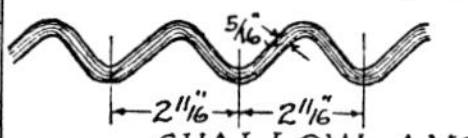

5/16"
2 11/16"
2 11/16"

5/16" thick, 26½" wide 42" & 63" long

SHALLOW ANGLE

For siding space T steel girts 5'-3 5/8" o.c.
Space roof purlins 5'-1" o.c.

WALL PAPERS & FABRICS

AMERICAN PAPERS	Trimmed Width	Notes	Length in yards in Commercial Single Rolls	Coverage of Commercial Single Roll: In Square yards	Coverage of Commercial Single Roll: In Square feet	American Wall Papers are generally sold as follows:
20" (so termed)	18"	Used most generally	8 yards	4 sq. yds.	36 sq. ft.	2 single (or 1 double roll) = 15 yds long
22" (so termed)	20"	Seldom used	7 yards	3.88 sq. yds.	35 sq. ft.	2 single (1 double roll) = 14 yds long
30" so termed	27"	Used generally	5 yards	3.852 sq. yds.	34.68 sq. ft.	3 single rolls = 15 yards long
30" so termed	27¾"	Used generally	5 yards	3.75 sq. yds.	33.75 sq. ft	3 single rolls = 15 yards long
30" so termed	30"	Seldom used	5 yards	4.166 sq. yds.	37.50 sq. ft.	3 single rolls = 15 yards long

Based on U.S. Dept. of Commerce, Bureau of Standards CS. 16-29

IMPORTED PAPERS	Widths	Trimmed Widths	Length in yards single roll	How sold	MISCELLANEOUS	Widths	Trimmed Widths	Length in yards single roll	How sold
English	22"	21"	1½ yards	1½ American roll	Washable wall fabrics	48" (also 34")	47"	3 yards	12 yards or 4 rolls
Swedish	22"	21"	7¾ yards	Single roll	Grass cloth	35"	34½"	4 yards	8 yards or 2 rolls
Swiss	32¾"	31"	5⅕ yards	Double roll 10⅖ yds.	Burlap	36", 54", 72"	—	———	30 yards, 50 yards
French & German	20", 22"	18", 21"	8 meters (8½ yds)	Single roll 8 meters	Wall canvas (prepared)	36"	—	———	50 yards
" " "	24½"	18½" to 21½"	" " " "	" " " "	" " "	48", 54", 84", 100"	—	———	30 yards usually
" " "	27", 30"	25½"	5 meters	Double roll (10 meters)	Scenic wall paper, strips	18", 20", 21", 22" etc.	—	———	6' to 12' long
" " "	33"	30½"	" "	" " " "	Note. A stick is used to designate 2 or more rolls sold in one piece				

VENETIAN BLINDS

Slat size	Use
2⅜" × 1/8"	General use
2" × 1/8"	Residential.
1¾" × 1/8"	Residential.
1½" × 1/8"	Rarely used.

Operation types	Max. window sizes
Single pulley	5'-0" wide, 40 sq. ft
Double pulley	12'-0" " , 100 " "
Roller lift	Large windows

These are the average M'f'rs recommendations and are variable

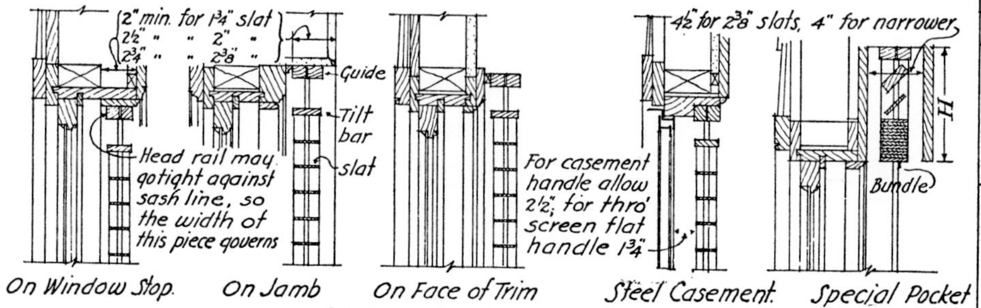

2" min. for 1¾" slat
2½" " " 2" "
2¾" " " 2⅜" "
Guide
Tilt bar
slat
Head rail may go tight against sash line, so the width of this piece governs
4½" for 2⅜" slats, 4" for narrower
For casement handle allow 2½"; for thro' screen flat handle 1¾"
Bundle
H
On Window Stop.
On Jamb
On Face of Trim
Steel Casement.
Special Pocket

SECTIONS THRO' HEAD Scale ¾" = 1'-0"

Pocket Height H

Slat	Height of Pocket
2⅜"	4"+1¼" per ft. of blind ht.
2"	4"+1½" " " " "
1¾"	4"+1¾" " " " "

Does not apply to large windows.

Metal housing type eliminates tilting bar and requires less pocket height than given above.

For Specifications, See "Architectural Specifications" - by Harold R. Sleeper

11

MECHANICAL, ELECTRICAL, AND PLUMBING

ELECTRICAL SYMBOLS

GENERAL OUTLETS

CEILING WALL

Ⓞ	—Ⓞ	Outlet
Ⓑ	—Ⓑ	Blanked Outlet
Ⓓ		Drop Cord
Ⓔ	—Ⓔ	Electrical Outlet for use only when circle used alone might be confused with other symbols
Ⓕ	—Ⓕ	Fan Outlet
Ⓙ	—Ⓙ	Junction Box
Ⓛ	—Ⓛ	Lamp Holder
Ⓛ$_{PS}$	—Ⓛ$_{PS}$	Lamp Holder with Pull Switch
Ⓢ	—Ⓢ	Pull Switch
Ⓥ	—Ⓥ	Outlet for vapor Discharge Lamp
Ⓧ	—Ⓧ	Exit Light Outlet
Ⓒ	—Ⓒ	Clock Outlet (Specify Voltage)

CONVENIENCE OUTLETS

Duplex Convenience Outlet

Convenience Outlet other than Duplex 1=Single, 3=Triplex, etc.

$_{WP}$ Weatherproof Convenience Outlet

$_{R}$ Radio Outlet

$_{S}$ Switch and Convenience Outlet

Ⓡ Radio and Convenience Outlet

Special Purpose Outlet (Describe in Spec.)

⊙ Floor Outlet

SWITCH OUTLETS

S	Single Pole Switch
S$_2$	Double Pole Switch
S$_3$	Three Way Switch
S$_4$	Four Way Switch
S$_D$	Automatic Door Switch
S$_E$	Electrolier Switch
S$_K$	Key Operated Switch
S$_P$	Switch and Pilot Lamp
S$_{CB}$	Circuit Breaker
S$_{WCB}$	Weatherproof Circuit Breaker
S$_{MC}$	Momentary Contact Switch
S$_{RC}$	Remote Control Switch
S$_{WP}$	Weatherproof Switch
S$_F$	Fused Switch
S$_{WF}$	Weatherproof Fused Switch

SPECIAL OUTLETS

Ⓞa,b,c etc.

—Ⓞa,b,c etc.

S a,b,c etc.

Any Standard Symbol as given above with the addition of a lower case subscript letter may be used to designate some special variation of Standard Equipment of particular interest in a specific set of Architectural Plans.
When used they must be listed in the key of Symbols on each drawing and if necessary further described in the Specifications.

PANELS, CIRCUITS & MISCELLANEOUS

▨ Lighting Panel

▨ Power Panel

——— Branch Circuit—Concealed in ceiling or wall

--- Branch Circuit—Concealed in floor

---- Branch Circuit—Exposed

→ Home Run to Panel Board. Indicate number of Circuits by number of arrows. Note: Any circuit without further designation indicates a two-wire circuit. For a greater number of wires indicate as follows: —╫— (3 wires) —╫—╫— (4 wires), etc.

━━ Feeders. Note: Use heavy lines and designate by number corresponding to listing in Feeder Schedule.

⊞ Under floor Duct and Junction Box. Triple System. Note: For double or single Systems eliminate one or two lines. This symbol is equally adaptable to auxiliary system layouts.

Ⓖ Generator

Ⓜ Motor

Ⓘ Instrument

Ⓣ Power Transformer. (Or draw to scale)

⊠ Controller

⊡ Isolating Switch

AUXILIARY SYSTEMS

▣	Push Button
◻	Buzzer
◻○	Bell
◇	Annunciator
◀	Outside Telephone
◁	Interconnecting Telephone
◁	Telephone Switchboard
Ⓣ	Bell Ringing Transformer
D	Electric Door Opener
F○	Fire Alarm Bell
F	Fire Alarm Station
✕	City Fire Alarm Station
FA	Fire Alarm Central Station
FS	Automatic Fire Alarm Station
W	Watchman's Station
W	Watchman's Central Station
H	Horn
N	Nurse's Signal Plug
M	Maid's Signal Plug
R	Radio Outlet
SC	Signal Central Station
◻	Interconnection Box
‖‖‖	Battery

—————— Auxiliary System Circuits Note: Any line without further designation indicates two-wire system. For a greater number of wires designate with numerals in manner similar to

——————12—No. 18 W—¾" C., designate by number corresponding to listing in Schedule.

◻a,b,c etc. Special Auxiliary Outlets Sub-script letters refer to notes on plans or detailed description in Specifications.

Prepared by Sub-Committee of A.S.A. Z32; have been submitted for approval as an American Standard to replace Symbols in A.S.A. C10-1924

HEATING & VENTILATING SYMBOLS

No.	Symbol	Description
1		HIGH PRESSURE STEAM SUPPLY PIPE MAIN.
2		LOW " " " " "
3		HIGH " " RETURN " " or DR.IP.
4		LOW " " " " " or H.W.Ret.
5		LOW " " DRIPS.
6		HOT WATER HEATING SUPPLY PIPE MAIN.
7		VACUUM PUMP DISCHARGE.
8		BLOW-OFF.
9		TUBULAR RADIATORS - PLAN.
10		TUBULAR " - ELEVATIONS.
11		WALL " - PLAN.
12		WALL " - ELEVATION.
13		STEAM or HEATING RISER - LOW PRESSURE.
14		RETURN RISER. " "
15		FIRST FLOOR RADIATOR CONNECTION.
16		PIPE COIL - PLAN.
17		PIPE " - ELEVATIONS.
18		INDIRECT RADIATOR - PLAN.
19		INDIRECT " - ELEVATION.
20		FLANGES.
21		SCREWED UNION.
22		ELBOW - LOOKING UP.
23		ELBOW - " DOWN.
24		TEE - " UP.
25		TEE - " DOWN.
26		GATE VALVE
27		GLOBE "
28		ANGLE "
29		ANGLE " STEM PERPENDICULAR.
30		LOCK SHIELD VALVE.
31		CHECK VALVE.
32		REDUCING VALVE.
33		DIAPHRAGM VALVE.
34		DIAPHRAGM " STEM PERPENDICULAR.
35		THERMOSTAT.
36		RADIATOR TRAP - ELEVATION.
37		RADIATOR " - PLAN.
38		EXPANSION JOINT.
39		SUPPLY DUCT - SECTION.
40		EXHAUST " - "
41		BUTTERFLY & DEFLECTING DAMPERS.
42		AIR SUPPLY OUTLET = AIR EXHAUST INLET.
43		VANES

Recommendations of Kimball & Cucci; Consulting Engineers

PLUMBING

PLUMBING SYMBOLS

PLAN	LINE	Band Initials	COLOR	
○	————————	SAN.	BLUE	SANITARY SEWER, SOIL & DRAIN LINE.
○	– – – – – –	V.S.	BLUE	VENT LINE.
◎	▬ ▬ ▬ ▬			TILE PIPE.
◉	—•—•—•—	C.W	WHITE	COLD CITY WATER.
◉	– – – – –	H.W	WHITE	HOT CITY WATER.
◉	– – – – –	C.R	WHITE	HOT WATER RETURN.
⊗	—×—×—×—	G	BROWN	GAS PIPE.
○	—••—••—••—	D.W	WHITE	ICE WATER SUPPLY.
○	—•••—•••—	D.R	WHITE	ICE WATER RETURN.
○	—/—/—/—	FL	RED	FIRE LINE.
⊕	—→—→—→—	I.W	GREEN	INDIRECT WASTE.
⊕	—ı—ı—ı—	I.S	GREEN	INDUSTRIAL SEWAGE.
◔	—\—\—\—	A.W	GREEN	ACID OR CHEMICAL WASTE.
Ⓐ	—·o—·o—·o—	A	GREY	AIR LINE.
Ⓥ	—oooo—oooo—	V	CREAM	VACUUM CLEANER. outlet= Vac
	—←—←—←—	R		REFRIGERATING LINE.
				GATE VALVES.
				CHECK VALVES.
	C.O.			CLEAN OUT.
	▣			FLOOR DRAIN.
	✕			SHOWER DRAIN.
	▣			FLOOR DRAIN & BACKWATER VALVE

Recommendations of Kimball & Cucci; Consulting Engineers.

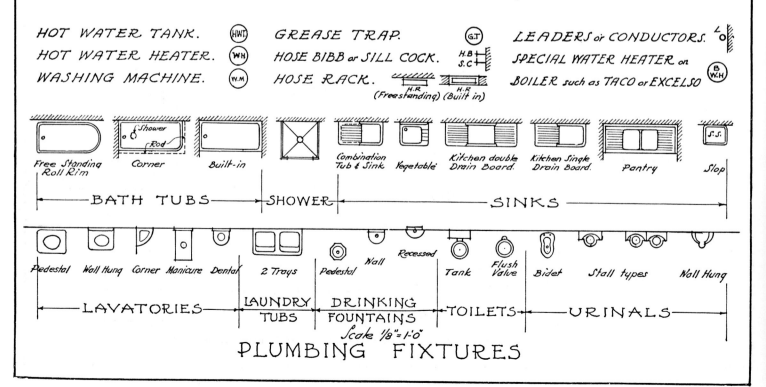

PLUMBING FIXTURES

DUCTWORK SYMBOLS

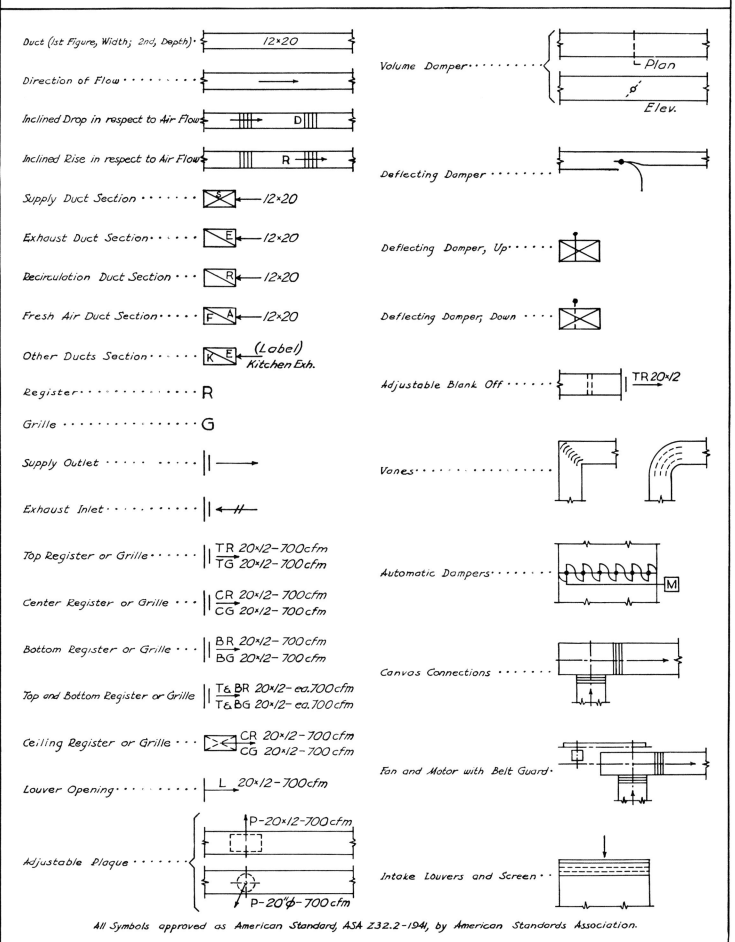

Duct (1st Figure, Width; 2nd, Depth)· — 12×20

Direction of Flow · · · · · ·

Inclined Drop in respect to Air Flow — D

Inclined Rise in respect to Air Flow — R

Supply Duct Section · · · · · · S ← 12×20

Exhaust Duct Section · · · · · E ← 12×20

Recirculation Duct Section · · · R ← 12×20

Fresh Air Duct Section · · · · F A ← 12×20

Other Ducts Section · · · · · K E ← (Label)
Kitchen Exh.

Register · · · · · · · · · · R

Grille · · · · · · · · · · · G

Supply Outlet · · · · · →

Exhaust Inlet · · · · · · ←

Top Register or Grille · · · · · TR 20×12 – 700 cfm
TG 20×12 – 700 cfm

Center Register or Grille · · · CR 20×12 – 700 cfm
CG 20×12 – 700 cfm

Bottom Register or Grille · · · BR 20×12 – 700 cfm
BG 20×12 – 700 cfm

Top and Bottom Register or Grille T&BR 20×12 – ea.700 cfm
T&BG 20×12 – ea.700 cfm

Ceiling Register or Grille · · · CR 20×12 – 700 cfm
CG 20×12 – 700 cfm

Louver Opening · · · · · · · L 20×12 – 700 cfm

Adjustable Plaque · · · · · · P – 20×12 – 700 cfm
P – 20"ϕ – 700 cfm

Volume Damper · · · · · · · · Plan
ϕ
Elev.

Deflecting Damper · · · · · · ·

Deflecting Damper, Up · · · · · ·

Deflecting Damper, Down · · · ·

Adjustable Blank Off · · · · · · TR 20×12

Vanes · · · · · · · · · · · · ·

Automatic Dampers · · · · · · · M

Canvas Connections · · · · · · ·

Fan and Motor with Belt Guard ·

Intake Louvers and Screen · ·

All Symbols approved as American Standard, ASA Z32.2-1941, by American Standards Association.

HEAT-POWER APPARATUS & REFRIGERATING SYMBOLS

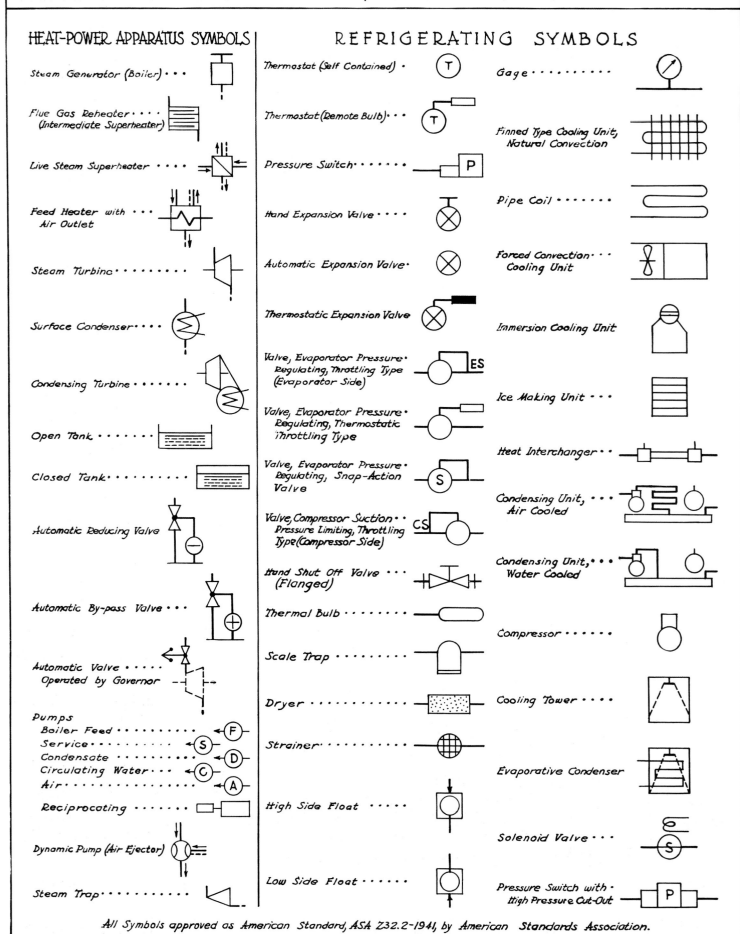

HEAT-POWER APPARATUS SYMBOLS

Steam Generator (Boiler) · · ·

Flue Gas Reheater · · · ·
(Intermediate Superheater)

Live Steam Superheater · · · ·

Feed Heater with · · ·
Air Outlet

Steam Turbine · · · · · · · ·

Surface Condenser · · · ·

Condensing Turbine · · · · · ·

Open Tank · · · · · · ·

Closed Tank · · · · · · · · ·

Automatic Reducing Valve

Automatic By-pass Valve · · ·

Automatic Valve · · · · ·
Operated by Governor

Pumps
Boiler Feed · · · · · · · · ·
Service · · · · · · ·
Condensate · · · · · · ·
Circulating Water · · ·
Air · · · · · · · · · · · ·
Reciprocating · · · · · · ·

Dynamic Pump (Air Ejector)

Steam Trap · · · · · · · · · ·

REFRIGERATING SYMBOLS

Thermostat (Self Contained) ·

Thermostat (Remote Bulb) · ·

Pressure Switch · · · · · · ·

Hand Expansion Valve · · · ·

Automatic Expansion Valve ·

Thermostatic Expansion Valve

Valve, Evaporator Pressure ·
Regulating, Throttling Type
(Evaporator Side)

Valve, Evaporator Pressure ·
Regulating, Thermostatic
Throttling Type

Valve, Evaporator Pressure ·
Regulating, Snap-Action
Valve

Valve, Compressor Suction · ·
Pressure Limiting, Throttling
Type (Compressor Side)

Hand Shut Off Valve · · ·
(Flanged)

Thermal Bulb · · · · · · ·

Scale Trap · · · · · · · ·

Dryer · · · · · · · · · · ·

Strainer · · · · · · · · · ·

High Side Float · · · · ·

Low Side Float · · · · · ·

Gage · · · · · · · · · ·

Finned Type Cooling Unit,
Natural Convection

Pipe Coil · · · · · · ·

Forced Convection · · ·
Cooling Unit

Immersion Cooling Unit

Ice Making Unit · · ·

Heat Interchanger · ·

Condensing Unit, · · ·
Air Cooled

Condensing Unit, · ·
Water Cooled

Compressor · · · · · ·

Cooling Tower · · · ·

Evaporative Condenser

Solenoid Valve · · ·

Pressure Switch with ·
High Pressure Cut-Out

All Symbols approved as American Standard, ASA Z32.2-1941, by American Standards Association.

ELECTRICAL

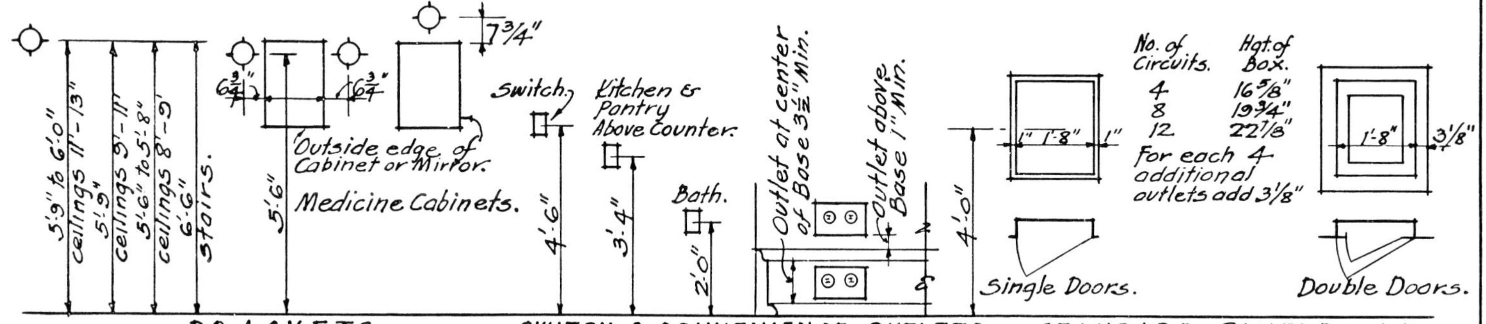

7¾"
5'9" to 6'0" ceilings 11'-13"
5'9" ceilings 9'-11"
5'6" to 5'8" ceilings 8'-9'
6'6" stairs.
6¾"
6¾"
5'6"
Outside edge of Cabinet or Mirror.
Medicine Cabinets.
Switch.
Kitchen & Pantry Above Counter.
4'6"
3'4"
Bath.
2'0"
Outlet at center of Base 3½" Min.
Outlet above Base 1" Min.
4'0"
1" 1'-8" 1"
No. of Circuits. Hgt. of Box.
4 16⅝"
8 19¾"
12 22⅞"
For each 4 additional outlets add 3⅛"
1'-8"
3⅛"
Single Doors.
Double Doors.

BRACKETS   SWITCH & CONVENIENCE OUTLETS   STANDARD PANELBOARDS.

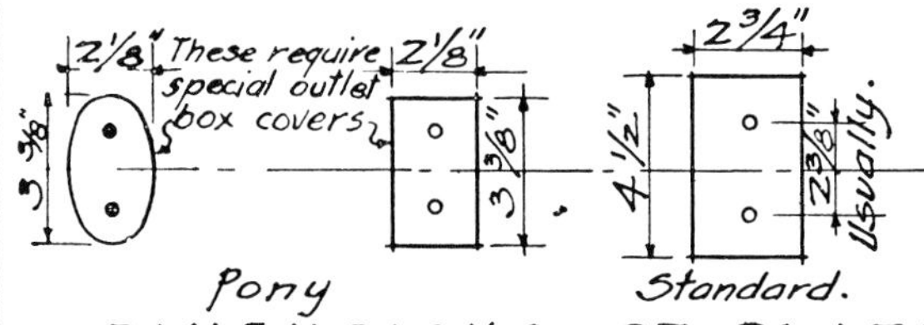

2⅛"
These require special outlet box covers
2⅛"
3⅝"
3⅜"
2¾"
4½"
2⅜"
Usually.
Pony
Standard.

Vertical Gangs.

Gang:	Height:	Width:
2	8⅛"	2¾"
3	11¾"	do.
4	15⅜"	do.
5	19"	do.
6	22⅝"	do.

For each additional gang add 3⅝"

Horizontal Gangs.

Gang:	Height:	Width:
2	4½"	4 9/16"
3	do.	6⅜"
4	do.	8 3/16"
5	do.	10"
6	do.	11 13/16"

For each additional gang add 1 13/16"
Spacing of screws: 1 13/16 o.c. 2⅜" Apart.

DIMENSIONS OF PLATES FOR SINGLE & CONVENIENCE OUTLETS

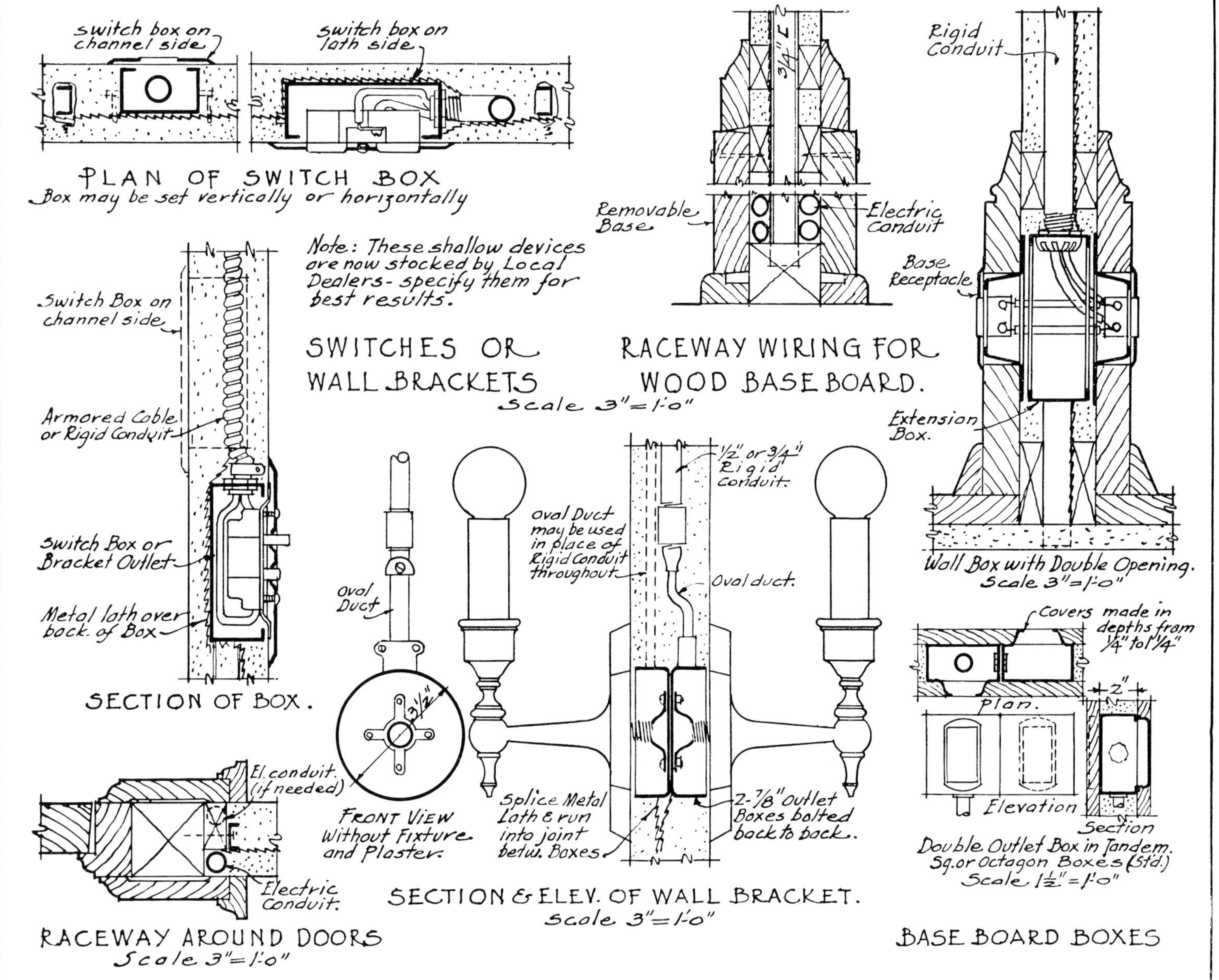

switch box on channel side
switch box on lath side
PLAN OF SWITCH BOX
Box may be set vertically or horizontally
3/4" L
Removable Base
Electric Conduit
Rigid Conduit
Base Receptacle
Extension Box.
Wall Box with Double Opening.
Scale 3"=1'-0"
Note: These shallow devices are now stocked by Local Dealers - specify them for best results.
Switch Box on channel side
Armored Cable or Rigid Conduit
Switch Box or Bracket Outlet
Metal lath over back of Box
SECTION OF BOX.
SWITCHES OR WALL BRACKETS
RACEWAY WIRING FOR WOOD BASE BOARD.
Scale 3"=1'-0"
½" or ¾" Rigid Conduit.
Oval Duct may be used in place of Rigid Conduit throughout
Oval duct.
Oval Duct
3½"
FRONT VIEW Without Fixture and Plaster.
Splice Metal Lath & run into joint betw. Boxes
2-⅞" outlet Boxes bolted back to back.
SECTION & ELEV. OF WALL BRACKET.
Scale 3"=1'-0"
El. conduit (if needed)
Electric Conduit.
RACEWAY AROUND DOORS
Scale 3"=1'-0"
Covers made in depths from ¼" to 1¼"
2"
Plan.
Elevation
Section
Double Outlet Box in Tandem.
Sq. or Octagon Boxes (Std.)
Scale 1½"=1'-0"
BASE BOARD BOXES

ELECTRICAL WORK IN 2" SOLID LATH & PLASTER PARTITIONS

CONDUITS

OVAL DUCT
Rigid conduit for wiring in plaster

$\frac{3}{32}$" $\frac{9}{32}$"

Size		
$1\frac{1}{2}$" .840	1-6	2-12	3-14
$\frac{3}{4}$" 1.05"	1-1	2-8	3-10
1" 1.315"	1-000	2-6	3-8
$1\frac{1}{4}$" 1.660"	1-4	2-2	3-3
$1\frac{1}{2}$" 1.90"			
2" 2.375"			
$2\frac{1}{2}$" 2.875"			
3" 3.50"			
$3\frac{1}{2}$" 4.00			
4" 4.50"			

OUTSIDE DIAMETERS OF STANDARD ELECTRICAL CONDUITS

Cut from 4" Conduit
Wgt.= .9 # per foot

Obsolete now but still available

ORANGEBURG (open bottom type)
Fibre Conduit Co. - To be used with cinder fill. Top of duct to have $\frac{3}{4}$" minimum coverage, 1" to $1\frac{1}{4}$" preferred. Must be placed on a concrete pad that is 1" wider on both sides. Outlets are inserted after floor is finished.
One size only- $4\frac{1}{2}$" x $2\frac{1}{4}$" outside dimension It is cut from a 4" conduit. Wgt.= 0.9 # per linear foot. Inside area 6 square inches.

$2\frac{5}{16}$ R $\frac{1}{16}$" $\frac{1}{4}$" $4\frac{1}{2}$"   2" R.

ORANGEBURG (closed Type)
Fibre Conduit Co. - One size only; to be imbedded in concrete slab. Top of duct to be $\frac{3}{4}$" min. from finished masonry floor, $1\frac{1}{2}$" to 2" preferred. Outlets are inserted after floor is finished. Wgt.= 1 lb. per linear ft. Inside area= 5 sq. inches. (Note that this type has rounded corners with $\frac{1}{8}$" inside radius. Smaller size is obsolete (3").

$2\frac{5}{16}$" R $\frac{1}{8}$ R

FIBREDUCT
General Electric Co. - To be installed in concrete slab. Top of duct to be $\frac{3}{4}$" min. 1" desirable from finished masonry floor. Outlets are inserted after floor is finished.
(Wt.= .78 # per ft.)   (Area= 3.05 sq. in.)
Fibre Conduit Co. also makes duct similiar & equal in dimensions to G.E. Fibreduct

$3\frac{3}{4}$" $3\frac{3}{8}$" $1\frac{1}{2}$"

STEEL DUCTS- To be imbedded in concrete. Where duct top is less than $1\frac{1}{2}$", $\frac{3}{4}$" coverage of masonry is required. Where duct top is more than $1\frac{1}{2}$", 1" coverage is required $1\frac{1}{4}$" is preferred. Outlets are set before floor is laid, usually 2'-0" O.C.
Nepcoduct- National Electric Products Corp.
   Two Sizes - $1\frac{3}{8}$" x $1\frac{7}{8}$" & $1\frac{3}{8}$" x $2\frac{7}{8}$".
Walker Bros. - system -
   Two Sizes - $1\frac{7}{8}$" x $1\frac{1}{4}$" & - $3\frac{1}{8}$" x $1\frac{1}{4}$"

Junction boxes 40' apart max.

$5\frac{1}{16}$' max. $2\frac{1}{16}$5

SPACING OF DUCTS

UNDERFLOOR DUCT SYSTEMS

ELECTRICAL CONDUIT & UNDERFLOOR DUCT SIZES

ELECTRIC LAMP BULBS

T-8
40 W.
med.

Lumiline or double ended lights made.
T-8 — 40 W. 11¾" long
T-8 — 30 W. 17¾" "   disc base
T-8 — 60 W. 17¾" "

LAMPS DRAWN ARE USUALLY STOCKED

EXPLANATION of LAMP NUMBERS
A = Standard shape 15-150 Watts   F = Flame.
PS = " " pear shaped.
S = Straight sided
G = Round.   T = Tubular.
The number signifies the bulb diameter in ⅛ inches.

OTHER ABBREVIATIONS USED HEREIN
For bases: Cand = Candelabra. Inter = Intermediate.
Med = Medium.   Mog. = Mogul.   W = Watt.
The lamps as shown are G. E. Madza.

SCALE = ½ FULL SIZE

Cand.
F-10
15 W.

Inter
T-6½
25 W.

A-25
med.
150 W.

also made
S-6, 6 w. cand.
1⅞" long.
S-14, 6 & 10 W.
med. 3½" long

inter
S-11
10 W.

A-23
med.
100 W.

A-21
med.
75 W.

A-19
med.
25 W.
and
40 W.
25 W. is 5/16"
shorter than this
50 W.
"60 W.
3/16 longer

A-15
med.
15 W.

med.
F-15
25 W.

med.
T-10
25 W.

PS-30
med.
200 W.

PS-35
Med. &
mogul
300 W.
Medium ⅝"
shorter
than this

PS-40
mogul
500 W.

25 W.
med.
G-18½

25 & 40 W.
med.
G-25

PS-52 is
13⅛" long O.A. & 6½" dia.
and is made in 750 & 1000 W.
1500 W.

15 W.

FLUORESCENT LAMPS

Watts	Length	Diameter
6	9	⅝"
14	15	1½"
15	18	1"
20	24	1½"
30	36	1"
40	48	1½"
100	60	2⅛"

Special lampholders and
auxiliary equipment required

Candelabra   Intermediate. Medium. Mogul.

TYPES of BASES
3" = 1'-0"

RADIATOR ENCLOSURES

Figures with % below enclosures indicate efficiency of the enclosures in relation to an exposed radiator which is assumed at 100% efficiency

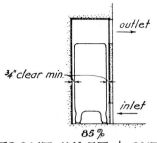

85%
FRONT INLET & OUTLET

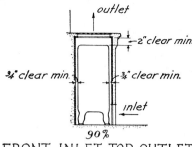

90%
FRONT INLET, TOP OUTLET

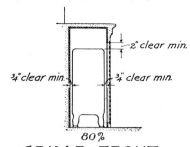

80%
GRILLE FRONT

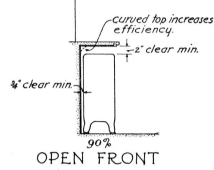

90%
OPEN FRONT

100%
SHIELDED FRONT

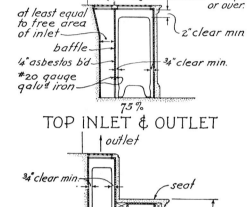

75%
TOP INLET & OUTLET

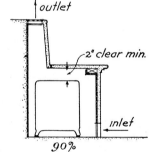

80%
FRONT INLET & OUTLET *under* SEAT.

85%
OPEN FRONT *under* SEAT

90%
FRONT INLET TOP OUTLET *with* SEAT

90%
FRONT INLET TOP OUTLET *with* SEAT

CURVE SHOWING GRILLE AREA REQUIRED *with* VARYING FREE AREA

Square inches of Grille area per sq.ft. radiation

% free area of Grille

Outlet

Inlet

Allow 6" clearance at each end of radiator except that for one pipe systems allow 6" on one end for valve and 3" on other end for air valve.
All enclosures lined with ¼" asbestos board covered with #20 gauge galvanized iron.
Provide 6"×6" access door for valve control, or extension stem through top of enclosure.
Provide damper and control for outlet grilles or slots for quick control.
All grilles may be replaced by slots and slots replaced by grilles.
For same efficiency maintain same free area when changing from slot to grille and vice versa.
All efficiencies approximate; deeper radiators give lower efficiencies; narrower radiators higher efficiencies.
For same height radiator increasing height of enclosure increases efficiency; lowering enclosures lowers efficiency.

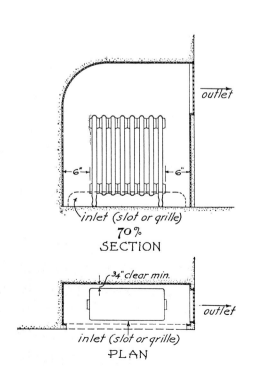

70%
SECTION

PLAN

FRONT INLET SIDE OUTLET

Compiled by Sullivan A. S. Patorno, Consulting Engineer, N.Y.C.

RADIATOR ENCLOSURES

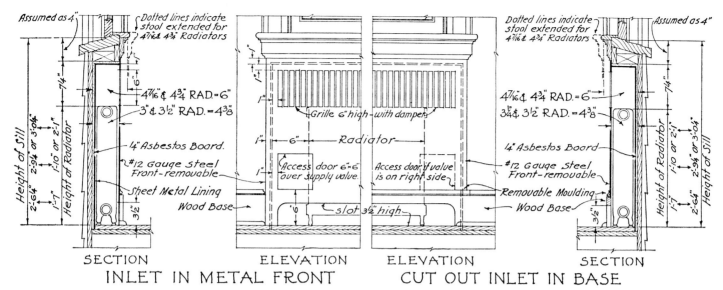

SECTION — INLET IN METAL FRONT
ELEVATION
ELEVATION
SECTION — CUT OUT INLET IN BASE

Grilles may be of any design. Reduction of free area reduces efficiency. Designs shown are 65% free area.

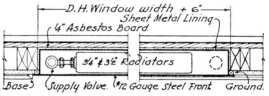

PLAN
PLAN

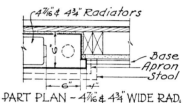

PART PLAN – 4⁷⁄₁₆ & 4¾ WIDE RAD.

FOR JUNIOR TYPE TUBULAR RADIATORS

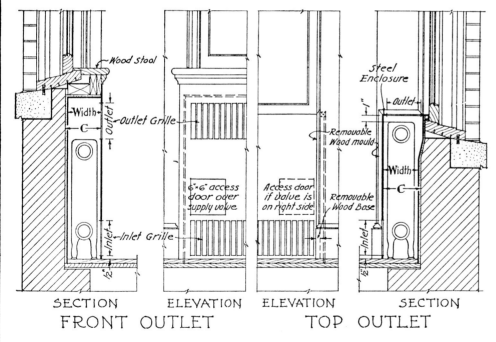

SECTION
ELEVATION
ELEVATION
SECTION

FRONT OUTLET
TOP OUTLET

Where supply valve is at top of radiator access door is to be set in outlet grille. Where top supply valve is used with sill grille provide valve with extended stem and plate or increase enclosure height to clear valve handle.

NO. OF TUBES	3		4		5		6		7	
Width	6¾"		8½"		10¼"		12¼"		13¾"	
C	7"		8¾"		10½"		12½"		14"	
Radiator Height	In-let	Out-let	In-let	Out-let	In-let	Out-let	In-let	Out-let	In-let	Out-let
13"									5"	6"
13½"									5"	6"
14"									5"	6"
16½"									6"	8"
17"									6"	7"
20"	5"	5"	5"	6"	6"	7"	6"	7"	8"	10"
23"	5"	5"	5"	6"	6"	7"	7"	8"		
26"	5"	6"	5"	7"	7"	8"	8"	9"	9"	11"
30"	6"	7"	7"	8"	8"	10"			10"	13"
32"	6"	7"	7"	8"	8"	10"	9"	12"		
36"	7"	8"	8"	10"	9"	12"			13"	16"
37"			8"	10"	9"	12"	11"	14"		
38"	6"	7"	8"	10"	9"	12"	11"	14"		

PLAN
PLAN

FOR STANDARD TYPE TUBULAR RADIATORS

Where supply valve is at top of radiator access door is to be set in outlet grille. Where top supply valve is used with sill grille provide valve with extension stem and plate or increase enclosure height to clear valve handle.

Compiled by Sullivan A. S. Patorno, Consulting Engineers, N.Y.C.

RADIATORS - CAST IRON TUBULAR

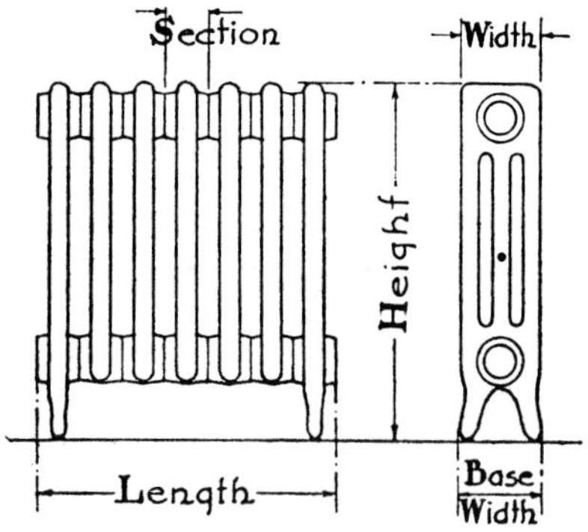

KEY to TABLE

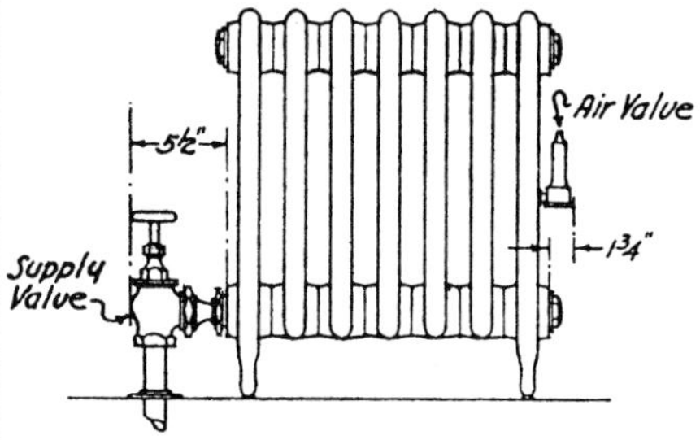

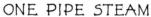

ONE PIPE STEAM

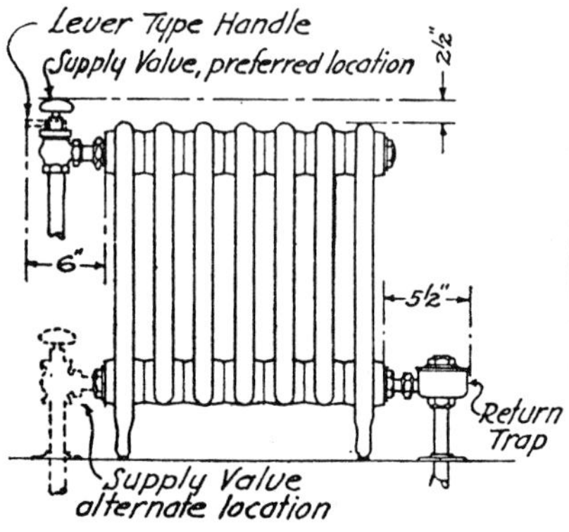

VAPOR or VACUUM

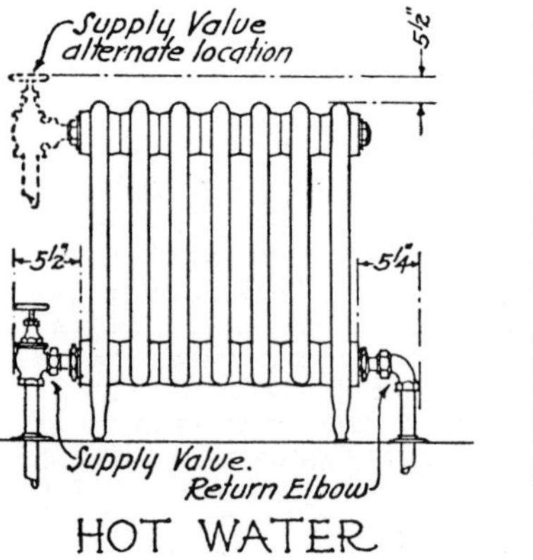

HOT WATER

All dimensions for valve clearances etc. maximum. Dimensions vary with size and make of valve trap etc.

NO. OF TUBES		3	4	5	6	7	JUNIOR 3	JUNIOR 4	JUNIOR 5	JUNIOR 6
S = LENGTH PER SECTION		2½"	2½"	2½"	2½"	2½"	1¾"	1¾"	1¾"	1¾"
Width	American	4 5/8"	6 5/16	8"	9 11/16	11 3/8	3½	4¾		7 7/8
	National	5 1/8"	6 13/16	8 7/16	9	12	3 3/8	4 9/16	5¾	7 7/8
	U.S.	4 5/16"	6¾	8 9/16	10 3/8	12 3/16	3¼	4 7/16	5 5/8	7 7/8
	Crane	4 5/8"	6 5/16	8	9 11/16	11 3/8	3½	4¾	6	7¼
	Burnham		6½	8½	10 5/16	12 1/8	3¼	4 7/16	5 11/16	6 15/16
Base Width	American	4¾"	6 7/16	8 1/8	9 13/16	11½	3½	4¾	—	7 7/8
	National	5 1/8"	6 13/16	8 7/16	9	12	3 3/8	4 9/16	5¾	7 7/8
	U.S.	5 1/8"	6 15/16	8¾	10 9/16	12 3/16	3¼	4 7/16	5 5/8	7 7/8
	Crane	4 5/8"	6 5/16	8	9 11/16	11 3/8	3½	4¾	6	7¼
	Burnham		6 5/8	8½	10 5/16	12 1/8	3¼	4 7/16	5 11/16	6 15/16
H = HEIGHT		SQUARE FEET PER SECTION								
13"	U.S.					2½				
13½"	National					2½				
14"	American					2½				
	Crane					2½				
	Burnham					2⅔				1.6
16½"	National					3				
	U.S.					3				
17"	American					3				
	Crane					3				
	Burnham					3¼				2.0
19"	American							1.6		2.3
	National							1.6		2.3
	U.S.							1.6		*2.3
	Crane							1.6		2.3
	Burnham							1.6		
20"	American	1¾	2¼	2⅔	3	3⅔				
	National	1¾	2.3	2.7	3	3.7				
	U.S.	1¾	2¼	2.67	3	3.67				
	Crane	1¾	2¼	2⅔	3	3⅔				
	Burnham		2¼	2⅔	3	3⅔				2.3
22"	American							1.8		
	National							1.8	2.1	
	U.S.							1.8	2.1	
	Crane							1.8	2.1	
	Burnham							1.8		
23"	American	2	2½	3						
	National	2	2½	3						
	U.S.	2	2½	3						
	Crane	2	2½	3						
	Burnham		2½	3					2.1	
25"	American						1.6	2.0		3.0
	National						1.6	2.0	2.4	3.0
	U.S.						1.6	2.0	2.4	3.0
	Crane						1.6	2.0	2.4	3.0
	Burnham						1.6	2.0		
26"	American	2⅓	2¾	3½	4					
	National	2⅓	2.8	3½	4	4.8				
	U.S.	2⅓	2¾	3½	4					
	Crane	2⅓	2¾	3½	4					
	Burnham		2¾	3½	4				2.4	3.0
30"	National	3 also U.S.	3½	4.4						
32"	American	3	3½	4⅓						3.7
	National									3.7
	U.S.		3½	4.33						3.7
	Crane	3	3½	4⅓						3.7
	Burnham		3½	4⅓					3.0	
36"	National	3 also U.S.	4.3	5						
37"	U.S.		4¼	5	6					
38"	American	3½	4¼	5	6					
	National				6					
	Crane	3½	4¼	5	6					
	Burnham		4¼	5	6					

*Width is 6 13/16"

Junior Type Radiators supplied in even numbers of sections only.

Manufacturers Names in Full

American = American Radiator & Standard Sanitary Corporation
Crane = Crane Company
Burnham = Burnham Boiler Corporation.
National = National Radiator Company
U.S. = United States Radiator Corp.

Compiled by Sullivan A. S. Patorno, Consulting Engineers., N.Y.C.

LIGHTNING PROTECTION

Symbol for down conductor •

Plan 110'-0" or less in perimeter; minimum of 2 down conductors. If over 110'-0" in perimeter, add 1 for each additional 50'-0" or fraction thereof.

Plan 300'-0" or less in perimeter; minimum of 2 down conductors. If over 300'-0" in perimeter add 1 for each additional 100'-0" or fraction thereof.

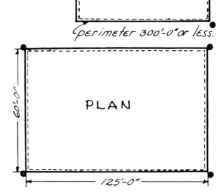

perimeter 110'-0" or less.

EXAMPLE
Perimeter 220'-0"
110'-0" perimeter; Two •
220'-0"–110'-0" = 110'-0"
110/50 = 2+1 = Three •
Total = Five •

EXAMPLE
Perimeter 410'-0"
300'-0" perimeter; Two •
410'-0"–300'-0" = 110'-0"
110/100 = 1+1 = Two •
Total = Four •

perimeter 300'-0" or less.

GABLE, GAMBREL, or HIPPED ROOFS
Scale: 1/64" = 1'-0"

FLAT, FRENCH or SAWTOOTH ROOFS

DOWN CONDUCTORS
REQUIRED for SQUARE or RECTANGULAR SHAPED STRUCTURES

ELL SHAPE
Add one •

T SHAPE
Add one •

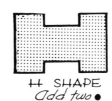
H SHAPE
Add two •

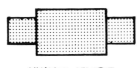
WING TYPE
Add one • per wing

In addition to the above requirements; On irregular shaped structures, the total number of down conductors shall be sufficient to make the average distance between them along the perimeter not greater than 100'-0".

EXTRA DOWN CONDUCTORS REQUIRED for IRREGULAR SHAPED STRUCTURES

PERSPECTIVE

If structure is over 60'-0" high; add one down conductor for each additional 60'-0" or fraction thereof, but not so as to cause down conductors placed about perimeter at intervals of less than 50'-0".

EXAMPLE
Flat roof; perimeter 340'-0"
By plan: 3 down conductors required. By elevation: 1 extra required because of height.
By plan: Three •
By elevation: One •
Total Four •

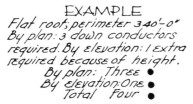
PLAN

Extra down conductors are not required if distance between is less than 50'-0". This plan does not have conductors at less than 50' intervals, so none can be omitted.

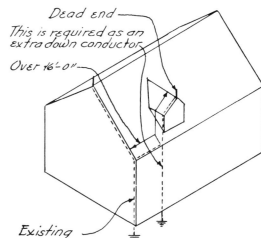

Dead end — This is required as an extra down conductor. Over 16'-0" — Existing

Install extra down conductors wherever it becomes necessary to avoid dead ends, or branch conductors ending at air terminals, which exceed 16'-0" in length, except that single down conductors descending flagpoles, spires & similar structures which are adjuncts of buildings shall not be regarded as dead ends, but shall be treated as air terminals.

EXTRA DOWN CONDUCTORS REQUIRED for STRUCTURES OVER 60'-0" HIGH

DEAD ENDS

Requirements for metal roofed or clad buildings, if sections are insulated from one another, are same as for buildings composed of non-conductive materials. When metal is continuous, terminals and conductors, if used, shall be bonded to it and grounded. Structures of steel frame or reinforced concrete construction need no protection if steel is connected and grounded.

LIGHTNING PROTECTION

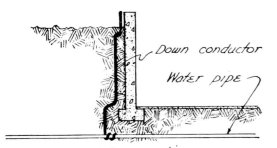

Down conductor

Water pipe

Ground connection to metal water pipe.

GROUNDING to PIPE

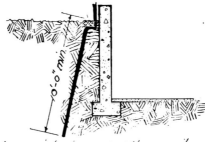

In moist clay or other soil of similar character as to electrical resistivity, extend rod into soil not less than 10'-0".

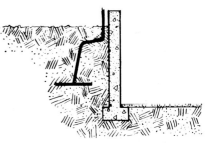

When soil is largely sand, gravel, or stones, enlarge electrodes by addition of rods, strips, or plates.

GROUNDING to DEEP SOIL

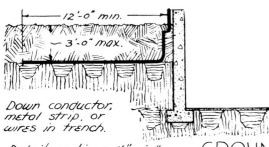

12'-0" min.

3'-0" max.

Down conductor, metal strip, or wires in trench.

Detail sections 1/8" = 1'-0"

Rock at least 1'-0" under grade. Maximum required trench depth 3'-0". Minimum 1'-0". If trench cannot be dug over 1'-0" in depth (because of rock), encircle building with a buried conductor and connect to all down conductors.

Connection to down conduct.

GROUNDING to SHALLOW SOIL

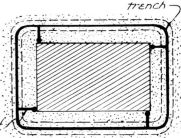

trench

Plan 1/32" = 1'-0"

SMOKE STACK

lead covering 25'-0"

uncovered conductor

guard 6'-0"

2'-0"

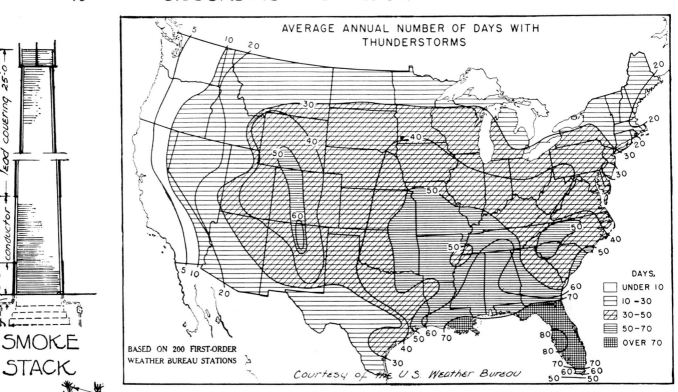

AVERAGE ANNUAL NUMBER OF DAYS WITH THUNDERSTORMS

BASED ON 200 FIRST-ORDER WEATHER BUREAU STATIONS

Courtesy of the U.S. Weather Bureau

DAYS.
UNDER 10
10-30
30-50
50-70
OVER 70

Terminals on highest parts. Main conductor down trunk.

Radial conductor in trench 1'-0" deep. Required: 3 for every main conductor. Need shallow network to prevent damage to roots.

Encircling conductor. Average 10'-0" to 25'-0".

TREE PROTECTION

Maximum protection; cone ABC. Minimum; ABD. Vertical conductor assumed to divert strikes which might fall in conical space. Cone of influence is not a zone of complete protection

CONE of INFLUENCE

LIGHTNING PROTECTION

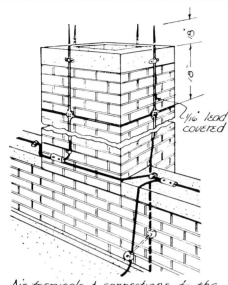

¹⁄₁₆" lead covered

Air terminals & connections to the
Top of coping conductor Terminals
must be within 2'-0" of each corner.
LARGE CHIMNEY

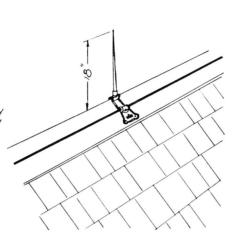

Air terminal and
ridge conductor.
ROOF RIDGE

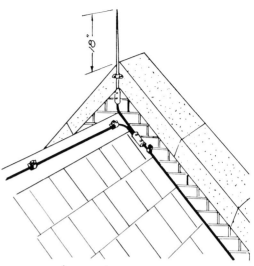

Air terminal & connections
to the roof conductor.
STONE GABLE

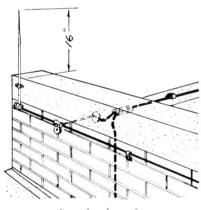

Conductor from
air terminal.
BELOW COPING

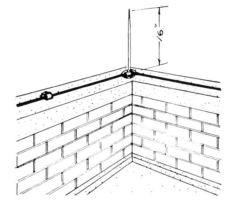

Conductor with corner air terminal.
Terminals must be within 2'-0" of corner.
TOP of COPING

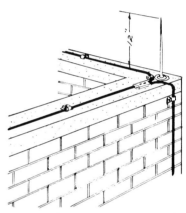

Conductor with corner air
terminal & down conductor.
TOP of COPING

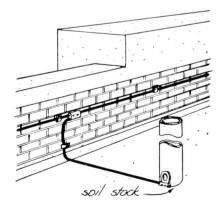

soil stack

Parapet & conductor to soil stack.
BOND from INSIDE

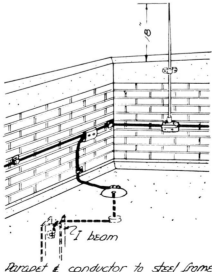

I beam

Parapet & conductor to steel frame.
BOND from INSIDE

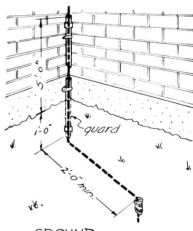

guard

GROUND
CONNECTION

EXPOSED TYPE

Details on this sheet are mainly applicable to commercial bld'gs.
Heavy solid lines indicate lightning conductors exposed to view.
Heavy dotted lines indicate lightning conductors hidden from view.

Courtesy of West Dodd Lightning Conductor Corp.

LIGHTNING PROTECTION

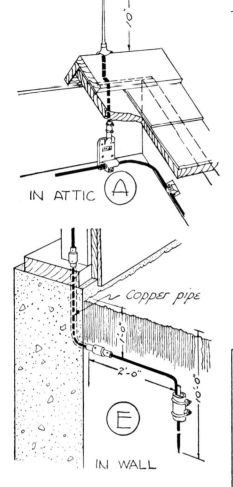

IN ATTIC Ⓐ

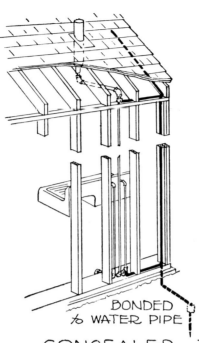

BONDED to WATER PIPE

CONCEALED TYPE
This type installed during construction.

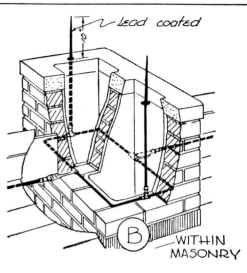

Lead coated

WITHIN MASONRY Ⓑ

Copper pipe

2'-0"

IN WALL Ⓔ

KEY to DETAILS

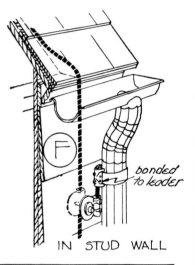

bonded to leader

IN STUD WALL Ⓕ

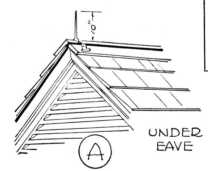

UNDER EAVE Ⓐ

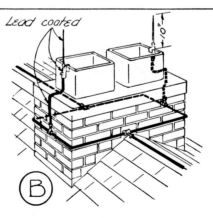

Lead coated

SEMI-CONCEALED TYPE Ⓑ

UNDER EAVE Ⓒ

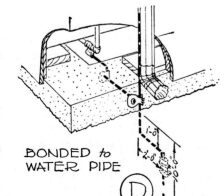

BONDED to WATER PIPE Ⓓ

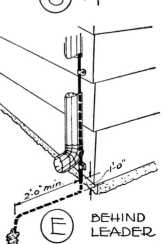

2'-0" min

BEHIND LEADER Ⓔ

All details on this sheet are applicable to residential buildings. Heavy solid lines indicate lightning conductors exposed to view. Heavy dotted lines indicate lightning conductors hidden from view.

Courtesy of West Dodd Lightning Conductor Corp.

PLUMBING FIXTURES

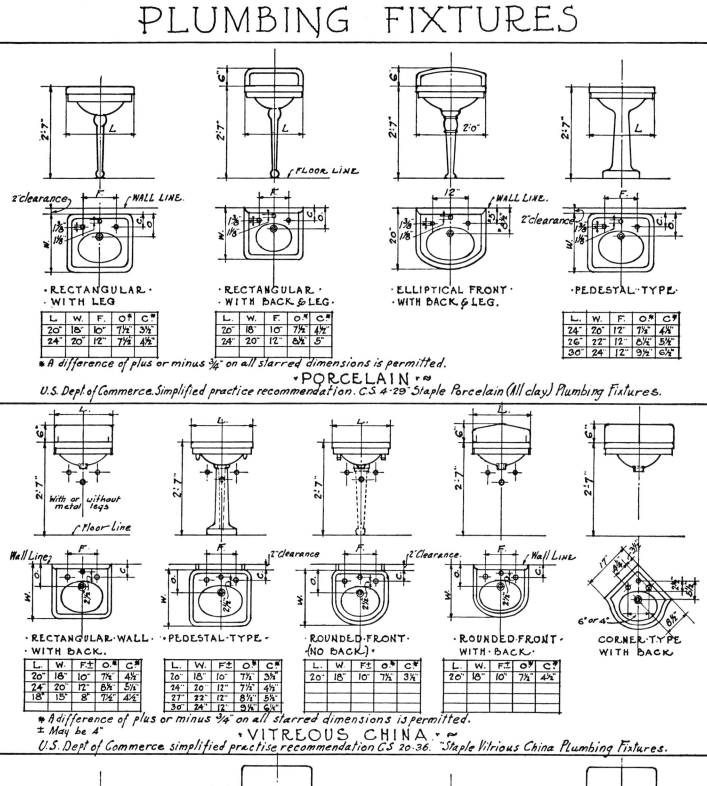

·RECTANGULAR· ·WITH LEG·

L.	W.	F.	O.*	C.*
20"	18"	10"	7½"	3½"
24"	20"	12"	7½"	4½"

·RECTANGULAR· ·WITH BACK & LEG·

L.	W.	F.	O.*	C.*
20"	18"	10"	7½"	4½"
24"	20"	12"	8½"	5"

·ELLIPTICAL FRONT· ·WITH BACK & LEG·

·PEDESTAL·TYPE·

L.	W.	F.	O.*	C.*
24"	20"	12"	7½"	4½"
26"	22"	12"	8½"	5½"
30"	24"	12"	9½"	6½"

* A difference of plus or minus ¾" on all starred dimensions is permitted.

·PORCELAIN·~

U.S. Dept. of Commerce. Simplified practice recommendation. C.S 4-29 Staple Porcelain (All clay) Plumbing Fixtures.

·RECTANGULAR·WALL· ·WITH·BACK·

L.	W.	F.±	O.*	C.*
20"	18"	10"	7½"	4½"
24"	20"	12"	8½"	5½"
18"	15"	8"	7½"	4½"

·PEDESTAL·TYPE·

L.	W.	F.±	O.*	C.*
20"	18"	10"	7½"	3½"
24"	20"	12"	7½"	4½"
27"	22"	12"	8½"	5½"
30"	24"	12"	9½"	6½"

·ROUNDED·FRONT· (NO BACK)·

L.	W.	F.±	O.*	C.*
20"	18"	10"	7½"	3½"

·ROUNDED·FRONT· ·WITH·BACK·

L.	W.	F.±	O.*	C.*
20"	18"	10"	7½"	4½"

CORNER·TYPE· WITH BACK

* A difference of plus or minus ¾" on all starred dimensions is permitted.
± May be 4"

·VITREOUS CHINA·~

U.S. Dept of Commerce simplified practise recommendation C.S 20-36. "Staple Vitrious China Plumbing Fixtures.

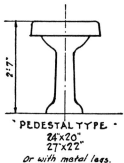

·PEDESTAL TYPE·
24"x20"
27"x22"
Or with metal legs.

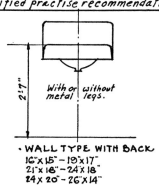

·WALL TYPE WITH BACK·
16"x15" — 19"x17"
21"x18" — 24"x18"
24"x20" — 26"x14"

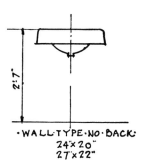

·WALL·TYPE·NO·BACK·
24"x20"
27"x22"

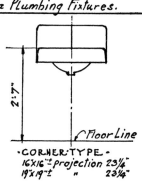

·CORNER·TYPE·
16"x16"± projection 23¼"
19"x19"± " 23¼"

· ENAMELED · IRON ·
~Sizes given are not standard, but those generally used.~

·~PORCELAIN;VITREOUS·CHINA·& ENAMELED IRON LAVATORIES·~SCALE:⅜"=1'·0"

PLUMBING FIXTURES

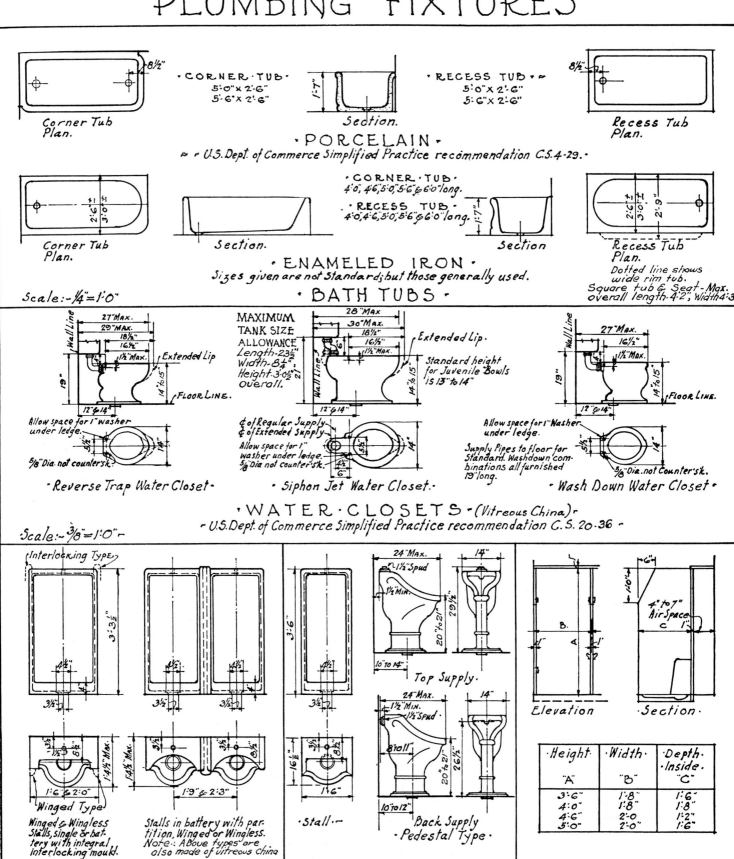

·CORNER·TUB·
5'-0"x 2'-6"
5'-6"x 2'-6"

·RECESS·TUB·~
5'-0"x 2'-6"
5'-6"x 2'-6"

Corner Tub Plan.

Section.

Recess Tub Plan.

·PORCELAIN·

~ - U.S. Dept. of Commerce Simplified Practice recommendation C.S. 4-29.·

·CORNER·TUB·
4'-0", 4'-6, 5'-0, 5'-6 & 6'-0 long.

·RECESS·TUB·
4'-0, 4'-6, 5'-0, 5'-6 & 6'-0 long.

Corner Tub Plan.

Section.

Section

Recess Tub Plan.

·ENAMELED IRON·
Sizes given are not Standard; but those generally used.

·BATH TUBS·

Dotted line shows wide rim tub. Square tub & Seat - Max. overall length-4'2", Width 4'-3

Scale:- 1/4 = 1'0"

MAXIMUM TANK SIZE ALLOWANCE
Length-23½"
Width-8½"
Height-3'-0½"
Overall.

Standard height for Juvenile Bowls is 13" to 14"

·Reverse Trap Water Closet·

·Siphon Jet Water Closet.

·Wash Down Water Closet·

·WATER·CLOSETS· (Vitreous China)·
- U.S. Dept. of Commerce Simplified Practice recommendation C.S. 20-36·

Scale:- 3/8 = 1'0"-

Interlocking Type.

Top Supply.

Elevation

Section·

Winged Type

Winged & Wingless Stalls, single or battery with integral interlocking mould.

Stalls in battery with partition, Winged or Wingless. Note: Above types are also made of vitreous china

·Stall·-

Back Supply
·Pedestal Type·

Height "A"	Width "B"	Depth Inside "C"
3'-6"	1'-8"	1'-6"
4'-0"	1'-8"	1'-8"
4'-6"	2'-0"	1'-2"
5'-0"	2'-0"	1'-6"

·PORCELAIN·
·U.S. Dept of Commerce Simplified·
·Practice, recommendation C.S. 4-29·

·VITREOUS·CHINA·-
·U.S. Dept. of Commerce Simplified·
·Practice recommendation C.S. 20-36·

·SLATE·-
·U.S. Dept. of Commerce Simplified·
·Practice recommendation·R-13-28·

·URINALS·
·Scale:- 3/8 = 1'0"·

·BATH TUBS· WATER·CLOSETS· & ·URINAL·STALLS·

BIBLIOGRAPHY

Preservation Assistance Division
National Park Service
Washington, DC

The subject of historic preservation technology is a broad one, encompassing not only information on how historic buildings were constructed but information on the techniques, materials, and methods for preserving these resources for future generations to appreciate and enjoy. It includes the study of building materials, both old and new; how these materials are worked and finished; the tools, techniques, and equipment used to construct and restore buildings; craft practices; the development of new structural and construction systems and of prefabricated and manufactured components; and the development of new technologies to facilitate preservation work.

This annotated bibliography provides a basic introduction to the literature of historic preservation technology; it is not a comprehensive listing of all publications on the subject. Omitted from the bibliography are articles from periodicals and single chapters from books. Those interested in the subject will find the following periodicals of particular interest:

APT Bulletin. Published quarterly by the Association for Preservation Technology, this periodical provides a wealth of information on state-of-the-art preservation and rehabilitation techniques, case studies, and the history of construction technology.

CRM Bulletin. Published by the National Park Service, this bimonthly journal contains a broad range of articles on cultural resource management. Since 1989 it has included a section entitled "Preservation Technology Update" which contains technical articles on preservation, repair, and maintenance techniques for historic properties.

Old-House Journal. This magazine was begun in late 1973 to share "how-to" information on rehabilitating and preserving older homes. Now a bimonthly, *Old-House Journal* provides a range of useful technical information, from paint stripping techniques to roofing practices.

Technology and Conservation Magazine. This journal is aimed at professionals working in or managing programs involving analysis, preservation, restoration, protection, and documentation of art, buildings and monuments, historic sites, and antiquities. Although published infrequently, its articles are usually of great interest.

Traditional Building. Begun in 1988, this bimonthly newspaper provides detailed technical information on building products intended for historic buildings. While the focus of this newspaper is not preservation technology, it frequently contains useful information for individuals involved in restoration and rehabilitation work.

Principles and Practices

CHAMBERS, J. HENRY. *Cyclical Maintenance for Historic Buildings.* Washington, DC: National Park Service, 1976.
This handbook provides a step-by-step process for building managers, architects, and others involved in the routine maintenance of historic properties.

CURTIS, JOHN OBED. *Moving Historic Buildings.* Nashville, TN: American Association for State and Local History, 1988.
Initially published by the National Park Service, this handbook establishes a methodology for planning, research, and recording prior to the move and addresses the siting, foundation construction, building assembly, and restoration work after a successful move has taken place.

FEILDEN, BERNARD M. *Conservation of Historic Buildings.* London: Butterworth & Co., Ltd., 1982.
This major work covers all aspects of maintenance and conservation of historic buildings. It includes chapters

264

on internal structural elements, internal temperature control, building inspections, inserting new systems into old building, fire and security, and sections on materials repair including woodwork, ironwork, plaster, paint, and glass. This is a very useful book for anyone who works with old buildings.

FRAM, MARK. *Well Preserved: The Ontario Heritage Foundation's Manual of Principles and Practice for Architectural Conservation.* Erin, Ontario: Boston Mills Press, 1988.

This is one of the most comprehensive compilations of preservation principles and practices available. Separate chapters address conservation standards and guidelines, archeology, project management, structural systems, exterior features, interior features, energy conservation, and new construction.

HANSON, SHIRLEY, and NANCY HUBBY. *Preserving and Maintaining the Older Home.* New York: McGraw-Hill Book Company, 1983.

Written for owners of historic houses, this book covers everything from identifying the style of the building to maintenance and repair. It is organized according to the building system or element and tells what problems to look for and how to fix them, in simple, clear language.

INSALL, DONALD W. *The Care of Old Buildings Today— A Practical Guide.* London: The Architectural Press, 1972.

This publication deals with maintenance of buildings according to system. A large portion is devoted to roofs, identifying areas of concern and providing assessment methods to determine it's conditions. Other topics included in the book are timber construction, stone decay and repair, metal work, glass, rain gutters, and church bells. Specifications for each system are provided, and annotated drawings pointing out areas where defects are likely to occur.

Interiors Handbook for Historic Buildings. Washington, DC: Historic Preservation Education Foundation, 1988.

Prepared for a national conference on appropriate interior treatments for historic buildings, cosponsored by the National Park Service, this handbook includes nearly 400 pages of technical papers as well as guidance for architects, developers, building managers, curators, and property owners. The contents address both rehabilitation and restoration issues, including inspection, evaluation and planning, architectural features and materials, systems and fixtures, space utilization and adaptive use, finishes and decorative accessories, and fire protection and building codes.

KAPLAN, HELAINE S., and BLAIR PRENTICE. *Rehab Right.* Berkeley, CA: Ten Speed Press, 1986.

This "how-to" manual was written for owners of older houses in Oakland, California; it is well-illustrated and clearly written and provides basic information on repair, rehabilitation, and restoration techniques.

LABINE, CLEM, and CAROLYN FLAHERTY (editors). *The*

Old-House Journal Compendium. Woodstock, NY: The Overlook Press, 1980.

Many of the articles compiled here form the first 8 years of the *Old-House Journal* and although somewhat dated, will be useful in various aspects of interior rehabilitation, including energy efficiency and insulation, wiring, heating and plumbing, plaster repair, floor and stair repair and refinishing, painting, restoring mantels and fireplaces, and repairing woodwork. The Compendium also includes numerous articles on 19th and early 20th century interior decorative styles, bathrooms and kitchens, and craft techniques such as stenciling and graining.

MICHELL, ELENOR. *Emergency Repairs for Historic Buildings.* London: English Heritage, 1988.

Commissioned by the Historic Areas Division of English Heritage, this book deals specifically with temporary repairs, which can be carried out easily and with minimum expense, and with care adequate to protect a building until permanent repairs can be made. It includes 12 well-illustrated case studies which describe specific repair techniques.

NATIONAL PARK SERVICE. *Respectful Rehabilitation: Answers to Your Questions about Old Buildings.* Washington, DC: The Preservation Press, 1982.

This book provides technical guidance to owners of historic houses on a wide range of specific preservation and maintenance problems.

Preservation and Conservation: Principles and Practices. Proceedings of the North American International Regional Conference, Williamsburg, VA, and Philadelphia, PA, September 10–16, 1972. Washington, DC: The Preservation Press, 1976.

This volume includes the full texts of essays prepared for the conference, documented with photographs and drawings. Chapters on wood, masonry and masonry products, metals, paints and varnishes, maintenance, standards, and education provide differing perspectives by architects concerned with the restoration of historic buildings and conservators involved with the preservation of materials and objects.

Preservation Briefs 1–21. Washington, DC: National Park Service, 1975–1989.

This ongoing series of technical leaflets produced by the National Park Service provides information on recognizing and solving common preservation problems. Topics covered to date are the cleaning and waterproof coating of masonry buildings, repointing mortar joints, conserving energy, historic roofing, historic adobe preservation, dangers of abrasive cleaning, historic glazed architectural terra cotta, aluminum and vinyl siding, the repair of historical wooden windows, exterior paint problems, rehabilitating historic storefronts, historic pigmented structural glass, the repair of historic steel windows, new exterior additions, historic concrete preservation, the use of substitute materials, identifying the visual aspects of historic buildings, rehabilitating historic interiors, the repair and replacement of historic wooden shingle roofs, the preservation of historic barns, and repairing historic flat plaster.

Rehabilitation Guidelines 1986. Volumes 1–11. Prepared by the National Institute of Building Technology, Inc., and the University Research Corporation, 1986.

This reprint of guidelines developed for the Department of Housing and Urban Development is designed for use with existing code by government and building officials, designers, inspectors, and builders.

The Secretary of the Interior's Standards for Historic Preservation Projects. Washington, DC: Preservation Assistance Division, National Park Service, U.S. Department of the Interior, 1985.

This guidance was developed for use by the National Park Service and state historic preservation offices in planning, undertaking, and supervising work undertaken on properties listed in the National Register of Historic Places. Separate sets of standards and guidelines are included for acquisition, protection, stabilization, preservation, rehabilitation, restoration, and reconstruction.

The Secretary of the Interior's Standards for Rehabilitation and Guidelines for Rehabilitating Historic Buildings. Washington, DC: Preservation Assistance Division, National Park Service, U.S. Department of the Interior, revised 1990.

These 10 standards are intended to serve as guidance in preserving the character-defining features in rehabilitation projects involving historic buildings. The accompanying guidelines assist in the application of the standards and provide a model process for owners, developers, and local officials to follow in planning and carrying out rehabilitation work.

SHOPSIN, WILLIAM C., AIA. *Restoring Old Buildings for Contemporary Uses: An American Sourcebook for Architects and Preservationists.* New York: Whitney Library of Design, 1989.

This handbook focuses on predesign and design issues of preserving and rehabilitating older buildings for continued and new uses.

SMEALLIE, PETER H., and PETER H. SMITH. *New Construction for Older Buildings: A Design Sourcebook for Architects and Preservationists,* New York: John Wiley & Sons, Inc., 1990.

Through text, case studies, and plentiful illustrations, this book provides a rich compendium of practical information for architects and designers working in the field of building expansion and rehabilitation. Addressing the application of new design to older, historic, and even prominent recent buildings, this sourcebook is a rich mine of ideas for designers seeking to create new construction while respecting the existing environment.

Materials

AMOROSO, GIOVANNI G., and VASCO FASSINA. *Stone Decay and Conservation: Atmospheric Pollution, Cleaning, Consolidation and Protection.* Materials Science Monographs, 11. Amsterdam: Elsevier Science Publishers B.V., 1983.

This is a highly scholarly publication which analyzes and develops current studies in the field of conservation and restoration of stone buildings and monuments of historic and cultural significance. Special attention is given to the deleterious influence on stone in industrial and urban environments which hasten natural deterioration.

ASHURST, JOHN, and NICOLA ASHURST. *Practical Building Conservation, English Heritage Technical Handbook, Volume 1: Stone Masonry.* New York: John Wiley & Sons, Inc., 1988.

This book tells how to recognize and diagnose problems in masonry walls. Routine maintenance procedures and repair methods are explained. Appropriate cleaning methods are prescribed for the various types of stone, and a list summarizes treatment procedures for removing stains and controlling organic growth.

ASHURST, JOHN, and NICOLA ASHURST. *Practical Building Conservation, English Heritage Technical Handbook, Volume 2: Brick, Terra Cotta and Earth* New York: John Wiley & Sons, Inc., 1988.

Since most deterioration of brick and terra cotta is caused by moisture, this book begins with a full explanation on the nature and control of dampness in buildings in order to properly evaluate problems and prescribe appropriate treatments. The rest of the book is devoted to specific repair and maintenance treatments, as well as testing and evaluation procedures for brick, terra cotta, and earth construction.

ASHURST, JOHN, and NICOLA ASHURST. *Practical Building Conservation, English Heritage Technical Handbook, Volume 3: Mortars, Plasters and Renders* New York: John Wiley & Sons, Inc., 1988.

This book explains the physical and chemical properties of lime and gypsum plasters and cements. Application techniques for interior and exterior uses are given along with repair methods for decorative and flat plaster, external renders, limewashes, and plaster ceilings. Case studies on cleaning and consolidation of plaster are included.

ASHURST, JOHN, and NICOLA ASHURST. *Practical Building Conservation, English Heritage Technical Handbook, Volume 4: Metals.* New York: John Wiley & Sons, Inc., 1988.

The properties of metals and causes of corrosion are explained in this book. Deterioration problems related to specific metals and installation details are given, along with repair and maintenance treatments for each.

COMMITTEE ON THE CONSERVATION OF HISTORIC STONE BUILDINGS AND MONUMENTS. *Conservation of Historic Stone Buildings and Monuments.* Washington, DC: National Academy Press, 1982.

This is a compilation of papers presented by scientists, preservation architects, engineers, and architectural historians in a meeting held at the National Academy of Sciences in February 1981. The objectives of the conference were to summarize the state of research on stone conservation and to define research needs and priorities.

GAYLE, MARGOT, DAVID W. LOOK, AIA, and JOHN G. WAITE. *Metals in America's Historic Buildings.* Washington, DC: Technical Preservation Services Division, Heritage Conservation and Recreation Service, U.S. Department of the Interior, 1980.

This volume provides a good overview of historic architectural metals and includes sections on lead, tin, zinc, bronze, copper, iron, nickel, steel, and aluminum. Part I, "A Historical Survey of Metals," focuses on identification and historic uses of architectural metals. Part II, "Deterioration and Methods of Preserving Metals," provides in-depth information on repair and preservation methods, and discusses each metal individually.

GRIMMER, ANNE E. *A Glossary of Historic Masonry Deterioration Problems and Preservation Treatments.* Washington, DC: Technical Preservation Services, National Park Service, 1984.

This booklet is generously illustrated and provides information of 22 common masonry deterioration problems and their known treatments. The source is intended for use both as a general reference tool and as on-site interpretive guide in the maintenance and preservation of historic structures.

GLIMMER, ANNE E. *Keeping It Clean: Removing Dirt, Paint, Stains, and Graffiti from Historic Exterior Masonry.* Washington, DC: Technical Preservation Services, National Park Service, 1988.

The author covers virtually every aspect of a cleaning project—identifying building materials to be cleaned and those that might be affected by cleaning, scheduling cleaning around other work, what to ask for in cleaning "specs," and what kind of test cleaning procedures to use. A useful chart summarizes cleaners and techniques.

LONDON, MARK. *Masonry: How to Care for Old and Historic Brick and Stone.* Washington, DC: The Preservation Press, 1988.

The first step in diagnosing deterioration in brick and stone is to know its causes, based on the properties of the material and nature of the building system. This book outlines an inspection process for identifying masonry problems and explains testing procedures to determine the exact cause. A preventive maintenance checklist is included, along with cleaning and repair techniques.

LYNCH, MICHAEL F., and WILLIAM J. HIGGINS. *The Maintenance and Repair of Architectural Sandstone.* New York: New York Landmarks Conservancy, 1982.

This 7-page bulletin is one of the few available publications to address this subject and includes traditional uses of the material in building, problems of decay, protection, and repair and replacement techniques.

MCKEE, HARLEY J. *Introduction to Early American Masonry: Stone, Brick, Mortar and Plaster.* Washington, DC: National Trust for Historic Preservation and Columbia University, 1973.

This book is an invaluable reference on historic masonry materials and how they have been used in American buildings. Information is included on stone quarries, brick patterns, mortar types, and bond patterns, as well as interior and exterior plastering.

SMITH, BAIRD M., AIA. *Moisture Problems in Historic Masonry Walls.* Washington, DC: Preservation Assistance Division, National Park Service, U.S. Department of the Interior, 1984.

This publication describes the physical and chemical nature of moisture problems in walls. Particularly useful for a maintenance program are the inspection and diagnostic procedures to determine the source and extent of problems and to identify areas of concern. Preservation treatments for common types of deterioration are given.

WINKLER, E. M. *Stone: Properties, Durability in Man's Environment.* New York: Springer-Verlag, 1973.

This book surveys the properties of stone that are pertinent to the architect's and engineer's needs. Chapters on natural deformations, color and color stability, the decay of stone, moisture, and weathering provide useful information to individuals involved in preserving historic masonry.

Features

BALLARD, CANDACE. *Working with Slate Roofs.* Ottawa, Canada: Heritage Canada Foundation, 1984.

This well-illustrated book covers both past and present uses of slate roofing and includes information on both repair and replacement work.

FERRO, MAXIMILIAN L., AIA, RIBA, and MELISSA L. COOK. *Electric Wiring and Lighting in Historic American Building: Guidelines for Restoration and Rehabilitation Projects.* New Bedford, MA: AFC/A Norteck Company, 1984.

This excellent publication is devoted to the subject of historic electric wiring, as well as historic lighting. While perhaps one fourth of the book deals with wiring, wire insulation, types of wiring systems, and a discussion of rewiring historic building, the rest of the book is composed of a well-illustrated chronology of fixtures, 1880–1930, from old lighting catalogs. These fixtures are classified as functional, gas/electric, artistic, scientific, and traditional.

FISHER, CHARLES E. (editor). *The Window Handbook: Successful Strategies for Rehabilitating Windows in Historic Buildings.* Washington, DC: Historic Preservation Education Foundation, 1986.

This compilation of technical information, assembled by the National Park Service and the Georgia Institute of Technology, includes guidance on the repair and reuse of historic windows and a series of well-illustrated case studies. Subjects include weatherization, double glazing, replacement sash and frames, and screens, awnings, and accessories. Cost details and product information are provided for each case study.

MEADOWS, ROBERT E. *Historic Building Facades—A Manual for Inspection and Rehabilitation.* New York: New York Landmarks Conservancy, Technical Preservation Services Center, 1986.

Written in response to a New York City law requiring periodic inspection of exterior walls, this guide is intended to promote the maintenance of facades while retaining all features. The first part identifies sources of deterioration and failure in faced elements and building materials. The rest is devoted to inspection techniques, evaluation and diagnosis, and planning for repairs.

SHIVERS, NATALIE. *Walls and Molding: How to Care for Old and Historic Wood and Plaster.* Washington, DC: The Preservation Press, 1990.

Written for homeowners and building managers, this book provides valuable information on early wall treatments, methods of repairing and replastering walls, guidance on recasting ornamental work, and techniques for painting, stenciling, and marbelizing.

History of Technology

JANDL, H. WARD (editor). *The Technology of Historic American Buildings.* Washington, DC: Foundation for Preservation Technology, 1983.

This collection of essays focuses on the history of building technology in the following areas: hand-forged iron builders' hardware, the evolution of the Chicago balloon frame, the invention of the I-beam, American cast-iron, the manufacture and use of architectural terra cotta, decorative metal roof, and exterior painting techniques of the 19th century.

PETERSON, CHARLES E. (editor). *Building Early America.* Radnor, PA: Chilton Book Co., 1976.

This important reference book contains papers from a 1976 symposium on the history of American building technology up to the Civil War. Included are chapters on such topics as 18th century frame houses of Tidewater, Virginia, brick and stone, roofing for Early America, window glass, the development of central heating, and early 19th century lighting. Also included are preservation case studies for Independence Hall, the University of Virginia, and the U.S. Capitol.

INDEX

The number in parentheses preceding a page number indicates the edition from which that material was taken.